THE MOST
RUSTED NAME
IN TRAVEL

Frommer's®

PORTUGAL

24th Edition

By Paul Ames

FrommerMedia LLC

FROMMER'S STAR RATINGS SYSTEM

Every hotel, restaurant, and attraction listed in this guide has been ranked for quality and value. Here's what the stars mean:

★	Recommended
★★	Highly Recommended
★★★	A must! Don't miss!

AN IMPORTANT NOTE

The world is a dynamic place. Hotels change ownership, restaurants hike their prices, museums alter their opening hours, and buses and trains change their routings. And all of this can occur in the several months after our authors have visited, inspected, and written about these hotels, restaurants, museums, and transportation services. Though we have made valiant efforts to keep all our information fresh and up-to-date, some few changes can inevitably occur in the periods before a revised edition of this guidebook is published. So please bear with us if a tiny number of the details in this book have changed. Please also note that we have no responsibility or liability for any inaccuracy or errors or omissions, or for inconvenience, loss, damage, or expenses suffered by anyone as a result of assertions in this guide.

Saint Jerome, legend has it, pacified a lion by removing a thorn from his foot. That's why there are a number of lion statues around the Jerónimos Monastery in Lisbon, including this fountain in the cloisters. PREVIOUS PAGE: Sidewalk cafes populate the streets of Lisbon and many have stupendous views.

CONTENTS

A LOOK AT PORTUGAL

Portugal is a mystery to most would-be travelers. It's far harder to pin down its public persona than other Western nations. Say the word "Italy" and a slew of images—pasta, hand gestures, suave clothing, and more—pop to mind. The same with "France," "Germany," or the "United States." But to understand Portugal, one must travel there. And listen to the nation's plaintive fado music, gorge on grilled sardines, and wander over rocky cliffs, through cutting-edge contemporary museums, winding cobblestoned alleys, and churches glittering with colonial-era gold. This book tells you how to do all of that and much more. In the following pages are just a few of the spectacular sights you'll see.

Go . . . and be dazzled.

– Pauline Frommer

The colorful, eclectic architecture of the Palácio Nacional da Pena, the most recognizable building in Sintra (p. 162).

LISBON

Lisbon is set on seven hills, meaning there's a gobsmacking view around most every corner. Pictured is the atmospheric Alfama district, which has some of the oldest buildings in the city (built on stronger stone, it wasn't as badly damaged as other neighborhoods during the 1755 earthquake).

A foodie mecca, Lisbon has a number of outdoor cafes, though few climb the hills as adeptly as this one does.

The Tram 28 line (p. 105), the most famous of Lisbon's iconic yellow trams, runs through Alfama, Baixa, Chiado, and other historic districts.

Climb the Arco da Rua Augusta triumphal arch for 360-degree views over the Baixa district (see p. 122).

Inaugurated in 1902, the imposing Elevador de Santa Justa towers over the Baixa and carries pedestrians up the Largo do Carmo in the Chiado.

Portugal's most distinctive music is fado, the urban blues of Lisbon, which comes close to encapsulating the nation's soul.

A UNESCO World Heritage Site, 16th-century Jerónimos Monastery is the city's most impressive building (p. 108).

The 1880s Mercado da Ribeira/Time Out Market (p. 105) is a historic produce, meat, and seafood market with a gourmet food hall.

The MAAT (Museum of Art, Architecture and Technology), which opened in late 2016, has transformed the cityscape with its sail-like roof jutting out over the river (p. 107).

The village of Óbidos (p. 193) is so pretty King Afonso II gave it as a wedding gift to his queen. It's a short day-trip from Lisbon.

Sintra Palace (p. 164) rests on a rocky outcrop surrounded by stunning gardens and can be seen for miles around.

A short distance from downtown Cascais, the Boca do Inferno, or Mouth of Hell (p. 150) is a natural rock cavern carved by the waves.

Known as the "River of Gold," the Douro wends its way from north-central Spain to Porto. In Portugal, its often-steep banks are terraced with the vineyards that produce the area's famous fortified wine.

Espigueiros, raised stone tomblike structures that are actually grain stores, are found near Parque Nacional da Peneda-Gerês (p. 396).

Opened in 1906, Livraria Lello in Porto is regarded as one of the world's most beautiful bookstores (p. 341).

With a permanent collection of more than 4,000 works by Portuguese and international artists, Serralves (p. 343) is one of Portugal's most important art museums.

A view of the colorful Ribeira neighborhood (p. 336). It has clung to this hillside since the Middle Ages.

The grand chambers of Porto's Palácio da Bolsa (p. 340), the former Stock Exchange, borrow decorative elements from ancient Rome, Renaissance Italy, and the court of Versailles.

The city's largely Romanesque Sé (Cathedral, p. 340) was begun in the 12th century.

Pop by for a cimbalino (shot of espresso) at the 1920s-era Café Majestic (see p. 342).

The Arco da Porta Nova (p. 391), a baroque triumphal arch, makes up part of the city walls of Braga.

You can't say you've been to Porto until you've tippled your way through a port tasting (see p. 339).

Guimarães' castle (p. 382), site of an important siege, is considered the birthplace of the nation.

Guimarães' Largo de Oliveira (Olive Tree Square, p. 383) is rich in history...and taverns. It's the place to be in the evenings.

A UNESCO World Heritage Site, the hilltop pilgrimage site of Santuário Bom Jesús do Monte is Braga's best-known landmark (p. 391).

SOUTHERN PORTUGAL

Near Lagos (p. 249), the coast is a wonderland of hidden lagoons, jutting rocks, and grottoes.

A falconer participates in a medieval festival in Silves.

From the heady heights of Marvão Castle (p. 290) visitors feel like they can see all of Portugal, and a good swatch of Spain, too.

Grilled sardines are a staple of Portuguese cuisine, their aroma wafting through old towns and along seaside promenades.

A pretty square in Lagos (p. 249). Today known for its beaches and relaxed vibe, its history is darker—as the place where the Atlantic slave trade began in the 1400s.

Stairs lead down to Praia do Camilo (p. 252), one in a series of stunning beaches south of Lagos.

The Algar de Benagil sea cave (p. 235), a natural sandstone formation near Portimão, can be explored via a boat tour or stand-up paddleboard.

Established in 1290, University of Coimbra (p. 299) is one of the oldest universities in the world. It dominates the Alta, or upper town of Coimbra.

Dramatically sited Praia de Carvoeiro beach is the focal point of Carvoeiro (p. 235), a resort town of the Algarve.

Throughout Portugal, you'll see important works from the many civilizations that once ruled this land. Pictured is a still-standing Roman-era bridge in Tavira.

The Castelo dos Mouros (p. 241) in Silves was the center of the Moorish empire until the Reconquista. All that's left are ruins.

Sagres (p. 255) was once considered the edge of the world. Hike to the lighthouse for a view of the vast Atlantic, and you'll understand why.

THE BEST OF PORTUGAL

Europe's West Coast is suddenly very fashionable. Portugal's 1,000 miles of shore and California-style climate are attracting travelers in record numbers. The buzz is justified. Beyond the glorious beaches, this ancient nation is crammed with heritage ranging from Stone Age graffiti to villages clustered beneath medieval castles and forests filled with romantic palaces. Its lifestyle is laidback; its food and wine fabulous. Five hundred years ago, Portuguese explorers opened up the world; now it's time to discover this little land of many wonders.

Mainland Europe's westernmost nation has few rivals as a land where climate, landscape, and history combine so effectively to satisfy travelers' wish lists. Atlantic breezes waft over beaches for every taste, from sheltered, family-friendly coves to strands of endless sand offering the continent's best surf. The capital **Lisbon** and second city **Porto** are among Europe's hippest cities, where the plaintive songs of traditional fado music or the guitars of student troubadours echo down medieval alleys that lead to waterfront nightclubs throbbing with the latest dance tunes.

Foodies can feast on a rich and varied cuisine that's rooted in tradition and dominated by superlative seafood and wines. Crammed into a country the size of Maine are 17 UNESCO cultural World Heritage Sites, ranging from the rolling hillside vineyards above the **River Douro** and the mysterious stronghold of the Knights Templar in **Tomar,** to historic cities like **Évora, Guimarães,** and **Angra do Heroísmo** in the Azores islands. If your goal is relaxing in a year-round subtropical springtime, **Madeira Island** is the place.

Those seeking a more active break can hike the mountain wildernesses of the **Peneda-Gerês National Park** or **Serra da Estrela** highlands; race speedboats to watch dolphins frolic off **Algarve** beaches; or play a round on world-class golf courses. All that combined with its reputation for safety, low crime, and warm hospitality have made Portugal one of Europe's hottest destinations.

CITIES Spread along the broad estuary of the River Tagus, **Lisbon** is the country's political, economic, and cultural heart. It enjoys more sunshine than Madrid, Rome, or Athens. Commuter trains run from downtown to Atlantic beaches in minutes. There are gilded theaters, treasure-packed museums, and atmospheric old neighborhoods that recall the 15th-century golden age of Portuguese discoveries. Second city **Porto** is fast catching up as a city-trip destination, thanks to its UNESCO World Heritage riverside heart, cultural scene, and established reputation as a capital of cool. The ancient university city of **Coimbra** is regarded as Portugal's most romantic, while regional centers like **Guimarães** and **Braga** in the far north, Évora in the **Alentejo** region, and **Funchal** on **Madeira** are treasure houses of tradition and culture.

COUNTRYSIDE For a small country, Portugal boasts a richly diverse landscape. The southern **Algarve** region is redolent of the Mediterranean, with balmy beaches, almond groves, and citrus plantations. Farther north in the vast rolling plains of the **Alentejo,** where black pigs feast on acorns under forests of cork oaks to produce fabulous hams. The land is punctuated by picture-perfect whitewashed villages. In the rugged interior of the central **Beiras** region, mainland Portugal's highest peaks are found in the **Serra da Estrella** mountain range, home to the country's only ski resort. Vine-covered slopes surround the **River Douro** inland from Porto, arguably the world's most beautiful wine region. Beyond, the northwest **Minho** region is verdant and dotted with elegant manor houses, while **Tràs-os-Montes** to the northeast is marked by starkly beautiful high plateaus and a cuisine as robust as its climate. **Madeira** is known as the island of eternal spring, and the nine islands of the **Azores** display dramatic volcanic landscapes surrounded by the blue Atlantic.

EATING & DRINKING The Portuguese love to eat, and restaurant attendance in the nation is among Europe's highest. Fortunately, eating out costs less here than just about anywhere in Western Europe. Portuguese cuisine isn't as well-known as it should be, perhaps because it depends heavily on fresh local ingredients—fish newly plucked from the Atlantic, a multitude of seasonal fruits and vegetables that ripen in the warm climate, beef raised on lush northern pastures, lamb nourished on spring flowers.

COAST The **Algarve** is Portugal's premier vacation region, its sheltered south coast is strung with beaches that range from flat, gently sloping sandbar islands (reached by bridge or boat close to the border with Spanish Andalusia) to the iconic coves hidden between honeycomb cliffs near the towns of **Lagos** and **Albufeira.** Unfortunately, some of the resort towns in the Algarve's central strip suffer from the excesses of mass tourism with strips of ugly high-rise condos and bargain-booze bars, but beyond the dramatic headland of Europe's most southwesterly point at **Sagres,** the coast changes. Wind and waves make the wild west a paradise for surfers and sailors. The world's biggest surfed waves crash ashore near the picturesque fishing port of **Nazaré.** Even along the west coast, however, there are sheltered beaches—the soft white sands and gentle bays just south of Lisbon at **Comporta** and **Arrábida** are a delight.

PORTUGAL'S best AUTHENTIC EXPERIENCES

- **Fado:** There are many places to experience Lisbon's unique fado music: from backstreet dives where the cook may step out of the kitchen to give voice to her emotions by bursting into song, to fancy clubs where you'll pay dearly to dine accompanied by a renowned diva, to concert halls packed with thousands of fans gathered to hear one of the genre's big stars. Fado's bluesy blend of voice and guitar strives to capture the pain of lost love and longing for homelands left behind, all bound up with the untranslatable feeling they call *saudade,* which is deeply bound up with Portugal's national character.
- **Market shopping:** Portugal's daily food markets have suffered from superstore competition, but most showcase an array of fresh products that make them a must for anybody interested in food. They are not for the faint-hearted: butchers' stalls proudly present glistering arrays of offal, and fishmongers cheerfully gut and scale the day's catch. Naturally grown fruits and vegetables may lack the shine and same-shape regularity of supermarket goods, but will taste oh so much better. Those in Setúbal, Funchal, and Olhão are among the best.
- **Hitting a hot tub:** Hot springs bubble up from Portugal's hills and plains. Spa resorts are scattered about the country. Some have roots going back to Roman times; many maintain an old-world elegance with splendid Belle Epoque hotels or Art Deco baths in marble, brass, and painted *azulejo* tiles. The charm can be a little faded in some places, but plenty have been restored to their full glory.
- **Downing a bica:** In a country whose former colonies included Brazil, Angola, and East Timor, it's no surprise that the country is hooked on coffee. Although you can find local equivalents of lattes and flat whites, the Portuguese mostly get their caffeine fix through tiny espresso shots known as a *bica*, or simply a *café*. If you want to blend in, eschew pavement terraces and join the locals lined up at the counter in countless cafes to knock back their *bicas*, quite possibly with a custard-filled *pastel de nata* or another treat from the selection of pastries on show. See p. 106.
- **Chilling on a beach:** While the English complain "it's not my cup of tea," the Portuguese say "*não é a minha praia*"—"it's not my beach." The phrase shows how central the beach is to Portuguese life. Inhabitants of Lisbon and Porto will rush out to the cities' suburban shores at weekends, even in mornings and evenings before and after work. Most beaches have cool bars or restaurants that serve up wonderful fresh shellfish or grilled fish. Surfers from around the world flock to ride the rollers along the west coast at places like Aljezur, Ericeira, and Peniche.
- **Wine tasting at a quinta:** Port wine from the Douro region has been a major Portuguese export for centuries, but the world has only recently

woken up to the wonders of the country's other wines: darkly brooding reds, playful white *vinho verdes* from the Minho, bubbly *espumantes,* sweet *moscatels.* Excellent tipples are produced the length and breadth of the country, but the Douro region's terraced hills stand out for their beauty. Sampling wines in one of the Douro's historic estates (*quintas*) while gazing out over the landscape is unforgettable.

- **Watching the sun set at the end of the earth:** The ancients believed the remote Sagres Peninsula at the southwestern tip of Europe was the end of the earth. Prince Henry the Navigator set up there to plot the Age of Discoveries. There are few better places to watch the sun go down. Crowds gather around the clifftop fort and lighthouse at nearby Cape St. Vincent to see the sun turn the sky orange before sinking beneath the waves. There's nothing but the Atlantic between here and New York. The cocktails served in the fortress cafe help keep out the sometimes chilly winds.
- **Party with the saints:** Lisbon's biggest party comes on June 13. To honor Saint Anthony (*Santo António*), its patron, the city engages in all-night revelry. The streets in the oldest neighborhoods fill with the whiff of sardines on the grill and the sound of guitars and accordions. Hordes of revelers quaffing beer and red wine dance into the wee hours. Celebrations are most intense in the district that wins the *marchas populares* contest, a singing costumed promenade down the capital's main boulevard. Eleven days later it's Porto's turn, on the night of Saint John (*São João*). The second-city's party includes a spectacular fireworks display over the Douro.
- **Walking a levada:** The island of Madeira is crisscrossed with more than 2,092km (1,300 miles) of hiking trails that follow narrow stone irrigation channels, known as *levadas.* Walking them offers wonderful views of the island's mountainous interior and out over the deep blue Atlantic all around. Many lead though the *Laurisilva* forest, what's left of the semitropical native vegetation that covered the island before Portuguese explorers arrived in 1419. It is now a UNESCO World Heritage Site. Among the most scenic is Levada do Caldeirão Verde, which snakes 4 miles though verdant glades and tumbling ocean views before arriving at a 91-meter (300-ft.) waterfall.
- **Taking to the waves on the Tagus:** Lisbon's cutest mode of public transport are the tiny streetcars that weave through the narrow streets. But the famed Tram 28 has fallen victim to its reputation and is now swamped with tourists. A more authentic journey would be to join the thousands of Lisbonites who commute from the south bank of the River Tagus into the city on little orange ferry boats called *cacilheiros.* For 1.30€ you can admire an unrivaled view of the Lisbon skyline as the boat chugs across for the 10-minute voyage to the dock at Cacilhas, where there's a welcoming row of riverside seafood restaurants.

PORTUGAL'S best VILLAGES & SMALL TOWNS

- **Tavira:** While much of the central Algarve coast has been scarred by mass tourism, the region's eastern and western extremities retain their charm. Nowhere more so than this little town, where noble 17th-century homes line the riverside, narrow streets are filled with restaurants and cafes, and small boats can whisk you to near-deserted island beaches. See p. 227.
- **Óbidos:** Clustered around its 12th-century castle, this is one of Portugal's best-preserved medieval towns. Its maze of cobbled lanes connects whitewashed houses with bright blue or yellow trim. The town is also famed for its bookshops, its sweet cherry liqueur, and the white sands of its lagoon that opens out into the Atlantic nearby. See p. 193.
- **Belmonte:** Birthplace of the explorer who discovered Brazil and home to a Jewish community that preserved its faith in secret through centuries of persecution, Belmonte is built from granite hewn from the remote central highlands. Among the rough stone buildings are a 13th-century castle and the ruined tower dating back to Roman times. See p. 328.
- **Amarante:** Inland from Porto, Amarante sits on a tree-lined curve in the River Tâmega. Its Renaissance-style riverside church, built with Spanish and Italian influences out of soft golden local stone, is surrounded by townhouses rising up the hillside and spreading along the riverbank. It is home to a fine luxury hotel, a surprising museum of modern art, and famed cafes serving sweet almond- and cinnamon-flavored pastries. See p. 365.
- **Marvão:** As dramatic locations go, this could hardly be better. Marvão is perched on a rocky crag rising 860 meters (2,800 ft.) out of the Alentejo plain. It stood as a frontier post for centuries, fought over by Celts and Romans, Muslims and Christians, Castilians and Portuguese. Inside its medieval battlements, the old whitewashed town has survived all those battles. Views are extraordinary, especially if you're there at dawn or sunset. See p. 290.
- **Angra do Heroísmo:** The history-packed capital of Terceira island in the Azores permits residents to choose from 18 authorized shades for painting their houses. The result is a riot of pastel facades huddled around a couple of Atlantic coves and framed by volcanic slopes covered in grass of the deepest green. The city was a key staging post for the Portuguese trading empire and served as an inspiration for colonial ports across Latin America. See p. 448.
- **Miranda do Douro:** Located on the edge of a canyon formed by the River Douro on Portugal's northeast frontier, Miranda has been a land that time forgot since 1762, when invading Spaniards blew up a big part of it and the authorities decamped farther from the border. Isolation has allowed the town to maintain its own unique language, Mirandese, and traditions like the war dance performed by local men wearing frilly skirts and striped

woolen socks. There's a sturdy stone cathedral and cobbled streets lined with centuries-old homes. It's also famed for steak. See p. 410.

- **Piodão:** Huddled on a terraced hillside in a remote corner of the Açor mountains in the center of the country, homes here are made from dark, almost black schist stone with slate roofs. In dramatic counterpoint is the little parish church, a wedding-cake confection in purest white with pale blue trim. At dusk, when the village glitters with yellow lights, it resembles a Neapolitan nativity scene. It's a great base for hiking the hills or sampling hearty highland dishes like goat slow-cooked in red wine. See p. 328.
- **Ponte de Lima:** Once a Roman outpost, Ponte de Lima lays claim to being the oldest village in Portugal. It's defined by the ancient stone bridge that arches over the slow-moving River Lima and connects the village to the slender tower of St. Anthony's Church on the west bank. Ponte de Lima is packed with historic mansions whose balconies overflow with summer flowers. It's set in the verdant hills of the Minho region and surrounded by baroque estates producing crisp *vinho verde* wines. See p. 386.
- **Mértola:** Clinging to a high ridge over the River Guadiana, this picturesque collection of white-painted houses surrounded by medieval walls was the capital of an Arab kingdom in the Middle Ages. Its parish church was a mosque with a multi-columned interior—a rare survivor of Islamic architecture in Portugal. Wandering its ancient streets, it's not hard to imagine its golden age as a cosmopolitan river port. The river provides swimming and kayaking opportunities, and local restaurants thrive on boar, hare, and other game hunted in the wild surroundings. See p. 290.

PORTUGAL'S best BEACHES

- **Porto Santo:** Madeira Island lacks beaches, but a 2-hour boat trip (or 15-min. flight) away is one of Portugal's best. The little island of Porto Santo boasts a 10km (6 mile) stretch of golden sand stretching around a bay of still blue water with views across the mountains of Madeira on the horizon. See p. 428.
- **Cabanas:** Cabanas is a little fishing village just outside the Algarve town of Tavira. After lunching in one of the great waterfront seafood joints, hop on one of the skiffs that skim across the blue lagoon to a sandbar island flanked with over 5km (3 miles) of soft yellow sand. See p. 229.
- **Praia da Marinha:** Coves of pale sand nestled beneath honeycomb cliffs, near the resort of Carvoeiro, this is one of the most iconic Algarve beaches. In summer, you won't have it to yourself, but its distance from the main resorts means it does not get as crowded as most along this stretch of coast. See p. 235.
- **Comporta:** A endless curve of platinum-blond sand in a bay of sapphire blue water. It's achingly beautiful, with the Arrábida hills in the distance. With the shabby-chic village of Comporta on the other side of the dunes, this is the most fashionable spot on the coast. Be careful you don't bump

into Madonna or Maria Sharapova as you head from the seafood desk to the water, and make sure you're inside before mosquito time around sunset. See p. 190.

- **Guincho:** In the lee of Europe's westernmost point at Capo da Roca, this broad expanse of sand is the most dramatic of the beaches in the Cascais-Sintra area west of Lisbon. Its exposure to Atlantic breezes whipping around the cape means that except on rare calm days, it's better for surfers and wind sports rather than laying out on the sand. But the views are dramatic, and there are excellent restaurants along the coast road. See p. 150.
- **Supertubos:** Portugal's surfer beach *par excellence*. Although the waves here are not as big as the record-breaking rollers up the coast in Nazaré, this strand, just south of the fishing town of Peniche, is renowned for the regularity of its perfect tubular waves crashing on to the soft sand. See p. 204.
- **Quiaios:** Look north from the Serra da Boa Viagem hills above the resort of Figueira da Foz and Quiaios beach stretches as far as you can see—an endless strip of sand backed by dunes and pine forest. There's a small village at the southern end, and beyond that, solitude. Care can be needed with riptides; check with the lifeguard. See p. 310.
- **Moledo:** Portugal's northernmost beach has long been a favorite for the in-crowd from Porto. A vast sandy expanse, it curves down from the River Minho that forms the border with Spain. It is overlooked by the conical outline of Mount Santa Tecla over the frontier and a 15th-century fort on a small offshore island. As with other northern beaches, the water can be cold, the wind fresh, and the mornings shrouded in mist, but there is no denying the wild beauty of the location. See p. 401.

PORTUGAL'S best HOTELS

- **Belmond Reid's Palace** (Funchal): The grand old lady of Madeira hotels was built in 1890s and was once the favored retreat of Sir Winston Churchill. Tea and scones are still served on the terrace at 5pm as a reminder of the time when the British upper set wintered here, but Reid's has managed to shed a one-time fusty image without losing any of its period charm or superlative service standards. It's wonderfully located amid cliff-top gardens overlooking the Atlantic. See p. 430.
- **Dá Licença** (Estremoz): Two guys from the Parisian antique and fashion world have transformed an Alentejo farmstead into a work of art. Each of the enormous, light-filled suites and rooms is decorated with great style using locally mined marble and unique pieces from their world-class collection of art nouveau furniture and design. There are private pools hewn from marble and views, citrus groves and thousands of olive trees and the opportunity to take dinner in art-themed private dining rooms. See p. 282.
- **Le Monumental Palace** (Porto):This long derelict 1920s palace has been rescued by French investors who have restored its Jazz Age glamor. It blends Belle Epoque, Art Nouveau, and Art Deco styles with sensitive

modern touches. The pavement-level cafe is again a city social hub; rooms are "grand hotel" elegant, and the deluxe spa ensures premium pampering on the main boulevard of Portugal's second city. See p. 348.

- **Palácio de Seteais** (Sintra): The Dutch ambassador owned one of the most romantic palaces in Portugal, built in the 1780s on a forested hillside in Sintra. They say the name came later: "Sete ais" translates as "seven sighs," apparently uttered by Portuguese nobles forced to sign a humiliating treaty here after an 1807 defeat by Napoleon's invading armies. Any sighing you're likely to do today will be from pleasure—at the views, the lavish gardens, the gloriously restored neoclassical building, and the chance to plunge into the lifestyle of the old-world aristocracy. See p. 166.
- **Pousada Palacio de Estoi** (Faro): Our pick from the Pousada chain of historic inns was built in the 1780s as a pleasure place for a viscount's palace. Its rococo domes and towers are painted in raspberry and lemon shades overlooking gardens filled with palms, fountains, and rows of statues. The central salon is a downsized version of the Versailles' Hall of Mirrors. In contrast, guestrooms are in the new wing built along minimalist-but-comfy lines by an award-winning architect. See p. 224.
- **Rio do Prado** (Óbidos): On the road from the white town of Óbidos to pristine west-coast beaches is this friendly eco-chic resort formed by concrete cubicles that blend into the grass. It might not sound tempting, but the bungalows are intriguingly crafted to allow in sunlight and decorated with sustainable good taste, with private patios, fireplaces inside and out, and theatrical stand-alone tubs. The garden is a delight, and the property's organic herb and vegetable plot supplies the restaurant. See p. 198.
- **Six Senses Douro Valley** (Lamego): Probably the most pampering you can get at any one place, this was the first European resort with the sensory overload approach of Asian luxury specialist Six Senses. It has acres of land among the Douro's riverside vineyards, a match of award-winning contemporary design with the charm of the original 19th-century mansion, great restaurants, and a superlative spa. See p. 375.
- **The Independente** (Lisbon): Lisbon has a reputation for some of the world's hippest hostels, and this is one of the best: at the heart of the action in the Bairro Alto nightlife zone and with great views over the city. It has basic dorm bunks for as little as 10€ including breakfast—and this in a palatial, early-20th-century residence originally built for the Swiss ambassador! A couple of cool restaurants are in the building along with a rooftop bar. There are also some charming private suites, for those who can afford to pay for privacy. See p. 79.
- **Verride Palácio Santa Catarina** (Lisbon): An 18th-century palace restored and renovated as one of the capital's most luxurious. You'll gape at marble arches, panels of antique tiles, and the monumental staircase. On the roof, the pool and bar/restaurant gift guests with 360-degree views over the rooftops and River Tagus. The king-size royal suites are draped in lemon-yellow

silk and stucco work like piped cream. It's regal but has a laidback and unstuffy feel. See p. 76.

- **Vidago Palace** (Chaves): Of all Portugal's grand old spa hotels, this is the grandest. Built in 1910 on the orders of King Carlos I, who wanted a resort to rival the best of Europe, it oozes Belle Epoque glamour. Built over natural spring waters reputed for their curative properties since Roman times, it is surrounded by 100 hectares (250 acres) of forested parkland. Inside, expect expanses of marble, silk wall hangings, and monumental staircases, all tastefully restored when the hotel reopened in 2010. The gourmet restaurant and 18-hole golf course are bonuses. It's an hour's drive from Porto in the heart of Trás-os-Montes. See p. 406.

PORTUGAL'S best RESTAURANTS

- **Belcanto** (Lisbon): Lisbon's finest fine dining, the flagship of star chef José Avillez with two Michelin stars. Avillez brings a refined but irreverent approach to his cooking, which is revolutionary but firmly rooted in Portuguese traditions. His exquisite tasting menus can feature radical reworkings of classics like roast suckling pig or the country's Sunday lunch favorite—*cozido* (a one-pot of boiled meats and vegetables). Recently expanded into bigger premises next door, it still keeps the elegant and intimate feel, on a plaza facing the opera house. See p. 87.
- **Casa de Chá da Boa Nova** (Porto): First the location: surging out of rocks lapped by the Atlantic surf. Then the building: Built as a teahouse in the 1960s, this low-rise concrete-glass-and-wood construction is an early masterwork by architectural genius Álvaro Siza Vieira. Then the food, produced by starred chef Rui Paula, whose ocean menu features scallop with black radish and red mullet with cashew and cassava. See p. 355.
- **Casa dos Passarinhos** (Lisbon): No visit to Portugal is complete without eating in a *tasca.* These are simple taverns, serving up hearty portions of traditional food to hungry workers. This is one of the best: just two simple dining rooms, which fill up quick. Garlicky bread mush with shrimp, deep-fried cuttlefish, and griddled steaks are among the specialties. See p. 95.
- **A Casa Guedes** (Porto): Sandwiches are big in Porto, and it's hard to beat the roast pork lathered with marinade and cooking juices and slapped into fist-size rolls in this retro hole-in-the-wall. If you really want to push the boat out, grab one with an added portion of creamy *queijo da serra* sheep's cheese. Wash down with cold *vinho verde* or a black beer. See p. 358.
- **Chico Elias** (Tomar): Chef Maria do Céu is in her eighties but still works the ovens to produce the slow-roasted dishes that make this rustic eatery, beside the UNESCO-listed Knights Templar stronghold, a temple of traditional food. You should call at least 24 hours in advance to order her best dishes like rabbit cooked in pumpkin or baked codfish with

acorn-sweetened pork. Celebrity photos on the walls bear witness to the timeless appeal. See p. 268.

- **Fialho** (Évora): The cooking of the Alentejo region is considered by many Portuguese to be the country's best. It's based on acorn-reared pork, free-range lamb, game in season, the finest olive oils, and organically grown produce. For more than 70 years, this family-run restaurant has been an ambassador for the region's authentic cruise. The roast lamb is sublime, the rice with wild pigeon delectable, the sliced black pork heavenly. A national treasure (p. 278).
- **Midori** (Sintra): For a Portuguese chef to win a Michelin star with Japanese cooking takes some doing. But Pedro Almeida has done just that, using the freshest local seafood to craft a fabulously creative fusion of East and West in a luxury resort set among forested hills outside Lisbon. His *kaiseki* fixed menus bring a parade of complex morsels like red mullet sashimi with butter sauce and miso, or nigiri of striped Algarve shrimp with finger lime. See p. 169.
- **O Sapo** (Penafiel): Before entering, loosen your belt. Better still, don't wear a belt. Portugal's north is famed for eating large, but this rustic place takes it all a step further. They'll start by loading your table with wooden platters filled with appetizers—smoked meats, cheeses, fried balls of salt cod, pigs'-ear salad, egg with cornbread, and so on. Just go with the flow, but remember to leave space for the mighty, meaty main courses. Help it down with the local red *vinho verde* served in china mugs. See p. 364.
- **Cervejaria Ramiro** (Lisbon): Bright, noisy, and invariably crowded, Ramiro is the monarch of the *marisqueiras*—specialty seafood restaurants. The idea is to order a succession of shellfish dishes: clams steamed with garlic and cilantro, whole crabs (you get a mallet to smash the claws), shrimp in various sizes, goose barnacles that must be wrestled from their leathery sheaths. It's traditional to follow up with a steak sandwich. Be prepared to stand in line, it's very popular. See p. 88.
- **Restinga** (Portimão): One of Portugal's great gastronomic pleasures is sitting at a beachside restaurant watching the waves roll up to the shore while tucking into expertly prepared seafood that was swimming about beneath those same waves a few hours before. There are many swell places to do that in the Algarve, but Restinga takes the concept a step further. It's located on a glorious beach and next to a shellfish-rich lagoon. Start with fried shrimp or fish soup, then settle down to a whole grilled bream, bass, or other fish as the main event. See p. 245.

PORTUGAL'S best PALACES & CASTLES

- **Palácio Nacional da Pena** (Sintra): An extraordinary 19th-century confection sitting atop the Sintra hills, this palace was built by King consort Ferdinand II, the German husband of Portugal's Queen Maria II. It boasts a potpourri of styles—Neo-Gothic, Moorish revival, imitation Renaissance, pastiches of Portugal's maritime-inspired Manueline—inspired by the romantic mountaintop fantasy castles of Bavaria. Painted in shocking reds and yellows, it looms over thick forests, a palace fit for fairytales. See p. 162.

- **Forte da Graça** (Elvas): As Portugal battled to regain its independence from Spain in the 1640s, the border town of Elvas held a key position on the road from Madrid to Lisbon. To fortify it, they brought in a German military architect, who built the biggest fort of its type in the world. A massive series of defensive walls and ditches circle the pretty, whitewashed town. The city fortifications and the aqueduct ensuring the inhabitants could get water even during a siege are a UNESCO World Heritage Site. See p. 284.
- **Casa de Mateus** (Vila Real): Familiar around the world to fans of the rosé wine that bears its name and image on the label, this is the most beautiful of the baroque manor houses scattered around the wine lands of northern Portugal. The reflecting pool out front perfectly duplicates the white-and-gray stone facade with its double staircase and decorative spires, partly the work of the great Italian architect Nicolau Nasoni in the 1740s. It's surrounded by delightful formal gardens. See p. 407.
- **Palácio de Mafra** (Mafra): This was originally supposed to be a convent, but King João V decided he'd spend some of his Brazilian gold-mine riches expanding it. The result is a monster-size mix of church and royal residence covering an area bigger than seven football fields. Completed in 1755, its vast yellow-painted facade dominates the little town of Mafra. Inside, the royal apartments and old hospital are well worth visiting, but the real treasure is the rococo library lined with almost 40,000 books dating back to the 14th century. UNESCO declared it a World Heritage site in 2019. See p. 171.

PORTUGAL'S best MUSEUMS

- **Museu Calouste Gulbenkian** (Lisbon): If you go to one museum in Portugal, this should be it. Whatever your taste in art—from ancient Egyptian funeral masks to French Impressionist paintings, Persian carpets to Lalique jewelry—you're sure to find something interesting. The remarkable collection was amassed by Armenian oil magnate Calouste Gulbenkian (1869–1955), who found a home in neutral Portugal during World War II. The museum complex also includes concert halls and a separate modern art museum, all housed in discreet 1960s buildings integrated into shady gardens that are a peaceful getaway in the heart of the city. See p. 116.
- **Museu Nacional do Azulejo** (Lisbon): Wherever you go in Portugal you'll see *azulejos*—painted ceramic tiles used to decorate buildings inside and out, from ancient churches to modern metro stations. The best place to understand this thoroughly Portuguese art form is this museum situated in a 16th-century convent in Lisbon's riverside Madre de Deus neighborhood. The collection contains tiles dating back over 600 years. Highlights include

a giant panel showing Lisbon before the great earthquake of 1755 and the convent church filled with tiles and gold leaf. See p. 113.

- **Serralves** (Porto): Porto's modern art museum is housed in a fine Art Deco villa and a purpose-built contemporary gallery designed by local architect Álvaro Siza Vieira. It holds a huge collection of Portuguese and international art from the 20th and 21st centuries and hosts temporary exhibitions, serving as the most dynamic cultural center in the north. Its latest big acquisition was more than 80 works by Spanish surrealist Joan Miró. See p. 343.
- **Museu Nacional de Arte Antiga** (Lisbon): The country's best collection of Portuguese and international painting is housed in a 17th-century palace high on a cliff overlooking the River Tagus. Much of the collection was brought together from monasteries and noble homes after the civil war of the 1830s. Among the highlights: the nightmarish *Temptations of St. Anthony* by Hieronymus Bosch; Japanese screen paintings showing the arrival of Portuguese mariners in the 16th century; and Nuno Gonçalves' *Panels of St. Vincent,* depicting Lisbon society at the time of the Discoveries. The gardens at the back offer peaceful views over the river. See p. 111.
- **Museu Colecção Berardo** (Lisbon): In the depths of the bunker-like Centro Cultural de Belém is a groundbreaking collection of modern and contemporary art. It was put together by Joe Berardo, an emigrant from Madeira who made a fortune in South Africa. The museum covers the greats of 20th-century art including Jackson Pollack, Roy Liechtenstein, and Giorgio de Chirico, along with cutting-edge artists of today. See p. 110.

PORTUGAL'S best CHURCHES & ABBEYS

- **Mosteiro dos Jerónimos** (Lisbon): Begun in 1502 in the riverside Belém district, this great monastery is the best example of the Manueline style developed in Portugal to combine late-Gothic and Renaissance architecture with motifs inspired by the great maritime voyages of discovery. Built from white limestone, the soaring nave of the main church building looks almost organic, like a coral-and-algae-crusted sea cave. Inside are the tombs of explorer Vasco da Gama and poets Luís de Camões and Fernando Pessoa. The cloister, decorated by fine Manueline stonework, is a delight. See p. 108.
- **Santa Maria de Alcobaça** (Alcobaça): Don't be fooled by the ornate baroque facade added in the 18th century. This church was founded in 1153 by Portugal's founding father, King Afonso Henriques. Inside, the slender, soaring nave is done in unadorned early-Gothic style, then newly imported from France by Cistercian monks. The church is the resting place of several medieval royals, among them King Pedro II and his murdered mistress Inês de Castro, whose tragic story has long inspired poets and musicians. Their extravagant tombs are treasures of Gothic stonework. See p. 196.

- **Igreja de São Francisco** (Porto): Porto's "Golden Church" doesn't look like much from its plain Gothic exterior. But inside it is a gilded grotto, shimmering from floor to ceiling with wood carvings coated in gold leaf, a technique known as *talha dourada* developed by Portuguese craftsmen in the 18th century when the precious metal was pouring in from Brazilian mines. The church dates back to 1244. Amid all the gold, the towering "Tree of Jesse" sculpture showing the family tree of Jesus is a standout. See p. 337.
- **Mosteiro da Batalha** (Batalha): In 1385, a Portuguese army defeated a much larger Spanish invasion force in a field south of Leiria, guaranteeing the country's independence for 200 years. To mark the victory, King João I, who led the troops, erected near the battlefield this masterpiece of the Flamboyant style of Gothic architecture. Using local limestone that glows golden in the setting sun, a succession of architects brought in influences from France, England, and beyond to make a unique construction. Unfortunately, 20th-century planners were less gifted, placing a busy highway close to the main facade. See p. 209.
- **Convento de Cristo** (Tomar): Another World Heritage Site, this convent in the pretty little town of Tomar once served as headquarters for the Knights Templar, who held off a siege by Arab forces in 1190. Around that time, they built a circular church at the center of the convent, taking as their model the Dome of the Rock in Jerusalem. Inside, it is richly decorated with Gothic sculptures and paintings. Successive Portuguese monarchs kept adding to the grandeur of the convent, particularly during the Discoveries period, adorning it with some of the best examples of Manueline stonework. See p. 265.

PORTUGAL IN CONTEXT

2

"Where the land ends and the sea begins" was how the great poet Luís Vaz de Camões defined his homeland in the 16th century. Portugal has always been shaped by the ocean. For centuries it turned its back on its often prickly Spanish neighbors and the rest of Europe. Instead, it reached out to continents beyond the Atlantic, gaining riches though maritime trade and forging Europe's first and longest-lasting colonial empire.

In Camões' day, Portuguese seafarers like Vasco da Gama and Ferdinand Magellan pushed back the boundaries of the known world, discovering routes to Africa, Asia, and America, laying the foundations for a global empire. Today's Portugal carries the legacy of that Age of Exploration, from the Brazilian gold that lines its churches to the diversity of the population, and the exotic touches that spice Portuguese cuisine.

The sea also provided an escape route. In hard times, millions of emigrants sailed for a better life, founding communities that today flourish as outposts of Portuguese culture, from Massachusetts to Macau, Paris to São Paulo.

Maritime expansion had a dark side. Portugal initiated the trans-Atlantic slave trade that lasted hundreds of years. Up to the 1970s, the dictatorship in Lisbon fought to cling to its overseas colonies. The wars left Portugal cut off from the European mainstream, economically backward, and culturally isolated. Since a peaceful 1974 revolution restored democracy, the country has taken huge strides toward modernity. Portugal joined the European Union in 1986 and adopted the euro as its currency in 1999. Today, Lisbon is fast developing as a tech hub. Tourism is booming, thanks to Portugal's reputation as a safe, easy-on-the-wallet destination, plus the timeless advantages of living on Europe's southwestern seaboard—from the endless sun-kissed beaches to superlative seafood and cities brimming with heritage.

PORTUGAL TODAY

For much of the past 100 years, Portugal has been out of step with the European mainstream. While World War II raged, it was peacefully neutral; while post-WWII democracies embraced unity, it labored under a "proudly alone" dictatorship; while other colonial powers dismantled their empires, it waged doomed wars against African independence movements up to 1975. Now, as much of Europe is racked by political turmoil, angry demonstrations grip the streets, and voters turn to insurgent parties, this nation of 10 million is a haven of contentment and stability.

The radical right has failed to make a mark in repeated elections; the radical left, which has been a fixture for decades, seems unable to emulate the breakthroughs of comrades in Spain and Greece. From 2015 to 2019 they supported a center-left government that has given the country a balanced budget for the first time in years and ensured Portugal remains among the most enthusiastic members of NATO and the European Union. In a system where most power lies with the prime minister, but the president can impose significant checks on government policy, politicians holding both posts have managed to cooperate amiably and maintain high levels of popularity, despite coming from rival political parties: one socialist, the other conservative.

The economy helps maintain this rosy scenario. Portugal was hard hit by international economic crisis in 2009. The shock cut short the progress Portugal had been making since the 1980s when it emerged from decades of dictatorship and years of post-revolutionary turmoil. From 2009 to 2013 the economy shrank by 8%. Unemployment hit record levels. Since 2015, however, the economy has bounced back. Talented youngsters who emigrated during the lean years have been tempted home, bringing new skills and experiences that are helping renew Lisbon's creative buzz.

Textiles, shoemaking, agriculture, and other traditional mainstays are winning markets with a new focus on high-quality production. Tourism has boomed, thanks in part to security fears in rival Mediterranean destinations. Tourism revenues doubled between 2012 and 2018 to total 16 billion€.

Lisbon and Porto have thriving tech scenes, boosted by the annual Web Summit, the world's biggest geek gathering which moved from Dublin to the banks of the Tagus in 2015, bringing in 11,000 CEOs. Porto-based online fashion retailer Farfetch became the country's first unicorn startup, valued at $5.8 billion at its 2018 flotation on the New York Stock Exchange. Volkswagen recently more than doubled production at its state-of-the-art plant south of Lisbon. Unemployment has halved since 2015, but many fear the recovery remains fragile given the national debt at over 120% of economic output.

It's not just big businesses that are investing. Foreign homebuyers are fueling a real-estate boom that has brought urban renewal in downtown Lisbon and Porto, but also pushed out many local residents; vacation rentals now account for over half of housing in some historic neighborhoods.

Portugal looks toward Europe, but retains close economic, political, cultural, and personal ties with its former colonies. Brazilians make up the biggest immigrant community. Angola is a major trade partner. International networking helped Portugal's push to have former Prime Minister António Guterres appointed secretary general of the United Nations in 2017.

The country is now firmly established as a European democracy unrecognizable from the poor, backward dictatorship of the early 1970s. Back then, under over 4 decades of authoritarian rule instituted by dictator António de Oliveira Salazar, Portuguese women were forbidden to travel without the permission of husbands or fathers, homosexuality was outlawed, and poor children left school illiterate with minimal education.

Today, women make up 35% of lawmakers (compared to 27% in Canada and 20% in the United States). Of the five main political parties, two are led by women. The mainly Roman Catholic nation legalized same-sex marriage in 2010 and gave gay couples equal adoption rights in 2016. Education is free and compulsory until the age of 18, and foreign students are flocking to its increasingly well-reputed universities.

LOOKING BACK: HISTORY

ANCIENT BEGINNINGS Legend has it Lisbon was founded by the Greek hero Ulysses, somewhat off course as he voyaged home from the Trojan War. Whether that's true or not, what *is* certain is that man and beasts have lived in Portugal for several millennia. Some of Europe's most spectacular dinosaur remains were unearthed at Lourinhã up the coast from Lisbon. Rock carvings in the Côa valley are among humanity's oldest known art. In the Iron Age, Celtic tribes traded with visiting Mediterranean seafarers—Phoenicians, Greeks, and Carthaginians.

The Romans began muscling in around 200 B.C. as part of their struggle with Carthage for Mediterranean supremacy. They met tough resistance from the Lusitanians, a Celtic tribe whose leader, Viriato, is Portugal's oldest national hero. As usual, the Romans won, but they named their new province

DATELINE

- **22000–10000 B.C.** Paleolithic people create some of the world's earliest art with rock carvings of animals in the valley of the Côa River.
- **210 B.C.** Romans begin takeover of the Iberian Peninsula.
- **139 B.C.** Local Lusitanian tribes and their leader Viriato defeated by the Romans after 15 years of resistance.
- **27 B.C.** Emperor Augustus creates the province of Hispania Ulterior Lusitania, comprising much of Portugal and western Spain.
- **A.D. 409** Germanic tribes begin invasion of Roman Iberia. The Visigoths gain control of Portugal.
- **711** Muslim warriors arrive in Iberia, conquering Portugal within 7 years.
- **868** County of Portugal created in today's Minho region by the Spanish kingdom of Asturias on land reconquered from the Muslims.

Lusitania after their defeated foes. For around 600 years, they built roads and cities, kept order, and eventually introduced Christianity.

INVASIONS FROM NORTH & SOUTH As Roman power waned, the Iberian Peninsula filled with Germanic folk. The Suevi ruled northern Portugal for 150 years. They were ousted in 588 by the Visigoths, who built a Christian kingdom covering Spain and Portugal, and made Braga a major religious center.

In 711, Islamic warriors crossed from North Africa. They took less than a decade to conquer almost the entire peninsula and would remain for more than 8 centuries. At times, Portugal formed part of powerful caliphates based in Cordoba, Seville, or Marrakesh. At others, local emirs ran independent Muslim kingdoms like those in the Algarve, Lisbon, and Mértola. Arabic influences are still felt in Portugal's culture, cuisine, and language.

PORTUGAL IS BORN In the early days, resistance to Muslim rule was led by the Kingdom of Asturias in the high mountains of northern Spain. Toward the end of the 9th century, land between the Minho and Douro rivers was reconquered and given the name Portocale after a Roman-era town close to today's Porto.

Christian knights from across Europe traveled to join the fight. One was Henry of Burgundy, given the title Count of Portugal in 1092 by his father-in-law, one of the kings of León. When Henry died young, his son, Afonso Henriques, took the title, but since the boy was just 3 years old, his mother Teresa got to rule the country.

As he grew, Afonso became unhappy with his mother's politics and love life, especially her cozy relations with a leading Spanish nobleman. The youngster led a rebellion by Portuguese nobles, defeated Teresa at a battle outside Guimarães, and in 1139 declared himself King Afonso I of Portugal.

1018 Arab rulers in the Algarve declare their emirate independent of the Muslim Caliphate in southern Spain.

1139 Afonso Henriques is proclaimed the first king of Portugal after leading a rebellion against his mother and her allies in the Spanish kingdom of Leon.

1147 After a 4-month siege, Afonso I captures Lisbon from the Arabs with the aid of northern European crusaders.

1249 Afonso III completes the *Reconquista*, taking the Algarve from the Muslims.

1290 Portugal's first university formed in Coimbra.

1373 Portugal signs treaty with England, forming the world's oldest surviving diplomatic alliance.

1383 King João I defeats Castilian invaders at the Battle of Aljubarrota, securing Portugal's independence.

1415 Henry the Navigator sets up a navigation school in Sagres. Portugal conquers Ceuta in North Africa, triggers era of overseas expansion. Madeira is discovered in 1419; the Azores in 1427.

continues

Impressed by Afonso's prowess battling the Muslims and his enthusiastic church construction program, the Pope confirmed Portugal's status as an independent kingdom in 1179.

THE RECONQUISTA With the aid of Northern European crusaders, Afonso expanded his kingdom southward. Lisbon was reconquered after a 4-month siege in 1147. Fighting ebbed and flowed, but Afonso Henriques' great-grandson, Afonso III, completed the Portuguese *reconquista* in 1249, driving the Muslims out of their last stronghold in Faro.

The danger now came from the east in the shape of the powerful Spanish kingdom of Castile. In 1385, Spanish king Juan I sent an invasion force of 30,000 to back his claim to the Portuguese throne. They were defeated at the **Battle of Aljubarrota** by much-outnumbered Portuguese forces in a struggle that preserved Portuguese independence and helped forge a national identity. Legend has it a woman baker joined the fray at a decisive moment, whacking several Castilian knights with heavy wooded bread trays. French cavalry backed the Spanish while English archers joined the defenders under the Anglo-Portuguese treaty of 1373—the world's oldest surviving diplomatic alliance. Victorious King João I built the magnificent Gothic monastery at Batalha, now a UNESCO World Heritage Site, to celebrate his win.

THE AGE OF DISCOVERY With its frontiers secured, Portugal started looking overseas. In 1415, João I opened the era of maritime expansion when he captured the city of Ceuta on the coast of North Africa. João's son, Henry, fought at the battle to win Ceuta from the Moroccans. He never voyaged farther, but would change the face of world history and be forever known as Henry the Navigator.

Henry gathered sailors and scholars on the windswept southwestern tip of Europe at Sagres to brainstorm on what may lay beyond. Using new

1434	Sea captain Gil Eanes rounds Cape Bojador, opening up the coast of West Africa.
1444	Portugal initiates Atlantic slave trade when 235 African captives are landed in the Algarve.
1484	Diogo Cão explores the Congo River.
1488	Bartolomeu Dias passes the Cape of Good Hope into the Indian Ocean.
1494	Portugal and Spain divide up the New World with the Treaty of Tordesillas.
1497	Manuel I orders Portuguese Jews to convert to Catholicism or leave.
1497–98	Vasco da Gama's first voyage to India, opening up East-West trade.
1500	Pedro Álvares Cabral is the first European to reach Brazil; Corte-Real brothers sail to Newfoundland.
1506	Lisbon Massacre: hundreds murdered in anti-Jewish pogrom.
1510	Afonso de Albuquerque conquers Goa, starting Portuguese colonization in India.

navigational technology and more maneuverable boats, the Portuguese sent out probing voyages that reached Madeira Island off the coast of Africa around 1420 and the mid-Atlantic Azores 8 years later.

A breakthrough came in 1434, when captain Gil Eanes sailed around Cape Bojador, a remote Saharan promontory that had marked the limits of European knowledge of the African coast. Eanes showed the sea beyond was not boiling and monster-filled, as was believed. The way was opened to Africa and beyond.

In the years that followed, Portuguese navigators pushed down the West African coast looking for gold, ivory, spices, and slaves. By 1482, Diogo Cão reached the mouth of the Congo River. In 1488, Bartolomeu Dias sailed past Africa's southern tip: He called it the Cape of Storms, but the name was quickly changed to Cape of Good Hope to encourage further voyages. That worked. Vasco da Gama traded and raided up the coast of east Africa before reaching India in 1498. World trade would never be the same. Over the next 4 decades, Portuguese explorers moved into southeast Asia, up the coast of China, and eventually into Japan. Along the way they set up trading posts and colonies. Portugal grew rich by dominating East-West exchanges and forging the first global empire. But the Portuguese also destroyed cities reluctant to submit to their power and frequently massacred civilians.

There were setbacks. In the 1480s, King João II rejected repeated requests to finance the westward exploration plans of a Genovese seafarer named Christopher Columbus, who eventually claimed the New World for his Spanish sponsors. And King Manuel I took a dislike to veteran Portuguese sea dog Fernão de Magalhães. Piqued, he crossed the border with his plans to reach Asia by sailing west and ended up leading the Spanish fleet that became the first to sail around the world. Later historians called him Ferdinand Magellan.

1542 Inquisition installed in Portugal, resulting in the execution of hundreds accused of practicing Judaism.

1542 Portuguese seafarers reach Japan.

1578 King Sebastião I killed in disastrous invasion of Morocco, leaving Portugal without an heir.

1581 Philip II of Spain proclaimed king of Portugal, ushering in 6 decades of Spanish rule.

1640 Portuguese nobles rebel, proclaim the Duke of Bragança as João IV; a 28-year war will restore independence.

1661 Princess Catarina de Bragança marries Charles II of England, gives him Mumbai and Tangiers as wedding presents, introduces the British to tea.

1697 The discovery of gold in southern Brazil makes João V Europe's richest monarch; he builds gilded palaces, churches.

1755 Earthquake destroys Lisbon, killing up to 50,000. Prime Minister Sebastião de Melo, Marquis of Pombal, leads reconstruction efforts.

continues

The Portuguese also moved west. Six years after Spain and Portugal agreed to divide up the world with the 1492 Treaty of Tordesillas, Pedro Álvares Cabral landed in Brazil, which conveniently lies on the eastern Portuguese side of the dividing line.

A small arched building in the Algarve coastal town of Lagos has a grim past. It is reputed to be the site of Europe's oldest African slave market, first used in the early 15th century. Early Portuguese settlers in Brazil began using captured natives as slaves, but as demands of sugar plantations and gold mines grew in the 17th and 18th centuries, more and more slaves were shipped from Africa. Slavery was abolished in Portugal itself in 1761, but it continued in its African colonies until 1869 and in Brazil until 1888, 66 years after the South American country's independence. Historians estimate Portuguese vessels carried almost 6 million Africans into slavery.

INDEPENDENCE LOST & RESTORED In 1578, Portugal overreached. King Sebastião I, an impetuous 24-year-old, invaded Morocco. He was last seen charging into enemy lines at the disastrous Battle of Alcácer Quibir, where a large slice of the Portuguese nobility was wiped out. Sebastião had neglected to father an heir before he set off. An elderly great-uncle briefly took over, but he was a cardinal known as Henry the Chaste, so when he died in 1580, Portugal was left without a monarch. King Philip II of Spain decided he could do the job. His army marched in, crushed local resistance, seized a fortune in Lisbon, and extinguished Portuguese independence for the next 60 years.

The Iberian union made Philip ruler of the greatest empire the world had ever seen, controlling much of the Americas, a network of colonies in Asia and Africa, and European territories that included the Netherlands and half of Italy. Spanish rule strained Portugal's old alliance with England: The Spanish Armada sailed from Lisbon, and Sir Francis Drake raided the Portuguese coast.

1807	Napoleon invades; British troops under Duke of Wellington will finally send him back to France in 1814.
1822	Brazil declares independence.
1828–34	War of the Two Brothers between liberal Pedro IV and conservative Miguel I leaves Portugal further weakened.
1856	First railroad opens in Portugal, but the 19th century sees economic decline and political instability.
1908	Carlos I and his son Crown Prince Luís Filipe are assassinated in Lisbon.
1910	Republican revolution overturns the monarchy.
1916	Portugal enters World War I on the Allied side.
1926	After years of political chaos, a military coup topples the Republic.
1932	António de Oliveira Salazar appointed prime minister, establishing a conservative dictatorship that will last over 4 decades.
1939–45	Portugal stays out of World War II. In France, diplomat Aristides de Sousa Mendes defies orders,

By 1640, the Portuguese had had enough. While Spain was distracted fighting France in the 30 Years War, a group of nobles revolted and declared the Duke of Bragança to be King João IV. It took 28 years, but the Portuguese eventually won the War of Restoration. An obelisk in one of Lisbon's main plazas commemorates the victory.

Meanwhile a new enemy, the Dutch, had seized some of Portugal's overseas territories. Malacca and Ceylon (today's Sri Lanka) were lost. Faced with such threats, João IV strengthened Portugal's British alliance by marrying his daughter Catherine of Bragança to King Charles II. Her dowry included Tangiers and Mumbai. Perhaps more significantly for the British, she introduced them to marmalade and the habit of drinking hot water flavored with a new-fangled Asian herb they called tea. In return, the British named one of their North American settlements in her honor: Queens.

Fortunately for the Portuguese, they managed to hang on to Brazil through these turbulent times. At the end of the 17th century, huge gold deposits were found inland from São Paulo. The gold rush made King João V the richest monarch in Europe. He used it to build the vast palace at Mafra and to line baroque churches up and down the country with glimmering gilt carvings.

DISASTER & DECLINE On All Saints' Day in 1755, churches were packed when Lisbon was struck by a great earthquake. The tremor was followed by a tsunami and raging fire. Much of the city was destroyed and up to 50,000 people are believed to have died. Reconstruction was led by Prime Minister Sebastião José de Carvalho e Melo, later Marquis of Pombal. He laid out Lisbon's downtown, or Baixa, in the grid pattern of sturdy, four-story buildings that remains today, although the Gothic ruins of the Carmo Convent were left overlooking the city as reminder of the quake's destructive force.

saving thousands of Jews by issuing visas to neutral Portugal.

1961 Insurgent attacks in Angola start 14 years of colonial war in Portugal's African empire; Indian army drives Portugal out of Goa.

1974 Almost bloodless revolution led by junior army officers topples the dictatorship.

1975 Portugal grants independence to five African colonies; brings home up to a million refugees; Indonesia invades the newly independent territory of East Timor.

1976 After a power struggle with leftist radicals, General António Ramalho Eanes is elected president, steers Portugal toward pro-Western path.

1980 Center-right Prime Minister Francisco de Sá Carneiro is killed in mysterious air crash.

1986 Portugal joins the European Union.

1987 Center-right Social Democratic Party under Prime Minister Aníbal Cavaco Silva wins electoral landslide.

continues

Pombal also battled to modernize the country. He curbed the powers of the Inquisition and expelled the Jesuit order. Foreign experts were brought in to expand industry and agriculture. Education and the military were reorganized.

Still, Portugal's days as a great power were already long gone when French troops marched in as part of Napoleon's grand design for European domination. The French met little resistance and the royal family fled to Rio de Janeiro. Harsh French rule, however, saw uprisings in Spain and Portugal. Eventually Portugal's old ally was able to land troops in support, and after a long campaign, the Duke of Wellington led a combined British and Portuguese army that drove Napoleon's forces back to France in 1814.

Portugal was much weakened. The decline was compounded when Brazil declared independence in 1822 and civil war broke out in the 1830s between the liberal King Pedro IV (also Emperor Pedro I of Brazil) and his conservative brother, Miguel I.

As Europe pushed ahead with industrialization in the 19th century, Portugal fell further behind, dogged by political instability and slipping into economic backwardness. Government debt mounted, pushing the state toward bankruptcy.

Unrest grew. In 1908, King Carlos I and his oldest son were assassinated in Lisbon's Praça do Comércio. Two years later, Lisbon erupted in revolution, the monarchy was overthrown, and the last king, Manuel II, left for exile in London.

The change of regime did little to ease Portugal's economic woes or political tensions. Over the next 16 years, there were no less than 49 governments. Portugal entered World War I in 1916 on the side of its old ally, Britain. Around 8,000 soldiers were killed fighting the Germans in France and Africa. Instability continued until a military coup in 1926 put an end to the first Republic.

1998 Millions flock to Lisbon for the EXPO '98 World's Fair; economic growth peaks at over 7%.

1999 Portugal becomes founder member of euro currency bloc; Portugal's last overseas territory, Macau, handed back to China after 442 years.

2004 Prime Minister José Manuel Barroso appointed President of the European Commission.

2011 Hit hard by euro-zone debt crisis, Portugal requests $86 billion IMF-EU bailout; prolonged recession, record unemployment.

2014 Banco Espírito Santo, Portugal's second-largest bank, collapses.

2015 Left wins narrow election victory; minority Socialist government takes power under Prime Minister António Costa, on pledge to roll back austerity.

2016 Cristiano Ronaldo leads Portugal to victory in Euro 2016 soccer championship, country goes wild; former Prime Minister António Guterres appointed U.N. Secretary General; Web Summit, world's largest tech fest, moves to Lisbon in symbol of Portugal's economic revival.

2017 Wildfires ravage the countryside across north and central Portugal, leaving more than 100 dead.

PEDRO & INÊS: A MEDIEVAL love story

Centuries before Shakespeare gave us Romeo and Juliet, Portugal was gripped by its own tale of star-crossed lovers.

Seeking Spanish alliances, King Afonso IV in 1339 married off his son and heir, Pedro, to Constance, a Castilian princess. Nineteen-year-old Pedro promptly fell in love with one of his new wife's ladies-in-waiting, a noblewoman named Inês de Castro. They began a very public affair and Inês bore Pedro three children.

King Afonso was outraged, frightened of offending the Castilians and worried about the influence of Inês' ambitious brothers. He pleaded with Pedro to break it off, then banished Inês to the Santa Clara Monastery in Coimbra. When all that failed to cool Pedro's passion, Afonso had Inês murdered. In Coimbra today, beneath the clear spring water that bubbles to the surface at the spot where she was decapitated, there's a red rock, supposedly forever stained by her blood.

Grief-stricken, Pedro revolted against his father. He captured two of the killers and personally ripped out their hearts. Pedro became king when Afonso died in 1357 and announced that he'd secretly married Inês before her death. On the day of his coronation, Pedro ordered Inês' corpse removed from its tomb, dressed in a regal gown, and crowned queen beside him. Portugal's nobles lined up to kiss the hand of the woman slain 2 years before.

The story has inspired poets, painters, and musicians from Camões to Ezra Pound. Today, Pedro and Inês lie side by side in ornate tombs within the great medieval monastery at Alcobaça.

DICTATORSHIP & DEMOCRACY The junta appointed António de Oliveira Salazar as finance minister in 1928. He became the dominant figure in Portugal's 20th-century history, establishing a dictatorship that ruled with an iron hand for over 4 decades. Prime minister from 1932, Salazar constructed a Fascist-inspired regime, the *Estado Novo,* or New State. He brought some order to the economy and managed to keep Portugal neutral during World War II. Dissent was suppressed and censorship strict. A secret police force—the PIDE—spread fear; opponents were jailed or worse.

In 1961, the regime was shaken by an Indian invasion of Goa, Daman, and Diu, Portugal's last colonies in South Asia. That same year, pro-independence forces launched attacks in Angola, starting a war across Portugal's African empire. Salazar struck back, dispatching ever more conscripts to fight rebel movements in Angola, Mozambique, and Guinea-Bissau. Proportionally, Portugal suffered more casualties in the colonial wars than the U.S. in Vietnam. The fighting drained the economy and left Portugal internationally isolated. Hundreds of thousands of Portuguese emigrants fled poverty, oppression, and conscription, mostly to France, Switzerland, and Luxembourg.

Salazar suffered a stroke in 1968 and died 2 years later, but the regime limped on. On April 25, 1974, a group of war-weary officers staged a coup and the people of Lisbon rose up to support the troops. Flower sellers in Rossio square handed out spring blooms to the young soldiers and sailors, so the

FOUR NAVIGATORS WHO CHANGED world maps

From 1415 to 1580, Portuguese explorers opened up the world for Europe, discovering new routes to Africa, Asia, and the Americas. They created a global empire and redrew world maps.

Bartolomeo Dias (ca. 1450–1500) was 38 and from a family of navigators when he led an expedition of three boats down the coast of West Africa in 1487. He failed in his mission to find the mythical Christian kingdom of Prester John, but became the first European to sail around the southern tip of Africa into the Indian Ocean. Dias was killed in a shipwreck off the Cape of Good Hope in 1500, while serving with Pedro Álvares Cabral on the expedition that reached Brazil.

Vasco da Gama (ca. 1460–1524) wasn't the first European to explore India—wealthy Europeans had been spicing their food with its cinnamon, pepper, and nutmeg for centuries—but the trade was controlled by price-hiking Venetian, Turkish, and Arab middlemen. By discovering the sea route in 1498, da Gama opened up direct trade between Europe and Asia. His adventures are celebrated in Portugal's national epic, *Os Lusíadas*, by swashbuckling 16th-century poet Luís de Camões. The two men are buried near each other in Lisbon's Jerónimos monastery. Da Gama died of malaria in 1524 in Kochi on his third voyage to India. Western Europe's longest bridge, an Indian seaport, and a leading Brazilian soccer club bear his name.

Brazil was first reached by accident in 1500, when the fleet of 13 ships commanded by **Pedro Álvares Cabral** (ca. 1467–1520) sailed too far west while heading down the coast of Africa on the new route opened by da Gama. At least that's the official story. Some believe the Portuguese already knew about Brazil but kept it quiet until they had concluded the 1492 Treaty of Tordesillas with Spain to divide the world along a line halfway between Portugal's Cape Verde outpost and the newly discovered Spanish territories in the Caribbean. Brazil was clearly in the Portuguese sphere. Cabral didn't stay long, but sailed on to Africa and India, becoming the first man to visit four continents. His birthplace in the pretty village of Belmonte and tomb in Santarém are much visited by Brazilian travelers.

In 1519, **Fernão de Magalhães** (ca. 1480–1521) was a 39-year-old veteran of the Portuguese Discoveries. He'd served 8 years in India, fighting against Turks, Arabs, and Indian states. He played a key role in the capture of Malacca, a hub for Portuguese power in southeast Asia, and was wounded at the siege of Azemmour in Morocco. Despite all this service, he managed to annoy King Manuel I. There were rumors he went AWOL, had rustled cattle, and engaged in shady deals with the Moroccans. Unable to get a ship in Lisbon, he went to Spain, where his stories of Spice Island riches convinced Emperor Charles V to send him on a mission to reach Asia by sailing west—avoiding the Portuguese-controlled eastern routes. Now known as Ferdinand Magellan, he led the fleet into the Pacific as far as the Philippines, where he was speared to death in a battle with local warriors. What was left of the expedition sailed on. Only one of the five ships made it back to Spain, the first to sail around the globe. In 2019, the 500th anniversary of his voyage was marked by a brief tiff between Portugal and Spain over which country can claim the glory of his legacy.

uprising was immortalized as the "Carnation Revolution." Censorship was lifted, exiles returned, and political prisoners were released to joyous scenes.

The revolutionaries, however, faced enormous difficulties. The wars were ended and independence hastily granted to the African colonies. Portugal then had to organize the evacuation and integration of a million refugees fleeing the new nations. Investors retreated as radical leftists ordered the nationalization of banks, industry, and farmland. For a while the country looked like it would veer toward communism.

Then, in 1976, the first presidential elections brought a moderate, General António Ramalho Eanes, to office. Socialist Party leader Mário Soares was elected prime minister the same year. Together they steered Portugal on a pro-Western course. It remained a loyal NATO ally and joined the European Union along with Spain in 1986. The previous year, Aníbal Cavaco Silva, leader of the center-right Social Democratic Party, won a landslide election on a pledge to free up the economy. The combined impact of EU membership and stable, business-friendly government led to an economic boom and rapid modernization. In 1999, Portugal handed Macau back to China, ending almost 600 years of overseas empire. Women's rights made giant strides. The successful hosting of the EXPO '98 World's Fair in Lisbon symbolized Portugal's emergence as a successful European democracy.

However, problems lay ahead. The rise of China and the EU's inclusion of new members from Eastern Europe exposed the Portuguese economy to competition it was ill-equipped to handle. The global financial crisis of 2008 hit hard. As the economy tanked and debt soared, the government was forced in 2011 to seek a bailout from the EU and International Monetary Fund to stave off bankruptcy. In exchange for a 78€-billion rescue package, creditors demanded tough measures to bring state finances under control. The economy stabilized, but at a high cost in unemployment, cuts to public services, and increased poverty. After elections in November 2015, a new Socialist government was narrowly elected under Prime Minister António Costa, promising to ease up on austerity.

In July 2016, spirits received an enormous boost from the victory of Portugal's national soccer team in the European championships. The first major success for a soccer-crazy nation triggered country-wide celebrations.

The last few years have seen an economic recovery fueled in a large part by tourism, which has taken off big time. An improved international financial climate has boosted exports and a thriving start-up scene has seen the emergence of strong new tech companies such as online fashion retailer Farfetch, which was valued at $5.8 billion when it was floated on the New York Stock Exchange in 2018. Symbolizing the economic comeback is the 2016 decision of Web Summit, the world's biggest tech event to make Lisbon its home.

Clouding the upbeat feeling were the forest fires that swept across the country in 2017, killing more than 100 people and leaving the country traumatized. Despite criticism of government handling of the fires, Costa's left-of-center government won big victories in local elections in 2017 and European Parliament elections in 2019.

PORTUGAL'S jewish heritage

In 1497, King Manuel I, the monarch behind the golden age of Portugal's Discoveries, married a Spanish princess, a political move designed to improve relations with the powerful neighbor. Spain's condition: Portugal had to get rid of its thriving Jewish community, as Spain had done 5 years before. Manuel agreed, ordering all Jews to convert to Catholicism or leave. Many fled, finding refuge in the Ottoman Empire, North Africa, France, and the Netherlands, where they built Amsterdam's splendid Portuguese Synagogue. Others stayed and became "New Christians."

They were still not safe. In 1506, a riot over Easter led to the murder of up to 2,000 *conversos* in what became known as the Lisbon Massacre. Manuel I had some of the perpetrators executed, but 30 years later the state institutionalized persecution when it set up a Portuguese branch of the Inquisition, tasked with hunting down heretics—especially converts suspected of maintaining Jewish practices in secret. The Inquisition ordered almost 1,200 burned at the stake over the next 2 centuries and was only abolished in 1821. Nevertheless, some crypto-Jews managed to cling to their faith. A community in the remote village of Belmonte practiced in secret into the 1980s. There is now a small but open community there with their own rabbi.

Jews began returning to a more tolerant Portugal in the 19th century. During World War II, neutral Portugal became a haven for many fleeing the Nazis. Although dictator António Oliveira Salazar tried to prevent Jewish refugees arriving in 1940 as Hitler's troops marched into France, the Portuguese consul in Bordeaux, Aristides de Sousa Mendes, defied orders and handed out visas, saving up to 30,000 lives. Salazar ruined his career and plunged his family into poverty, but Sousa Mendes is today regarded as a national hero.

President Mário Soares formally asked for forgiveness for past persecution in 1989. In 2015, Portugal's parliament passed a law offering citizenship to the descendants of Jews expelled from the country. Today there are small Jewish communities, mostly in Lisbon, Porto, and Madeira Island, but recent genetic studies suggest that up to 20% of Portugal's population may have Jewish ancestry.

ART & ARCHITECTURE

From prehistoric carvings to world-class contemporary buildings, Portugal is packed with art and architecture that reflect the country's history and unique style. A country the size of Maine, it has 14 UNESCO World Heritage Sites—four more than the entire United States.

ANCIENT BEGINNINGS Discovered in the 1990s and saved from destruction during a dam-building project, the outdoor rock carvings in the **Côa valley** form some of humanity's oldest art. The oldest of the enigmatic animal depictions date back to 22000 B.C. A state-of-the-art hilltop museum explains the site and arranges visits to the rocks.

Portugal is dotted with standing stones and prehistoric tombs. The most complete include the **Almendres Cromlech,** made up of circles of almost 100 menhirs near Évora that dates back to 6000 B.C., and the **Great Dolmen of Comenda da Igreja,** a Stone-Age burial site outside Montemor-o-Novo.

Northern Portugal contains some of Europe's best-preserved remains of fortified hilltop villages built by ancient Celts. Those of **Citânia de Briteiros** near Guimarães and **Monte Mozinho** close to Penafiel are well worth a visit.

FROM ROMAN TO ROMANESQUE During 600 years of occupation, the Romans built cities, roads, and villas across the country. To get an idea of life in Roman Portugal, visit **Conímbriga,** 16km (10 miles) south of Coimbra, where the remains of a complete settlement have been excavated complete with baths, forum, theater, and mosaic-decorated private homes. Other Roman monuments include the 1st-century **Temple de Diana** in Évora, a bridge constructed during the reign of Emperor Trajan that's still used in **Chaves,** and the well-preserved remains of ancient Coimbra beneath the **Museu Machado de Castro.**

Few physical traces remain of the Germanic peoples who flowed in after the Romans, although the **Chapel of São Frutuoso** in Braga is of Visigoth origin. The pretty town of **Mertola** in the Alentejo region was briefly the capital of an Arab kingdom. Its mosque was converted into the parish church but still offers the best example of Islamic architecture in Portugal. Several medieval castles also bear witness to Portugal's Muslim past, notably that in **Silves** and the hilltop **Castelo dos Mouros** in Sintra.

As the *reconquista* gathered pace in the 10th century, churches in the European Romanesque style sprang up across northern Portugal. The cathedrals of Braga and Lisbon date from this time, but **Sé Velha** in Coimbra is where the Romanesque style is at its purest, with fewer later additions. The **Rates Monastery** near Póvoa de Varzim is one of the oldest Romanesque buildings. Others can be discovered along the **Romanesque Route** (*Rota do Românico*) linking over 50 churches and other monuments in the hills east of Porto. The granite **Domus Municipalis** (municipal house) in Bragança is a rare example of civic architecture to survive from the period.

Portugal's most remarkable Romanesque building forms the core of the **Convent of Christ** in Tomar. The circular 12th-century church was built by the Knights Templar who had their base here. They copied it from the ancient churches in Jerusalem that the knights had visited during the Crusades. The whole magnificent complex, which includes later medieval and Renaissance additions, is a UNESCO World Heritage Site.

THE GOTHIC ERA The history of the Gothic style in Portugal is bookended by two fabulous monasteries, built just 25km (14 miles) apart. **Alcobaça Monastery** was built in the 12th century, its white stone arches following the pure, unadorned style imported from France by the Cistercian order of monks. Although the church's exterior was significantly modified in the baroque era, the interior remains a hugely atmospheric medieval monument. Constructed 2 centuries later to celebrate a famous victory over invading Spaniards, **Batalha Monastery** is a flamboyant example of the ornate late

Gothic style, bristling with statues, spires, and richly decorated arches. Lit by the setting sun, its limestone facade glows golden. Both monasteries are now UNESCO Sites.

Between these two masterpieces, major Gothic churches were built all around the country; the **Church of São Francisco** in Porto, **Évora Cathedral,** and the ruined **Carmo** convent in Lisbon are among the best. However, **Santarém,** high on the north bank of the Tagus River, holds the title "capital of Gothic," thanks to the sheer number of medieval churches there.

PORTUGAL'S UNIQUE MANUELINE STYLE Named for King Manuel I, the monarch behind Portugal's Era of Discoveries, the Manueline style is unique to Portugal. It combines elements of medieval Gothic and the new ideas of the Renaissance, but adds elements inspired by Portugal's adventures on the high seas. Maritime motives become an integral part of the architecture—shells, ropes, branches of coral, and navigational instruments, as well as exotic touches brought back from distant lands.

Best-known among the Manueline monuments are the iconic **Torre de Belém** fortress guarding the Tagus River in Lisbon's Belém neighborhood and the neighboring **Jerónimos Monastery,** a spectacular building containing the tombs of explorer Vasco da Gama, poets Luís de Camões and Fernando Pessoa, as well as King Manuel himself.

Other fine examples of the Manueline style can be found in Tomar's Convent of Christ, the **Royal Palace** in Sintra, and the **Monastery of Jesus** in Setúbal.

The Discoveries period also saw a flowering of Portuguese painting. The country's most cherished artwork is **Nuno Gonçalves**' giant *Panels of Saint Vincent,* which contains portraits of 60 people, a cross-section of 15th-century society, from nobility (including Henry the Navigator) to friars and fishermen. It alone justifies a visit to Lisbon's Museu Nacional de Arte Antiga.

Another renowned painter of the Discoveries period is **Grão Vasco,** best known for his sumptuous religious works. Many are displayed in the excellent Grão Vasco museum in his hometown of Viseu.

BAROQUE GOLD The drama and exuberance of the baroque style were embraced across the Catholic world in response to austere Protestant values. Nowhere was this truer than in Portugal and its empire, where the wealth pouring in from Brazilian gold fields in the 17th and 18th centuries fueled a spending spree on ornate churches and palaces.

Two specifically Portuguese art forms thrived in this period: *talha dourada* (wood carving gilded with gold leaf), and the glazed ceramic tiles known as *azulejos*. The combination of the intricately carved altars gleaming with gold and the soft blue-and-white tiles make church interiors of this period uniquely beautiful. Wonderful examples can be found in the **São Roque** church in Lisbon, the church of **Santa Clara** in Porto, or the tiny church of **São Lourenço de Almancil** in the Algarve. Elsewhere, baroque architects demand an upward gaze: The 75-meter (246-ft.) tower of the **Clérigos** church is a symbol of the city of Porto, while Braga and Lamego both have hilltop churches reached by monumental stairways.

A RICH handicraft tradition

Aside from high art, Portugal retains a wealth of regional handicraft traditions. The small town of **Arraiolos** in the Alentejo is famed for carpets, woven from local wool into designs that reflect the flowers of the region. Hand-painted pottery from **Coimbra** is refined and colorful, based on designs from the 15th and 16th centuries. Artists around **Barcelos** in the Minho have always produced ceramic figures: demons, saints, and the rooster, which has become a national symbol. Delicate golden filigree jewelry is a specialty of **Viana do Castelo,** while **Castelo Branco** is famed for silk embroidery and **Madeira** for lacework. Many countries produce decorated ceramic tiles, but in few places are they so central to the folk-art tradition as *azulejos* are to Portugal. They appear on buildings ranging from ancient churches to brand-new subway stations. Even the sidewalks can be works of art. The *calçada portuguesa* technique uses small cubes of white and black limestone to make patterned pavements that are found around Lisbon and other Portuguese cities—Rossio square in the heart of the capital is one fine example.

Secular art also thrived in the baroque era, including the **Queluz Royal Palace,** the **Palácio de Mateus** vila near Vila Real, and the splendid **Joanina Library** in Coimbra University. Putting all the others into shade, however, is the enormous **Mafra Palace,** built by King João V, north of Lisbon. It covers an area larger than seven football fields, filled with sumptuous ballrooms, churches, a hospital, and a library lined with 36,000 volumes. The 4 decades of construction feature prominently in *Baltasar and Blimunda*, one of the best novels by Nobel Prize–winning author José Saramago.

Portugal's greatest sculptor emerged during this period—**Joaquim Machado de Castro** (1731–1822), whose works grace many churches and plazas, including the statue of King Jose I on horseback in the center of Lisbon's Praça do Comércio.

RECONSTRUCTION & ROMANCE After the excesses of the baroque era, the Marquis of Pombal imposed his sober-minded architectural vision after the great earthquake of 1755. The prime minister ordered the rebuilding of Lisbon's **Baixa** district in an orderly grid pattern of solid, unadorned blocks. In the Algarve, an entire town, **Vila Real de Santo António,** was laid out in this Pombaline style.

Architecture in the 19th century looked backward. Ancient Athens inspired neoclassical buildings like Lisbon's **Dona Maria National Theater** or the **São Bento palace,** which houses the parliament. Other styles looked closer to home. The sumptuous **Arab Room** in Porto's Stock Exchange is a gilded Moorish fantasy. Nostalgia for the Age of Discovery saw the development of a neo-Manueline fashion represented by Lisbon's **Rossio station,** or the delightfully romantic **Buçaco Palace,** a royal residence that's now a luxury hotel surrounded by lush forest. The Romantic movement in Portuguese architecture reached its peak with the completion in 1854 of the mountaintop

PORTUGUESE ART'S armenian connection

Lisbon's art scene owes an inestimable debt to an Armenian-born philanthropist named Calouste Gulbenkian. One of the first to appreciate the potential of Middle East oil, Gulbenkian amassed a fortune in the early 20th century.

He settled in neutral Lisbon in 1942 to escape WWII. When he died 13 years later, Gulbenkian thanked his adopted homeland by leaving much of his wealth to a foundation to promote culture, education, and science. Located in a one of Lisbon's loveliest gardens, the Gulbenkian Foundation remains a driving force behind the arts. Its concert halls offer some of the city's best classical, jazz, and world music.

The Gulbenkian Museum is a must-see attraction housing the tycoon's wonderfully diverse collection—from ancient Egyptian statuary to French Impressionist masterpieces, fine Ming vases to exquisite Persian rugs. Its collection of Fabergé jewelry is dazzling. The modern art museum at the Gulbenkian showcases Portuguese and international works from the 20th and 21st centuries.

Pena Palace in Sintra, a multicolored potpourri of styles devised by Ferdinand, the German prince married to Queen Maria II.

Industrialization was slow coming to Portugal, but building the railroads created a network of stations decorated with exquisitely painted *azulejo* tiles. The stations in Aveiro, the Douro wine town of **Pinhão,** and **São Bento** in Porto are among the prettiest. The railway also graced Porto with a magnificent iron bridge over the Douro. The **Maria Pia Bridge** (p. 347) was built in 1877 by a French engineer named Gustave Eiffel, who went on to build a certain tower in Paris. At the time, it was the world's longest single-arch bridge. Nine years later, a colleague of Eiffel's built an even longer span just next door: the double-decker **Dom Luís I Bridge.** Portugal's other great iron structure of the Industrial Age is the **Santa Justa Elevator,** a startling 13-meter (43-ft.) tower that offers vertical transportation between Lisbon's downtown and the chic shops of the Chiado district.

Despite political turmoil and economic decline, the arts flourished in the 19th century. Talented naturalist painters included **José Malhoa** (1855–1933), best known for his depictions of fado singers and boozers in Lisbon taverns, and **Columbano Bordalo Pinheiro** (1856–1929), arguably Portugal's greatest painter, whose impressionistic portraits captured intellectual life in the capital. Columbano's dandyish brother, **Rafael Bordalo Pinheiro** (1846–1905), a sculptor, created fantastical ceramic works that range from plates and bowls decorated with animal and plant motifs to comic figurines caricaturing figures of the day. His works remain hugely popular and are still produced in the factory he built in Caldas da Rainha.

20TH CENTURY The most influential figure in Portuguese modern art was **Amadeo de Souza Cardoso** (1887–1918), a daring figure who painted bold, bright canvases, flirting with cubism, futurism, and abstraction. Souza Cardoso was cut down young by the Spanish flu epidemic, but international interest in his work was revived in 2016 by a major exhibition in Paris.

Other 20th-century giants in Portuguese art include **José de Almada Negreiros** (1889–1970), a non-conformist much influenced by the Italian futurist movement; and **Maria Helena Vieira da Silva** (1908–92), who worked mostly in Paris. She was the first woman to be awarded France's Grand Prix National des Arts. Her abstract works recall Portuguese *azulejos,* endless libraries, and the winding alleys of Lisbon.

During the early years of the Salazar dictatorship, architecture was much influenced by the grandiose ideas emanating from Fascist Italy and Nazi Germany, although softened by a Portuguese touch recalling the country's medieval or maritime past. Modern extensions to **Coimbra University,** the **Monument to the Discoveries** jutting into the river at Belém, and the **Praça Francisco Sá Carneiro** in Lisbon showcase the *Estado Novo* style.

Later, the Porto School of Architecture produced a crop of designers whose cool, modernist buildings have won worldwide acclaim. **Álvaro Siza Vieira** (b. 1933) is the best known. His clean white cubic buildings grace cities around the world. Work started on the 85-year-old's first New York City skyscraper in 2019. In Portugal, his landmark buildings include the Serralves contemporary art museum in Porto and the Portuguese Pavilion in Lisbon's Parque das Nações district. **Eduardo Souto de Moura** (b. 1952) is a fellow winner of the Pritzker Prize, considered architecture's "Nobel." The soccer stadium in Braga carved into the rock walls of a quarry is among his most distinctive works.

Contrasting with the geometric purity favored by the Porto School, Lisbon architect **Tomás Taveira** (b. 1938) made an eye-catching contribution to the capital's skyline in the early 1980s with his giant Amoreiras shopping and residential center, whose oddly shaped towers in pink, black, and silver are monuments to then-trendy postmodern style.

ART TODAY The arts scene today is thriving. Contemporary works are showcased in important new galleries like the **Berardo Museum** (see p. 110) in Lisbon's Belém district, the **Serralves** (p. 343) center in Porto, and the **MAAT** museum (p. 107) that opened in the fall of 2016.

Joana Vasconcelos (b. 1971) is perhaps the contemporary artist who has gained most international recognition, after three appearances at the Venice Biennale. She uses colorful textiles, crochet, and lacework to cover and distort familiar Portuguese objects, from ceramic shellfish to a Tagus riverboat.

Paula Rego (b. 1935) divides her time between London and Cascais, where there's a museum designed by Souto de Moura is dedicated to her work. Her paintings often reflect a sinister, fairytale world populated by powerful, muscular women.

Lately, Lisbon has gained a reputation as a center of graffiti art, including towering works covering abandoned apartment blocks that greet visitors on the way into town along Avenida Fontes Pereira de Melo. **Vhils** (b. 1983) is Portugal's most renowned urban artist. His haunting portraits carved into the side of buildings have sprung up around the world from San Diego to Sydney, Beijing to Bogota, as well as locations around Lisbon.

BOOKS

The ideal literary companion to a visit to Portugal is a guide by the country's only Nobel Prize in Literature winner, José Saramago. In 1979, Saramago set out on a meandering drive from north to south seeking the soul of his homeland's history and culture. His ***Journey to Portugal*** is an intimate, highly personal portrait that reaches into the lives of the Portuguese people.

For an up-to-date survey, ***The Portuguese: A Modern History*** by the Associated Press Lisbon correspondent Barry Hatton looks at how history has shaped today's Portugal. The country's love of soccer, the significance of fado, and the importance of good eating are all included in this excellent introduction.

History

Before his death in 2012 at the age of 92, José Hermano Saraiva was Portugal's best-known historian, a familiar face to millions thanks to his TV series on the country's past. Saraiva's ***Portugal: A Companion History*** provides a sweeping saga of the land you're about to visit.

A Concise History of Portugal by David Birmingham is a readable, short overview, while Malyn Newitt's ***Portugal in European and World History*** puts the story in the wider international context. Hatton's latest book ***Queen of the Sea*** is a highly readable history of Lisbon, packed with intriguing details, from the career of the black matador who wowed the bullrings of Spain, to the cavorting of the kings who kept harems in a Lisbon convent.

A wide range of books focuses on Portugal's Age of Discovery. ***Conquerors: How Portugal Forged the First Global Empire*** by Roger Crowley is a rip-roaring account of Portugal's expansion into the Indian Ocean, which isn't shy in portraying the brutality of the early colonial enterprise. Indian historian Sanjay Subrahmanyam's ***The Portuguese Empire in Asia*** presents an epic alternative to Eurocentric views of the Discoveries.

For gripping accounts of great voyages, try ***The Last Crusade: The Epic Voyages of Vasco Da Gama*** by Nigel Cliff, ***or Over the Edge of the World: Magellan's Terrifying Circumnavigation of the World*** by Laurence Bergreen.

Portuguese Literature

The earliest poems in the Portuguese language emerged from the troubadours of the old kingdom of Galicia, one of the Christian states fighting Muslim rule in the Iberian Peninsula. The written language was refined in the Middle Ages by the chroniclers of the royal reigns. The first great Portuguese literature emerged in the 15th century, by playwright Gil Vicente, whose works range from moral tales with a maritime theme to bawdy comedies.

Born in 1524, Luís de Camões is the towering figure in Portuguese letters and considered one of the greats of world literature, up there with Shakespeare, Dante, and Cervantes. His epic poem ***Os Lusíadas*** is a heroic retelling of the voyages of discovery. A swashbuckling one-eyed veteran of Portugal's

FIVE ESSENTIAL portuguese reads

Five of the best by Portuguese authors:

The Crime of Father Amaro by José Maria de Eça de Queirós: Written in 1875, this tale of forbidden passion between a young priest and an innocent girl in the provincial city of Leiria still has the power to shock.

The Year of the Death of Ricardo Reis by José Saramago: This deeply atmospheric book set in dictatorship Lisbon during the 1930s evokes the mysterious world of poet Fernando Pessoa.

Os Lusíadas by Luís de Camões: Portugal's national epic was written in 1572 by the seafaring poet whose statue stares down on Lisbon's Chiado district. Inspired by Homer's *Odyssey,* Camões tells a heroic tale of Portugal's voyages of discovery through the eyes of Vasco da Gama, embellished by encounters with giants, seductive nymphs, and Greek gods.

The Book of Disquiet by Fernando Pessoa: This posthumously published literary oddity has become a cult favorite. A meandering reflection on life and Lisbon, it is at turns funny and sad. It was chosen as one of the 100 greatest books ever in a survey of world authors.

The Return by Dulce Maria Cardoso: Set in 1975, this novel by one of Portugal's best current writers tells of the trauma of the *retornados,* the up to one million Portuguese who fled Angola and other newly independent African nations at the end of Portugal's colonial wars. It was a 2016 PEN Award winner for translated books.

overseas adventures, Camões is a national hero whose death is commemorated on June 10 as the national holiday.

The Portuguese novel came of age in the 19th century, and the greatest author of the age was José Maria de Eça de Queirós. A diplomat, his novels about Portuguese society blend biting satire with often dark tragedy dealing with controversial themes like incest, adultery, and clerical abuse. ***The Maias*** and ***The Crime of Father Amaro*** are his most powerful novels.

Poet Fernando Pessoa is a unique figure. Considered a founder of modernist literature, his writings are mystical and deeply philosophical, but struck a chord with his compatriots, who rate him second only to Camões among their literary greats. ***A Little Larger Than the Entire Universe: Selected Poems*** gives a selection of his works translated into English.

Among modern writers, José Saramago stands out as the Portuguese language's only winner of the Nobel Prize for Literature. A lifelong Communist who had a sometimes testy relationship with the authorities, he is widely revered. When he died in 2010, 20,000 attended his funeral. Saramago's novels like ***The Elephant's Journey*** and ***Baltasar and Blimunda*** delve into Portuguese history. ***Blindness*** and ***The Double*** are dark parables of modern life.

Successful contemporary works available in English include David Machado's ***The Shelf Life of Happiness,*** a heartwarming tale set in the recession-hit 2000s; ***What Can I Do When Everything's On Fire?*** by veteran intellectual António Lobo Antunes; and ***In Your Hands,*** a saga covering the lives of three generations of Portuguese women by Inês Pedrosa.

Foreign Fiction Set in Portugal

Lisbon's curious position in World War II as a neutral port filled with refugees and spies has inspired many novels. The best is ***The Night in Lisbon*** by the German anti-Nazi writer Erich Maria Remarque, who was himself a refugee. ***Estoril*** by Dejan Tiago-Stankovic is set in the same period and tells the story of a Serbian spy believed to be the real-life model for James Bond.

Italian author Antonio Tabucchi, a frequent Nobel Prize contender, had a long love affair with Portugal. His novel ***Pereira Declares*** is a story of intrigue set in 1930s Lisbon. Another classic with a Lisbon setting is ***Confessions of Felix Krull,*** about a visiting con artist by German Nobel-winner Thomas Mann, who unfortunately died before writing the ending.

Recent books include ***Alentejo Blue,*** a series of tales set in the rural south by award-winning British writer Monica Ali; ***The Last Kabbalist of Lisbon,*** a best-seller by Richard Zimmer focusing on a Jewish family during the persecutions of the 16th century; and ***Like a Fading Shadow,*** a fictionalized account of James Earl Ray's attempt to hide from American justice in Lisbon after the murder of Martin Luther King, written by Spanish novelist Antonio Muñoz Molina.

FOOD & DRINK

The recent international discovery of Portugal's healthy and delicious cuisine has triggered a sudden blooming of cookbooks and food guides. Manhattan-based culinary superstar George Mendes has penned a mouthwateringly beautiful tribute to the cooking of his homeland in ***My Portugal.*** His near namesake Nuno Mendes—a giant in London's restaurant scene—has produced a recipe-packed homage to his hometown in ***My Lisbon. Food of Portugal*** by Jean Anderson is an excellent introduction for anybody wanting to cook up a taste of the country, while Maria de Lourdes Modesto's encyclopedic ***Traditional Portuguese Cooking*** is a sacred text in many Portuguese kitchens.

Combining recipes with travelogue are ***Eat Portugal*** by Célia Pedroso and Lucy Pepper, and ***The Portuguese Travel Cookbook*** by food blogger Nelson Cavalheiro.

For the secrets of Portugal's most complex tipples, try Richard Mayson's ***Port and the Douro,*** and ***Madeira: The Mid-Atlantic Wine*** by Alex Liddell.

MUSIC

Portugal's most distinctive music is **fado,** the urban blues of Lisbon that comes close to encapsulating the nation's soul. Fado traditionally involves a singer, male or female, accompanied by two guitarists, one playing the familiar classical guitar, called a *viola* in Portuguese, the other plucking the unique, tear-shaped *guitarra Portuguesa*. With 12 steel strings, the Portuguese guitar can, in the right hands, produce an amazing range of sound.

The word "fado" means "fate." Although not all fado songs are melancholic, the music is deeply associated with *saudade,* an untranslatable word that implies longing for lost loves and distant homelands. It is a sentiment ingrained in the national character since the days when long sea voyages and successive waves of emigration carried the Portuguese to the far corners of the globe.

Fado has its roots in the bars and bordellos of Lisbon's docklands and the tightly packed old neighborhoods of Alfama and Mouraria. **Maria Severa,** the earliest fado great, was a renowned lady of the night in early-19th-century Lisbon. The music's disreputable origins are summed up in the painting *O Fado* by José Malhoa, on show in Lisbon's Fado Museum.

Early in the 20th century, fado went mainstream. Although some maintained a bohemian edge, fado singers moved from backstreet bars to boulevard theaters, radio studios, and movie sets. Many *casas de fado*—fado houses—became chic restaurants. The Salazar dictatorship sought to sanitize fado, censoring lyrics and seeking to promote conservative values though the music.

Towering above all this was **Amália Rodrigues,** fado's biggest name. From a poor background, she began singing as a teenager in the 1930s and became fado's first global star. She sang lyrics penned by the nation's greatest poets and popularized the song "April in Portugal," later covered by the likes of Louis Armstrong, Bing Crosby, and Eartha Kitt.

Boosted by radio, cinema, and later TV, fado singers became household names. When Amália died in 1999, the government declared 3 days of national mourning. The crowds who packed Lisbon streets for her funeral were calculated in the hundreds of thousands. The emotion shown for the diva's passing sparked a revival of interest in fado and thrust a new generation of singers into the limelight.

Young singers like **Mariza, Camané,** and **Ana Moura**—who has sung with the Rolling Stones—have gone on to international success. Suddenly fado is sexy again. Alongside the posh, sometimes stuffy fado houses, new hip venues have sprung up. Uninhibited new stars are experimenting, adding piano, bass, and saxophone to the traditional guitars, blending elements of jazz, tango, and bossa nova. Current sensations include **Carminho, Aldina Duarte, Raquel Tavares,** and the exuberant **Gisela João,** hailed by some as the best voice since Amália.

The university city of Coimbra (see p. 294) has its own distinctive form of fado. There, it's traditionally sung only by men, and the songs tend to have a lighter, more romantic feel, dating back to the days when lovesick students would sing nocturnal serenades beneath the windows of their latest flames.

A number of Portuguese pop bands have used fado and other folk elements to create a modern sound rooted in tradition. The most successful was **Madredeus,** whose haunting sound has won them an international following.

Portugal's musical traditions go way beyond fado. From the powerful male-voice choirs formed by miners and farm workers in the southern Alentejo to the Celtic-tinged bagpipe music of the north, each region has a distinctive sound.

Singer-songwriters rooted in the folk tradition, but also taking in outside influences from French chanson to American protest songs, evolved in the 1960s and 1970s to produce a highly politicized sound in opposition to the long dictatorship. The major figure was **José "Zeca" Afonso,** whose songs range from biting political satire to lyrical evocations of the Portuguese countryside. When revolutionary soldiers seized the state radio station in the early hours of April 25, 1974, they played his banned song "Grândola, Vila Morena" over the airways as a signal to comrades to move to the next phase of the uprising that restored democracy. Zeca died in 1987, but other veterans of that era, like **Sérgio Godinho, Vitorino,** and **Júlio Pereira,** remain popular performers.

Portuguese jazz has its spiritual home in Lisbon's Hot Club de Portugal, an archetypal basement dive that's been bopping since the 1940s. Portuguese jazz musicians who have made international splashes include vocalist **Maria João** and pianist **Mário Laginha.** In 2017, jazz singer **Salvador Sobral** became a national hero when he became Portugal's first winner of the Eurovision Song Festival, crooning a soulful ballad in complete contrast to the event's usual kitsch offerings.

Portugal's close ties with its former colonies mean that Lisbon nights echo with the sounds of Brazilian samba, Cape Verdean mornas, and Angola's sensual kizomba music. The riverside B.Leza club is a legendary venue for live African music. Over the past decade, **Buraka Som Sistema,** a group from Lisbon's northern suburbs, has found international success with its blend of techno beats and Angolan rhythms.

For classical music, the Lisbon-based **Gulbenkian Orchestra** is tops. In the north, Porto's Casa da Música is a major venue. Lisbon's gilded 18th-century São Carlos theater is the premier opera venue, while the modern Teatro Camões is home to the prestigious National Ballet Company.

A final word should go to **pimba,** a style scorned by city cool kids but wildly popular at rural festivals. It's strangely similar to Germany's Schlager music, involving singers belting out saucily suggestive up-tempo dance numbers backed by electric organ, guitar, and accordion. Performers tend to be curvaceous blondes or middle-aged guys flanked by scantily clad dancing girls.

FILM

The good news for film fans heading to Portugal is that theaters there run movies in the original language with subtitles, rather than dubbing them. That means English-speakers are free to enjoy the latest Anglophone flicks in a mega-mall multiplex, in Lisbon's cool *Cinemateca* movie museum, or in the capital's few intimate arthouse theaters.

Portugal's own movie industry was long dominated by one man, **Manoel de Oliveira,** who died in 2015 at the age of 106 as the world's oldest working director. Oliveira's often slow-moving and melancholic adaptations of literary works were loved by critics, less so by mass audiences. The most accessible of his movies is his first, *Aniki-Bóbó,* a tale of street urchins in 1940s Porto.

Two of the best recent films that have been hits with both critics and audiences have been *Os Maias,* **João Botelho's** adaptation of the great 19th-century novel, and *The Gilded Cage,* a heartwarming comedy about Portuguese emigrants in Paris, by the promising young actor/director **Ruben Alves.**

THE LAY OF THE LAND

3

Portugal is a roughly drawn rectangle on Europe's southwestern seaboard. It's about 550km (350 miles) from north to south, 200km (110 miles) from east to west. To the north and east it's bordered by Spain. On the south and west it's bathed by the Atlantic Ocean. There are two Atlantic island groups: Madeira lying off the coast of Morocco; and the nine Azores islands, a third of the way to Atlantic City.

As a general rule, the landscape north of the River Tagus is hilly and often rugged, while the south has softly rolling plains. Over 80% of Portugal's 10.5 million people live in districts bordering the ocean, while the interior is thinly populated.

Within that general picture, regions vary greatly. The **Algarve** occupies the southern coastal strip. Separated from the rest of the country by low forested hills, it basks in a Mediterranean-type climate that facilitates the growth of orange, lemon, fig, and almond trees and draws tourists to its sheltered, south-facing beaches.

Above it lays the **Alentejo,** a region that covers a third of the country. Here the endless, sun-soaked grasslands bring to mind the African savannah, but with the baobabs replaced with umbrella pine, cork oak, and olive trees, and, instead of herds of antelope, flocks of sheep or black pigs rooting around for acorns. The Alentejo's whitewashed towns and villages are among the country's most beautiful, and the coast here is fringed with wild surfing beaches. Even in the Alentejo there are occasional hill ranges, like the Serra de Grândola overlooking the coast or the Serra de São Mamede topped by the stunning fortified town of Marvão overlooking the Spanish border.

The River Tagus, known in Portugal as the Tejo, cuts the country in half. "Alentejo" means "beyond the Tagus." The river rises deep in Spain and reaches the Atlantic just downstream of Lisbon. East of the capital, the flat Tagus valley is characteristic of the **Ribatejo** region. This is cattle country. Local festivals feature bullfights and displays of horsemanship by *campinos,* the local cowboys, sporting red vests and green tasseled caps. Much of the old province of Estremadura, along the coast north of Lisbon, has been rebranded as the **Oeste** (West). It features a gentle landscape filled with vineyards, apple and pear orchards, and hills topped with stubby white windmills. The hills of Sintra create a cool, lush microclimate that's resulted in the growth of thick rainforest, while the Arrábida range south of Lisbon has Mediterranean weather and overlooks some of the country's best beaches.

The **Beiras** form a vast region covering the center of the country. The coastal strip (Beira Litoral) is cultivated and low lying, including the marshlands of the Aveiro lagoon and the Bairrada wine region, but the Beira Interior is made up of austere landscapes of boulder-strewn plateaus and bare mountains. The mainland's highest peaks are in the Serra da Estrella, reaching almost 2,000m (6,500 ft.). The land here has an epic grandeur. Rough-hewn villages and the few cities preserve a hearty cuisine and age-old handicraft traditions. Cutting a green swath through the region is the valley of the River Mondego, the longest wholly Portuguese river.

The far north is made up of two contrasting regions. To the northwest, the **Minho** is green, its hills covered with trellised vineyards and dissected by fast-flowing rivers. It's well populated, a center for the textile and footwear industries. Farther east lies remote **Trás-os-Montes,** a region whose name means "beyond the mountains." Here, life can be harsh; locals sum up the climate as "nine months of winter, three months of hell." The high plains are bare and empty, but starkly beautiful. Girdling the north, the River Douro flows from the Spanish border to the Atlantic near Porto. Farthest east it forms the frontier and cuts a deep canyon where vultures and eagles soar. Downstream, its banks are cultivated to grow grapes, creating perhaps the world's most beautiful wine region.

Finally, the **Azores** islands are nine specks of grass-covered volcanic rock rising from the Atlantic, containing Portugal's highest mountain (the astounding volcano of Pico) and a unique variety of landscapes and culture. Subtropical **Madeira** enjoys a climate of year-round spring. Its mountainous interior and thick forests are a paradise for hikers.

WHEN TO GO

Summer is the most popular season, when it can seem that half of Europe is heading to Portugal's beaches. July and August are the hottest, most expensive, and most crowded months in the Algarve and other beach destinations. Although Atlantic breezes generally keep the coast relatively cool, if you are planning to tour in the interior, it can get seriously hot—topping 100°F (40°C). Humidity, however, is usually low. You get better deals if you go in September or June, when the weather is still good.

Portugal's climate is similar to California's. Lisbon is Europe's sunniest capital, and along the coast the country enjoys mild winters and warm summers. Average temperatures range from 77°F (25°C) in summer to about 58°F (14°C) in winter. Spring can be a great time to visit, when wildflowers paint Algarve clifftops, Alentejo pastures, and northern hillsides with color. Temperatures are more extreme inland. Winters in the northern hills can be bitter, snowfall is common, and there is some (limited) skiing in the Serra da Estrela

Lisbon's Average Daytime Temperature (°F & °C) & Monthly Rainfall (Inches)

	JAN	FEB	MAR	APR	MAY	JUNE	JULY	AUG	SEPT	OCT	NOV	DEC
Temp. (°F)	57	59	63	67	71	77	81	82	79	72	63	58
Temp. (°C)	14	15	17	19	22	25	27	28	26	22	17	14
Rainfall	4.3	3.0	4.2	2.1	1.7	0.6	0.1	0.2	1.3	2.4	3.7	4.1

mountains. Winter can also bring delights. In February, groves of almond trees are covered in snow-white blossoms in Trás-os-Montes and parts of the Algarve. Cool but sunny winter days can be best for exploring the cities or playing a round of golf on one of the Algarve's many excellent courses.

Madeira has its own subtropical climate and boasts year-round springtime. When it rains on one side of the island, you can often escape to sunshine on the other side, with a short scenic drive over the mountainous interior. Weather in the Azores is mild, but unpredictable. July and August are the driest months and the best for viewing the islands' famed hydrangea blooms.

Lisbon and Estoril enjoy 46°F (8°C) to 65°F (18°C) temperatures in winter and temperatures between 60°F (16°C) and 82°F (28°C) in summer.

Public Holidays

New Year's Day (Jan 1); **Carnival** (Feb or early Mar—dates vary); **Good Friday** (Mar or Apr—dates vary); **Freedom Day** (Apr 25); **Labor Day** (May 1); **Corpus Christi** (May or June—dates vary); **Portugal Day** (June 10); **Assumption** (Aug 15); **Republic Day** (Oct 5); **All Saints' Day** (Nov 1); **Restoration of Independence** (Dec 1); **Immaculate Conception** (Dec 8); **Christmas Day** (Dec 25). The **Feast of St. Anthony** (June 13) is a public holiday in Lisbon, and the **Feast of St. John the Baptist** (June 24) is a public holiday in Porto.

Events

Where Spain has its fiesta, Portugal has *festa.* There are countless traditional celebrations held up and down the country. Just about every village has a *festa* of some sort. Many have a religious origin, based on a pilgrimage (*romaria*) to honor a local saint. Others are feasts created around a prized local product. In the Algarve, for example, **Lagos** celebrates traditional almond, fig, and carob cakes in July; **Portimão** and **Olhão** hold two of the biggest food-based festivals at the height of the summer season in August, the former focused on sardines, the latter on shellfish. More modest is the Festival of Sweet Potatoes held in November in the pretty west-coast town of **Aljezur.** The pattern is repeated up and down the country. Some such events are humble: where villagers carry a holy statue through the streets, attend a church service, and then follow up with a communal barbecue, performance by the local folklore group, and a wine-fueled *baile* (dance). Others go on for several days, attracting big-name performers and crowds of visitors.

The bigger festivals are concentrated in the summer, but there is always plenty going on in Portugal. Kicking off the year, Madeira's capital, Funchal, hosts one of Europe's most spectacular **New Year's Eve** parties, with the city streets strung with colored lights and a dazzling firework display over the bay. February sees **carnival** celebrations around the country. Many are rather less-glamorous imitations of Rio. Once again, Funchal's is the biggest: Madeira islanders claim their emigrants took the carnival tradition to Brazil. For a more authentic experience, head to northern villages like Podence in Trás-os-Montes or Lazarim, near Lamego, where young men still act out pagan traditions by dressing in bizarre colored costumes, donning devilish masks, and chasing girls around the streets.

Easter is an altogether more solemn occasion, especially in the religious center of Braga, where **Holy Week** processions feature masked marchers and bejeweled floats along with fireworks, folk dancing, and torchlight parades. Students in Coimbra's ancient university will paint the city red in early May with the **Queima das Fitas** celebrations, when they mark the end of the school year by burning the colored ribbons worn to designate their faculties, then get down to nights of serious partying.

Early May also sees the **Festas das Cruzes,** in Barcelos, where since 1504, women dress in gold-adorned regional costumes as part of a procession over streets strewn with millions of flower petals. May 13 sees the start of the pilgrimage season in **Fátima,** where many Catholics believe the Virgin Mary appeared to shepherd children in 1917. Pope Francis attended the centenary of the apparitions in 2017. Pilgrims flock to the Fátima shrine all year round, but the main gatherings are on the 13th of every month between May and October.

Recently, Portugal has emerged as a popular venue for rock festivals, drawing the biggest international names. Highlights include **Nos Alive** and **Super Bock Super Rock,** held in July near Lisbon, and the **Nos Primavera Sound,** held in June in Porto. The **Rock in Rio** festival is held every other May in Lisbon; the next is in 2020. Recent performers have included Bruce Springsteen, Ed Sheeran, and Katy Perry.

Street parties to celebrate Lisbon's patron saint, **Santo António,** on June 12 and 13, are a joyous celebration. Neighborhoods compete to produce the best *marcha,* a musical promenade in costume down the Avenida da Liberdade, then head home to eat grilled sardines, drink red wine or sangria, and dance the night away in squares decked with fairy lights and paper decorations. Similar scenes are repeated in Porto when the second city honors **São João** on June 23 and 24. The Azores island of Terceira celebrates St. John with the 10-day **Sanjoaninas** festival in late June. Portugal's biggest agricultural fair, the **Feira Nacional da Agricultura,** is held every June in Santarém, the heart of cattle country. Expect bullfights, displays of horsemanship, and opportunities to consume heaps of regional food.

Farther down the River Tagus, Vila Franca de Xira holds its **Festa do Colete Encarnado,** featuring Pamplona-style bull-running through the riverside streets, in early July. Portugal's bullfighting season reaches its height in the summer. There are weekly performances at Lisbon's exotic Campo

Pequeno ring. Unlike in Spain, the bulls are not killed in Portuguese bullfighting, but the spectacle can be disturbing for animal lovers.

One of the most striking traditional events is the **Festa dos Tabuleiros,** held every 4 years in Tomar, which features a procession of young women in traditional costume balancing trays laden with 30 stacked loaves of bread, decorated with flowers and topped with crowns. The next is due in early summer 2023.

The Portuguese **soccer season** runs from August through May. Catching a *clássico* game between the top clubs—Benfica, Sporting Lisbon, or FC Porto—in a packed stadium of impassioned fans is a powerful experience, showing just how deeply engrained the love of club is for most Portuguese.

September sees the **Romaria da Nossa Senhora** festival in Nazaré, Portugal's most famed fishing town, where a sacred statue is carried to the sea, followed by folk dancing, singing, and bullfights. A relatively recent tradition is the **Santa Casa Alfama** festival in September, where top fado singers perform in venues throughout Lisbon's Alfama neighborhood.

Horse lovers should head to Golegã in early November for the **Feira Nacional do Cavalo,** a celebration of all things equine, where the beautiful *Lusitano* breed holds pride of place. **Christmas** (*Natal*) is a family affair. Midnight masses fill churches up and down the country.

EATING & DRINKING

In his delectable cookbook *My Lisbon,* Chef Nuno Mendes gets to the heart of the Portuguese diet. "Simplicity sums up the best of Portuguese cooking: taking fantastic produce and letting its own natural flavor be the main player on the plate," he writes. "Ours is one of the most overlooked cuisine in Europe, and I believe it is time to truly shout about the food of Portugal."

DINING CUSTOMS Most Portuguese breakfast lightly: milky coffee with toast, fresh bread rolls with preserves, perhaps a pastry—variations on croissants are common, sometimes filled with ham and cheese, an innovation considered scandalous by the French.

Short shots of espresso, known here as *bica,* are ingested throughout the day, often accompanied by the sweet, sticky pastries on show in all cafes. In Lisbon, custard tarts (*pasteis de nata*) are the calorie fix of choice.

Lunch is often the main meal of the day, and working people fill restaurants throughout the week to tuck in. Portions in traditional restaurants are large. In all but the poshest places, it's completely acceptable to share a main course or ask for a half-portion (*meia-dose*). Aside from their printed menus, most restaurants offer dishes of the day (*pratos do dia*), which are usually a good bet, with market-fresh products at a bargain price.

Many people will take *lanche* in the afternoon—a light meal with tea or coffee. Dinner is usually eaten between 8pm and 9pm, although Spanish-style late-night dining is catching on. People drink wine with both lunch and dinner.

In restaurants, waiters often bring a selection of appetizers unbidden—they can range from a few olives or bread with a pot of sardine pâté, to an array of cheeses, sausage, and seafood. Most of the time, you'll be charged a cover fee for what you eat (so say "no" if you don't want any of these nibbles).

CUISINE Portuguese cooking is one of Europe's best gourmet secrets. There's great regional variation, with a more Mediterranean feel to Algarve cuisine and heartier, meatier options as you go farther north and farther away from the coast.

The Portuguese are among the world's biggest fish eaters. The coastal waters produce a rich variety of seafood that is served super-fresh in markets and restaurants up and down the country. One of the country's great treats is enjoying fresh, charcoal-grilled fish—gilt-head bream (*dourada*) and bass (*robalo*) are among the most popular species—with a splash of olive oil and lemon juice and a glass of chilled white wine in a beachside restaurant. Fish served this way is usually priced by weight on the menu.

Long considered the most humble of fish, sardines (*sardinhas*) are grilled in the streets during the summer season, bringing a pungent scent to the old neighborhoods of Lisbon and other cities. They are eaten by the boatload during Lisbon's Santo Antonio festival in June and are a particular specialty in the fishing ports of the Algarve. They are usually accompanied by roasted bell peppers, green salad, and boiled potatoes drenched in olive oil, and best washed down with cold beer or red wine. Fresh sardines should only be eaten during the summer season, when they are at their fattest. After the weather turns cooler, sardines come from a can.

Another much-cherished fish dish is *caldeirada,* the Portuguese version of bouillabaisse, a fish stew enriched with tomatoes, bell peppers, and potatoes. Hake (*pescada*) is eaten "boiled with everything" (*cozida com todos*), meaning potatoes, carrots, green beans, and a boiled egg. In Madeira and the Algarve, tuna steaks (*bifes de atum*) are a specialty, pan-fried in olive oil with garlic and onions.

Despite the panoply of fresh local seafood, Portugal's favorite fish is cod, caught in the waters of Norway or Iceland and preserved by drying and salting. *Bacalhau,* or salt cod, is as close to the Portuguese soul as soccer or fado music. It dates back to pre-refrigeration times, when salting enabled *bacalhau* to become a staple on long sea journeys or deep into the interior of the country. They say Portugal has more ways of serving *bacalhau* than there are days in the year. Popular versions include *bacalhau à brás,* a Lisbon treat with scrambled eggs, olives, and fries; *pastéis de bacalhau,* fishcakes often served with black-eyed peas; and *bacalhau com broa,* crumbled with cornbread.

Shellfish is generally excellent, best enjoyed in specialist restaurants called *marisqueiras,* which are often bright, busy places where customers slurp cilantro-and-garlic-steamed clams (*amêijoas à bulhão pato*) from their shells, smash crab claws with mallets to get at the flesh within, or pry shrimp in spicy sauce from their shells with fingers sticky. There's a tradition of finishing off a seafood feast with a steak sandwich, or *prego*. A classic shellfish main

A COFFEE survival guide

From Brazil to East Timor, many of Portugal's former colonies happened to produce wonderful coffee (*café*), so coffee culture runs deep. The Portuguese imbibe inordinate amounts of the stuff in an array of styles. Here's what to order:

Bica: Thimble-size shots of strong black espresso. Portugal's default option; if you ask for *café*, this is what you get.
Café cheio: As above, but slightly less strong, a full espresso cup.
Café pingado: A *bica* with a drop of milk.
Garoto: Espresso cup of half-coffee, half-milk.
Café duplo: A double espresso.
Abatanado: Large black coffee.
Galão: Weak milky coffee like a caffe latte, served in a tall glass.
Meia de leite: Big cup of half-milk, half-espresso, like a café au lait or flat white.
Café com cheirinho: Shot of black coffee topped up with *aguadente* (firewater).

course is *arroz de marisco,* a pot of rice and seafood in broth flavored with garlic, cilantro, tomato, and just a touch of *piri-piri*—a fiery chili sauce of African origin that's a favorite condiment in Portugal.

Piri-piri is also used to spice up spit-roasted chicken, one of Portugal's most successful culinary exports, served in specialty restaurants known as *churrasqueiras.*

Portuguese pork is among some of the world's best. Black pigs roam semi-wild in the plains of the Alentejo region, feasting on the acorns that fall from the region's cork forests. The *porco preto* meat they produce is fabulous. The region's signature dish, *carne de porco à Alentejana*, combines red-pepper-marinated pork with clams. The black pigs also produce superlative hams (*presunto*) and an array of sausages, including paprika-spiced *chouriço*, cumin-flavored blood puddings (*morcela*), and soft, smoky *farinheiras*. All of these porky pleasures are combined in *cozido à portuguesa*, an artery-stopping one-pot that's become the national dish. It can include hunks of beef, pigs' ears, chicken, cabbage, turnips, chick peas, carrots, potatoes, squash, and beans, as well as an array of spiced sausages.

Lamb (*borrego*) is another Alentejo specialty, served grilled, fried, or in hearty stews. Goat is more common in the center and north; a succulent meat, it usually comes in the form of roasted young kid (*cabrito assado*), although around Coimbra older goats or sheep are slow-stewed in red wine to make *chanfana*. Beef is good in the north; the *posta Mirandesa* is a succulent steak served in Trás-os-Montes, but the Atlantic island of Madeira also boasts a beefy signature dish in the shape of *espetada*, cubes of garlic-rubbed meat skewered on a laurel branch and roasted over hot coals.

The Portuguese have a weakness for offal. Tripe stewed with beans (*tripas à moda do Porto*) is Porto's favorite dish. Lisbon prefers liver sautéed in white wine (*iscas*). Pig's feet, stomachs, ears, and snouts will all find their way into hearty stews.

Soups are a common way of starting a meal. The most popular, especially in the north, is *caldo verde,* a green broth made from cabbage, sausage, potatoes, and olive oil. Typically southern, *açorda alentejana* is made from simmered bread, poached eggs, cilantro, and a ton of garlic. *Sopa da pedra* is a meal in itself from the Ribatejo region, combining meat, beans, sausage, and just about every conceivable ingredient except the stone (*pedra*) from which it gets its name.

Portuguese cheeses deserve to be better known internationally. The best is *queijo da serra:* Made from sheep's milk in the high central mountains, it is rich and creamy, fabulous on freshly baked rye bread. Similar but more delicate is *queijo de Azeitão* from the hills south of Lisbon. *Queijo de São Jorge* is a hard cow's milk cheese made in big wheels in the Azores. Soft, unaged white cheeses called *queijo fresco* are often served as an appetizer.

Fruit ripened in Portugal's sunny climate is fabulous. Bananas and passion fruit from Madeira, pineapple from the Azores, cherries from the central mountains, juicy Rocha pears from the far west, and honey-sweet figs from the Algarve are just some of the treats. If your tooth is still sweeter, traditional Portuguese desserts promise calorific overload. Many are based on old convent recipes using eggs, almonds, and the cinnamon that explorers of the 15th century went to such great lengths to bring from the East.

Portugal's ties with its former colonies have spiced up the local cuisine: Brazilian shrimp *moquecas*, curries from Goa, or Angolan chicken *muamba* are all imported additions to Lisbon menus.

Recently, a new generation of younger chefs has been building on the country's traditional cuisine to forge modern adaptations of cherished additions and win international accolades. Leading the pack is **José Avillez,** whose Belcanto restaurant (p. 87) became Lisbon's first with two Michelin stars.

WINE For years, international interest in Portuguese wine (*vinho*) was largely limited to cheap-and-cheerful rosé and the complex Porto and Madeira fortified wines. In recent decades, however, the world has woken up to the full range of terrific tipples made under Portugal's unique blend of Atlantic and Mediterranean conditions.

Strong yet sophisticated reds produced from the beautiful terraced hillsides along the Douro or the rolling, sun-soaked Alentejo plains have drawn admiration from critics and drinkers around the world. Great wines are also produced in the valleys of the Dão, the coastal Bairrada region, and the flatlands flanking the Tejo River east of Lisbon. Tangy whites made from *arinto* grapes or sweet *Moscatel* dessert wines are made on the edge of Lisbon's suburbs. Fresh white wines known as *vinho verdes* from the verdant hills of the northwest make an excellent partner for seafood. Even the Algarve, whose wines were once mocked as good only for unsuspecting tourists, is now producing quality reds and whites.

Port remains the most alluring of Portugal's wines. It was invented in the age of sailing ships, when exporters added brandy to Douro wines to prevent them from spoiling during the long sea journey to England. Quality controls exist since at least the 17th century. Drier white ports are traditionally sipped as an aperitif before meals, the sweet red tawny and ruby ports are served with dessert or cheese, and rare vintage wines from selected years are saved for special occasions. Wines produced on the volcanic island of Madeira are similarly fortified and aged and also range from drier aperitifs to sweet dessert wines.

BEER & OTHER DRINKS The beer (*cerveja*) market in Portugal has long been a duel between Lisbon's *Sagres* and Porto's *Super Bock,* both refreshing lagers, best served chilled. Lately, there's been a craft beer revolution with breweries such as *Sovina, Letra,* and *Dois Corvos* edging onto the scene with some tasty thirst-quenchers.

The wine industry has a long distillery tradition resulting in fiery liquors like *bagaço* and *bagaceira,* which are clear, powerful, and similar to Italian grappa, or barrel-aged *aguardente velha,* at its best a wonderfully warming after-dinner tipple that can rival French cognac.

Many regions have their own special drinks: *Poncha* is a potent mix of local rum and lemon from Madeira; *ginja* is a sweet cherry liqueur knocked back in hole-in-the-wall Lisbon bars; the Algarve has a firewater made from a forest fruit called *medronho; Licor Beirão* is an herby liqueur from the Beiras.

Mineral water is commonly drunk, bottled from springs around the country. Waiters will inevitably ask if you want it *com gas* (sparkling) or *sem gas* (still), *fresca* (cold) or *natural* (room temperature). The Compal range of fruit drinks can make a healthier alternative to international soda brands.

SUGGESTED PORTUGAL ITINERARIES

4

Portugal is a relatively compact country, and major road investments over the past few decades mean fast highways have cut driving times even to the most remote regions. Despite its size, there's a great variety of landscapes, from the rolling plains of the Alentejo to sun-kissed resorts along the coast and the rugged highlands of the north and center, where rough-hewn granite towns rise out of the hillsides.

Whether you race along the *autostradas* or prefer pottering along country roads or discovering the country by rail, traveling around Portugal can be a delight. Driving from Lisbon, in less than 3 hours you can be bronzing on a beach in the Algarve or sipping port in a riverside bar overlooking Porto.

Yet it would be a mistake to spend your holiday rushing from point to point. Portugal is a land that lends itself to taking things easy. If you've got a week, spend time exploring Lisbon, the historic and happening capital that is the heart of the country's cultural life; take a relaxed ride out to nearby attractions, driving through forested hills or vine- and orchard-covered countryside to view World Heritage Sites within an hour or so of the city; chill on a beach, admire the view from a cliff-top lighthouse, or settle down to a seafood lunch.

If you've more time, or are on a return trip, move north to the great city of Porto, or to smaller but culturally rich cities such as Braga or Guimarães, the beautiful wine regions of the Douro and Minho, or the wild landscapes of Peneda-Gerês National Park. Or go south, passing through the Alentejo's picturesque cities and villages, gastronomic temples, and landscapes redolent of the African savannah before reaching the Algarve's beaches.

The following itineraries assume that you'll be traveling by car outside the main cities. You can do most of it by train or bus, but it will take longer to get from place to place. *Boa viagem!*

Lisbon and Around & Northern Delights

LISBON & AROUND IN 1 WEEK

This tour will give you time to get an impression of the capital, from its medieval heart to futuristic new riverside districts, plus take in some of the surrounding area, reaching no less than six World Heritage Sites without spending more than an hour per day on the road.

Days 1, 2 & 3: Lisbon ★★★

Lisbon is the cultural highlight of Portugal. As the capital and biggest city, it is packed with cultural attractions, great restaurants, and exciting nightlife. It has a fabulous river-mouth location and maintains timeless traditions and a unique maritime heritage while reaching out to the world as a dynamic, cosmopolitan metropolis.

DAY 1

9am: Start by getting your bearings. The best place to do that is from **Castelo de São Jorge (St. George's Castle;** p. 98). From the ramparts of this hilltop fortress you get stellar views over the city's neighborhoods. The castle is the cradle of the city and traces its roots back to Roman, Arab, and Crusader times. Spend an hour up there checking out the view, soaking up the history, and relaxing in the gardens.

10am: Next, head down to the Alfama (p. 118), a casbah-like ancient neighborhood tumbling down to the broad River Tagus. The warren of lanes is imbued with the plaintive sounds of fado music and the whiff of sardines on the grill. Take a couple of hours getting lost here, wandering into baroque churches like the splendid São Vicente de Fora (p. 99), with its panels of *azulejo* tiles and rooftop views.

Noon: After admiring the view over Alfama's rooftops from **Portas do Sol** (p. 101) square, walk downhill following the tram line, pausing for a quick look at the **Sé,** Lisbon's fortress-like cathedral (p. 102) built in 1147, before reaching the downtown **Baixa** (p. 102) district. Rebuilt on a grid pattern after the devastation of a 1755 earthquake, this is the administrative and commercial heart of the city. Opening out onto the river is **Praça do Comércio** (p. 102), one of Europe's great city squares, surrounded by grand ministerial buildings linked by a triumphal archway. Running inland is **Rua Augusta** (p. 122), a pedestrianized shopping street built in the harmonious 18th-century Pombaline style. Pause to take a picture of the **Elevador de Santa Justa,** a 19th-century iron elevator whisking shoppers uptown. Grab **lunch** at one of the restaurants popular with locals in the parallel street, **Rua dos Correeiros.**

2pm: Nearby is the busy **Rossio** square (p. 122), the hub of the downtown bustle. From there, head uphill again to the **Chiado** district (p. 102), an uptown, upscale shopping area that's thrived since the 18th century, with its old-world stores, gilded theaters, and historic cafes, like **A Brasileira** (p. 106), serving up shots of coffee (or something stronger) to artists and poets since 1905. Walk there up **Rua do Carmo** and **Rua Garrett,** which are steep but have some of the best shops.

4pm: Hopefully, you'll be energized by that shot of coffee, so continue to climb. Head up **Rua da Misericórdia** to visit the **Igreja de São Roque** church. Spend an hour inside admiring one the city's great baroque interiors and the attached museum.

5pm: Just behind the church is the **Miradouro de São Pedro de Alcântara,** a leafy viewpoint where you have another spectacular view of the city, this time looking across to the castle where you started the day. If you have the energy, walk uphill just a little bit farther to the **Jardim do Príncipe Real,** a garden surrounded by some of the city's trendiest boutiques, bars, and restaurants. The Arabesque architecture of the 19th-century **Embaixada** building may contain Europe's coolest shopping mall.

7pm: Drag your shopping bags into the **Pavilhão Chinês** bar for a cocktail among the extraordinary collection of vintage bric-a-brac before dinner.

DAY 2

10am: Start the day at the **Museu Nacional de Arte Antiga** (p. 111). You should spend a couple of hours here; it houses the country's best collection of old masters. Take coffee in the riverside garden and cafe.

Noon: Head along the river to the **Belém** district, a UNESCO World Heritage Site packed with monuments and museums. After lunch at one of the riverside restaurants near the **Monument to the Discoveries,** stroll along the river to the **Torre de Belém.** The white tower has guarded the entrance to the city since 1514 and is its most recognizable symbol. Skip the queues lined up to visit the less-than-overwhelming interior.

2pm: Walking past the vast stone buildings of the **Belém Cultural Center,** head now to the **Jerónimos Monastery** (p. 108), which dates to the early 1500s and is the most impressive church in the country, containing the tomb of explorer Vasco da Gama.

4pm: Time for refreshments. Next door to the monastery are the scrumptious, custard-filled tarts served at the **Pastéis de Belém** cafe (p. 106), dating from 1837. You can beat the crowds lining up for takeout by taking yours at a table inside with coffee or tea.

4:30pm: Finish your visit to Belém with a visit to the **National Coach Museum** (p. 111), featuring one of the world's greatest collections of Cinderella-style carriages.

DAY 3

10am: Time to get modern. After all that history, the **Parque das Nações** comes as a shock. Built to house the EXPO '98 World's Fair, it's a showcase of contemporary architecture spectacularly located on the broadest expanse of the River Tagus. The highlight here is the **Oceanário** (p. 113), arguably the world's paramount aquarium. A multistoried treasure trove devoted to ocean life; it features creatures from huge sharks circling the main tank to tiny iridescent jellyfish. You'll need a whole morning to visit the aquarium and to stroll among the modern architecture.

2pm: After lunch, head back into town to the **Calouste Gulbenkian Museum** (p. 116), an awe-inspiring collection of artwork—from 3,000-year-old Assyrian sculptures to French Impressionist masterpieces—all amassed by an Armenian oil magnate. The museum buildings are integrated into soothing landscaped gardens, and there's a separate modern art museum.

4pm: Up the hill from the Gulbenkian complex, the top of **Parque Eduardo VII** provides yet another stunning viewpoint over the city, from which the world's biggest Portuguese flag is flown. Walk down and you come to **Avenida da Liberdade,** the city's swankiest boulevard, over 1km (⅔ mile) of leafy walkways, grand buildings, and luxury brands.

Day 4: Sintra ★★★

9am: Head out to **Sintra** (p. 157). Packed with palaces, this little town in the thickly wooded hills west of Lisbon has for centuries been an escape from the summer heat for the capital's elite.

11am: A hilltop fantasy built in the 19th-century Bavarian mode, **Palácio da Pena** (p. 162) was the dream of the German husband of Portugal's Queen Maria II. The views are amazing. Spend a couple of hours visiting the palace and strolling the romantic gardens.

1pm: The whole Sintra area is a World Heritage Site. After lunch in the town, drive west through the lush semitropical vegetation dotted with aristocratic abodes. Pass through the charming little wine village of **Colares** until you reach **Cabo da Roca** (p. 163), a blustery promontory that is Europe's most westerly point.

3pm: If the weather is good, dip down to the beach of **Praia da Adraga,** enclosed between soaring cliffs, to soak up some rays.

5pm: Return to Sintra via the **Parque e Palácio de Monserrate,** a fairytale, Arabian-inspired palace surrounded by semitropical parkland that inspired Lord Byron and Hans Christian Andersen. Overnight in Sintra.

Day 5: Mafra ★★, Óbidos ★★★, Alcobaça ★★★ & Nazaré ★★

10am: It's a 20-minute drive north from Sintra to **Mafra** (p. 170), home to the vast palace and monastery built by King João V, using riches acquired from an 18th-century Brazilian gold rush. The sheer scale of it is mind-boggling. You'll need a couple of hours to tour the inside, including the library, which holds 36,000 leather-bound books, some over 500 years old.

Noon: Next stop, Óbidos (p. 193), 40 minutes farther north through the vineyards and apple and pear orchards of Portugal's far west. Surrounded by high walls, this is one of the country's best-preserved medieval towns. It's filled with whitewashed houses, their doors and windows decked out in deep blue and yellow. Take lunch in the town.

3pm: From here, it's a short hop to the **Mosteiro de Alcobaça** (p. 196), founded in 1153 by Portugal's first king, Afonso Henriques, in the unadorned Gothic style newly imported from France. Entering the interior is like stepping into the Middle Ages. The little town of Alcobaça is also renowned for its brightly colored **chintz fabrics** and the heavenly treats based on centuries-old convent recipes sold by **Alcôa** pastry shop (p. 202).

6pm: Take an evening stroll around the clifftop heights of **Nazaré** (p. 205), a picturesque fishing port 20 minutes to the west. Then finish the day with a hearty fish stew before overnighting in Nazaré.

Day 6: Batalha ★★★ & Tomar ★★★

9:30am: It's a 30-minute drive from Nazaré to the monastery at **Batalha** (p. 209), the first of two medieval UNESCO World Heritage Sites you'll visit today. Executed in flamboyant Gothic style, Batalha was built in golden stone as a tribute to a Portuguese victory over invading Spaniards in 1385.

Noon: Another 40 minutes heading inland takes you to the pretty riverside town of **Tomar** (p. 262). After lunch in one of the restaurants in the pretty downtown, head up to the **Convento de Cristo** (p. 265), a fascinating complex of buildings dating back to the 12th century. It was once a stronghold of the Knights Templar. The architecture of the round church at the center was inspired by their crusading ventures to Jerusalem. Spend the night in Tomar.

Day 7: Coimbra ★★★

9am: Leave early to make the hour-long drive through thick forests of eucalyptus to the romantic city of **Coimbra** (p. 294), where you'll spend the day.

10am: You'll need a couple of hours to visit Portugal's oldest **university,** dating back to 1290, including the ceremonial rooms, jail for unruly students, and the magnificent baroque **library.**

Noon: Wander down the narrow old street of the upper town, taking care descending steep **Rua Quebra Costas** (backbreaker street), popping in for a look at the Romanesque **cathedral.** When you reach the busy **Baixa** commercial district, grab lunch at historic **Café de Santa Cruz.**

2pm: Move next door to the church bearing the same name as the cafe, then lose yourself in the maze of narrow streets making up the Baixa and enjoy an amble through the romantic gardens beside the **River Mondego.**

4pm: Uphill again, spend a couple of hours in one of Portugal's best provincial museums, the **Museu Machado de Castro** (p. 299). Be sure to explore the remains of the Roman city in the basement.

6pm: Catch an early-evening performance of Coimbra's own amorous version of **fado** music at **Fado ao Centro,** where they'll explain the music's significance and serve a glass of port at the end.

THE BEST OF PORTUGAL IN 2 WEEKS

You can return to Lisbon from Coimbra in a couple of hours but if you have time, head north. A second week will open up the delights of Porto and the Douro wine region.

Days 1–7

Follow the itinerary suggested above.

Days 8 & 9: Porto ★★★

Porto (p. 331) is an hour's drive from Coimbra. Both banks of the **River Douro** (p. 335) will keep you occupied on the first day.

DAY 8

10am: On the northern bank, the **Ribeira** district is Porto's most traditional neighborhood. Behind a row of high-fronted, brightly painted merchants' houses lining the quayside are a warren of alleys strung with washing, where you'll stumble on architectural landmarks like the gold-lined **São Francisco** church (p. 337) and the **Bolsa** (p. 340), or stock exchange, with its sumptuous **Arabian Salon** (p. 340). Afterward, grab lunch at one of the cool restaurants in **Largo de São Domingos.**

2pm: Walk up the pretty **Rua das Flores** shopping street. At the top, peek at the tiled hall of **São Bento** railway station, and then continue up the hill to the **Sé,** Porto's cathedral, where you'll want to look in at the richly decorated cloisters and admire the view from the patio out front. Then walk across the upper level of the double-decked **Dom Luís I bridge** (p. 347), whose mighty ironwork spans the Douro. Now you are in **Vila Nova de Gaia** (p. 335), home of port wine.

4pm: Take the **cable car** to the waterfront and admire the ***barco rabelo*** boats that once hauled wine barrels, now moored in the Douro. Along the riverfront and rising up the bank are dozens of centuries-old warehouses where ports are blended, then left to age. Most **port lodges** offer **tasting tours.** Among the best are the 300-year-old **Taylor's** cellars up the hill.

DAY 9

9am: After that wine, it's time for coffee. The city of Porto has some fabulous old cafes. The most opulent is **Café Majestic** (p. 343), founded in 1921. After your caffeine shot, wander out onto **Rua de Santa**

Catarina (p. 342), the main shopping street in Porto's uptown **Baixa** district (p. 341).

11am: Visit the **Bolhão market,** a colorful collection of stores selling the city's favored foodstuffs, which was due to reopen in May 2020 after 2 years of renovation, and the traditional stores in the street around it. Lunch on Porto's famed *francesinha* sandwiches in a nearby cafe.

1pm: Continue your uptown tour, admiring **Avenida dos Aliados** (p. 341), the city's grandest boulevard, fronted with Belle Epoque buildings leading up to the tower of **City Hall,** the soaring **Clérigos** church tower (p. 343), and the intriguing **Lello bookstore** (p. 341).

2pm: Head to the leafy **Boavista district** (p. 343) where, among patrician villas, the **Serralves** (p. 343) cultural complex contains a cutting-edge modern art museum surrounded by parkland.

4pm: If the weather is fine, carry on to the coast to promenade along the oceanfront at **Foz** (p. 349) or swim on one of the suburb's sandy beaches.

8pm: Return to Boavista in the evening to catch a concert at the **Casa da Música** (p. 362).

Day 10: Braga ★★

10am: Make the 40-minute drive out to Portugal's spiritual capital, **Braga** (p. 388).

11am: Braga has been a center of Christianity since Roman times and is home to **Portugal's oldest cathedral** (p. 392), founded in 1070. After a visit, spend the rest of the morning exploring downtown around **Praça da República** and **Rua do Souto.** Be sure to get coffee at an iconic cafe like **A Brasileira** or **Vianna.**

2pm: After lunch, head up to the 18th-century church of **Bom Jesus do Monte** (p. 391) looming over the city at the summit of a 116m (380-ft.) baroque staircase. The sanctuary is surrounded by gardens filled with statues, lakes, and grottoes.

4pm: Back in town, visit the **Museu dos Biscainhos** museum for a taste of the 18th century. The building has been preserved as a noble home, complete with ornamented ceilings and walls with panels of tiles and paintings. Spend the night in one of Braga's fine hotels.

Day 11: Ponte de Lima ★★ & Peneda-Gerês National Park ★★★

9am: Drive northeast through the green, vine-covered slopes of ***vinho verde*** wine country.

10am: Pull into the delightful wine town of **Ponte de Lima** (p. 386), with its medieval bridge arching over the River Lima.

Noon: You reach Portugal's most spectacular wilderness area, the **Peneda-Gerês National Park** (p. 396). Spend the rest of the day exploring Portugal's only national park, 700 sq. km (270 sq. miles) of rugged highland: boulder-strewn plateaus, mountains, forests of oak and pine, and valleys carved by fast-flowing rivers. Wolves, boar, and wild horses roam. The human geography is also fascinating. The area is studded with granite villages, where longhorn cattle, sheep, and goats are raised, and rural life seems little touched by the 21st century. Sinister stone structures, looking like tombs raised on pillars, are everywhere: They are actually grain stores, known as *espigueiros*. The clusters of them around the villages of **Soajo** and **Lindoso** (p. 396) are striking. Fortunately, you can find modern comforts in plenty of fine hotels and inns around the region.

Day 12: Guimarães ★★★

10am: Moving south, head to **Guimarães** (p. 380), another of Portugal's World Heritage cities. It's the cradle of the nation, birthplace of the first king, Afonso Henriques, in 1109, and Portugal's first capital. "Guimarães is Portugal, the rest is just what we conquered," locals like to say.

11am: The founding father's **hilltop castle** still looms over the city, along with a Renaissance-era **royal palace** (p. 382).

1pm: Head downtown for lunch, then explore the tangle of cobbled lanes and plazas—like **Largo da Oliveira** and **Largo do Tourel**—lined with centuries-old granite homes, often painted in bright tones, sporting wrought-iron balconies or glass-fronted verandas.

3pm: The arts scene got a boost when the city was made European Cultural Capital in 2012, and it remains vibrant, so try to catch the latest contemporary art show at **Centro Cultural Vila Flor.**

4pm: Guimarães is a center for Portugal's fashionable **footwear** industry, so leave some time to pick up a bargain in one of the city's outlets.

Days 13 & 14: The Douro Wine Region ★★★

For the final 2 days in the north, you'll be in the **Douro wine region** (p. 372), another UNESCO World Heritage Site.

DAY 13

9am: Drive south from Guimarães, stopping in the lovely riverside town of **Amarante** (p. 365) to check out the Renaissance church of **São Gonçalo.**

Noon: Continue the precipitous decline to the big river. At Mesão Frio you'll see the Douro winding its way through a distinctive landscape of terraced hills covered with grapevines. Follow the winding riverbank until **Peso da Régua** (p. 376), where you can have lunch and discover the secrets of winemaking at the **Museu do Douro** museum (p. 376).

3pm: Cross the bridge to the south bank and visit the town of **Lamego** (p. 369), with its remarkable mountaintop church, before overnighting in one of the wine estates or wine-themed hotels, where you can sample the nectars without having to worry about driving.

DAY 14

9am: Hopefully your head is clear in the morning, because you will start with a twisting drive along the **N-222** (p. 371) riverside road, which has been called the world's most scenic route. There are also plenty of wineries to visit along the way.

Noon: Make a short detour to visit the charming wine village of **Pinhão** (p. 370) before rejoining the N-222 as it climbs through the heart of the wine region—stopping to enjoy tastings at the estates you pass.

3pm: Vila Nova de Foz Côa is the last UNESCO site on the tour, with its **prehistoric rock carvings** (p. 377) that date back more than 20,000 years. This is a chance to get up close and personal with some of humanity's earliest art, both at the riverside sites and in the excellent **museum** that's an architectural landmark in its own right.

SOUTHERN PORTUGAL FOR 2 WEEKS

An alternative to heading north out of Lisbon would be to discover the attractions of mainland Portugal's two southernmost regions, the Alentejo and the Algarve. They are very different. The Alentejo, taking up a third of the country, is mostly rolling farmland broken up by occasional hill ranges. Amid vineyards, olive groves, and forests of cork oak are some of the country's best-preserved historic towns and villages, painted white to reflect the sun which pushes summer temperatures over 40°C (100°F). The Algarve is separated from the rest of the country by a range of scrub-covered hills running east-west. It enjoys a Mediterranean-style climate where almond and citrus trees thrive. The beaches on the sheltered southern coast are among Portugal's biggest draws for visitors.

On this tour by car, we're assuming you'll want to spend some time chilling on those beaches, so we've have spaced out the sightseeing accordingly.

Days 1, 2 & 3

Follow the Lisbon schedule at the start of "Lisbon & Around in 1 Week," above.

Days 4 & 5: Comporta ★★ & Alcácer do Sal ★★

Heading south out of Lisbon, you cross the red-painted **Ponte 25 de Abril** suspension bridge high above the River Tagus toward the outstretched arms of the **Cristo Rei** statue (p. 188) on the south bank. It's less than an hour to the handsome town of **Alcácer do Sal** on the banks of the River Sado. Whitewashed Alcácer is an ancient center for rice production. It's surmounted by a convent wrapped in a castle that's now a luxurious hotel overlooking the rice fields. Spend a couple of hours there before joining the sun-worshipers on the fine **sandy beaches** 30 minutes farther west. The beaches curve south for almost 60km (40 miles) from the headland of **Tróia** to the fishing port of **Sines.** The village of **Comporta** and its beaches have become the "in" place for Lisbonites (and international celebrities) to escape for the weekend. If you have the cash, bed down at rustic-chic **Sublime Comporta** resort.

Days 6, 7 & 8: Lagos & the Western Algarve ★★★

To get to the Algarve, it will take you 2 hours down the A2 toll highway. Head to **Lagos** (p. 249), the best town in the western Algarve, which you'll make your base for the next 3 nights.

Day 6: Explore the town that was the center for Portugal's 15th-century voyages of discovery. The old town lies within the walls that once protected it from pirates. It retains its charm, although Lagos' popularity with a youthful surfer crowd means it's hopping on summer nights. Lagos is surrounded by **beaches,** quiet coves among honey-colored cliffs, curving dune-backed strands, and deep blue lagoons.

Day 7: Drive out to the headland fortress of **Sagres** (p. 255), Europe's southwestern tip, where Prince Henry the Navigator established his headquarters for launching the Discoveries. It is a wild atmospheric space. Try to be there for the spectacular sunsets. North of Sagres are some of Europe's best surf beaches.

Day 8: Drive inland through orange groves to spend the morning in the former Moorish capital of **Silves** (p. 241) with its mighty medieval fortress. After lunch, head south to the coast. In the tiny cove of **Benagil** you can pick up a skiff that will take you to amazing **sea caves** carved into the sandstone and the beach at **Praia da Marinha,** arguably the most beautiful in Portugal.

Days 9 & 10: Tavira & the Eastern Algarve ★★★

Slow down and relax. The eastern Algarve, close to the border with Spain's Andalusia region, is known as the **Sotavento,** meaning "sheltered from the wind"—in contrast to the breezy west. Beaches here, many of them on long, sandbar islands, are tranquil and have warmer water. **Tavira** (p. 227) is a sweet town, with manor houses lining the banks of the Gilão River and streets filled with restaurants and cafes. There are plenty of good places to stay here and excellent beaches to explore. Be sure to take a boat tour in the marshy **Ria Formosa** reserve, a magnate for birdwatchers.

Day 11: Mértola ★★

Before leaving the Algarve coast, look in on **Vila Real de Santo António** (p. 232), a border town built after the 1755 earthquake, which is a rare example of 18th-century town planning. Then head north following the River Guadiana for about an hour to **Mértola** (p. 290), one of Portugal's

South for 2 Weeks of Culture & the Coast

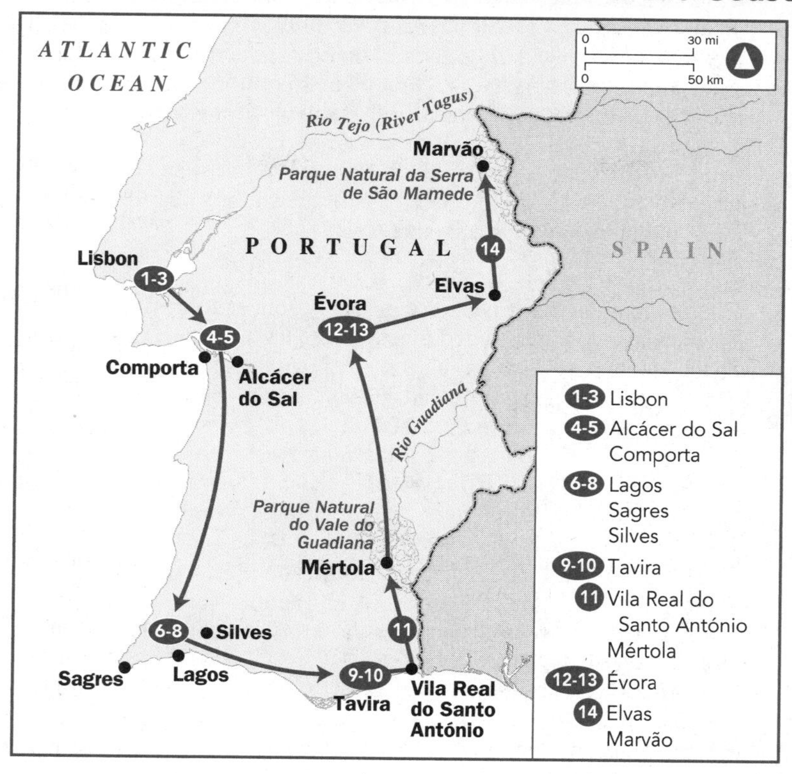

most beautiful villages. Strung out on the crest of a ridge, its white houses and crenellated battlements are perfectly reflected in the river's still blue waters. This was once the capital of an Arab emirate and a busy medieval trading hub. Its parish church is one of the few in Portugal that still clearly shows the signs that it was once a mosque.

Days 12 & 13: Évora ★★★

It's a 2-hour drive north to Évora**,** the majestic capital of the Alentejo, a UNESCO World Heritage city. Take the slow road, winding your way through picturesque villages like **Serpa, Moura,** and **Monsaraz,** which occupies a spectacular location overlooking the **Alqueva** reservoir, Western Europe's largest man-made lake.

Arriving in Évora in the late afternoon, spend your time moseying around its white-painted heart, admiring the medieval fortifications and 16th-century aqueduct before preparing to feast on Alentejo food in one of the city's excellent restaurants.

Next day, start out in the main square, the **Praça do Giraldo,** once a scene of executions and the horrors of the Inquisition, now an elegant focal point for city life and serious coffee drinking. Spend the rest of the morning visiting the 12th-century **cathedral**—being sure to admire the views from the roof—and the **Temple of Diana,** whose columns form one of the best-preserved Roman ruins in the Iberian Peninsula.

In the afternoon, visit the **Igreja de São Francisco,** which, besides being an impressive example of Portugal's "maritime discoveries–inspired" Manueline architecture, is best known for a chapel with walls made from human skulls and other bones.

Day 14: Elvas ★★★ & Marvão ★★★

For the final day, visit two very different frontier fortress towns. First **Elvas,** whose defenses, built during Portugal's war of independence from Spain in the 1640s, are the biggest of their type in the world. A giant complex of overlapping walls and ditches encircles the ancient city on the old road leading to Lisbon from Madrid. It's also a World Heritage Site.

Just over an hour to the north, **Marvão** perches on a spur of rock surging 860 meters (2,800 ft.) above the plain. It was fought over since ancient times due to its commanding position over the lands below. Inside its stone walls, the town of red-tiled, white-walled houses seems to grow out of the rocks. There's a peaceful atmosphere now, but it's easy to imagine as a battlefield between Celts and Romans, Christians and Moors, and Spanish invaders versus the British redcoats helping defend Portugal in the 1760s.

A WEEK IN LISBON WITH KIDS

Day 1

Lisbon is pretty much unique among European capitals in having summer-long sunshine, plus suburbs featuring broad sandy beaches and regular Atlantic rollers ideal for surfing. So rather than drag the kids around museums, get them enrolled in one of the city's many surf schools. That way they spend the mornings having fun in the waves, you get to do cultural stuff undisturbed by the complaints of bored juniors, and you can all spend some quality time together in the afternoons.

Carcavelos Beach, just a 20-minute train ride from downtown, is ideal for beginners, but there are beaches within a short drive from Lisbon to suit all standards.

In the afternoon, it's time to discover what lies beneath the waves. The **Oceanário** (p. 113) is a delight for all ages, but children will marvel at its range of sea life. The aquarium also organizes special events such as concerts for young children, or sleepovers where kids (and parents) can spend the night next to the shark tank. You'll need at least a couple of hours to explore the Oceanário.

Lisbon with Kids

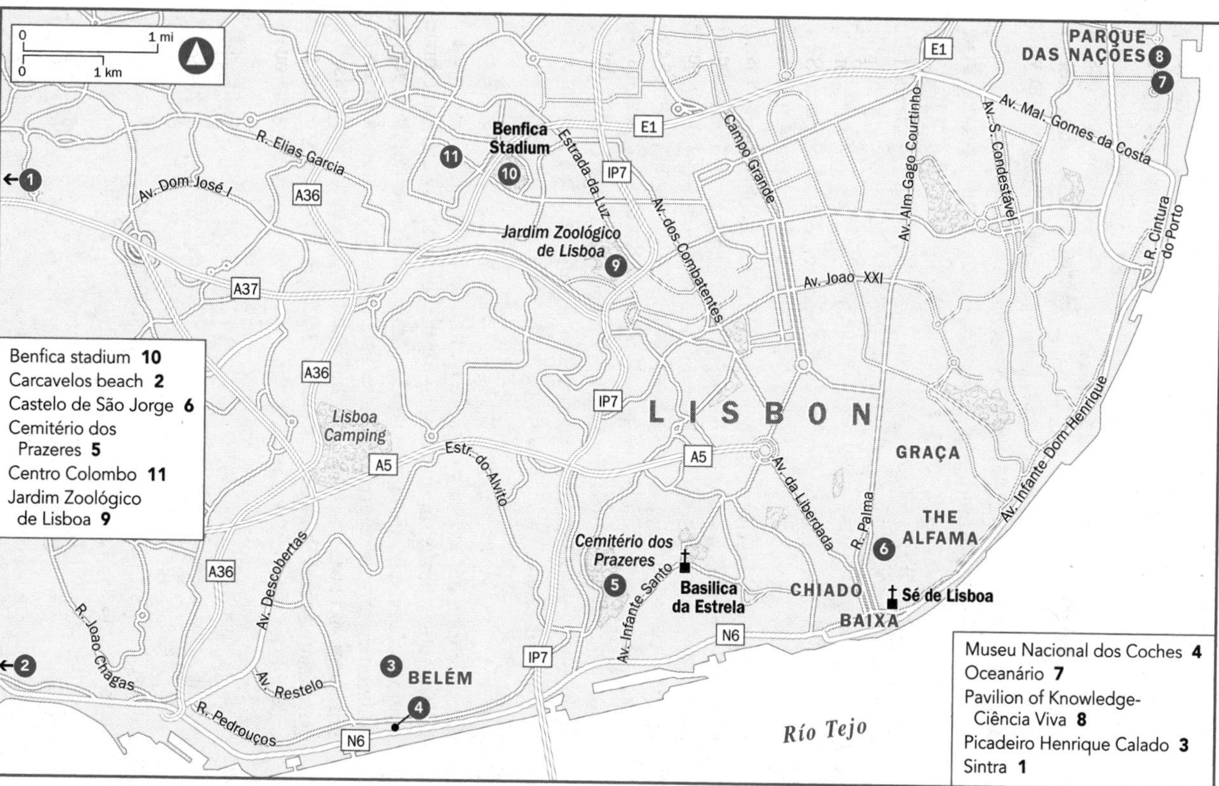

Day 2

After the morning at surf school, spend the afternoon on dry land. Take the kids to **Castelo de São Jorge** (**St. George's Castle;** p. 98) so they can admire the view, roam the ramparts, and imagine the days of the Romans, Moors, and Crusaders who lived and battled there. Then head down the castle hill and up the next slope to the **Graça** neighborhood to catch **Tram 28** (p. 105), the most iconic line of Lisbon's vintage yellow streetcars (*eléctricos*). It will likely be crowded with tourists, but the eléctrico remains a fun way to see the city as it rattles down the narrow lanes of the **Alfama** neighborhood, scoots through **Baixa**'s streets, passes the posh shops of **Chiado,** and finally ends at the **Cemitério dos Prazeres**, Lisbon's largest cemetery. Few tourists venture here, but the 19th-century necropolis, with its massive family tombs, makes for an intriguingly spooky visit. Don't miss the pyramid built by Dom Pedro de Sousa Holstein, Duke de Palmela, believed to be Europe's biggest private mausoleum.

Day 3

In the afternoon head for the zoo. The **Jardim Zoológico de Lisboa** (p. 117) has been around for 132 years and contains over 2,000 animals from 300 different species. At least one you're unlikely to see anywhere else—the **Iberian lynx**—is the world's rarest cat, struggling to survive with the help of a conservation program in the wild lands of southern Spain and southeastern Portugal. The zoo is a much-loved attraction for Portuguese schoolchildren who come to see the rare red pandas or the "enchanted woods," where exotic birds fly in the open air.

Day 4

Take the train out to **Sintra** (p. 157). High up in the hills to the west of Lisbon, this was the summer retreat for the royal family and their aristocratic entourage. Among the thickly forested hills are fairytale palaces and secret gardens to explore. Make like 18th-century nobles and hire a horse-drawn carriage to take you through the forests to the gates of the phantasmagorical **Palácio da Pena** (p. 162).

Day 5

Sport Lisboa e Benfica, better known simply as **Benfica,** is one of the world's great soccer clubs, twice European champions. In fact, it's believed to be the world's biggest club in terms of membership, with almost 160,000 paid-up fans. Catching a home game can be a tremendous experience, especially if they are playing against cross-town rivals Sporting or northern upstarts FC Porto. If you can't get to a match, you can still tour the **Estádio da Luz** stadium and visit its state-of-the-art **museum** dedicated to the club's 112-year history, in which its greatest player, Eusébio (1942–2014), plays a starring role.

Next door to the stadium is one of Europe's largest shopping malls, the **Centro Colombo,** offering 119,725 square meters (1.3 million sq. ft.) of retail therapy. There are 340 stores, 60 restaurants, nine movie screens, and a bowling alley. It's all vaguely themed around the Portuguese Era of Discoveries.

Day 6

Lisbon's coach museum, the **Museu Nacional dos Coches** (p. 111), has one of the world's greatest collections of historical carriages. It is Portugal's most visited museum and contains Cinderella-style carriages dating back to the 16th century. The oldest was used to bring King Filipe II from Madrid to Lisbon during the Spanish occupation, and the most exuberant is a gold-covered vehicle given as a gift to the Pope from a Portuguese king in 1715. It's housed in a new building that opened in 2015 in Lisbon's riverside **Belém** district.

Nearby in the **Picadeiro Henrique Calado** you can watch some 18th-century-style horsemanship. This arena is where the Portuguese School of Equestrian Arts holds its daily training and weekly performances, with horses and riders clad in period costumes to conjure up the displays they once put on to entertain the royal family. The **Lusitano** horses used in the performances are a unique Portuguese breed.

Day 7

Head back out to the riverside **Parque das Nações** district packed with modern architecture. Apart from the **Oceanário** (p. 113), kids will love the **Pavilion of Knowledge–Ciência Viva,** an interactive science museum, where they can engage in an array of experiments, including riding a bike on a tight rope. It's loads of fun. After that, take a ride in the cable cars that run high above the riverbank, giving a splendid view over Europe's longest bridge. Be warned: The area also contains another big shopping mall.

SETTLING INTO LISBON

5

Lisbon is the gateway to Portugal, the nation's capital, its biggest city and a vibrant cultural hub. Long a sleeping beauty, the city is now firmly established as a must-see European destination. Bathed in milky light, the ancient hills of Europe's sunniest capital overlook the shimmering estuary of the river Tagus just before it flows into the Atlantic. Lisbon has been a global meeting place since its explorers and traders reached out around the world in the 15th century.

Today, it's changing fast, as trendy boutiques, gourmet restaurants, and chic hotels spring up to serve the tourists who fill its winding lanes and 18th-century avenues. Some fear it's losing its soul, but the city's unique character endures. Find it in the impassioned strains of fado music echoing down the alleys of Alfama, the fishmongers hawking sardines in the Ribeira market, or the gentle sway of ferry boats carrying commuters across the broad river. For visitors the city offers a potent emotional mix. You can surf ocean rollers in the morning, peruse exquisite art in the afternoon, and then dine alfresco beneath castle walls once guarded by Roman legionnaires, Arab warriors, and crusader knights.

TOP THINGS TO DO Like Rome, Lisbon is built on seven hills, each ringed by viewpoints (*miradouros*) where you can contemplate the city laid out before you, the vast estuary, and distant hills: The *miradouro* at **São Pedro de Alcântara** (p. 101) is a good place to start. Eat seafood in bustling *marisqueiras* (seafood restaurants) like **Ramiro** (p. 88). Rattle through lanes in a vintage street car; **Tram 28** (p. 105) is the most sought after, but other routes are less crowded. Grab some great art: from the masterpiece-filled **Gulbenkian** (p. 116) and **Ancient Art** (p. 111) museums to cutting-edge collections at the **MAAT** (p. 107) or **CCB** (p. 110). Refresh your wardrobe in the hip **Príncipe Real** (p. 126) district, where an Arabian Nights–style palace maybe the world's prettiest shopping mall. Sip *bicas* (shots of strong espresso) at the bar where poets and artists have dallied for over a century. Explore the monumental **Belém** (p. 71) neighborhood redolent of the great Age of

Lisbon

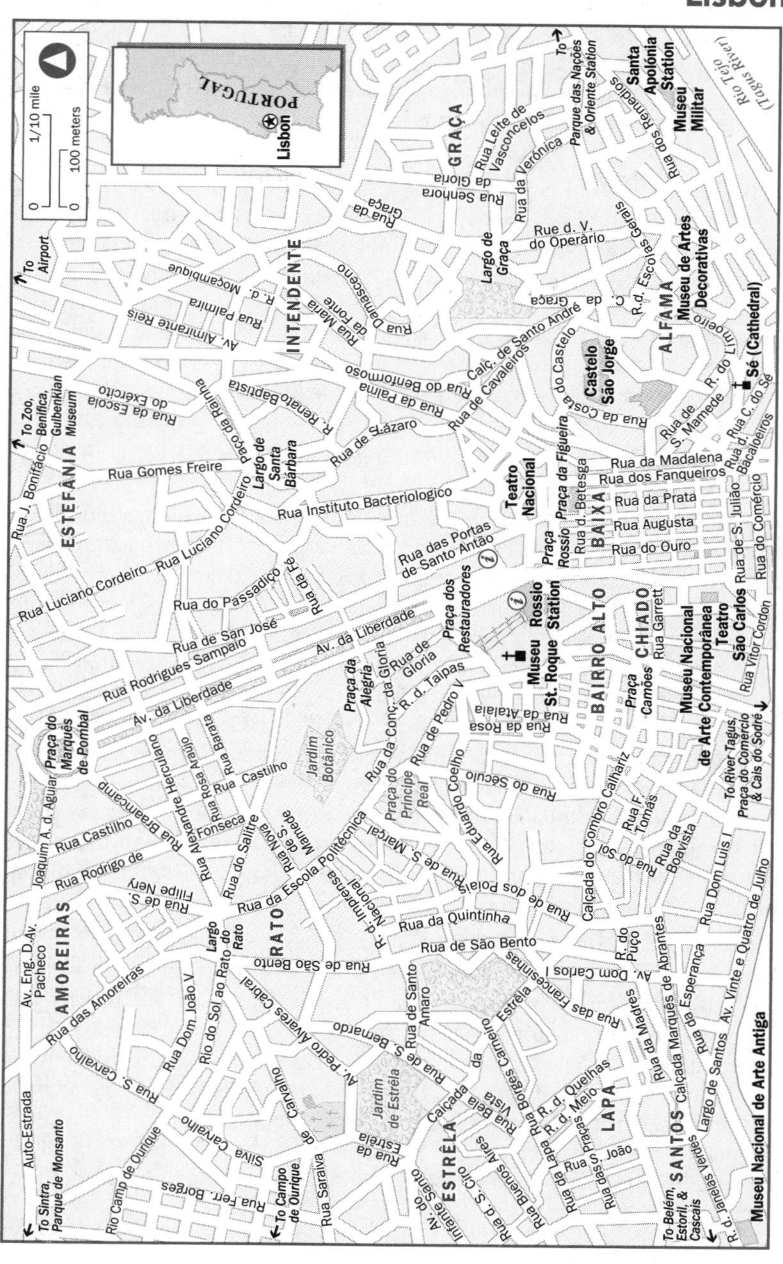

PORTUGAL
Lisbon
0 1/10 mile
0 100 meters
To Airport
To Zoo, Benfica, Gulbenkian Museum
To Sintra, Parque de Monsanto
To Campo de Ourique
To Belém, Estoril, & Cascais
To River Tagus, Praça do Comércio & Cais do Sodré
To Parque das Nações & Oriente Station
Rio Tejo (Tagus River)
GRAÇA
INTENDENTE
ESTEFÂNIA
AMOREIRAS
RATO
ESTRÊLA
LAPA
SANTOS
BAIXA
BAIRRO ALTO
CHIADO
ALFAMA
Santa Apolónia Station
Museu Militar
Museu de Artes Decorativas
Sé (Cathedral)
Castelo São Jorge
Teatro Nacional
Rossio Station
Museu St. Roque
Museu Nacional de Arte Contemporânea
Teatro São Carlos
Museu Nacional de Arte Antiga
Jardim Botânico
Jardim de Estrêla
Praça do Marquês de Pombal
Praça dos Restauradores
Praça Rossio
Praça da Figueira
Praça da Alegria
Praça do Príncipe Real
Praça Camões
Largo de Santa Bárbara
Largo de Graça
Largo do Rato
Av. da Liberdade
Rua das Portas de Santo Antão
Rua Instituto Bacteriologico
Rua Gomes Freire
Rua Luciano Cordeiro
Rua do Passadiço
Rua de San José
Rua Rodrigues Sampaio
Rua Castilho
Rua Braamcamp
Rua Alexandre Herculano
Rua da Escola Politécnica
Rua de São Bento
Rua da Quintinha
Rua Garrett
Rua do Ouro
Rua Augusta
Rua da Prata
Rua dos Fanqueiros
Rua da Madalena
Rua do Comércio
Rua de S. Julião
Rua do Século
Rua da Rosa
Rua da Atalaia
Rua da Misericórdia
Calçada do Combro
Av. Dom Carlos I
Rua Dom Luís I
Av. Vinte e Quatro de Julho
Calçada Marquês de Abrantes
Largo de Santos
Rua dos Remedios
Rua da Verónica
Rua Leite de Vasconcelos
Rua Senhora da Glória
Av. Almirante Reis
Rua da Palma
Rua do Benformoso
Rua de Cavaleiros
Calç. de Santo André
Rua de S. Lázaro
Rua Rodrigo da Fonseca
Rua Dom João V
Rio do Sol ao Rato
Rua das Amoreiras
Rua Saraiva de Carvalho
Rua Silva Carvalho
Auto-Estrada
Rua de Buenos Aires
Rua da Lapa
Rua das Janelas Verdes

Discoveries. Go nose-to-nose with sharks and rays at the colossal **Oceanário** (p. 113) aquarium. Dance the night away in the clubs of **Cais do Sodré.** Save some energy for the best Lisbon activity: losing yourself in a stroll around the streets and alleys of the old city where every curve can reveal a surprise, be it a church lined with baroque gold; a "hospital" that's treated broken dolls since 1830; or another stunning view of the expanse of blue water that holds the city in an eternal embrace.

SHOPPING **Avenida da Liberdade** has been Lisbon's chicest shopping street since 1879. Inspired by Paris's Champs Élysées, this tree-lined boulevard boasts 1,200 yards of designer stores, theaters, and upscale eateries. More eclectic shopping experiences can be found in older neighborhoods like the **Baixa, Chiado,** or **Príncipe Real.** The Baixa has a street almost entirely devoted to tiny retro stores selling buttons and ribbons, as well as some of the best specialist wine and gourmet stores. Chiado's treasures include the world's oldest bookshop and a tiny boutique dedicated to exquisite handmade leather gloves. Príncipe Real is a fashionistas' delight. For mall rats, the city is ringed by huge modern shopping centers: **Amoreiras** is the poshest and most architecturally distinctive.

DINING Lisbon's food scene has been transformed. A generation of young chefs such as José Avillez and Henrique Sá Pessoa have refined and modernized Portuguese cuisine, winning the city of constellation of newly minted Michelin starts. The city's historic ties means Lisbon has always had an exotic mix of restaurants serving cuisine from places like Brazil, Mozambique and Goa, but lately there's been an explosion of international eating options meaning you can get excellent pizza, ceviche, mezze, or braised sea cucumber. Thankfully, traditional Portuguese food is still available either in hole-in-the-wall *tascas* (taverns) or decades-old temples to tradition, where white-suited waiters will supply you with city favorites like fava beans sautéed with peppery *chouriço* sausage and cilantro, or shredded salt-cod mixed with scrambled egg, fried potatoes, and black olives. Then, of course, you must track down the source of Lisbon's most successful culinary export, the cinnamon-dusted custard tarts, known as *pastéis de nata*.

NIGHTLIFE & ENTERTAINMENT Lisbon's legendary nightlife includes riverside discotheques featuring Europe's top DJs, rooftops where you can toast the sunset, and whimsical antique-filled cocktail bars. The **Bairro Alto** and **Cais do Sodré** districts hold the greatest concentration of nightspots. To get an authentic taste of Lisbon's unique fado music, it's best to go late when most tourists head for their hotels but true aficionados emerge. Cinema buffs will love that Portugal doesn't dub, but shows subtitled films in their original language. The **São Carlos** opera house is a rococo treat; the **Gulbenkian** orchestra offers world-class classical music, and the **Teatro Camões** showcases avant-garde dance.

LISBON YESTERDAY & TODAY

In his hit *Lisboa Menina e Moça,* fado legend Carlos do Carmo croons an erotic paean to his hometown, likening this "city-woman" to a lover who has seduced him by the purity of her light. Lisbon is a sensual city, easy to fall in love with. Seen from the river, the gentle curves of its hills are clad in a harmonious architectural mix where gothic towers and baroque church fronts blend with the Enlightenment rigor of its 18th-century downtown.

Sunlight from the expanse of slow-flowing river reflects onto limestone walls and paving stones giving Lisbon a "white city" nickname. Close up, you'll find it's full of colors. Centuries-old government ministries, mansions, or apartment blocks can be painted in burgundy, cornflower-blue, or lemon-yellow. Even the skyline's most intrusive modern addition—the towers of the Amoreiras shopping mall—are a technicolor tribute to 1980s taste.

Be prepared for a sensory overload. Another favorite song claims "it smells good, it smells of Lisbon": you can catch the scent of orange blossom, laundry freshly hung from wrought-laundry balconies, or cinnamon sprinkled on oven-hot pastries. Tastes and sounds will be a multicultural mix. Lisbon was the first global city; its cuisine is fused with cinnamon, cumin, and cilantro. Shots of thick black coffee are knocked back at countless neighborhood pastry shops. The soundtrack will include the cries of gulls, rattling of streetcars, and fado music mixed with rhythms from Brazil and Africa, the throb of Portuguese hip-hop from the suburbs. Feel the cool of marble bars in 19th-century cafes or the sun-warmed *azulejo* tiles on the walls of a baroque church.

Of course, you also get the horns of backed up traffic, the whiff of blocked drains and uncollected trash, and the babble of tourists from around the world. Lisbon is not a museum, but the capital of a modern European state with all the issues facing big cities around the world. Despite the changes, travelers will discover a place of great beauty: laidback, welcoming, and affordable.

The history of Lisbon can be told in four landmarks. Let's start with **Castelo de São Jorge** (p. 98), the city's cradle, whose crenelated ramparts are immediately visible on one of the highest of the city's shills. Humans have lived here since at least the 8th century B.C. Celtic tribes and Phoenician, Greek, and Carthaginian traders all had defensive outposts before Roman colonizers erected a fort to defend their seaport of Olisippo. After them came a succession of Germanic tribes, including the Christian Visigoths who ruled from their capital in Toledo for almost 150 years, before they were defeated by Muslim armies who swept in from North Africa and captured Lisbon in 714. Under Arab rule, the city spread down the hillside in the current neighborhoods of Alfama and Mouraria, whose narrow winding lanes still recall the medinas of North African cities. Remains of the Moorish fortifications (*Cerca Moura*) can still be seen today, but most of the medieval walls you see were built after the 1147 capture of the city by Portugal's first king, Afonso I Henriques, with the help of crusaders from northern Europe. The siege of Lisbon was a turning point in the Reconquista wars, confirming Afonso's leadership and setting the Christian forces on course for victory, although it would be another 100 years before they captured the whole of the country. In 1255, King Afonso III, grandson of the country's founder, transferred the capital from Coimbra to Lisbon, and the castle became a royal residence. It was named after St. George (*São Jorge*) only in the 14th century, after King João I married an English princess, the legendary dragon-slayer being England's patron saint.

Next up, the **Mosteiro dos Jerónimos,** a symbol of Portugal's Age of Discoveries. The 15th-century monastery is the city's best example of the flamboyant Manueline style of architecture, named for King Manuel I who oversaw Lisbon's transformation from a medieval town on the margins of Europe to the capital of a global empire. The man who perhaps did most to bring about that change lies buried inside: Vasco da Gama, who prayed on this spot the night before he left on the first sea journey from Europe around Africa to India. The Discoveries made Portugal rich and powerful, as Asian spices, African ivory, and Brazilian gold flooded into Lisbon. Long viewed as a golden age, the era is now questioned by historians given Portugal's role in launching the Atlantic slave trade and European colonialism. Foreign travelers at the time were amazed at the variety of produce and people in Lisbon. By the mid-16th-century, estimates suggest, over 10% of the city's population was black, both slaves and free. A visiting Flemish painter produced cityscapes showing Africans carrying out menial tasks, but also mixed-race couples dancing together and a black horseman in colors of the knightly Order of Santiago.

Manuel's reign also saw the expulsion of Portugal's Jewish community who had thrived in Lisbon since Roman and Arab times. Under pressure from Spain, in 1496 he ordered all Jews to convert to Catholicism or leave. Those who chose to stay were persecuted by the Inquisition. For more than 250 years, it tormented converts suspected of clinging to the Jewish faith and executed almost 500 people in *autos-de-fé* in Lisbon. A monument near Rossio square marks the spot where the Inquisition carried out its deeds. In 2019, the city council approved plans for a memorial to the victims of slavery on Lisbon's waterfront.

Our third landmark is the vast riverside plaza officially named **Praça do Comércio.** Even when Portugal was in decline as a world power in the 18th century, its overseas territories continued to bring in riches, notably in the form of Brazilian gold, which financed the construction of lavish churches and palaces around the capital. It all came crashing down on November 1, 1755, when Lisbon was hit by a massive earthquake. Tremors were felt around Europe but it devastated the Portuguese capital, where it was followed by a tsunami and fire that left the city a gutted, charred shambles. Up to 90,000 were believed to have died. Cometh the hour, cometh the man: Prime Minister Sebastião José de Carvalho e Melo, better known as the Marquis of Pombal, took charge of the reconstruction efforts. He rebuilt downtown Lisbon along modern lines, inspired by the rational ideas of the Enlightenment.

Praça do Comércio became the centerpiece of the new capital, with grand government buildings in an austere classical style that became known as Pombaline. From it runs a grid of straight streets and identical buildings making the Baixa district unlike the heart of any other European city. Informally, Lisbonites still refer to the square as Terreiro do Paço (Palace Yard) after the royal residence that stood there before the quake laid it low.

Pombal tried to modernize the country as well as its town planning, but his reforms were too little, too late. Left behind by the Industrial Revolution, Portugal entered the 19th century in deep decline. When Napoleon's troops conquered Lisbon in 1807, the royal family escaped in the nick of time on British ships and transferred the capital to Rio de Janeiro. Brazil's independence and a civil war in the 1830s hastened Portugal's decline.

In 1908 King Carlos II and his oldest son were assassinated in Praça do Comércio and 2 years later, a republic was proclaimed from the balcony of City Hall. More chaos followed until dictator António de Oliveira Salazar took power in 1932. He managed to keep Portugal neutral during World War II, when Lisbon became a nest of spies and a haven for refugees.

By the 1960s, however, Portugal was at war: Lisbon's quaysides saw the tearful departure of troops ships headed for colonial conflicts in Angola, Mozambique, and Guinea Bissau. Poor and isolated, Portugal was an outcast in democratic Europe. That began to change as dawn broke on April 25, 1974 to reveal armored cars and young soldiers taking up position in Praça do Comércio. The revolution launched by junior officers immediately won the hearts of Lisbon's citizens, who took to the streets and decorated the soldiers' guns with carnations from the flower stalls on Rossio. Portugal was set on the path to democracy.

The soaring towers and cutting-edge architecture of **Parque das Nações** symbolize modern Lisbon. The district was built to house the Expo '98 World Fair, which drew 11 million visitors to the city on the 500th anniversary of Vasco da Gama's arrival in India. It was a brash statement of a newly confident country. The new landmarks included Europe's then-longest bridge, towering blocks of upscale apartments, shopping malls, exhibition halls, theatres, and a railway station designed by Spanish architectural superstar Santiago Calatrava. It embodied Lisbon's transformation since the 1974 revolution. After some years of revolutionary turmoil, the country emerged as a stable parliamentary democracy. In 1986, it joined what would become the European Union, along with neighboring Spain. EU funds and foreign investment fueled an economic boom with new roads and infrastructure springing up around the country. The party had fizzled out by the mid-2000s and Lisbon, like the rest of Portugal, was hard hit by the world economic crisis. The capital, however, has been at the forefront of a recovery since 2015, with tourism and foreign investment fueling a booming property market.

Today, the city is the heart of an urban area that's home to 2.8 million people. Its airport struggles to keep up with the demand for visitors flying in to enjoy its attractions. Neighborhoods in the old center that were once picturesquely rundown are spruced up with facades brightly painted or covered in new *azulejos*. The downside of the renewal is that those districts are losing their character. Residents are forced out as demand for vacation apartments pushes up rents; unique stores and cafes that have served neighborhoods for generations are replaced with souvenir shops and hipster watering holes that look like they're transplanted from New York's Williamsburg or London's Shoreditch. Like in Prague and Barcelona, you'll find old timers who'll tell you Lisbon's not what it was, but its sun-drenched beauty endures and, if you know where to look, there's still charm aplenty in the streets and squares, along with marvelous museums, fabulous (and still affordable) food and wines, and amazing architecture for all tastes from early medieval to startlingly modernist.

ORIENTATION

When to Visit

Lisbon is a year-round destination, but the summer months of July and August are the busiest, when tourists flock in, temperatures sizzle, and *Lisboetas* leave on vacation. June is a party month when Lisbon city celebrates its patron, Saint Anthony. It's great for atmosphere with street parties and open air concerts on warm evenings, but not ideal if you seek peace and quiet. Winter is calmer, when hotels are cheaper, temperatures cool (January averages 12°C/53°F), and cultural programs are in full swing in museums and theaters. April and May are many people's favorites as the weather warms and markets fill with strawberries and juicy loquats, but they can be showery. September and October see the city still warm and fizzing with energy after the summer break.

Arriving

BY PLANE Lisbon's **Humberto Delgado Airport** (www.aeroportolisboa.pt; ✆ **21/841-35-00**), is Portugal's main entryway, serving almost 30 million passengers in 2018. It's an important hub for flights from Europe to Brazil and Africa and has an increasing number of direct routes to North America (p. 465). The smaller Terminal 2 handles mostly low-cost departures within Europe. There are plans to open a second airport by 2022 on the site of a military air base in Montijo, across the river Tagus from downtown.

The current airport is conveniently just 6.5km (4 miles) from the heart of the city. A cheap and easy way to the center is the **Aerobus** (www.aerobus.pt; ✆ **21/850-32-25**) shuttle service running on two lines into the city center and a third, less frequent, line to the Sete Rios bus terminal. Lines 1 and 2 stop close to main downtown landmarks and hotels. They operate daily every 20 minutes from 8am to 9pm and take approximately 30 minutes to reach the center. Tickets cost 4€ from the stand outside Arrivals, or 3.60€ online.

The airport **Metro** station is part of the red line, connecting with central Lisbon in Alameda (green line), Saldanha (yellow line), or São Sebastião (blue line) stations. A single journey costs 1.40€ plus 0.50€ for the reusable Viva Viagem Card (p. 73).

Taxi passengers line up outside the Arrivals hall. The parking lot in front of Departures is the place to meet drivers from **Uber** or other ride hailing firms. Taxi fares to downtown should be around 15€, with supplements at night and an extra 1.60€ for each piece of luggage. Watch the meter, because taxi drivers frequently try to hike prices for unsuspecting visitors.

BY TRAIN Lisbon's few international train connections (p. 467) arrive at the **Oriente** station in Parque das Nações and **Santa Apolónia** close to Alfama. Both are on the metro and have taxi ranks. Mainline trains to Porto and the north also depart from there. Trains from the Algarve and Alentejo arrive at the **Sete Rios** and **Entrecampos** stations. Bookings on domestic routes can be made on the website of **CP** (www.cp.pt) the national rail company, which also has details of fares, routes, and timetables

BY BUS Intercity domestic and international buses (p. 468 and 471) terminate at the **Terminal Rodoviário de Sete Rios** (www.rede-expressos.pt; **© 21/358-14-72**) which is next to **Jardim Zoológico** subway station, where you can catch a 10-minute metro ride to downtown.

BY CAR If you are arriving by car (p. 466), try to avoid rush hour when there are a number of bottlenecks, notably on the Ponte 25 de Abril bridge. If you can, book accommodation with private parking, because parking lots are expensive, street parking is limited, and foreign-registered cars left overnight in downtown streets are a preferred target for thieves looking for valuables inside.

Visitor Information

The official **Lisbon Tourism Association** (www.visitlisboa.com) has 13 **"Ask Me Lisboa"** information points around the city, including on Praça do Comércio (**© 21-031-2810**) and in **Palácio Foz** on Praça dos Restauradores (**© 21/346-33-14**). Both are open daily 9am to 8pm. If you are planning some intensive museum visiting, consider the **Lisbon Card** run by the tourist board. It includes free public transport and free (and sometimes fast-track) access to 35 museums and attractions, including A-list destinations like Jerónimos monastery and the Museu Nacional de Arte Antiga, as well as reductions on selected tours and stores. Adult prices range from 20€ for 24 hours or 42€ for 72 hours, with reductions for children. They are available online at the Visit Lisbon site, or from any of their stores and information points.

City Layout & Neighborhoods

Lisbon is the westernmost capital of continental Europe. Atlantic beaches start a 20-minute train ride away from downtown. It's spread out along the north bank of the Tagus, the longest river on the Iberian Peninsula, where it broadens into an estuary almost 20km (12 miles) wide before narrowing again just before it reaches the ocean. Like Rome, Lisbon is built on seven hills, but as the city spread it took in more rises and valleys. That makes walking tough on the calves but easy on the eye, as you discover more and more viewpoints over the city and the river. Here's a pick of Lisbon's most interesting neighborhoods.

BAIXA The city's downtown core, Baixa was laid out in a grid of rectangular blocks after the earthquake of 1755. It's bookended by two plazas: **Praça do Comércio,** whose arcaded government offices and sidewalk cafes open out onto the Tagus; and **Rossio** (officially Praça de D. Pedro IV) the city's favorite meeting place, featuring waves of black-and-white paving, the **National Theater,** fountains, and a towering column in honor of King Pedro. The lattice of busy streets running between them is a unique example of 18th-century town planning and a major shopping hub. Although tourist-oriented stores are increasingly taking over, it's still packed with enchanting curiosities: from generations-old stores selling buttons and ribbons to grocers backed with strings of spicy sausage and bags of aromatic coffee, and splendid old cafes like **Confeitaria Nacional** (p. 106). The grandest, most harmonious (and most touristy) street is pedestrianized **Rua Augusta,** which ends in a triumphal arch leading into Praça do Comércio. Among the Baixa's curiosities are the **Elevador de Santa Justa** (p. 105) and the fire-damaged **Igreja de São Domingos** church. **Praça da Figueira** is another fine square with interesting stores and cafes.

ALFAMA, SÉ & CASTELO Immediately east of Baixa is the hill where Lisbon began. It's crowned by **Castelo São Jorge** and the medieval lanes of the Castelo neighborhood that surrounds it. They contain some fine hotels and the **Fundação Ricardo do Espírito Santo Silva,** a living museum with artisans' workshops. On the slope leading up to the castle, the **Sé** neighborhood takes its name from the fortress like 12th-century Cathedral (Sé). It's traversed by the famed **Tram 28** line along a street lined with antique and handicraft shops. At its foot, **Campo das Cebolas** is a plaza lined with cafes, restaurants, and historic facades like **Casa dos Bicos.** Next door, **Alfama** is Lisbon's most characteristic district. Its steeply winding streets are the spiritual home of fado music and, although fast gentrifying, it remains highly atmospheric. Among Alfama's many churches, grand **São Vicente de Fora** contains wonderful azulejos, and **Santa Engrácia** holds the tombs of Portugal's great and good. Both have sweeping river vistas from their rooftops, but Alfama's best view is from **Largo Portas de Sol**—especially if you get (or stay) up for sunrise.

CHIADO, BAIRRO ALTO & PRÍNCIPE REAL The hill on the other side of Baixa is for shopping and partying. **Chiado** has been a chic shopping district since the 19th century. On its streets nestle venerable shops like the tiny **Luvaria Ulisses** glovemaker and **Livraria Bertrand,** the world's oldest working bookshop. There are also splendid old cafes, grand theaters like the **São Carlos opera house,** and the **National Museum of Contemporary Art.** Among the attractive squares, **Praça Luís de Camões** is a popular meeting place, and **Largo do Carmo** fronts the gothic arches of the **Convento do Carmo,** an atmospheric museum amid ruins left by the 1755 earthquake.

Bairro Alto means "high neighborhood"—the name refers to its hillside elevation rather than the impact of substances consumed in the bars and clubs that line its narrow alleys. Amid the booze joints are some cool bars, fine restaurants, and fado houses. Across the road, **São Roque** church has a golden interior of baroque carvings. **Príncipe Real,** spread out around the shady gardens of the same name, is the premier fashionista hangout, packed with eclectic boutiques and yet more cool bars. The **Miradouro de São Pedro de Alcântara** has iconic views over the city and **Praça das Flores** (Square of Flowers) is as pretty as its name.

CAIS DO SODRÉ, SANTOS & ALCÂNTARA **Cais do Sodré** is the other main nightlife district, down by the river. Its nocturnal focus is bar-lined Rua Nova do Carvalho, better known as "**Pink Street**" for its rose painted asphalt. During the day, the big attraction is the **Time Out Market,** an always-packed gourmet hall, and its neighbor the traditional **Ribeira Market** with its morning displays of fish and fruit. Riverside **Santos** has more bars and design stores, but its must-see is the **Museu Nacional de Arte Antiga,** a 17th-century palace housing a world-class collection of old masters. Farther along the river and in the shadow of the **Ponte 25 de Abril** bridge, **Alcântara** is an old working-class district that's making the most of its industrial heritage with **LX Factory,** a jumble of hip stores, bars, and restaurants installed in a derelict printworks and the **Museo do Oriente,** a superb collection of Asian art housed in a 1940s warehouse.

BELÉM Memories of the Discoveries abound in **Belém.** Spread out amid riverside gardens are the unmissable **Jerónimos Monastery** and the **Torre de Belém,** perhaps Europe's most photogenic fortress. There's a 1960s **Monument to the Discoveries** in the grandiose style preferred by the Salazar dictatorship, and a **Maritime Museum.** More recent attractions include the **Centro Cultural de Belém** (CCB), which holds theaters and a fine modern art collection, the **Coach Museum** and the spanking-new **MAAT** contemporary art center. Portugal's president lives in a pretty pink palace overlooking the river and, of course, there is the cafe that opened in 1837 to serve the custard and cinnamon treats known as **Pastéis de Belém.**

AVENIDA & AVENIDAS NOVAS Back downtown, head north from Rossio and you'll hit the **Avenida de Liberdade**, Lisbon's swankiest boulevard since 1879. It's over a kilometer (1,000 yards) long, with trees, ponds, and pavements down the center and boutiques, banks, shopping malls, and theaters along both sides. It's the place to flex your credit card. Oddly enough, it also contains the headquarters of the Portuguese Communist Party in a striking Art Deco building. At the top is **Parque Eduardo VII,** the biggest city center park. Farther out toward the airport is the **Avenidas Novas** district laid out in the 19th and early 20th centuries. It has more shopping, historic cafes like **Pastelaria Versailles,** and quirky buildings like the arabesque **Campo Pequeno** bullring. But by far, the biggest draw is the **Gulbenkian Museum,** with amazing art surrounded by a tranquil garden.

ESTRELA, LAPA & CAMPO DE OURIQUE Uphill from Santos, the tony **Lapa** neighborhood is filled with mansions holding embassies and ambassadorial residences. Neighboring **Estrela** is centered around the **Basílica da Estrela,** a white-domed baroque church from the 18th century and the **Jardim da Estrela** gardens, a favorite place for Lisbon families to cool off in summer. Nearby **Campo de Ourique** is a village within the city: Built largely in the early 20th century on a flat plateau, it contains some fine Art Deco buildings, a gourmet market, and excellent shops and cafes away from the tourist trail (even though it's the terminus of **Tram 28**). The **Cemitério dos Prazeres,** Lisbon's oldest cemetery, is here; a stroll among the popular trees and grand 19th-century tombs is a peaceful escape from the urban bustle.

MOURARIA, GRAÇA & INTENDENTE At the other end of tramline 28 is **Graça,** a bustling, quintessentially Lisbon area atop one of the tallest hills. A leafy terrace in front of the baroque **Convento da Graça** is one of the best places to enjoy a drink with a view. Tumbling down the hill is the medieval Arab neighborhood of **Mouraria,** whose maze of alleys echoes to the sound of *fado*. It leads down to **Intendente,** once a seedy red-light district, now fast upcoming, particularly around **Largo do Intendente Pina Manique,** home to the tiled facade of **Viúva Lamego,** one of the city's best ceramic stores. **Largo Martin Moniz** is a focus for Lisbon's Chinese and South Asian communities; around it are Asian groceries and some tasty hole-in-the-wall eateries.

PARQUE DAS NAÇÕES Strung out along the Tagus at Lisbon's northeastern extremity, **Parque das Nações** is a modernist counterpoint to the city's retro charms. It holds Lisbon's most-visited attraction, the **Oceanário,** one of the world's biggest and best aquariums, containing a panoply of sea life from huge rays to tiny fluorescent jellyfish. The whole neighborhood was developed on a former industrial site for the 1998 World's Fair. Among all the architecture is an interactive **science museum** that kids will love, a big shopping mall, casino, theaters showcasing dance and music, towering hotels, and some first-class riverside restaurants.

GETTING AROUND

Central Lisbon is relatively compact and walking is a joy, although because of the hills it can be hard on the feet. There's a clean, safe, and efficient subway system, and the trams and buses can be a delight to ride through the historic streets. Traffic gets jammed at rush hour, driving in narrow old town streets is challenging, and parking hard to find except in expensive parking lots. Public transport is a better option. Taxis are plentiful, easy to hail, and cheap compared to many other European cities. Uber and other ride-hailing services are available. Ferries can take you to destinations across the Tagus, and suburban trains run out to Cascais and Sintra. There's a plethora of tourist-related transport options: from tuk-tuks to bikes and electronic scooters.

One Card, Many Rides

For most modes of public transport in Lisbon and surrounding areas, you can use the **Viva Viagem card,** which can be bought at ticket booths and machines at metro stations as well as the post office, most newsagents, and other shops bearing MOB and Payshop logos. They cost just 0.50€ and can be charged up with amounts from 3€ to 40€ through a system called zapping. Using the card, a single ride costs 1.31€. The amount is deducted from your card when you touch it on a contact pad as you enter and leave metro or train station platforms, or board the bus. In comparison, a single ticket for the metro costs 1.45€ and a bus ride is 2€ if you buy a ticket on board. The cards can also be used on suburban trains like those heading to Cascais and Sintra, ferry boats crossing the Tagus river, and Lisbon's iconic trams and funiculars. You must buy a card for each person traveling. They are valid for a year, if you are planning a return trip. Alternatively, you can buy a daily card offering unlimited 24-hour travel for 6.40€ for the bus, street car, and metro, or 10.55€ if you add suburban train services, for example to Cascais and Sintra. Avoid buying your ticket at the ever-crowded Cais do Sodré railway station.

METRO The Metro (www.metrolisboa.pt), Lisbon's clean and modern subway, is the quickest and easiest way to get around. There are four lines identified by colors: red, yellow, blue, and green. Many of the metro stations are clad in tiles decorated by modern artists and are attractions in their own right. The Olaias, Parque, and Cidade Universitária stations are recommended. The Metro operates daily from 6:30am to 1am.

BUS, TRAM, TRAIN & FERRY The city bus company **Carris** (www.carris.pt) runs an extensive network that gets to places the metro doesn't reach. Carris also runs street cars (***eléctricos***), often using little yellow trollies dating back to the early 1900s, which have become a major attraction for visitors (annoying regular users who often find them too crowded on their commute to work). Other public transport options include the suburban rail lines run by the **CP** rail company (www.cp.pt) departing from Cais do Sodré station for the beach resorts of the Cascais coast, and to Sintra from Rossio station. For a cheap, off-the-beaten track adventure and great views of Lisbon, take the little orange **ferry boats** or fast catamarans that leave from Cais do Sodré, Terreiro do Paço, and Belém to the south bank of the Tagus.

FUNICULARS & ELEVATORS Carris runs a trio of cute funiculars that will haul you up to elevated districts: **Glória,** which goes from Praça dos Restauradores to Rua São Pedro de Alcântara; **Bica,** from Rua da Boavista in Santos to the Bairro Alto; and **Lavra,** from the eastern side of Avenida da Liberdade to Campo Mártires da Pátria. There's also the **Elevador de Santa Justa,** an iron landmark constructed in 1902 and a stylish way (although you'll have to queue) to rise from Baixa to Chiado. A pair of newer elevators will take you from Baixa to Castelo (they aren't so picturesque, but are free and will save your feet).

TAXIS & RIDE HIRE Taxis are plentiful, relatively cheap and easily hailed in the street in all but the busiest times. A 15-minute trip from riverside Praça do Comércio to the cool Campo de Ourique neighborhood will cost around 5€, for example. For a radio taxi, call ✆ **21/811-90-00** (www.retalis.pt). **Uber** and other ride hailing services such as Bolt and Cabify also operate. **Tipping** cab drivers is not obligatory, but most travelers will round up to the nearest euro, or add a euro or so on longer trips.

[FastFACTS] LISBON

See also "Fast Facts" on p. 471.

Currency Exchange Currency-exchange booths at the Santa Apolónia station and at the airport are open 24 hours a day. But ATMs run by the Multibanco network offer better rates. They operate in English, and there are almost 3,000 around the city.

Dentists Among dental practices orientated to foreign visitors are: **São Dente** (www.saodente.pt; ✆ **21/397-00-96**) at Rua Borges Carneiro 20B in Lapa; and **Medidental** (www.medidental.pt) with clinics in Alcantâra (✆ **21/590-06-20**) and Campo do Ourique (✆ **21/139-00-01**).

Drugstores Pharmacies (*farmácias*) normally open Monday to Friday 9am to 7pm, and Saturdays 9am to 1pm. Most in the center will have staff who speak English. A list of "farmácias de serviço" that stay open late and on Sundays are listed on the windows of all pharmacies and on the website www.farmaciasdeservico.net.

Hospitals & Doctors The U.S. embassy has a list of hospitals and doctors: (https://pt.usembassy.gov/u-s-citizen-services/doctors). Good private hospitals include **Hospital da Luz** (www.hospitaldaluz.pt; ✆ **21/710-44-00**) and **CUF** (www.saudecuf.pt/en; ✆ **21/112-17-17**). The English-speaking team at **International Medical Clinic of Lisbon** (www.cmil.pt; ✆ **21/351-33-10;** located at Av. Sidónio Pais 14 beside Parque Eduardo VII) offers general and specialized services.

Internet Access Lisbon is a wired-up city. Most restaurants, cafes, and hotels have free Wi-Fi (just ask for the password). There's also free Wi-Fi on buses, the metro, and in several public buildings.

Lost Property The Interior Ministry runs an interactive web page for locating lost property (https://perdidoseachados.mai.gov.pt), but it's only in Portuguese. Failing that, the Lisbon police lost property office is at **Secção de Achados da PSP,** Praça Cidade de Salazar Lote 180 in the Olivais Sul district near the airport (✆ **21/853-54-03;** open Mon–Fri 9am–12:30pm and 1:30–4pm). If you've lost something on a CP train, call customer service at ✆ **70/721-02-20.**

Luggage Storage & Lockers Lisbon **airport** runs a baggage storage system near the P2 car park (✆ **21/841-35-94**). It's open 24/7. Prices start from 3.36€ per day for luggage less than 10kg. There are coin-operated lockers at the following Lisbon **train stations:** Cais do Sodré, Lisboa Oriente, Lisboa Santa Apolónia, Rossio. and Sete Rios, with a 24-hour limit. Among several private storage operators are **City Lockers** (www.citylockers.pt), which has lockers in Rossio metro station and in the parking lots at Martin Moniz and Praça da Figueira; or **Luggage Storage Lisbon** (www.luggagestoragelisbon.com; ✆ **21/346-03-90**), which has storage in the Chiado and Parque das Nações areas. Online storage booking services like **Stasher** (www.stasher.com) and **Bagbnb** (www.bagbnb.com) also operate in Lisbon with local partners.

Police For emergencies call ✆ **112.** There is a "tourist police" unit dealing with travelers' problems based in the pink Palácio Foz building in Praça dos Restauradores (✆ **21/342-16-23** or ✆ **21/340-00-90**).

Safety Violent crime against tourists is rare, but pickpocketing and theft from parked cars are problems. Don't leave valuables in cars if you can avoid it, even during daylight. **Pickpockets** and bag snatchers tend to focus on crowded areas where there are lots of tourists. The Chiado district and the Portas do Sol viewpoint in Lisbon are hotspots. They also operate on public transport: Take special care on packed Lisbon streetcars. If you are robbed, it's best to report it to the police. They may not put out an all-points alert, but they will return stolen documents which frequently show up dumped by criminals after they've emptied purses and wallets of cash. Foreigners are frequently approached by shady characters offering cocaine or marijuana. What they sell is usually fake. They can seem intimidating and appear to operate with impunity. It's best to politely say "no, thanks" and walk away.

Taxes Lisbon (and Cascais) imposes a 2€ city tax on hotel bills on a per-person, per-night basis for all visitors over 13, up to a maximum 7 nights.

WHERE TO STAY

Lisbon has a wider range of accommodations than ever before. New hotels are sprouting up all the time, often in tastefully restored historic buildings. Unfortunately, as Lisbon's popularity grows, so do the prices. Short-term rentals have also expanded rapidly in Lisbon, with over 18,300 vacation apartments—known as *Alojamento Local*—registered between 2013 and 2019. They cater to all budgets, are often in restored historic buildings, and can offer practical alternatives to traditional hotels. Check out platforms like Airbnb.com and HomeAway.com.

Baixa & Chiado

EXPENSIVE

Martinhal Chiado ★★ This elegant city center five-star hotel is dedicated to families. Parents will enjoy the cool, clean design incorporated into a 19th-century mansion block. Kiddies will love the colorful family apartments, climbing wall, Xbox sessions, and pajama parties. There are supervised, complimentary kids-club activities for different age groups from early morning 'til 10pm. You can lunch with the offspring in the fun cafe serving Italian food and decorated with a vintage three-wheeler micro-car; then head out to dinner in the chic Chiado restaurants close by while the hotel's babysitters look after junior. The owners developed the family-friendly concept after traveling with their own four children, and have sister hotels and resorts in Cascais and the Algarve.

Rua das Flores, 44. www.martinhal.com. ✆ **21/850-77-88.** 37 units. 244€–650€ studios and apartments. Metro: Baixa-Chiado. Private parking 25€ for 24 hours, reservation required. **Amenities:** Restaurant; kid's club; indoor play room; babysitting; free Wi-Fi.

Memmo Príncipe Real ★★ Lisbon's second Memmo hotel maintains the group's high standards. It blends into the hillside down a tiny lane leading out of one of Lisbon's trendiest neighborhoods. Breathtaking views, elegant contemporary design in local limestone and painted tiles, and specially commissioned artworks. All rooms have Bang & Olufsen TVs and Hermes toiletries. Some have balconies overlooking the city and outdoor fireplaces. The stylish restaurant has modern Portuguese cuisine with influences from Asia, Brazil, and Africa.

Rua D. Pedro V, 56 J. www.memmohotels.com. ✆ **21/901-68-00.** 41 units. 270€–554€ doubles. Tram 24. Paid parking 30€ daily. **Amenities:** Restaurant; bar; outdoor pool; free Wi-Fi.

Pousada de Lisboa ★★★ This flagship addition to the Pousada chain of historic inns occupies a strategic location on riverside Praça do Comércio, in the heart of downtown. The sturdy, pastel-painted building is typical of the Pombaline style and was once Portugal's Interior Ministry. Its interior is filled with artworks and artifacts, including a number of works by the abstract painter Nadir Afonso. After decades of neglect, a 9€-million restoration program transformed the regal building into a first-class downtown accommodation. It has an indoor pool, a fine steak restaurant, and made-in-Portugal Castelbel toiletries in marble bathrooms. Orchids on the breakfast tables are a nice touch.

Praça do Comércio, 31-34. www.pousadas.pt/pt/hotel/pousada-lisboa. ✆ **21/040-76-40.** 90 units. 233€–429€ doubles. Metro: Terreiro do Paço. **Amenities:** Restaurant; bar; indoor swimming pool; spa; gym; massage service; babysitting; free Wi-Fi.

Verride Palácio Santa Catarina ★★★ Opened in 2017, this restored palace was an immediate success. Madonna reportedly loved it so much she wanted it for her Lisbon home. Robert De Niro and the Queen of Belgium were also among early guests. Built in the 1750s, the palace occupies a skyline-dominating site and one of the city's best viewpoints. Marvel at the marble archways, stucco ceilings and panels of antique tiles, all clustered around a monumental 18th-century staircase. On the roof, the pool and fashionable bar/restaurant offer jaw-dropping, 360-degree views. If you can afford it, the huge royal suites are decked out in lemon-yellow silk and stucco work like piped cream. It's grand, but the ambience is relaxed and unstuffy. Glorious floral arrangements are the work of the part-owner Dutch flower merchant.

Rua de Santa Catarina, 1. www.verridesc.pt. ✆ **21/157-30-55.** 19 units. 299€–1,000€ doubles; 850€–3,000€ suites. Tram: 28. **Amenities:** 2 restaurants; bar; outdoor pool; sun terrace; library; babysitting; free Wi-Fi.

MODERATE

Casa Baltazar ★★★ This classy bed-and-breakfast is a secret hideaway in the heart of the city. It's located in a discreet townhouse owned by the same family since 1882. They also own the Confeitaria Nacional, Lisbon's oldest (and arguably best) pastry shop, which guarantees a treat at breakfast time. Rooms blend modern art with antique furnishings. The best have private terraces with hot tubs and panoramic views over the Baixa and St. George's

Lisbon Accommodations

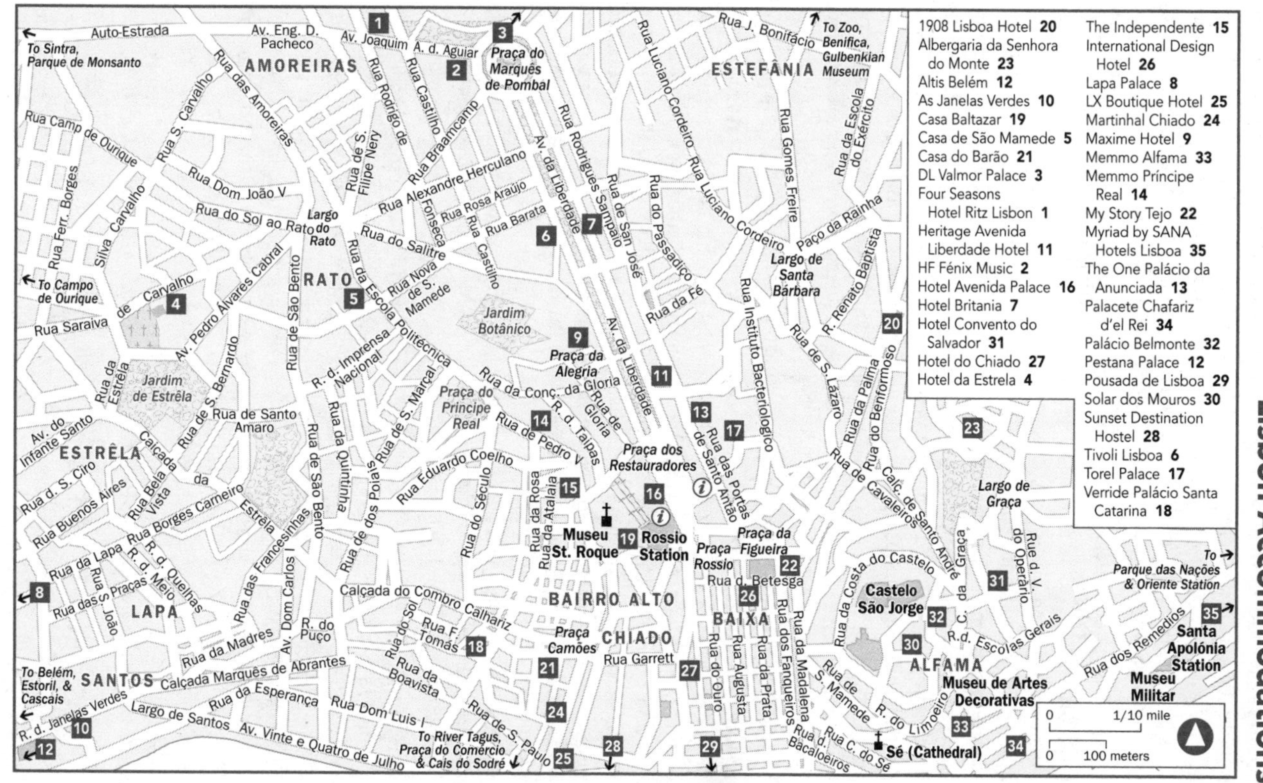

Castle. It's a 2-minute walk from Rossio square or the Carmo ruins. There's a secret garden with lawn, loungers, and pool. Inside, a cozy lounge comes with honesty bar, art books, and quirky ceramics.

Rua do Duque, 26. www.casabalthazarlisbon.com. ✆ **91/708-55-68.** 19 units. 160€–350€ doubles; 195€–340€ suites. Tram: 24. Free parking (reservation required). Adults only. **Amenities:** Heated outdoor pool; sun terrace; garden; Jacuzzi; bar; free Wi-Fi.

Casa do Barão ★★★ The "Baron's House," an aristocratic residence built after the 1755 earthquake, is now a friendly, family-run bed-and-breakfast, a haven in a quiet side street just off the bustle of Chiado. Rooms are spacious and white-painted with soft drapes, period prints, and marble bathrooms. Some are decorated with Bordallo Pinheiro ceramics. The top suites and rooms have private terraces and spectacular views. There's a courtyard pool, and you can breakfast in a secret garden filled with tropical vegetation. Complimentary port and muscatel wines await in the library.

Rua da Emenda, 84. www.casadobarao.com. ✆ **96/794-41-43.** 12 units. 105€–290€ doubles; 260€–390€ suites. Tram: 28. Public parking nearby. Adults only. **Amenities:** Bar; outdoor swimming pool, garden; free Wi-Fi.

Hotel do Chiado ★★ Occupying the two upper floors of a building restored by Pritzker Prize–winning Álvaro Siza Vieira after fire ravaged many of the Chiado's historic stores in 1988, Hotel do Chiado has a hard-to-beat location. Top-floor rooms have private lawns offering amazing views over the city and river. You can also admire the vista over cocktails on the terrace of the rooftop bar amid blooming bougainvillea and wildflowers. Rooms are comfortably sized and furnished in modern-classic style with sober natural tones, and they're just an elevator ride from the designer stores and centuries-old shops below.

Rua Nova do Almada, 114. www.hoteldochiado.pt. ✆ **21/325-61-00.** 39 units. 119€–353€ double. Parking 12€ daily, reservation required. Metro: Baixa-Chiado. **Amenities:** Bar; sun terrace; free Wi-Fi.

International Design Hotel ★★ From the floor-to-ceiling windows of the bar or the private balconies in suites and superior rooms, guests enjoy unique views over Rossio square, Lisbon's favorite meeting spot for centuries. Opened in the 1920s, the hotel received a total makeover in 2009. The exterior features creamy columns, lilac walls, and intricate wrought-iron railings. Inside it's hyper-hip, with modern art and colorful design features. Rooms are decorated according to Pop, Tribal, Urban, or Zen themes. The second-floor Bastardo restaurant is a favorite for Lisbon trendsetters.

Rua da Betesga, 3. www.idesignhotel.com. ✆ **21/324-09-90.** 55 units. Doubles 77€–324€. Metro: Rossio. **Amenities:** Restaurant; bar; garden; babysitting; free Wi-Fi.

LX Boutique Hotel ★★ Once the emblematic Hotel Braganza, a hang-out for Lisbon's 19th-century literary set: it features prominently in José Saramago's novel *The Year of the Death of Ricardo Reis*. Reborn in 2010 as this cool boutique hotel, the LX maintains a historic ambience behind the sky-blue exterior. Each floor is themed—one is dedicated to poet Fernando Pessoa, another to fado music, with rooms featuring photos of guitars and singers. Interiors have bold colors, stripes, and floral prints. Standard rooms are rather small, but gain in size, light, and river views as you get higher up. The ground floor has a restaurant renowned for sushi, although for breakfast it serves goodies from the nearby Tartine bakery. For better or worse, the hotel is smack in the middle of Lisbon's nightlife action.

Rua do Alecrim 12. www.lxboutiquehotel.com. ✆ **21/347-43-94.** 61 units. 140€–275€ double; 409€–439€ suite. Metro: Cais do Sodré. **Amenities:** Restaurant; bar; babysitting; free Wi-Fi.

INEXPENSIVE

The Independente ★★★ This cool operator combines a hip hostel offering bargain bunks with elegantly bohemian rooms and suites. The hostel and four suites are set in the artfully decorated Belle Époque former home of the Swiss ambassador; 18 more suites fill in the palace next door. The location is hard to beat, overlooking one of the best panoramic views, on the edge of Bairro Alto nightlife and the chic shopping zones of Príncipe Real and Chiado. In mixed and single-gender dorms for 6, 9, or 12, furniture is Nordic minimal, the cotton sheets crisp and clean. There's a spacious kitchen and a light-filled lounge hosting movie nights and occasional live music. Separately, they offer private rooms and suites offering a taste of offbeat luxury. There are two excellent restaurants on site, including The Insolito on the roof. The group has recently opened an offshoot, The Indy, in the fast upcoming Intendente quarter.

Rua S. Pedro de Alcântara 81. www.theindependente.pt. ✆ **21/346-13-81.** 33 units. 94€–234€ double; 10€–34€ dorm bunks. Tram 24. **Amenities:** Bar; 2 restaurants; free Wi-Fi.

My Story Tejo ★ The hotel reception greets guests with a funky mix of bare brick and contemporary wood and glass. This youthful hotel is just a short walk from Rossio. It was made by combining two smaller hotels in a building that contains the remains of a Roman wall and Pombaline arches. Rooms are simple but comfortable with modern pine furniture, soft-wool blankets, and white cotton sheets. They are a bit on the small side (taller guests should take care if they take an attic room) but many have high windows and balconies facing the bustling street, and some have castle views.

Rua dos Condes de Monsanto, 2. www.mystoryhotels.com. ✆ **21-886-6182.** 130 units. Doubles: 87€–254€. Metro: Rossio. **Amenities:** Restaurant; bar; free Wi-Fi.

Sunset Destination Hostel ★★ Downtown accommodation with a riverside rooftop pool for less than 20€ a night? Sounds impossible? Well if you don't mind bunking down in a dorm, it's perfectly feasible here. One of Lisbon's premium hostels is perfectly located for exploring downtown, hitting the nightlight hotspots, and escaping to the beach. It's located upstairs from the Cais do Sodré station, where trains depart along the coast to Cascais. There are electronic lockers, a funky design featuring French comic strip art, bikes to hire, surf school trips, and other activities. All in an Art Deco gem of a building within staggering distance of the bars on Pink Street. Double rooms with private bathrooms are available.

Praça do Duque de Terceira. www.sunset-destination-hostel.lisbon-hotel.org. ✆ **21/099-77-35**. 20 units. 53€–125€ double; 19€–46€ dorm. Metro: Cais do Sodré. **Amenities:** Bar; outdoor pool (Apr–Sept); sun terrace; shared kitchen; lockers; free Wi-Fi.

Alfama & East of Center

EXPENSIVE

Palacete Chafariz d'el Rei ★★★ Between Alfama and the river, this theatrical oddity was built by a coffee tycoon in a turn-of-the-20th-century style known as Brazilian Nouveau. A 2-year restoration respects the hotel's heritage, with stucco ceilings, polychrome tiled floors, and tropical plants. Rooms are spacious, overflowing with crystal chandeliers, hardwood antiques, and velvety drapes. The terrace garden filled with flowering plants is a delight for taking afternoon tea.

Travessa Chafariz del Rei 6. www.chafarizdelrei.com. ✆ **21/888-61-50.** 6 units. 263€–580€ suites. Metro: Terreiro do Paco. **Amenities:** Garden; terrace; library; babysitting; free Wi-Fi.

Palácio Belmonte ★★ There are hotels with history, and then there is the Palácio Belmonte. The Romans built one of the towers, and another two were erected over a thousand years ago when the Arabs ruled Lisbon. The noble palace chambers linking them together were constructed in the 15th century and once were home to the family of explorer Pedro Álvares Cabral, who led the first European expedition to Brazil. The current French owner invested 26€-million into turning the palace into an ultra-luxurious hotel with 10 suites. Each is unique and furnished with original antiques, and most have fabulous views. There are bathrooms clad in rare gray marble with walk-in showers, sunken baths, and their own panoramic vistas. One tower-topping bedroom boasts 360-degree views high above the city; others have private terraces where you can take your organic, freshly prepared breakfast. The walled garden has luxuriant vegetation, a swimming pool, and a waterfall. Walls are coated with more than 3,000 18th-century tiles. The French restaurant is a gourmet treat. There's a minimum 2-night stay, but you'll want more.

Páteo Dom Fradique 14. www.palaciobelmonte.com. ✆ **21/881-66-00.** 11 units. 650€–3,100€ suites. Free parking. **Amenities:** Restaurant; bar; outdoor pool; sun terrace; library; garden; sauna; massage services; babysitting; free Wi-Fi.

MODERATE

Memmo Alfama ★★★ Set your alarm early, because this hotel has the best sunrise views over the Alfama and the Tagus. The infinity pool is brick-red, matching the rooftops of the old neighborhood tumbling down the hillside below. The hotel is tucked away down a cul-de-sac lined with citrus trees behind the 12th-century cathedral. There's a mural outside by street artist Vhils. Modern furniture in soft creams and browns blends with ancient interior features like portions of ancient stone wall or domed baker's ovens transformed into cozy sitting rooms. Bedrooms come with Egyptian linen sheets, LED TVs, and Apple charging docks.

Travessa das Merceeiras, 27. www.memmohotels.com. ✆ **21/049-56-60.** 42 units. 157€–4,220€ doubles. Tram: 28. **Amenities:** Bar; outdoor pool; babysitting; free Wi-Fi.

Myriad by SANA Hotels Lisboa ★★★ Soaring 23 floors out of the River Tagus in the ultra-modern Parque das Nações district, the light-filled rooms of this landmark built in 2012 enjoy fabulous sunrises. There's a bold red-and-black design running through the rooms and public spaces, and a towering atrium complete with jellyfish-shaped chandeliers. The whole thing has a distinctly Dubai feel. Views get more spectacular as you rise toward the penthouse spa and fitness center. The deck of the River Lounge bar is the place to enjoy a waterfront port and tonic. All rooms feature a hammock seat beside the panoramic window, where it feels like you're floating over the Tagus. Basque multi-Michelin-star-winner Martin Berasategui oversees the 50 Seconds restaurant, 120 meters over the Tagus.

Cais das Naus, Lote 2.21.01. www.myriad.pt. ✆ **21-110-7600.** 186 units. 146€–413€ double. Metro: Moscavide. Private parking 15€ daily. **Amenities:** Restaurant; bar; indoor swimming pool; spa; fitness room; babysitting; free Wi-Fi.

Solar dos Mouros ★★ This tasteful, artsy micro-hotel sits below the walls of the São Jorge Castle in the oldest part of the city. It has an intimate atmosphere and offers panoramic terraces perfect for a glass of port or plate of *petiscos* (snacks) while enjoying the sunset over the city and river below. Rooms feature bold color schemes and modern art—many by owner Luís Lemos. If you can, grab the deluxe suite with vast private balconies and unique marble-clad bathroom with a view.

Rua Milagre de Santo António 6. www.solardosmouroslisboa.com. ✆ **21/885-49-40.** 11 units. 132€–275€ double; 325€–365€ suites. Adults only. Tram: 28. **Amenities:** Bar; snacks; terrace; massage services; free Wi-Fi.

INEXPENSIVE

Albergaria da Senhora do Monte ★ It's off the beaten track, a bit dated and with rooms on the small side, but this little place has bedroom views among the best in town. Perched on a hilltop in an old neighborhood served by Tram 28, the inn makes a fine budget option. The best rooms have balconies and big windows overlooking the city and river. All guests can enjoy the vistas from the top-floor breakfast room. It's cozy with a family home vibe, but can be a bit tough to get to on foot up on its hilltop perch.

Calçada do Monte 39. www.albergaria-senhora-do-monte.inlisbonhotels.com. ✆ **21/886-60-02.** 28 units. 84€–144€ double. Nearby private parking 20€ daily. Tram: 28. **Amenities:** Bar; terrace; free Wi-Fi.

Hotel Convento do Salvador ★★ Amid the medieval lanes of Alfama, this old convent has been converted into a hotel with Scandinavian-style minimalist rigor. There's a hip bar and a spacious patio for chilling on summer evenings. The white walls are enlivened by colorful works by contemporary Portuguese artists. There are family and reduced-mobility rooms.

It's also a hotel with a social conscience, proud of its environmental credentials and supporting children in need. Several rooms have river views.

Rua do Salvador, 2B. www.conventosalvador.pt. ✆ **21-887-2565.** 43 units. 97€–193€ double. Tram: 28. Nearby public parking 15€ daily. **Amenities:** Bar; garden; sun terrace; library; babysitting; free Wi-Fi.

Belém & West of Center

EXPENSIVE

Altis Belém ★★ This marble-clad cube of modernist luxury is so close to the waterfront it feels like you're on a cruise liner floating down the River Tagus. It sits in the Belém district within sight of the iconic white tower, the UNESCO-rated Jerónimos Monastery, and the galleries and concert halls of the Centro Cultural de Belém. Despite all the history around it, the hotel is rigorously contemporary. The bar and lounge have clean black-and-white lines with liberal use of leather furniture and hardwood decks. Natural light is a big feature in the public and guest rooms, thanks to floor-to-ceiling windows opening out onto the water. All the rooms are spacious and airy with great views. A top perk: the panorama from the rooftop pool. Downstairs, the Spa by Karin Herzog has 1,000 square meters (10,764 sq. ft.) where you can relax with a massage, sauna, or Turkish bath, or work out in the gym or dynamic pool. After burning up the calories, treat yourself in the Michelin-starred Feitoria restaurant.

Doca do Bom Sucesso, Belém. www.altishotels.com. ✆ **21/040-02-00.** 50 units. 176€–468€ double; 486€–846€ suite. Tram 15. Free parking, reservation required. **Amenities:** 2 restaurants; bar; outdoor pool; spa; sauna; hammam; jacuzzi; indoor pool; sun terrace; garden; fitness center; massage services; free Wi-Fi.

Lapa Palace ★★★ Back in the 1880s, the Count of Valenças made his palatial home the glittering center of Lisbon's high society. The city's best artists were invited to decorate its grand salons and ballrooms, and a lush tropical garden was laid out where the in-crowd could stroll beside streams and waterfalls. Since 1992, the count's palace has been one of the capital's most luxurious hotels, favored by royalty, presidents, and movie stars. The 109 rooms are all individually decorated, in keeping with the building's heritage, with themes ranging from rococo to Art Deco. The palace is located among the embassies and mansions of Lapa district on a hillside with broad views across the Tagus. The outside pool, set amid the tranquil greenery, is kept at a constant 25°C (77°F) from May through September, and there's a fully equipped spa, gym, and indoor pool center. The gourmet restaurant features five-star variations on Portuguese cuisine. Most rooms are in a modern six-story wing, but continue the palatial decor.

Rua do Pau da Bandeira 4. www.lapapalace.com. ✆ **21/394-94-94.** 109 units. 340€–755€ double; 755€–2,800€ suite. Free parking. Tram 25. **Amenities:** 2 restaurants; bar; babysitting; children's play area; fitness center; indoor and outdoor pools; spa; massage service; sauna, hammam; free Wi-Fi.

Pestana Palace ★★★ This temple of five-star luxury is in the Romantic Revival Valle-Flor palace, constructed by a marquis who made a fortune in

African cocoa. The main building contains a succession of ever-more-opulent salons filled with Louis XV furniture, gilt-framed oil paintings, crystal chandeliers, windows bright with stained-glass nymphs. Built in 1905, the palace and its magnificent gardens are protected national heritage sites. Most of the guest rooms are located in two modern wings overlooking the tropical flora, but there are four opulent suites in the main palace. Most rooms are elegantly modern, with hardwood trim, *trompe l'oeil* detailing, and upholstered headboards. Between Belém and downtown, it's a bit out of the way, but there's a free shuttle bus four times a day.

Rua Jau 54. www.pestana.com. ✆ **21/361-56-00.** 190 units. 184€–485€ double; 489€–3,005€ suite. Parking 17€ daily. **Amenities:** Restaurant; bar; babysitting; exercise room; Jacuzzi; spa; indoor and outdoor pools; garden; sun terrace; sauna, business center; chapel; free Wi-Fi.

MODERATE

As Janelas Verdes ★★ This boutique hotel in an 18th-century mansion was once a hangout of novelist José Maria Eça de Queiros, whose 19th-century epic *The Maias* is partly set nearby in "green windows street." Designer Graça Viterbo has given it a comfortably contemporary feel in keeping with the literary history. Rooms have modern facilities and period charm, with wood furnishings and pastel drapes on the tall windows. There are two honesty bars and a cozy top-floor library with a fireplace and terrace. The mansion's ivy-clad garden is a lovely spot for breakfast, and all the masterpieces of the Museu de Arte Antiga are just next door.

Rua das Janelas Verdes 47. www.asjanelasverdes.com. ✆ **21/396-81-43.** 29 units. 139€–650€ double. Parking 10€. Tram: 15, 25. **Amenities:** Bar; garden; terrace; library; free Wi-Fi.

Hotel da Estrela ★★ In a quiet neighborhood featuring one of Lisbon's most beautiful gardens is this luxury boutique hotel. It's located in the former palace of the Counts of Paraty, a historic Brazilian town. The interiors feature quirky, colorful designs that reference old-style school rooms. They are the brainchild of Miguel Câncio Martins, the designer behind Paris' Buddha Bar and the Pacha in Marrakech. All the spacious rooms have views over the city, the River Tagus, or the hotel's own peaceful garden. For a real treat, book one of the Hästens suites kitted out by the Swedish firm reputed to make the world's most comfortable beds. There's an excellent restaurant, Book, where customers choose how much they want to pay. Many of the efficient young staff are graduates from the next-door hotel school.

Rua Saraiva de Carvalho, 35. www.hoteldaestrela.com. ✆ **21/190-01-00.** 19 units. Doubles 110€–190€; suites 125€–219€. Parking 15€ daily. Metro: Rato. **Amenities:** Restaurant; bar; garden; terrace; babysitting; free Wi-Fi.

Avenida & North of Center

EXPENSIVE

Four Seasons Hotel Ritz Lisbon ★★★ Back in the 1950s, dictator António de Oliveira Salazar decided Lisbon needed a modern five-star hotel. The Ritz was the result. Still a modernist icon, it's a byword for service and luxury overlooking Eduardo VII Park. The lounge contains one of the best private collections of 20th-century Portuguese art; the Varanda restaurant is among the city's finest; there's a vast spa and a bar that remains the rendezvous of choice for the Lisbon elite. An extra bonus is the rooftop running track and fitness center 10 stories over the city. Rooms feature mahogany canopied marquetry desks and satinwood dressing tables, and plush carpeting. Try for one of the rooms with a private terrace overlooking the park.

Rua Rodrigo de Fonseca 88. www.fourseasons.com/lisbon. ✆ **21/381-14-00.** 282 units. 575€–830€ double; 1,145€–3,950€ suite. Private parking 40€ daily. Metro: Marquês de Pombal. **Amenities:** 2 restaurant; 2 bars; spa; indoor pool; Pilates studio; fitness center; massage services; rooftop running track; free Wi-Fi.

The One Palácio da Anunciada ★★★ Walk into the lobby and you're met by a symphony of colors from the marbled floors and walls, stained-glass windows, stucco ceilings, and extravagant floral arrangements. Opened in 2019, this five-star occupies a once-abandoned 16th-century palace. Barcelona-based designer Jaime Beriestain has blended the building's history with a stripped-down design in dazzling white that's softened by subtle greys and warm colors in the rooms and suites. There are 2,500 square meters (3,000 sq. yards) of garden, including a pool and sun terrace forming a welcome oasis, just a block from bustling Avenida da Liberdade. A highlight is the 100-year-old dragon tree. A grey-marble-clad spa, high-tech gym, two elegant bars, and a gourmet restaurant in one of the palace's noble salons round out the package.

Rua das Portas de Santo Antão, 112-134. www.hotelstheone.com. ✆ **21/041-23-00.** 83 units. 220€–458€ double; 288€–668 suite. Private parking 30€ daily. Metro: Restauradores. **Amenities:** Restaurant; 2 bars; spa; gym; sun terrace; outdoor pool; babysitting; free Wi-Fi.

Tivoli Lisboa ★★ This Lisbon landmark has been attracting visiting politicians, artists, and stars since the 1930s. The lobby oozes old-world elegance with marble columns and velvet armchairs in rich, deep tones. It's long been the preferred meeting spot for Lisbon's business elite. New owners gave this grand dame a facelift in 2016, installing the sumptuous Anantara spa, a traditional Portuguese beer-and-shellfish restaurant and, more recently, hip Seen restaurant on the rooftop Sky Bar, already one of the capital's hottest spots on summer evenings. Rooms are big and airy, overlooking the tree-lined avenue or the lush garden and pool below. They are decorated in modern classic style with easy-on-the-eyes shades predominating. Portuguese movie icon Beatriz Costa liked it so much, she lived there for 30 years.

Av. da Liberdade 185. www.tivolihotels.com. ✆ **21/319-89-00.** 285 units. 325€–685€ double; 514€–932€ suite. Parking 17.50€ daily. Metro: Avenida. **Amenities:** 2 restaurants; 3 bars; spa; massage services; sauna; fitness center; outdoor pool; garden; terrace; babysitting; free Wi-Fi.

MODERATE

1908 Lisboa Hotel ★★ There's a clue to this place's vintage in this splendid Art Nouveau construction, whose restoration and reopening in 2017 symbolized the regeneration of the once-seedy Intendente neighborhood. Room decor is restrained and comfortable. For a real treat, book the duplex suite in the dome that crowns the building. The cool Infame restaurant shows off the building's original features. There are regular displays by contemporary artists. This is a perfect base for exploring the new shops and restaurants of the exciting neighborhood, which is just a short walk from downtown.

Largo do Intendente Pina Manique, 6. www.1908lisboahotel.com. ✆ **21-880-4000.** 36 units. 119€–309€ double. Private parking nearby 20€ daily, reservation required. Metro: Intendente. **Amenities:** Restaurant; bar; free Wi-Fi.

DL Valmor Palace ★★★ Lisbonites were delighted to see new life breathed into this iconic building, which had lain abandoned for over a decade before being transformed into this charming boutique hotel in 2019. Located on busy Avenida da República, the two-story mansion scooped up the city's top architecture prize when it was built in 1906 as home for the Viscountess of Valmor. It served for many years as a businessman's club and fine restaurant. A tasteful restoration maintains the romantic ambiance with heavy drapes and oriental rugs, chandeliers and empire-style wall paintings. A little out of downtown, but close to the Gulbenkian museums.

Av. da República 38. www.dearlisbon.com. ✆ **21/249-71-87.** 12 units. 79€–247€ double; 121€–285€ suite. Metro: Campo Pequeno. **Amenities:** Garden, terrace; free Wi-Fi.

Heritage Avenida Liberdade Hotel ★★ This boutique hotel combines the 18th-century grandeur of the original building with understated contemporary style. With its sumptuous sofas, low lighting, and sweet scent, the foyer is as relaxing as the spa and pool downstairs. Rooms feature stylish wallpaper, chaises longues, large, cool en-suites, and city center views. Some have French windows opening onto Juliet balconies overlooking the Avenida. Bedding is cloud-like—we love the array of pillows.

Av. da Liberdade 28. www.heritageavliberdade.com. ✆ **21/340-40-40.** 41 units. 162€–600€ double. Public parking nearby 15€ daily, reservation needed. Metro: Restauradores. **Amenities:** Bar; exercise room; indoor pool; babysitting; free Wi-Fi.

Hotel Avenida Palace ★★ The Avenida Palace first opened in 1892 as a typical grand hotel in the European fin-de-siècle style. Full of atmosphere, the hotel hosted well-heeled refugees from the Spanish Civil War, undercover agents during World War II, and stars of screen and stage in the '50s and '60s. It later fell on hard times, but has since had its glamor restored. The neoclassical landmark is strategically located between Rossio Square and the start of Avenida da Liberdade, close to all the city center attractions. The public rooms are glittering confections of gilt, crystal, and marble. An English-style bar in hardwood and worn leather is famed for its cocktails, and 5 o'clock tea with scones is served by white-coated waiters in the palatial main salon. This is a genuine classic in the heart of the city.

Rua 1 de Dezembro 123. www.hotelavenidapalace.pt. ✆ **21/321-81-00.** 82 units. 181€–287€ double; 307€–700€ suite. Limited free parking. Metro: Restauradores. **Amenities:** Bar; babysitting; exercise room; free Wi-Fi.

Hotel Britania ★★ Built in the 1940s by famed Portuguese architect Cassiano Branco, this hotel is an Art Deco gem. It has been restored to enhance its original 1940s style, with a dash of contemporary design. The location on a quiet road off the Avenida da Liberdade means you can escape the city traffic and retreat to the clubby bar, library, and lounge, warmed in winter by an open fire. Original decor includes murals in the bar, expanses of marble, and porthole windows. Inside is an old barber's shop converted into a small museum.

Rua Rodrigues Sampaio, 17. www.heritage.pt. ✆ **21/315-50-16.** 32 units. Doubles 112€–746€. Parking 15€ daily. Metro: Avenida. **Amenities:** Bar; library; free Wi-Fi.

Maxime Hotel ★★ Lisbon's sexiest hotel opened in 2018. Name and decor pay tribute to Maxime Dancing, once Lisbon's most notorious nightspot which occupied the ground floor from the 1940s until its demise in 2011. Throughout, the hotel is inspired by the old Maxime's. There are blow up black-and-white photos of dancers in stockings and bodices, a bondage-themed room decorated with handcuffs and black feather dusters, and cabaret shows featuring standup comics and burlesque entertainers in the restaurant/bar that occupies the old nightclub. It could have turned out sleazy, but instead the atmosphere is cheeky but sophisticated. Even so, probably better for a romantic getaway *à deux* than a family vacation. It's set in a verdant square, just a few steps from Lisbon's grandest boulevard.

Praça da Alegria, 58. www.maximehotellisbon.com. ✆ **21/876-00-00.** 75 units. Doubles 119€–254€. Metro: Avenida. **Amenities:** Restaurant; bars; terrace; garden; free Wi-Fi.

Torel Palace ★★ This charming boutique hotel occupies a pair of 1900s mansions in a noble, but little-visited hilltop district overlooking Avenida Da Liberdade. One is painted in bold blue, the other a soft pink. Decor in the rooms reflects that mix of primary or pastel shades. All the rooms are named after Portuguese royalty. Our favorite is Dona Amélia, with royal blue walls and astounding views from the veranda. Between the two buildings is a leafy garden patio paved with traditional tiles and a pool that makes up for its small size with a hillside location and great views. Recent additions include a private villa and the innovative Cave 23 restaurant.

Rua Câmara Pestana, 23. www.torelboutiques.com. ✆ **21-829-0810.** 26 units. Doubles 120€–420€. Parking 15€ daily. Metro: Avenida (then take the funicular). **Amenities:** Restaurants; bars; outdoor pool; garden; sun terrace; babysitting; free Wi-Fi.

INEXPENSIVE

Casa de São Mamede ★★ This solid, yellow-painted townhouse was built in 1758 as a magistrate's home and has been a hotel since 1948. It's great value for money on the edge of the happening Príncipe Real district. The good-sized rooms are individually decorated. Some may feel a tad old-fashioned, but most have a stylishly uncluttered historical style, and all have private bathrooms. Breakfast is served in a sunny second-floor dining room decorated with antique tiles. Service is friendly and attentive.

Rua da Escola Politécnica 159. www.casadesaomamede.pt. ✆ **21/396-31-66.** 28 units. 99€–224€ double. Metro: Rato; Tram 24. **Amenities:** Free Wi-Fi.

HF Fénix Music ★ The best of a row of mid-20th-century hotels run by the HF group just across from Eduardo VII Park. This one has a musical theme. Each room is decorated according to a style from jazz to classical to fado. There are live bands and DJ sets beside the rooftop pool and bar, where there's a city view that's the envy of many more expensive hotels. High-tech sound systems allow guests to turn their rooms into a personalized disco. The check-in desk is shaped like a drum kit and the bar's a piano keyboard.

Rua Joaquim António de Aguiar, 5. www.hfhotels.com. ✆ **21/049-65-70.** 109 units. 81€–193€ double. Metro: Marquês de Pombal. **Amenities:** Bar; outdoor pool; sun terrace; free Wi-Fi.

WHERE TO EAT

Baixa & Chiado

EXPENSIVE

100 Maneiras ★★★ INTERNATIONAL Sarajevo-born chef Ljubomir Stanisic is a star in Portugal. He judges TV cooking contests, fronts food documentaries and played Gordon Ramsey's role in Portugal's version of "Kitchen Nightmares." He's also an excellent cook. His restaurant (which means "100 ways") underwent its own makeover in 2019, moving down the road to a new Bairro Alto location with a mildly spooky modern-gothic interior. For the new menus, Stanisic has reached back to his Bosnian roots, serving Balkan treats like peppery ajvar and creamy kajmak along with Belenga island barnacles, amberjack, and other fishy treats plucked from the Portuguese ocean. Stanisic takes an iconoclastic approach, incorporating cough sweets, garlic, and hay into his desserts. This is a true original.

Rua do Teixeira 39. www.restaurante100maneiras.com. ✆ **21/099-04-75.** Reservations recommended. Tasting menu 80€–110€. Daily 7pm–2am. Metro: Baixa-Chiado.

Belcanto ★★★ CREATIVE PORTUGUESE Lisbon's most famous fine-dining experience boasts two Michelin stars and is a regular fixture in the world's top 50 restaurants rankings. Belcanto is the flagship of celebrity chef José Avillez's flotilla of eateries spread around the Chiado and Baixa. In 2019 it moved from its cozy-but-cramped location in front of the São Carlos opera house to take over a more spacious neighbor with domed brick ceilings and more natural light. The discreet charm and exquisite food remain. It's not cheap, but Avillez's irreverent take on Portuguese classics is unique. New dishes introduced with the move include braised red mullet with squid rice, liver sauce, vegetable roe, and cuttlefish-ink aioli; and roasted, hay-smoked pigeon with foie gras and hazelnut-cinnamon sauce. Go for the tasting menus for a special treat, and sample from the incomparable wine list.

Largo de São Carlos,12. www.belcanto.pt. ✆ **21/342-06-07.** Reservations required. Main courses 50€; tasting menus 165€–185€. Tues–Sat noon–3pm 6:30–11pm. Metro: Baixa/Chiado.

Gambrinus ★★ PORTUGUESE Gambrinus is resolutely old school, its menu unchanged for years and its dining room classically styled, with leather chairs under a beamed cathedral ceiling (we always try to nab the little table beside the fireplace at the raised end of the room). The restaurant is renowned for its seafood bisque, its lobster dishes, and the seafood *cataplana* (a traditional dish from the Algarve cooked in a copper pot). Those are all pricey, but you don't have to break the bank to dine here: Sitting at the counter (*barra*), the menu is affordable, featuring *petiscos* (Portuguese snacks) if you feel like a mid-afternoon or late night nibble.

Rua das Portas de Santo Antão 23. www.gambrinuslisboa.com. ✆ **21/342-14-66.** Reservations recommended. Mains 18€–38€. Daily noon–1:30am. Metro: Rossio.

MODERATE

Aqui Há Peixe ★★ SEAFOOD The name of this stylish restaurant in the heart of one of the Chiado's prettiest squares translates as "Here there are fish"—and so there is, a lot of it, freshly caught and selected by Chef Miguel Reino from Lisbon's markets. On our last visit, we started with one of the few fish not lately plucked from Portuguese waters (anchovies from off Spain's northern Cantabrian coast), but followed up with a whole Atlantic turbot for two, served with rice cut with tangy rapini greens, followed up with vanilla ice cream doused in a thick fig syrup. There's meat if you must: The Brazilian-style *picanha* steak is excellent.

Rua da Trindade 18A. www.aquihapeixe.pt. ✆ **21/343-21-54.** Reservations recommended. Mains 16€–45€. Tues–Fri noon–3pm, 7–11pm. Metro: Baixa/Chiado.

Cervejaria Ramiro ★★★ PORTUGUESE This place has been popular since opened by a Spanish immigrant in the 1950s, but after the late Anthony Bourdain raved about it on TV, lines stretch down the street. It's noisy, crowded and chaotic, but the wonderous seafood makes it all worth it. The usual routine is to take a series of shellfish plates, say clams with garlic and cilantro; grilled giant shrimp, leathery goose barnacles, or a football-sized crab served with a mallet to smash through the claws. Wash everything down with icy draft beer or *vinho verde* and follow up with a steak sandwich (*prego*). Try to find space for the fresh mango. They don't take phone reservations. To avoid the queues, eat early (or late). Like with most such joints, the seafood is sold by the kilo. For lobster, crab and other larger critters ask the waiter in advance how much you're likely to pay.

Av. Almirante Reis,1. www.cervejariaramiro.pt. ✆ **21/885-10-24.** Main courses 13€–38€. Tues–Sun noon–midnight. Metro: Intendente.

Fidalgo ★★ PORTUGUESE With its marble-clad walls and displays of standout Portuguese wines, Fidalgo is a class apart from the tourist traps and cheap-booze joints that have infested much of the Bairro Alto. It's been operating to a loyal clientele since the 1950s. The cuisine is classical Portuguese with daily specials that can include rare treats like rice with salted cod cheeks

Lisbon Restaurants

- 100 Maneiras **10**
- Adega da Tia Matilde **3**
- Aqui Há Peixe **18**
- Belcanto **16**
- Café Buenos Aires **19**
- Cantina LX **12**
- Cantinho do Aziz **22**
- Casa dos Passarinhos **1**
- Cervejaria Ramiro **9**
- Comida de Santo **7**
- Darwin's Café **12**
- Dom Feijão **4**
- Estórias na Casa da Comida **2**
- Fidalgo **17**
- Gambrinus **20**
- Ibo **15**
- Jesus é Goês **8**
- João do Grão **21**
- Marítima de Xabregas **24**
- Monte Mar **13**
- Nune's Real Marisqueira **12**
- The Old House **24**
- Olivier Avenida **5**
- O Pitéu **23**
- O Polícia **4**
- Os Tibetanos **6**
- Pap' Açorda **14**
- Rabo D'Pexe **4**
- Rio Maravilha **12**
- Senhor Peixe **24**
- Soajeiro **11**

or char-grilled boar. There are over 250 wines to choose from, so let Sr. Eugénio guide you to the perfect match with your dish.

Rua da Barroca 27. www.restaurantefidalgo.com. ✆ **21/342-2900.** Mains 11€–18€. Mon–Sat noon–3pm, 7–11pm. Metro: Baixa-Chiado.

Ibo ★★ MOZAMBICAN/PORTUGUESE Little-known beyond the Portuguese-speaking world, the cooking of Mozambique blends African roots with Asian and European influences with delicious results. This upscale restaurant serves up a posh version of the East African nation's delicately spiced cuisine, with prices to match. Set in a former salt warehouse, it enjoys a prime riverside view from where to watch the come and go of Tagus boats. The emphasis is on seafood. Start with crab and mango salad, move on to shrimp curry with okra, and finish up with papaya stuffed with ewe's milk cream cheese. Wash it down with 2M beer imported from Maputo, or some chilled Douro white wine.

Armazém A, Porta 2, Cais do Sodré. www.ibo-restaurante.pt. ✆ **96/133-20-24.** Reservations recommended. Mains 18€–33€. Tues–Fri 12:30–3pm, 7:30–11pm; Sat 12:30–3pm, 7:30pm–1am; Sun 12:30–3:30pm. Metro: Cais do Sodré.

Monte Mar ★ PORTUGUESE/SEAFOOD In summer, diners flock to this fish restaurant's deck jutting out over the river Tagus. This is the little sister of a famed seashore restaurant in Cascais and shares its reputation for serving the freshest Atlantic seafood in a stylish waterfront setting. You can eat fish for cheaper in Lisbon, but it's hard to match the river views, or the quality of seafood. The house specialty is tempura-style hake with cockle rice, but other fine choices include squid and shrimp on a skewer, or swordfish steak, as well as the catch of the day grilled, oven-baked, or salt-baked. Among the meat selection, *iscas* (liver) is typically Lisbon. They also operate a riverside oyster bar through the summer. There are other offshoots in Troia and Time Out Market.

Rua da Cintura, Armazém 65. www.mmlisboa.pt. ✆ **96/334-29-83.** Mains 17€–32€; Tues–Sun noon–11:30pm. Metro: Cais do Sodré.

Pap' Açorda ★ PORTUGUESE To dodge the crowds at the Time Out Market food hall, head upstairs to this airy space on the first floor of the old market building. Hip since the 1980s, when it was based in the Bairro Alto, the Pap'Açorda serves top-notch Portuguese dishes with a dash of innovation. It moved downhill to the market in 2016, taking up a space designed by the trendy Aires-Mateus architectural team. You can order rice with baby cuttlefish and Azores cheese or paprika-spiced black pork tenderloin, but chef Manuela Brandão's signature is naturally *açorda,* a traditional mash of bread, seafood, eggs, coriander, garlic, and olive oil. Finish with their famous chocolate mousse, thick and rich and oh so good.

Mercado da Ribeira, 49, Av. 24 de Julho. www.papacorda.com. ✆ **21/346-48-11.** Reservations recommended. Mains 14€–36€. Sun, Tues, Wed noon–midnight; Thurs–Sat noon–2am. Metro: Cais do Sodré.

INEXPENSIVE

Café Buenos Aires ★ INTERNATIONAL Founded by an Argentine-Portuguese couple, the interior of this cozy cafe resembles a Parisian bistro. Lit by yellow street lamps, the terrace offers romantic views over the Baixa. Dishes reflect the owners' origins, like Argentine steak with chimichurri sauce or Portuguese salt cod in olive oil with sweet potatoes. There are occasional live tango nights. Fresh salads and pastas make it a great stop for a light lunch, too.

Calçada do Duque 31 B. www.cafebuenosaires.pt. ✆ **21/342-07-39**. Mains 10€–26€. No credit cards. Mon–Fri 6pm–1am, Sat–Sun noon–1am. Metro: Baixa/Chiado.

João do Grão ★ PORTUGUESE Take care dining in the Baixa district. While good traditional restaurants survive, there are plenty of rip-off joints with hidden charges and substandard food. This place, whose name translates as "Johnny Chickpea," is the real deal. It's been serving honest Portuguese comfort food for well over 100 years. Nobody seems to be sure exactly when it opened up under the building's 18th-century arched ceiling, but it featured in a popular 1940s musical hit. It fills with die-hard regulars, families from the suburbs, and tourists. They enjoy an ever-changing menu featuring seasonal specialties, but the salt-cod (*bacalhau*) dishes are a fixture, including mixed with scrambled egg and fries (*à brás*) or plain boiled with those chickpeas (*cozido com grão*).

Rua dos Correeiros 222. www.joaograo.pai.pt. ✆ **21/342-47-57.** 7.90€–15€. Summer: Mon noon–3:30pm, 6–10pm, Tues–Sun noon–10pm; Winter: Daily noon–3:30pm, 6–10pm. Metro: Rossio.

Alfama & East of Center

MODERATE

Marítima de Xabregas ★★ PORTUGUESE Since 1966, hungry families have been gathering in this warehouse-sized dining space tucked away in the docklands between downtown and the Parque das Nações. The three amigos who pooled their funds to launch the place are still in charge over half-a-century later. They oversea huge charcoal-fired grills that are constantly filled with favorites like steak on the bone or slabs of codfish to be served with smoky skin-on potatoes. The more adventurous can try eel stew, a specialty from up the Tagus or (on Thurs only) *cozido*—Portugal's cherished boiled meat dinner. Portions are big, ordering a portion to share between two is the norm.

Rua Manutenção, 40. www.restaurantemaritimadexabregas.com.pt. ✆ **21/868-22-35.** Mains 10€–17€. Sun–Fri 7am–11pm. Bus: 728/759.

The Old House ★★ CHINESE Lisbon has become a popular European base for wealthy Chinese, with the happy consequence that the city has grown a number of very good Chinese restaurants. This one serves gorgeously presented Sichuan cuisine in a stylish dining hall decorated with red lanterns and blue ceramics, private rooms and a shady riverside terrace. The owners see themselves as ambassadors for Chinese culture and their encyclopedic menu features dishes hard to find in Europe, like tea shrimp or chicken with Chinese yam. Appropriately, its address translates as "pepper street."

Rua Pimenta 9. www.theoldhouseportugal.pt. ✆ **96/932-27-71.** Mains 8€–59€. Daily noon–3pm, 7–11pm. Metro: Oriente.

Senhor Peixe ★ SEAFOOD "Mr. Fish" is the name and fish is very much the game in this riverside restaurant that opened 20 years ago out among the modernist architecture of the Parque das Nações district. Its slogan is "Setúbal in Lisbon," a reference to the southern port whose famed fish market is the source of the piscatorial pleasures served up here. Most people go for charcoal-grilled catch of the day, be it seabass, gold-eyed bream, red mullet, or whatever, but there are other specialties such as a sloppy pasta stew with wreckfish (*cherne,* a highly-prized white fish), or Setúbal favorite fried cuttlefish with fries.

Rua da Pimenta 35. www.senhorpeixe.pt. ✆ **21/895-58-92.** Mains 15€–28€. Tues–Sun noon–3:30pm, 7–10:30pm; Sun noon–3:30pm. Metro: Oriente.

INEXPENSIVE

Cantinho do Aziz ★★ MOZAMBICAN This backstreet, family-run restaurant serves up the exotically delicious cuisine of Mozambique, a coconut and chili infused blend of African, Indian, and Portuguese flavors. It's been a favorite in the hillside Mouraria district since the 1980s, and Chef Jeny Sulemange launched her own cookbook in 2019. Try crab curry, shrimp with okra, or baby goat with toasted coconut. Three things that are hard to resist but it might be better to go easy on: iced 2M beer shipped in from southern Africa, Chef Jeny's fiery piri-piri sauce, and the oh-so-sweet cashew-fruit mousse for dessert.

Rua de S. Lourenço 5. www.cantinhodoaziz.com. ✆ **21/887-64-72.** Mains 9€–19€. Daily noon–11pm. Metro: Martim Moniz.

O Pitéu ★ PORTUGUESE Run by the same family since the 1960s, this is a typical neighborhood restaurant: decorative tiles on white walls, paper tablecloths, soccer game on the TV. It buzzes with the chatter of regular customers and curious newcomers wandering in from the nearby terminus of Tram 28 up in the trendy Graça neighborhood, just a short walk away from one of Lisbon's most spectacular view points. There's a wide daily range of traditional Portuguese dishes, but for many the highlight is fried fish served with tomato rice. Finish up with Siricaia, an eggy dessert from the Alentejo that's accompanied by syrupy preserved plums.

Largo da Graça, 95-96. www.restauranteopiteu.pt. ✆ **21/887-10-67.** Mains 10€–20€. Mon–Fri noon–3:30pm, 7–10:15pm. Tram: 28.

Belém & West of Center

MODERATE

Darwin's Café ★★ INTERNATIONAL Enjoying a spectacular waterfront location in the Champalimaud Center for the Unknown, a cutting-edge science center and architectural landmark, this vast white space is dominated by evolutionary-inspired modern art with giant, multicolored prints of 19th-century zoological tracts on the walls. Mediterranean and Portuguese influences mingle on an international menu that includes the likes of shrimp and octopus risotto with sundried tomato, and salt cod under a corn-bread crust. They have a lighter menu for snacks on the riverside terrace and are open for *lanche,* Portugal's version of afternoon tea. Darwin's is a short walk from the Torre de Belém.

Champalimaud Center for the Unknown, Av. Brasília. www.darwincafe.com. ✆ **21/048-0222.** Mains 15€–27€. Mon 12:30–3:30pm; Tues–Sun 12:30–3:30pm, 4:30–6:30pm & 7:30–11pm. Tram: 15.

Nune's Real Marisqueira ★★ PORTUGUESE/SEAFOOD One of the best fish restaurants in the city, Nune's is a welcome escape from the bustle of Belém's tourist attractions—just follow the tram line out of town. This upscale seafood joint serves up superlative shellfish alongside fresh char-grilled fish plus a number of signature dishes like John Dory filets served with roe or grouper arroz (Portuguese risotto). It's more expensive than most such places, but the stream of regular local customers know that you pay for quality. There's meat too, its aged steaks are justly famed.

Rua Bartolomeu Dias 112. www.nunesmarisqueira.pt. ✆ **21/301-98-99.** Mains 11€–45€. Tues–Sun noon–midnight. Tram: 15.

Rio Maravilha ★★★ INTERNATIONAL Climb to the top floor of what was an old printworks, to discover this uber-trendy post-industrial space. Expansive views over the river await, as does some of the city's most interesting food. An innovative blend of Portuguese and Brazilian influences pervades the frequently changing menu. We've particularly enjoyed broiled shrimp with pureed manioc or salt cod with caramelized turnips and miso. The atmosphere is relaxed and sharing is encouraged. The bar, with its irreverent polychrome statue reaching out to Cristo Rei across the river, is the coolest place amid all the cool hangouts in LX Factory.

Rua Rodrigues Faria, 103. www.facebook.com/riomaravilha.lxfactory. ✆ **96/602-82-29.** Mains 14€–25€. Tues–Thurs 12:30pm–2am; Fri–Sat 12:30pm–3am; Sun 12:30–midnight. Tram:15.

INEXPENSIVE

Cantina LX ★★ PORTUGUESE A canteen for print workers for generations back in the days when LX Factory was actually a factory rather than Lisbon's hippest post-industrial shopping, eating, and cultural hub. Cooking is traditional with the occasional twist—try dishes like slow-cooked pork cheek with asparagus "migas" (a bread-based accompaniment), or tuna steak with fennel and spinach. The decor is a homely junkyard jumble of recycled furniture and tools left behind by workers dating back to the 1840s. There's a cocktail bar and a leafy terrace out back.

R. Rodrigues Faria 103. www.cantinalx.com. ✆ **21/362-82-39.** Mains 12€–17€. Sun–Mon, Fri noon–11pm; Tues–Thurs, Sat noon–3pm, 7:30–11pm. Tram: 15.

Soajeiro ★★ MADEIRAN/PORTUGUESE This hole-in-the-wall does a range of Portuguese standards, but the crowds who pack in every lunchtime are drawn by one dish: *espetada*. A specialty from the owner's Madeira island home, it comprises cubes of tender, garlic-infused beef skewered on laurel branches, then grilled over hot coals. Served with red-pepper salad, fries, and (on baking days) garlic-infused *bolo do caco* (a Madeiran flat-bread). This traditional *tasca* (tavern) is extremely popular with people working in the neighborhood, so get there early to avoid the lines. For dessert there's passion-fruit pie, and do try a *poncha,* the potent island cocktail of rum and lemon juice.

Rua do Merca-Tudo, 16. ✆ **21/397-53-16**. Mains 8€–11€. Mon–Sat noon–3pm. Tram: 25.

Avenida & North of Center

EXPENSIVE

Estórias na Casa da Comida ★ CONTEMPORARY PORTUGUESE Occupying the ground floor of an old townhouse off one of Lisbon's must atmospheric squares, this joint oozing old-world charm has been a standout on the Lisbon restaurant scene for 40 years. It's built around a courtyard garden and decorated with ceramics tiles and French Empire furnishings. Chef João Pereira's creations add a contemporary touch to Portuguese tradition. Dishes vary with the seasons, but regular delicacies include blackbelly rosefish with corn-broth and razor clams, chestnut soup with wild mushrooms and truffle, or peasant stuffed with quince. The cellar contains an excellent selection of wines and the atmosphere is ideal for a romantic tête-à-tête.

Travessa das Amoreiras 1. www.casadacomida.pt. ✆ **21/386-08-89.** Reservations recommended. Mains 24€–30€; tasting menus 50€–65€; Mon–Sat 7–midnight. Metro: Rato.

Olivier Avenida ★★ MEDITERRANEAN Chef Olivier was a pioneer in Lisbon's food revolution, blending classical French techniques with fresh local produce. His flagship restaurant continues to pull in a glamorous crowd (a former prime minister, several ambassadors, and a scattering of telenovela stars were on show last time we visited). The food is a sophisticated fusion of French, Italian and Portuguese, creating dishes like scallops gratin with truffle and duck magret in port wine.

Rua Júlio César Machado, 7. www.restaurantesolivier.com. ✆ **21/317-41-05.** Mains 18€–55€. Mon–Fri 12:30–3pm, 7pm–1am; Sat 7pm–1am. Metro: Avenida.

MODERATE

Adega da Tia Matilde ★ PORTUGUESE We once overheard a Portuguese father here telling his son, "Food like this will make a man out of you." Indeed, it's a great place to sample the savory and hearty specialties of Ribatejo, including *cabrito assado* (roast mountain kid), *arroz de frango* (chicken with rice), *pato corado com arroz* (duck rice), and pungent *caldeirada* (fish stew). The Portuguese love this large, busy place in the Praça de Espanha area—foreign visitors are rare.

Rua da Beneficência 77. www.adegatiamatilde.com. ✆ **21/797-21-72.** Main courses 10€–31€. Mon–Fri noon–4pm, 7:30–11pm; Sat noon–4pm. Metro: Praça d'Espanha. Bus: 31.

Comida de Santo ★ PORTUGUESE/BRAZILIAN From your first drop of caipirinha to the last spoonful of papaya puree, this is a tropical tastebud adventure. One of Lisbon's oldest Brazilian restaurants, it's inspired by the cooking of Salvador da Bahia famed for its use of coconut, lime, and delicate spices. Typical dishes include *vatapá*, made with fish, palm oil, cashew nuts, and dried shrimp; or cured beef with cassava and catupiry cheese.

Calçada Engenheiro Miguel Pais, 39. www.comidadesanto.pt. ✆ **21/396-33-39.** Mains 12€–18€. Wed–Mon 12:30–3:30pm, 7:30–midnight. Metro: Rato. Bus: 758/730.

Dom Feijão ★★★ PORTUGUESE This is hallowed ground for lovers of true Portuguese cuisine, so book in advance, because local families often besiege this retro open-plan dining room off the Avenida de Roma shopping street. Like many in this mid-20th-century neighborhood, it's rooted in the robust cooking of northern Portugal, serving baked turbot or roast young goat. Nobody is quite sure how it got the name, which translates as "Sir Bean."

Largo Machado de Assis, 7D. www.domfeijao.com. ✆ **21/846-40-38.** Mains 10€–17€. Mon–Sat noon–3:30pm, 7–10:30pm. Metro: Roma.

O Polícia ★★ MEDITERRANEAN Named for the ex-cop who founded it in 1900, this discreet little gem has a decor and menu that seems little changed in decades. The classic Portuguese food is consistently good, but you're in for a special treat if baked porgy (*pargo no forno*) is on the specials board. Close to the Gulbenkian Museum, this place is popular for business lunches.

Rua Marquês Sá da Bandeira, 112A. www.restauranteopolicia.com. ✆ **21/796-35-05.** Mains 12€–17€. Mon–Fri noon–3pm, 7–10pm; Sat noon–3pm. Metro: São Sebastião.

Rabo D'Pexe ★★ AZOREAN/JAPANESE Portugal's mid-Atlantic Azores islands are renowned for wonderful seafood and free-range beef. This place serves it up, flying in 80% of its fish and meat from the archipelago. Fish takes pride of place. You can choose spectacular array of species in the ice tray, then watch them prepare it the open kitchen. As well as traditional Portuguese preparations, there are expert sushi chefs on hand if you want it raw. Dishes are beautifully presented in a light-filled interior.

Avenida Duque de Ávila 42. www.rabodpexe.pt. ✆ **21/314-16-05.** Mains 12€–25€. Sun–Thurs noon–11:30pm; Fri–Sat noon–midnight. Metro: Saldanha.

INEXPENSIVE

Casa dos Passarinhos ★★ TRADITIONAL PORTUGUESE Solid comfort food at affordable prices—that's the promise of good *tascas* like this one, and it's a potent draw. Even more alluring: the idea of cooking for yourself. *Bife na pedra* (steak on the stone)—it comes raw for you to grill on a hot stone—is very popular here. It's smoky and smelly but also lots of fun. If you don't want to work for your supper, the octopus is recommended, as is the tuna steak and Iberian pork (called *secretos*). Arrive before 1pm or you'll have to wait, as that's when local workers arrive for lunch.

Rua Silva Carvalho 195. www.casadospassarinhos.com. ✆ **21/388-23-46.** Mains: 7.95€–17€. Mon–Sat noon–3pm and 7–10:30pm. Bus: 758.

Jesus é Goês ★ GOAN Culinary exchanges between India and Portugal have been producing delicious results for 500 years. Nowhere more fruitfully than in the state of Goa, a Portuguese outpost until the 1960s. Chef Jesus Lee recreates the tropical charm and tangy flavors of his homeland in the brightly colored shrine to gastronomic intermingling. Try shrimp masala or spiced cilantro chicken. On no account should you miss the date-filled samosas with ginger and cardamom ice-cream.

Rua de São José, 23. ✆ **21/154-58-12.** Mains 8€–19€. Tues–Fri noon–3pm, 7–11pm; Sat noon–3pm, 7pm–midnight. Metro: Restauradores.

Os Tibetanos ★ VEGETARIAN When it opened in the 1980s, this was the first vegetarian restaurant in Lisbon, and 20 years later, it's still going strong. The decor and cuisine pay tribute to the people of Tibet, offering several variations on the stuffed Himalayan dumplings known as *momos.* There is a range of other internationally inspired dishes that change with the seasons, but could include oven-baked tofu steaks with goat's cheese and pesto, or beetroot pancakes with roasted squash.

Rua do Salitre 117. www.tibetanos.com. ✆ **21/314-20-38.** Mains 8€–13€. Mon–Fri 12:15–2:45pm, 7:30–10:30pm; Sat 12:45–3:30pm, 8–11pm; Sun 12:45–3:30pm, 7:30–10:30pm. Metro: Restauradores.

EXPLORING LISBON

6

Lisbon's historic center is compact. Most attractions can be reached by foot or by hopping onto the historic streetcars, elevators, and funiculars. Safe and mostly efficient public transport and relatively cheap taxis will get you to farther-flung attractions like historic Belém, modernist Parque das Nações, or the Gulbenkian museum. To really see the city, allow at least 3 days, more if you make side trips to Sintra and Cascais (see chapter 7).

SUGGESTED ITINERARIES

For more extended itineraries, not only of Lisbon, but Portugal itself, refer to chapter 4.

If You Have 1 Day

Take a stroll through Alfama, Lisbon's most evocative *bairro* (neighborhood). Visit the 12th-century **Sé** (cathedral) and take in a view of the city and the River Tagus from the **Miradouro Santa Luzia** belvedere. Climb to the **Castelo de São Jorge.** Then, head out to Belém to visit the **Mosteiro dos Jerónimos,** stroll along the river to **Torre de Belém,** and take in the modern art at the **Berardo Collection Museum.** Be sure to try a *pastel de Belém* (custard tart) in the historic cafe of the same name.

If You Have 2 Days

On **Day 2,** start by checking out the food on show at **Mercado da Ribeira,** then stroll along the waterfront to **Praça do Comercio** to begin a walking tour through **Baixa** and **Chiado** to peruse the historic shopping streets. Stop for a shot of coffee at **Café A Brasileira** before walking up to the ruined **Convento do Carmo** and gold-lined **São Roque** church, and take in the view at **Miradouro São Pedro de Alcântara.** After lunch in the hip **Príncipe Real** neighborhood, cram in some culture at the **Gulbenkian Museum** and relax in its delightful gardens. In the evening, go full circle to enjoy the gourmet experience at **Time Out Market** and some **Cais do Sodré** nightlife.

If You Have 3 Days

Head east to spend the morning by the river at **Parque das Nações** to admire the modern architecture and visit the **Oceanário,** an awe-inspiring aquarium. Enjoy fish in a different way over lunch at **Senhor Peixe** before crossing town to admire the magnificent old masters at the **Museu Nacional de Arte Antiga.** Wrap up the afternoon with a visit to the hip **LX Factory** area of stores, cafes, and bars, and a wander along the Tagus for more cutting-edge design at the **MAAT** contemporary art museum.

CASTELO & ALFAMA

Let's start in the cradle of Lisbon, its ancient hilltop fortress and the emblematic hillside quarter where a warren of lanes connects Renaissance palaces, baroque churches, and taverns emitting the scent of barbecued sardines and the plaintive melodies of fado.

Castelo de São Jorge ★★★ CASTLE This is the best place to get your bearings on a first visit to Lisbon. From its hilltop perch, virtually the whole city is laid out before you, from the medieval alleyways beneath the ramparts to the 18th-century blocks of the Baixa and gleaming modern towers in the distance.

Nowadays the castle is a peaceful green oasis. Come in the early morning or evening when there are fewer visitors and it's more like a tranquil garden than a fortress. There are pathways shaded by venerable olive, pine, and cork trees, peacocks hopping among the ruins. The setting sun adds another dimension to the extraordinary **views ★★★** over the city and the shimmering waters of the Tagus. It wasn't always so serene. Standing on the ramparts, it's not hard to imagine the mayhem in 1147, when the troops of Portugal's first king Afonso Henriques joined forces with northern European crusaders to successfully lay siege to the castle and end over 4 centuries of Muslim rule. When Lisbon replaced Coimbra as Portugal's capital in 1255, the castle became a royal palace, and many of the walls you see today date from that period. Later it served as a military base and a prison.

Within the walls there's an archeological site where secrets of past centuries are still being unearthed; a neat little **museum ★** showing the history of the castle through Roman coins, Iron Age pottery, and Moorish ceramics; and an odd **camera obscura ★** in one of the towers, which uses a lens and looking glasses to zoom in on city landmarks. Kids will enjoy the regular weekend re-enactments of battles and medieval pageantry, not to mention the after-dark tours to observe the castle's abundant **bat population.** There's a good restaurant: the **Casa do Leão** (mains 18€–31€), located in the remnants of the old royal palace, plus a range of snack options inside the castle, although their opening hours can be a little unpredictable. With over 2 million visitors in 2018, the castle was Portugal's most visited national monument, so buying tickets in advance via the website is advised to avoid lines at the entrance in peak times. Guided tours run up to nine times a day.

Rua de Santa Cruz do Castelo. www.castelodesaojorge.pt. ✆ **21/880-06-20.** 10€ adults; 5€ youngsters 13–25; 8.50€ over 65s; free for children under 13. Mar–Oct daily 9am–8:30pm; Nov–Feb daily 9am–5:30pm. Bus: 737. Tram: 12, 28.

Fundação Ricardo do Espírito Santo Silva ★★ MUSEUM If you can tear yourself away from the views at the Portas do Sol miradouro, the crimson-painted palace across the road has something rather special. Behind the baroque facade, the perfectly preserved interior of the **Palácio Azurara** houses an array of furniture, textiles, tiles, porcelain, and glassware that offers a fascinating insight into 18th-century aristocratic life. Even more fascinating are the **workshops ★★★** where craftsmen and women preserve centuries of knowhow in silver plating, leather book binding, cabinetmaking, and 15 other decorative arts. The collection and the workshops are run by a foundation set up by banker Ricardo Espírito Santo Silva (1900–1955) with the aim of keeping traditional crafts alive. You can book tours of the ateliers to watch the artisans in action, purchase their work, including reproductions of the museum exhibits, even take a lesson in one of the crafts (5€ a lesson, booking required). In 2019, the foundation opened the **Manufactum,** a store in Chiado (Rua do Alecrim 79) retailing contemporary pieces made by its craftspeople.

Largo das Portas do Sol 2. www.fress.pt. ✆ **21/881-46-00.** 4€ adults, 2€ students under 25; free for children under 12. Guided visits 8€; workshops 10€. Both need to be booked in advance. Wed–Mon 10am–5pm. Tram: 12, 28. Bus: 737.

Igreja da São Vicente de Fora ★★★ CHURCH Portugal's first king, Afonso I Henriques, raised a first church here on the site of his camp during his successful siege of Arab-held Lisbon; the tombs of a couple of Teutonic knights who helped can be seen inside. Construction of the current grand late-Renaissance building begun in 1583, during Portugal's 6-decade Spanish occupation, the involvement of Spanish and Italian architects reflected in the style.

Ironically, it holds the tombs of the Braganza royal family, who kicked the Spanish out and ruled from 1627 to 1910. Fourteen monarchs are buried there, together with their consorts and children. When you visit the **somber pantheon ★★,** look for the eerie weeping statue over the caskets of King Carlos I and Crown Prince Luís Felipe, assassinated at Praça do Comércio in 1908.

The monastery-church takes its name from St. Vincent, one of Lisbon's patrons, and from the fact that it was outside (*fora*) the city walls. Its white limestone facade dominates Alfama's skyline. There are great views from the **rooftop ★★.** The interior is filled with baroque paintings and sculptures, and there's a magnificent marble-clad **sacristy ★** and an intricate **altarpiece ★** by sculptor Joaquim Machado de Castro. The greatest treasure, however, are the around **100,000 blue-and-white tiles** (*azulejos*) **★★★** painted with historical scenes and illustrations of the fables published in the 1600s by French writer

Jean de La Fontaine, full of crafty foxes, rapacious magpies, and greedy bears. The tiles form one of the best examples of this particularly Portuguese artform. Guided tours can be booked via the "Património" section of the website.

Largo de São Vicente. www.patriarcado-lisboa.pt. ✆ **21/888-56-52.** 5€ adults; 2.50€ youngsters 12–21 and over 65s; free for under 12s. Tues–Sun 10am–5pm; Sun 9am–12:30pm and 3–5pm. Tram: 28. Bus: 712 or 728.

Igreja e Museu de Santo António ★ CHURCH The rest of the Christian world may know him as St. Anthony of Padua, after the Italian city where he died; *Lisboetas* venerate the saintly friar as one of their own. His festival day on June 13 is the city's biggest party. Anthony is believed to have been born in 1195 where this pretty baroque church now stands next to Lisbon Cathedral (p. 102). The museum recounts the story of his life and holds relics of the saint. The saint's reputed talents as a matchmaker mean he is especially revered by young couples, and mass weddings are held in the cathedral on the eve of his saint's day.

Largo de Santo António da Sé. www.museudelisboa.pt. ✆ **21/581-85-30.** Museum admission 3€; 1.50€ over 65s; free for students, under 12s and all Sun before 2pm. Church: Mon–Fri 8am–7pm, Sun–Sat 8am–8pm. Museum Tues–Sun 10am–5:30pm. Tram: 12, 28; Bus: 714, 732, 736, 737, 760.

Museu do Aljube Resistência e Liberdade ★ MUSEUM This grim building was a prison dating back to the Middle Ages—its name comes from the Arabic for pit. From 1928 to 1965, the Salazar dictatorship detained and tortured political prisoners here. It's now a moving museum of "Resistance and Freedom" showing the history of the dictatorship, the suffering of prisoners held, and the underground resistance movement that eventually triumphed in the democratic revolution of 1974.

Rua de Augusto Rosa, 42. www.museudoaljube.pt. ✆ **21-581-8535.** Admission 3€; 2.60€ over 65s; 1.50€ youngsters 13–25; free under 12s. Tues–Sun 10am–6pm. Tram 12, 28; Bus 737.

Museu do Fado ★★ MUSEUM The museum dedicated to Lisbon's favorite musical genre (p. 34) is a short walk from Rua dos Remédios, one of Alfama's most typical streets, lined with cute stores and some well-known fado bars. The museum is situated in a former water-pumping station close to the river. With visual displays and a great soundtrack, it tells how the music evolved from the melody of dockside mean streets to a UNESCO World Heritage treasure. Galleries feature interactive presentations, old guitars, theater bills and artworks, including national treasure José Malhoa's 1910 portrait of bohemian tavern life *O Fado* ★★★. Check the website for the program of live performances organized in the museum and venues around the city. There's a well-stocked shop with CDs and a good cafe/restaurant.

Largo do Chafariz de Dentro, 1. www.museudofado.pt. ✆ **21/882-3470.** Admission 5€; 2.50€ youngsters from 12 to 25; 4.30€ over 65s; free for under 12s. Tues–Sun 10am–5:30pm. Tram: 28; Bus: 728, 735, 759, 794.

THE best VIEWS

Lisbon's hilly waterside topography offers many opportunities for fabulous panoramas. Each *miradouro* (belvedere) provides a different angle over the city and the Tagus; many have alfresco cafes. Here are five of our favorites:

Miradouro das Portas do Sol ★★★ Alfama is spread before you in one of the most photogenic views of Lisbon, featuring russet rooftops, church towers and domes, and conveniently placed palm trees against the river's blue backdrop. Adding to the charm, little yellow street cars rattle by every few minutes. It's wonderful at sunrise, but at all times watch out for pickpockets. Tram: 12, 28.

Miradouro de Santa Catarina ★★ This one looks directly down to the river, and sunsets are spectacular. There are lawns and a couple of cafes. It's a popular spot for young people, who gather in the evenings to drink beer and listen to street musicians. It's looked over by the brooding statue of Adamastor, a mythical giant who haunts the Cape of Good Hope in the epic poem *Os Lusíadas*. Nearby is the picturesque Bica neighborhood with its famed funicular. Largo Santa Luzia. Tram 28; Bus 734.

Miradouro de Santa Luzia ★★ Wander down through the charming lanes of the Castelo neighborhood to discover this viewpoint suspended over the river. It's shaded by purple bougainvillea and surrounded by *azulejos*. Below are the red rooftops of Alfama. The panoramic viewpoint is backed by a pretty little church belonging to the knightly Order of Malta. Hidden behind it is a staircase leading to a little terrace bar with its own unique vista. Largo Santa Luzia. Tram 28; Bus 734.

Miradouro de São Pedro de Alcântara ★★ Just beside the Bairro Alto, this broad belvedere has a leafy garden and views across to Castelo de São Jorge, Graça, and the hill of Santana. Across the road is a convent interior beautifully decorated with azulejos. Rua São Pedro de Alcântara. Tram 24; Bus 758.

Miradouro de Sophia de Mello Breyner Andresen ★★ Atop the hill of Graça, the pine-shaded spot lays the city at your feet, from the gardens of Castelo São Jorge to the distant river and a tangle of narrow lanes in medieval Mouraria district just below. Commonly known as Miradouro da Graça after the handsome baroque church behind, it was named after poet Sophia de Mello Breyner Andresen (1919–2004). Try a sundowner from the little kiosk cafe. Calçada da Graça. Tram 28; Bus 734.

Panteão Nacional ★ CHURCH The National Pantheon is the final resting place of many of Portugal's great and good. Aside from the presidents and poets buried here, you can visit the tombs of fado legend Amália Rodrigues (1920–1999), soccer great Eusébio (1942–2014) and Gen. Humberto Delgado, an opposition hero murdered by the dictatorship's secret police in 1966. That was the year this white-domed church—also known as Igreja de Santa Engrácia—was finished, almost 300 years after work began. Portuguese still refer to never-ending tasks as *obras* (works) *de Santa Engrácia*. Richly decorated in multicolored marble, the interior also has monuments to (but not the remains of) Discoveries-era heroes, including Henry the Navigator and Vasco da Gama. There are spectacular views from the roof. If you come on a

Tuesday or Saturday, combine a visit here with shopping at the Feira da Ladra (p. 127) flea market next door.

Largo de Santa Clara. ✆ **21/885-48-20.** Admission 3€ adults, 1.50€ ages 15–25, free for children under 14; free for all Sun after 2pm. Tues–Sun 10am–5pm; closed holidays. Tram: 28.

Sé de Lisboa ★★ CHURCH Chances are you'll do a double take on first sight of Lisbon's medieval cathedral. It looks more like a fortress than a place of worship. Lisbon's new Christian rulers built the church on the site of a mosque (itself constructed over an ancient Visigothic church) after taking the city in 1147 but made sure it could serve as defendable sanctuary in case of a Muslim counterattack. An English crusader-turned-bishop named Gilbert of Hastings was put in charge of the works.

Although damaged by the 1755 earthquake, the Sé remains an impressive example of Romanesque architecture with a barrel-vaulted ceiling and arched upper-level gallery. Graceful Gothic additions were made in later centuries. Most notable are the airy **cloisters ★★**, but restoration work and archeological excavations means they are closed until at least 2020.

Among the treasures inside are the font where St. Anthony is said to have been christened in 1195; the 14th-century Gothic **chapel of Bartolomeu Joanes ★**, a wealthy merchant; and **14th-century sarcophaguses ★** holding the remains of nobleman Lopo Fernandes Pacheco and his book-reading wife Maria Villalobos. There are frequent performances of Portuguese classical guitar music in the sacristy.

Largo da Sé. ✆ **21/886-67-52.** Free admission Mon-Sat 9am–7pm, Sun 9am–8pm. Tram: 12, 28. Bus: 737.

BAIXA & CHIADO

The Baixa is the commercial heart of old Lisbon, its handsome plazas connected by a grid of streets lined by solid five-story building erected after the 1755 earthquake. Climbing up the hill to the west, Chiado's elegant shops, theaters, and cafes recall the days of 19th-century artists and poets, while neighboring Bairro Alto and Príncipe Real are today's hip nightlife and shopping hubs.

Convento do Carmo & Museu Arqueológico ★★ MUSEUM No other Lisbon museum conveys so well the sensation that you've wandered into a living relic to become a witness to history. You enter into the **ruined nave ★★★** of a Gothic church, originally built in 1389, that has stood in a state of partial collapse since the earthquake of 1755, when many parishioners died inside.

In a stark monument to nature's destructive power, the pointed Gothic arches point skyward like the ribs of a skeletal whale. The church was the center of a convent that was built in the 14th century by Nuno Álvares Pereira, the kingdom's richest nobleman and a military hero for defeating Spanish invaders at the battle of Aljubarrota (p. 18). When construction was

0 1/10 mile
0 100 meters
Academia das Ciencas
Rua do Século
Rua N. do Loureiro
Rua S. Boaventura
Rua de São Pedro Alcântara
Glória Funicular
LISBON
Estação do Rossio
Rua Soriano
Rua da Rosa
Trav. da Queimada
Rua Santa Catarina
Rua da Atalaia
Rua da Barroca
Rua do Norte
Rua das Gáveas
Rua da Misericórdia
BICA Funicular
Rua das Chagas
Rua Nova da Trindade
Pr. Luis Camões
Largo do Carmo
Rua Trindade
Largo do Chiado
Rua Garrett
Rua do Carmo
Rua das Flores
Rua de São Paulo
Rua do Alecrim
Rua Duque de Bragança
Rua Capelo
Rua Ivens
Rua Serpa Pinto
Rua Nova do Almada
Rua do Crucifixo
Rua do Ouro
Rua Augusta
Rua de S. Nicolau
Rua Vitor Cordon
Rua da Conceição
Pr. Duque da Terceira
Pr. do Município
Church
Elevador de Santa Justa 6
Café A Brasileira 7
Convento do Carmo Museo Arcqueológico 5
Mercado da Ribiera/ Time Out Market 2
Museu de São Roque/ Igreja de São Roque 1
Museu Nacional de Arte Contemporânea 3
Teatro Nacional de São Carlos 4
Lisbon
PORTUGAL

completed, Álvares Pereira gave away his wealth and lived there as a humble monk. Pope Benedict made him a saint in 2009.

The magnificent church tumbled like most of Lisbon in 1755, and its soaring nave was left as a memorial to quake victims. Surviving structures at the back rooms contain the **Archeological Museum ★★**, whose exhibits include 6th-century Jewish gravestones, an Egyptian sarcophagus, and a pair of spooky Peruvian mommies.

In summer, concerts, plays, and open-air movie screenings are held in the ruins, which are even more evocative in the evening light. The entrance is on one of the Chiado's prettiest squares. Next door, guarded by soldiers in plumed helmets, is the headquarters of the National Republican Guard (GNR) where the remnants of Portugal's 46-year dictatorship surrendered to revolutionary forces in 1974.

Largo do Carmo. www.museuarqueologicodocarmo.pt. ✆ **21/346-04-73.** Admission 5€, 4€ students and seniors; free under 14s. May–Sep Mon–Sat 10am–7pm; Oct–Apr Mon–Sat 10am–6pm. Metro: Baixa-Chiado. Tram: 28. Bus: 758.

Igreja de São Domingos ★ CHURCH This church was never fully repaired after a devastating fire in 1957. Scorched walls and soot-blacked columns stand where once were baroque paintings and gilded carvings. Its eerie atmosphere is accentuated by a dark history.

In Easter 1506, an argument broke out in the church between a Jewish man who had recently converted to Christianity and other worshipers in what was then one of the biggest churches in Lisbon. The dispute sparked a pogrom against Lisbon's Jewish community. Before King Manuel sent the royal guard to quell the violence, an estimated 2,000 Jews were murdered.

More horrors were to come. Manuel's successor João III invited the Holy Inquisition to Portugal. This became the inquisitors' church. Hundreds of suspected heretics were burned at the stake over the next 250 years, many in the square facing the church. Most victims were "New Christians"—Jews who converted to avoid being exiled from the country.

In 1987, President Mário Soares asked the Jewish community for forgiveness and in the 2000s, a memorial was placed in front of the church and a ceremony declared Lisbon a "City of Tolerance" open to all races and religions.

Largo de São Domingos. ✆ **21/342-82-75.** Free. Daily 7:30am–7pm. Metro: Rossio. Bus: 711, 732, 736, 746, 759, 783.

Igreja e Museu de São Roque ★★★ CHURCH From the plain white facade it's hard to guess at the treasures within. The interior is a masterpiece, combining artforms that Portugal made its own: *azulejo* tiles and *talha dourada* (gold-covered wood carving). Both reached their peak when a gold rush in Portugal's Brazilian colonies made King João V one of the richest monarchs in 18th-century Europe.

The church is lined with side chapels gleaming with gold, but its crowning glory is the **Chapel of St. John ★★★** which the king ordered from Rome and shipped here at enormous cost. It is a rococo fantasy in lapis lazuli, agate,

TRAMS, elevators & FUNICULARS

Lisbon provides some vintage transport solutions to help footsore travelers (and locals) overcome its hilly terrain. Its trams, elevators, and funiculars date back to the turn of the 20th century. They're run by the Carris public transport company and can be accessed with the **Viva** transport card (p. 73).

Elevador de Santa Justa ★★★
Inaugurated in 1902, this imposing iron structure towers over the Baixa and continues to haul pedestrians up the Largo do Carmo in the Chiado. Contrary to local lore, Gustave Eiffel had no role in its construction, although the ornate 45m (148-ft.) structure definitely shares style-points with his Parisian tower. Be prepared to queue, but there are great views from the top. Runs daily 7am to 9pm in winter and until 11pm summertime.

Tram 28 ★★★ The little yellow street cars that rattle around the city are one of Lisbon's most recognizable symbols. Many of the trams (*eléctricos*) date back to 1901 when the network was first installed. Running through Alfama, Baixa, Chiado, and other historic districts, line 28 is a travelers' must-do. It's always crowded, and you should watch out for pickpockets on board. Runs weekdays from around 6:30am to 11pm, starting a bit later on Saturdays and staying in the shed on Sunday. Other trolley lines include No. 15 along the river to Belém and No. 24 heading from Chiado through Príncipe Real and Amoreiras.

Ascensor da Bica ★★ The most photogenic of three 19th-century funicular rail cars running up Lisbon's hills, this one was installed in 1892 and takes about 5 minutes to lug passengers from Rua de São Paulo, just behind Ribeira market, through the picturesque Bica neighborhood to Bairro Alto (Mon–Sat 7am–9pm; Sun 9am–9pm). The other yellow-painted *ascensors* are **Glória** running from the start of Avenida da Liberdade to Bairro Alto; and **Lavra** from just off Avenida da Liberdade (next to the excellent Solar dos Presuntos restaurant) to the charming, but little-visited Santana district.

alabaster, Carrara marble, gold, ivory, and more. Look up too at the 16th-century painted **ceiling ★★**, the only one of its kind in Portugal, and the **sacristy ★★** lined with baroque paintings.

The church was a headquarters of the Jesuits, the wealth and power of which led the Marquis of Pombal to kick them out of the country in the 1750s because of a perceived threat to Portugal's secular rulers. A **museum ★★** adjacent to the church tells the order's story and includes a notable collection of religious art. Don't miss the ivory sculpture of the Crucifixion, a fine example of the 17th-century East-West crossover art produced in Portugal's Indian colonies.

Largo Trindade Coelho. www.museu-saoroque.com. ✆ **21/323-50-65.** Museum 2.50€; free for over 65s, under 14s, students, and all on Sun before 2pm. Oct–Mar: Mon 2–5:30pm, Tues–Sun 10am–5:30pm; Apr–Sept: Mon 2–6:30pm, Tues–Wed and Fri–Sun 10am–6:30pm, Thurs 10am–7:30pm. Tram: 24. Bus: 758.

Mercado da Ribeira/Time Out Market ★★ MARKET Lisbon's main food market was built in the 1880s and topped with a distinctive white

FIVE historic CAFES

Cafes are an essential part of Lisbon life. Traditionally they are also *pastelarias* (pastry shops) meaning you can always get freshly baked cakes to go with your *bica* (espresso). Unfortunately, many neighborhood cafes are closing, often to be replaced by bland imitations of international hipster joints. Thankfully this historic quintet is looking good for a few more years:

A Brasileira ★★★ Lisbon's most-famous cafe opened in 1905 and got its name from the coffee shipped from Brazil. It's said the *bica* was invented here. A longtime favorite with writers and artists—including poet Fernando Pessoa, whose statue sits on the pavement terrace—paintings from 1960s habitués decorate the mirrored interior. Make like a local and knock back your (0.70€) shot of coffee standing at the bar, rather than join the tourists paying much more outside.

Rua Garrett, 120. www.abrasileira.pt. ✆ **21/346-95-41.** Daily 8am–2am. Metro Baixa-Chiado.

Confeitaria Nacional ★★★ One of Europe's oldest pastry shops, this place is little changed since it opened in 1829. Its display of homemade pastries will tempt the most calorie-conscious. Locals stand in line at Christmas time for its *bolo rei* (king of cakes) heavy with crystalized fruit. There are eggy sponge cakes called *austríacos* in memory of WWII refugees from Austria who left the recipe. Among the creamy and chocolatey delights, our favorites are unassuming aniseed-flavored crescents called *meia-luas*.

Praça da Figueira, 18. www.confeitarianacional.com. ✆ **21/342-44-70.** Mon–Thurs 8am–8pm; Fri–Sat 8am–9pm; Sun 9am–9pm. Metro: Rossio.

Martinho da Arcada ★★ In the middle of the action, surrounded by government ministries on riverfront Terreiro do Paço, this joint has been serving thirsty *Lisboetas* since 1782. There's a bar with a couple of tables for snacks, beer, or coffee, an elegant dining room out back, and an esplanade under the arcades. City workers pop in through the day to refuel, and it's always been a literary hangout, favored by poet Fernando Pessoa.

Praça do Comercio, 3. www.martinhodaarcada.pt. ✆ **21/887-92-59.** Daily 7:15am–11pm. Metro: Terreiro do Paço.

Pastéis de Belém ★★ This tile-covered cafe/bakery founded in 1837 is famed for the little custard tarts (known as *pastéis de nata*) that have become one of Portugal's best-known culinary exports. This is where they were invented to bring in income for cash-strapped monks. Skip the (always long) lines for takeaway by grabbing a table in the waiter-service back room where the tarts come warm from the oven and ready for you to sprinkle them with cinnamon. You can always ask them to add a to-go box to your bill.

Rua de Belém, 84–92. www.pasteisdebelem.pt. ✆ **21/363-74-23.** Daily 8am–11pm. Tram 15.

Pastelaria Versailles ★★★ Lisbon's most beautiful cafe opened in 1922 on one of the new boulevards built for the expanding city. Its gleaming mirrors, carved woodwork, and stained glass recall the French palace of the same name. Waist-coated waiters whisk trays of tea and homemade pastries to crowds of regular customers. They also serve full meals. Recently opened branches are in Belém and at Lisbon Airport.

Avenida da República 15-A. ✆ **21/354-63-40.** Daily 7:30am–11:45pm.

onion-dome. The traditional side has morning displays of flowers and rows of stalls loaded with seasonal produce (strawberries in April, peaches in July, etc.). Side aisles have butchers' counters gleaming with steaks and offal and fishmongers offering everything from baby squid to swordfish the size of small submarines. Supermarkets and gentrification have robbed the market of some of its bygone bustle, but it remains a window into the soul of the city. Avoid Mondays, when there is no fish catch and many stalls are closed. On the western side of the market hall, a gourmet food court launched by *Time Out* magazine has become one of Lisbon's most-visited attractions. Diners can choose from around 40 restaurants, bars, and stores. Their offerings range from intricate dishes fashioned by Michelin-starred chefs, to sushi, pizza, and Portuguese nibbles like deep-fried cod cakes. There are stores to buy wine, cheese, or chocolate, plus cooking workshops and music into the small hours.

Avenida 24 de Julho. www.timeoutmarket.com. ✆ **21/395-1274.** Traditional market: Mon–Sat 6am–2pm. Time Out Market: Sun–Wed 10am–midnight; Thurs–Sat 10am–2am. Metro: Cais do Sodré. Tram: 15, 25. Bus: 706, 720, 728, 732, 738, 760.

Museu Nacional de Arte Contemporânea ★ MUSEUM Popularly known as the MNAC or Museu do Chiado, the official title of this fine museum is a little misleading because as well as hosting exhibitions of contemporary artists, the permanent collection presents a panorama of Portuguese art from mid-19th-century Romanticism to eclectic 21st-century works.

Among our favorite pieces, look for works by José de Almada Negreiros, Amadeo de Souza-Cardoso, Columbano Bordalo Pinheiro, José Malhoa, and Paula Rego. Housed in a sprawling building that was formally a Franciscan convent and then a cookie factory before being transformed into a museum during the 1990s. The impressive architecture features a sculpture-filled atrium and garden (although the garden cafe had closed as we went to press).

Despite a recent expansion into a neighboring building (creating a second entrance on Rua Capelo), there's not enough space to display all 5,000 works, so the collection is regularly rotated.

Rua Serpa Pinto 4. www.museuartecontemporanea.gov.pt. ✆ **21/343-21-48.** 4.50€, 2.25€ students and over 65s, free for under 12s. Tues–Sun 10am–5:30pm. Metro: Baixa-Chiado. Tram: 28.

BELÉM, SANTOS & ALCÂNTARA

Among the riverside gardens of Belém, you'll find Lisbon's paramount monuments to the Discoveries era, but also exciting modern art and architecture, as well as a range of restaurants and cafes. Portugal's president has his palace there. Between Belém and downtown, Santos and Alcântara offer a mix of hip shopping and nightlife as well as a couple of top-flight museums.

MAAT ★★ MUSEUM The Museum of Art, Architecture and Technology is a spectacular new addition to the Lisbon art scene. Opened in 2016, the building, designed by British architect Amanda Levete, rises like a soft white wave over the Tagus, transforming this stretch of Lisbon's waterfront. It set records for Lisbon museum attendance in its first week, when natives rushed to view its swooping architectural panache.

The new building connects and contrasts with **Centro Tejo ★★,** a 20th-century power plant next door, which is also open to visitors as a museum of electricity and hosts regular art exhibitions among the furnaces and turbines.

MAAT showcases the collection of the EDP power company based on 21st-century Portuguese artists and hosts regular temporary exhibitions within its curvilinear galleries, with a focus on links between contemporary art, new media, and technology. The choices are not to everybody's taste, but even those with no stomach for contemporary art will enjoy strolling up to the grass-covered roof and taking in the views.

Avenida de Brasília, Central Tejo. www.maat.pt. ✆ **21/002-81-30.** 5€, 2.50€ students and over 65s, free for under 18s and unemployed. Free for everyone the first Sunday of the month. Combined ticket with the Central Tejo powerplant 9€. Wed–Mon 11am–7pm. Train: Belém. Tram: 15. Bus: 728, 714, 727, 729, 751.

Mosteiro dos Jerónimos ★★★ CHURCH If you visit one monument in Lisbon, this should be it. A UNESCO World Heritage site, this 16th-century monastery is the city's most impressive building. That's no secret, so go early or late to avoid the longest lines.

Like the nearby Torre de Belém, the monastery was built on the orders of King Manuel I and is the city's most expressive showcase of the Manueline architectural style named after the monarch (p. 28). It's a grandiose expression of the newfound wealth and glory that came with Portugal's maritime expansion. Manuel paid for it with the so-called "pepper tax" on spices shipped from the East.

From outside, the **south portal ★★** is the visual centerpiece of the limestone facade, an extraordinary shrine-like doorway carved with saintly figures and Portuguese heroes intertwined with the twisted ropes and exotic vegetation that characterizes the Manueline style. Visitors enter through the **west portal ★**, built by French sculptor Nicolas Chantereine, a more discreet but equally ornate entrance, featuring figures of Manuel and his queen, Maria of Aragon.

Once you're in, the **three-aisled church ★★★** is an immediate showstopper. Slender columns like ship's masts bloom into flower-like supports for the web of tracery on the vaulted ceiling, a masterpiece by Spanish architect Juan de Castillo. Among the **tombs of royalty and Portuguese worthies ★★**, those of King Manuel (1469–1521), explorer Vasco da Gama (1460–1524), and poet Luis de Camões (1524–80) standout. At the far end is the **capela-mor,** the main chapel, built in marble under the orders of Queen Catarina of Austria in 1571 with panels of Mannerist paintings.

Other highlights include the **cloisters ★★★** decorated with Manueline carvings and the **refectory ★★,** whose walls are lined with 17th-century *azulejos*. The cloisters hold tombs of great writers including poet Fernando Pessoa (1888–1935). In the 19th century, somebody had the bright idea of

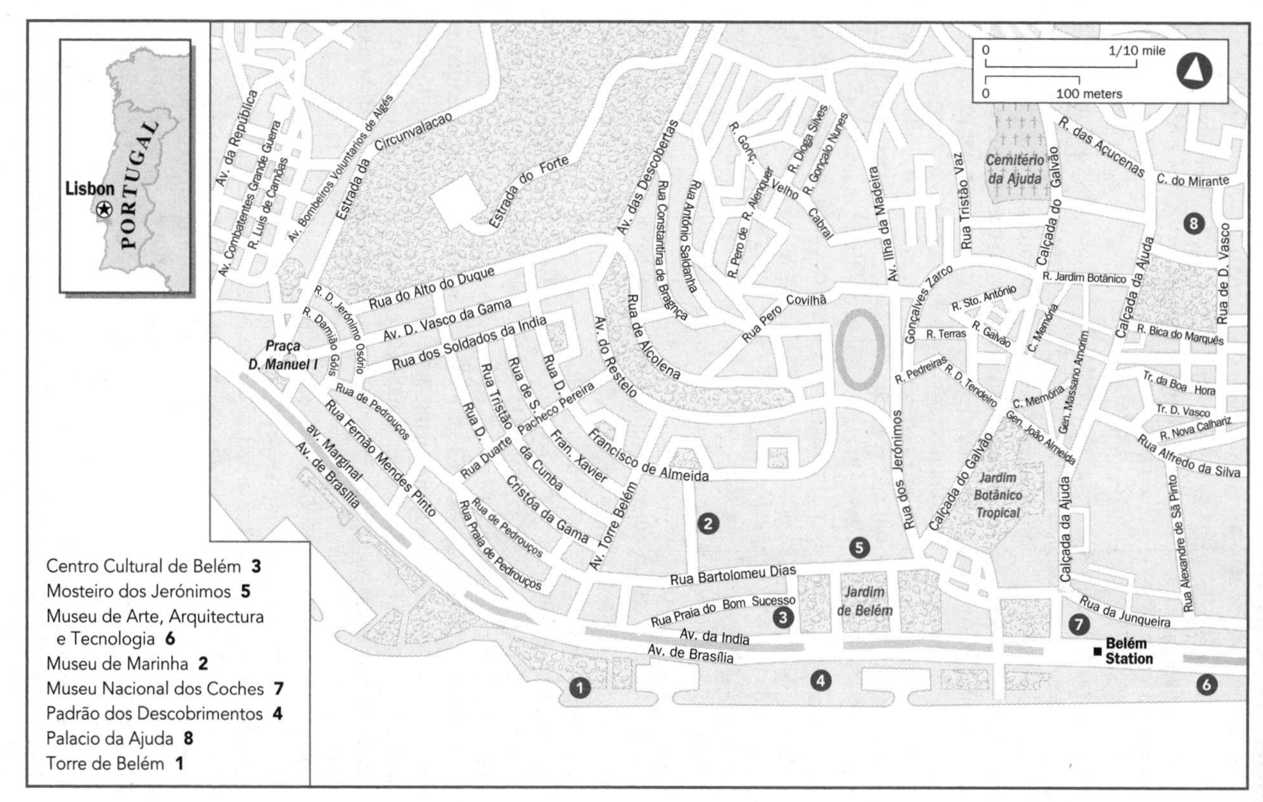
Centro Cultural de Belém 3
Mosteiro dos Jerónimos 5
Museu de Arte, Arquitectura e Tecnologia 6
Museu de Marinha 2
Museu Nacional dos Coches 7
Padrão dos Descobrimentos 4
Palacio da Ajuda 8
Torre de Belém 1
0 1/10 mile
0 100 meters
PORTUGAL
Lisbon
Belém Station
Jardim Botânico Tropical
Jardim de Belém
Cemitério da Ajuda
Praça D. Manuel I
Calçada da Ajuda
Calçada do Galvão
Rua dos Jerónimos
Rua Bartolomeu Dias
Rua Praia do Bom Sucesso
Av. da India
Av. de Brasília
Av. Torre Belém
Av. do Restelo
Rua de Alcolena
Av. das Descobertas
Av. Ilha da Madeira
Rua Tristão Vaz
Rua da Junqueira
Rua Alexandre de Sá Pinto
Rua Alfredo da Silva
Rua de D. Vasco
Estrada do Forte
Estrada da Circunvalacao
Rua Fernão Mendes Pinto
av. Marginal
Rua do Alto do Duque
Av. D. Vasco da Gama
Rua dos Soldados da India
Francisco de Almeida
Rua Pero Covilhã
Rua Constantina de Bragança
Rua António Saldanha

appending a long two-story annex to the facade of the building in the then-fashionable neo-Manueline style. It now holds the **National Archaeology Museum ★** (where you can buy tickets for Jerónimos from automatic vending machines) and the **Maritime Museum ★★** (p. 117).

Praça do Império. www.mosteirojeronimos.pt. ✆ **21/362-00-34.** 10€, 5€ over 625s, free for under 12s. Oct–Apr Tues–Sun 10am–5pm; May–Sept Tues–Sun 10am–6pm. Train: Belém. Tram: 15. Bus: 714, 727, 728, 729, 751.

Museu Colecção Berardo ★★★ MUSEUM In the depths of the bunker-like Centro Cultural de Belém (CCB) is a world-class collection of modern and contemporary art assembled by Joe Berardo, an emigrant from Madeira who made a fortune in South African gold. In the 1990s, he struck a deal with the Portuguese government to place his treasures on public view in this modern architectural landmark across from Jerónimos Monastery.

The collection is divided into two parts. The first features sculpture and painting from 1900 to 1960 and is a who's who of 20th-century art, littered with works by Picasso, Miró, Pollack, Bacon, Warhol, and many, many more. The post-1960 section covers the latest movements of contemporary creativity from minimalism to Arte Povera and traumatic realism. There's a 2m (6-ft.) robot made from flickering TV screens by Nam June Paik, some Portuguese barnyard S&M from Paula Rego, and a life-size plastic sheepdog by Jeff Koons. The museum has a challenging program of temporary exhibitions of Portuguese and international artists.

The CCB is Portugal's biggest cultural space and has a packed program of concerts, plays, and other events (p. 138) as well as a couple of good restaurants and interesting shops.

Praça do Império. www.museuberardo.pt. ✆ **21/361-2878.** 5€, 2.50€ students, over 65s and youngsters 7–18, free for under 7s and for all on Sat. Daily 10am–6:30pm. Train: Belém. Tram: 15. Bus: 714, 727, 728, 729, 751.

Museu do Oriente ★★ MUSEUM Down by the docks, just next to the Alcântara station, is a windowless white warehouse built in the 1940s to store salt cod. In 2008, it was transformed into a museum to celebrate Lisbon's 5 centuries of cultural and commercial exchanges with Asia. The dark spaces inside feature eclectic collections ranging from larger-than-life statues of Jesuit martyrs to traditional Korean costumes, Indian shadow puppets, suits of Samurai armor, or ritual masks from East Timor. Temporary exhibitions showcase contemporary Asian artists or focus on more treasures from the storerooms. The cultural program ranges from concerts of Japanese flute music to Bollywood movie evenings. Visitors can sign up for workshops for adults and children; themes include Chinese kite-making, yoga, or Japanese manga drawing. The top-floor restaurant is reputed to serve the best brunch in town.

Avenida Brasília, Doca de Alcântara. www.museudooriente.pt. ✆ **21/358-52-00.** 6€; 3.50€ over 65s; 2.50€ students; 2€ youngsters 6–12; free under-6 and for all Fri 6pm–9:30pm. Open Tues–Thurs and Sat–Sun 10am–5:30pm; Fri 10am–9:30pm. Train: Alcântara. Tram: 15, 18. Bus: 714, 738, 742.

Museu Nacional de Arte Antiga ★★★ MUSEUM Portugal's finest collection of old masters is housed in a clifftop 17th-century palace and adjacent convent backed by grassy, sculpture-filled garden where visitors can enjoy 180-degree harbor views while enjoying coffee or lunch from the self-service restaurant/cafe.

Inside, the National Museum of Ancient Art is focused on Portuguese and European art from the 15th to 19th centuries. Masterpieces include the nightmarish ***Temptations of St. Anthony*** by Hieronymus Bosch ★★★; Francisco de Zurbarán's full-body **portraits of the 12 Apostles ★★★;** a wickedly seductive ***Salomé*** by Lucas Cranach ★★★; and a pair of golden 16th-century **Japanese screen paintings ★★★** depicting Portuguese sailors arriving in Nagasaki. For many Portuguese, however, the museum's greatest treasure item is the ***Panels of St. Vincent*** **★★★,** a massive 1470s work by Nuno Gonçalves depicting Lisbon society—from fishermen to royalty—at the time of the Discoveries.

Besides the world-class painting collection, there are rooms filled with goldware, ceramics, antique furniture and textiles from around Europe and the lands visited by Portuguese explorers. Don't miss the **Belém Monstrance ★★★,** a solid gold creation crafted by playwright Gil Vicente in 1506 with gold brought home by Vasco da Gama from the coast of East Africa on his way back from the first sea voyage to India. Diverse objects from West Africa, India, Persia, China, and Japan also recall Portugal's overseas ventures.

Rua das Janelas Verdes 95. www.museudearteantiga.pt. ✆ **21/391-28-00.** 6€; 3€ over 65s; free under 12s. Tues–Sun 10am–6pm. Tram: 25. Bus: 713, 714, 727.

Museu Nacional dos Coches ★★ MUSEUM Every child who visits the National Coach Museum here must dream about hiding until midnight to find out if the gleaming gold carriages turn into pumpkins. This is one of Europe's finest collections of horse-drawn coaches and one of the most visited museums in the country. It was founded in 1905 to showcase the carriages of the aristocracy and royal family. The oldest coach on exhibit carried King Phillip III of Spain on a visit to Lisbon in 1618. The golden carriage—shipped from Vienna by Emperor Joseph I for his sister Maria Anna's 1708 wedding to Portugal's King Joao V—is the most fairytale-like. Others among the rococo contraptions were used by popes, nobles, and crowned heads from Portugal and around Europe, but there's no evidence any of them ever rushed a kitchen maid with missing glass slipper home from a ball.

Controversially, in 2015 the museum was moved into a vast ultra-modern building across the road from its original atmospheric home in the old royal stables (which can still be visited). Still, it remains one of Portugal's most-visited museums.

Avenida da Índia 136. www.museudoscoches.gov.pt. ✆ **21/073-23-19.** 8€, (10€ if you include the royal stables); 4€ (5€ with stables) for over 65s; free for under 12s. Tues–Sun 10am–5:30pm. Train: Belém. Tram: 15. Bus: 714, 727, 729, 751.

Padrão dos Descobrimentos ★ MONUMENT The 50m-high (164-ft.) Discoveries Monument was first erected in the 1940s by Portugal's Fascist-inspired dictatorship to celebrate the Age of Discovery. It remains a striking landmark jutting like the bow of a *caravela* sailing boat over the waters of the Tagus. From the bow to the stern, the pure white monolith is lined with outsized statues of Discoveries-era heroes including Vasco da Gama and Ferdinand Magellan. They are led by Henry the Navigator standing proud atop the prow. The original temporary structure was replaced by the current concrete-and-limestone monument in 1960 to mark the 500th year after Henry's death. Among the sculptures on the west side is Gomes Eanes de Zurara's poignant description of the 1444 sale of the first Africans carried to Portugal as slaves. In another sign of the Discoveries' darker associations, the giant compass rose laid out before the monument was a 1960 gift to the Salazar dictatorship from the apartheid government of South Africa. There are temporary exhibitions inside and views over Belém and the river from the terrace.

Av. de Brasília. www.padraodosdescobrimentos.pt. ✆ **21/303-19-50.** 6€; 5€ over 65s; 3€ youngsters 13–18; free under 12s. Mar–Sept daily 10am–8:30pm; Oct–Feb Tues–Sun 10am–5:30pm. Train: Belém. Tram: 15. Bus: 714, 727, 728, 729, 751.

Palacio da Ajuda ★★ PALACE In the aftermath of the 1755 earthquake, King José I was so shaken up he refused to live under masonry and ordered the building of a wooden cabin, known as the "royal shack" on a hillside above Belém. When she succeeded to the throne, his daughter Queen Maria I wanted something grander, ordering the construction of a colossal neo-classical palace in white stone. Work hardly got underway when Napoleon invaded, and the royals fled to Brazil. Then came Civil War (1828–1834). Then the money ran out. All that left the palace looking from one side like a grand rival to London's Buckingham Palace, from the other like an abandoned construction site. Still the royal family lived there until booted out by a republican revolution in 1910. It makes an impressive visit with the sumptuous salons fully furnished with regal trappings, as if they were expecting the monarch to return at any moment. Particularly imposing is the banqueting room where the president still holds state dinners. In 2016, a 21€-million plan was announced to finish the construction by building a west wing to hold the crown jewels, currently stashed in vaults. It's unlikely to be open before 2021, and there will be closures of some rooms during the construction work. Behind the palace, Lisbon's oldest **Botanical garden ★** laid out in 1768 is a festival of exotic flora with a 2€ admission fee.

Largo da Ajuda. www.palacioajuda.gov.pt. ✆ **21/363-70-95.** 5€; 2.50€ students and over 65s; free under 13s. Thurs–Tues 10am–5:30pm; Train: Belém. Bus: 729, 732, 742.

Torre de Belém ★★ MONUMENT This graceful white tower set on the bank of the Tagus is Portugal's most recognizable landmark. Now a World Heritage site, it was constructed in 1520 and is a prime example of the Discoveries-era Manueline architecture (p. 28), standing close to where the explorers' boats set to sea.

Although it looks more decorative than warlike, it was built to defend the entrance to Lisbon and saw action in the 1830s when its cannons fired on French ships intervening in Portugal's Civil War. The park surrounding it is a shaded place where you can contemplate the castellated tower and carvings of ropes, regal domes, shields, and intricate statues. However, the mostly empty interior can be a little underwhelming, especially if you've had to endure the long lines to get in. Spend a moment to contemplate the next-door memorial to soldiers killed in Portugal's 1961–1974 colonial wars.

Avenida de Brasília. www.torrebelem.gov.pt. ✆ **21/362-0034.** 6€; 3€ over 65s and students; free under 12. Oct–Apr Tues–Sun 10am–5pm; May–Sept Tues–Sun 10am–6pm. Train: Belém. Tram: 15. Bus: 714, 727, 728, 729, 751.

PARQUE DAS NAÇÕES & XABREGAS

On the city's northeastern edge, Parque das Nações is a complete contrast with old Lisbon, a planned neighborhood which since the 1990s has replaced old docks and industrial space with ultra-modern architecture, including cultural and entertainment centers, shopping malls, hotels, and restaurants. The main draw is undoubtedly the amazing aquarium, but there's much more to do and see. On the way there, the old dockside districts of Xabregas, Beato, and Marvila are fast up-and-coming.

Museu Nacional do Azulejo ★★ MUSEUM Wherever you travel around Portugal you'll see *azulejos.* The painted ceramic tiles are used to decorate buildings inside and out, from medieval churches and baroque palaces to modern metro stations. The best place to understand this thoroughly Portuguese artform is this museum, situated in a gem of a 16th-century convent in an out-of-the-way riverside neighborhood. The collection traces the history of Portuguese tiles over 600 years. Highlights include a **giant panel ★★** showing Lisbon before the great earthquake of 1755, and above all the fabulous **convent church ★★★** decorated with blue-and-white tiles and carvings covered in gold leaf. Don't let the outdated and malfunctioning website put you off; the museum really is worth a visit.

Rua da Madre de Deus 4. www.museudoazulejo.gov.pt. ✆ **21/810-03-40.** Adults 5€, 2.50€ students with ID and over 65s, free for under-13s. Tues–Sun 10am–5:30pm. Bus: 718, 742, 794.

Oceanário de Lisboa ★★★ AQUARIUM Arguably the most spectacular aquarium on the planet, this opened as the focal point of the 1998 World's Fair and remains the city's most popular indoor attraction. At the core of the ultra-modern riverside building is a 1.3-million-gallon tank, 23 feet deep and holding over 100 species of sea life including sharks, rays, barracuda, and a slow-moving ocean sunfish weighing in at over 1 ton.

Floor-to-ceiling panels enable visitors to stay nose-to-nose with these creatures as they circle the main tank to visit the four corner towers, representing life in the Atlantic, Indian, Antarctic, and Pacific oceans.

ART on the STREETS

Lisbon is scarred by senseless graffiti splattered on churches, historic monuments, trains, businesses, and private homes, but among the dross are dozens of outstanding murals that make the city a leading European street-art hub. There are organized tours that will take you to some of the best-known spots: try www.alternativelisbon.co or www.lisbonstreetarttours.com. Alternatively, just keep your eyes open as you wander the city. Among the most eye-catching works are the portrait of fado legend **Amália Rodriques** by Vhils at Calçada do Menino de Deus, 1-3 in Alfama; the house-size **Racoon** created by Bordallo II out of auto parts near Rua Bartolomeu Dias, 43, just behind Belém Cultural Center; the **tribute to Portugal's 1974 democratic revolution** by U.S. artist Shepard Fairey at Rua Natália Correia 11; and the murals by an international group of artists covering a **whole block of abandoned buildings** halfway down Avenida Fontes Pereira de Melo. Far from the beaten track but well worth a visit is **Quinta do Mocho,** a tough neighborhood on the far side of Lisbon airport where tenement blocks are decorated with almost 70 murals in what's believed to be Europe's biggest urban art space. Tours can be arranged at www.greentrekker.pt.

You start your visit on the surface, ogling penguins, puffins, brilliantly colored frogs, and playful sea otters. Then you spiral down through startlingly different ecosystems, discovering psychedelically colored cuttlefish, jewel-like wrasse and puffers, and shoals of luminous jellyfish.

It's a delight for all ages, beautifully laid out and well explained. For a night to remember, you can book your kids for an overnight sleepover party next to the shark-filled tank. The Oceanário isn't cheap, but fees support its scientific, education, and conservation work.

Esplanada d. Carlos I. www.oceanario.pt. ✆ **21/891-70-00.** 16€, 11€ children 4–12 and over 65s, free for under 4s. Family tickets 42€. Apr–Oct daily 10am–7pm, Nov–Mar daily 10am–6pm. Metro: Oriente; Bus 728.

ESTRELA, CAMPO DO OURIQUE & AVENIDAS NOVAS

Less visited than the city's ancient core, central Lisbon's northern districts offer verdant avenues, cool gardens, excellent shopping, restaurants, and some fascinating museums and monuments.

Aqueduto das Águas Livres ★★★ MONUMENT The Águas Livres aqueduct is an engineering marvel whose giant arches stride over 11 miles into the city. Built in the 18th century, it survived the 1755 earthquake and carried water to Lisbon until the 1960s. It's still run by Lisbon's water company and is part of its network of museums and monuments, including pumping stations and vast underground cisterns.

A walk across the soaring arches is a unique experience. It's about 1km (about 1,000 yards) each way from the main entrance in Campolide to the end in the Monsanto park. The walkway over the aqueduct used to be a regular access for rural people heading into the city, where in the 1830s, dozens fell victim to serial killer Diogo Alves, who would throw them into the valley 60 meters (almost 200 f.t) below. After his execution, Alves' head was preserved for scientific research and remains on show at the university medical facility.

Among the reservoirs that form part of the water museum, the **Mãe d'Água ★★** (Mother of Water) is a vast cistern that feels like a flooded cathedral with columns supporting the high, arched roof emerging from the waters.

Aquaduct: Calçada da Quintinha 6. www.epal.pt. ✆ **21/810-02-15.** 3€; 1.50€ students and over 65s, free under 12s. Tues–Sun 10am–5:30pm. Bus: 742, 751, 758. Mãe d'Água: Praça das Amoreiras 10. 3€; 2.50€ students and over 65s; free under 12s. Tues–Sun 10am–12:30pm and 1:30–5pm. Metro: Rato. Bus: 706, 709, 713, 758, 720, 727, 738, 774.

Basílica da Estrela ★ CHURCH The twin bell towers and white dome of one of Lisbon's biggest religious buildings recall the baroque churches of Rome. It was built in 1779, on the orders of Queen Maria I who is buried inside. A nativity scene containing over 500 cork and terracotta figures by 18th-century sculptor Joaquim Machado de Castro is a main attraction amid Italian paintings and multicolored marble. More than 100,000 people packed the church and surrounding streets for the funeral of fado diva Amália Rodrigues in 1999. Across the road, the **Jardim da Estrela ★** is one of the city center's most relaxing parks, featuring ponds and shady tropical plants.

Largo da Estrela. ✆ **21/396-09-15.** Free. Daily 8.45am–8pm.Tram: 25, 28. Bus: 713, 773, 774.

Cemitério dos Prazeres ★★ MONUMENT This graveyard is the end of the line for westbound travelers on Tram 28. Opened in the 1830s, Prazeres cemetery is Lisbon's largest. An improbable attraction maybe, but it is a historic and absorbing place to visit, featuring lane after lane lined with cypress trees and ornate mausoleums built to house the remains of Portugal's most distinguished families. A white pyramid built in 1849 for the family of the Dukes of Palmela is Europe's largest private mausoleum and is replete with masonic symbolism. The cemetery lies on the edge of the leafy Campo de Ourique neighborhood, which makes a pleasant place to stroll with many cafes, restaurants, and Art Deco buildings.

Praça São João Bosco. ✆ **21/396-15-11.** Free. Winter 9am–4:30pm. Summer 9am–5:30pm. Tram: 25, 28. Bus: 701, 709, 774.

Fundação Amália Rodrigues Casa Museu ★ MUSEUM On a street where you can find Portugal's parliament and Lisbon's best collection of antique shops is the home of fado's greatest singer (p. 35). This three-story ochre house has been left largely as it was when Amália lived here, up to her death in 1999 at the age of 79. The guide tells the story of her rags to riches story through thousands of the diva's personal items including swanky dresses, jewelry, and portraits. Poignantly, the star's pet parrot still lives in the kitchen and occasionally says "*olá*" to visitors. It's a fascinating insight into the star's lifestyle. In the summer from 5–7pm there are live fado performances in the patio cafe behind the house.

Rua de São Bento 193. www.amaliarodrigues.pt. ✆ **21/397-18-96.** 5€; 3.50€ students and over 65s; free under 5s. Daily 10am–6pm. Metro: Rato. Bus: 707, 727.

Museu Calouste Gulbenkian ★★★ MUSEUM One of the world's greatest private art collections was amassed by Armenian oil magnate Calouste Gulbenkian (p. 30). Thanks to Gulbenkian's discerning taste, many of the foundation's 6,000 items are masterpieces. The museum treads a path through almost every era in the history of art. There are funeral masks from ancient Egypt and Assyrian carvings made in 888 B.C. You'll discover rare Greek vases and Roman jewels, Persian rugs, Ottoman ceramics, and Armenian Bibles sumptuously illustrated in the 1620s. One gallery overflows with Japanese and Chinese porcelain, the next features furniture and tableware from the palaces of French kings and Russian czars.

Rembrandts, Turners, and Manets shine among the **European art ★★★.** Among our favorites are a wistful ***Portrait of a Young Woman*** painted in 1490 by Florentine master Domenico Ghirlandaio and a wintery Claude Monet landscape, ***The Thaw.*** The final room is devoted to the gem-encrusted genius of Art Nouveau designer **René Lalique ★★★.**

All this is held in a low-lying 1960s building that also holds concert halls, conference rooms, and temporary exhibitions. Its **landscaped gardens ★★** are filled with wild birds, leafy paths, and tumbling steams, making a perfect place to escape the city bustle. On the other side of the garden, a separate museum holds the **Modern Collection ★★,** considered the most complete collection of 20th-century Portuguese art and a big selection by international artists. The same ticket gets you into both. There are good cafe/restaurants in both museums and in the gardens.

Av. de Berna 45. www.gulbenkian.pt. ✆ **21/782-30-00.** 10€; 5€ for under 25s and over 65s. Free for under 12s and for all Sunday after 2pm. Wed–Mon 10am–6pm. Metro: Sebastião or Praça de Espanha. Bus: 713, 716, 726, 742, 746, 756.

LISBON FOR KIDS

The display of aquatic life at the **Oceanário de Lisboa** (p. 113) is indisputably Lisbon's No. 1 attraction for kids (and for many adults), but there's much else to keep children happy, from trips to suburban beaches on the Cascais coast (p. 147), to a hands-on science museum, "dragon boats," and equine dancing displays.

Escola Portuguesa de Arte Equestre ★★ RIDING SCHOOL Horse lovers will delight at the dressage skills performed regularly by the Portuguese School of Equestrian Art. The shows are held in a specially designed riding ring just up the road from Belém's National Coach Museum (see p. 111). Wearing 18th-century aristocratic outfits, riders mounted on beautiful

Lusitano horses execute a series of precise routines to uphold an ancient tradition of Portuguese equestrian expertise. It's considered one of the "big four" such riding schools alongside those of Vienna, Saumur in France, and Jerez, Spain. Spectators can attend hourlong training sessions mornings Tuesday through Saturday at 10am, or attend grand gala nights held the final Friday of every month at 9:30pm. Check in advance for other times.

Calçada da Ajuda, next to No. 23. www.arteequestre.pt. ✆ **21/923-73-00.** Training sessions 8€–12€; Gala nights 25€–38€. Metro: Belém. Tram: 15. Bus: 728, 714, 727, 729, 751.

Jardim Zoológico de Lisboa ★★ ZOO Lisbon's Zoo has been charming kids for over 130 years. It holds over 2,000 animals from 300 different species. One that you're unlikely to see anywhere else is the Iberian lynx—the world's rarest cat struggles to survive in the wild of southern Spain and southeastern Portugal. The pair here are part of a conservation program.

The zoo fell on hard times in the 1980s but has turned itself around and is now a modern and much-loved animal park, where Portuguese children flock to see rare red pandas, a dolphin show, or the "enchanted woods" where exotic bird fly in the open air. It's designed to let visitors get as close as possible to the animals and includes a cable car that whisks visitors over the enclosures.

Praça Marechal Humberto Delgado. www.zoo.pt. ✆ **21/723-29-00.** 22€, 16€ seniors, 15€ kids 3–12, free under 3s. Summer daily 10am–6:45pm; Winter 10am–5:15pm. Metro: Jardim Zoológico. Bus: 701, 716, 726, 731, 746, 754, 755, 758, 768, 770.

Museu de Marinha ★★ MUSEUM The Navy Museum is one of the best of its kind in Europe, a tribute to Portugal's one-time domination of the high seas. It's installed in the west wing of the Mosteiro dos Jerónimos. Grabbing the limelight are five 18th-century royal galleys, their bows decorated with gilded dragon figureheads. The grandest of all, built in 1784, ferried the royal family to a British fleet as they fled to Brazil just before Napoleon's troops captured Lisbon. It was last used in 1957 to give Queen Elizabeth II of England a trip on the Tagus. The museum has an important collection of artifacts from the Age of Discoveries, including a battered statue of Archangel Raphael which Vasco da Gama carried on his voyages to India. There's also the seaplane piloted by Carlos Gago Coutinho and Artur de Sacadura Cabral on their first flight between Europe and South America in 1922. The Navy runs a number of other visitor attractions, including the next-door **Planetarium ★** and a 19th-century frigate, the ***Dom Fernando II* ★,** across the river in Almada. It's fun to visit by taking one of the little orange ferry boats from Cais do Sodré to Cacilhas.

Praça do Império. www.ccm.marinha.pt/pt. ✆ **21/097-73-88.** 6.50€, 3.25€ kids 4–12, over 65s, free for under 4s. Oct–Apr: Daily 10am–4:30pm; May–Sept: Daily 10am–5:30pm. Train: Belém. Tram: 15. Bus: 714, 727, 28, 729, 751.

Pavilhão do Conhecimento-Ciência Viva ★★ MUSEUM This wonderfully interactive science museum lets the little ones simulate an astronaut jump, ride a bike on a high-wire, build a bridge they can walk over, and any number of other gee-whiz experiments. The building was one of the highlights of Expo '98 in the Parque das Nações district. It brims with interactive exhibits that are educational, but still a bundle of laughs for youngsters and their parents.

Largo José Mariano Gago 1. www.pavconhecimento.pt. ✆ **21/891-71-00.** 9€, 7€ youngsters 12–17, 6€ seniors and kids 3–11, free under 3s; 24€ families (2 adults and with kids up to 17). June–Aug: Mon–Fri 10am–5:30pm, Sat–Sun 11am–6:30pm; Sept–May: Tues–Fri 10am–5:30pm, Sat–Sun 11am–6:30pm. Metro: Oriente. Bus: 728.

Telecabine Lisboa ★ CABLE CAR Built (like most of Parque das Nações) for the World's Fair in 1998, the cable car pulls you along over the riverbank, 100 feet up, offering spectacular views over the Tagus and the area's modern architectural landmarks, such as the graceful Vasco da Gama bridge (Western Europe's longest at 7.6 miles), the towering Myriad Hotel, and the egg-like Altice Arena. It's close to the Oceanário, the Ciência Viva science museum, and the Vasco da Gama shopping mall. The trip lasts about 10 minutes.

Passeio de Neptuno. www.telecabinelisboa.pt. ✆ **21/895-61-43.** One-way ticket 4€; 2.60€ kids 5–12 and over 65s; free under 5s. Spring and fall daily 11am–7pm; summer 10:30am–8pm; winter 11am–6pm. Metro: Oriente. Bus: 728.

CITY STROLLS

Lisbon is a walker's delight; the city's principal neighborhoods abound with major sights and quiet glimpses into daily life.

WALKiNG TOUR 1 ALFAMA

START:	**Praça do Comércio.**
FINISH:	**Costa da Castelo.**
TIME:	**2 hours.**
BEST TIMES:	**A day when it's not too hot.**
WORST TIMES:	**When the mercury tops 30°C.**

The streets of Alfama are best traversed on foot, even if that means some steep hills. If it's too tiring, hop on Trams 28 or 12, which clatter through the narrow streets.

From Praça do Comércio head east along Rua da Alfândega.

1 Igreja da Conceição

Built in the 1500s on the site of a synagogue, this once-grand church was almost completely destroyed by the 1755 quake. The magnificent Manueline doorway survives complete with floral designs, mythical beasts, and maritime mementoes.

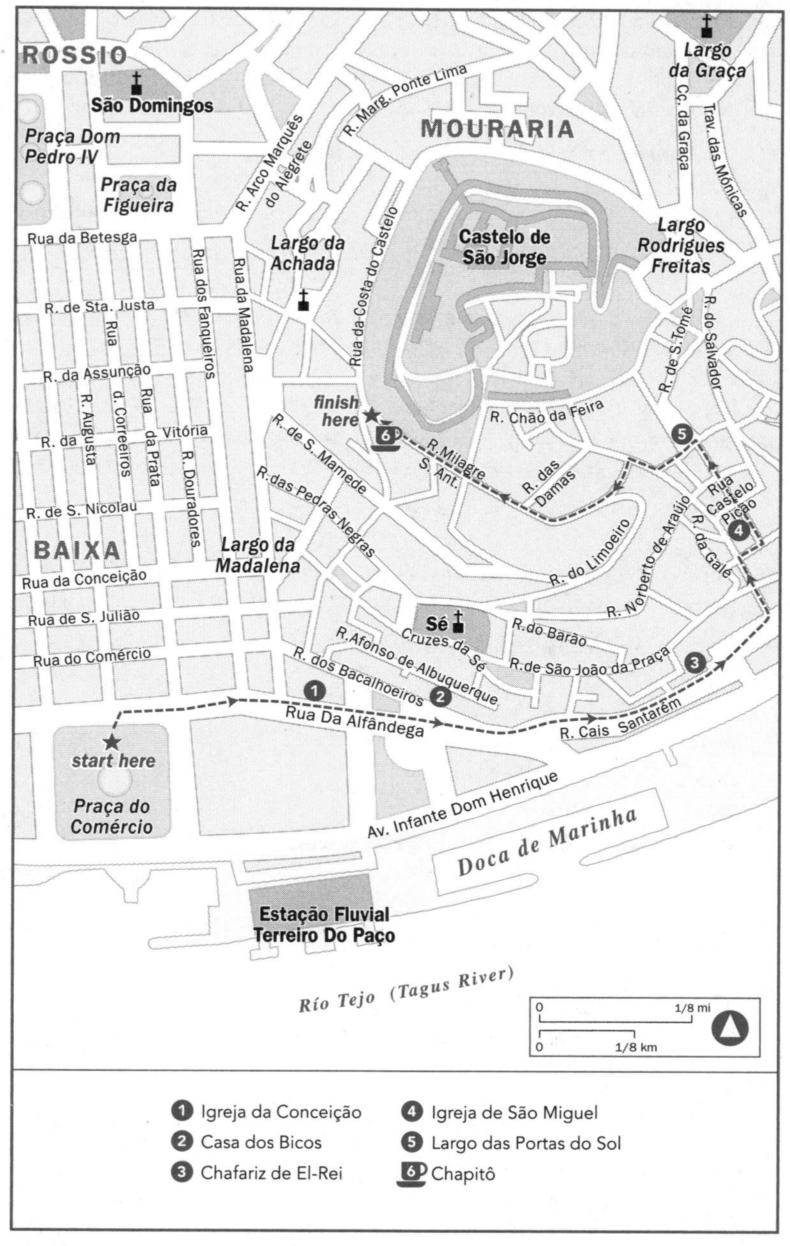

1 Igreja da Conceição
2 Casa dos Bicos
3 Chafariz de El-Rei
4 Igreja de São Miguel
5 Largo das Portas do Sol
6 Chapitô

Continue on Rua da Alfândega until it opens onto Campo de Cebolas:

2 Casa dos Bicos

This noble residence built in 1523 has a facade of stone spikes inspired by Renaissance Italy. It hosts a foundation dedicated to José Saramago, the Nobel-winning novelist who died in 2010. His ashes are buried under the olive tree out front.

Keep heading east on Rua Cais de Santarém.

3 Chafariz de El-Rei

The facade dates from 1864, but this is one of the oldest drinking fountains in Lisbon, opened in 1487. Noble households and the India fleet tanked up with water here.

Take the alley on the left, then stairs leading up to Rua Judaria, in the heart of the old Jewish quarter, pass Largo de São Rafael on to Rua de São Miguel.

4 Igreja de São Miguel

It's a pity this pretty white church in the heart of Alfama only opens Wednesday and Friday 4 to 6pm and Sunday 8 to 10am. Inside, it's a jewel box of gilded 17th-century wood carvings.

Wind your way uphill, north along steps and lanes until you reach:

5 Largo das Portas do Sol

This is one of the best vistas in Lisbon, busy with street performers. Look beyond the statue of St. Vincent toward the rooftops and river (p. 101).

Turn west along Rua de Santiago and Largo dos Lóis until you reach Costa da Castelo.

6 Chapitô

You deserve a break. A circus school may not seem like the most relaxing place, but it has an excellent restaurant with lovely views over the city and a shady patio cafe. ✆ **21/888-01-54.**

WALKING TOUR 2 BAIXA, THE CENTER & THE CHIADO

START:	**Praça do Comércio.**
FINISH:	**Elevador de Santa Justa.**
TIME:	**3 hours.**
BEST TIMES:	**Any sunny day except Sunday.**
WORST TIMES:	**Monday to Saturday from 7:30 to 9am and 5 to 7pm; Sunday, when shops are closed.**

This tours also starts in:

1 Praça do Comércio

One of Europe's most beautiful squares, looking out over Tagus, it was the nerve center of Portugal's maritime empire. The royal palace that stood here was destroyed by the 1755 earthquake. In its place are sturdy

Walking Tour: Baixa to Intendente

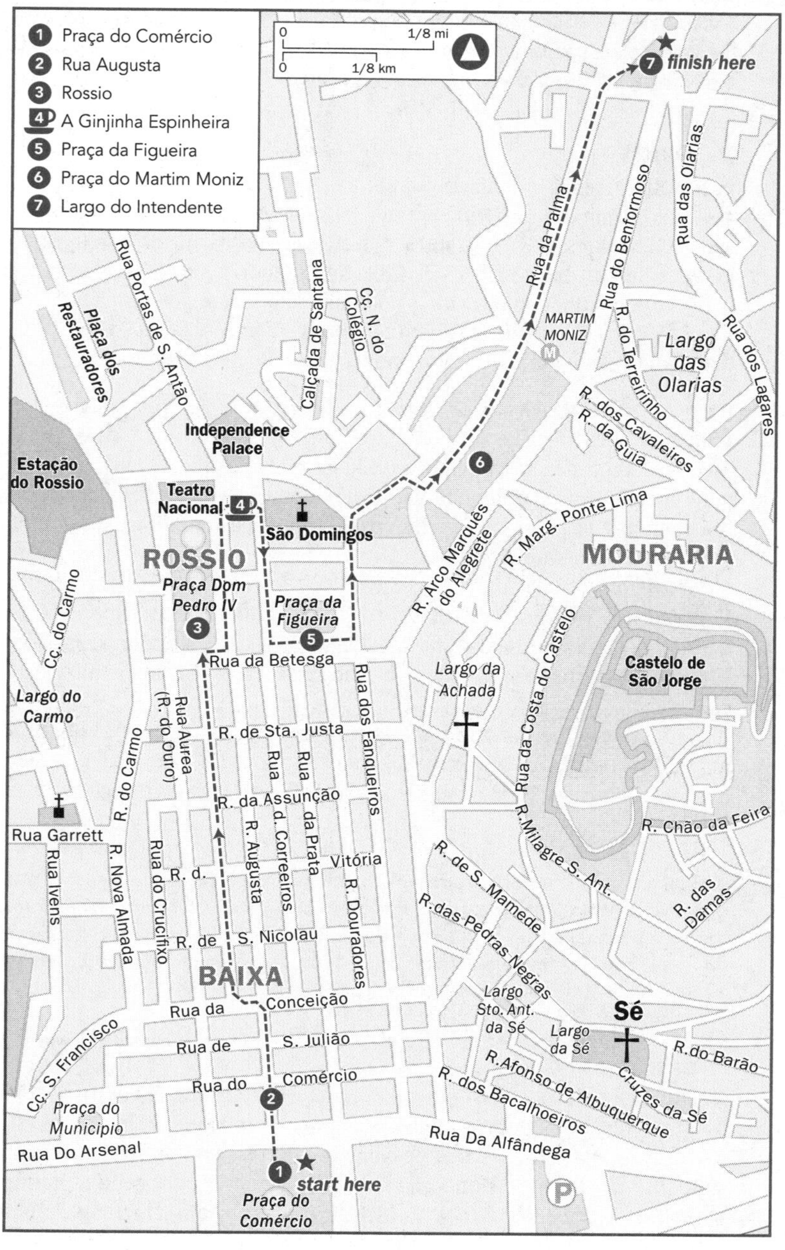

white towers bookending rows of pastel-painted government ministries. Long arcades cover cafes and restaurants. To the east, the **Lisbon Story Centre** (www.lisboastorycentre.pt) gives an interactive explanation of the city's history, complete with mock quake. A horseback **statue of King José I** (1714–77) dominates the center of the plaza.

Head north along:

2 Rua Augusta

Facing the river is a triumphal arch, the **Arco da Rua Augusta,** which you can climb for 2.50€ to enjoy 360-degree views over the Baixa. Through the arch is Rua Augusta, a bustling pedestrianized thoroughfare in the heart of the grid-plan district. Sadly, tourist traps have replaced many of the authentic old stores and cafes, but some gems survive, like **Casa Pereira da Conceição,** selling coffee and fans; fabrics store **Londres Salão;** and 1913 wine store and grocer **Casa Macário.**

Continue on Rua Augusta until you reach:

3 Rossio

This is Lisbon's version of Times Square or Piccadilly Circus, an energetic meeting place complete with fountains, sidewalk cafes, and traditional shops. The black-and-white paving inspired imitations around the Portuguese-speaking world from Rio to Macau.

Rossio's official name is Praça Dom Pedro IV, after the king of Portugal and first emperor of Brazil, whose statue stands atop a 90-ft. column. An urban legend has it that the statue actually represents Emperor Maximilian of Mexico and was recycled after his 1867 execution.

Check out the historic **Café Nicola** and (the outside of) **Animatógrafo do Rossio,** just under the archway at the southern end: The movie house dating from 1908 must be the world's prettiest porn joint.

4 Take a Break

A Ginjinha, Largo de São Domingos, 8. Turn into the square just east of the Dona Maria II National Theater to find this hole-in-the-wall serving *ginjinha*—a cherry liquor that's a favorite Lisbon tipple. It invented the drink and has been serving it over the marble counter since 1840. If you want your little glass to include macerated cherries, ask for it "com elas."

Head south along Rua Dom Antão de Almeida into:

5 Praça da Figueira

One of Lisbon's most harmonious squares, it is surrounded by five-story houses typical of the post-1755 earthquake Pombaline style. It's dominated by an equestrian statue of King João I. On the north side is a tiny store, the **Hospital de Bonecas** (The Dolls Hospital) has been repairing broken toys since 1830 (www.hospitaldebonecas.com). Frequent gourmet markets are held in the square.

Take Rua Dom Duarte to:

6 Praça do Martim Moniz

This sprawling plaza is surrounded by ugly modern buildings, but it's the focus of one of the city's most lively and diverse communities. There are Chinese and Indian groceries and restaurants, and regular markets and concerts at weekends. The **Mercado Oriental de Lisboa** is a food court serving snacks from Vietnam, Japan, Macau, and other Asian destinations.

Follow Rua Palma and Avenida Amirante Reis to:

7 Largo do Intendente

Until a few years ago, this was the capital's sleaziest red-light district and a place to avoid after dark. Now it's one of the most fashionable spots, with original stores like **A Vida Portuguesa** (p. 131) and **Viúva Lamego** (p. 127); the beautifully restored Art Nouveau **Hotel 1908** (p. 84); cafes, restaurants, craft markets, and street performers. And **Tram 28** passes just next door, so no need to walk back.

ORGANIZED TOURS

There's a vast array of tours available by bus, boat, bike, tuk-tuk, Jeep, amphibious vehicle, etc. Here's a selection: **Yellow Bus Tours** (www.yellowbustours.com; ✆ **21/850-32-25**) has hop-on-hop-off circuits in an open-top double-decker, which is a good way to discover the main sights in a hurry; it also has boat tours. **Lisbon Walkers** (www.lisbonwalker.com; ✆ **21/886-18-40**) has a knowledgeable team of walking tour guides that includes art historians, architects, and journalists. **Lisbon Explorer** (www.lisbonexplorer.com; ✆ **21/362-92-62**) has a range of walks including "Hidden Lisbon" and "Jewish Lisbon." **Storic** (www.storic.pt; ✆ **93/588-20-64**) really gets into the city's history, while **Culinary Backstreets** (www.culinarybackstreets.com) uncovers gastronomic secrets.

SPORTS & OUTDOORS

For beaches, watersports, and golf, you'll do best to head out of the city to Cascais, Sintra (see chapter 7) or south of the Tagus (see chapter 8).

FITNESS If you're looking for a gym, the low-cost chain **Fitness Hut** (www.fitnesshut.pt) has two dozen units scattered around the city and allows daily or weekly membership. The excellent **Academia Life Club** (www.academia.jazzy.pt; ✆ **21/393-40-20**) down by the river in Santos allows you to sign up for daily or weekly membership. To keep fit in the open air, the **riverside path** running west along the river from Cais do Sodré for 6.5km (4 miles) to Torre de Belém is excellent for jogging, walking or cycling, as is the 2.5km (1.5-mile) **Corredor Verde** (Green Corridor) running from Parque Eduardo VII to the Monsanto forest park. There are a number of card-operated bike rental operators in the city, or go to a specialist like **Lisbon Bike Rentals** (www.lisbonbikerentals.com; ✆ **30/050-19-96**) based in Cais do Sodré.

Some hotels recommended in chapter 5 allow non-guests to use their health clubs for a fee. It's always best to call in advance. Outside of the hotels, a worthwhile fitness club is **Ginásio Keep Fit,** Av. João Crisóstomo 6 (✆ **21/793-15-36;** 18€ for one-time use; Mon–Fri 8am–10pm, Sat 10am–2pm; bus no. 58; Metro: Saldanha).

PARKS & GARDENS Although the historical center is densely packed, there are some wonderful green spaces around the city, from cozy urban gardens to Europe's largest city park. Here are some of our favorites:

Jardim Botânico ★★★ A haven of biodiversity in the heart of the city. Lisbon's botanical garden first opened in 1878 but underwent a major facelift in 2018. It cleaves to a hillside above Avenida da Liberdade, allowing visitors to glimpse views across town as they explore the vegetation. Over 1,500 species, including specimens like the *árvore-do-imperador* (emperor's tree), threatened with extinction in its native Brazil, and cycad plants around since the dinosaurs. The gardens are run by the next-door **Natural History and Science Museum ★,** also well worth a visit.

Rua da Escola Politécnica 56/58. www.museus.ulisboa.pt. ✆ **21-392-1800.** 3€; 1.50€ youngsters 10–18, over 65s; free under 10s. Daily, Oct–Mar 9am–4:30pm; Apr–Sept 9am–7:30pm. Metro: Rato. Tram: 24. Bus: 758, 773.

Jardim do Palácio Fronteira ★★★ Out in the suburb of São Domingos de Benfica, this has been listed among the world's most beautiful gardens. Formally laid out are spectacular displays of *azulejos,* fountains, and statues on the edge of Monsanto forest. Descendants of the Marquis of Fronteira still live in the 17th-century palace, but it too can be visited in morning guided tours.

Largo de São Domingos de Benfica, 1. www.fronteira-alorna.pt. ✆ **21/778-20-23.** 4€. Mon–Fri 10am–7pm, Sat 10am–1pm. Bus: 770.

Parque Eduardo VII ★★ Rising up in an extension of Avenida da Liberdade, central Lisbon's biggest green space was named after Britain's King Edward VII, who visited in 1902. From the top, there's an uninterrupted view from geometric hedge patterns running down the center of the park to the tree-lined Avenida and beyond to the Tagus and the Arrábida hills in the distance. The country's biggest Portuguese flag also flaps from a 35m (115-ft.) pole. Behind is the intimate Jardim Amália Rodrigues named for the late fado singer and an outdoor cafe beside a cooling pond. The park looks best in May/June when the jacaranda trees fill with purple blossoms. On the western side of the park are a collection of hothouses filled with exotic vegetation.

Free. Open 24 hr. Metro: Parque, Marquês de Pombal. Bus: 713, 726, 742, 744, 746.

Parque Florestal de Monsanto ★★ Europe's largest urban woodland covers over 4 square miles of hilly land on the city's western edge, 10% of Lisbon's total area. It's full of natural, wild vegetation including oak and umbrella pine, through which run biking, hiking, and riding trails, plus adventure parks with ropeways through the trees, picnic spots, and playgrounds. Pay a visit to the UFO-like Panorâmico de Monsanto, a modish restaurant in the 1960s, now a graffiti-strewn ruin (look for the portrait of murdered Brazilian rights activist Marielle Franco by artist Vhils) but open to the public for its sweeping views.

Information Estrada do Barcal, Monte das Perdizes. ✆ **21/817-02-00.** Free. Open 24 hr. Bus: 711, 724, 770.

Praça das Flores ★★ This little square (the name means "Square of Flowers") contains one of Lisbon's loveliest public gardens, shaded with magnolia and lime trees, with a little fountain in the middle. It's favorite place of locals to unwind. Around are some great restaurants and cafes: the city's widest selection of craft beer at Cerveteca Lisboa; Persian treats at Cafeh Terhan; and glorious home-made gelato from Nanarella (go on a Thursday when they make Cassata Siciliana using *requeijão*—a creamy ricotta-like cheese from the hills south of Lisbon.

Metro: Rato. Tram: 24; Bus: 773.

SPECTATOR SPORTS Lisbon is a city divided by soccer. Almost everybody has a fanatical devotion to one of the top local clubs: **Benfica** or **Sporting** (just a few eccentrics support Belém-based Belenenses). Catching a match between the red-shirted "eagles" of Benfica and Sporting's green-clad "lions" (or a match pitching either of them against northern upstarts FC Porto, nicknamed the "dragons") is a great Lisbon experience. Derby tickets sell out fast, but attending any game involving the big clubs is fun.

Benfica (www.slbenfica.pt) is a two-time European champion forever associated with one of the game's all-time greats, Eusébio da Silva Ferreira. If you can't catch a game, check out the club museum at the Estádio da Luz stadium (Av. Eusébio da Silva Ferreira Porta 9; ✆ **21/721-950;** Metro: Alto dos Moinhos, Colégio Militar-Luz).

Based a short way away on the airport ring road, **Sporting Clube de Portugal** (www.sporting.pt) has less silverware, but lays claim to launching the career of the biggest superstar in today's game: Cristiano Ronaldo, who features prominently at the club museum in José Alvalade Stadium (Rua Prof. Fernando da Fonseca; ✆ **21/751-61-64;** Metro: Campo Grande).

Besides soccer, both clubs run teams in basketball, track, volleyball, and other sports that are often among the best in Europe.

One sport the clubs don't do is bullfighting. If you're into that, head to the **Praça de Touros do Campo Pequeno.** The bullring is a startling construction in vivid red, capped with onion domes in an 1890s approximation of the Arabian style. Unlike in Spain, bulls are not killed in Portuguese bullfights, but they are stabbed by horsemen (and, occasionally, horsewomen) armed with barbed spears. There are calls for a ban. The building holds a museum explaining bullfighting history and offering tours of the ring. The building also holds a shopping mall, cinema, and restaurants (www.campopequeno.com; ✆ **21/799-84-50;** Metro: Campo Pequeno).

LISBON SHOPPING

SHOPPING AREAS **Príncipe Real** is Lisbon's most-fashionable shopping district with cool boutiques, antiques shops, and design emporiums. **Avenida da Liberdade** is a grand boulevard, filled with high-end fashion. The **Baixa** is a traditional shopping zone, now a mix of international brands, quirky traditional stores, and tourist traps. Up the hill to **Chiado,** Rua do Carmo and Rua Garrett are filling up with international chains, but there are still plenty of characterful local stores clinging on, including its renowned antique bookstores. The **Rua de São Bento** near the parliament is another area to hunt out antiques. Away from downtown, the leafy **Alvalade** and **Campo de Ourique** neighborhoods have an attractive mix of stores and excellent food markets. There's a plethora of large, modern **malls** ringing the city center.

Shopping A to Z

ANTIQUES & ART

Cavalo de Pau Antiguidades ★ This enchanting store in the heart of the São Bento antiques district has a mix of vintage goods and their own retro designs, plus ceramics and art objects from around the world: from Kenyan basketry to Indian fabrics. Rua de São Bento 164. www.cavalodepau.pt. ✆ **21/396-66-05.** Tram: 28.

Galeria 111 ★★ A leading light on the art scene since the 1960s and a driving force behind Portuguese contemporary art, they host cutting-edge exhibitions and a wide selection of works by artists from Portugal and beyond, including world-renowned Paula Rego. The gallery also sells drawings, etchings, silk screens, lithographs, art books, and postcards. Campo Grande 113. www.111.pt. ✆ **21/797-74-18.** Metro: Entre Campos.

Miguel Arruda ★★ Top-class antiques beautifully presented in a palatial townhouse. The store is in an 18th-century building with 500 square meters (5,382 sq. ft.) of goodies ranging from baroque furniture crafted from Brazilian hardwood, to delicate Chinese porcelain and saintly Church statues. Rua de São Bento, 356. www.arruda.pt. ✆ **91/465-01-65.** Tram: 28.

Solar ★★★ Lisbon's oldest antiques shop lays claim to the title of world's biggest dealer in antique *azulejos* (ceramic tiles). The store in Príncipe Real has been run by the same family since the 1940s, a treasure trove with pieces dating back to the 15th century. ***Tip:*** Always buy tiles from a reputable dealer to make sure you're not handling stolen goods. Rua D. Pedro V, 70. www.solar.com.pt. ✆ **21/346-55-22.** Tram: 24.

BOOKS

Bertrand ★★★ Officially the world's oldest bookstore (there's a Guinness certificate by the entrance), opened in 1732 and still going strong. This wonderful store has a maze of little rooms, a cafe, and a selection of English books and magazines. Hallowed ground for generations of literary *Lisboetas,* it was a hangout for many of the city's great writers. It has branches around the country. Rua Garrett 73. www.bertrand.pt. ✆ **21/347-61-22.** Metro: Chiado.

THE robber woman's MARKET

One of Lisbon's most enjoyable shopping (or just browsing) experiences is the **Feira da Ladra ★★** (it translates as the female thief's market) held on Tuesday and Saturday (9am–6pm) on the Camp de Santa Clara, a broad open space behind Alfama's Igreja de São Vicente de Fora. Lisbon's colorful and always lively flea market features an endless array of bric-a-brac, handicrafts, plain old junk, and some genuine antiques. Some of the better stuff can be found in the old covered market building in the center of the square, where there are fashionable boutiques, ceramics stores, and antiques shops. There are plenty of eating and drinking spots around.

Ler Devagar ★★★ A standout in the post-industrial LX Factory cultural zone, this huge bookshop is in an old printshop, with books (new and second-hand) stacked around the disused presses. Hanging from the high ceiling is a flying bicycle installation that's become a favorite on Instagram. There's a limited selection of books in English. The cafe is hip and holds regular conferences, book launches, and live music performances. Rua Rodrigues Faria 103. www.lerdevagar.com. ✆ **21/325-99-92.** Train: Alcantara-Mar. Tram: 15, 18.

Palavra de Viajante ★★ Travelers will love this little place nestled beneath the arches of a typical 18th-century building. All the books are arranged by country, so from Albania to Zimbabwe you can find novels, guides, histories, etc. The selection is multilingual, with many choices in English. The staff give the impression of having read every book on their shelves. If you want a romance set in Lisbon, they'll know what to pick. Rua de São Bento, 34. www.palavra-de-viajante.pt. ✆ **21/195-63-40.** Tram: 28.

CERAMICS, POTTERY & TILES

Fábrica Sant'Anna ★★ They've been making *azulejos* since 1741, making this the oldest tile company, and still going. They're all handmade and exquisite, from individual tiles to the elaborate panels covered in still life or pastoral scenes. They also sell ceramic pots, vases, and basins. The flagship Chiado store has itself been going for 100 years. You can also visit the factory near Belém to buy direct or even book a lesson to make your own. Rua do Alecrim 95. www.santanna.com.pt. ✆ **21/342-25-37.** Metro: Baixa-Chiado.

Viúva Lamego ★★★ A special place, this store, open since 1849, is covered in gloriously colorful *azulejos*. Its tiles cover buildings around the country, including many of Lisbon's metro stations. They are much sought after by artists, architects, and designers: In 2019 a swimming pool covered with their tiles opened in Edinburgh, designed by artist Joana Vasconcelos. Its selection includes both traditional and contemporary designs of the highest quality. There's a second store at the factory in Sintra. Largo do Intendente 25. www.viuvalamego.com. ✆ **21/885-24-08.** Metro: Intendente. Tram: 28. Bus: 8.

DEPARTMENT STORES & SHOPPING MALLS

Amoreiras Shopping ★★ When it opened in the 1980s, the eye-catching post-modernist architecture sparked controversy with this colorful modification of Lisbon's skyline. But it quickly became the in place to shop and remains the poshest of Lisbon's malls, with more than 219 stores, 50 restaurants, and seven cinema screens. International brands from Accessorize to Zara are represented, plus a scattering of Portuguese designers. Book a ticket to the top floor for one of the best views of Lisbon. Av. Eng. Duarte Pacheco. www.amoreiras.com. ✆ **21/381-02-00.** Metro: Rato, Marquês de Pombal.

Centro Colombo ★ When it opened in 1997, this was Europe's biggest shopping center. It holds more than 420 retailers beside the soccer stadium out in the Benfica district. You can buy everything from Lion King pajamas to a 48,000€ gold-and-diamond broach ring crafted by jeweler David Rosas. Av. Lusíada. www.colombo.pt. ✆ **21/711-36-36.** Metro: Colégio Militar.

El Corte Inglés ★ The stylish Lisbon branch of this Spanish department store chain is a favorite with expats thanks to the international edibles in the basement supermarket. The store also features 13 floors with swank selections of fashion, perfumery, tech gadgets, and much more. There's a big range of eating options from tapas bar to gourmet restaurants run by some of the city's top chefs. Av. António Augusto de Aguiar, 37. www.elcorteingles.pt. ✆ **70/721-17-11.** Metro: São Sebastião.

Embaixada ★★★ There is no other mall like this. Housed in a 19th-century Moorish-style palace that was once an embassy (hence the name), the grand salons and colonnaded courtyard hold stores that pay tribute to Portuguese design from eco-design furniture to trendy updates of traditional mountain garb; steamy beachwear to organic cosmetics. Besides the shopping, there are a couple of classy restaurants, a gin bar hosting fado evenings, and the city's sexiest staircase. Praça do Príncipe Real, 26. www.embaixadalx.pt. ✆ **96/530-91-54.** Tram: 24.

CHINA & GLASSWARE

21PR Concept Store ★ This showcase for Portuguese and international creativity fills a delightfully jumbled store packed with art books, designer jewelry, quirky accessories, and much else. A browse in this delightful space should be part of any retail therapy trip to Príncipe Real. Praça do Príncipe Real, 21. ✆ **21/346-94-21.** Tram: 24.

Casa dos Tapetes de Arraiolos ★★ The little town of Arraiolos in the Alentejo (p. 275) region south of Lisbon has a centuries-old tradition of weaving carpets from local wool. This is the artisans' outlet in the capital. Their intricate patterns are often inspired by local flowers and wildlife and are influenced by oriental designs. The hand-sewn rugs take months to make and don't come cheap, but here you can guarantee they are genuine and not Asian-made imitations that are now widely sold. Rua da Imprensa Nacional, 116E. www.casatapetesarraiolos.com. ✆ **21/396-33-54.** Metro: Rato. Tram: 24.

Cutipol ★ The combination of timeless skills and modern design lies behind the global success of this Portuguese cutlery maker. The flagship store of the family-run business in Chiado is a tableware treat, with elegant designs in silver, stainless steel, gold-plate, and resin. The Goa and Bauhaus ranges by designer José Joaquim Ribeiro are among the most sought-after. Rua do Alecrim, 84. www.cutipol.pt. ✆ **21/322-50-75.** Metro: Baixa-Chiado.

Vista Alegre ★★★ The Vista Alegre factory near Aveiro (p. 317) has been producing fine porcelain since 1824. This gem of a store in the core of the Chiado elegantly displays its range of classic and contemporary designs. They work with leading chefs, artists, and designers to produce unique pieces. Also available are top-class crystalware from the group's Atlantis factory. As a sign of the brand's iconic status, Portugal's government often presents Vista Alegre gifts to visiting heads of state. Largo do Chiado 23. www.vistaalegre.pt. ✆ **21/346-14-01.** Metro: Baixa/Chiado. Tram: 28.

FASHION

A Outra Face da Lua ★★ Walk into this cavern of vintage and you'll be assailed by color. The retro clothes range from 1920s flapper dresses to '70s disco chic. It's delightfully eccentric (they have a thing for aloha shirts and kimonos). There's also costume jewelry, hats, and handbags. Film, TV, and theater crews often scour this place looking for period costumes. A pity though that they closed the friendly cafe/bistro to make room for more clothes. Rua da Assunção 22. www.aoutrafacedalua.com. ✆ **21/886-34-30.** Metro: Rossio.

Azevedo Rua ★★★ Portugal's oldest hatter has headwear you'd want to leave on in any occasion. The shop is little changed since the owner's great grandfather opened it on Rossio Square in 1886. Kings of Spain, presidents of Portugal, and poet Fernando Pessoa got their headgear here. Aside from a head-spinning selection of men's and women's hats and caps, there are some fine gentlemen's canes. Praça Dom Pedro IV, 69, 72–73. www.azevedorua.pt. ✆ **21/342-75-11.** Metro: Rossio

Dama de Copas ★★ Shocked by the discovery that 90% of women wear ill-fitting bras, two Polish immigrants created "Queen of Hearts," offering a personalized bra fitting and consulting service, plus an expanded range of sizes to ensure a perfect fit from A to K. Their fitted lingerie concept took off and they now have stores across Portugal and Spain, besides expanding into beachwear, nightwear, and gym-wear. This shop in the Baixa is the original and offers unparalleled underwear expertise. Rua de Santa Justa 87. www.damadecopas.com. ✆ **21/195-59-97.** Metro: Rossio.

Kolovrat 79 ★★ Bosnian-born Lidija Kolovrat is one of Lisbon's top designers. Her boutique in trendy Príncipe Real buzzes with vivid shades and audacious shapes for men and women as she drives to turn dressing up into "an act of self-empowerment." This is a must for daring urban butterflies. Rua Dom Pedro V, 79. www.lidijakolovrat.com. ✆ **21/387-45-36.** Tram: 24.

Pelcor ★★ Yes, cork is fashion. Portugal is the world's biggest producer of cork, and almost everything in this stylish Príncipe Real shop is made from the naturally produced bark. If you think cork is only for bottle stoppers, this will quickly change your mind. Choose from handbags, umbrellas, hats, belts, and much more. Pátio do Tijolo, 16. www.pelcor.pt. ✆ **21/886-42-05.** Tram: 24.

Story Tailors ★★ If you're not afraid of ruffles, bold patterns, and unusual dress cuts, this is the store for you. Designers João Sanchez and the late Luís Branco created this space over three floors of an 18th-century Chiado townhouse to showcase designs that are flirty, shapely, and like nothing you'll find elsewhere. The off-the-rack designs and a made-to-measure service for men and women are popular with stars of stage and screen. Calçada do Ferragial, 8-10. www.storytailors.pt. ✆ **21/343-23-06.** Metro: Baixa-Chiado.

FOOD & DRINK

A Carioca ★★★ Take a deep breath when you squeeze into this 1930s Art Deco Chiado gem. The aroma of coffee is overwhelming. It's a place for connoisseurs, with single origin grinds from places like East Timor or São Tomé, as well as house blends. We love their Tavares blend (60% Arabica, 40% Robusta) originally made for the posh (18th-century) restaurant up the road. The shop is decorated with painted panels recalling the exotic East. It also sells tea from the Azores and a variety of chocolates, plus coffee and tea-making accessories. Rua da Misericórdia, 9. ✆ **21/346-95-67.** Metro Baixa-Chiado.

Conserveira de Lisboa ★★ Portugal is a canned fish superpower and this 1930s store is the place to stock up on a pungent piscatorial present. Tuna, sardine, anchovy, and squid are just some of the critters pressed into their retro-style tins. The type of fish varies by the season, and there are several sauces; try the *picante* with hot chilis. You can bring them back to the U.S. and Canada with no problem. They also have outlets close to Bairro Alto and in Time Out Market. Rua dos Bacalhoeiros, 34. www.conserveiradelisboa.pt. ✆ **21/886-40-09.** Metro: Terreiro do Paço; Tram 28.

Garrafeira Nacional ★★ This Baixa wine shop was founded in 1927 and has one of the biggest and best selections of wine in Portugal. If you have 14,900€ to spare, grab a 1795 bottle of Madeira. Find that a bit steep? The experts here will guide you to the right bottle, starting with a very drinkable white from south of the Tagus for just 1.80€. As well as the vast choice of Portuguese wines, they stock rare whiskeys, cognacs, and other liquors. The company has other shops around town, but this flagship is the best-stocked. Rua de Santa Justa 18. www.garrafeiranacional.com. ✆ **21/887-90-80.** Metro: Rossio.

Manteigaria Silva ★★★ Whiffs of salt cod, cured ham, and ripe cheese will rush you when you enter this grocery dating back to 1890. It's a taste of old Lisbon. They take their food very seriously here, presenting artisan products from around the regions, such as tangy Azorean hard cheese to smoked sausages from Tràs-os-Montes or preserved plums from Elvas in the Alentejo. The fabulous selections of ham are sliced paper thin with the hand-turned

Berkel slicer. They also have stalls in Time Out Market and the Bairro de Avillez gourmet village in Chiado, but the original store has more variety and lower prices. Rua Dom Antão de Almada 1 C/D. www.manteigariasilva.pt. ✆ **21/342-49-05.** Metro: Rossio.

Manuel Tavares Lda ★ This is a heavenly food and wine emporium, founded in 1860. Behind a traditional wood-framed shopfront, it's teeming with goodies: a superb collection of Portuguese wines, liquors, and brandies; a baffling array of sausages and cheese; and tray after tray of dried fruits. There are juicy Algarve figs, pine nuts embalmed in honey, salted almonds begging to be matched up with a chilled glass of white port. It's easy to find on the smallest street in Lisbon linking Rossio to Praça da Figueira. Rua da Betesga 1 A–B. www.manueltavares.com. ✆ **21/342-42-09.** Metro: Rossio.

GIFTS & SOUVENIRS

A Arte da Terra ★★ Step down into the old stables behind Lisbon's cathedral and you find this unique space dedicated to Portuguese handicrafts. The horses' stone feeding troughs have been converted into display units for regional products from embroidery to ceramics, wine to woodcarving. They also hold regular exhibitions and showcase the work of young artists and artisans. And Tram 28 stops just a few paces away on its way up to Alfama. Rua de Augusto Rosa. www.aartedaterra.pt. ✆ **21/274-59-75.** Tram: 28.

A Vida Portuguesa ★★★ In 2007, journalist Catarina Portas opened a store in the Chiado to preserve and promote traditional Portuguese merchandise. It's been a runaway success, and now there are four "The Portuguese Life" shops in Lisbon and another in Porto. They serve as a time capsule, with retro brands whose styling recalls a bygone age. Over 6,000 authentic products are on offer from wine to toilet paper, shepherds' blankets to cereals in 1930s boxes, or shiny Bordallo Pinheiro ceramic creatures. Both this original Chiado store and the biggest outlet in hip Intendente are wonderful, old-style emporiums where the goods are beautifully presented. Rua Anchieta 11. www.avidaportuguesa.com. ✆ **21/346-50-73.** Metro: Baixa/Chiado.

Caza das Vellas Loreto ★★★ Two centuries ago, dozens of candlemakers flourished around Praça Luís de Camões. This is the last survivor, dating from 1789 and one of the oldest and most beautiful shops in the city. It sells aromatic handmade candles, and the tiny interior feels like an intimate Gothic chapel, with arched wood panels and a pervasive aroma of beeswax. There are candles of every shade, size, and aroma. Among the bestsellers is the exotically spiced "Samarcande." Rua do Loreto 53–55. www.cazavellasloreto.com.pt. ✆ **21/342-53-87.** Metro: Baixa/Chiado. Tram: 28.

Claus Porto ★★★ Prepare for sensory delight. Installed in an old Chiado pharmacy, it showcases the fragrant soaps and perfumes made by this firm in Porto since 1887. It's renowned for the colorful retro packaging and luxurious soapmaking traditions. Claus Porto works with top international perfumers to create scents inspired by the Portuguese countryside. Its male grooming range, Musgo Real, dates back to the 1930s, with a splendid Art Deco look. There's a fancy barber shop downstairs if you want to book a hot-towel shave. They opened a second store in the Baixa in 2019. Rua da Misericórdia, 135. www.clausporto.com. ✆ **91/721-58-55.** Metro: Baixa-Chiado; Tram: 24.

JEWELRY

Leitão & Irmão ★★★ It's almost 150 years since Emperor Pedro II of Brazil made these guys his court jeweler, but they are still going strong. From traditional filigree to contemporary designs, from engagement rings to silver plates—over the decades they've made swords for kaisers, wedding gifts for princesses, and chalices for popes. Their silverware is of the highest quality and the jewelry designs a mix of traditional and contemporary. You can order bespoke pieces from their Bairro Alto workshop. Aside from the flagship in Chiado, store they have three branches. Largo do Chiado 16. www.leitao-irmao.com. ✆ **21/325-78-70.** Metro: Baixa-Chiado.

Maria João Bahia ★★ Internationally renowned designer Bahia still takes inspiration from her Portuguese homeland. Her creations in sterling silver, pure gold, and quality gems are sold around the world, but her nerve center is this handsome Pombaline building. Its five floors contain Bahia's workshop and exhibition spaces as well as the boutique. Her sometimes playful designs often reference Portuguese icons—take the diamond-encrusted white gold sardine necklaces. Av. da Liberdade 102. www.mariajoaobahia.pt. ✆ **21/324-00-18.** Metro: Avenida.

W. A. Sarmento ★★ Goldsmiths gave the name to one of the main streets running through the Baixa. Today this is one of the last surviving on Rua Áurea (aka Rua de Ouro). At the foot of the Santa Justa elevator, W. A. Sarmento has been in the hands of the same family since 1870. They are one of the most distinguished silver- and goldsmiths in Portugal, specializing in lacy filigree jewelry, including charm bracelets. The shop, which was remodeled in the 1940s by architect Cassiano Branco, is a go-to place to buy treasured confirmation and graduation gifts. It showcases the work of young jewelry artists as well as traditional designs. Rua Áurea 251. www.ourivesariasarmento.pt. ✆ **21/342-67-74.** Metro: Rossio.

LINEN & EMBROIDERY

Príncipe Real Enxovais ★★★ Here they sell linens for the tables of royalty and stars. Princess Grace of Monaco, Jackie Kennedy, Michael Douglas, and various other crowned heads and Hollywood A-listers are among the customers. Victor Castro, whose mother Cristina Castro founded the store in 1938, recalls how Amália Rodrigues would drop by to sing to the women who continue to embroider to order. It produces some of Europe's finest tablecloths, bed and bath linen, as well as bridal and christening wear. Rua da Escola Politécnica 12–14. www.principereal.com. ✆ **21/346-59-45.** Tram 24.

Teresa Alecrim ★★ This store bears the name of the owner, who founded it in the 1980s to present her refined embroideries and traditional house linens. You'll see sheets, pillowcases, towels, and bedcovers in plain and patterned cotton, plus monogrammed damask cotton hand towels. The handmade baby wear will ensure your little cherub is the cutest in the nursery. Rua Nova do Almada, 76. pt.teresaalecrim.com. ✆ **21/342-18-31.** Metro: Baixa-Chiado.

MUSIC

Discoteca Amália ★ In the age of Spotify and Deezer, this is a survivor: a hole-in-the-wall record shop specializing in fado on vinyl or CD. Named after the legendary diva Amália Rodrigues, it also stocks today's hot names like Gisela João, Raquel Tavares, and Carminho, as well as other musical genres. You can get a sample from their "fado truck," which pumps out tunes while parked on nearby Rua do Carmo. Rua Aurea, 274. ✆ **21/342-09-39.** Metro: Baixa-Chiado.

SHOES & LEATHER GOODS

Cubanas ★ Don't let the name fool you; these shoes for men and women are 100% Portuguese. They are exported around the world, but the best place to buy their stylish-but-fun (and affordable) footwear and handbags is right here. Largo Rafael Bordallo Pinheiro, 31 A. www.cubanas-shoes.com. ✆ **91/237-45-16.** Metro: Baixa-Chiado.

Fly London ★★ Portugal is second only to Italy as an exporter of quality footwear, and this hyper-trendy brand played a large role in establishing its reputation. Under the slogan "don't walk, fly," their shoes are sold in over 3,000 outlets from Greece to Greenwich Village (where they have their own store on Bleecker Street). It's hard to miss the store on Lisbon's poshest avenue: It has a giant bat over the door (although, as we were going to press, they were planning a new, bigger store on the same boulevard). Av. da Liberdade, 230. www.flylondon.com. ✆ **91/059-45-64.** Metro: Avenida.

Luís Onofre ★★★ Michelle Obama, Kat Graham, and Paris Hilton are among the big names spotted stepping out in shoes made by this tony Portuguese designer. A third-generation shoemaker, Onofre blends time-honored techniques and leading designs to create shoes that don't come cheap—a pair of black, studded stilettos in his summer 2019 collection retails at 495€ but are an undoubted fashion statement. Avenida da Liberdade, 247. www.luisonofre.com. ✆ **21/131-36-29.** Metro: Marquês de Pombal.

Luvaria Ulisses ★★★ Opened in 1925, this teeny boutique sells the finest handmade leather gloves. The store is renowned for the quality of its service and raw materials, which include cashmere linings for winter gloves. One of the last surviving independent retailers on the once-charming Rua do Carmo, its thumb-size interior is wood-lined and decorated with original panels showing fashionable young flappers trying on their new gloves. Rua do Carmo, 87-A. www.luvariaulisses.com. ✆ **21/342-02-95.** Metro: Rossio.

LISBON ENTERTAINMENT & NIGHTLIFE

Lisbon has a vibrant cultural and nightlife scene. So, whether you want to relax to a top classical orchestra, be thrilled by opera in a gilded theater, or sip exotic cocktails before dancing the night away (or all of the above) the riverside capital has it all. The epicenters of Lisbon's *vida nocturna* are in the **Bairro Alto** and around **"Pink Street"** (Rua Nova de Carvalho) in Cais do Sodré, but there are hotspots spread around the city.

City Hall publishes a monthly **"Agenda Cultural Lisboa"** that you can pick up at hotels, museums, and tourist offices, or consult online (www.agenda lx.pt). An alternative is to consult the "What's On" section of the city tourist office website (www.visitlisboa.com) or its publication **"Follow Me Lisboa."** The Portuguese site of ***Time Out*** magazine (www.timeout.pt) also has good listings of cultural events. There are several online booking services, including **TicketLine** (www.ticketline.sapo.pt) and **BOL** (www.bol.pt), which both have sites in English. You can also buy tickets from **FNAC** stores or from its website (bilheteira.fnac.pt).

One important thing for **film** fans is that unlike in many European countries, Portugal generally shows movies in their original language, with subtitles, rather than dubbing Hollywood into the local lingo.

Bars, Pubs & Clubs

B.Leza ★★★ This mythical club is the place to strut your stuff to Angolan kizomba, Cape Verdean funaná, and other sensual rhythms from Portuguese-speaking Africa. Opened in the 1990s in a derelict palace, it moved in 2012 to this renovated quayside warehouse. The environment is more modern, but energy levels from the DJs and live bands are unabated. Other musical styles from samba and fado to reggae are often featured. There's usually a 10€ cover charge for live music. On Sundays it hosts regular dance classes for anyone hoping to sharpen their moves. Cais da Ribeira Nova, Armazém B. ✆ **21/010-68-37.** Wed–Thurs 10:30pm–4am; Fri–Sat 10:30pm–5am; Sun 6pm–2am. Metro: Cais do Sodré.

British Bar ★ Not a typical expat bar, this place opened in 1919 to pump suds for British mariners and thrived when Cais do Sodré was a notorious rendezvous for sailors and ladies of the night. The neighborhood's morphed into Lisbon's hot nightlife hub, but the pub's smoky ambiance is little changed as it serves up international beers to curious newcomers, seasoned locals, and bohemian types who have always frequented it. The bar starred in the cult 1980s movie *Dans la Ville Blanche*. There are regular displays of contemporary art in the windows. Look out for the surreal timepiece behind the bar. Rua Bernardino Costa 52. ✆ **21/342-23-67.** Daily noon–4am. Metro: Cais do Sodré.

CINCO Lounge ★★ Cocktail bars don't come any chicer. Located in Príncipe Real, CINCO features a dazzling array of over 100 fiendishly inventive drinks. Founded in 2005 by British mixologist Dave Palethorpe with the aim of restoring "the lost art of polite drinking," the place is elegant but relaxed with the most flattering lighting in town. Try a "Finders Keepers," a blend of gin, lime, agave syrup, mint, lemongrass, and ginger ale, served in a sealed tin can—it was voted Lisbon's most original cocktail. Rua Ruben A. Leitão 17A. www.cincolounge.com. ✆ **21/342-40-33.** Daily 9pm–2am. Tram: 24.

Finalmente Club ★★ This famed late-night dive has been shaking its stuff since 1976. It's the place where gay men in Lisbon gravitate after a long evening in the Bairro Alto. There's a hardworking, hard-drinking bar area; a dance floor crowded with bodies of all shapes and sizes; and a small stage where the famed drag shows kicks off at 3am. If you fancy joining them, Monday night is new talent night. Rua da Palmeira 38. www.finalmenteclub.com. ✆ **21/347-99-23.** Daily 12:30–6am. Bus 773.

Hot Clube de Portugal★★★ Hep cats head here. This archetypal basement dive is one of Europe's oldest and most-respected jazz clubs, bopping since the 1940s. According to legend, the youthful founders would grab musicians off planes that in those days stopped over between Paris and New York. When fire devastated the original building in 2009, they built a replica a few doors up. It runs a renowned school for musicians and is still the capital's coolest joint. Praça da Alegria, 48. www.hcp.pt. ✆ **21/346-03-05.** Tues–Sat 10pm–2am. Metro: Avenida.

Lux Frágil ★★ Lisbon's hottest club celebrated its 20th birthday in 2018 but shows no sign of losing its youthful buzz. Occupying a former warehouse overlooking the Tagus, it has a laidback upstairs bar, an outdoor terrace, and a river-level dance floor where some of the world's top DJs lay down a frenetic beat. Its reputation means you should be early or famous to make sure of getting in. Av. Infante Don Henrique, Armazém A, Cais da Pedra a Sta. Apolónia. www.luxfragil.com. ✆ **21/882-08-90.** Thurs–Sun 11pm–6am. Metro: Santa Apolónia.

Musicbox Lisboa ★ Featuring international and Portuguese bands alternating with DJ sets, Musicbox is a cultural icon for Lisbon nighthawks. It's renowned for rock, but the program is diverse, ranging from house and funk to African and Brazilian beats. Monday's "Fresh Prince" nights are popular for old school hip-hop nostalgics. Everything happens in a cavernlike space under a much-Instagrammed archway on "Pink Street." Rua Nova de Carvalho 24. www.musicboxlisboa.com. ✆ **21/347-31-88.** Daily 11pm–6am. Metro: Cais do Sodré.

Park ★★ Urban life would be better if all multistory parking lots were crowned by rooftop bars. This is one of Lisbon's hippest places for outdoor tipples. It's perched six stories above the Bairro Alto with extraordinary river views. The entrance is a little hard to find; just take the car park elevator to the top. Deckchairs and potted plants give it a chilled, garden feel. It offers burgers, R&B sets, and cocktails, and a great place to sip at a goblet filled with white port wine and tonic. No reservations and it can get crowded, especially around sunset. Calçada do Combro 58. ✆ **21/591-40-11.** Mon–Sat 1pm–2am. Tram: 28.

Pavilhão Chinês ★★★ Like stepping into a labyrinthine Victorian curiosity cabinet, walls here are lined with bric-a-brac, regiments of lead soldiers, shoals of ceramic sea creatures, busts of long-departed European aristocracy. One of the discreetly lit salons is filled with military headgear, another has flights of vintage model aircraft. Opened in 1986 in a 100-year-old grocery store, the "Chinese pavilion" is like an eccentric gentleman's club, complete with billiards room. The drinks list is an inch-thick work of art. Try the "Summer in Madeira," which mixes brandy, passionfruit, grenadine, and sparkling wine. Check out their Facebook page for times of occasional fado performances. Rua Dom Pedro V 89. www.facebook.com/pavilhaochineslisboa. ✆ **21/342-47-29.** Mon–Sat 6pm–2am; Sun 9pm–2am. Tram: 24.

Pensão Amor ★★★ With the decadent air of an Edwardian bordello, this hip bar recalls Cais do Sodré's shady past—although the real brothels that once filled the building were never this fancy. The crimson interior is laden with erotic artworks. There are crystal chandeliers and velvet sofas, shimmering curtains, and quiet side rooms suggestive of intimate encounters (one holds a sex shop, another an erotic bookstore). It's laidback during the day but heats up after dark, with an eclectic program that can include burlesque shows, live jazz, funky DJ sessions, or literary discussions. The bar staff make a mean pisco sour. Packed at weekends. Rua do Alecrim 19. www.pensaoamor.pt. ✆ **21/314-33-99.** Sun–Wed 2pm–3am; Thurs–Sat 2pm–4am. Metro: Cais do Sodré.

Procópio ★★ This charming little watering hole with a 1920s feel is hidden in a back street next to the lovely Jardim das Amoreiras. A longtime favorite of journalists and politicians, it has a plush, Art Nouveau interior and bluesy soundtrack, making it perfect for enjoying a quiet drink or one of their famed toasted sandwiches. Guests sit on tufted red velvet, surrounded by stained glass and ornate brass hardware. Alto de São Francisco 21. www.barprocopio.com. ✆ **21/385-28-51.** Mon–Fri 6pm–3am; Sat 9pm–3am. Metro: Rato.

Red Frog ★★ With its New York speakeasy vibe, the Red Frog was the first Portuguese joint to make it onto the World's 100 Best Bars list. It's renowned for its flabbergastingly attractive cocktails, presented more like works of art than booze. Sample the "Spiced Rusty Cherry": made with Venezuelan rum, Portuguese sour cherry liqueur, vanilla, chocolate, and spiced smoke. Like all the best speakeasies, the door is locked; you buzz to enter. In 2019, the owners opened a colorful offshoot, Monkey Mash, around the corner in Praça da Alegria. Rua do Salitre 5A. ✆ **21/583-11-20.** Mon–Thurs 6pm–2am; Fri–Sat 6pm–3am. Metro: Avenida.

Silk ★★ Perhaps the city's most exclusive club, there are stunning views from this place on the rooftop of a seven-floor Chiado mansion, making it the ideal place to sip champagne, gulp designer sashimi, and watch the sunset. As the night progresses, and particularly at weekends, things heat up, with DJs spinning dance sets into the wee small hours. You should book ahead. There's also a cafe service from noon to 5pm. The dress code means you don't show up in your gym shorts and flip-flops. Rua da Misericórdia 14. www.silk-club.com. ✆ **91/300-91-93.** Tues–Wed 7pm–1am; Thurs 7pm–1:30am; Fri–Sat 7pm–4pm. Metro: Baixa-Chiado.

Toca da Raposa ★★ After years of mixing cocktails in London, Constança Raposo Cordeiro returned to set up the "vixen's lair," her own bar in Chiado. The ceiling is low, the furniture bright, and the bar made from a block of pink marble. They don't do "normal" cocktails, but forage for seasonal herbs and vegetables to formulate original drinks named after animals. The "fox" is made from tequila mixed with peppers and cauliflower, the "horse" with Madeira-island rum, carrot, peach, and mint. 45 Rua da Condessa. ✆ **96/546-32-62.** Tues–Sun 6pm–2am. Metro: Baixa-Chiado.

Topo ★★ Things don't look too promising when you enter a rather gloomy shopping mall filled with Chinese textile stores and an Indian grocery. But head to the top floor and you'll find one of Lisbon's best rooftop bars featuring cool music, great views of St. George's Castle, and food that reflects the area's diversity. There's also an intoxicating mix of classic and creative cocktails (try the "Dragon Square" with spiced rum and ginger beer). Topo's success has spawned a couple of subsidiaries in posher parts of the city, but the original remains the most atmospheric (and less visited by tourists). Centro Comercial Martim Moniz, Piso 6, Praça do Martim Moniz. ✆ **21/588-13-22.** Sun–Wed 12:30pm–1am. Fri–Sat 12:30pm–2am. Metro: Martim Moniz.

Trumps ★★ Absolutely nothing to do with any present or past U.S. president, this is Lisbon's biggest and hottest gay venue and has been around for almost 40 years. It features a cafe, bars, and dance halls over two floors. The decor is a mixture of metal, glitter, and neon lighting downstairs; black floors and trendy chandeliers upstairs. The music is pop/house, plus there are regular shows with everything from flame breathers to drag. Young gay fashionista men and women make up most of the crowd, but straight friends are welcome. Rua da Imprensa Nacional 104B. www.trumps.pt. ✆ **91/593-82-66.** Metro: Rato.

Vestigius ★★★ Over 200 wines are available for sipping in this warehouse, with a terrace lapped by the waters of the Tagus. The interior is artfully shabby chic, designed by owner Esmeralda Fernandes and spread over two floors. Staff are friendly and knowledgeable. They also have over 40 gins, cocktails and excellent meals from brunch through snacks, pizza, and more elaborate seafood dinners. This is a good place for watching the little orange ferry boats chug across the river. Rua da Cintura do Porto de Lisboa, Armazém A17 www.vestigius.pt. ✆ **21/820-33-20.** Sun–Thurs 11am–11pm; Fri–Sat 11am–midnight. Metro: Cais do Sodré.

Casino

Casino Lisboa ★ This smaller sister to the famed casino in Estoril is closer to the city center, in the modern, riverside Parque das Nações district. Run by the same Macau-based group, it offers similar attractions including blackjack, baccarat, and poker tournaments. Visitors can enjoy four bars and three restaurants serving Portuguese or Chinese food. Leading fado singers and other top Portuguese acts perform at the Casino's theater, and there are frequent art exhibitions. Alameda dos Oceanos, 45. ✆ **21/892-90-00.** Sun–Thurs 3pm–3am; Fri–Sat 4pm–4am. Metro: Oriente.

Concert Venues, Opera & Theater

Centro Cultural de Belém ★★ Besides holding one of Lisbon's foremost modern art collections (p. 110), the huge CCB has a performing arts center with two auditoriums boasting excellent acoustics. There's a wide-ranging program featuring national and international stars of classical music, jazz, fado and roots music, plus theater and contemporary dance performances. Praça do Império. www.ccb.pt. ✆ **21/361-24-00.** Tram: 15.

Cineteatro Capitólio ★★ This 1930s Art Deco landmark hosts an eclectic program of Portuguese and international acts from hip hop to flamenco, Portuguese heavy metal to Emmy-winning standup comedians. It's located in the Parque Mayer, once Lisbon's thriving variety theater scene. Parque Mayer. www.capitolio.pt. ✆ **21/138-53-40.** Metro: Avenida.

Gulbenkian Música ★★★ Another of Lisbon's multifaceted arts hubs, the Gulbenkian center has first-class concert facilities as well as its art collections (p. 116). The foundation's orchestra and choir are globally respected and play with visiting international stars. The focus is on classical music, but there are also regular shows with jazz and folk musicians from around the world, plus Lisbon's own fado. Operas beamed in live from the New York Met are a popular attraction. In the summer, there are alfresco performances in amphitheater set among the Gulbenkian's wonderful gardens. Av. de Berna 45. www.museu.gulbenkian.pt. ✆ **21/782-30-00.** Metro: São Sebastião.

Teatro Camões ★★ Part of the legacy of the Expo '98 World's Fair, this riverside white-stone-and-glass theater is home to the Companhia Nacional de Bailado (National Ballet Company) out in the Parque das Nações district. The repertoire ranges from classical to contemporary, but the CNB's international reputation is based mainly on trailblazing modern dance. Passeio do Neptuno. www.cnb.pt. ✆ **21/892-34-77.** Metro: Oriente

Teatro Nacional de São Carlos ★★★ A grand opera house built after the 1755 earthquake with an imposing neoclassical facade and a lavish rococo interior. The opera season usually runs from October through to May. It's wise to book in advance. Most seasons, the program mixes the classical cannon with a couple of new works. The theater also hosts the Orquestra Sinfónica Portuguesa, which has a full concert program running through fall and winter. Rua Serpa Pinto 9. www.tnsc.pt. ✆ **21/325-30-45.** Metro: Baixa-Chiado.

Teatro Nacional D. Maria II ★ Portugal's national theater shows superior drama in a splendid 19th-century auditorium. Almost all performances are in Portuguese without subtitles, but guest troupes occasionally perform in other languages. Praça de Dom Pedro IV. www.tndm.pt. ✆ **21/325-08-00.** Metro: Rossio.

Fado Clubs

Fado (p. 34) is to Lisbon what tango is to Buenos Aires or jazz to New Orleans, an earthy urban sound that's deeply engrained in the soul of the city. You can hear fado in posh *casas de fado* over expensive dinners; in backstreet dives where amateur crooners. or sometimes even cooks and waiters will belt out a tune; or in concert halls where a new generation of singers like Mariza, Gisela João, and Ana Moura draw thousands of fans. As a general rule, the later you go the more they fill up with Portuguese aficionados.

A Baiuca ★ This is for *fado vadio*—vagabond fado, which means the singers are amateurs singing for the sheer enjoyment of it. The quality of the singing, food, and service can be indifferent, but the atmosphere is always special and the guitarists excellent. Squeeze around one of the tiny tavern's communal tables, order up some simple food and red wine, and sit back as the waiters, cook, and various neighbors step up to sing. Anyone talking during the singing should expect to be aggressively hissed. 20 Rua de São Miguel. ✆ **21/886-72-84.** Wed–Mon 8pm–midnight. Tram: 12, 28.

Adega Machado ★★ A Bairro Alto landmark since 1937, with its idiosyncratic tiled facade showing musical scenes, this is a refined place for dinner with live fado under the eye of Marco Rodrigues, a leading guitarist and singer, who played a key role in reviving the house. The food is expensive, with mains around 30€, but you can opt for snacks. This is a place with real tradition, where Amália Rodrigues once sang and European royalty listened. A good initiation is their "fado in the box" sessions, featuring an hour of music and snacks daily at 5pm. The owners have two other houses, the nearby Café Luso and Timpanas in Alcântara. Rua do Norte 91. www.adegamachado.pt. ✆ **21/342-22-82.** Daily 7:30pm–2am. Tram: 24.

Clube de Fado ★★ Founded by virtuoso guitarist and composer Mario Pacheco in a prime location in an old house with vaulted ceilings behind the cathedral, this is a top-quality venue. Pacheco himself often plays, joined by famed house singers like Sandra Correia and Maria Ana Bobone. The food (mains 22€–33 €) sometimes struggles to match the music, but this is one of the places where the fado stars (not to mention the likes of Cristiano Ronaldo) come to listen to fado. Rua São João da Praça, 86–94. www.clube-de-fado.com. ✆ **21/885-27-04.** Daily 8pm–2am. Tram: 12, 28.

Mesa de Frades ★★ Another place loved by fado devotees, it was launched in 2006 by guitarist Pedro Castro in a chapel covered with handsome 18th-century *azulejos*. You'll need to book in advance to secure a table for dinner (fixed three-course menu for 60€, excluding drinks), or you can do like the locals, and squeeze in to standing-room-only spots and enjoy the singing and drinking into the late night. If you are lucky, you'll catch some of fado's biggest names popping in for an impromptu jam session. Celeste Rodrigues, sister of fado legend Amália, sang here regularly until she died in 2018 at the age of 95. Rua dos Remédios, 139A. ✆ **91/702-94-36.** Daily 8pm–2:30am. Metro: Santa Apolónia.

Povo ★★ This youthful tavern stands out among the more raucous nightlife on Cais do Sondré's famed "Pink Street." From Tuesday to Sunday, 8:30 to 11pm, it showcases young fado singers on 3-month residencies. On Monday nights, fado takes a break, replaced with live poetry readings. The ambiance is more relaxed than in older fado houses; food is tasty and affordable, based on typical *petiscos* (snacks) to share. They range from deep-fried shrimp balls at 2€ each to octopus salad at 12€. After the fado, there are late-night DJ sets. Rua Nova do Carvalho, 32–36. www.povolisboa.com. ✆ **21/347-34-03.** Metro: Cais do Sodré.

Senhor Vinho ★★ Step back in time in this *casa do fado* opened in 1975 by celebrated singer Maria da Fé. The rustic-chic decor and groups of besuited diplomats and business types among the diners recall bygone times. The biggest draw is Aldina Duarte, one of today's best fado voices, but there are also excellent upcoming *fadistas*. Food is traditional, with mains like rabbit or monkfish rice for around 30€. The singing starts at 9pm. Rua do Meio à Lapa, 18. www.srvinho.com. ✆ **21/397-26-81.** Mon–Sat 8pm–2am. Tram: 25, 28; Bus: 713, 773.

Tasca do Chico ★★★ In this hallowed ground for fado fans, the photos lining the walls show that just about anybody who's anybody in modern fado has stood up and opened their lungs here. It's an unassuming tavern serving snacks, sandwiches, and jugs of wine (its flame-grilled *chouriço* sausages are famed). *Fado vadio* at its best, it gets packed most evenings, especially since Anthony Bourdain gave it his seal of approval on TV. Go late to increase your chances of catching a big-name star dropping by to sing unannounced. There's a second Chico branch in Alfama. Rua do Diàrio de Notícias, 39. ✆ **96/133-96-96.** Sun–Thurs 7pm–1:30am; Fri–Sat 7pm–3am. Metro: Baixa-Chiado.

Film

Cinema City Alvalade ★ This delightful neighborhood movie house has an agreeable mix of Hollywood blockbusters and European films on its four screens. There's a cool bar/cafe out front, decorated with a 1950s mural depicting artistic endeavors and antique film posters. It's how movie theaters were before they moved to shopping malls. The group also has another cinema under the Campo Pequeno bullring. Avenida de Roma, 100. www.cinemacity.pt. ✆ **21/841-30-43.** Metro: Alvalade.

Cinema Ideal ★★ Portugal's oldest cinema opened in 1904 but has had a checkered past. It was once a porn joint and lay derelict for years before reopening in 2014 as the only regular movie house in the city's historic center. It mostly shows European arthouse movies, which is challenging if you can't read the Portuguese subtitles, but when there are English-language films, this is undoubtedly the coolest hangout for cinephiles. Rua do Loreto, 15-17. www.cinemaideal.pt. ✆ **21/099-82-95.** Metro: Baixa-Chiado. Tram: 28.

Cinemateca Portuguesa ★★★ More than just a cinema, this is a museum, archive, exhibition center, and bookshop, housed in a palatial 19th-century building. It generally shows three or four films a day on two screens. A typical bill could include a dark silent drama from 1920s German, a '50s Hollywood epic, or '60s British sci-fi. On warm evenings, it's great to have a pre-movie drink or meal on the rooftop bar (although it's closed in August). Rua do Loreto, 15–17. Rua Barata Salgueiro, 39. www.cinemateca.pt. ✆ **21/359-62-62.** Metro: Avenida.

CASCAIS, SINTRA & MAFRA

Head west along the road or railway that hugs the Tagus shore, and less than 20 minutes out from downtown Lisbon you hit the first of a chain of golden beaches that stretches along to the posh resort towns of Estoril and Cascais. Continue along the coast on a road that climbs upward to the high cliffs at mainland Europe's western-most point. Behind you are the forest-clad Serra de Sintra hills, described by Byron as a "glorious Eden." Lisbon's nobles fled here to avoid the summer heat, building a sprinkling of palaces that earned Sintra its UNESCO World Heritage status. There's another World Heritage site a few miles north at the great convent-palace complex at Mafra. On the coast here, Ericeira is a paradise for surfers and seafood lovers.

The area to the west of Lisbon is a fascinating mix of history, heritage, and leisure opportunities. Sintra is the top attraction, its spectacular landscape of thickly wooded hills filled with a fairy tale mix of castles and palaces, including an ancient Moorish fortress, 19th-century romantic fantasies, and a royal retreat from the 1400s.

Cascais is known as the city of fishermen and kings. Portugal's royals made the then-fishing village famous when they turned a seaside fortress into a holiday home in the late 19th century. In the decades that followed, its neighbor Estoril became the fashionable bathing spot for the pre-jet set, sprouting a casino and palatial hotels. In World War II and its aftermath, the area was awash with spies and well-heeled refugees. Today, Cascais remains one of the richest cities in Portugal, blending a rich cultural life with its role as a millionaires' hideaway.

Of the region's palaces, none is more grandiose than the vast convent and royal palace at Mafra. Built in the 18th-century with the revenue from Brazilian gold, it covers an area equivalent to 5½ football fields and contains one of Europe's greatest libraries. In 1910, when republican revolutionaries seized power in Lisbon, the royal family fled from Mafra to the fishing port of Ericeira, then on to exile in England. Today, that whitewashed village is a lively meeting place for surfers drawn by the regular waves along the coast.

All along the coast there are great seafood restaurants popular with Lisbonites heading out for Sunday lunch. Wine lovers will appreciate the few but tasty reds and whites produced around the village of Colares and the fortified sweet wines grown inland from Carcavelos, the best beach along the Costa do Sol.

ESTORIL ★

25km (15 miles) W of Lisbon

This fashionable resort, with its beautiful beaches, has a long history as a home away from home for expats of all nationalities. The coast here is sometimes called the Portuguese Riviera and the Costa dos Reis (Coast of Kings). Tourism began here in the 19th century when fashionable society decided sea bathing was good for the health. The construction of a spa resort, casino, and luxury hotels led to Estoril developing as an international leisure destination. Wealthy refugees from across Europe flocked to Estoril in the first half of the 20th century, fleeing the Spanish Civil War, World War II, and the Communist takeover of eastern Europe, including the royal families of Spain, Italy, Romania, Bulgaria, Greece, and Yugoslavia. Movie stars and cultural giants from Zsa Zsa Gabor to Antoine de Saint-Exupéry also languished in what one called "a sad paradise," hoping for passage to the United States. Portugal's WWII neutrality also turned Estoril's grand hotels and casino into a nest of espionage. The hotels filled up with refugees again in 1975, as hundreds of thousands of Portuguese fled from Angola and other newly independent African colonies. Today, Estoril retains an exclusive air. The casino is the biggest in Europe and the town is filled with fancy villas and fine restaurants, making this much sought after by foreign homebuyers from Brazil and China notable among the longer-established ex-pat communities. The town is part of Cascais municipality.

Essentials

ARRIVING

BY TRAIN Up to five trains an hour leave Lisbon from Cais do Sodré, taking 26 minutes to reach Estoril. But it's better you buy your ticket, known as a Viva Viagem card (p. 73), in advance to avoid the huge queues. It's also better you choose the zapping option because a one-way trip costs you less this way, 1.90€, than if you buy a ticket to Estoril, 2.25€. Trains operate daily 5:30am to 1:30am. Details on: www.cp.pt.

BY BUS From Lisbon take the train. But if you're coming to Estoril from Sintra, the 418 bus is your best bet. It leaves every hour, takes about 30 minutes and costs 3.30€. For more details check the Scott Urb company site: www.scotturb.com.

BY CAR From Lisbon, head west on Avenida Marginal (EN6). It's a scenic trip that hugs the coast, but can be slow when it's busy, and scary when traffic lightens and local speedsters accelerate around the curves. It should take about 35 minutes, if not too busy. An alternative is the A5 toll highway that runs inland.

VISITOR INFORMATION

The Cascais Tourism Board is based at Edifício do Centro de Congressos do Estoril 3, C, Av. Clotilde, Estoril (www.visitcascais.com; ✆ **21/466-62-30**), but the main Visitor Center is in Cascais, on Praça 5 de Outubro (✆ **91/203-42-14**). It's open 9am to 6pm in winter, 9am to 8pm in summer.

Exploring Estoril

Estoril is short on museums and monuments, but it is a pleasant place to stroll, soak up the rays, or hang out in the shops, cafes, and gardens. The main focus is the **Jardim do Estoril** ★, an oblong of lawns and palm trees stretching about 300 meters (yards) down from the casino to the beach.

It's linked with shops and arcades on the eastern side by the historic hotel Palácio (see p. 145) and the modern congress center. At the bottom is the resort's main beach **Praia do Tamariz** ★, a wedge of golden sand with cafes and restaurants. It's flanked by a couple of idiosyncratic buildings, the castle-like **Forte da Cruz** (www.fortedacruz.com) and the pointy-towered, lemon painted **Vila Tamariz Beach Club** and restaurant, which belongs to Sintra's uber-swanky Penha Longa resort (p. 166). Next door the **Reverse Beach & Pool Lounge** (www.reversepoolandbeach.com; ✆ **21/152-57-13**) offers cocktails, sushi, and a pool, just in case the Atlantic's too cold, or you don't want sand between your toes.

A seaside **promenade** ★ (*paredão*) makes a pleasant walk a few meters east to the smaller **Praia da Poça,** or westward to Cascais, 2km (1¼ miles) away. On the first floor of Estoril's disactivated 1940s post office (Correios) building there's **Espaço Memória dos Exílios** ★, a small exhibition space and library dedicated to the refugees and exiles who passed through from 1936 to the 1960s (Av. Marginal, 7152; ✆ **21/481-59-30;** free admission; Mon–Fri 10am–6pm). Visitors with a sweet tooth should step next door to **Pastelaria Garrett** ★, a cafe open since 1934, whose majestic pastries once tempted many of those exiled royals (Av. de Nice, 53; ✆ **21/468-03-65;** Wed–Mon 8am–7pm).

Among the beaches between Lisbon and Estoril, the best is **Praia de Carcavelos** ★★, a long, broad expanse of sand guarded by a mighty 16th-century fortress. It's a 15-minute walk from Estoril and 25-minute train ride from Cais do Sodré.

SPORTS Other than the beach, the big activity here is golf. A fixture in Estoril since 1940, **Clube de Golfe do Estoril** (Av. da República; www.clubegolfestoril.com; ✆ **21/468-01-76**) is one of the oldest in the country, its roots dating back to the 1920s. It was favored by aristocrats and exiled royals and hosted international championships. These days it's dissected by the A5 motorway and hemmed in by urban development, but the course designed by Scotland's Mackenzie Ross remains an excellent play, lined with pine and eucalyptus and with sea views. There's a splendid 1940s clubhouse and a highly reputed academy.

THE NAME'S popov, duško POPOV

Neutral Portugal was one of the few places in WWII the Allies and Axis had easy access to people from the other side. In Estoril, spies mingled with refugees and travelers who flocked to its hotels and casino. Among the agents passing through was a young British operative named **Ian Fleming.** He was sent to keep an eye on a Yugoslav playboy called **Duško Popov,** a double agent who convinced the Nazis he was one of theirs, but fed them fake information while supplying the British with the real thing. Always elegant, a notorious womanizer and player for high stakes in the casino, Popov made an impression on the Brit. Fleming created **James Bond** in his 1953 novel *Casino Royale* with distinct similarities between Popov and 007. Although he switched the action to France, the book's gambling scenes were inspired by what Fleming witnessed at the tables of Estoril. Popov's story is told in fictionalized form in *Estoril: A War Novel*, by Serbian-Portuguese **Dejan Tiago Stanković**. Fittingly, scenes from the 1969 Bond movie *On Her Majesty's Secret Service* was filmed in the Palácio and other locations around Estoril and Lisbon.

The **Clube de Ténis do Estoril** (Av. Conde de Barcelona; www.ctestoril.pt; ✆ **21/466-27-70**) opened in 1945. It is the country's most prestigious, with 18 courts and top-level facilities, including a pool, gym, and restaurant. It hosts regular big-name tournaments, including the annual Millennium Estoril Open, an ATP tour event held in the spring.

Carcavelos beach has gentle but regular waves that make it ideal for learning to surf. There are a number of **surf schools** offering classes in English for all ages, including www.carcavelossurfschool.com, www.angelsurfschool.com, and www.theblueroom.pt. The latter is run by pro Frederico "Kikas" Morais when he's not traveling the world in the WSL Men's Championship.

SHOPPING As might be expected, there are some fine upscale shopping opportunities among the leafy avenues and posh villas of Estoril. For an eccentric experience, enter the **Cabinet of Curiosities** (Av. de Nice 68; www.viterbo-id.com; ✆ **21/464 62-43**). In a warren of small rooms, designer Gracinha Viterbo displays handpicked decorative objects in a magical environment. Up in the verdant Monte Estoril neighborhood, **Cura** (Av. Sabóia, 915; ✆ **91/244-68-90**) is the place for cool summer clothes and accessories; while **Espace Canelle** (Arcadas do Parque, 52H, Avenida Clotilde; www.espacecannelle-shop.com; ✆ **21/466-21-41**) is a beautiful store selling top international fashion designs in the arcades besides Estoril gardens. Foodies will like **Quinta do Saloio** (Av. Nice, 170; www.quintadosaloio.com; ✆ **21/098-79-58**), a grocery with excellent cheese, canned fish, wines, olive oil, and other specialties.

In July and August, the resort holds an open-air handicrafts fair, the **Feira do Artesanato,** near the casino and open from 6pm until midnight. In addition to regional food, stalls sell handicrafts from all parts of Portugal.

Where to Stay

EXPENSIVE

Palácio Estoril ★★★ Many hotels use the "Palace" label, but few merit it as much as this grand 1930s landmark. It's spent decades hosting crowned heads, princes and presidents and retains a regal air with Pompeian columns, regency-style furnishing and crystal-lit dining halls. There's a gallery with photos and memorabilia from the old days, but the Palácio is no museum. Regular upgrades ensure its opulent, old-world charm is matched with up-to-the-minute amenities, including the Asian-inspired Banyan Tree Spa and high-tech gym. The splendid outdoor pool is surrounded by gardens backing onto those of the casino, the beach is just across the road and the golf course minutes away.

Rua Particular. www.palacioestorilhotel.com. ✆ **21/464-80-00.** 161 units. 156€–414€ double; 256€–589€ suite. Free parking. **Amenities:** 2 restaurants; bar; babysitting; concierge; golf course nearby; outdoor and indoor pools; room service; spa; sauna; fitness center; animals admitted; free Wi-Fi.

MODERATE

Estoril Eden ★ Perched over the coast at Monte Estoril, between Estoril proper and Cascais, this typically mid-20th-century tower is dated but good value for money. Rooms come equipped with kitchenettes. It's worth paying extra to get one with an oceanview balcony, as the vistas over Cascais bay are immense. There are more coast views from the outdoor pool and sun lounge (Praia das Moitas beach is a 5-min. walk down the hill). In the unlikely event that the sun's not shining, there's also indoor pool.

Avenida Saboia 209, Monte Estoril. www.hotelestorileden.pt. ✆ **21/466-76-00.** 162 units. 77€–177€ double; 164€–277€. Parking 15€ daily. **Amenities:** Indoor and outdoor pools; garden; sun terrace; gym; sauna; massage service; restaurant; bar; babysitting; free Wi-Fi.

Hotel Inglaterra ★★ The curved lemon-and-cream facade of this historic gem looks toward the coast from a slight hill. It was built as a palatial private home toward the end of the 19th century, with five stories of Belle Epoque styling. It was recently renovated by Swedish fashion designer Corine Henriksson, a discreet modern wing also added. Decor includes ostrich plume lampshades and tailor's dummies perched on windowsills (quirkily charming or just plain spooky, depending on your point of view). Rooms range from cool and functional in the modern part, to spectacular bay-windowed suites each with themed colors, whimsical furnishings, and views across Cascais Bay. One is a shocking scarlet love suite, but our favorite on the fifth floor has soft shades of grey and the best view. There's an outdoor pool, children's playground, and access to the spa of the next-door Palácio.

Rua do Porto 1. www.hotelinglaterra.com.pt. ✆ **21/468-44-61.** 70 units. 59€–289€ double; 144€–384€ suite. Free parking. **Amenities:** Restaurant; 2 bars; babysitting; bikes; children's center; concierge; exercise room; outdoor pool; room service; free Wi-Fi.

INEXPENSIVE

Blue Boutique Hostel ★★ This pale blue, 100-year-old former family villa has made a habit of picking up international kudos. It enjoys a prime location in the São João de Estoril neighborhood, a short walk to sheltered Praia da Azarujinha beach. The azure decor continues in the (mixed and female-only) dorms, private doubles, and suites (only the latter have private bathrooms). All types of rooms are cheery and have bright quality beds, wooden floors, and whitewashed walls. Many of the rooms have Atlantic views, and the gardens are filled with beanbags and deckchairs for relaxing in the sun. Surf and yoga packages are available.

Av. Marginal, 6538. www.blueboutiquehostel.com. ✆ **21/466-30-06.** Doubles 34€–84€; 15€–24€ bed in dorms; 45€–188€ suites. Free parking (w/reservation). **Amenities:** Garden; sun terrace; bike hire; kitchen; bar; massage service; free Wi-Fi.

Where to Eat

Cimas Restaurante ★★ INTERNATIONAL/PORTUGUESE Another place linked to Estoril's espionage history, this mock-Elizabethan cottage overlooking the bay opened in 1941 as an English pub. In the 1950s, the Cima family took it over and turned it into the gastronomic reference point on the coast, a favorite with exiled royalty, political leaders, and visiting celebrities (dictator Marcelo Caetano celebrated his birthday here *en famille* every year). The Cimas are still in charge, the decor very British, and the food French-influenced Portuguese. The fish is always excellent, but it's best known for game dishes like woodcock flambé or hare with butterbeans. The crêpes suzette will make you wish you'd gone easy on the hare.

Avenida Marginal 276, Monte Estoril. www.cimas.com.pt. ✆ **21/468-12-54.** Reservations recommended. Mains 18€–58€. Mon–Sat 12:30–4pm, 7:30–11pm.

Eduardo das Conquilhas ★★ PORTUGUESE/SEAFOOD Tucked away on a backstreet near the Parede station, a couple of stops before Estoril, this is the favorite beer-and-shellfish joint for inhabitants of the *linha* (as the Lisbon-Cascais line is called). *Conquilhas* are tiny-but-tasty clams from the Algarve, and Eduardo is the octogenarian who started the place over half a century ago. Much of the seafood comes from their own tanks, and the usual thing to do is order a selection to share around the table, be it shrimp, clams, and lobster or exotic creatures like goose barnacles or periwinkles. There are other dishes including steak or salt-cod. It's big, bright, and busy, and recently spawned an offshoot in the market at Carcavelos.

Rua Capitão Leitão 118-A, Parede. www.eduardodasconquilhas.com. ✆ **21/457-33-03.** Mains 8€–20€. May–Sept: Tues–Sun noon–1am; Oct–Apr: Tues–Sun noon–midnight.

Estoril Mandarim ★★ CHINESE The Macau-based owners behind Estoril Casino gave themselves the mission of bringing the finest Cantonese cuisine to the gaming house. The result is this restaurant featuring refined oriental décor, views over the park from its glass facade and terrace, and an infinite list of dishes from the team led by Chef Dong Wei. Splashing out dishes include bird's nest soup with crab and braised abalone in oyster sauce, but there are less extravagant choices such as Cantonese roast duck, or pork and squid with water-chestnut. They offer a fine selection of Portuguese wines.

Casino Estoril, Avenida Dr. Stanley Ho. www.casino-estoril.pt. ✆ **21/466-72-70.** Mains 11€–150€. Wed–Sun noon–3pm, 7–11pm.

Estoril Entertainment & Nightlife

CASINO Estoril's nightlife revolves around Europe's biggest casino. A little piece of Macau by the Atlantic, it's the capital region's glitziest entertainment center. There are vast gaming rooms offering roulette, blackjack, Caribbean stud Baccarat and French bank dice, as well as regular poker tournaments. Punters pulling on the 1,110 slot machines helped the casino generate 64 million€ in gaming revenues in 2018. Beside the gambling, the casino's **Salão Preto e Prata** is a dining and showroom featuring cabaret dances and regular performances by international stars. **Lounge D** has fado, flamenco nights and DJ sets, and frequent performances by some of the biggest names in Portuguese music. The casino runs the **Tamariz** outdoor discotheque down by the beach until 6am on summer nights, while the **Jézebel** dance club takes over in the winter. There are four restaurants and five bars, plus regular art exhibitions. Under 18s are banned from the gaming rooms and you may be asked to show ID. The casino opened in 1931 as the epitome of Estoril coast glamor—the building you see now was mostly built in the 1960s.

Avenida Dr. Stanley Ho. www.casino-estoril.pt. ✆ **21/466-77-00.** Daily 3pm–3am.

CASCAIS ★★

34km (21 miles) W of Lisbon

For much of its history, Cascais was little more than a fishing village, modest trading post and military base whose fortress guarded the maritime approaches to Lisbon. Then in the 1870s, the royal family got into the then-upcoming habit of taking the sea air, turning the old citadel into a summer residence. Portugal's penultimate monarch Carlos I was a bon vivant who loved sailing, hunting and other outdoor pursuits, and turned the village into a favored hideaway. Fashionable society soon followed, and smart villas sprouted out around the coastal community. More expansion followed when the railway arrived in 1889. By the time of World War II, Cascais was an international resort and exiled royalty flocked here; the Spanish, Italian and Romanian royal families making it their homes for decades.

Today, Cascais is Portugal's fifth-largest municipality, with 212,000 people, its citizens are in fourth place in terms of spending power. The city center is tightly packed in the narrow streets around the still active fishing port and a quartet of sandy beaches. An arts district has grown up around the old citadel. Green spaces abound, and the poshest neighborhoods stretch out west along the rocky coast to the point of Cabo Raso. Many of today's millionaires head for the Quinta da Marinha neighborhood, popular with soccer stars, bankers, and increasingly wealthy Brazilians, whose arrival in large numbers has given Cascais a "Europe's Miami" tag. Farther round the coast, just before the windswept cliffs of continental Europe's westernmost point, the huge Praia do Guincho is one of Portugal's most spectacular. Many of Cascais' best fish restaurants lie along the coast road to Guincho. The city has a vibrant cultural life, organizing a major summer jazz festival and hosting some dynamic museums.

Essentials

ARRIVING

BY TRAIN Up to five trains an hour trains leave Lisbon from Cais do Sodré, taking 40 minutes to reach Cascais. Using the **Viva Viagem** zapping cards (p. 73), a one-way trip costs 1.90€; it's 2.25€ if you buy an individual ticket. Trains operate daily 5:30am to 1:30am. Details on www.cp.pt.

BY BUS Buses from Lisbon are impractical, considering the low cost and convenience of the frequent trains. But if you're coming to Cascais from Sintra, take the 403, 417, or 418 busses; the trip takes between 30 minutes and 50 minutes depending on the route. Tickets purchased on board will cost 4.15€, but the trip is much cheaper if you use the zapping cards. Info at www.scotturb.com.

BY CAR Depending on traffic, it should take between 40 minutes to an hour to reach Cascais from Lisbon along the scenic Avenida Marginal (EN6) along the coast, less on the A5 toll highway.

VISITOR INFORMATION

The Visitor Center (www.visitcascais.com; ✆ **91/203-42-14**) is on Praça 5 de Outubro in the tile-covered old town hall and is open winter 9am to 6pm; summer 9am to 8pm.

Exploring Cascais

Coming from the rail station, it's a short walk through the narrow streets to the seafront. There are four beaches in the city center, of which **Praia dos Pescadores** ★ is the most photogenic, surrounded by grand townhouses and noble villas. In summer all the beaches will be teeming, and you may feel like a trip to **Santini** ★ (Av. Valbom 28F; www.santini.pt; ✆ **21/483-37-09**), the city's much-loved Italian ice-cream maker since 1949 (although there too you'll need to wait in line). From the beach follow the uphill curve toward imposing **Citadela** ★ fortress (Av. Dom Carlos I), guarding the harbor since the 16th century. Portugal's presidents still regularly use the former royal summer house within the walls, but it's open to visitors for free and also contains a luxury hotel (see p. 153), shops, and art galleries.

Past the citadel are a couple of interesting museums. The **Museu do Conde de Castro Guimarães** ★ (Av. Rei Humberto II de Itália, ✆ **21/481-54-01**) is

Cascais & Environs

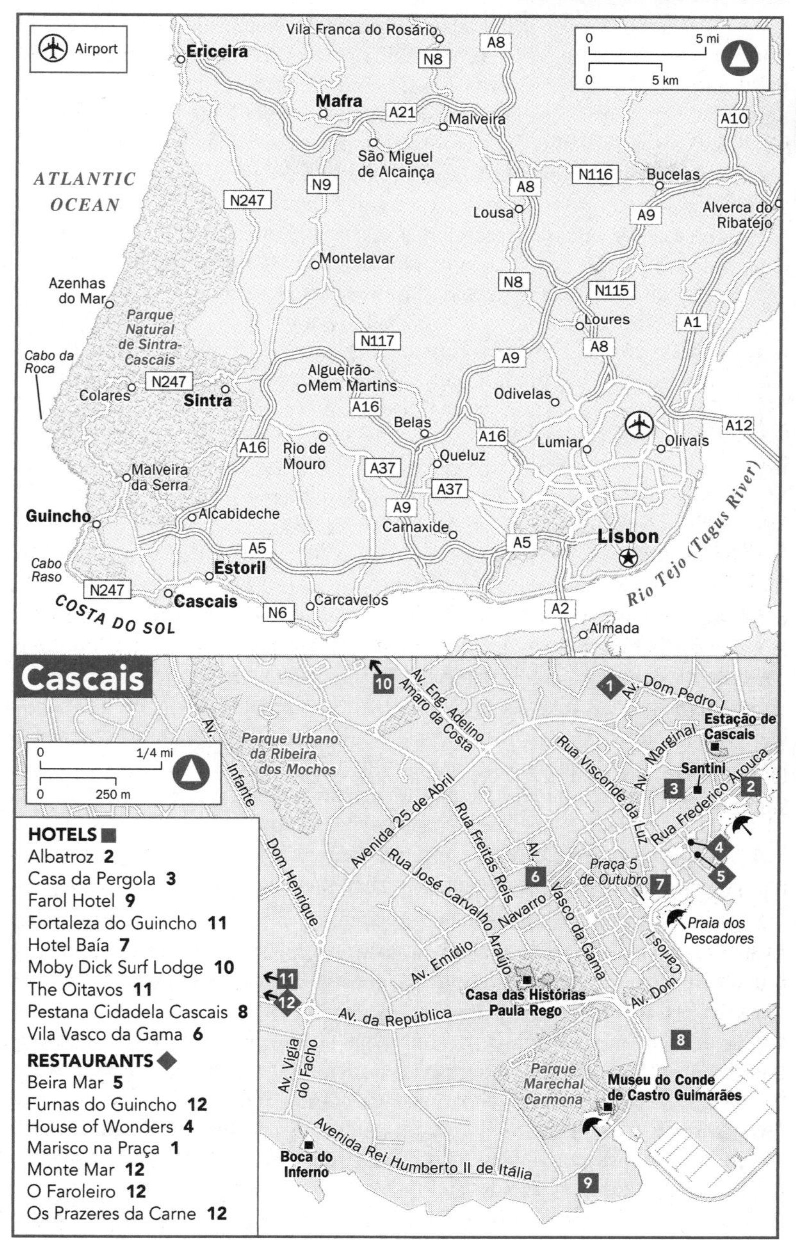

housed in a mock-Manueline mansion built in 1900 and packed with an aristocratic collection of antiquities, including Indo-Portuguese furniture and books from the 1500s. Across the road is an achingly beautiful cove whose still waters reflect another eclectic 1900s building, the **Casa Santa Marta** (Rua do Farol de Santa Marta; ✆ **21/481-53-83**), and a candy-striped blue-and-white lighthouse. They are both open to visit. Britain's former King Edward VIII and his American wife Wallis Simpson were among the royals who once stayed here. Both museums are open Tuesday to Sunday, 10am to 6pm.

Heading inland, cross **Parque Marechal Carmona,** the town's sprawling park, where an organic produce market is held on Saturday mornings. On the other side is Cascais' best museum, the **Casa das Histórias Paula Rego ★★** (Av. da República, 300; www.casadashistoriaspaularego.com; ✆ **21/482-69-70**), dedicated to Portugal's greatest living artist. Born in 1935, Rego spent much of her childhood around Cascais and maintains close ties to the city even though she's lived much of her life in London. The museum gives an overview of her work, from early abstractions to the disquieting portraits of powerful women for which she has become best known. The striking building with its twin red pyramids was designed by Pritzker Prize–winning architect Eduardo Souto de Moura. The museum opens Tuesday to Sunday, 10am to 5:45pm; admission is 5€, 2.50€ students and over 65s, free for under 18s.

Back on the coast, a bracing 10-minute walk leads to the Mouth of Hell **(Boca do Inferno) ★**, a natural rock cavern carved by the waves. Breakers continue to pound the cavern, creating a thunderous tumult of surf and foam. A sign recalls how British occultist Aleister Crowley faked his death here in 1930 then turned up 3 weeks later at a Berlin art exhibition.

From here you can hike 5 miles, hire a bike, or catch a bus (405, 415) to Guincho. You'll follow the stark rocky coastline dotted with lighthouses, fortresses, and fish restaurants on one side and a millionaires' row of condos, hotels, and golf courses on the other. At the end, **Praia do Guincho ★★★** is a stunning soft-sand beach, half-a-mile long, broad and backed by the Sintra mountains and Cabo da Roca (p. 163), Europe's western extremity. It's usually gusty here, making the beach better for wind- and kite-surfing than laying in the sun.

SPORTS The Quinta da Marinha area, among the dunes stretching west along the Atlantic from Cascais, boasts two excellent golf courses. **Oitavos Dunes** (www.oitavosdunes.com; ✆ **21/486-06-00**) was included among the world's top 100 courses by *Golf* magazine in 2018, the only Portuguese course to make it. One of just two European courses by U.S. architect Arthur Hills, the par-71 courses crosses bare dunes and wooded areas shaded by umbrella pine, with ocean views and the Sintra hills as a backdrop. The **Quinta da Marinha** course (www.quintadamarinha.com; ✆ **21/486-01-00**) just to the north was carved out by legendary designer Robert Trent Jones, Sr., with ocean dunes, pine woods, and those easy-on-the-eye Sintra hills as you tread the 5.870 meters of this par-71. Hole 3, featuring wide Atlantic views, is the course signature.

Guincho offers more board sport opportunities. **Bar do Guincho** (www.bardoguincho.pt) on the beach has a wave center to support boarders and is home to the **Moana Surf School** (www.moanasurfschool.com; ✆ **96/444-94-36**) offering surf and kite-board classes. **Surf Cascais** (www.surfcascais.com; ✆ **21/245-59-12**) also offers classes at Guincho and other nearby beaches.

SHOPPING There are plenty of chic and offbeat shopping opportunities to be uncovered in the narrow street of downtown just inland from Cascais beaches. **White and Voodoo** (Travessa da Alfarrobeira, 2A; www.whiteandvoodoo.com; ✆ **21/822-69-88**) offers fashions for the beach-and-party lifestyle with their own brand and original designers in the heart of downtown. Fashion followers will also love heading up the stairs to the boho concept store **Zöe by Pavlia Tomic** (Rua da Palmeira 4; ✆ **96/130-16-45**) or picking out designer jewelry at **Galeria 50/50** (Rua Frederico Arouca 192A; www.galeria5050.weebly.com; ✆ **21/486-17-16**). Cascais' Brazilian connection is represented by **Casa Pau Brasil** (Av. Valbom 16; ✆ **21/160-88-64**) with dozens of brands from across the south Atlantic, from Lenny Niemeyer beachwear to Granado tropical cosmetics. They also have a store in Lisbon's Príncipe Real neighborhood.

Inside the Citadela is a bookstore with a heart: **Déjà Lu** (Av. Dom Carlos I; ✆ **92/405-82-38**) sells a multilingual range of secondhand books, with proceeds going to young peoples' charities. It's upstairs from the Taverna da Praça bar. For a nautical souvenir of your stay, try **Happy Sardine** (Travessa dos Navegantes 15; ✆ **96-668-37-62**), whose gifts are "50% handmade by local artists, 90% made in Portugal, 100% made with love and happiness."

Market lovers should not miss the **Mercado da Vila** (Rua Padre Moisés da Silva 29), the city's food market where the fish, fruit, and meat stores are now mixed with bars and restaurants. Go in the morning for the traditional food stalls; the rest stays open late at weekends. Every Wednesday, the central **Jardim Visconde da Luz** turns into a sprawling market selling a mix of antiques and flea-market stuff. If you're travelling with mall rats, **Cascais Shopping** (Estrada Nacional 9, Alcabideche; www.cascaishopping.pt; ✆ **21/012-16-28**) is a 10-minute drive (or take buses 400, 406, 417, 418, 455, 456, or 462) from Cascais center, with over 158 stores and 52 dining options.

Where to Stay

Cascais is a posh place, top heavy with upscale accommodations, but there are a few easier-on-the-credit card options.

EXPENSIVE

Albatroz ★★★ This monument to aristocratic opulence reopened in the summer of 2019 after a major facelift directed by local designer Graça Viterbo (p. 144). She's introduced daringly bold colors and a mix of classic and modern art to the rooms and public spaces of a palatial hotel that's been the most sought-after location in downtown Cascais since the 1960s. The hotel sits on a clifftop above Praia da Conceição beach, presenting great views over the coast. It's made up of two 19th-century palaces raised by noble families as they joined the royals in opening summer houses on the coast—the more modern "white building" is in beach chalet style. It gets just about everything right, from the fresh papaya at breakfast time to the stylish wooden loungers beside the seafront pool, and the dedication to personalized service with a smile. The owners also operate the Vila Cascais guesthouse overlooking Fisherman's Beach.

Rua Frederico Arouca 100. www.thealbatrozcollection.com. ✆ **21/484-73-80.** 51 units. 125€–464€ double; 425€–691€ suite. Free parking. **Amenities:** Terrace; outdoor pool; bike hire; yacht hire; restaurant; bar; babysitting; free Wi-Fi.

Farol Hotel ★★ If your aim is chilling in style, this is the place for you. The "lighthouse hotel" is set in a four-story 19th-century mansion built for viscounts and marquises, but has some sleek modernist additions. It boasts a perfect location on the rocky coastline just south of downtown. Gentle surf laps up against the expansive sun terrace around the pool. Rooms are all different, often the work of top Portuguese designers. Some are minimalist in white, chrome, and mirrored glass; others are lush confections of crimson and gold. All fill with natural light, but try to get one facing the ocean where the vistas are amazing. Bathrooms are blessed with hydromassage tubs (ah!). There are two restaurants, one serving sushi, the other Mediterranean-inspired dishes. Sunset drinks on the terrace bar are a must. After that, shimmy into the night as the DJ sets get underway at the summer-only cocktail bar on the rocks.

Avenida Rei Humberto II de Italia 7. www.farol.com.pt. ✆ **21/482-34-90.** 33 units. 149€–400€ double; 421€–649€ suite. Free parking. **Amenities:** Garden; terrace; outdoor pool; bike rental; 2 restaurants; 2 bars; massage service; babysitting; free Wi-Fi.

Fortaleza do Guincho ★★★ This Relais & Châteaux hotel originated in the 17th century as a fort within cannon range of the westernmost point of the Eurasian landmass. From the coast road approach, the yellow-painted facade looks bunkerlike and forbidding, but pass through the imposing stone gateway and the interior is filled with light from the covered patio, arched windows, and terrace opening out over the Atlantic. You can gaze on the Sintra hills, cliffs of Cabo da Roca and the surf rolling on to Praia do Guincho. Rooms feature curved stone ceilings, pastel colors, and *azulejo*-tiled bathrooms. Try to get an upper-floor room with sea-facing balcony if you can. Antiques scattered around the public rooms are in keeping with the architecture. The Michelin-starred restaurant is one of the main attractions. Chef Gil Fernandes does wonders with the local seafood, which you can tuck into while watching the sun turn the watery horizon to gold.

Estrada do Guincho. www.fortalezadoguincho.com. ✆ **21/487-04-91.** 27 units. 127€–362€ double; 244€–572€ suite. Free parking. **Amenities:** Sun terrace; free bikes; restaurant; bar; babysitting; free Wi-Fi.

The Oitavos ★★ This is all about wide open spaces. It's surrounded by dunes and forests of umbrella pine. Views stretch across to the ocean and mountains (Y-shaped architecture ensures every room sees the Atlantic). Built by architect José Amaral Anahory in rigorously contemporary glass and steel, it's white and full of light. Rooms are at least 40 square meters (430 sq. ft.) with floor-to-ceiling glass opening onto private balconies. On your doorstep is one of the world's top-rated golf courses (see p. 150). There's a luscious spa and swimming pool surrounded by an expansive terrace. A free shuttle bus will whisk you to Cascais or the beach in summer. A collection of restaurants under the eye of French chef Cyril Devilliers serves up Gallic-influenced Atlantic cuisine (or sushi, if you prefer).

Rua de Oitavos, Quinta da Marinha. www.theoitavos.com. ✆ **21/486-00-20.** 142 units. 146€–281€ double; 484€–1,496€ suite. Parking 15€ daily. **Amenities:** Terrace; garden, golf; bike hire; tennis; outdoor and indoor pools; spa; hammam; sauna; massage service; 4 restaurants; bar; babysitting; free Wi-Fi.

Pestana Cidadela Cascais ★★ In the 16th-century Fortaleza de Nossa Senhora da Luz, this member of the Pousada chain provides a rival to the Albatroz in the downtown luxury category. Created by architects Gonçalo Byrne and David Sinclair, the hotel integrates organically into the fort's massive bulwarks. They made the citadel an "art district," and there's modern art in all the rooms and public spaces, from a copy of Dali's "Mae West lips" sofa to abstract lobby paintings by Nadir Afonso and quirky Bordallo Pinheiro ceramics. Rooms are a blend of clean white lines, soft greys, and splashes of color. Most have a sea view. The "authors' rooms" have original art and the most distinctive designs. The terraces of the bar and restaurant (and some of the rooms) spill out into the citadel courtyard (Portugal's president maintains a residence on the other side of the quad). There's a pool with Atlantic views, a fine restaurant, and a spa. If there's a criticism, it's that it all feels a bid cold and impersonal, but that may wear off with age.

Cidadela de Cascais, Avenida D. Carlos I. www.pestanacollection.com. ✆ **21/481-43-00.** 126 units. 124€–412€ double; 196€–371€ suite. Public parking nearby 7€ daily. **Amenities:** Sun terrace; outdoor and indoor pool; spa; sauna; fitness room; massage service; 2 restaurants; bars; free Wi-Fi.

MODERATE

Hotel Baía ★★ This well-managed mid-range hotel could hardly be more central. You just have to cross the road to feel the sand of Fishermen's Beach between your toes, while the shops of downtown are right behind. It's run by the third generation of the family that founded it in 1962. Its five floors contain contemporary furnishings, with wooden panels and bright colors. Many rooms are decorated with photos of early-20th-century Cascais. Rooms can be on the small side, but half of them enjoy lovely sea views and balconies. None, however, can match the view from the rooftop Blue Bar, one of the best spots to enjoy a drink along the coast, looking down on the beach and the lights of the town. There's also an upper-floor indoor pool with a view, and the street-level restaurant does a renowned Sunday brunch.

Passeio Dom Luis I. www.hotelbaia.com. ✆ **21/483-10-33.** 113 units. 75€–184€ double; 126€–304€ suite. Parking 10€. **Amenities:** Sun terrace; indoor pool; restaurant bar; free Wi-Fi.

Vila Vasco da Gama ★★ Given its reputation as "Portugal's Hamptons," finding moderately priced accommodation in Cascais can be difficult. This romantic neo-Manueline villa in a leafy residential neighborhood a short walk from the downtown shops and beaches is an excellent solution. It's a pleasant amalgam of Old World charm and modern design. Some of the rooms are smallish, and one in the attic with a sloping attic roof won't be to everybody's taste, but all feature bold patterns and colors, stripped wooden floors, smart TVs, and ultra-comfortable bedding. The bar, lounge, and breakfast rooms are stylish and hidden from the street; there's a lovely garden and pool. The free-to-use mountain bikes are perfect for heading down the coast to Guincho.

Av. Vasco da Gama 21. www.villavascodagama.com. ✆ **93/367-10-20.** 12 units. 94€–182€. Public parking nearby 7€ daily. **Amenities:** Garden; free bikes; outdoor pool; bar; babysitting; free Wi-Fi.

INEXPENSIVE

Casa da Pergola ★★ Warning: Guests frequently fall in love with this place. The graceful 19th-century villa has whitewashed facades offset by colorful tiles framing the windows. The garden is a floral delight with bougainvillea, venerable rose bushes, and seasonal flowerbeds lovingly tended by the owners. Inside the house feels like a much-treasured, antiques-filled family home. Which is just what it is. Patrícia Gonçalves maintains the house where she grew up and which her great-grandfather bought over 100 years ago. The family opened it up to guests in the 1980s. Rooms are individually themed and named for the colors and flowers that inspire their decor. Children are not allowed. A memorable breakfast is served in the garden or the pastel-painted dining room. Make sure you're around between 7 to 8pm, when they serve the complementary port.

Av. Valbom 13. www.pergolahouse.pt. ✆ **21/484-00-40.** 10 units. 62€–172€ double. **Amenities:** Garden; free Wi-Fi

Moby Dick Surf Lodge ★★ The white whale gave its name decades ago to a cozy guesthouse in this hill village above Guincho beach. Now it's been transformed into a laidback, free-spirited surfer lodge. There are boards on the walls, a jumble of new and old furniture, hammocks in the garden, and a friendly young staff. It's not luxurious, but it's fun. The beach is 5 minutes away, and they organize a range of surf-camp packages that mix wave classes with trips to discover the region. In addition to regular doubles they have family/group rooms with bunks. Minimum 3-night stay during summer peak times.

Rua do Cabo, 1, Malveira da Serra. www.mobydick.pt. ✆ **91/572-07-13.** 7 units. 59€–79€ double. Free parking nearby. **Amenities:** Garden; bike hire; surf school; table tennis; free Wi-Fi.

Where to Eat

The Cascais coast is renowned for its seafood restaurants, popular with Lisbonites, especially at weekends.

Beira Mar Restaurante ★★ PORTUGUESE/SEAFOOD The city's classic traditional seafood restaurant. The dining room is wood-paneled and cozy, if a bit gloomy. If the weather's good, go for the flower-decorated terrace that spills onto the traffic-free plaza. Under the same management since 1973, it is the sort of timeless place focused on simple cooking, the best ingredients, and impeccable service that Portugal does so well. They do good steaks and game in season, but seafood is the thing here. Sole Meunière or bass baked in a salt crust are among the specialties.

Rua das Flores 6. www.restaurantebeiramar.pt. ✆ **21/482-73-80.** Reservations recommended. Mains 17€–34€. Wed–Mon noon–4pm and 7pm–midnight.

Furnas do Guincho ★★ PORTUGUESE/SEAFOOD Diners are so close to the sea here, you might expect a gilt-head bream or red mullet to jump onto your plate. Instead you order them by weight almost as fresh as that and wait for them to be expertly charcoal-grilled. If you don't fancy whole fish, go for one of the specialties, like octopus and sweet potato cooked in a *cataplana* (an Algarvian implement, something like a cross between a wok and a pressure cooker), or a monkfish-and-shrimp skewer. Start out with clams, shrimp, or *bruxas,* a tiny, ugly-but-delicious species of slipper lobster that's an expensive Cascais delicacy. The house white is very quaffable at 13€ a bottle.

Estrada do Guincho. www.furnasdoguincho.pt. ✆ **21/486-92-43.** Reservations recommended. Mains 15€–25€. Mon–Fri 12:30–6pm, 7:30–11pm; Sat–Sun 12:30–11pm.

House of Wonders ★ VEGETARIAN This happy, hippy vegetarian and vegan house in the heart of town features a maze of bright (really bright) rooms (selling handicrafts and stuff, as well as food) and an especially wonderful rooftop. The owner is Dutch and the chefs (one of whom is Syrian) serve a glorious Middle Eastern–inspired buffet of mezze-style dishes. The menu changes daily, but could include sweet potato with coriander and ginger, shakshuka, or tomato tarts. They do breakfasts, daily fresh juices, herbal teas, cocktails, and craft beers.

Largo da Misericordia 53. ✆ **91/170-24-28.** Main courses 8€–12€; buffet 15€–18€. Daily 10am–10pm.

Marisco na Praça ★ PORTUGUESE/SEAFOOD While some traditional seafood joints can be expensive and just a tad stuffy, this place that opened in 2016 in the Cascais market is hip, happening, and excellent value for money. You can pick what you want from the maritime goodies packed on the ice trays and wait for them to bring it to you on the terrace or spacious dining room—the catch varies day by day, but the choice is usually enormous, with up to seven species of shrimp. Alternatively choose a dish from the blackboard, which might include white-bean stew or oven-baked salt-cod. In 2018, they opened a second outlet down by the marina.

Rua Padre Moisés Silva. www.marisconapraca.com. ✆ **21/482-21-30.** Mains 11€–15€. Daily noon–midnight.

Monte Mar ★★ PORTUGUESE/SEAFOOD Eat fish direct from the market while surf splashes against the panoramic windows. Built right on the black rock separating the Guincho road from the Atlantic, this is among the best of a succession of great seafood restaurants following the coast from Cascais. The signature dishes include rock-lobster crepes, tempura hake served with tartar sauce, and rice cooked with tomato and cockles (this is a Cascais specialty served in many of the town's restaurants). Popular with Lisbon families driving out for Sunday lunch, they have opened two branches in the capital, on the Tagus riverfront in Lisbon and in Time Out Market.

Avenida Nossa Senhora do Cabo. www.mmcascais.pt. ✆ **21/486-92-70.** Reservations recommended. Mains 16€–32€. Tues–Fri noon–10pm; Sat–Sun noon–midnight.

O Faroleiro ★★★ PORTUGUESE/SEAFOOD The view, the fish, the service, the decor all make this place out at Guincho one of our favorites. Windows wrapped around the red-tiled building ensure all-encompassing vistas of the beach, cliffs and hills (the sunsets . . .). The fish (order by the kilo and have it grilled) or shellfish (a must-have is the sloppy seafood rice with lobster) is of the highest quality. Service is old-school, with white-shirted waiters who will know which local wine should accompany your fried turbot and whether a whole spider crab *ao natural* is too much for a starter (go for it!). The room is spacious and bright, lined with weathered board and fish-related handicrafts. A downside? It may be a detail, but they need to clean the salt spray from the windows more regularly—it messes with the sunset.

Estrada do Guincho. www.faroleiro.com. ✆ **21/487-02-25.** Reservations recommended. Mains 19€–33€. Daily 12:30–4pm and 7:30–11pm.

Os Prazeres da Carne ★ BRAZILIAN/INTERNATIONAL If you are looking for a break from all the Cascais fish, try this carnivores' cabin on the shore just beyond Boca de Inferno. The name means "pleasures of the flesh" and they import their beef from South America to help Cascais' sizable Brazilian community overcome any homesickness for *picanha, maminha, bife de chorizo,* or other juicy cuts fresh from the barbecue. Filet steak is the specialty, served with a multiplicity of sauces from port wine and peppers to vodka, caviar, and cream. To go the whole hog, there's a couple of Argentine Malbecs among the fine list of Portuguese reds and, of course, they mix caipirinhas to sip on the sea-hugging veranda before you attack those steaks.

Avenida Nossa Senhora do Cabo, 101, Quinta São José da Guia. www.osprazeresdacarne.pt. ✆ **21/484-33-34.** Mains 12€–20€. Tues-Sun 12:30–3pm and 7:30–11pm; Mon 7:30–11pm.

Cascais Entertainment & Nightlife

There's a cool little movie house, **Cinema da Villa,** with a varied international program on its five screens. It also has a DVD and poster store, bar, and children's play area located in the CascaisVilla Shopping Center close to the station (Av. D. Pedro I Lote 1; www.ocinemadavilla.pt; ✆ **21/588-73-11**).

Downtown is always lively on summer evenings, particularly around Praça 5 de Outubro and Praça Camões, where there are several British and Irish bars, but Cascais isn't really a nightlife hotspot. The rooftop **Blue Bar** is open to midnight above the hotel Baía, and the **Bar on the Rocks** which bops to 1am (2am on Fri and Sat) at the Farol Hotel (see p. 152) are both cool places for a drink with music. For live jazz, blues, and bossa nova, head to the city-center **Cascais Jazz Bar** (Largo Cidade de Vitória 36; www.cascaisjazzclub.pt; ✆ **962/773-470**). It's open Thursday to Sunday, 9:30pm to 12:30am.

SINTRA ★★★

30km (18 miles) NW of Lisbon

Sintra is one of those rare places where the hand of nature and the hand of humankind come together to craft a masterpiece. The Serra de Sintra is a small mountain range rising to 529m (1,736 ft.) west of Lisbon, between the capital and the Atlantic. It has a microclimate, cooler than the capital with high rainfall and a damp mist that frequently settles on the hills. This means things grow here, almost anything. The hills are lush with vegetation, bursting with over 900 species of native and exotic plants in its forests and gardens.

Ancient peoples called this range the mountains of the moon, home of the hunter goddess Diana. Now the hills are sprinkled with the work of passing generations. One peak is topped by an Arab fortress built to watch for invaders; another has a troglodyte convent carved into its rock by Franciscan monks seeking solitude in the 1500s; a third is capped by a fairytale palace to rival any in Bavaria, dreamed up by a German prince. Portugal's medieval royals built a spectacular palace in the little village of Sintra to escape from the heat of Lisbon's summer. Over centuries, Portuguese aristocracy, affluent eccentrics, and foreigners followed them to erect fantastic palaces and magnificent gardens.

It's always attracted artistic types, from Lord Byron, Richard Strauss, and Hans Christian Andersen to Madonna, who went house hunting in the hills in the late 2010s. The most romantic of romantic poets, Byron famously called Sintra a "glorious Eden" and complained his pen was incapable of describing its "dazzling" views. These days it's a somewhat crowded Eden—as one of Portugal's most visited places, you'll have to be prepared to put up with crowds at the main palaces and monuments. Going outside the summer, early, and during the week will help. Despite the crowds, the UNESCO World Heritage site is an outstanding place to visit, and the 56 square miles of nature reserve that cover the mountains provide plenty of opportunities for solitude. Besides all the heritage, Sintra produces some fine wine on the lower slopes toward the ocean, and its wild coastline has excellent beaches and seafood.

Essentials

ARRIVING

BY TRAIN Sintra is a 40-minute ride from the Estação do Rossio in downtown Lisbon. The first train leaves Lisbon at 5:41am and the last from Sintra to the capital departs at 12:20am. Using the Viva Viagem card's zapping function (p. 73), a one-way trip costs 1.90€; buy a single ticket and it's 2.25€. For info: www.cp.pt.

BY BUS From Lisbon, it's better to go by train. Coming from Cascais, take the 417, 418, or 403 bus. The trip takes between 30 minutes and 50 minutes depending on the route (403 is slower). Tickets purchased on board will cost 4.15€, but the trip is much cheaper if you use the zapping cards. Info at www.scotturb.com.

BY CAR Depending on traffic, it takes between 35 minutes to an hour to reach Sintra from Lisbon along the A37 toll highway, while the A16 should get you there from Cascais in less than 40 minutes. Slower, but far more attractive is to take the N247 coast road from Cascais past Guincho, one of Europe's most scenic drives (p. 163).

VISITOR INFORMATION

The tourist board (www.sintraromantica.net) has its main visitor office at Praça da República 23 (www.cm-sintra.pt; © **21/923-11-57**). It's open daily 9:30am to 6pm (until 7pm in Aug). There are also posts at Sintra railroad station and at Cabo da Roca.

Exploring Sintra

Coming from the station, it's a pleasant 10-minute walk to the Palácio Nacional de Sintra at the heart of the town, surrounded by gardens, villas, shops, and restaurants. However, unless you are a dedicated hiker, you'll need transport to visit most of the other main attractions that are scattered through the hills.

Bus 434 runs in a circuit taking in the station, center of town, Palácio Nacional da Pena, and the Castelo dos Mouros, plus the picturesque village of São Pedro. The 435 goes to many of the other sights, including Monserrate, Regaleira, Seteais, and the wine village of Colares. The 434 route is not included in the Viva card ticketing system, and the trip to Pena will cost 5.50€. Details from the **Scotturb** bus company: www.scotturb.com. There's also a little tourist train that makes a 45-minute tour, including Pena, the Moors' Castle, and Regaleira for 8€, 5€ for children 5 to 12 (www.comboiodesintra.pt; © **91/825-80-01**). You can also grab taxis from stands at the station or near the Palácio Nacional de Sintra.

A more romantic, and more expensive, way to visit the palaces is by **horse and carriage.** A 3-hour roundtrip up to Pena with **Sintratur** costs 230€ and needs to be booked 3 days in advance, but they offer a series of cheaper routes and bespoke rides to see more of Sintra's charm (www.sintratur.com; © **93/823-28-87**). Less heavy on the purse are the carriage rides through the Pena gardens once you get up there. You can hop on the coach making a regular tour for 3.50€, buying tickets at the palace gates; or pre-book an exclusive 1-hour ride for 75€ from the palace administrators (www.parquesdesintra.pt).

If you're heading to the coast, it's fun in summer to take the **little red street car,** dating from 1904, that rattles through the forest for 45 minutes to reach the beach at Praia das Maçã. As of 2019, it makes the round trip three times a

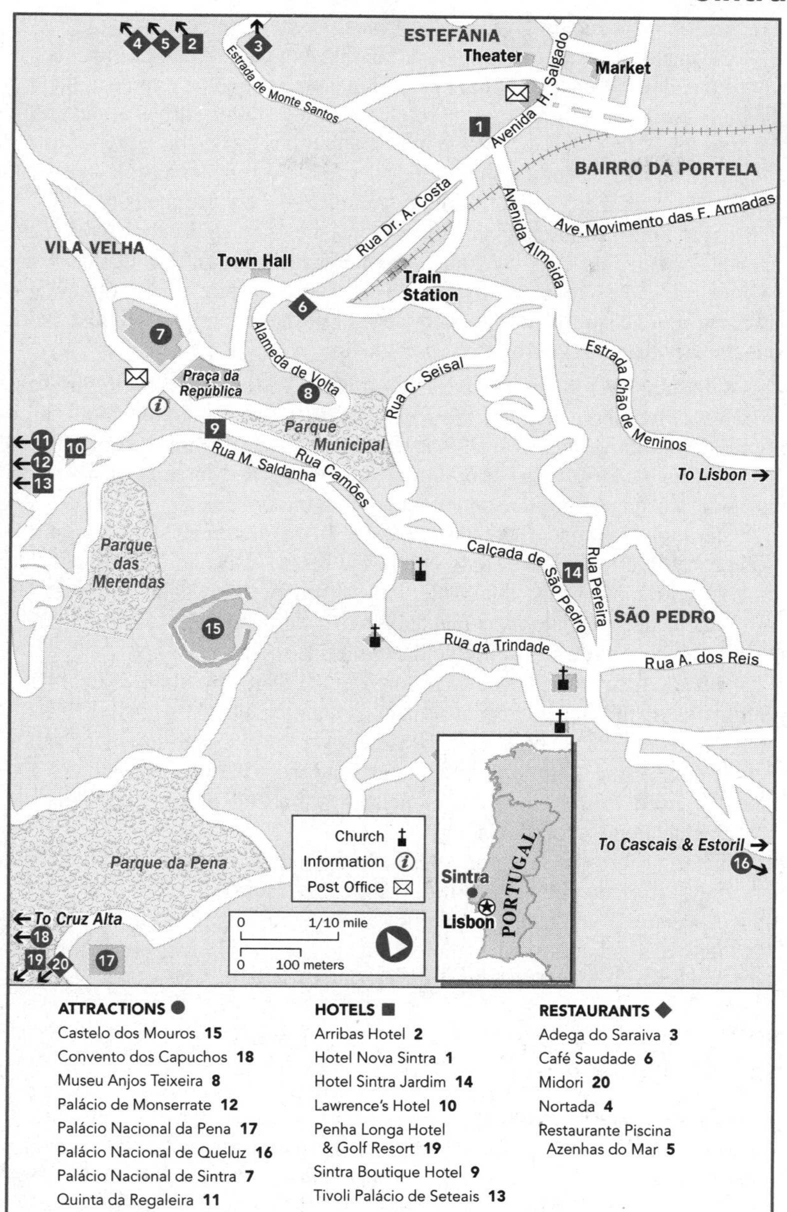

ATTRACTIONS ●
Castelo dos Mouros **15**
Convento dos Capuchos **18**
Museu Anjos Teixeira **8**
Palácio de Monserrate **12**
Palácio Nacional da Pena **17**
Palácio Nacional de Queluz **16**
Palácio Nacional de Sintra **7**
Quinta da Regaleira **11**

HOTELS ■
Arribas Hotel **2**
Hotel Nova Sintra **1**
Hotel Sintra Jardim **14**
Lawrence's Hotel **10**
Penha Longa Hotel & Golf Resort **19**
Sintra Boutique Hotel **9**
Tivoli Palácio de Seteais **13**

RESTAURANTS ◆
Adega do Saraiva **3**
Café Saudade **6**
Midori **20**
Nortada **4**
Restaurante Piscina Azenhas do Mar **5**

day, leaving the Vila Alda–Electric House at 10:20am, 12pm, and 4pm. Weekdays, you buy the 3€ tickets from the Vila Alda (✆ **96/133-03-91**), which has exhibitions about the trolleys. On weekends purchase on board.

A car makes it easier to get around the hills, but parking can be difficult. If your hotel doesn't have parking, one option is to leave your vehicle at the big **24-hour parking lot** next to the Portela de Sintra station. It has a maximum daily fee of 1.50€ and is a 2- to 4-minute train or bus trip to the center of town. If you leave your car in the street, don't leave any valuables visible—as with other areas with many tourists, thieves and pickpockets operate here.

Most of Sintra's museums and monuments are operated by the government agency **Parques de Sintra-Monte da Lua,** which has an excellent website (www.parquesdesintra.pt; ✆ **21/923-73-00**); you can buy tickets online at a discount. Purchasing joint tickets for several of the attractions will also work out cheaper than paying for each individually.

Castelo dos Mouros ★★ MONUMENT Vertigo sufferers might want to think twice about making the trip up to this Castle of the Moors, high (really high) above the town. It was constructed in the 8th and 9th centuries by Lisbon's Arab rulers as a mountaintop fortress and lookout post to give advance warning of invaders approaching by land or sea.

Excavations still underway have revealed Iron Age remains, showing there was probably a fort up here long before the Moors. Despite the impregnable look of its double walls, the castle was sacked by Norwegian crusaders in 1109 and 4 decades later was handed over to Portugal's first king, Afonso I Henriques, without a fight after he'd captured Lisbon.

The battlements were partially restored in the 1840s by Sintra-loving King Ferdinand II, turning them into today's romantic ruin. At 412m (1,352 ft.) above sea level, it's the best place for views over the city of Sintra in the valley below, Pena Palace on the opposite peak, and the Atlantic Ocean in the distance. Viewed from below, the crenelated silhouette of its 1,000-year-old battlements are an evocative sight.

You can visit **archaeological sites** to see remains of a **Muslim village** and a medieval Christian **burial ground.** Walking the ramparts can be tiring on the feet, especially if you hike up to the **Royal Tower** (which has the best views), but there is a cafeteria and visitor center to recover. If you are feeling fit, there's a 45-minute walking trail through the forest that will take you here from downtown Sintra.

Estrada da Pena. www.parquesdesintra.pt. ✆ **21/923-73-00.** 8€ adults, 5€ over 65s, youngsters 6–17, free under. Daily 9:30am–7pm. Bus 434.

Convento dos Capuchos ★★ RELIGIOUS SITE Deep in the forest, this strange 16th-century convent has a lost world feel. Franciscan monks carved it into the rocks where, for over 250 years, their little community lived an isolated, troglodyte existence in moss-covered, **cork-lined cells.**

King Felipe II of Spain, then the most powerful man in Europe, trekked up here in 1581 after adding Portugal to his conquests. He declared there were two places he esteemed most in his vast realm: the Escorial Monastery outside Madrid for its richness, and this place for its poverty. For many current visitors, it recalls the home of the Hobbits.

The place has its origins in a battle on the coast of India. After a 1546 victory over the Sultan of Gujarat, Portugal's fourth Viceroy of India, João de Castro, was in line for a gift from his king. "A rock and six trees" was all he wanted and this is what he got. As his dying wish he ordered the building of this monkish retreat on the land.

Over 7km (around 4½ miles) from Sintra and off the bus route, it's hard to reach without a car. But the warren of cells and passageways make for a fascinating visit. The monks lined the monastery walls with cork for insulation and used seashells to decorate. Among the points of interest are the **"door of death"** marked with skull and crossbones, a **church** decorated with colored stone, and the tiny nearby **cave** where a friar named Honório is said to have spent the last 30 years of his life (he lived to 100). The area around is rich in plant life and there are a number of **forest trails.** With luck, you'll spot one of the majestic Bonelli's eagles who glide over these hills searching for prey.

Estrada N247-3, Colares. www.parquesdesintra.pt. ✆ **21/923-73-00.** 7€, 5.50€ over 65s and youngsters 6–17. Daily 9:30am–7pm.

Museu Anjos Teixeira ★ MUSEUM Tucked away in a deep valley below the chimneys of Palácio da Vila, this tiny museum is dedicated to Pedro Augusto dos Anjos Teixeira, a sculptor little known outside his native Sintra (and Madeira island, where he lived for several years). His work in the neo-realist style popular in the mid-20th century features muscular fishing and farming folk, languid nudes, and a variety of animals in copper and plaster. There's a room dedicated to his father Artur Anjos Teixeira, also a sculptor. Pedro had his studio in this building, a former watermill.

Azinhaga da Sardinha. www.cm-sintra.pt. ✆ **21/923-88-27.** 1€, .50€ students; free under 17s and over 65s. Tues–Fri 10am–6pm; Sat–Sun noon–6pm.

Palácio de Monserrate ★★ PALACE "A scene from 1001 Nights, a fairytale vision," was how Hans Christian Andersen described this arabesque palace emerging from the Sintra forests. Like Quinta da Regaleira and Seteais Palace (see below) this is one of Sintra's great privately built homes.

It was raised in the 1860s by Francis Cook, a British merchant, on the site of an earlier palace that had once been home to Byron's fabulously wealthy, gothic novelist buddy William Beckford.

Like many Brits at the time, Cook was enthused by romantic conceptions of Portugal's Islamic past that inspired him to build this Oriental-style villa—with an interior that recalls Granada's Alhambra. He wasn't opposed to taking on other influences, bits of Beckford's neo-gothic pile survive, and the central red dome was modeled on the Renaissance Duomo in Florence.

After years of abandon, Monserrate was lovingly restored to its Moorish glory in the early 2000s, complete with stucco ceilings, alabaster fountains, and gilded columns. The palace is surrounded by a fabulous landscaped

park ★★★ filled with spooky statues, grottoes, ornamental ponds, and exotic vegetation, including giant ferns from New Zealand and a plantation of Mexican agave.

Rua Barbosa do Bocage. www.parquesdesintra.pt. ✆ **21/923-73-00.** 8€; 6.50€ youngsters 6–17, over 65s; free under 6s. Palace 9:30am–6:15pm; Park 9:30am–7pm. Bus: 435.

Palácio Nacional da Pena ★★★ PALACE This magical mountaintop castle is the most recognizable building in Sintra. Its peculiar silhouette of domes and towers can be seen for miles around, but close up it's even more eccentric with Moorish domes, pointed towers, crenelated turrets, Manueline arches, doorways defended by demonic statues. Everything comes in a candy-colored array of shades from shocking pink to brimstone yellow.

Comparisons are often made to the Neuschwanstein schloss in Bavaria, which inspired Disney's Cinderella castle, but Pena predates it by 30 years. Similarities, however, are not coincidental: both were built by German kings stirred by romantic 19th-century visions of the Middle Ages. Pena was a labor of love for Prince Ferdinand of Saxe-Coburg and Gotha-Koháry (1816–1885), who became king consort of Portugal after his marriage to Queen Maria II.

Ferdinand was captivated by the forested hills of Sintra and their medieval memories, so he built this extraordinary pastiche, mixing bits of just about every era in Portugal's architectural history. The inside provides a glimpse into the domestic life in the last years of the monarchy. It's packed with period furnishings and portraits. Standouts include the **kitchens,** the **noble hall** (later the royal billiard room), and the high-arched **reception room.** Remains of the 16th-century monastery that once stood here can be seen in the **church and cloisters.** There are touching reminders of King Carlos I, who was gunned down in 1908 by republican assassins. Paintings in many of the rooms show that the monarch was a talented artist. Be sure to walk the pathway around the **palace walls,** which offer immense views. "I know Italy, Sicily, Greece, and Egypt, and I've never seen anything as good as Pena," was the opinion of composer Richard Strauss (1864–1949). "It's the most beautiful thing I've ever seen."

The palace rests on a rocky outcrop surrounded by stunning **gardens** that range from formal French-style lawns and flowerbeds to thick forests filled with exotic flora brought from around the world. In a valley in the extreme west of the gardens, you can find an Alpine chalet with a romantic story. After the death of Queen Maria II, the widowed Ferdinand fell for American opera singer Elise Hensler (1836–1929). Defying social convention, they married. Elise was made a countess and they lived quietly in the **Chalet da Condessa d'Edla,** entertaining artists and cultivating their gardens. Visits to the restored chalet and the couple's gardens are included on the Pena entry ticket.

Estrada da Pena. www.parquesdesintra.pt. ✆ **21/910-53-40.** 14€; 13€ youngsters 6–17, over 65s; free under 6s (Park-only 7.50€; 6.50€ youngsters 6–17, over 65s). Palace 9:30am–6:15pm; park 9:30am–7pm. Bus 434.

TAKE THE high ROAD

If you've got wheels, the coastal road from Lisbon to Sintra via Cascais is a great drive, taking in some spectacular views and out-of-the-way sights.

Head west past **Belém** on the N6 road, popularly known as the Marginal. You'll soon have the broad mouth of the Tagus before you, with each curve revealing ocean vistas reaching across to the south shore at Costa da Caparica. The first of Lisbon's urban bathing beaches appears at **Caxias ★**, along with a string of defensive forts, culminating at the massive **São Julião de Barra ★** at Carcavelos. It still belongs to the army and is not open to visits.

After Estoril and Cascais, follow the signs to **Guincho** along the N247, where the road passes through exposed dunes and bare rock before starting to climb through forest hills after turning past Guincho beach. After the village of **Malveira da Serra,** you'll have wonderful views behind you toward Cascais. To enjoy the view without risking an accident, turn off to the right toward **Santuário da Peninha ★**, a pilgrimage spot since the Middle Ages, high over the coast with a splendid marble-lined chapel. Seafarers' families would come to pray to the Virgin Mary for the safety of loved ones at sea. Go back to the N247 until the turning for **Cabo da Roca ★★**. Here you stand at mainland Europe's westernmost point, a dramatic spot where the Sintra mountains meet the Atlantic in a series of soaring cliffs. A lighthouse stands 500 feet above the waves. "Where the land ends and the sea begins" says a plaque quoting 16th-century seafaring poet Luís de Camões. Walks along the clifftops can be blustery, so stay within the safety rails. A bit further along, the forest gives way to vineyards. At **Casal Santa Maria ★** you can visit a historic estate and sample the crisp white wines produced at Europe's most westerly vineyard (reservations required: www.casalstamaria.pt; **✆ 91/111-18-50**).

If you fancy a dip in the ocean or are feeling hungry, take a detour to **Praia da Adraga ★★**, a lovely beach hidden among the cliffs, with a simple but outstanding fish **restaurant ★★★** (www.restaurantedaadraga.com; **✆ 21/928-00-28;** closed Tues). Refreshed, head east toward the wine village of **Colares.** If you come at the weekends there will be a **farmer's market** selling local produce by the road in Almoçageme, near the turning for **Praia Grande** (another fine beach). After Colares, head up the valley and you'll soon be in Sintra.

Palácio Nacional de Queluz ★★★ PALACE This pleasure palace between Lisbon and Sintra was built in the middle 18th century as a summer residence for the royal family. Although now surrounded by highways and suburban sprawl, Portugal's "mini-Versailles" is a charm-soaked rococo gem. The exterior is a pastel confection in blue, yellow, and ochre, with white trim piped on like wedding cake icing. Inside you can wander through **Queen Maria I's Boudoir,** admiring the marquetry floors and painted panels of romping children; gasp at the gilded carvings in the **Royal Chapel;** and let your imagination run wild thinking of the sumptuous receptions once held in the mirror-lined **Hall of Ambassadors.** There are splendid colonial-inspired *azulejos* in the **Sala das Mangas.** The **King's Bedroom,** decorated with illustrations from *Don Quixote,* is where Pedro I, the emperor who led Brazil to independence, was born and died. It was all meticulously restored after fire ravaged the palace in the 1930s.

The government still uses it occasionally for state occasions and important guests, including U.S. Presidents Eisenhower, Carter, and Reagan, as well as Queen Elizabeth II of Great Britain, Prince Charles and Princess Diana, all of whom have spent a night or two among the tropical frescos, Flemish tapestries, and cabinets bulging with Chinese porcelain.

Especially lovely are the 16 hectares (40 acres) of **gardens** where blossoming mauve petunias and red geraniums highlight the topiary. Lakes, tile-line canals, and statues abound. Look out for the cages where the royals kept their menagerie of lions, tigers, and monkeys. The palace did not bring only happy memories for the monarchy however: In her later years Maria I was secreted away here to hide her insanity from the people of Lisbon.

There's a fine hotel, the **Pousada Palácio de Queluz,** located in an 18th-century annex with renowned restaurant **Cozinha Velha** in the old palace kitchens.

Largo Palácio de Queluz. www.parquesdesintra.pt. © **21/434-38-60.** 10€; 8.50€ youngsters 6–17, over 65s; free under 6s. Daily 9am–6pm. Train: Queluz-Belas. Bus: 101.

Palácio Nacional de Sintra ★★★ PALACE The outlandish Palácio da Pena may be better known, but this is Sintra's greatest historical treasure. An agreeably eclectic jumble of a building, the palace can trace its origins back over 1,000 years when the Muslim emirs of Lisbon had a residence here. It's better known locally as the *Palácio da Vila* (Town Palace) to distinguish it from the upstart royal abodes scattered around.

Grabbing everybody's attention as soon as they arrive in Sintra are the duo of champagne-bottle-shaped **chimneys** dominating the skyline. A glance at the ox-size spits in the hearths of the huge tile-lined royal **kitchen** explains why they needed those 33m (108-ft.) smokestacks.

Portugal's first king, Afonso I Henriques, moved into the palace after he conquered Lisbon in 1147. Over the following centuries, successive additions created today's architectural mishmash of styles from Moorish to Manueline, Gothic to Renaissance.

Behind the white facade, highlights include the ***Sala das Pegas*** (Magpie Room). Its multitude of black-and-white birds were painted on the ceiling on the order of King João I (1385–1483) to represent all the gossiping ladies at court after his English wife Philippa of Lancaster found him kissing one of them. The grand ***Sala dos Cisnes*** (Swan Room) where João held regal receptions was apparently decorated in honor of his brother-in-law King Henry IV of England. One of the grandest is the ***Sala dos Brasões,*** capped with a dome bearing the coats of arms of 72 noble families. The whole thing makes a fascinating tour through Portugal's history, from the courtyards full of Hispano-Moorish *azulejos* to the bedchamber where King Afonso VI was imprisoned for 9 years after being ousted by his brother, finally dying there in 1683.

Largo da Rainha Dona Amélia. www.parquesdesintra.pt. © **21/910-68-40.** 10€, 8.50€ over 65s, youngsters 6–17, free for under 6s. Daily 9:30am–6:30pm. Bus: 434, 435.

Quinta da Regaleira ★★ PALACE Among all the palatial homes peppering the Serra hills, none is more mystifying than this one. It was built in 1910 by António Carvalho Monteiro, a mining and coffee mogul known as "Millions Monteiro" for the fabulous wealth he built up in Brazil. Monteiro was something of a mystic, and together with Italian architect Luigi Manini he created this gothic tangle of towers, spires, and gargoyles filled with mysterious symbols linked to alchemy, magic, Templar knights, and secret societies.

It's surrounded by lush tropical gardens where paths uncover dramatic statues, grottoes, and fountains. Most bizarre of all is the **"Initiation well,"** a 90-foot pit with a staircase spiraling down into the bowels of the earth. The Quinta hosts regular concerts and theater productions (in keeping with the nature of the place, performances based on the works of Edgar Allan Poe have been particularly popular). They also organize guided tours after dark once a month between April and September, but tickets sell out fast.

Rua Barbosa do Bocage, 5. www.regaleira.pt. ✆ **21/910-66-50.** 8€, 5€ children 6–17, seniors 65–79, free under 6s and over 80s. Apr–Sept Daily 9:30am–7pm; Oct–Mar Daily 9:30am–5pm. Bus 435.

SHOPPING

History-rich Sintra has been a repository of salable Portuguese charm since the dawn of modern tourism. The narrow streets on the hillside across from Palácio da Vila (round Rua das Padarias) are traditionally the place to shop for souvenirs, but tourist traps have supplanted many of the old vendors of authentic linen and ceramics. Root around and you can still find original places. Try **Páteo de Titão** (✆ **91/406-53-53**) on Arco do Terreirinho for tiles, pottery, blankets, and other handicrafts; or **Pó de Arroz** (✆ **21/923-20-09**), for offbeat design and handicraft at 14 Rua Dr Alfredo da Costa.

Some of Sintra's best souvenirs are edible. The town is renowned for some time-honored pastry recipes. Best-known are the *queijadas de Sintra,* tiny baked cheesecakes spiced with cinnamon. There are a number of venerable producers, but one of the best is **Piriquita** (www.piriquita.pt; ✆ **21/923-06-26**) on Rua das Padarias, which has been serving them up (including to the royal family) since 1862. You can try them at the cafe, then grab some to go.

The **São Pedro** neighborhood has antiques shops and other independent stores, but is best on the second and fourth Sunday of every month, when it holds a centuries-old **street market** where you can buy handicrafts, clothes, antiques, and piping hot *pão com chouriço* (bread packed with slices of spicy sausage inside).

Farther afield, some of Portugal's best ceramics are made in the village of Abrunheira by **Viúva Lamego** (www.viuvalamego.com; ✆ **21/915-09-79**), a manufacturer since 1849. The outlet at its factory at 39 Rua Thilo Krassman is a less-pretty (but potentially less expensive) alternative to their historic Lisbon store (p. 127). On the other side of Sintra, there's a scattering of noteworthy stores in villages close to the coast. **Coisas da Terra** (www.coisasda terra.pt; ✆ **21/928-03-62**) is a beautiful space selling art, antiques, textiles, and other temptations at 31 Avenida Dr. Brandão de Vasconcelos in Almoçageme. In the pretty nearby village of Pé da Serra, you'll find **Flores do Cabo** (839 Estrada dos Capuchos; https://flores-do-cabo.business.site; ✆ **91/445-08-58**), a concept store selling everything from tribal rugs to organic wines.

Where to Stay

EXPENSIVE

Penha Longa Hotel & Golf Resort ★★★ You could quite happily live here for a fortnight without feeling any desire to step off the grounds. Choose between eight restaurants whose range of cuisines spans the globe. Two have Michelin stars. The spa rivals the restaurants in picking up awards: In 2019 the World Luxury Awards voted its Thai-inspired facilities the best in Southern Europe. The championship golf course is rated among Europe's finest, with the forested hills of Sintra as a backdrop. If you do get bored, there's a second 9-holer for variation. You can ride, walk the hills to discover traces of a medieval monastery and royal residence, and swim in the indoor or outdoor pools. Rooms are at least 50 square meters (540 sq. ft.) and stylishly laid out, with forest views and luxuries ranging from Bluetooth hi-fi connections to Asprey toiletries and Egyptian cotton linens. Did we mention it's a short drive from this forest hideaway to Sintra, Cascais, and Lisbon?

Estrada da Lagoa Azul, Linhó. www.penhalonga.com. ✆ **21/924-90-11.** 194 units. 169€–467€ double; 295€–1,512€ suite. Free parking. **Amenities:** Garden; terrace; golf; tennis; squash; bike hire; games room; indoor and outdoor pools; spa; fitness center; sauna; jacuzzi; hammam; 8 restaurants; 4 bars; babysitting; children's play area; free Wi-Fi.

Tivoli Palácio de Seteais ★★★ Seteais is simply sublime. If it weren't in the "Where to Stay" section, this 18th-century palace would be up there among Sintra's must-see sights. In an elegant neo-classical design, it was built as a residence for a Dutch ambassador in 1787. Lord Byron wrote poetry in the gardens when he was the guest of a flamboyant marquis who turned it into a party destination. In later years, Agatha Christie, Brad Pitt, and Mick Jagger have enjoyed its charms. The building is in two wings linked by a grand stone archway. The rooms and salons are designed in keeping with the period with chandeliers, heavy drapes, and 18th-century "Dona Maria" style furnishings, and there are wonderful gardens and views along the coast and up the hills to Pena. In the excellent restaurant are delightful original frescos by Jean-Baptiste Pillement. The bar specializes in local Colares wines. The Asian-style Anantara spa occupies an old dovecote.

Rua Barbosa do Bocage 8. www.tivolihotels.com. ✆ **21/923-32-00.** 30 units. 273€–499€ double. Free parking. **Amenities:** Garden; terrace; bike hire; tennis; outdoor pool; spa; massage services; restaurant; bar; babysitting; free Wi-Fi.

MODERATE

Arribas Hotel ★★ Okay, so you're not amid Sintra's historic charms; you're right on the golden sand of Praia Grande beach, lulled to sleep by the rolling surf, and where you can enjoy one of Europe's biggest and most dramatic saltwater swimming pools (open May–Sept). That pool is a huge attraction, 100m (328-ft.) long and right next to the beach (loungers close to the edge may get the occasional shower of refreshing sea spray). The clean white, mid-20th-century modern lines of the hotel curve around the pool in five tiered stories. It all feels very Bondi Beach. The rooms have Atlantic views and were all refurbished in 2017. Decor is functional and comfortable without winning too many style points. It's a scenic 25-minute drive into historic Sintra. Prices drop dramatically in winter when the pool is closed.

Av. Alfredo Coelho 28, Praia Grande. www.arribashotel.com. ✆ **21/928-90-50.** 58 units. 61€–212€ double. Free Parking. **Amenities:** Sun terrace; outdoor pool; games room; restaurant; bar; free Wi-Fi.

Lawrence's Hotel ★★ The oldest hotel in the Iberian Peninsula was opened by English innkeeper Jane Lawrence in 1764 when Sintra was already a draw for romantic travelers. Byron began work on his masterpiece *Childe Harold's Pilgrimage* here, and it features in the classic Portuguese romantic novel *The Maias*—in 1888 author José Maria de Eça de Queirós was already calling it "old Lawrence's." Not that it's dated. The four-story, pale yellow building has been regularly renovated. Rooms are airy and bright like a Victorian summer house, with wooden floors (terracotta in the bathrooms), floral fabrics, and marble fixtures. Some have four-poster beds, fireplaces and, of course, panoramic views. It's like staying in an upscale family home in the center of old Sintra. There's a fine restaurant (famed for partridge pie), cozy bar, and a pátio perfect for afternoon tea.

Rua Consigliéri Pedroso 38–40. www.lawrenceshotel.com. ✆ **21/910-55-00.** 16 units. 139€–194€ double; 192€–305€ suite. Limited parking nearby 20€ daily, reservation required. **Amenities:** Terrace; restaurant; bar; babysitting; free Wi-Fi.

Sintra Boutique Hotel ★ This relative newcomer may have the least original name around, but it enjoys a privileged location in a row of typical pastel-painted townhouses just a 2-minute walk from the main square. Rooms have a fairly standard modern design in soft shades of beige and cream, enlivened with some witty touches. Each is based on a theme relating to the town (e.g., 109 is inspired by the epic poem *Os Lusiadas* and features a leather-bound copy; 201 has an antique gramophone in honor of soprano Elise Hensler, who captured the heart of King Ferdinand). Some rooms look out onto the chimneys of *Palácio da Vila* or the green valley running through the town. Be sure to try the typical *travesseiro* and *queijada* pastries.

Rua Visconde de Monserrate, 40. www.sintraboutiquehotel.com. ✆ **21/924-41-77.** 18 units. 110€–183€ double; 201€–247€ suite. Free parking. **Amenities:** Restaurant; bar; exercise room; room service. Free Wi-Fi in some rooms and public areas.

INEXPENSIVE

Hotel Nova Sintra ★★ Don't be put off by the unimposing entrance in a row of shops. Up the stairs and off the street, this amiable 1875 villa is a haven in the Estefânia neighborhood: away from the tourist crush, but just a 15-minute stroll to the *Palácio da Vila*. In the same family for four generations, the canary-colored house has a pátio where you can soak up the sun or seek shade under low-hanging plane trees. The lounge and breakfast room are decorated with comfy leather armchairs, vintage radios, and black-and-white townscapes. They warn you the cheapest rooms are very small, but even they come with king-size beds and arched windows looking onto forest views. The best and biggest come with *azulejo* headboards and flower-bedecked private verandas.

Largo Afonso de Albuquerque 25. www.novasintra.com. ✆ **21/923-02-20**. 9 units. 78€–147€ double. Free street parking nearby. **Amenities:** Terrace; garden; bar; free Wi-Fi.

Hotel Sintra Jardim ★★ In the bucolic village of São Pedro, this rose-colored mid-19th-century stone house was commissioned as a summer home for a family of Lisbon blue-bloods. The parents of the current owners transformed it into a delightful guesthouse back in the 1940s. Gardens overflowing with greenery are the definition of peaceful, apart from the occasional splash from the pool over by the lawn. The rooms feature floral bedspreads and Victorian-style furnishings. Some of the decor and facilities are a bit dated, but this leafy oasis is a real bargain.

Travessa dos Avelares 12. www.hotelsintrajardim.pt. ✆ **21/923-07-38.** 15 units. 67€–102€ double. Free parking. **Amenities:** Garden; terrace; bike hire; games room; outdoor pool; bar; babysitting; free Wi-Fi.

Where to Eat

Adega do Saraiva ★ PORTUGUESE Head out to the village of Nafarros, a 15-minute drive northwest from Sintra, and get ready for a genuine Portuguese eating experience far from the tourist crowd. Be prepared to loosen your belt a notch or two. This is no frills eating. There's a cafe out front, then you squeeze down a back alley where customers stand in line and staff ferry trays laden with roast meat from the kitchens. The two simple dining rooms have paper table cloths and yellowing newspaper clippings lauding the place. Although they do fish dishes, notably chargrilled salt-cod with baked potatoes, it's the meat that draws the lunchtime crowds. The signature is roast lamb or kid, served in "big, medium, or small" portions (unless your name is Shrek, small is usually enough for two) and served with piles of roast potatoes and rice. It's usual to gulp down flagons of the house red and finish up with traditional Sintra cinnamon cheesecake.

Largo do Paquete, Nafarros. ✆ **21/929-01-06.** Mains 10€–18€. Mon–Sat 12:30–3:30pm, 7:30–10pm; Sun 12:30–3:30pm.

Café Saudade ★ CAFE Despite (or because of) its dependence on tourism, central Sintra doesn't have a lot of good dining options. Locals prefer to head into Lisbon, the coast, or villages around. This popular cafe is an exception, ideal for a pit stop on a long day of sightseeing. It has a hip flea-market decor and incredibly charming staff. It's the perfect spot for breakfast (try the "Saudade": condensed milk with two shots of espresso sided by a pastry), brunch, or a light lunch (salad with fresh cheese and canned sardines, or cured ham on local "saloio" bread). Not gourmet fare, but the delicious cakes are newly baked and salad ingredients fresh from the ground. There's a smart wine list too, making it the perfect place for a late-afternoon tipple. "Saudade" means a deep state of longing or nostalgia, something you may well feel after leaving this place.

Av. Miguel Bombarda, 6. ✆ **21/242-88-04.** Sandwiches and salads 3€–11€. Brunch 16€–19€. Thurs–Tues 8:30am–7pm.

Midori ★★★ JAPANESE/FUSION Some people might think that slapping a sliver of raw seabass on a ball of sticky rice is all you need to consummate a marriage between Portugal's Atlantic seafood and the gastronomic arts of Japan. Chef Pedro Almeida knows better. He's earned a Michelin star with his brilliantly creative blend of East and West. It's best to go for one of kaiseki fixed menus and put yourselves in the hands of the super-attentive staff as they bring you a parade of intricately assembled dishes like red mullet sashimi with butter sauce and miso; or nigiri of striped Algarve shrimp with finger lime. The name Midori means "green" and refers to the views over to the Sintra hills from the glass walls of the dining room. There's an exceptional wine list to match the masterpieces on the plates.

Penha Longa Golf & Resort Hotel, Estrada da Lagoa Azul. www.penhalonga.com. ✆ **21/924-90-11.** Reservations required. Mains 31€–134€; tasting menus 96€–263€. Tues–Sat 7:30–10:30pm.

Nortada ★★ PORTUGUESE/SEAFOOD This longtime favorite of ours sits high on the clifftop above Praia Grande. You can select your fish from the ice tray on the way in, then settle down on a terrace caressed by the sea air (the restaurant takes its name from the north wind that blows here in summer) and contemplate the rolling Atlantic as you wait. Take a whole bream or bass butterflied, grilled, and served with one of their signature sauces, like garlic and cilantro, or herbs and lemon; or go for a Brazilian-style *moqueca* of shrimp with coconut. Chilled Malvasia wine from the Casal Santa Maria vineyard just up the road will wash it down just nicely.

Av. Alfredo Coelho 8, Praia Grande. www.restaurantenortada.com. ✆ **21/929-15-16.** Reservations recommended. Mains 11€–29€. Wed–Mon noon–11pm.

Restaurante Piscina Azenhas do Mar ★★★ PORTUGUESE/SEAFOOD It's a challenge to find a more dramatically located restaurant. The stone-and-glass structure is carved into the foot of a cliff, with the hamlet of Azenhas do Mar stacked up behind it. There's a triangle of beach below, and the surf almost laps against the panoramic windows, while sunlight reflects on an oceanfront swimming pool. The food matches the setting. Seafood and grilled fish are among the freshest and best prepared in the region. Specialties include scarlet *carabineiro* shrimp with garlic and cilantro rice, or tuna steak with sweet-potato chips. Adventurous eaters should start out with a plate of *percebes* (goose barnacles) freshly pried from the cliffs. It's a 20-minute drive from central Sintra. Arrive in time for the glorious sunset.

Azenhas do Mar. www.azenhasdomar.com. ✆ **21/928-07-39.** Reservations recommended. Mains 18€–38€. Daily noon–10pm.

Sintra Entertainment & Nightlife

Sintra is blessed with an excellent cultural center, the **Centro Cultural Olga Cadaval** (www.ccolgacadaval.pt; ✆ **21/910-71-10**) on Praça Dr. Francisco Sá Carneiro, which has a diverse theater and music program. Together with the Queluz palace, it's one of the main venues for the **Festival de Sintra** (www.festivaldesintra.pt) which brings world-class classical music to the town every fall. Throughout the year, but particularly in summer, there are evening events in some of Sintra's iconic settings. In August, the **Splendor in the Grass** festival turns the lawns of Monserrate into a magical open-air cinema every night. The 2019 edition featured Hollywood classics from *Casablanca* to *Terminator*. Another summer festival is **Aura** (www.aurafestival.pt) in early August, which fills the night-time streets and gardens with spectacular light effects. Check with the Tourism Office (www.sintraromantica.net; ✆ **21/923-61-14**) to find out what's on when you're visiting.

Sintra isn't much of a party town in terms of bars and clubs. The best-known bar is the **Casa do Fauno** (www.casadofauno.wordpress.com; ✆ **91/484-49-23**), a medieval-themed pub with live music at 10pm on Saturdays. It's at Caminho dos Frades 1, a 20-minute walk out of downtown.

For an original night out, sign up for a **nocturnal walk.** There are various operators that guide groups under the moonlight on tours that range from spooky saunters to uncover history and legend (www.miguelboim.com), to nighttime nature trails up in the hills (www.trilhosnocturnos.com).

MAFRA ★★ & ERICEIRA ★

40km (25 miles) of Lisbon

The little town of Mafra has one real attraction, but it's a big one: The Royal Building of Mafra is a combination of convent, library, basilica, and palace covering 40,000 square meters (48,000 sq. yards), a massive monument to King João V and his Brazil-based riches. The royal hunting grounds (Tapada de Mafra) are now a nature reserve and can also be visited.

The area's other main attraction is the pretty fishing and surf center of Ericeira, 9km (6 miles) away, with excellent beaches and lively restaurants.

The rolling countryside around here is dotted with stubby white windmills on the hilltops and is famed for the *saloio* bread made from flour they used to grind. Sophisticated Lisbonites had a tradition of mocking the rustic folk from around here as simple-minded and gullible *saloios*.

Essentials

ARRIVING

BY TRAIN There are three direct trains a day making a direct trip from Lisbon's Santa Apolonia station to Mafra, taking about an hour. Lisbon-area **Viva Viagem** (p. 73) passes are valid on the trains, or you can buy a one-way ticket for 3.80€. Mafra station is a long way from the town, and the bus may be a better bet. There is no train to Ericeira. Info is at www.cp.pt.

BY BUS **Mafrense buses** (www.mafrense.pt) from both Sintra and Lisbon serve Mafra and Ericeira. At least one bus per hour leaves Lisbon's Campo Grande Station between around 6:30am until just before midnight. It takes about 1¼ hour to reach Mafra, stopping just in front of the palace, then continues another 30 minutes or so to Ericeira. There are faster trips that go direct to Ericeira, skipping Mafra and other intermediate stops. Tickets costs around 6€. From Sintra, there's one bus per hour. The trip takes 1 hour and costs around 4€ one-way.

BY CAR From Lisbon, the A8 and A21 highways should get you to Mafra in about 40 minutes, with another 10 minutes or so along the A21 getting you to the beaches at Ericeira.

VISITOR INFORMATION

Mafra City Hall (www.cm-mafra.pt) runs the tourist office at Avenida das Forças Armadas, 28 (✆ **26/181-71-70**), just next to the palace; daily 10am to 1pm and 2 to 6pm. The office in Ericeira is at Praça da República, 17 (✆ **26/186-31-22**). It's open daily (July–Aug 10am–8pm; June and Sept 10am–7pm; Oct–May 10am–6pm).

Exploring the Area

The Royal Building is definitely worth making an excursion out from Lisbon or Sintra, or a stopover if you are driving north. Beyond the palace-convent, there's not a great deal to see in Mafra, although the little town makes a pleasant stroll, and there are plenty of cafes laid out in the square in front. Beach bums will love Ericeira; the town has invested heavily in promoting itself as a laidback surfer destination. It has a lively, youthful buzz in summer and great seafood.

Aldeia-Museu José Franco ★ CURIOSITY This peculiar and rather wonderful place was the work of a village potter who in the 1940s started spending his spare time building and collecting stuff. José Franco's dream was to create a place where traditions of his region would be preserved and enjoyed for future generations. By the time he died in 2009 at age 89, Franco had assembled this hamlet composed of full-size and miniature buildings—typical homes, working wind- and water-mills, workshops, and much more. They are filled with agricultural implements, ceramics, and other rustic bric-a-brac covering 2,500 square meters (almost 3,000 sq. yards). You can snack on hot rolls stuffed with *chouriço* sausage from Franco's bakery, drink wine at his tavern, and marvel at the labors of a humble man who turned his dream into reality. Brazilian writer Jorge Amado would visit him whenever in Portugal. Popular with families—Franco also constructed a kids' play area in a mock castle.

N116, Sobreiro. www.cm-mafra.pt. ✆ **26/181-54-20.** Free. Summer 9:30am–7pm; winter 9:30am–6pm.

Real Edificio de Mafra ★★★ PALACE/RELIGIOUS BUILIDING This huge baroque structure, the brainchild of King João V (1707–1750) is so complex, nobody seems to know what to call it. It's known variously as the

Palace of Mafra, the Convent de Mafra, or the Basilica of Mafra. UNESCO seemed to solve the dilemma by calling it simply the Royal Building of Mafra (*Real Edifício de Mafra*) when it bestowed it with World Heritage status in 2019.

Seen from out front, the edifice is dominated by the white columns, towers, and dome of a soaring church in the baroque style then popular in Rome ("one of the most relevant sites of Italian baroque outside Italy," according to UNESCO). Extending for over 200 meters (over 650 ft.) on each side is the yellow-painted facade of the royal palace culminating in stubby, three-story towers where the king and queen lived. Behind, the quadrangular construction is completed by the convent designed to house 300 friars, and the great library.

The ensemble is a monument of extraordinary grandeur, "the materialization of absolute power," according to UNESCO. The numbers are staggering: An army of 45,000 workers was mobilized to build it over 13 years (an estimated 1,350 were killed in the construction); it holds 880 rooms covering a floor area the size of 5½ football fields; there are 4,500 doorways and windows. The private apartments of the king and queen are so far apart from one another that a trumpeter would alert her majesty when João was coming to call.

All this was made possible by a Brazilian gold rush that turned João V into one of the world's richest monarchs. Sparing no expense, he engaged artists and artisans from around Europe. The 92 church bells were founded in Antwerp (they still regularly ring and can be heard 24km [15 miles] away); marble was shipped from Carrera; paintings and sculptures ordered from Rome. German architect Johann Friedrich Ludwig was in charge of creating one of the grandest royal residences in Europe, which he capped with a 60m (200-ft.) white cupola.

Visitors take in the sumptuous royal apartments and palatial reception rooms laden with tapestries, swirling ceiling paintings, and antiques showing how generations of the ruling family lived—up to the day in 1910 when young King Manuel II spent his last night here before fleeing into exile from Ericeira after republican revolutionaries seized Lisbon. Convent visits are more austere, featuring the monks' cells, kitchen, refectory, and an eye-opening 18th-century infirmary. The barrel-vaulted church is cavernous, covered in multicolored local stone and dripping with baroque sculpture. However, the highlight is João's great collection of **36,000 leather-bound books,** one of the great libraries of Europe containing volumes dating back to the 15th century. *Baltasar and Blimunda,* one of the best novels by Nobel Prize–winning author José Saramago (1922–2010), is set against the backdrop of Mafra's construction and will give you a feel for the period.

Terreiro Dom João V. www.palaciomafra.gov.pt. ✆ **26/181-75-50.** 6€ adults, 3€ over 65s and students with ID, free for children under 15. Wed–Mon 9:30–4:45pm (the infirmary and religious art gallery close for lunch 12:45–2pm); the basilica has a separate entrance with free admission, daily 9:30am–12:45pm, 2–5:30pm.

Tapada de Mafra ★ PARK King João also ordered the creation of hunting grounds behind the palace where he and his offspring could chase deer and boar. There is evidence of their enthusiasm for this in the palace's macabre trophy room. Today, the walled 1,2000-hectare (3,000-acre) estate is a nature reserve open to the public. Lisbon families head out on weekends to see herds of red and fallow dear, plus the wild boar rooting around the forest of oak, pine, eucalyptus, etc. If you're lucky, smaller animals like the genet or Egyptian mongoose will make an appearance. Bird life is abundant. Unfortunately, they don't make visits easy. The entrance is a 10-minute drive from the palace, and there's a rather complex ticketing system, with options from walks along marked trails to a 10€, 2½-hour package including a tour in a little train that leaves twice a day at 10am and 15am, a falconry display, and a detailed explanation of the reserve's beekeeping activities.

Portão do Codeçal, N9-2. www.tapadademafra.pt. ✆ **26/181-42-40.** 4€. Daily 9:30am–5pm.

World Surf Reserve Ericeira ★★ BEACHES In 2011, Ericeira became the second place, after Malibu, to declare itself a World Surf Reserve (www.savethewaves.org) devoted to preserving the nature and surf culture of its beaches. It covers seven beaches running for 8km (5 miles) up the coast. What this means in practice is a little unclear, but Ericeira is definitely one of Europe's top spots for surfers, and its beautiful sandy beaches—less crowded than those around Cascais—are well worth a visit, whether you surf or just want to enjoy the sun and the ocean. Our favorite *praias* (beaches) include **Ribeira d`Ilhas,** which has a cafe and support structures for surfers including board and wetsuit hire; and **São Lourenço,** overlooked by the tasty Golfinho Azul restaurant. Ericeira itself is a pretty and lively whitewashed fishing port, with fine restaurants and a town beach sheltered from the waves.

Where to Stay

Casa Paço D'ilhas ★★ The nucleus of this delicious B&B is an 1869 country house lovingly restored by a pair of Belgian surf buddies who fell in love with the coast here. Digs include rooms in the main house and a series of rustic outbuildings. They range from small, hostel-style rooms with a shared bathroom to deluxe family apartments. All are awash in sunlight, with large windows, wooden ceilings, boho furnishings, and exotic knick-knacks. Our favorite is *Casa Privada,* an apartment with wood-paneled living space, three bedrooms, and a very cool bathroom. So much more than a surf shack, it offers a "holistic leisure experience." Within walking distance of great beaches and seafood restaurants, and a 10-minute drive from Ericeira, the B&B closes from mid-November to mid-March, although you can call to make exceptional bookings. They have minimum-stay requirement of 1 week in July through August and 2 nights in June and September.

Estrada da Junceira, Paço de Ilhas. www.casapacodilhas.com. ✆ **96/005-53-61.** 7 units. 50€–85€ double; apartments 120€–155€. Free Parking. **Amenities:** Garden; terrace; bike hire; surf equipment hire; barbeque; kitchen; 2 outdoor pool; yoga classes; surf school; bar; children's play area; free Wi-Fi.

Vila Galé Ericeira ★★ Overlooking the beaches and the waters of the Atlantic, this is the westernmost hotel in continental Europe, built right on the rocky shore. The five-story building was originally built as an escape for well-to-do Lisbon families in the 1950s. It's been undergoing a renovation but maintains the retro style that recalls seaside holidays of a bygone era. (Some may complain it's a bit old-fashioned.) Typically Portuguese glazed tiles have been used effectively. Bedrooms have quality dark-wood furnishings and beds, and perky striped curtains and comforters; over half enjoy an Atlantic view. In summer there are Friday evening "sunset parties" with music on the terrace.

Largo dos Navegantes. www.vilagale.pt. ✆ **26/186-99-00.** 202 units. 82€–258€ double. Limited free parking. **Amenities:** Garden; terrace; games room; 3 outdoor pools; spa; fitness center; sauna; hammam; Jacuzzi; massage service; restaurant; 2 bars; children's play area; free Wi-Fi.

Where to Eat

Esplanada Furnas ★★★ PORTUGUESE/SEAFOOD The formula is simple, but unbeatable: a glass-fronted wooden building on the surf-lashed rocks; super-fresh fish, charcoal-grilled, served with new vegetables drizzled with olive oil; chilled local white wine; expert service. This is the best in town and one of our regular haunts. The service is expert and the decor pleasingly nautical. You should book, especially at weekend lunchtimes. Prices below for main courses only refer to the three steak dishes—seafood is sold by weight, and you choose the fish you want from the ice tray. Prices may vary with the catch, but 49€ per kilo is par for noble white fish like turbot, gilt-head bream, or king fish. They'll also do fish baked in the oven or under a salt crust, if you're bored with grilled.

Rua das Furnas 2 www.m.restaurantefurnasericeira.com. ✆ **26/186-48-70.** Mains 16€–27€. Daily noon–4pm, 7–10pm.

Viveiros do Atlântico ★★ PORTUGUESE/SEAFOOD The road running through the village of Ribamar is lined with giant restaurants specializing in seafood. They do grilled fish, but shellfish is really the thing. In this one, up and running since the 1980s, you enter through an arch decorated with pebbles and seashells into a 120-seater round dining room looking out toward the Atlantic horizon. On the side in rows of tanks, critters still in their shells sit unsuspecting of your intentions toward them. Big brown crabs, spiny lobsters, oysters, razor clams, and up to six species of shrimp are just some of the mollusks and crustaceans on the menu. Have a mixture simply cooked in a *mariscada* or get them served up in an *arroz de marisco* (the soupy seafood rice dish from this coastline). It fills up with local families, especially for weekend lunches.

Estrada Nacional 247 31, Ribamar. www.viveiros-atlantico.com. ✆ **26/186-03-00.** Mains 12€–28€. June–Aug: Tues–Sun noon–11:30pm; Sept–May: Wed–Sun noon–11pm.

THE SETÚBAL PENINSULA & COMPORTA

8

The wedge of land immediately south of Lisbon was, until recently, little visited by international travelers. But it has some of Portugal's best beaches, fine scenery, pockets of fascinating heritage, and excellent vineyards. A pair of iconic bridges take highway and rail traffic across the broad Tagus estuary to the Setúbal Peninsula, and a flotilla of ferry boats zip back and forth across the river, carrying multitudes of commuters and a growing number of curious visitors.

The region's main city, **Setúbal ★★**, is a workaday seaport whose main attractions include one of the country's best fish markets, a magnificent Manueline church, and seafood restaurants scattered around its quayside and handsome main avenue. Head west out of Setúbal and you enter the **Parque Natural da Arrábida ★★★**, a protected natural area where hills covered in Mediterranean scrubland drop abruptly down to a necklace of white-sand crescent beaches with still, turquoise waters. It's one of the most beautiful landscapes in Portugal. On the northern slopes of the hill range, the villages of **Azeitão ★★** and the castle town of **Palmela ★** are centers of wine production, most notably of the sweet Moscatel variety.

Further west, **Sesimbra ★** has developed into a sought-after beach resort. In contrast to its summer crowds, you'll find solitude at the desolate **Cabo Espichel ★★** with its clifftop church and lighthouse. At **Praia do Meco ★★** you'll find the southern extremity of an unbroken strand of golden sand running for over 30km (20 miles) up the coast. To the south it's wild and popular with nudists. Continuing north, you reach **Costa da Caparica ★**, just across the river from Lisbon, a cheerfully developed urban beach backed by rows of big, bustling restaurants and much frequented by locals from the south-bank suburbs. In contrast, you'll find Portugal's chicest beaches just across the river Sado from Setúbal, where the **Península de Troia ★★** pokes a thin sandy finger into the water. At its base, the village of **Comporta ★★** has become hyper-fashionable. If you don't mind bumping into Madonna, Maria Sharapova, Carla Bruni, or other celebs on the beach (not to mention the mosquitos), the endless white sands are paradisiacal.

SETÚBAL ★★

45km (33 miles) SE of Lisbon

Setúbal is one of Portugal's most important seaports, sitting on the north bank of the river Sado just before its broad estuary reaches the Atlantic. Despite the boats passing in and out, the estuary waters are clean enough to bathe in and attract pods of dolphins hunting for seafood. They are a common sight for passengers on the ferry across to Troia.

The city has a pretty downtown with narrow streets and handsome early-20th-century houses radiating from its broad central boulevard, **Avenida Luísa Todi.** Fish dominates the local cuisine for reasons that become particularly apparent when you visit the fabulous covered market.

Legend has it the city was founded by the grandson of Noah. What's sure is that the Romans were active in a settlement called Cetóbriga, with remains of their fish-salting industry found around the banks of the Sado. It was captured by the Portuguese in 1217, ending centuries of Arab rule, and put up a fight against the takeover of the country by Spain's King Felipe II in 1580. The victorious Spanish monarch visited a couple of years later and showed the locals who was the boss by building the Castelo de São Filipe fortress, which still looms over the town.

Today Setúbal has around 120,000 residents. Its most famous sons are the romantic (and sometimes rather racy) poet Manuel Maria Barbosa du Bocage (1765–1808), whose statue stands atop a towering column in the grandest downtown square, and soccer coach José Mourinho (b. 1962) who played as goalie for the local club before winning hat-loads of championships, leading the likes of Real Madrid, Chelsea, and Inter Milan.

Essentials

ARRIVING

BY TRAIN The **Fertagus** (www.fertagus.pt) rail company runs trains every 30 minutes from Lisbon's Roma-Areeiro station across the Ponte do 25 de Abril (25th of April Bridge) to Setúbal. The trip takes just under an hour and costs 4.55€.

BY BUS Bus lines 561, 562, 563, 565, and 583 operated by the **TST** company (www.tsuldotejo.pt) run from Lisbon's Praça de Espanha to Setúbal, with departures once or twice an hour. The fastest is 561, taking just over 50 minutes. The **Rede Expressos** (www.rede-expressos.pt) inter-city bus company also has about 15 departures a day from Lisbon's Sete Rios station, taking 45 minutes and costing 6€.

BY CAR It should take about 40 minutes from Lisbon to Setúbal on the A6 highway over the April 25 Bridge. An alternative is the A12 over the equally

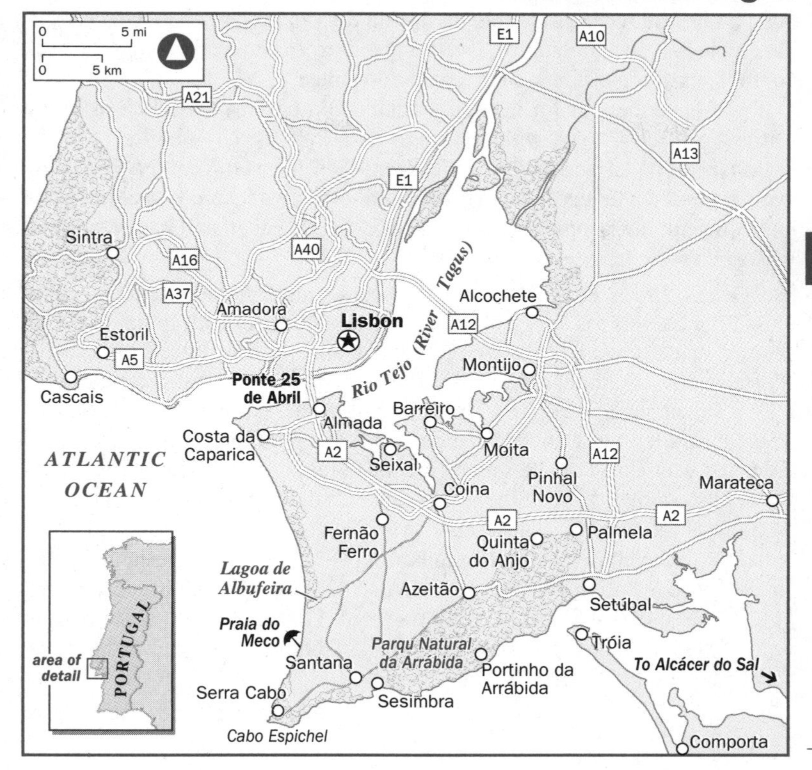

spectacular Vasco da Gama bridge, which is usually about 10 minutes slower coming from downtown, but is faster if you're coming from the north or east of Lisbon, or (as frequently happens) traffic is snarled. Both roads and bridges carry tolls.

VISITOR INFORMATION

Setúbal City Hall (www.mun-setubal.pt) opened an excellent visitor center, the **Casa da Baía (✆ 26/554-50-10)**, in a bright blue 18th-century building that long served as the city orphanage. It's packed full of information and exhibitions about the city, its beaches, and the natural charms of the Sado bay, and offers a cool cafe and store. It's on the main avenue and something of a tourist attraction in its own right.

Exploring Setúbal

Setúbal's downtown makes a pleasant, undemanding stroll. Start out on **Avenida Luisa Todi,** the main drag, which has a tree-lined walkway running down the center and is lined with attractive 18th-, 19th-, and early-20th-century buildings, many covered with *azulejos*. The old town runs off to the north in a series of narrow lanes, leading to **Praça Bocage,** with its monument to the poet; a fine 16th-century church, the **Igreja de São Julião;** and the arcades of the city hall. A recent initiative has promoted street art around the city: Check out the faux-*azulejo* facade in Praça Teófilo Braga.

If you have the legs for it, the 20-minute climb up to **Castelo São Filipe** fortress will reward you with amazing views over the city and the bay. The star-shaped citadel was built by the Spanish in the 16th century. For many years it housed a luxury hotel, but structural problems forced it to close. Now, you can walk the ramparts, visit an *azulejo*-lined chapel, and have a glass of *moscatel* on the terrace of a new bar.

Igreja de Jesús ★★ CHURCH Setúbal's most important monument is one of the earliest examples of Manueline architecture, built in the late-15th century, an early work by Diogo de Boitaca, one of the architects of Lisbon's Mosteiro dos Jerónimos. The ornate star-ribbed ceiling of the main chapel is a clear precursor of Jerónimos, embellished by the addition of 17th-century *azulejos*. Barley-twist columns, rope-like tracery, and decorative bosses all point the way ahead of the unique architectural style inspired by the Portuguese Discoveries. "One of the most beautiful small churches that I have ever seen," was the view of Hans Christian Andersen, who dropped by in 1866. Adjacent to the church is the city museum packed with art treasures, notably an altarpiece featuring 14 paintings by Jorge Afonso (1470–1540), the leading light of the so-called Setúbal Primitive school. The church and museum spent years closed for refurbishing work which was continuing as we went to press, despite a partial reopening in 2018.

Praça Miguel Bombarda. ✆ **26/553-78-90.** 2€. Free for children under 16 or adults over 65. Tues–Sat 9am–1pm and 1:30–5:30pm.

Mercado do Livramento ★★★ This is possibly the best produce market in mainland Portugal. While supermarket competition has reduced traditional markets in many cities to pale shadows of their former selves, Setúbal's citizens ensure theirs thrives, turning up daily to stock up on provisions within the *azulejo*-clad walls of its enormous hall. There are 132 stalls and 44 shops selling seasonal fruit and vegetables (local oranges and Palmela apples are famed), delicacies like creamy Azeitão ewe's cheese or cured meats from the Alentejo, but most spectacular is the fish section. There's a dumbfounding assortment of denizens of the deep freshly landed by the city's fleet. Amid noble tuna and exclusive oysters, look for the displays of Setúbal's favorite catch: the humble cuttlefish.

Av. Luísa Todi 163. ✆ **26/554-53-92.** Free. Tues–Sun 7am–2pm.

OUTDOOR ACTIVITIES

SPORTS The landscape around Setúbal has sprouted several golf courses. Among the highest-rated are two at the **Aroeira Clube de Golfe,** the biggest golf complex around here, with fairways set between avenues of pine near the cliffs at Fonte da Telha, and their sister club **Quinta do Perú** up near Azeitão (www.orizontegolf.com). Their splendid 72 par amid the dunes at **Troia Golf** (www.shotelscollection.com) is also ranked among the country's best, with a third hole that architect Robert Trent Jones, Sr. describes as one of the finest he's ever designed.

BOAT TRIPS Getting onto the still blue waters of the Sado is one of the great pleasures of Setúbal, where you can enjoy the scenery of Troia's sandbars and the Arrábida hills, with the added bonus of bumping into the bay's resident dolphin community. Reliable operators include **Vertigem Azul** (www.vertigemazul.com), which runs sunset wine cruises as well as dolphin cruises, and **Sado Emotion** (www.sadoemotion.pt), whose trips include drop-offs at remote beaches and nature tours to see flamingo colonies up river.

WALKING The countryside around Setúbal has some great hiking trails, either up into the hills or along the banks of the Sado. Some of the best are around the **Molina da Mourisca** (✆ **26/578-30-90**), a restored tide mill in a nature reserve up the river. Check with the Casa da Baía visitor center for maps and details.

SHOPPING

Setúbal's downtown (Baixa) is relatively untouched by tourism, and many individual and traditional stores endure in its narrow streets. The city's best-known product is wine (see p. 182). The surrounding countryside produces excellent reds, whites, rosés, and sweet *moscatel* varieties. There's a wide and excellent choice at **Mercado do Vinho** (✆ **96/950-37-47**), at Avenida Luisa Todi, 115. For the uninitiated, they do a taster pack featuring tubes of three different *moscatels*. A special place to pick up local products is the **Mercearia Confiança** in the old fisherman's neighborhood of Troino (Praça Machado dos Santos; ✆ **91/358-88-87**), where the owner has preserved the family grocer's store from 1926 as a place where clients can pick up vintage Portuguese products, from soaps to chocolate, and enjoy a coffee or toasted sandwich with Azeitão cheese. Nearby at 34 Rua Vasco da Gama, **Pedaços de Mar** (✆ **26/553-30-19**) specializes in handicrafts constructed with flotsam, from driftwood sculptures to seashell jewelry. Just behind City Hall, at Rua dos Almocreves 82, **Rota dos Saberes e Sabores** retails original ceramics and other handicrafts (earrings made from miniature *azulejos* are a bestseller) in a space that also includes a cafe and homemade pastries. Farther afield, **Fortuna** (✆ **21/287-10-68**) is a ceramics factory and school in the village of **Quinta do Anjo,** northeast of Setúbal.

Where to Stay

MODERATE

RM Guest House ★★ Taking fashionable to a whole new level, this downtown guesthouse themes all its rooms on icons of haute couture. So you can stay in a room dedicated to designer Roberto Cavalli, with exotic prints and a black leather headboard, or the Angels room inspired by Victoria's

Secret. The rooms are small, but impeccably stylish, and feature LCD TVs; Molton Brown toiletries; and cotton sheets, towels, and robes by Lameirinho of Portugal. It's located on Setúbal's leafy central boulevard, and many of the rooms have iron balconies overlooking it. A short walk takes you to the Livramento market and the waterfront.

Avenida Luisa Todi 59. www.rmguesthouse.pt. ✆ **26/540-01-19.** 7 units. 100€–175€ double. **Amenities:** Free bikes; bar; babysitting; free Wi-Fi.

INEXPENSIVE

Hotel do Sado Business & Nature ★ This hilltop mansion offers a restaurant and roof terrace and many of its rooms enjoy big-time views over the city, hills, and bay. It promotes itself as Portugal's first allergy-friendly hotel, with special rooms for guests with respiratory allergies, and gluten- and lactose-free menus. It also has rooms adapted for travelers with disabilities and families. Room decor is comfortable if unexciting, with drapes and throws in warm colors and stone features in the bathrooms.

Rua Irene Lisboa 1. www.hoteldosado.com. ✆ **26/554-28-00.** 66 units. 70€–120€ double. Free parking. **Amenities:** Garden; terrace; bike hire; games room; massage services; restaurant; bar; babysitting; free Wi-Fi.

Where to Eat

Museu do Choco ★ PORTUGUESE/SEAFOOD Cuttlefish thrive in the waters of Setúbal's bay. They are the favorite food both of the people of the city and the dolphins who hunt offshore. The name of this swish place on the main avenue translates to the "museum of cuttlefish" and, although it serves the rubbery creatures in a variety of ways (and even some other fish and meat), what draws the crowds is the city's signature dish *choco frito*—strips of deep-fried cuttlefish served with fries and a pot of mayo. There are joints serving this dish around the city, but this is one of the best, with the fish (actually it's a mollusk) tender and lightly breaded. There is an actual "museum" section within the restaurant, displaying photos and some of the frightening-looking tackle used by Sado fishing folk.

Avenue Luísa Todi 49. www.museudochoco.pt. ✆ **93/736-00-61.** Mains 9€–16€. Daily noon–11pm.

O Miguel ★★ PORTUGUESE/SEAFOOD Just across from the fishing harbor, this city institution serves up traditional dishes with an emphasis on fresh seafood in a sophisticated setting decorated with stone walls, wine bottles, and maritime motifs. It's very popular for dishes like grouper broth with clams, or fried turbot with razor-clam rice. It also has an interesting range of nibbles to start your meal, like fried skate or marinated sardines. Its special take on Setúbal favorite *choco frito* features a plate-size cuttlefish fried whole, rather than sliced into strips.

Avenida José Mourinho, 16. www.restauranteomiguel.pt. ✆ **26/557-33-32.** Mains 10€–18€. Daily noon-11pm.

BEACHES & mountains

Head west out of Setúbal and you are immediately surrounded by a marvel of nature. The **Parque Natural da Arrábida ★★★** is a natural reserve covering 108 square kilometers (42 sq. miles) of smooth hills running parallel to the coast. It possesses a Mediterranean microclimate and is covered in scrubland with over 1,000 species of plant. Springtime is a floral explosion. Peaks ascend to almost 500m (1,650 ft.) providing marvelous vistas across the bay to the white sands of Tróia and Comporta. James Bond fans may recognize the scenic road from the dramatic final scenes of *On Her Majesty's Secret Service*. What attracts most visitors are the beaches. As the hills drop to the sea, they meet a chain of coves combining new moons of pale sand and clear still waters. Among them, **Portinho da Arrábida ★★★** is the best-known, a symphony in blue, green, and white; **Galapinhos ★★★** has been voted the most beautiful in Europe; **Albarquel ★★** is within walking distance of the city. They get very crowded at peak times, leading City Hall to ban traffic from June 15 to September 15 on the narrow coast road. There are buses instead. Adding to all the natural beauty is the 16th-century convent **Convento da Arrábida ★★**, a cluster of white walls and terracotta roofs set on the green hillside. Visits are by appointment only (www.foriente.pt; ✆ **21/219-76-20**). Although the landscape is now protected, it was disfigured by a cement factory built in 1904 and still functioning. It's a shock when you drive past, but not noticeable on the beaches or up in the hills.

Setúbal Entertainment & Nightlife

The **Fórum Municipal Luísa Todi** (www.forumluisatodi.pt; ✆ **26/552-21-27;** Avenida Luísa Todi, 61-67) is the main cultural hub, a 1960s auditorium named, like the avenue, for a local girl who became an operatic superstar in the 1700s, wowing the crowned heads of Europe with her arias. Its shows range from classical to jazz and fado, a well as classic cinema nights. Another cherished institution is the **Cinema Charlot** (www.medeiafilmes.com; ✆ **26/552-24-46;** Travessa das Pedras Negras, 1-5), an independent movie house showing the latest blockbusters and obscure arthouse flicks.

Among the bars, **Moscatel de Setúbal Experience** (Largo do Bocage, 49) turned a historic cafe into a place to discover the city's renowned tipple while watching the world go by on Praça de Bocage. Jazz fans should head to **Jazzmine** (✆ **26/511-79-50;** open Fri–Sat 6pm–1am, and Thurs 'til 11pm, at Coronel Guilherme Portugal 17). The best-known dance club is **Absurdo** (www.barabsurdo.com; ✆ **91/983-89-78;** Av. José Mourinho, 24). In summer, Setúbal's nightlife heads to the beach, with sunset parties and late-night DJ sets. Praia de Albarquel gets particularly lively. The biggest party takes place in late July/early August with the 16-day **Feira de Sant'Iago** (www.feiradesantiago.pt), a centuries-old fair with bands, DJs, and a fun fair, as well as handicraft and food markets.

AZEITÃO ★

14km (8 miles) W of Setúbal; 30km (19 miles) S of Lisbon

Azeitão is the collective name for a cluster of bucolic villages in the heart of Setúbal's wine country. In among Vila Fresca de Azeitão, Vila Nogueira de Azeitão, Brejos de Azeitão, and Vendas de Azeitão is a sprinkling of *quintas* (estates) producing some excellent wine (www.vinhosdapeninsuladesetubal.org). The region is particularly renowned for its whites, but there are some fine red, rosé, and sparking varieties. However, the jewel in their intoxicating crown are the *moscatéis*. Like Port and Madeira, these are sweet wines fortified with brandy and served generally as an aperitif or to accompany dessert (they go down great with chocolate).

Vila Nogueira is the biggest of the Azeitão villages. It's traditional white houses are strung out along one long road lined with shops and cafes where you can buy wine, but also sample the area's other specialties: *queijo de Azeitão,* a buttery sheep-milk cheese that uses thistles grown in the hills to coagulate the milk in an ancient dairy technique; and *torta de Azeitão,* a sponge cake with a meltingly good yolk-and-cinnamon filling. At **Casa dos Tortas** ★ you can try them in a retro store/cafe dating back to 1910, alongside a glass of moscatel (Praça da República 37; ✆ **96/914-69-96;** closed Mon).

In Vila Fresca de Azeitão is one of the region's best ceramics workshops: **São Simão Arte** ★ (www.saosimaoarte.com; ✆ **21/218-31-35**). A visit will allow you to see (and buy) *azulejos* produced by local artisans. In nearby Palmela, be sure to visit the **castle** ★★, now partially a luxury hotel but still open for free visits (see p. 183).

Essentials

ARRIVING

BY BUS TST buses 554 and 755 between Lisbon's Praça de Espanha and Setúbal stop in Vila Fresca and Vila Nogueira. They take about 50 minutes from the capital, 20 minutes from Setúbal. From Setúbal, the 230, 770, and 783 also run to Azeitão.

BY CAR If you really want to explore the vineyards, a car will make things much easier. From Lisbon, take the A6 highway over April 25 Bridge, then leave at exit 2 to take the N10 to Azeitão. It should take about 40 minutes if traffic is fluid. From Setúbal, it's an attractive 20-minute drive through the hills on the N10.

VISITOR INFORMATION

There's a tourist office in Vila Nogueira de Azeitão: Praça da República 47 (✆ **21/218-07-29**).

Quinta Visits

There are several *quintas* open to visitors up among the vine-covered hills. A good place to start is the **Casa Mãe da Rota de Vinhos** ★ (www.rotavinhospsetubal.com; ✆ **21/233-43-98**), located in the main square of Palmela. It has maps showing routes linking the estates as well as a shop where you can buy the complete range of local wines, taste a few, and try local treats.

José Maria da Fonseca ★ WINERY This is one of Portugal's biggest wine producers and a family brand since the 1830s. The facade of its winery, decorated with colored tiles, dominates the high street in Vila Nogueira. A tour will take in the 19th-century family mansion, the winery, and cellars filled with oak barrels, where some of their oldest *moscatéis* have been maturing for over 100 years. At the end you can sample a selection, make some purchases in the atmospheric store, or grab a glass and a meal in their wine bar: By The Wine (they have another with the same name in Lisbon on Rua das Flores).

Rua José Augusto Coelho 11, Vila Nogueira de Azeitão. www.jmf.pt. ✆ **21/219-89-40.** 5€. Apr–Oct: daily 10am–noon, 2:30–5:30pm; Nov–Mar: daily 10am–noon, 2:30–4:30pm. Booking recommended.

Quinta da Bacalhôa ★★★ PALACE/WINERY Undoubtedly the grandest of the region's *quintas* and one of the great country houses of Portugal, the Tuscany-inspired architecture of this early 16th-century house was a pioneer of Renaissance styles. Aristocratic owners included the family of Afonso de Albuquerque, Portugal's first viceroy of India. His son laid out the classical gardens. The building and the grounds are stunning with arcaded terraces, elaborate topiary, reflecting pools, and one of the best displays of *azulejos*. Two Americans played key roles in the estate's development: Orlena Scoville, who acquired the place in the 1930s and oversaw its restoration; and her grandson Thomas Scoville, whose development of Bordeaux-inspired red wines in the 1970s marked a turning point in the modernization of the industry. The estate is now part of the empire of Madeiran millionaire Joe Berardo (p. 315). Excerpts from his extensive art collection (including contemporary Asian sculpture, medieval ceramics and Art Nouveau objects) are on show in the house, gardens, and winery/museum (which can be visited separately from the palace). The winery store opens daily 10am to 6:30pm.

Winery/Museum: Estrada Nacional 10, Vila Nogueira de Azeitão. www.bacalhoa.pt. ✆ **21/219-80-60.** 3€. Guided tour only: daily 10:30, 11:30am, 2:30, 3:30, 4:30pm. Palace: ✆ **21/218-00-11.** 8€. Guided tour only: Mon–Sat 10am, 3pm. Booking recommended. Combined ticket for both 10€.

Where to Stay

Pousada Castelo Palmela ★★ This extraordinary hotel is set in a medieval castle perched on a rocky crag 230m (755 ft.) above a plain stretching across to Lisbon. It can be clearly seen from the capital over 40 kilometers (25 miles) away. The strategic position made the castle a key part of the Portuguese defensive line after they captured it from the Moors in the 12th century, and in 1482 it became headquarters of the Order of Santiago. The cells of the monkish knights have been enlarged so rooms are at least 22 square meters (237 sq. ft). They're furnished in classic style with plaid throws, *azulejo*-clad bathrooms, and clay-tiled floors. Breakfast in the old cloisters, looking on to the orange trees in the patio, are excellent, but dining in the monks' refectory can be a bit gloomy, if historic. It goes without saying that the views are extraordinary: either south to the sea, or west toward the lights of Lisbon.

Avenida dos Cavaleiros de Santiago e Espada, Palmela. www.pousadas.pt. ✆ **21/235-12-26.** 28 units. 99€–199€ double; 189€–259€ suite. Free parking. **Amenities:** Garden; terrace; restaurant; bar; free Wi-Fi.

Where to Eat

Pérola da Serra ★ PORTUGUESE Since its founding in 1965, this no-frills roadside eatery up on a hillside between Palmela and Azeitão has built a dedicated following with its solid home cooking. It's well off the beaten track, and the cooking makes few concessions to modish tastes. The reputation of this "pearl of the mountains" is based on chargrilled fish and meat and its *tachinhos* (little pans" featuring stews like chickpeas with seafood) or *caldeirada* (a rich mixed fish stew with peppers and potatoes). Run by the Rodrigues family for three generations with "every client is a friend" as its motto, it's a bustling, happy, noisy place, particularly at lunch times.

Rua Dr. Bernardo Botelho 46, Palmela. www.peroladaserra.pt. ✆ **21/235-02-40.** Mains 10€–18€; Wed–Mon noon–3pm, 7–10pm.

SESIMBRA ★

40km (22 miles) S of Lisbon; 25km (15 miles) W of Setúbal

Set on a curving bay near the southwestern tip of the Setúbal peninsula, Sesimbra benefits from a beautiful location. It has calm, crystalline bathing waters, a fishing tradition ensuring great seafood, and an appealing old quarter below a Moorish castle. Still, recent rapid construction on the slopes of its narrow valley can make the little town seem a bit claustrophobic, especially in summer when crowds pack the town-center beaches.

It's most attractive features are out of town; beaches can be wild and windswept on the west coast, or sheltered South Sea Island lookalikes on the south. Between them, the remote headland of Cabo Espichel is certainly worth a detour.

Essentials

ARRIVING

BY BUS TST buses 207 and 260 take about an hour to reach Sesimbra from Lisbon's Praça de Espanha. There's roughly one bus an hour. Bus 230 takes about the same time to arrive from Setúbal. The rides costs around 4€.

BY CAR From Lisbon, cross the Ponte do 25 de Abril bridge and continue on the A2 highway. Take exit 2 and follow the N378 into Sesimbra. It should take about 1 hour. From Setúbal, the drive is about 40 minutes via the N10 to Azeitão, then the N379. The road down into Sesimbra gets very busy in summer, and parking can be a challenge.

VISITOR INFORMATION

The **tourist office** is in the harborside Fortaleza de Santiago fort (Rua da Fortaleza; www.visitsesimbra.pt; © **21/228-85-40**). June to mid-September, open daily 9:30am to 11:30pm; late-September 9:30am to 8pm; and October to June 9:30am to 6:30pm. There's also a post at Cabo Espichel (© **21/228-85-40**) open only in summer 11am to 5pm.

Exploring Sesimbra

Sesimbra sits in valley tapering down to a picturesque **harbor ★**, surrounded by green hills. Its bay is fronted by two sandy beaches, **Praia do Ouro** and **Praia da Califórnia.** It's an important fishing port, and during the summer you can watch fishermen using the ancient technique of ***arte xávega* ★**, hauling nets onto the beach by hand. Onlookers are welcome to help out. It happens June to September on Thursdays, 7pm on Praia da Califórnia.

To find out more about Sesimbra's intimate relationship with the ocean, visit the little **Maritime Museum ★** (© **93/842-74-79;** closed Mon) in the beautifully restored **Fortaleza de Santiago ★**, a 17th-century fort right on the beach that also contains an open-air cafe specializing in local craft beer. The fortifications around town bear witness to a bellicose past: In 1601 the bay witnessed a major battle between English ships sent by Queen Elizabeth I and a fleet of Spanish galleys.

High above the city is the much older **Castelo de Sesimbra ★** (© **21/268-07-46**). Built by the Moors in the 9th-century, the castle was captured by Portugal in 1199 after several battles. Visiting its long battlements, medieval chapel, and five towers is free and gives amazing ocean views, but can be hard on the calves. You'll also need strong legs to walk to lovely **Praia da Ribeira do Cavalo ★★**; surrounded by cliffs, blessed with white sand and transparent water, this beach earns Caribbean comparisons (the chill Atlantic will quickly dispel those illusions when you dip your toes). Its reachable by a 3km trail, or you can hire a kayak or boat in Sesimbra (www.ludyesfera.com; © **91/785-28-35**).

Drive 16km (10 miles) farther west to the headland of **Cabo Espichel ★★**, a remote and mystical place that has had religious appeal since pagan times. Christians started trekking out to this desolate edge-of-the-world spot after the *Reconquista* to pay homage to the Virgin Mary. In the 18th century, a striking baroque church was built on the clifftop along with rows of rooms for pilgrims' lodgings. Look out for the strange, pointy-roofed chapel containing blue-and-white 18th-century tiles. There's also a lighthouse built in 1790. Signs point out dinosaur footsteps imprinted on the rocks. If you don't have a car, the 201 bus from Sesimbra sometimes runs to the cape, but check with the driver, because sometimes they stop at the village of Azóia an hour's walk away (and check that there's a bus back).

North of Espichel there are more fabulous beaches. **Praia do Meco ★★** is part of a strip of unbroken sand stretching for about 6km (4 miles). It's popular with nudists in more remote areas. Take care with bathing; the waves can be wild and currents tricky even in the shallows. Follow the lifeguards' instructions and only swim when they fly the green flag. For calmer swimming, head further up the coast to **Lagoa de Albufeira ★★**, a calm lagoon backed by gentle dunes.

OUTDOOR ACTIVITIES Sesimbra's clear waters have made it a major **diving** center. A number of operators offer underwater excursions and lessons, including **Dive Club Cipreia** (www.diveclubcipreia.com; ✆ **21/595-99-76**) and **Haliotis** (www.haliotis.pt; ✆ **91/058-61-32**). The biodiversity around an artificial reef formed by a freighter that sunk in 1989 off Espichel is a particular draw. **Fishing** off the coast is also popular: try **Bolhas Tours** (www.bolhastours.com; ✆ **91/065-85-55**).

SHOPPING There's a colorful **food market** at Rua da República 10 (Tues–Sun 7am–2pm) where venders display fruit, fish, cheese, and other goodies. A good place to pick up local Azóia cheese and other produce is the weekend farmers' market at the **Moagem de Sampaio** (✆ **21/228-82-06**), a flourmill-turned-museum in the hamlet of Sampaio. The tourist board runs a store, **Loja Yes Sesimbra** in Fortaleza de Santiago, selling branded souvenirs including tins of locally caught fish.

Where to Stay

Quinta do Miguel Okay, so you have to share the 12,000 square meter (3-acre) gardens with the owners' pet peacocks as you head out to the pool or hot tub. Apart from that, this is the place for solitude. In contrast to the big resort hotels and summer crowds in Sesimbra, you'll find a quiet country estate with villas, studios, and a loft decorated in a less-is-more, rustic-chic style. The espresso machine, hi-fi, and a couple of raw-wood furniture pieces are all that disturbs the whiteness of the studio room. There are more colors and subtle use of marble, driftwood, and other natural materials in the other lodgings. At a 20-minute walk to the waves at Praia do Meco and a 20-minute drive to Sesimbra, book early—it sells out fast.

Rua do Casalinho, Aldeia do Meco. www.quintadomiguel.com. ✆ **91/947-61-29.** 7 units. 150€–210€ double. Free parking. **Amenities:** Garden; outdoor pool; Jacuzzi; free Wi-Fi.

SANA Sesimbra Hotel ★★★ Slap in the center of town on the palm-lined beach promenade, this cool, white, Art Deco–inspired seven-story hotel has the best location in town. The lobby is lined with natural wood, stone, and traditional paving. Rush to the sky lounge gazing down on to the beach, bay, and city rooftops. While you're there, enjoy the hot tub, pool (heated and covered in winter), and bar. Top-quality mattresses and bedding will ensure you'll slumber soundly, lulled by the waves (try get a room that faces the sands or a suite with curved private balcony). While awake, you'll enjoy the nautical slant of the decor (lots of navy-and-white stripes and photos of seagulls), the bathroom featuring local breccia stone, and the fruit-heavy breakfast in the beach-level restaurant. They organize excursions in a traditional sailing boat.

Avenida 25 de Abril. www.sesimbra.sanahotels.com. ✆ **21/228-90-00.** 100 units. 82€–237€ double; 139€–273€ suite. Parking 12€ daily. **Amenities:** Restaurant; 2 bars; terrace; indoor and outdoor pools; terrace; bike hire; fitness center; sauna, Jacuzzi, hammam; massage service; babysitting; free Wi-Fi.

Where to Eat

Bar do Peixe ★★ PORTUGUESE/SEAFOOD The name means "Fish Bar" and although they'll slap a steak on the barbeque if you're so inclined, fish is the big deal at this beach bar on the white sands at Meco (the nudist beach is just next door, but customers will be wearing trunks and bikinis, at least, on the deck or glass-fronted dining room). The chef picks up fish daily from Sesimbra market, and you can choose what you want from the ice box and pay by weight. Prices range from 45€ per kilo for white sea bream to 68€ per kilo for red emperor bream—allow for 300g–500g per person. Summer Sundays they have sunset parties with live music or chilled DJ sets.

Praia do Meco (Moinho da Baixo). www.bardopeixe.pt. ✆ **96/728-21-17.** Mains 16€–180€. Mon, Wed, Thurs 11am–7pm; Fri–Sun 11am–9pm.

Restaurante Ribamar ★★ PORTUGUESE/SEAFOOD The people of Sesimbra boast about the special conditions of the water where the Sado mixes with the cold Atlantic, and the ancestral techniques of their fishermen ensure they serve the best fish in the world. Offering evidence in favor of that argument are several excellent downtown restaurants. This beachfront place run by the Chagas family since 1950 is our favorite. Their "rich soup" (*sopa rica*) of seafood flavored with saffron (at 40€ for two) is a regular winner at the annual fish festival in Lisbon. Other standouts include swordfish and grilled black-scabbard fish, two species regularly caught in the deep waters off Cape Espichel.

Av. dos Náufragos 29. www.restauranteribamar.pt. ✆ **21/223-48-53.** Reservations recommended. Mains 9€–20€. Daily noon–4pm, 7–11pm.

COSTA DA CAPARICA & SOUTH BANK TAGUS ★

10m (16 miles) SW of Lisbon

Costa da Caparica is to Lisbon what Rockaway Beach is to New York City, a big, busy urban beach town, popular with surfers, and families from the nearby high-rise neighborhoods. There's golden sand and a popular boardwalk backed by cheap-and-cheerful food joints: Just expect grilled sardines and dishes of tiny snails (delicious with icy beer) instead of tacos and lobster rolls.

As you move down the coast south from the town of Costa da Caparica, the beach gets less crowded and less urban. It also goes through a series of character changes as different strips are preferred by a youthful party crowd, families with kids, gay men, foodies, nudists, surfers, and seekers of solitude, before it reaches the Lagoa da Albufeira lagoon 16km (10 miles) to the south.

Along the south bank of the Tagus inland there are a series of dormitory suburbs that face Lisbon across the river. They are short on A-list attractions, but some have pleasant riverside cores and excellent traditional restaurants. Catching one of the little commuter ferries is a fun excursion out of Lisbon.

Essentials

ARRIVING

BY FERRY & BUS TST 153, 155, and 161 run from Lisbon over 25 April Bridge to Costa da Caparica with up to five buses per hour leaving from Praça de Espanha, Praça Areeiro, or Marquês de Pombal. An alternative is to take the ferry from Cais do Sodré to Cacilhas, then bus 124 or 135 to the beach; or the ferry from Belém to Trafaria and hop on bus 129 (you can also walk from Trafaria—30 min. to the beach). ***Tip:*** Bikes go free on the Trafaria ferry; rent one in Lisbon and it's a short ride to the boardwalk.

BY CAR It can take as little as 23 minutes from downtown Lisbon to Costa da Caparica via the Ponte do 25 de Abril, A2 and A38 highways, but if you are going on a summer weekend, expect heavy traffic.

VISITOR INFORMATION

The **tourist office** is on the boardwalk at the junction with Rua dos Pescadores (✆ **21/290-00-71;** Mon–Sat 9:30am–1pm, 2:30–5:30pm; closed weekends Oct–Mar).

Exploring Caparica & the South Bank

Caparica is all about its **beaches** ★. At the northern end, closer to Lisbon, it's busy and popular with families and youngsters from the blue-collar suburbs inland. There's always a cheerful buzz in the summer as venders selling *bolas de Berlim* (custard-filled doughnuts) crisscross the sands crying "*olha a bolinha!*"

To get up and down the coast there's a **"micro-train"** ★ (www.transpraia.pt; ✆ **21/290-0706**) that has hauled sunseekers along its rails since 1960: it starts from Praia Nova, at the southern edge of the urbanized part of the seafront, then runs south to the surfer's beach at **Fonte da Telha.** It runs through the summer from 9am with the last return at 7:30pm. If you go all the way, tickets are 8.50€ return (4€ for children). As it chugs along parallel to the unbroken stretch of board sand, you can hop off at stops along the way, including **Praia da Rainha,** popular with families; **Praia do Castelo,** which pulls in a younger crowd; or blustery **Nova Vaga,** which lures kite-surfers. **Praia da Bela Vista** allows naturism as does **Praia 19,** one of Europe's best-known gay beaches.

Away from the beach, the best-known visitor attraction on what Lisbonites call the "outra banda" (other side) is **Cristo Rei** ★ (✆ **21/275-10-00**), the Rio-like statue of Christ that looks across at Lisbon from its pedestal 104m (304 ft.)

above the Tagus. It was built during the Salazar dictatorship to give thanks that Portugal had not been dragged into World War II. You can catch an elevator that will take you to the foot of the statue for a divine **view ★★★** over the red towers of the April 25 Bridge, with Tagus and all Lisbon laid out below. It's open every day from 9am to 6:30pm and costs 6€, 3€ for children and over 65s. Reach it by taking the ferry to Cacilhas and catching the 101 bus, which takes 20 minutes.

The trip to Cacilhas from Cais do Sodré on one of the **little Orange ferry boats ★★★** is a quintessential Lisbon experience, made by thousands of commuters every day. It takes 10 minutes and is the cost of a metro ride (you can use the Viva Viagem tickets). Besides views of Lisbon, Cacilhas' downtown area has some pleasing old streets, a riverside walkway, and a 19th-century warship, the ***Dom Fernando II,*** which can be visited as part of the Navy Museum (p. 117). Among the other south bank towns: **Seixal** has an agreeable downtown and good restaurants reachable by a fast ferry from Lisbon. White-painted **Alcochete,** located at the end of the Vasco da Gama bridge, has a bull-fighting tradition and hosts **Freeport Fashion Outlet** (www.freeportfashionoutlet.pt; ✆ **21/234-35-01**), a bargain-hunter magnet.

Where to Stay

EXPENSIVE

Quinta Tagus Village ★★ Who needs to stay in that big, noisy city, when you can see the best of Lisbon from the comfort of your pool or breakfast table? That's the reality at this hilltop abode on the south bank of the Tagus directly across from Belém. The apricot-painted mansion is surrounded by lawns and pine forests dropping to the blue expanse of the river and city beyond. Spacious rooms are individually designed in bold style, with offbeat features: huge mirrors; black-and-white striped walls, or floor-to-ceiling wine-racks. It's a slog to Lisbon (at least a 25-min. drive), but they do have a helicopter service. There's also a fine restaurant.

Quinta do Tagus, Montinhoso, Monte de Caparica. www.quintadotagus.com. ✆ **21/295-43-59.** 18 units. 110€–320€. Free parking. **Amenities:** Restaurant; bar; outdoor pool; free bikes; terrace; garden; massage service; babysitting; free Wi-Fi.

Where to Eat

Atira-te ao Rio ★ INTERNATIONAL The restaurant with the best view of Lisbon is called "Throw Yourself in the River": an invitation to hop on a boat across the Tagus to reach this little quayside hideaway. The vistas are so good (especially at sunset) that you may not care about the food. Thankfully, there's an exciting menu that includes sushi and ceviche, pork loin with sweet potato, and a peppery stew of fresh cod and shrimp. For a happy ending: guava mousse with strawberry and peanut. It's a 10-minute stroll from Cacilhas ferry.

Cais do Ginjal, 69, Almada. Atira-te ao Rio. www.atirateaorio.pt. ✆ **21/275-13-80.** Mains 14€–26€. Daily noon–11pm, 7–10:30pm.

O Barbas–Catedral ★ PORTUGUESE This is important: Don't go into this beachside restaurant wearing green. The extravagantly bearded owner has turned the place into a shrine to soccer club Benfica (they play in red, bitter rivals Sporting wear green). It's one of the iconic eateries on the Caparica boardwalk: big, bustling, and boisterous (especially when there's a match on TV). Go with the flow and order the fisherman's stew, monkfish *cataplana,* or a mixed grill of Alentejo black pork. And don't forget to cheer if the Reds score.

Rua. Pedro Álvares Cabral 25, Costa da Caparica. ✆ **21/290-01-63.** Main courses 9€–18€. Daily noon–11pm.

COMPORTA ★★

60km (37 miles) SW of Lisbon; 20km (12 miles) S of Setúbal

Until recently, Comporta was little more than a mosquito-ridden village beside some rice paddies in a remote corner of Portugal. Now the village is filled with hippy-chic stores and cool hotels frequented by international celebrities. The reason: an endless strip of vanilla-colored sand wrapped around a sheltered bay with a line of hills on the horizon. The beaches curve north along the forested slender Tróia sandspit tipped with a modern resort. In contrast, the white-painted river town of Alcácer do Sal, has millennia of history symbolized by its formidable hilltop castle.

Essentials

ARRIVING

BY TRAIN & BUS Trains run from Lisbon to Grândola taking about an hour. From there the 8346 bus makes a 40-minute run to Comporta twice a day, Monday to Friday. Or take the Lisbon-Setúbal train, then the ferry to Tróia and wait for a bus to Comporta (www.rodalentejo.pt).

BY CAR It's much easier and takes about 1 hour via the 25 April Bridge to highway A2; exit 8 for Alcácer, then link up to the N253 west to Comporta. Or take the Setúbal-Troia ferry (www.atlanticferries.pt) and drive south 20 minutes.

VISITOR INFORMATION

In the village of Carvalhal, south of Comporta, the tourist office (✆ **91/999-26-81**) is open July to September 9:30am to 1:30pm, 2:30 to 5:30pm. Alcácer's office on Largo Luís de Camões (✆ **26/500-99-87**) opens daily 9am to 5pm.

Exploring the Area

Alcácer do Sal's ★★ photogenic cluster of typically Alentejo, chalk-white houses and churches sits reflected in the waters of the Sado. The maze of medieval streets runs up to a **castle** ★★ that was once a mighty Muslim stronghold. It's now a luxury hotel (see below) but is still open for visits. The town's name combines the Arab word for castle with a reference to the salt trade which was important here since Roman times. Look out for the storks' nests on towers and rooftops.

The road to Comporta traverses rice paddies and forests of umbrella pine. Make a detour to the village of **Carrasqueira ★** where fishermen built an extraordinary network of quays and piers on rickety wooden stakes. **Comporta ★★** itself is made up of mostly modern white houses. It took off as a jet-set retreat after a society magazine reported on the sojourns of a high-profile banking family. Now it's filled with trendy cafes serving avocado brunches and boutiques peddling designer beach-wear or rustic decor. It has a certain boho allure, but the main attraction is its unbroken arc of **beach ★★★** running for almost 50km (30 miles) from the tip of Tróia to the lagoon at Santo André. **Praia da Comporta**, **Praia do Carvalhal,** and **Praia do Pego** (Madonna's favorite, apparently) are all gorgeous and feature beach bars with sun beds and straw umbrellas for rent, but you can easily walk a bit to find an untouched, deserted stretch. Watch out for mosquitos that rise at dusk from the rice fields.

The beach curls around the tip of the Tróia peninsula like the head of a match. Here there's a **modern resort ★** complete with golf course, marina and high-rise hotels and apartments. There are also **Roman ruins ★**, including the remains of a 1st-century fish-salting factory (www.troiaresort.pt; ✆ **93/903-19-36;** admission 5€; Tues–Sun 10am–1pm, 2:30–5:30pm).

Where to Stay

EXPENSIVE

Sublime Comporta ★★★ One of the hottest places in Europe right now, these deluxe wooden cabins, spacious suites, and rooms boast Nordic-minimalism-meets-beachcomber-chic design. Some have fireplaces, private pools, and exclusive decks. It's all spread around a broad expanse of pine and cork-oak forest. Its restaurants serve gourmet homegrown organic grub, and the heavenly spa uses local rice, salt, and flowers in its aromatic and beauty treatments. A downside? You'll need to take the car (or borrow a bike or horse) to get to the beach 10km (6 miles) away.

N261-1, Muda. www.sublimecomporta.pt. ✆ **26/944-93-76.** 34 units. 225€–480€ double; 285€–480€ suite; 700€–2,550€ cabin. Free parking. **Amenities:** Garden; terrace; bikes; tennis; 3 restaurants; 2 bars; indoor and outdoor pools; fitness center; spa; sauna; massage service; babysitting; free Wi-Fi.

MODERATE

Pousada de Alcácer do Sal ★★ Here's another hilltop castle-turned-hotel in the reliably historic Pousada chain. The medieval battlements once saw battles between Arab defenders and Viking raiders, but the interior reflects more peaceful times when the old fortress was converted into a convent for Poor Clare nuns. In keeping with the ascetic past, the rather small rooms are soberly furnished with dark wood and warm fabrics. Some have original features like Gothic archways, or balconies looking toward the Sado and rice fields. The garden and outdoor pool are surrounded by ramparts.

Rua Convento de Araceli, Alcácer do Sal. www.pousadas.pt. ✆ **26/561-30-70.** 35 units. 86€–179€ double; 180€–289€ suite. Free parking. **Amenities:** Garden; terrace; outdoor pool; games room; restaurant; bar; free Wi-Fi.

Where to Eat

Ilha do Arroz ★★ PORTUGUESE This laidback lounge on Comporta beach takes its name from the area's big crop: rice (*arroz*). It's owned by one of the biggest rice (and wine) producers and is an offshoot of their bigger restaurant (Museu do Arroz) in the village. This one has the advantage of sea air and views over to the Arrábida hills across the bay. Seafood-meets-rice dishes are the thing to go for, such as *arroz de tamboril* (with monkfish) *or arroz de lingueirão* (razor clams). Try typical Alentejo *encharcada* (heavy on cinnamon, eggs, and almond) for dessert and drink a fruity Herdade da Comporta white.

Praia da Comporta. ✆ **26/549-05-10.** Mains 16€–20€. Wed–Mon 11am–11pm.

Porto Santana ★★★ PORTUGUESE We're big fans of this riverside restaurant facing Alcácer across the Sado. Known as "Gino's Tavern" to generations of locals, or Lisbonites stopping off on their way to the beach, it serves authentic Alentejo cuisine, including *sopa de cação,* a tangy main-course soup made with dogfish; *canja de amêijoa* (clam broth with spinach and rice); or *ensopado de borrego* (lamb stew). There's a family atmosphere and decor is old style: dark wooden furniture, paper tablecloths, and local handicrafts. Try to get a seat in the main dining room overlooking the river.

Senhora Santana, Alcácer do Sal. ✆ **21/562-25-17.** Mains 9€–18€. Fri–Wed 12:15–3:15pm, 7:15–10:15pm.

OESTE & FÁTIMA

The region running along the coast between Ericeira and the Mondego river is endowed with undeveloped beaches, characterful fishing communities at Peniche and Nazaré, landscapes filled with orchards and vineyards, and one of the country's most beautiful small towns in Óbidos. There's a brace of World Heritages sites in the medieval monasteries of Batalha and Alcobaça. Nearby, the 20th-century Catholic shrine at Fátima draws millions of pilgrims annually.

The name Oeste, meaning "West," is a recent invention to promote the region that covers the northern part of the old province of Estremadura, which used to stretch down to Lisbon and Setúbal. The coastline here is also known as the *Costa da Prata* (Silver Coast). It's marked by untamed **beaches ★★** that draw surfers from around the world, like **Praia dos Supertubos ★★** near Peniche or Nazaré's **Praia do Norte ★★**, where winter brings world-record waves. There are more tranquil bathing spots in a couple of charming lagoons. History buffs visit the two UNESCO-protected monasteries built at opposite ends of the gothic period: the **Mosteiro de Alcobaça ★★★** with its pure, white lines, and the ornate **Mosteiro da Batalha ★★★**. The white town of **Óbidos ★★** has the best of both worlds, with fabulous beaches and first-class golf just beyond its heritage-filled ramparts. At **Fátima ★** even non-Catholics will be impressed by the devotion of pilgrims who come from around the world to the spot where the Virgin Mary is said to have appeared to three shepherd children during World War I. The area is renowned for seafood, Lisbon-region wines, and apples and pears that are exported around the world.

ÓBIDOS ★★

85km (55 miles) N of Lisbon

Enclosed within 1,565m (1,712 yards) of medieval walls, Óbidos is a picture-perfect town. Its houses have terracotta roofs and whitewashed walls framed with broad strips of blue, yellow, or peach. Bougainvillea pours over garden walls and homeowners take pride in decorating their windows with flowers.

The city has ancient roots with the usual procession of Celts, Romans, Visigoths, and Arabs before it came under Portuguese rule in 1149. Supposedly as a sign of Óbidos' great beauty, a tradition developed among medieval monarchs to give ownership of the town to their brides as a wedding gift, hence it's nickname of *Vila das Rainhas* (Town of Queens).

These days, the city is a major tourist lure, you will find it crowded particularly along **Rua Direita,** the old town's cobbled main street, which is lined with souvenir shops. However, you can get a feel for the city's history by wandering the narrow backstreets or walking the ramparts. A recent development is Óbidos' designation as a "city of literature" hosting an autumn **international book fair** (www.obidosvilaliteraria.com) and sprouting bookshops and literary-themed galleries, bars, and hotels. It's also big on chocolate and cherry liqueur. Outside the walls, the **Lagoa de Óbidos ★★★** lagoon provides gentle bathing waters that contrast with the surf-battered beaches more common along this coast. The coast is fast developing with the construction of new hotels and a cluster of golf courses.

Essentials

ARRIVING

BY TRAIN There are three trains a day from Lisbon's Entrecampos station, which crawl along the Linha do Oeste line, taking a little over 2 hours to reach Óbidos. One-way tickets cost 8.50€. Info: www.cp.pt.

BY BUS Buses take about an hour from Lisbon's Campo Grande bus station. Rodoviária do Oeste (www.rodoviariadooeste.pt) runs about 30 buses weekdays between 7am and midnight, about half that at weekends. Tickets are 7.95€, with discounts for children and seniors.

BY CAR The A8 toll highway will get you there from Lisbon in 1 hour. There are a couple of big parking lots outside the walls. Don't leave anything valuable visible in the car; they are favored hunting grounds for thieves.

VISITOR INFORMATION

Óbidos Tourist Office lies outside the old town on Rua da Porta da Vila, near the main parking (www.rt-oeste.pt; ✆ **26/295-92-31;** May–Sept: daily from 9:30am–7pm; Oct–Apr: Mon–Fri 9:30am–6pm, Sat–Sun 9:30am–12:30pm, 1:30–5:30pm).

Exploring the Town

Before you walk into the old town, check out the 3km (1.8-mile) aqueduct built in the 16th century to bring water to the town. The main gate into the walled town is **Porta da Vila ★**, which zigzags to confound invaders and is decorated by *azulejos* from the 1750s. Once you're through the stone staircase, on your left will take you up onto the ***muralhas*** **★★** (walls), which offer great views over the city and surrounding countryside. Climb down into Largo de Santiago, where a church rebuild after the 1755 earthquake has been turned into **Livraria de Santiago ★** (✆ **93/907-97-07**), the most original of the town's bookshops. Part of the ancient **castle ★**—which last saw action in 1808 against Napoleon—is now a hotel (see p. 197), but much remains open to the public and can be visited daily 9am to 5pm.

Oeste

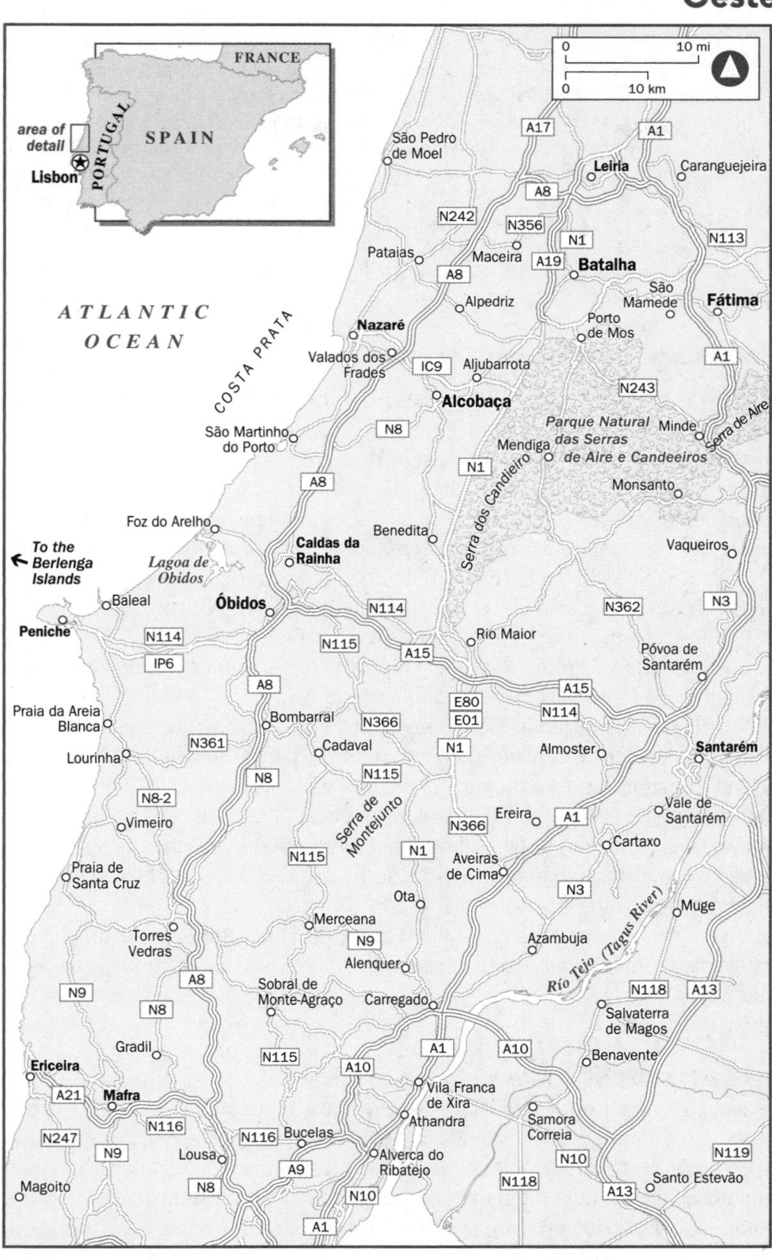

9
OESTE & FÁTIMA | Óbidos

BUDDHAS AGAINST barbarity

A 15-minute drive south of Óbidos lies one of Portugal's most surprising sights. The **Bacalhôa Buddha Eden ★★** is Europe's largest Asian garden, covering 35 hectares (86 acres) amid rolling wine country. It's filled with hundreds of statues of the Buddha, sitting, standing, and reclining among pagodas, lakes, and ornamental flora. It was created by millionaire Joe Berardo as an act of protest against the 2001 destruction of ancient Buddha statues by the Taliban in Bamiyan, Afghanistan. Located on the grounds of the 16th-century wine estate **Quinta dos Loridos,** it also features other examples of Berardo's art collection including several works by artists from Zimbabwe and dozens of cobalt-blue copies of the Xi'an Chinese warrior statues. There's also a wine store and restaurant (Quinta dos Loridos, Bombarral; www.bacalhoa.pt; ✆ **26/260-52-40;** admission 5€, free for under 12s; daily 9am-5:30pm).

Head down Rua Direita, past the souvenir shops and fellows dressed in medieval garb, until you reach **Igreja de Santa Maria ★★**, a Renaissance church overlooking a square of the same name. It's the most impressive of the town's many churches, filled with *azulejos,* painted ceilings, and gilded altars. There are two standouts inside: a Renaissance **tomb ★** by French sculptors Jean de Rouen and Nicolas de Chantereine; and paintings of Josefa of Óbidos (1630–1684). The church opens daily (Apr–Sept 9:30am–12:30pm and 2:30–7pm, closing at 5pm in winter). Free admission.

Back on Rua Direita, make a stop at No. 28, home of the **Mercado Biológico de Óbidos ★**, which combines an organic food market and bookshop specializing in secondhand, travel, and cookbooks. You may find it hard to resist a drop of ***ginjinha,*** the sour cherry liqueur for which the region is famed. Most of the stores along Rua Direita will offer you a sip in a chocolate cup (you then eat the cup). This is a very recent "tradition," but pleasant nevertheless. If you want to buy a bottle but are baffled by all the brands, **Oppidum** (www.ginjadeobidos.com)—made by a father-and-daughter team from locally grown fruit—is one to watch for.

If you find the crowds and tourist traps on Rua Direita a bit much, just amble down one of the side streets and lose yourself amid the less-traveled alleyways.

Outdoor Activities

WATERSPORTS The swirls of sugar-white sand emerging from the cerulean shallows of **Lagoa de Óbidos ★★★** make Portugal's biggest lagoon one of the most photogenic sites on the coast. Its still waters are a relaxing alternative to the surf rolling onto most beaches along the Oeste coast. The two main beaches are near the mouth of the lagoon at **Bom Sucesso,** on the south bank, and **Foz do Arelho** on the more developed north shore. On both sides, the beaches curve onto the ocean side so you can toggle between the rollers and the calm lagoon. Besides bathing, the lagoon is perfect for learning watersports. The **Escola de Vela da Lagoa** (www.escoladeveladalagoa.com; ✆ **26/297-85-92**) runs classes ranging from sailing to canoeing and kitesurfing. The bar in their waterside cabin is great for a snack or drink.

GOLF Golf is a booming affair along the coast west of Óbidos, with four highly rated courses set alongside luxury resorts in the once untouched countryside. Designed by Cynthia Dye, **West Cliffs** (www.westcliffs.com; ✆ **26/224-98-80**) offers an ocean view from every hole. It's been rated the best in central Portugal. "One of continental Europe's most invigorating sequences of holes," was the opinion of Britain's *Golf World* magazine on **Praia d'el Rey** (www.praia-del-rey.com; ✆ **26/290-51-00**), including it in ontinental Europe's top 30 courses. **Royal Óbidos** (www.royalobidos.com; ✆ **26/296-52-20**) was designed by five-time major-winner Steve Ballesteros. The **Guardian Bom Sucesso** (www.guardiangolf.net; ✆ **26/296-53-11**) course is renowned for its panoramic final three.

Shopping

As well as the liquid and literary purchases suggested above, there's a studio at Rua Direita 95 called **Oficina do Barro ★** (✆ **96/567-52-21**) where you can watch artisans making delicate *verguinha* ceramics that resemble the texture of a woven basket. The town also holds a big Christmas market, a "Medieval Market" in July and August, and a springtime Chocolate Festival.

Where to Stay

EXPENSIVE

Pousada de Óbidos, Castelo de Óbidos ★★ Here you'll be staying amid more than 1,000 years of history. The castle is one of the best-preserved medieval monuments in Portugal. Parts date from the 9th century. A hotel since 1951, it was the first Pousada opened in a historic building and remains one of the chain's best. Rooms can feature gothic arches, bare stone walls, wood-beamed ceilings, and centuries-old colored tiles. Tasteful additions such as pink-stone bathrooms ensure comfort while respecting the heritage. The downside of the architecture is that room size varies a lot and some are very small. Those in the newer Casa do Castelo wing tend to be larger. The Manueline windows of the famed restaurant open onto a spacious patio. Lobby and lounge are filled with tapestries, suits of armor, and other medieval accoutrements.

Paço Real. www.pousadas.pt. ✆ **26/295-50-80.** 16 units. 146€–310€ double; 410€–450€ suite. Free Parking. **Amenities:** Restaurant; bar; bikes; massage in room on request; free Wi-Fi.

MODERATE

Evolutee Hotel ★★ Set 20 minutes' drive from Óbidos, this modern oceanfront resort hotel is all about light and color. Sunshine pours in through the four-story windows of the reception and into rooms looking out over the golf course, the Atlantic and lagoon beyond. Inside, there are XXL reprints of baroque oil paintings, rainbow-hued quilts, and *azulejo*-filed bathrooms.

Those blue-and-white tiles give a special look to the long, thin outdoor pool and in the sumptuous Manderley spa. In contrast, the indoor pool looking across to the sea is in black tiles and textured grey marble. There are Castelbel creams and soaps and Troy speakers waiting for your music.

Cabeço da Serra, Vau. www.marriott.com/lisdr. ✆ **26/224-02-20.** 39 units. 98€–178€ double; 218€–410€ suite. Free parking. **Amenities:** Garden; terrace; bike hire; golf; indoor and outdoor pools; fitness center; spa; sauna; hammam; Jacuzzi; restaurant; bars; babysitting; free Wi-Fi.

Rio do Prado ★★★ Half-submerged concrete bunkers with decor involving recycled crates, driftwood, and rusting iron may not sound like dream accommodations, but make no mistake: This is one of the nicest places to stay in the whole country. The eco-chic resort is on a backroad from Óbidos to the lagoon, about 10 minutes' drive from town and a short bike ride to the beach. Driving by, you may miss its collection of bungalows integrated into the landscape with grass and moss covering the flat roofs. Ingenious skylights and glass-fronted facades ensure the open-space suites fill with natural light. The smallest are 45 square meters (48 sq. ft.), way bigger than most European rooms. They feature private patios, fireplaces inside and out, and polished concrete tubs forming an island in the room. A garden filled with umbrella pine, dwarf oak, and reed-ringed ponds contains the pool and spa. Greenhouses supply the excellent restaurant with organic herbs and veg. Service is relaxed and friendly.

Rua das Poças, Arelho. www.riodoprado.pt. ✆ **26/295-96-23.** 20 units. 142€–205€ suite. Free parking. **Amenities:** Garden; terrace; bike hire; outdoor pool; spa; sauna; hammam; restaurant; bar; library; free Wi-Fi.

INEXPENSIVE

Casa d'Óbidos ★★ This carefully restored 19th-century mansion is just outside the city walls, with extensive gardens and views over to the castle. The estate is decorated in typical Óbidos style: white facades offset by mustard trim. You can take a double or twin room in the antiques-filled main house (some have clawfoot baths and high-boarded "Dona Maria" beds), or pick from the four more rustic, self-contained cottages in the grounds, which offer good value for families. Breakfast in the main house is a treat of hams, jams, fruit, and fresh-baked bread and pastries (you get to have it on your own in the cottages).

Quinta de São José. www.casadobidos.com. ✆ **26/295-09-24.** 10 units. 73€–95€ double. Cottages 73€–183€. Free parking. **Amenities:** Garden; outdoor pool; tennis; games room; free Wi-Fi.

Casas de São Thiago ★ Simple, value-for-money accommodation is what you get in this yellow-and-white manorial guesthouse set amid the narrow town-center streets. It's comfortable and quiet, if old-fashioned, with lots of *azulejos* and dark wooden furniture. The smallish whitewashed rooms have private bathrooms and wood- or iron-framed beds draped with fabrics typical of nearby Alcobaça. The personalized hospitality here makes you feel like

CERAMIC city

Just 6.5km (4 miles) from Óbidos, **Caldas da Rainha ★** lacks the medieval charm of its little neighbor but it's a pleasant, relaxing town filled with leafy gardens (notably **Parque Dom Carlos I ★**, open daily 7am–10pm) and cheerful architecture that recalls its days as a Belle Epoque spa. The central focus is **Praça da República,** popularly known as Praça da Fruta (fruit plaza) due to its **daily farmers' market ★**. The city was founded by Queen Leonor in the 15th century after she stumbled upon the benefits of its thermal waters (the town's name means "queen's baths"). You can still take the waters at **Hospital Termal das Caldas da Rainha** (www.termas centro.pt; ✆ **26/224-00-12**), the treatment center she founded. Leonor ordered the construction of a fine church adjacent to the spa, **Nossa Senhora do Pópulo ★** containing beautiful hand-painted *azulejos* and an outstanding early-16th-century triptych of the Crucifixion under a triumphal arch of the temple. Caldas' biggest claim to fame, however, is ceramics. The **Fábrica de Faianças Artísticas Bordallo Pinheiro ★★** factory, created in 1884 by Raphael Bordallo Pinheiro, is still going strong, turning out the outlandish designs of this flamboyant artist. His gleaming frogs, flights of swallows, angry cats, and soup terrines in the form of giant tomatoes or cabbage leaves were once considered kitsch, but are now globally sought-after. The factory and outlet store are on Rua Rafael Bordallo Pinheiro (www.bordallopinheiro.com; ✆ **26/283-93-80;** open Mon–Sat 10am–7pm, Sun 2–7pm). Caldas also has a **Ceramics Museum ★** and a trail through the city featuring outsize versions of Bordallo Pinheiro creations, including a statue of **Zé Povinho** (Joe Public), Portugal's bearded everyman.

you're staying in a private home. Breakfast in the sun-dappled courtyard is a bonus.

Largo de São Tiago 1. www.casas-sthiago.com. ✆/fax **26/295-95-87.** 14 units. 53€–75€ double. **Amenities:** Free Wi-Fi.

The Literary Man-Óbidos Hotel ★★ This bibliophile heaven is more a library with rooms than a hotel. There are over 45,000 volumes housed in a former convent that claims to be the world's biggest literary hotel. Visitors are encouraged to read or buy books (proceeds go to charity), or contribute to the multilingual collection. Rooms are small (they were once nuns' cells) and are either traditionally decorated with iron beds and *azulejos* or in eco-modern style with salvaged wood packaging and ultra-smooth cement finishes (it has the same owners as Rio do Prado, above). Guests can take breakfast outside on the deck or in the book-lined restaurant, which also serves dinners that range from traditional Portuguese to Japanese-style Kamado grills. The bar has almost as many gins as books. Its sister restaurant, The History Man, serves traditional food in a cool town-center location with garden.

Rua Dom João de Ornelas. www.theliteraryman.pt. ✆ **26/295-92-17.** 30 units. 72€–145€ double; 115€–195€ suite. **Amenities:** Garden; terrace; restaurant; bar; cookery classes; library; free Wi-Fi.

AVOID THE drunkosaurus

Brandy and dinosaurs sounds like an explosive mix, but they are the main attractions (together with sandy beaches) of **Lourinhã ★**, a little town 32km (20 miles) south of Óbidos. The coast here contains one of Europe's richest deposits of dinosaur fossils, including a nest with over 100 eggs, remains of Torvosaurus (a carnivore that made T-Rex look wimpy), and a previously unknown predator now called Lourinhanosaurus. In 2018, the town opened **Dinoparque ★** (www.dinoparque.pt; ✆ **26/124-31-60**), a theme park featuring 180 full-size models scattered though woodland, plus displays of the actual finds and interactive galleries. It's a major hit with kids. Located in the village of Albelheira and open daily (June–Sept 10am–5:30pm; Mar–May 10am–4:30pm; Oct–Feb 10am–3:30pm). Admission is 13€, 9.90€ children 4–13; free under 4s. Some people have (apparently seriously) asked for their money back after discovering there are no actual live dinosaurs. They may have had a drop of the town's other claim to fame: *aguardente Lourinhã*, which like Cognac and Armagnac is a protected brandy label. Find all about it with a tour of the **Adega Cooperativa ★** (www.doc-lourinha.pt; ✆ **26/142-21-07**) a producers' cooperative where you can have a sip or two and make some purchases. Just don't down too much before you head to **Praia de Areia Branca ★**, a fine but frequently rough nearby beach.

Where to Eat

A Nova Casa de Ramiro ★ PORTUGUESE This revival of an old favorite in the medieval town, just below the defensive walls, has a cozy, basement feel with the room dominated by four man-size clay amphoras. Its classic menu puts an emphasis on hearty meat and salt-cod (*bacalhau*) dishes. Baked rice with duck is the house signature, but there are excellent steaks (try one *à Portuguesa* with a white wine and garlic sauce) and *bacalhau com natas* (with cream). Finish up with the chocolate dessert made with 76% cocoa and served with tropical fruits.

Rua Porta do Vale. ✆ **96/726-59-45.** Mains 16€–70€. Tues–Fri noon–3pm, 7–11pm; Sat–Sun 1–4pm, 7–11pm; Mon 7–11pm.

Covão dos Musaranhos ★★ PORTUGUESE Clams (*amêijoas)* are an integral part of the Portuguese diet, and this little shack down a forested track on the south bank of Lagoa de Óbidos is where some of the best can be eaten. They are harvested directly from the lagoon's sands, and regulars will tell you they have a unique flavor. Much of the other stuff on the menu comes from the shallow waters too, like razor clams, cuttlefish, or eels (served crispy fried or in a peppery stew). From a bit farther afield come ingredients for dishes like salt-cod in a cornbread crust or barbecued rabbit. Enjoy everything on the deck overlooking the blue lagoon. Lunch (or early dinner) only.

Quinta do Bom Sucesso, Vau. ✆ **26/296-99-30.** Mains 8€–16€. Daily 10:30am–8pm.

O Traçadinho ★ PORTUGUESE/ITALIAN This simple village restaurant, a 5-minute drive from Óbidos, can be found in a typical white-and-blue house that looks little changed from when it opened as a grocery/tavern (and reputedly smuggler's hangout) in the 1920s. There have been some changes—notably the addition of pizzas and pasta dishes to the menu—but it still does quality versions of traditional dishes, many using the region's famed fruit. A meal could start with black pudding with caramelized apple, move on to game sausage with apple puree and kale, and finish up with pears cooked in red wine.

Estrada da Capeleira 44, Capeleira. www.tracadinho.restaurantesdeobidos.com. ✆ **26/295-94-89.** Mains 5.50€–18.50€. Thurs–Tues 11am–10pm.

Tribeca ★ PORTUGUESE/INTERNATIONAL The name is as unexpected as the concept: a Parisian-style brasserie, named for a NYC neighborhood, and serving French, Italian, and Portuguese food in a village on the old road between Óbidos and Peniche. Surprisingly it works. The vintage posters for *Bières de la Meuse* and *Rhum Negrita* make you feel like you've stepped from the Atlantic coast to the Boulevard St. Germain. The food works on local seafood with a Gallic twist, with a constantly changing specials list including the likes of sole fillets with lemon risotto or salt-cod strudel; as well as French and Italian classic dishes including *coq au vin, linguine alla vongole,* and entrecôte steaks imported from Argentina. Enjoy a *kir royal* to start, then it's *bon appetit.*

Avenida da Serrana 5 Serra d'El-Rei. www.tribeca-restaurante.com. ✆ **26/290-94-61.** Mains 14€–38€. Tues–Sun 12:30–2:30pm, 7–10:30pm; Mon 7–10:30pm.

ALCOBAÇA ★★

120 (75 miles) N of Lisbon; 40km (25 miles) NE of Óbidos

Alcobaça is an amiable little town surrounded by vineyards and orchards (the local apples are particularly good) and renowned for **ceramics,** vibrant **chintz** fabrics, and sweet, sticky **cakes.** There is, however, one overwhelming reason to come here: the amazing **12th-century monastery ★★★**.

Essentials

ARRIVING

BY BUS From Lisbon's Sete Rios station, **Rede Expresso** has seven departures daily for Alcobaça, taking 1 hour, 40 minutes. Tickets start at 10.20€. Info: www.rede-expressos.pt. **Rodoviária do Oeste** (www.rodoviariadooeste.pt) also has two departures from Campo Grande in Lisbon on weekdays, just one at 7:30pm on weekends and holidays. The fare is 9.90€.

BY CAR On the A8 highway, it should take about 80 minutes from Lisbon, 30 minutes from Óbidos.

VISITOR INFORMATION

The **Alcobaça Tourist Office** is in Rua 16 de Outubro, 7 (www.cm-alcobaca.pt; ✆ **26/258-23-77**). It's open daily 9am to 12:30pm, and 2 to 5:30pm.

Exploring the Town

Mosteiro de Alcobaça ★★★ RELIGIOUS SITE The baroque overlay imposed on the facade in the 18th century gives no warning of the glories awaiting visitors inside this UNESCO World Heritage site. The great **nave ★★★** extends for 100m (330 ft.) in a succession of unadorned white-stone arches that soar upward over 20m (66 ft.). It is Portugal's first and largest gothic church and one of the finest anywhere in the early-gothic style. Regardless of your beliefs, it's hard not to sense the spirituality permeating the immense space. Portugal's first king, Afonso I Henriques, ordered it built in 1178 to give thanks for a victory over the Moors on the banks of the River Tagus.

Contrasting with the simplicity of the church, two ornate **gothic tombs ★★★** face each other across the transept. They hold the remains of tragic lovers, King Pedro I and his murdered mistress Inês de Castro, who was crowned queen after her death in 1355 (p. 23). The sarcophagi are the greatest examples of Portuguese gothic sculpture, decorated with Bible scenes, fantastic beasts, and weeping angels. Behind Pedro's tomb is a Romanesque-style **Royal Pantheon ★★** containing tombs of older monarchs. Their presence indicates the political importance of the monastery and its community of Cistercian monks.

On the eastern side is the **Cloister of Silence ★★★**, with delicate arches surrounding a square garden. The lower level was completed in 1311 on the orders of King Dinis, known as the "Farmer King" for promoting agriculture. Additions during the 16th-century reign of King Manuel include a second tier of arches and a sacristy in the style that bears his name. Look for the rhinoceros gargoyle—an exotic Discoveries-era touch. More architectural marvels continue beyond the cloisters: There's a graceful, column-filled **dormitory ★★★** and **refectory ★★★** together with an extraordinary, tile-clad **kitchen ★★★**, complete with towering chimney and a brook diverted to run through it.

Praça 25 de Abril. www.mosteiroalcobaca.gov.pt. ✆ **26/250-51-20.** 6€, 3€ over 65s, students with ID; free for under 12s. Daily Apr–Sept 9am–6:30pm, Oct–Mar 9am–5:30pm.

Shopping

Any medieval monks stepping out of the monastery today would soon be confronted by the sin of gluttony. Across the broad, sunny square is **Pastelaria Alcôa** (www.pastelaria-alcoa.com; ✆ **26/259-74-74**), a famed pastry shop. It's won "world's best *pastel de nata*" awards, but the specialty are *doces conventuais,* sweet morsels based on centuries-old convent recipes. The bestsellers are golden cones of eggy delight called *cornucopias.* Try them with coffee on their cafe terrace. There's also an outpost in Lisbon's Chiado.

Another Alcobaça claim to fame are *chitas*—cheerful chintz fabrics with floral motifs and bold stripes of color made in the town since the 15th century, inspired by styles from India. At **Made in Alcobaça** (Praça 25 de Abril 64; ✆ **26/258-54-02**) they have a dazzling selection of fabrics, plus *chita*-based gifts ranging from lampshades to beach bags. Find traditional blue, yellow, and white Alcobaça ceramics at **Casa Alcobaça,** next to the monastery on Praça Dom Afonso Henriques 6; or modern porcelain designs at the factory outlet of **SPAL** (www.spal.pt; ✆ **26/258-13-39**), one of Portugal's leading tableware producers, just out of town on Ponte da Torre, Valado dos Frades. Alcobaça's *ginjinha* (cherry liquor) rivals that of Óbidos; look for the **M.S.R.** brand, making the genuine article since 1930.

Where to Stay

MODERATE

Challet da Fonte Nova ★★ Past the palm trees and ornate iron gate, there's a tropical feel to this patrician 1870s villa. Its architecture is inspired by the *fazendas* of Brazil, where the then-owners accumulated a fortune before returning home. The rose-painted guesthouse is a 4-minute stroll to the monastery. It's furnished with impeccable taste: beds in the 18th-century "Dona Maria" style, handpainted bathroom tiles, and Castelbel toiletries. The old house radiates charm, but some of the rooms are a little cramped, especially on the second floor. There's more space and similar old-world elegance in the new-wing rooms and suites. To relax, enjoy the spa or billiards in the basement room. Excellent breakfast with fresh fruit.

Rua da Fonte Nova 8. www.challetfontenova.pt. ✆ **26/259-83-00.** 9 units. 85€–130€ double; 107€–142€ junior suite. Free parking. **Amenities:** Garden; terrace; games room; bar; spa; free Wi-Fi.

INEXPENSIVE

Real Abadia, Congress & Spa ★ This lowkey, modern hotel offers value-for-money pampering in rolling countryside, a 5-minute drive from the town center. It's a place to relax. You can sit by the pool contemplating the distant hills and goats grazing nearby. Indoors, the spa features a pool surrounded by stone walls and arches that recall the monastery cloisters. The bright rooms also feature local references with *chita* throws on beds, ceramic apples, and a suite named for lovers Pedro & Inês. Two suites are adapted for less-able travelers.

Rua da Escola, Capuchos. www.realabadiahotel.pt. ✆ **26/258-03-70.** 32 units. 71€–98€ double; 84€–148€ suite. Free parking. **Amenities:** Garden; terrace; free bikes; library; indoor and outdoor pools; restaurant; bar; spa; sauna; hammam; massage service; children's play area; babysitting; free Wi-Fi.

Solar da Cerca do Mosteiro ★★ The location could hardly be better: You can almost reach out and touch the monastery towers from the citrus-filled garden, poolside, or breakfast terrace. The main house dates from the 1860s, built on land once cultivated by the monks. There's a magnificent hardwood staircase spiraling up to the rooms. Our favorite is the Reis (king) suite featuring a four-poster bed, wooden ceiling, and private sauna. There are two beautifully decorated apartments housing up to seven guests.

Rua Dr. Francisco Zagalo 3. www.solardomosteiro.com. ✆ **26/250-53-10.** 8 units. 81€–110€ double; 104€–220€ suites and apartments. Free parking. **Amenities:** Garden; terrace; bike hire; library; outdoor pool; bar; babysitting; free Wi-Fi.

PORTUGAL'S other islands (& MORE BEACHES)

You've heard of Madeira and the Azores, how about the **Berlengas**? This craggy archipelago lies 10km (6 miles) off the coast. The islands are a nature reserve inhabited by thousands of seabirds, but the main island, **Berlenga Grande ★★**, is open to visits. The 30-minute trip from the fishing town of Peniche is notoriously choppy, but queasiness will be rewarded by the chance to explore the pristine wilderness. Among operators making the trip, **Viamar** (www.viamar-berlenga.com; ✆ **26/278-56-46**) has the biggest (and most stable) boat.

They drop you off in a natural harbor with a narrow but lovely butter-colored beach and glassy water. Grab a snack in the fishermen's shacks before hiking the trails around the 1.5km (almost 1-mile) long island. Toward the southwestern tip, a slender footbridge meanders over the waves to a rock capped by the 17th-century **Forte de São João Batista ★★**, looking altogether like a set from *Pirates of the Caribbean*. The fort was frequently attacked by real pirates as well as Turkish, French, and Spanish warships. These days, it's an inn where you can get basic (and cheap) accommodation (www.berlengas.org; ✆ **26/275-02-44**). There's also a campsite and rooms in some of the fishermen's huts. You can take a small boat tour to visit maritime caves under the island or go diving.

Peniche ★ itself is worth a visit. On the tip of a peninsula, its massive 16th-century fortress was used by the Salazar dictatorship as a prison for political opponents. In 1960, Communist Party leader Álvaro Cunhal and nine comrades famously escaped from the high-security wing. The **National Museum of Resistance and Freedom ★** (www.museunacionalresistencialiberdade-peniche.gov.pt; ✆ **92/414-51-03**) opened there in 2018. Peniche is Portugal's wave capital, boasting a dozen surf beaches including **Praia Supertubos ★★★**, which hosts World League championships. Then there's seafood: Among several great restaurants, our favorite is **Tasca do Joel ★★** (www.tascadojoel.pt; ✆ **26/278-29-45**).

The Oeste has endless beaches, generally much less crowded than those in the Algarve, but often wild with rolling surf. Among our favorites are **Santa Cruz ★★** near Torres Vedras; **São Pedro de Moel ★★**, a pretty seaside village; **São Martinho do Porto ★★**, which is sheltered from the waves in a shell-shaped bay; and wild **Osso da Baleia ★★** near the castle town of Pombal.

Where to Eat

António Padeiro ★★ PORTUGUESE Back in the 1930s, professional soccer players needed to supplement their wages, so António Padeiro opened a bakery and later started serving snacks in the basement. The business developed into an Alcobaça institution. Today run by his granddaughter, it's one of the best places in the region for traditional food. Smart but folksy decor features local ceramics, antique radios, and a salted cod in a gilt frame. The food is rooted in regional cuisine—notably the Alcobaça traditional specialty of slow cooking chicken in a clay pot (*púcara*). Here the signature is a posher version using partridge (although they do it with chicken too). To finish up they have a heavenly array of sticky, syrupy desserts based on old convent recipes: We're particularly partial to one called *barriga de freira* (nun's belly).

Rua Dom Mauro Cocheril 27. www.antoniopadeiro.com. ✆ **26/258-22095.** Mains 10€–15€. Daily noon–3pm, 7–10pm.

NAZARÉ ★★

125km (75 miles) N of Lisbon; 16km (10 miles) W of Alcobaça

In 1948, a 20-year-old New York City photographer named Stanley Kubrick traveled to Portugal on assignment for *Life* magazine. He was fascinated by the hardscrabble lives of the fishing folk in Nazaré. Kubrick's moody black-and-white shots of women in black, men in plaid hauling nets, and ragged children grinning for the lens set a trend. Over the following years, many of the world's top photographers, including Henri Cartier-Bresson and Bill Perlmutter, beat a path to this fishing town on the western edge of Europe to capture the resilience of a people who daily braved the foaming ocean in little high-prowed boats.

Those images spread the name of Nazaré around the world. Despite the poverty, a growing number of visitors came to visit. Portugal's dictatorship heavily promoted this most-typical of fishing towns, and gradually tourism replaced fishing as the economic mainstay. The old women in black, brandishing homemade "Room Free" signs, became more visible than men hauling nets. The spectacular cliffs and whitewashed, red-roofed town is still there, and a few locals still dress in their **traditional costumes.** But these days Nazaré is better known for the 30m (98-ft.) waves that crash onto **Praia do Norte ★★★**, which daredevil surfers ride into the world record book.

Come in summer and you won't see the big rollers and will fight for elbowroom among holidaymakers packing the grid of narrow streets and candy-striped beach tents on the broad sands of the **town-center beach ★★**. Still, the city has many charms, not least the upper town, **Sitio ★★★** with its clifftop plaza, religious heritage, and stunning views.

Essentials

ARRIVING

BY BUS **Rede Expressos** (www.rede-expressos.pt) runs six to eight buses daily from the Sete Rios station in Lisbon. The trip lasts 1 hour 50 minutes and fares start at 11.40€. Around 1 bus per hour makes the 20-minute trip from Alcobaça.

BY CAR It's about 90 minutes from Lisbon, up the A8 toll highway until exit 22. From Alcobaça, the IC-9 highway will get you there in less than 20 minutes if traffic's clear.

VISITOR INFORMATION

There are two **Tourist Offices:** one in the downtown market on Avenida Vieira Guimarães (✆ **26/256-11-94**); the other on Largo Nossa Senhora de. Nazaré up in Sítio (✆ **93/042-48-60**). Both open daily (July–Aug 9am–8pm; May–June, Sept 9:30am–1pm, 2:30–7pm; Oct–Apr 9:30am–1pm, 2:30–6pm).

Exploring the Village

Nazaré is a town of two parts. Downtown is dominated by the **Praia de Nazaré ★★**, a wide beach over 1.5km (almost 1 mile) long. In summer, the northern end is covered with rows of colorful striped tents (*barraquinhas*) which you can rent for 7€ a day. There will be a few fishing boats on the beach and likely some men and women wearing traditional clothing, fixing nets, or selling souvenirs—although these days there's a commercial harbor at the southern end of the town, with more productive but less picturesque fishing vessels.

Behind the beach, the tightly packed grid of **Bairro dos Pescadores ★** (fishermen's neighborhood) is lined with white houses, restaurants, and souvenir shops. The costumes can come as shock. Nazaré may have invented the mini-skirt: the women wear seven layers of skirt, but they are all cut above the knee to enable them to wade into the shallows to help with the catch. Men sport floppy elongated caps and thick plaid shirts and pants in many colors. You'll spot women in the costume selling nuts, figs, cookies, and dried fish on the boardwalk and up in the plaza in Sítio. During festivals more will be dressed up, including around Easter, when they play a version of dodgeball on waterfront Praça Sousa Oliveria. Take a look at the fish and fruit in the **Mercado Municipal ★** (Av. Vieira Guimarães; Tues–Sun 8am–1pm) before catching the **Funicular ★** that runs from Rua do Elevador up the cliff to Sítio. It takes a couple of minutes to climb 318m (1,043 ft.) and costs 1.50€ for an adult one-way.

Like a giant balcony, the **Miradouro do Suberco ★★★** viewpoint by the main square of **Sítio** juts out over the cliff with sensational views over the red tiles of the town, expansive sand, and endless Atlantic horizon. Vertigo sufferers shouldn't get too close to the edge.

If you walk west along Estrada do Farol, you'll reach a headland with a fortress and lighthouse at the tip. This is where the awe-inspiring shots of surfers riding monster swells are filmed. A submerged offshore canyon creates conditions for waves of over 30 meters in winter (Feb is the best time to catch them). After U.S. surfer Garrett McNamara smashed the world's highest ride record in 2011 on a 24m (78-ft.) breaker. **Praia de Norte ★★★** just north of the headland has become a mecca for big-wave riders. On the way down to the lighthouse, a bizarre statue of a stag-headed surfer references a 12th-century legend when the Virgin Mary is supposed to have rescued a huntsman who'd ridden his horse off the cliff in pursuit of a deer. An imposing baroque church, **Santuário de Nossa Senhora da Nazaré ★** commemorates the event and is the site of annual pilgrimage in early September, accompanied by a program of concerts, folk dancing, and bullfighting.

SHOPPING Nazaré is filled with shops offering souvenirs to visitors. One absolutely genuine place is **Casa Dos Escoceses** (Praça Dr. Manuel Arriaga 14; ✆ **26/255-26-13**), which despite its name (it means House of Scots), is a thoroughly local institution selling the rough tartan fabrics used to make Nazaré (fisher)menswear. They also have off-the-peg traditional shirts which make original gifts and effective winter warmers. **Carbel Artesanato,** on the seafront at Avenida da República 56 (✆ **96/637-35-00**) has a good selection of handicrafts from around Portugal at reasonable prices. For surf-inspired fashion, local brand **Praia do Norte** has a downtown boutique at Avenida Manuel Remígio (www.praiadonorte.com.pt).

Where to Stay

MODERATE

Mar Bravo ★ On the seafront and corner of a lively plaza, a recent overhaul gave this hotel a fresh, contemporary look. Rooms are bigger than most in the neighborhood. All have sea views; most have private verandas. Decor features white walls, bleached wood floors, and drapes in pastel ocean shades. Parking is an advantage in a city that gets very busy in summer. The location can be noisy at night.

Praça Sousa Oliveira 71. www.marbravo.com. ✆ **26/256-91-60.** 16 units. 67€–195€ double. Free parking nearby, with reservation. **Amenities:** Restaurants; bar; free Wi-Fi.

INEXPENSIVE

By the Sea ★ The name says it all. You practically step out onto the sand from this B&B in a newly restored mid-century modern building on the corner of a busy downtown square (it can be a noisy at night). Rooms are compact but cheerfully decorated with stripes and swirls of vivid colors. Many have little balconies. A rooftop terrace with a hot tub is a real bonus.

Travessa da Capitania 3. www.by-the-sea.pt. ✆ **26/228-50-27.** 15 units. 50€–110€ double; 60€–120€ family suite. Parking nearby 10€ daily, reservation required. **Amenities:** Terrace; Jacuzzi; free Wi-Fi.

Hotel Magic ★★ Nazaré is not overflowing with characterful accommodation, so this youthful place is a breath of fresh air. A 3-minute walk from the beach, it's the coolest place in town. Behind the curved, white facade of a three-story Art Deco–inspired townhouse, its rooms are smallish but stylishly and individually decorated with evocations of local life: wall-size color photos of fisherfolk costumes, seagull collages, abstract patterns inspired by traditional fabrics. They also have four self-contained apartments.

Rua Mouzinho de Albuquerque, 58. www.hotelmagic.pt. ✆ **26/256-90-40.** 31 units. 60€–150€ double. Free parking nearby. **Amenities:** Bar; free Wi-Fi.

Hotel Miramar Sul ★ Views are great at this bright, modern four-story hotel on a hillside overlooking the sea, but it's a 3km (1.8-mile) uphill hike back from the beach. Recover in an ample outdoor pool-with-a-view (there's also kid's paddling pool and a smaller indoor pool in a glass room with more ocean views). Standard rooms are on the small side but have window doors opening to private balconies. Most have sea views. Banal furnishings are brightened by cherry-red throws and drapes. Junior suites offer more space and bigger balconies.

Caminho Real. www.miramarnazarehotels.com. ✆ **26/255-00-00.** 71 units. 55€–155€ double; 88€–189€ junior suite. Free parking. **Amenities:** Garden; terrace; bike hire; indoor and outdoor pools; restaurant; bar; kid's club; free Wi-Fi.

Where to Eat

A Celeste ★★ PORTUGUESE/SEAFOOD Dona Celeste, who runs this little seafront place with energy and good humor, is way past retirement age. Food lovers everywhere will hope she'll carry on for many more years. From her kitchen, Celeste is a guardian of the region's seafood traditions. Her *caldeirada* (a mixed fish stew that's Portugal's equivalent to French *bouillabaisse*) is nationally famed. Other delights include beans with shrimp and grilled horse-mackerel with *migas* (a mix of cornbread, kale, and black-eyed peas). Not that Celestre is afraid to innovate: The menu features a very un-Portuguese sesame salad created for surf hero Garrett McNamara, a regular whose wave-defying exploits are immortalized on the walls.

Av. da República, 54. ✆ **26/255-16-95.** Mains 9€–15€. Daily 12am–11pm.

Aki-D'el-Mar ★★ PORTUGUESE/SEAFOOD Whether you start with *amêijoas à Bulhão Pato* (clams in garlic and cilantro) or *sapateira recheada* (stuffed crab), then move on to *açorda de lagosta com gambas* (a garlicky bread-based dish with lobster and shrimp) or *arroz de marisco* (mixed seafood rice), you can rest assured that you'll be getting the freshest, best-prepared shellfish around in this renowned beachfront *marisqueira* (seafood restaurant, in case you couldn't guess).

Avenida Manuel Remígio, 8. www.akidelmar.com. ✆ **26/282-43-00.** Mains 11€–20€. Daily noon–midnight.

Taverna 8 ó 80 ★ PORTUGUESE/MEDITERRANEAN This cozy seafront place started life as a tapas bar but has evolved into serving full meals. The daily menu ranges from Portuguese classics to Mediterranean-slanted dishes, like hake in saffron sauce and shrimp lasagna. You can enjoy small plates, like seabass ceviche and blood-sausage with pineapple, as tapas or appetizers. Many people start out with a G&T—there are over 80 gins to choose from.

Avenida Manuel Remigio, Edifício Atlântico, Loja 8. ✆ **26/256-04-90.** Mains 12€–22€. Wed–Mon noon–3:30pm, 6:30–10:30pm.

BATALHA ★★

120km (75 miles) N of Lisbon; 30km (20 miles) E of Nazaré

Outside the Iberian Peninsula, few people have heard of the **Battle of Aljubarrota.** Yet the 1385 clash between Portugal and Spanish invaders would have a lasting impact on world history. Portugal's against-the-odds victory made King João I the country's undisputed ruler and secured its borders for almost 200 years. Freed from outside threat, João's son Henry (later called The Navigator) was able to divert the energies of Portugal's ruling class overseas, triggering the Age of Discoveries.

João made sure the battle was commemorated in style, ordering construction of a flamboyant gothic monastery, the **Mosteiro da Batalha ★★★**

(literally the Monastery of the Battle) near the site. Now a UNESCO World Heritage site, it rivals Alcobaça as the country's most glorious gothic church. The near neighbors are a contrast in styles. Batalha's soft stone glows golden in the sunlight, its ornate tracery, pinnacles and sculpture-filled arches are the antithesis of Alcobaça's pale simplicity. There's not much else to see in the little town, except for a state-of-the-art **Interpretation Center ★** built on the battlefield to explain the history behind the conflict.

Essentials

ARRIVING

BY BUS The **Rede Expressos** bus (www.rede-expressos.pt) takes 2 hours to make the trip from Lisbon's Sete Rios station. There are five daily departures between 7am and 7pm. Fares start at 11.40€

BY CAR From Lisbon, the fastest option is the A1 toll highway. Leave at Exit 5 for Aveiras/Alcoentre, and continue on the N366 until it merges with the N1/IC2, which runs inexplicably close to the monastery facade.

VISITOR INFORMATION

The **Batalha Tourist Office** (www.descobrirbatalha.pt; ✆ **24/476-51-80**) is on Praça Mouzinho de Albuquerque, just alongside the monastery. It's open daily (10am–1pm, 2–6pm).

Exploring Batalha

Centro de Interpretação da Batalha de Aljubarrota ★ MUSEUM Aljubarrota was one of those medieval battles where, in the telling of the victors at least, a plucky band of patriotic yeomen defeated an overwhelming force of haughty invading bluebloods. In Portugal's case, the defenders include the "sweethearts wing," made up of students from Coimbra university and a baker woman who dispatched several Castilian knights with the heavy wooden shovel she normally used to lift loaves from the oven. This high-tech visitors center has films and displays to explain all the daring-do and allows you to explore the battlefield firsthand.

Avenida Dom Nuno Álvares Pereira 120, Calvaria de Cima. www.fundacao-aljubarrota.pt. ✆ **24/480-00-60.** 7€; 5€ youngsters 13–17, over 65s; 3.50€ children 6–12; free under 12s. Tues–Sun 10am–4:30pm.

Mosteiro da Batalha ★★★ RELIGIOUS SITE It's best to get your first look at Batalha in late afternoon when fading sunlight immerses the glorious stonework in honeyed light. But come anytime and the monastery is an awesome sight. The main facade stretches for over 100m (330 ft.) but is dominated by the **western portal ★★★**, a pointed arch lined with six rows of gothic statues (78 in all) featuring saints, prophets, angels, and biblical kings, surrounding a sculpture of Christ enthroned. Walk through the doors and more of that golden stone towers up in pairs of columns 32m (105 ft.) high that reach down the great **nave ★★★** for over 80m (88 yards). On sunny days, patterns of blue, mauve, and amber will filter onto the stone floor from the

15th-century stained-glass windows. The architect, known only as Huguet, made the church unusually narrow to accentuate the height of his vaulted ceiling.

To the right of the entrance is the **Founder's Chapel ★★★** where, beneath a lacy network of stone tracery and starry arches, lie the tombs of João I and his English queen, Philippa of Lancaster. Their hands are linked to symbolize the alliance between their countries, which survives as the world's oldest. Around the walls of the octagonal chapel are the final resting places of the couple's descendants, including Prince Henry the Navigator. Head down the aisle and take a door to the right, which will lead you to the ***Capelas Imperfeitas*** **★★** (Unfinished Chapels), commissioned by King Duarte in 1437 but never finished. Roofless (the floor is slippery on rainy days), they are a stumpy but impossibly intricate monument in the Manueline style executed by Diogo de Boitaca, architect of Lisbon's Jerónimos monastery.

The **Royal Cloisters ★★★** reflect the transition from the gothic to the Manueline style. Looking onto a formal garden are over two-dozen arches with embroidery-like stonework enlaced with floral motifs and Portugal's *Cruz de Cristo* emblem. The **Chapter House ★★★** is considered an architectural masterpiece due to the gravity-defining scale of its columnless star-vaulted ceiling. Sentries stand guard permanently here over the tombs of two unknown soldiers killed in World War I. A second cloister was built in the 16th century in less extravagant gothic style.

Back outside, the sword-swinging horseman whose statue stands next to the monastery is **Nuno Álvares Pereira** (1360–1431), the hero who led Portuguese troops at Aljubarrota. Look up to at the 380 **gargoyles** perched around the roof; they include grotesque, exotic, and disturbing characters. Among them is one supposed to represent a native of the newly discovered Americas.

Largo Infante Dom Henrique. www.mosteirobatalha.gov.pt/en. ✆ **24/476-54-97.** 6€, 3€ students and over 65s; free under 12s. Daily Apr–Oct 15 9am–6pm; Oct 16–Mar 9am–5:30pm.

Where to Stay

MODERATE

Hotel Villa Batalha ★ Sleek lines, groovy wallpaper, sinewy lamps, and lots of polished steel announce that this is a hotel of today. The interior space floods with natural light, and most bedrooms open onto private balconies. Some overlook the monastery. That view is also available through the glass walls surrounding the indoor pool, an essential element of a spa where you can get a hot-stone massage or exfoliating lava rub—just the thing after a hard day of sightseeing. The restaurant specializes in locally sourced dishes, like salt-cod with *chícharo* beans or Alcobaça apple pie. Throughout, there's a high level of accessibility for disabled guests.

Rua Dom Duarte I. www.hotelvillabatalha.com. ✆ **24/424-04-00.** 93 units. 79€–99€ double; 107€–183€ suite. Free parking. **Amenities:** Garden; terrace; golf; restaurant; bar; indoor pool; sauna; hammam; Jacuzzi; massage service; free Wi-Fi.

A royal SPA

There's little left of the royal palace where Saint Isabel, Portugal's holy queen, reputedly came to sip the spring water, but Monte Real remains a grand place to take the waters. Built in 1926, the **Palace Hotel Monte Real ★★** is one of Portugal's noble spa hotels. Restored to its former glory amid the pine forests in the valley of the river Lis, the salmon-colored palace makes a great place to unwind. The spa is one of the most complete and luxurious in the country with a range of treatments and massages, also open to non-guests. The separate, historical thermal center, whose natural hot springs have been valued since Roman times, was undergoing a facelift as we went to press and was due to open rejuvenated. The hotel's spacious rooms spread from the main building into a modern wing facing the pool and the extensive forested grounds. It's a 10-minute drive from the city of Leiria and its hilltop castle or to the sandy beach at **Praia da Vieira ★★**, renowned for its seaside restaurants, including **Cantinho do Mar ★★** (✆ **24/469-58-11**), whose *arroz da marisco* (seafood rice) is one of the best in the land.

Rua de Leiria, Monte Real. www.termasdemontereal.pt. ✆ **24/461-89-00.** 101 units. 55€–180€; 114€–175€ suite. Free parking. **Amenities:** Garden; terrace; free bikes; tennis; outdoor pool; gym; spa; sauna; hammam; Jacuzzi; restaurant; bar; children's play area; free Wi-Fi.

INEXPENSIVE

Hotel Casa do Outeiro ★★ If you get the right room here, you'll wake up to look upon the monastery from your private terrace. If not, don't worry too much: The monastery is only a 5-minute walk away and you can gaze out over the rolling countryside from beside the pool. Rooms are white with big splashes of color from modern paintings and handicrafts (which you can buy from the little shop). It's homelike and friendly. Breakfast with homemade jams and pastries is served by the pool when the sun's out.

Largo Carvalho do Outeiro 4. www.hotelcasadoouteiro.com. ✆ **24/476-58-06.** 23 units. 55€–111€ double. Free parking. **Amenities:** Children's play area; exercise room; outdoor pool; free Wi-Fi.

Where to Eat

Burro Velho ★ PORTUGUESE The restaurant's called "Old Donkey," but thankfully that's not one of the items on the menu. Instead expect aged steaks, Alentejo black pork, or Brazilian-style *picanha.* Fish dishes are equally renowned in this popular place behind the monastery in an unassuming row house. Rice with lobster (steep at 85€ for two) or baked octopus are among the saltwater treats. Let the expert host guide you around his extensive, and excellent, wine list.

Rua Nossa Sra. do Caminho 6A. www.burrovelho.com. ✆ **24/476-41-74.** Mains 9€–42€. Mon–Sat noon–3pm, 7–10pm.

FÁTIMA ★

128km (8 miles) N of Lisbon; 20km (12 miles) E of Batalha

Ironically, one of the most significant modern pilgrimage sites in the Catholic Church takes its name from a Muslim princess, herself named for the daughter of the Prophet Muhammad. At a rocky highland field outside the village of Fátima, three poor shepherd children said they were visited by a vision of the Virgin Mary over a period of months, starting on May 13, 1917. The church and secular authorities at first tried to suppress the story, but news spread and crowds flocked to the site. By the time of the last appearance, tens of thousands of people gathered. Many reported seeing the sky turn brilliant colors and the sun dance in a zig-zag motion. In a world rocked by uncertainty as the Great War and Russian Revolution raged, millions were fascinated by the secret messages the Virgin was said to have passed on to the children.

Over the years, Fátima's fame as a pilgrimage site spread. A small chapel, a statue of Mary, and a hospital were built. By the 1930s, the Church had recognized the visions as "worthy of belief" and the **Basilica of Our Lady of the Rosary of Fátima ★** was built with a vast outdoor prayer space, curving colonnade, and a 65m (213-ft.) tower, capped with a crown of bronze weighing 7,000 kilograms (7.7 tons), based on the one which the Virgin is supposed to have worn. Pilgrims continue to flock here in huge numbers. In 2017, the centenary of the events, 9.4 million came, including Pope Francis. He canonized two of the shepherds, Francisco and Jacinta Marto, who both died in the influenza epidemic that swept Europe after WW1. Their cousin, Lúcia dos Santos, became a nun and died in 2005 at the age of 97.

Fátima today is no longer the village of the early 1900s. A second, larger basilica, the **Basílica da Santíssima Trindade ★★**, was inaugurated in 2008 to cope with the flow of pilgrims. There are dozens of hotels and hostels, religious institutions, a wax museum, and countless retail outlets selling religious artifacts and souvenirs. Despite the commercialization, it can be an impressive experience to watch the throngs of pilgrims, many of whom walk for miles and complete the final stretch on their knees. The biggest crowds gather on the anniversary of the first and last visions, May 13 and October 13.

Essentials

ARRIVING

BY BUS Up to six buses an hour leave Lisbon's Sete Rios station daily for the approximately 90-minute trip. One-way tickets are 12.20€. For schedules: www.rede-expressos.pt.

BY CAR Take the A1 toll highway from Lisbon. Leave at Exit 8 for Fátima. It should take 1 hour, 20 minutes. From Batalha it takes about 25 minutes on the N362.

VISITOR INFORMATION

The **tourist office** is at Avenida Dom José Alves Correia da Silva 213 (✆ **24/953-11-39;** Mon–Fri 9am–1pm, 2–5pm; Sat–Sun 9am–1pm, 2–6pm).

GOING underground

Between Fátima and Alcobaça is a highland nature reserve, the **Parque Natural das Serras de Aire e Candeeiros ★★**, encompassing more than 30,000 hectares (74,132 acres) of moors and scrubland. The sparsely settled landscape is crisscrossed by trails linking lakes, waterfalls, canyons, and rocks imprinted with dinosaur footprints. Details at www.natural.pt. There are park offices in **Rio Maior** (Rua Dr. Augusto César Silva Ferreira; ✆ **24/399-94-80**) and **Porto De Mós** (Alameda D. Afonso Henriques; ✆ **24/449-19-04**).

The park's biggest attraction are the **Grutas de Mira De Aire ★★** (www.grutasmiradaire.com; ✆ **24/444-03-22**), a complex of caves and caverns running for 11km (almost 7 miles) through the limestone hills. They are among the most impressive in Europe, with a technicolor array of stalactites and stalagmites, weird rock formations and streams babbling through natural chambers. Open daily. Tickets for the hour-long guided tours are 6.90€, 4.10€ for children 5 to 11, free for younger kids. There's also a fun swimming complex next door with several pools, slides, and flumes.

On the northern edge of the park, the village of **Minde** is famed for its colorful, woven **wool blankets ★**. A workshop (*Atelier de Tecelagem*) is open for visits and has an online store (www.caorg.pt; ✆ **24/984-00-22**). A curiosity at the park's southern tip are the **Salinas Naturais de Rio Maior ★** where salt has been produced the same way since the 12th century. The evaporation pans are unusual: Far from the sea, they are fed by saline underwater streams seven times more salty than the Atlantic. The jumble of wooden huts and walkways around the pans make for a fascinating visit, particularly in late summer when there are dazzling piles of fresh salt. Among the shacks are stores to buy salty souvenirs, snacks, or a meal—try broiling your own steak on a heated slab of rock-salt (www.salarium.pt; ✆ **91/876-18-50**).

Info at www.visitfatima.pt. The **Shrine of Fátima** website (www.fatima.pt) provides detailed information in English on how to visit.

Exploring the Town

The religious sites of Fátima are centered around a spot called Cova da Iria, where the Virgin is said to have appeared to the three little shepherds. The central square is bigger than St. Peter's in Rome, and on major pilgrimage days it will be choked with visitors. Between May 13 and October 13 you will see small groups of pilgrims from across Portugal dressed in high-visibility vests tramping roads toward the shrine. On those days, marking the beginning and end of the apparitions, a statue of the Madonna passes through the crowd between about 10am and 12:30pm, as tens of thousands of white handkerchiefs flutter in the breeze. There are candlelit processions every night at 10:15pm, most impressive during a major pilgrimage.

The focal point is the tiny, white **Chapel of the Apparitions ★**, built in 1923 on the exact spot where the mother of Jesus is supposed to have appeared beside an oak tree. The chapel was rebuilt after the original was dynamited by sceptics in 1922. The chapel lies under a porch built in 1982 on a visit by Pope John Paul II.

Dominating the square is the great tower of **Basílica de Nossa Senhora do Rosário ★**, built between 1928 and 1954 and surrounded by a colonnade composed of 200 columns. Inside, the church is lined with colored Portuguese marble and packed with mosaics and statues. The tombs of Lúcia, Francisco, and Jacinta lie within. With the original basilica too small to hold the multitudes, a second, the **Basilica of the Most Holy Trinity ★★**, was built from 2004 to 2007 at the other end of the square. The low, white building designed by Greek architect Alexandros Tombazis has space for almost 9,000 worshipers, making it one of the world's largest churches. Among the artworks is a 50m (164-ft.) mosaic in terracotta and gilt behind the altar designed by Slovenian artist Marko Ivan Rupnik. Cova de Iria also has many religious statues and museums. The **Wax Museum** (*Museu de Cera*) is among the most visited, with dozens of figures telling the Fátima story (www.mucefa.pt; ✆ **24/953-93-00**). Amid the trees on the southside of the square is a segment of the **Berlin Wall,** illustrating the belief of many pilgrims that prayers here helped bring about the fall of communism in Eastern Europe.

A 15-minute drive east of Fátima, the town of **Ourém ★** boasts an impressive 12th-century castle and a pleasant core of medieval streets.

SHOPPING Fátima overflows with shops selling statues of the Virgin Mary and other religious souvenirs. The **Praceta de São José,** to the north side of the basilica square, has many small, traditional stalls, while the **Centro Comercial Fátima** (www.fatimashoppingcenter.com; ✆ **24/953-23-75**) holds a vast selection of religious items and secular handicrafts on Estrada de Leiria 108, the road heading out of town to the north.

Where to Stay

If you want to stay in the town, it's best to book well in advance on major pilgrimage days. Be aware the room prices skyrocket around the 13th of the month for every month from May through October.

Aurea Fátima Hotel Congress & SPA ★ Opened in 2017, this six-story hotel has an eye-catching black-and-gold striped exterior and continues the color scheme inside with gilt juxtaposed with dark backgrounds in the reception area and spacious rooms. Design icons like white-leather Barcelona chairs are matched with black-and-white photos and saintly statues. Pluses are the big, stone-lined bathrooms and an excellent breakfast with an emphasis on fresh fruit and pastries. It's a short walk to the sanctuary.

Avenida Dom José Alves Correia da Silva 279. www.aureafatimahotel.fatima-hotels.com/pt. ✆ **24/953-17-50.** 108 units. 58€–305€ double; 103€–523€ suite. Free parking. **Amenities:** Garden; terrace; 2 restaurants; bar; spa; gym; sauna; hammam; Jacuzzi; massage service; free Wi-Fi.

Dom Gonçalo & Spa ★ There's pampering for pilgrims at this family-oriented place, a 10-minute walk from the Sanctuary. Among the spa treatments is a 55-minute massage for sore backs and feet tired from walking.

Accommodation is divided between contemporary "design" rooms with floral prints and white-tiled bathrooms and the "classic" rooms of 1980s design with heavier wooden furniture and tawny brown bathrooms. Beds are comfy and there are bigger family rooms. The heated indoor pool is relaxing after a day of touring. Prices shoot up on pilgrimage peaks. The restaurant is one of the best in town: Try the Chateaubriand steak.

Rua Jacinta Marto 100. www.hoteldg.com. ✆ **24/953-93-30.** 71 units. 69€–350€ double. Free parking. **Amenities:** Garden; terrace; children's play area; restaurant; bar; bikes; indoor pool; spa; gym; sauna; hammam; Jacuzzi; massage service; free Wi-Fi.

Luz Charming Houses ★★★ This feels a million miles from the crowds in Fátima, but it's just a 20-minute walk (or 5-minute ride on the free bikes) from the sanctuary. In a complete hamlet of restored rural houses surrounded by woods and a garden bursting with oak, olive, and fig trees, rosemary and heather, the rustic-chic rooms and suites look like they've jumped from the pages of *Architectural Digest* with their tasteful blends of colors and textures: polished cement, natural wood, lace and linen. The main house has a store selling crafts, plus a lounge and breakfast room, and an honesty bar. Fairy lights sparkle by the swimming pool, and you can get a range of massages in a candle-lit cave.

Rua Principal 78, Moimento. www.luzhouses.pt. ✆ **24/953-22-75.** 15 units. 111€–155€ double; 160€–240€ suite. Free parking. **Amenities:** Garden; terrace; free bikes; outdoor pool; bar; massage service; babysitting; free Wi-Fi.

Where to Eat

Tasquinha ★ PORTUGUESE Don't be put off by the bland, canteen-like interior of this basement eatery in the shadow of the sanctuary: Locals swear this has some of the finest cooking in town. It's best-known for steaks, which come in a number of guises including swimming in cream sauce or topped with dripping *queijo da serra* sheep's cheese, but the grilled shrimp and codfish with cornbread crust have their fans.

Rua Monfortinos. www.tasquinhafatima.com. ✆ **24/953-34-46.** Mains 8€–24€. Daily noon–3:30pm and 7:30–10:30pm.

Tia Alice ★★ PORTUGUESE In the basement below an inconspicuous roadside house on the outskirts of town is a restaurant that been listed among the best in the country. The room is lined with rough stone walls, but the decor is sophisticated with soft lights and white-table linen. In the kitchen, Tia (aunty) Alice Marto prepares superlative versions of regional cuisine, and everybody from presidents to Nobel Prize winners to superstars of Brazilian music have come to try. Creamy oven-baked salt-cod with shrimp or veal roasted in the wood-fired oven are among the specialties. Book in advance on weekends.

Rua do Adro, 152. ✆ **24/953-17-37.** Reservations required. Main courses 18€–20€. Tues–Sat noon–3pm and 7:30–9pm; Sun noon–3pm. Closed last 3 weeks of July.

THE ALGARVE

The Algarve's golden beaches are what put Portugal on the international tourism map. Its south-facing coast is sheltered from the Atlantic rollers that pound the western seaboard; its climate and landscape are Mediterranean in feel. Citrus orchards and groves of fig and almond trees give it the "garden of Portugal" tag. In no other region does the legacy of Roman and Arab rule run as deep. Recently, however, mass tourism has left a more visible mark. Outsize resorts and high-rise strips scar parts of the coast, but if you know where to look, it's easy to discover beaches, villages, and landscapes where the sunny Algarve charm shines as brightly as ever.

10

When Portugal was a monarchy, its ruler was known as king, or queen, of Portugal and the Algarves. The title reflects a separateness that lingers. Ranges of low, forest-covered mountains run east-west from the coast to the Spanish border, forming a barrier to the rest of the country. Although the hills are only 900m (2,960 ft.) at their highest point and are easily traversed on the fast highway from Lisbon, the land on the other side is different. Its climate is gentler, its southern slopes bathed by sunshine, sheltered from the influence of the North Atlantic. The landscapes and culture can feel closer to Spain's Andalusia region to the east than they do to the rest of Portugal.

North to south, the Algarve can be divided into three distinct strips. The mountains are covered with dwarf oak, *maquis* shrubland and eucalyptus, easily visited in the west where the highland town of Monchique has spas and hearty restaurants, wild and inaccessible in the eastern Serra do Caldeirão. Sloping gently southward, the *barrocal* is characterized by orange and lemon plantations, groves of olive, fig and almond, carob and pomegranate. Then there is the coast with its fishing ports and resorts, and an array of beaches, from scalloped coves and endless sandbar islands to the wild surfer hangouts on the west coast.

The coast also has a distinct east-west divide. From Albufeira east to the Spanish border, the *Sotavento* is sheltered from the Atlantic winds. Its waters tend to be warmer, its beaches long placid strips of pale sand backed by dunes and lagoons. To the west, the *Barlavento* is more exposed, although the region's trademark honeycomb cliffs shelter sandy cove beaches until the coast turns the

The Algarve

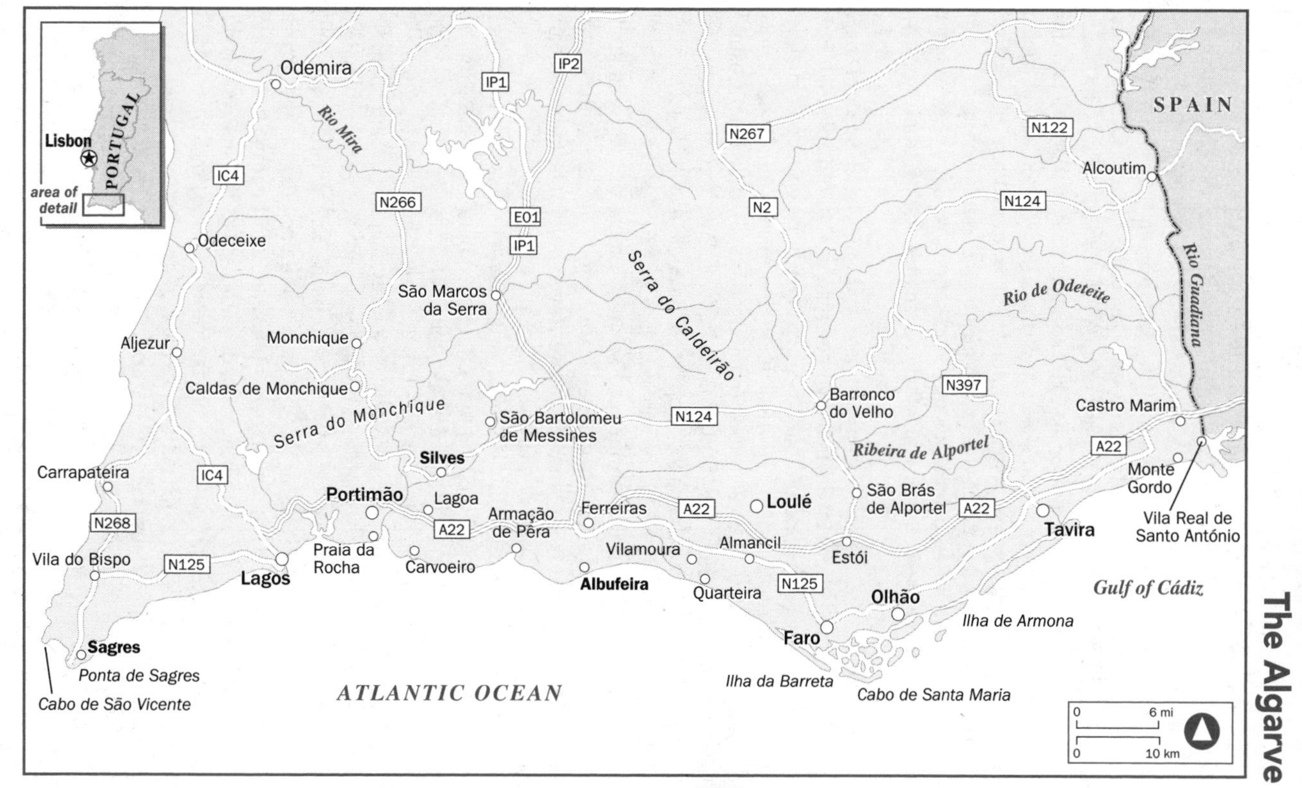

PORTUGAL
Lisbon
area of detail
Odemira
Rio Mira
IP1
IP2
N267
N122
SPAIN
Alcoutim
IC4
N266
E01
IP1
N2
N124
Odeceixe
Serra do Caldeirão
Rio Guadiana
São Marcos da Serra
Rio de Odeleite
Aljezur
Monchique
Caldas de Monchique
N397
Barronco do Velho
Castro Marim
Serra do Monchique
São Bartolomeu de Messines
N124
Ribeira de Alportel
A22
Silves
Monte Gordo
Carrapateira
IC4
São Brás de Alportel
Portimão
Lagoa
Loulé
Ferreiras
A22
A22
Tavira
Vila Real de Santo António
N268
Armação de Pêra
A22
Almancil
Vila do Bispo
N125
Praia da Rocha
Vilamoura
Estói
Lagos
Carvoeiro
Albufeira
N125
Gulf of Cádiz
Quarteira
Olhão
Ilha de Armona
Faro
Sagres
Ponta de Sagres
Ilha da Barreta
ATLANTIC OCEAN
Cabo de Santa Maria
Cabo de São Vicente
0
6 mi
0
10 km

corner at Europe's southwestern-most point into the surf-pummeled shore of the Costa Vicentina Natural Park.

Historically, as well as geographically, the Algarve falls under Mediterranean influence. Traders and settlers from ancient Greece, Phoenicia (today's Lebanon), and Carthage (in today's Tunisia) left traces before the Romans brought the region into their empire. Ruins of Roman temples, baths, and industrial enterprises can still be seen. Arabs ruled the Algarve for 538 years, from 711 until Portugal's King Afonso III took Faro in 1249. That's 100 years more than in Lisbon and almost 400 years longer than in Porto. The Arab influence can be seen in the architecture of the Algarve's white, flat-roofed houses with their distinctive pointed chimneys, in the agriculture and cuisine, in the very name of the region—*al-gharb* means "the West" in Arabic.

The historical turning point that's most marked the modern Algarve came in the late 1960s with the arrival of cheap charter flights from Northern Europe.

Before then, the region's balmy climate and sun-kissed beaches were already attracting a select international following. The still-splendid Bela Vista Hotel opened in 1934 on Praia da Rocha beach. Its guestbook includes the likes of exiled King Umberto II of Italy after World War II and Cuban dictator Fulgencio Batista, who took refuge in Portugal after Fidel Castro's takeover. At the height of the Beatles' fame in 1968, Paul McCartney and his soon-to-be wife Linda escaped to Alvor, where he could wander unrecognized on the largely tourist-free beaches and even jam with the hotel band.

Big name international celebrities and political leaders still vacation in the Algarve, but they tend to stay in closeted luxury resorts that divide the central strip of the southern coast with towns overflowing with cheap-booze bars, fast-food joints, and towering apartment blocks.

Years ago, Portuguese officials looked at the uncontrolled construction on Spain's Costa del Sol and pledged to avoid the neighbor's mistakes. But the lure of tourist lucre proved too great, and much of the natural beauty of the coast between Faro and Alvor has been bulldozered into overdevelopment. Even there, it's not all bad. Some resorts are lowkey, landscaped and luxurious with starred gourmet restaurants and world-class golf. You can find fabulous beaches and pockets of the old Algarve even in the center, but many of the region's highlights these days are on the extremities. Towns like Tavira, Olhão, and Vila Real de Santo António in the east, and Lagos and Sagres in the west have some of the best beaches and retain a sense of history and genuine Algarve character, although they are far from untouched by tourism. Faro, the regional capital, has a rich cultural heritage. Nature lovers can take a boat to explore the Ria Formosa lagoon, a protected reserve, or the River Guadiana that forms the frontier with Andalusia. There are excellent hiking trails, notably along the wild west coast or through the interior. And, if you avoid the tourist traps, the Algarve has some of the best food in Portugal, based largely on its fresh seafood peppered with influences from the Mediterranean cuisine of Spain and North Africa.

FARO ★★

280km (174 miles) S of Lisbon; 200km (125 miles) W of Seville, Spain.

Faro is the Algarve's administrative and cultural capital. With around 60,000 people, it's the region's nearest thing to a big city. Faro Airport is the international gateway to the Algarve, receiving over 8 million passengers a year. Most don't hang around, but head out directly to the resorts.

That's a pity because Faro deserves a look. It is an attractive and historic city overlooking the flat blue waters of the Ria Formosa lagoon. The oldest part is Vila Adentro, encircled by ramparts dating back to Roman, Byzantine, and Moorish times. It's crammed with pristine white streets, squares lined with orange trees, and historic buildings topped with triangular, terracotta-tiled roofs. Outside the walled city, the downtown area spreads north and east from the harbor gardens in a mix of simple, single-story cottages, 17th-century townhouses, early 1900s neo-Moorish palazzos, and dazzling white churches.

Faro's city walls tell a story. The Arab city was twice sacked by northern European crusaders on their way to the Middle East in the hundred years leading up to its eventual conquest by the Portuguese in 1249. In the 16th century, it was devastated by English corsairs led by Robert Devereux, Earl of Essex, a favorite of Queen Elizabeth I (until she changed her mind and had his head lopped off). In the 1830s, its parapets saw fighting between liberals and absolutists in Portugal's civil war. During a period of peace in 1487, Samuel Gacon, a member of Faro's then-numerous Jewish community, introduced a printing press. The first book printed in Portugal was in Hebrew script, the so-called Faro Pentateuch. One copy survives: Looted by Essex's buccaneers, it rests in London at the British Museum.

Essentials

ARRIVING

BY PLANE The opening of Faro International Airport (www.aeroporto faro.pt) in 1966 transformed the Algarve into a region of large-scale tourism. It's built on a sandy peninsula east of the city and has twice undergone major overhauls enabling it to handle current traffic levels, which in summer is around 25,000 passengers a day. As we write, a weekly flight from Canada's **Air Transat** (www.airtransat.com) from Toronto was the only intercontinental connection, but Faro is a major destination for European airlines. Looking at its timetable gives you an idea of the travelers you'll meet in the Algarve: There are flights from 23 British airports, 12 French, 11 German, and 5 each from Ireland, Poland, and the Netherlands. If you are traveling from elsewhere in Portugal, **TAP** (www.flytap.pt) has up to four daily flights making the 45-minute trip from Lisbon, with one-way prices around 70€; Ireland's **Ryanair** (www.ryanair.com) has one or two daily runs from Porto, sometimes charging as little as 15€ for the 70-minute trip.

From the airport, the local **Proximo** (www.proximo.pt; ✆ **28/989-97-00**) bus company has lines 14 and 16 providing a roughly twice-an-hour service between downtown and the airport between 5am and midnight. The trip takes 20 minutes in normal traffic, and the 2.25€ tickets can be bought directly from the drivers. They stop at the train station, then terminate at the main bus station at Avenida da República, 5. From there you can link up with the regional bus line **EVA Buses** (www.eva-bus.com; ✆ **28/989-97-60**) for connections to other Algarve destinations. EVA also has buses twice a day between Faro airport and the Spanish cities of Seville, Huelva, and Ayamonte. Seville is reached in about 4 hours and costs 20€.

There's a full selection of **car hire** options at Faro airport, including Avis, Hertz, Sixt, and Budget. Taxis in Portugal are painted black-and-green, or in some cases cream. The rank is outside Arrivals. It should cost around 12€ to downtown, although there will be extra charges for trips at night or weekends as well as for baggage. **Ride hailing apps** Uber, Bolt, and Cabify operate in Faro and elsewhere in the Algarve. There are also a number of direct transfer companies offering **shuttles to resorts** around the Algarve from the airport; check www.faroshuttlebus.com, www.hoppa.com, or www.terravision.eu.

BY TRAIN From Lisbon, Algarve-bound trains can be boarded at Oriente, Entrecampos, or Sete Rios stations. There are five daily direct trains to Faro, taking around 3 hours and costing from 22€. Over a dozen regional trains make the trip along the Algarve coast each day, stopping at Faro. To get to Vila Real de Santo Antonio on the Spanish border takes just over an hour and costs 5.25€. Details on: www.cp.pt.

BY BUS **Rede Expressos** (www.rede-expressos.pt) has 16 daily buses from Lisbon's Sete Rio station. The trip takes between 3 and 4 hours and fares start from 19€. The company also runs five buses from Seville that take about 3 hours and cost from 17€.

BY CAR From Lisbon, the drive takes about 2 hours 40 minutes on the A2 and A22 toll roads. Coming from Spain, the trip from Seville is along the A49 to the frontier, then the A22. It takes about 2 hours 15 minutes. Be aware that Portugal's automatic toll system works on the A22, so you should check if your rental car is equipped with an electronic device to automatically charge the toll, or register your vehicle with the system (p. 468).

VISITOR INFORMATION

The **tourist office** is at Rua da Misericórdia 8–11 (✆ **28/980-36-04**). It's open daily 9:30am to 5:30pm. There is also one at the airport (✆ **28/981-85-82**). The city hall has excellent tourist information in English on its website: www.cm-faro.pt.

Exploring Faro

Convento de Nossa Senhora da Assunção ★★ MUSEUM You get two attractions for the price of one here. First the building itself, a splendid Renaissance-style convent dating to the 16th century; secondly the surprisingly good **municipal museum** with objects and exhibitions explaining the history of the city and its art. The convent was battered in the English raid and by the 1755 earthquake but remains a graceful construction with a double-tiered **cloister,** colorful dome, and the pyramidal roofs typical of the eastern Algarve. The museum houses remnants from Roman (check out the sad sea god in the excellent mosaics) and Muslim Faro, plus a fine collection of old master paintings from the 16th to the 20th century. They frequently hold fado performances. The museum is just behind the cathedral in the heart of the ancient **Vila Adentro,** with plenty of sidewalk cafes nearby.

Largo Dom Afonso III 14. ✆ **28/987-08-29.** 2€, 1€ over 65s, youngsters 13–26, free under 12s. Tues–Fri 10am–6pm, Sat–Sun 10:30am–5pm.

Igreja do Carmo ★ CHURCH Despite high-rise construction nearby, the twin bell towers and baroque yellow-and-white facade of this 18th-century church are a striking landmark on the Faro skyline. Inside, the nave is lined with glittering rococo chapels covered with gold leaf and a procession of baroque statues by local carver Manuel Martins. What draws most visitors, however, is a **spooky chapel** at the back with walls made entirely by human bones. It was built in 1816 and contains over 1,200 skulls, believed to be the remains of monks. As with the bigger *Capela dos Ossos* in Évora, it was built as a reminder of the transient nature of life. A sign above the door says: "Wait here to consider that you too will end in this state."

Largo do Carmo. ✆ **28/982-44-90.** Free; 2€ for bone chapel. Summer: Mon–Fri 9am–6pm, Sat 9am–1pm; Winter: Mon–Fri 9am–5pm, Sat 9am–5pm.

Jardim Manuel Bivar ★ GARDEN These harborside gardens filled with shady semi-tropical vegetation have been the social heart of Faro since the 19th century. Open on the eastern side to the marina, an inlet of the Ria Formosa lagoon, the garden is surrounded on the three other sides by some of the city's most significant real estate. Just beyond its northern tip are the 18th-century **Alfândega** (Customs House) and the **Palácio Bivar,** an aristocratic property built in the neoclassical style. At the corner of Rua Dom Francisco Gomes, a pedestrian shopping street, is the **Café Aliança** (✆ **91/635-90-30;** open daily noon–midnight). It dates back to 1908 and still recalls its glory days as the city's intellectual hangout. The 1893 **bandstand** in the center of the garden is another popular local meeting point. Overlooking the garden halfway down its western flank is the **Banco de Portugal** building, a fine example of the 1920s fashion for architecture that mixes and matches Moorish and Manueline motifs. Next door, the **Misericórdia** is a church and former hospital built by Italian architect Francesco Fabri, the man behind many notable constructions in Portugal post-1755 earthquake. He also designed the grand **Arco da Vila** archway leading into the walled city (see below). Beside it is one final grand facade, the neoclassical **Civil Government Building** erected in the 1860s.

Praça Dom Francisco Gomes. Free. Open daily, 24 hours.

Mercado Municipal ★★ MARKET Like many cities, Faro has sought to breathe new life into its market hall by adding new stores, cafes, and restaurants to the traditional stalls. Given the size of its expansive Art Deco–inspired building, it's gone even further by installing tax and other government offices. Visitors will be more interested in the colorful fresh produce section, where locally caught fish; plus figs, almonds, honey, fresh peaches, juice-packed oranges and other Algarve produce, flowers; freshly baked bread and pastries take pride of place. The market is a dynamic space with frequent events, from chocolate festivals and show-cooking with celebrity chefs, to all-night DJ sets. The roof has a bar and organic herb garden.

Largo Doutor Francisco Sá Carneiro. www.mercadomunicipaldefaro.pt. ✆ **28/989-72-50.** Free. Market stalls daily 7am–3pm; Food court 7am–midnight.

Muralhas ★ HISTORIC MONUMENT Faro's city walls wrap themselves around the Vila Adentro and span historical eras. Much of the fortification we see today was built in the 9th century. Some are even older: two **pentagonal towers** on the eastern side (facing the main city parking lot) were built by the Byzantines, who held Faro before the Arab conquest. Nearby, the **Arco do Repouso** is one of the best-preserved city gates, built during the Almohad Empire. Its name means Arch of Rest because it's said King Afonso III rested there after capturing the city in 1249. According to legend, a Muslim girl in love with one of the besieging Portuguese knights opened the gate to the invaders. She was cursed by her father and her spirit is supposed to haunt the gate. The most spectacular gate, however, is the **Arco de Vila,** a towering edifice on the western side built after the 1755 earthquake and frequently home to nesting **white storks.** Under the arch is the last surviving Arab-style **horseshoe doorway** built in the 11th century. Details below are for the **visitor center** in the Arco de Vila with displays about city history and views from the roof. The walls can be climbed at any time, free of charge.

Rua da Misericórdia 8. ✆ **28/989-72-50.** Free. Daily 9am–6pm.

Sé Catedral ★★ CHURCH Faro's cathedral stands in the city's comeliest square, surrounded by the harmonious 18th-century facades of the **Bishop's Palace** and **Seminary** and lined with rows of orange trees. A Roman temple and mosque once stood on the site of the Gothic- and Renaissance-style cathedral, whose truncated tower is a reminder of the building's mauling at the hands of English arsonists in 1596 and the earthquake in 1755. Still, there's plenty to see inside the high-arched doorway. It's packed with 17th-century tiles, gilded baroque carvings, and Italian oil paintings. The huge **pipe-organ,** German-made in 1715, is richly decorated in red-and-gold chinoiserie painting. Among several remarkable chapels, that of **Nossa Senhora do Rosário**—with intricate goldwork, floor-to-ceiling *azulejos,* and statues of two African incense bearers—stands out.

Largo da Sé. ✆ **28/980-75-90.** 3.50€, 2.50€ over 65s and students 15–25, free under 15s. Feb–Nov: Mon–Fri 10am–6pm, Sat 9:30am–12:30pm; Dec–Jan: Mon–Fri 10am–5:30pm, Sat 9:30am–12:30pm

OUTDOOR ACTIVITIES Stretching along the coast for over 60km (37 miles) on either side of Faro, the **Ria Formosa ★★★** is a protected wetland system of blue lagoons, white-sand barrier islands, and wildlife-rich marshes. It's a complete contrast with the built-up beach resorts farther west, a place where you can hike wetland trails or kayak through the shallows surrounded by silence broken only by lapping waves and seabird screeches. To the seaward side, the sandbar islands offer peaceful beaches of fine, ivory-colored sand. **Praia de Faro ★★** is the most accessible, just beyond the airport and reachable by the No. 16 Airport bus over a narrow road bridge. **Ilha Deserta ★★★** (aka Ilha Barreta) is a more serene option. As the name implies, it's basically a desert island with protected status. The only construction is a famed restaurant (see p. 224). The sand can get a little crowded where the shuttle boats (www.ilhadeserta.com; ✆ **91/877-91-55**) from Faro drop off near the restaurant, but walk a little on the sand and you can find acres of space. Boats leave from a jetty at the southern end of Faro's old town. The fastest take 15 minutes and cost 10€. Other island beaches can be reached from Olhão and Tavira (see below). Beyond the beaches, there are a number of choices for plunging into Ria's natural wonders, from birdwatching tours to kayak hires and sunset cruises. Among the eco-tour operators in Faro offering boat or hiking trips, **Formosa Mar** (www.formosamar.com; ✆ **91/872-00-02**) has a 2-hour nature tour for 25€ where you can look for flamingos and other birdlife from a traditional fishing skiff; and **Lands** (www.lands.pt; ✆ **28/981-74-66**) will take you out in a solar-powered boat for a 45-minute sunset cruise for 15€.

SHOPPING Faro's downtown is fighting back. Faced with competition from out-of-town malls, local shopkeepers have gotten together to produce an excellent online guide (www.baixadefaro.pt) to shopping and dining in the city's **Baixa** (downtown). The main retail streets run inland from the quayside gardens, like Rua Francisco Gomes, Rua Santo António, or Rua Rebelo da Silva. They are mostly pedestrian-only and lined with 18th- and 19th-century buildings. Check out **Carminhos Artesanato,** Rua Santo António 29 (✆ **28/982-65-22**) or its neighbor **Arca de Santo António** (✆ **28/982-72-38**), at No. 19, for handicrafts. **António Manuel** (www.antoniomanuel.pt; ✆ **28/982-24-74**) has a chic selection of international fashion brands at Rua Santo António 46; and **Garrafeira Soares** (www.garrafeirasoares.pt; ✆ **28/982-02-23**) has a vast choice of Portuguese wine at Rua 1 de Maio 5.

Where to Stay

MODERATE

Eva Senses Hotel ★★ The Eva hotel has loomed in a white, seven-story block over the yachts bobbing in Faro's marina since the early days of Algarve tourism. A recent facelift has given its rooms a new sheen, with white-cotton bedclothes and robes matched with bold colors on the walls and furniture fabrics. The best rooms have views over the harbor and the lagoon. The lobby is full of white light; a fitness club comes equipped with Techno-Gym hardware; and the bar beside the rooftop pool has become Faro's "in" place for sunset cocktails. A penthouse restaurant offers breakfast with a view.

Av. da República 1. www.ap-hotelsresorts.com. ✆ **28/900-10-00.** 134 units. 66€–205€ double; 129€–300€ suite. **Amenities:** Terrace; bike hire; outdoor pool; spa; gym; sauna, hammam; massage services; restaurant; 2 bars; babysitting; free Wi-Fi.

Mercedes Country House ★ Get away from it all at this family-run villa amid the fruit trees of the Barrocal agricultural lands, a 20-minute drive to downtown or the beaches. The house is a modernist, rectilinear construction in white with lots of glass. A couple of traditional Algarve pointed chimneys give it a regional touch. Floors are in cool grey tiles and bleached planking. Throws, cushions, and bathroom *azulejos* bring splashes of color. The rooms all have sliding glass doors opening out onto the patios or lawns. The owners take pride in their range of Portuguese wines and homecooked meals made using vegetables and herbs grown organically on the property.

Local do Medronhal. https://mercedescountryhouse.com. ✆ **28/999-12-07.** 9 units. 108€–135€ double. Free parking. **Amenities:** Garden; terrace; outdoor pool; massage services; restaurant; bar; games room; babysitting; free Wi-Fi.

Pousada Palacio de Estoi ★★★ Conceived as a viscount's palace in the 1780s, this outrageous rococo confection of domes and towers in lemon, raspberry, and cream bursts out of the hillside looking south toward Faro. It is a spectacular place to stay. You can sip local liqueurs beneath the wedding cake stucco and cherub-adorned ceiling of a salon inspired by the Hall of Mirrors in Versailles, then stroll a garden filled with fountains, palm trees, and classical statues (rest in the pavilion filled with *azulejos* portraying risqué embraces between satyrs and lusty wenches). Guest rooms offer an escape from the baroque overload: In a discreet wing added in 2009, they have clean modern lines designed by architect Gonçalo Byrne and decor in shades of brown and ivory. Each has a private terrace overlooking the pool and surrounding groves of oranges and almonds. Faro is 10km (6 miles) away.

Rua São José, Estoi. www.pousadas.pt. ✆ **28/999-01-50.** 63 units. 103€–320€ double; 205€–380€ suite. Free parking. **Amenities:** Garden; terrace; bike hire; indoor, outdoor pools; spa; sauna, hammam; massage services; restaurant; 2 bars; babysitting; free Wi-Fi.

Where to Eat

Estaminé ★★★ PORTUGUESE/SEAFOOD A short boat ride from Faro's old town, this nationally famous restaurant is the only building on a deserted beach island (see p. 223). The setting is lovely, isolated amid the open spaces of sand and sea. Architecture is sustainably stylish, with wide windows, broad dark-wood decks, and a solar-powered kitchen. It's been dishing up seafood with a distinct Algarve accent since the 1980s, showcasing dishes like fried baby sole with cilantro rice, oven baked tuna, or *xerém* (cornmeal mash with seafood). If Crusoe and Friday had this place, they would never have wanted to be rescued. Lunch only.

Ilha Deserta. www.ilhadeserta.com. ✆ **91/781-18-56.** Mains 18€–25€. Mon–Sat noon–3pm, 7–11pm.

Faro e Benfica ★★ PORTUGUESE/SEAFOOD A *marisqueira* (seafood joint) that grew out of the local supporters association of Lisbon's Benfica soccer team, the location is hard to match, at the edge of the dock with views across the marina to Faro's downtown (if you can tear your eyes from the game showing on the wall-mounted TVs). They show seafood the same respect they give to the team. It's super fresh, and skillfully prepared in line with Algarve tradition. Choice depends on what's been hauled from the Atlantic that day, but a meal could kick off with sautéed cuttlefish roe, move on to a wing of skate bathed in garlic-infused olive oil, and finish up with a cinnamon-rich *Dom Rodrigo* to sweeten your shot of coffee. Just don't express your undying love of FC Porto before you ask for a table.

Doca de Faro. ✆ **28/982-14-22.** Mains 14€–21€. Mon–Sat 12:30–3:30pm, 7:30–11:30pm, Sun 12:30–3:30pm.

Tertúlia Algarvia ★★ PORTUGUESE Opened in 2013 by a group of friends who wanted to preserve the Algarve's gastronomic heritage, Tertúlia spills out onto a romantic terrace located on a lovely square in the Vila Adentro. Though there's some fusion at play here, the fare is mostly traditional, like mackerel filets with tomato and basil sauce, or the *cataplana* with octopus, cockles, and sweet potato. In addition, Tertúlia offers cooking lessons, workshops, and seminars about the region's cuisine. It also has a store where you can take away Algarve souvenirs from ceramics to sea salt. Be sure to take a look at the ancient cistern the owners found on the premises.

Praça Afonso III 13-15. www.tertulia-algarvia.pt. ✆ **28/982-10-44.** Reservations recommended in summer. Mains 13€–20€. Sun–Thurs noon–11pm, Fri–Sat noon–midnight.

Faro Entertainment & Nightlife

Finding highbrow culture can be difficult in much of the Algarve, but the regional capital boasts two excellent theaters. Even if you have no intention of catching a performance, you should take a look into the **Teatro Lethes** (www.teatrolethes.com; ✆ **28/987-89-08**), whose horseshoe tiers were inspired by Milan's La Scala. The theater was installed in 1845 in a long-derelict Jesuit college. It's a real gem and open for guided tours. While the plays in Portuguese may be challenging to non-speakers, there's a rich variety of music and dance that ranges from fado to blues, classical to belly dancing. **Teatro das Figuras** (www.teatrodasfiguras.pt; ✆ **28/988-81-00**) has a similarly assorted program but on a much bigger scale. It was built by architect Gonçalo Byrne in 2005 as a state-of-the-art cultural center housed in a massive white-stone block. A typical month could feature Russian classical ballet, chart-topping French pop, and a live-action children's musical based on a Dreamworks animated smash.

Faro's primary party zone is just north of downtown around **Rua do Prior** and **Rua Conselheiro Bívar**, where bars are wall-to-wall, and it rocks into the wee small hours. A couple of bars riding Portugal's craft-beer wave are **Grain's 864** (www.grainsbrewpub.com; ✆ **91/285-71-25**), open noon 'til 2am

DISCOVER THE seafood CAPITAL

The Algarve's biggest fishing town, **Olhão ★★** was the last on the coast to be discovered by tourism. Only recently have visitors ventured in significant numbers into its maze of narrow streets fronted with square-lined, flat-roofed cottages, inhabited by the families of those who set out to sea to bring back tuna and sardine, ply the lagoon for shellfish, or work in the canneries.

Artists, however, have long been drawn by the cubist white blocks stacked one upon the other like the casbahs of North Africa. To really appreciated the urban landscape, climb the tower of **Nossa Senhora do Rosário ★**, the unusual, double- porticoed 17th-century church. Admission costs 1€ and its open Tuesday to Saturday from 10am to 6pm, with a break for lunch between 12:30 and 3pm. Olhão's biggest attraction are the twin **market halls ★★★** (www.mercadosdeolhao.pt; ✆ **28/909-06-64**) built in red-brick and iron in 1916 down on the harbor front. One is dedicated to fish and has the most variety in the region, including things rarely seen elsewhere, like *muxama,* cured tuna eaten sliced like ham; or *litão*, a skinny little shark that's dried and eaten on special occasions. The other hall has meat and seasonal fruit and vegetables. Saturday mornings are best, when farmers come to town to sell their produce and home-bakers bring fresh cakes, like the sticky, caramel filled *folar de Olhão.* Among the colorful fishing boats bobbing in the harbor, you can catch a ferry to the sandbar islands of **Culatra ★★★** and **Armona ★★★** with miles and miles of soft sand and gentle waters.

To sample Olhão seafood, try **Sabores da Ria ★★** (✆ **96/347-94-72**) in the little square just behind the market, or **O Horta ★★** (www.restauranteohorta.pt; ✆ **28/972-42-15**) just down the waterfront. If you want to spend longer enjoying Olhão's salty charms, the **Real Marina Hotel and Spa ★** (www.realmarina.realhotelsgroup.com; ✆ **28/909-13-00;** doubles 62€–175€) provides pampering with a pool and spa overlooking the Ria Formosa. For one week in August, Olhão holds the Festival do Marisco (www.festivaldomarisco.com), a seafood-themed party that involves massive intakes of mollusks and crustaceans, plus late-night concerts by top artists from Portugal and Brazil.

on Travessa dos Arcos; and **Boheme** (www.boheme.pt; ✆ **28/914-25-45**) with similar hours at 2 Rua Conselheiro Bivar. The city's coolest cocktail and wine bar is **Columbus** (www.barcolumbus.pt; ✆ **91/777-62-22**) on the main harborside square, 13 Praça Dom Francisco Gomes, where nights are divided between the brick-arched interior and the terrace out front. Signature mixes include the *gold sour,* mixing Johnnie Walker Gold Label, pumpkin preserve, Madeira wine, vanilla, lemon, and egg white. You can go on drinking them from noon 'til 4am.

Faro nightlife revs up for 4 days in July when the city hosts one of Europe's largest **biker rallies** (www.motoclubefaro.pt; ✆ **28/982-38-45**). As well as thousands of motorcyclists from around the continent, the event involves international bands, 24-hour bars, erotic shows, tattoo competitions, and other fun stuff for guys and girls in denim and leather.

TAVIRA ★★★

306km (190 miles) SE of Lisbon; 36km (22 miles) E of Faro.

Tavira is the most attractive town in the Algarve. Nowhere along the coast does the hand of humankind and the hand of nature combine to produce an urban landscape so easy on the eye. The River Gilão runs through the town, tightly framed on one bank by terracotta-roofed palazzos and bordered on the other by palm-lined gardens. On either side of the arched Moorish bridge, narrow streets and leafy squares alternate, surrounded by a dazzling mix of historic buildings painted in Persil-white, draped in bougainvillea, or coated in multihued *azulejo* tiles. Just beyond the town, the Gilão river flows into the Ria Formosa lagoon, a patchwork of islets and inlets, limpid water and powdery sand, where you can find long stretches of nearly deserted beach.

Tavira has always been an artsy haunt and, until recently, was largely bypassed by the Algarve tourism wave. It still has a more cultured feel than many coastal towns, but has very much been "discovered." It's particularly popular with the French who come not just to visit but to buy homes in the town, near the beaches or amid the citrus- and fig-scented countryside. You can chew on *baguettes* and *pains au chocolate* from an artisan French baker or dine on camembert and *magret de canard* in a Parisian-style bistro. Although it's on the Atlantic, Tavira has a decidedly Mediterranean feel. The city of 20,000 was a major force behind a successful drive to have the Mediterranean diet declared a part of world heritage by UNESCO. It holds an annual celebration in September showcasing the food and culture from around the Mediterranean.

Essentials

ARRIVING

BY TRAIN Trains from Faro take about 35 minutes and cost 3.20€. There are about a dozen daily departs starting at 7:50am until 10:12pm. From Lisbon, you change in Faro to catch the eastbound Algarve line. Details on www.cp.pt. Tavira station is less than 10 minutes' walk to the city center.

BY BUS There are over a dozen direct buses from Lisbon on the **Rede Expressos** (www.rede-expressos.pt) network. Fares start at 19€ for the around 4-hour tip. For direct **shuttle buses** from Faro airport, check www.faroshuttlebus.com or www.hoppa.com. Fares start from 12.40€ per person. **EVA** (www.eva-bus.com) has almost hourly buses from Faro's downtown bus station during working hours, charging 4.50€ for the hour-long trip.

BY CAR It should take around 2 hours 40 minutes from Lisbon on the A2 and A22 toll roads. Faro is 30 minutes away.

VISITOR INFORMATION

The **tourist office** is at Praça da República, 5 (✆ **28/132-25-11**) Monday to Friday 9am to 5pm, Saturday 9am to 1pm and 2 to 5pm, Sunday 9:30am to 1pm and 2 to 5pm.

Exploring Tavira

The city's focal point is the seven-arched **Ponte Velha ★★** bridge spanning the slow-flowing waters of the River Gilão. It's commonly known as the Ponte Romana, but is now generally believed to have been built by the Arabs rather than the Romans, and has been much modified in the 17th-century. It makes a perfect spot to gaze downriver at the palaces and gardens on either bank, particularly in the twilight, when city lights start to sparkle on the water.

On the western bank, the bridge runs into Praça da República ★, a triangular plaza flanked by the colonnade of City Hall, the river, and a row of sidewalk cafes. At No. 5, the **Núcleo Museológico Islâmico ★ ✆ 28/132-05-70**) is a small museum tracing Tavira's Islamic history. It contains a clay vase, remarkably decorated with tiny human and animal figures, which was pieced together after it was discovered in an 11th-century garbage dump. Admission is 2€, open Tuesday to Saturday 9:15am to 12:30pm and 1:30 to 4:30pm. Just behind, the **Igreja da Misericórdia ★★** (**✆ 28/132-05-00**), built in the 1540s, is the most impressive of Tavira's 37 churches. The rather dumpy exterior is embellished by a splendid Renaissance doorway. Inside, it's chockfull of golden carvings, blue-and-white *azulejos,* and Italian baroque paintings. Entry costs 2.50€ (although you can purchase a combined ticket for 4€ that will also get you into the Santa Maria church up the hill). Open Tuesday to Saturday: summer 10am to 12:30pm and 3 to 18:30pm; winter 9:30am to 12:30pm and 2 to 5:30pm.

Across the square is the **Museu Municipal de Tavira ★★** (www.museumunicipaldetavira.cm-tavira.pt; **✆ 28/132-05-40**), housed in one of the city's grandest palaces, which dates back to the 16th century. Its creamy white facade is offset with pale grey stone frames around the 20 windows and the main doorway topped with baroque flourishes and coats of arms. Its eclectic collection ranges from Phoenician ritual items linked to the worship of Baal, to golden church chalices, painted wagon wheels, and modern artworks. Admission costs 2€, or 1€ for over 65s and students; free for under 8s. A combined ticket with the Islamic museum is 3€. Open Tuesday to Saturday, 9:15am to 4:30pm.

Up the hill from the museum is an oddity: the **Torre de Tavira ★** (www.torredetavira.com; **✆ 28/132-25-27**), a concrete water tower planted on the city's highest hill in the 1930s and a rare eyesore on the Tavira skyline. Rather than demolish the now-obsolete installation, the city installed a lift taking visitors into the blackened tank for a *camera obscura* show using mirrors and lenses to project 360-degree real-time images of the city onto the circular walls. Admission is 5€, 4€ for over 65s and students; 3€ for children; Monday to Friday 11am to 2:30pm. Strangely enough, the Spanish city of Cadiz down the coast has a similar show in a tower they call Torre Tavira, which can make things confusing if you're looking it up online.

Next door, the **Igreja de Santa Maria do Castelo ★** (**✆ 93/132-78-72**) is another of Tavira's gleaming white churches. It's believed to have been built on the site of a mosque after the conquest of the city, in 1242, by the Order of Santiago. Paio Peres Correia, who led the attack, is said to be buried inside, although a church in Spain also claims to hold his bones. A Manueline chapel, *azulejos,* and gold carvings are inside, plus views from the bell tower. Admission is 2.50€. Summer: Monday to Friday 10am to 1pm and 2 to 9:30pm, Saturday 10am to 5pm; Winter: Monday to Friday 10am to 1pm and 2pm to 5pm; Saturday 10am to 1pm.

On the other side of Largo, Abu-Otmane square is the entrance to the **Castelo de Tavira** ★, which like most castles in the Algarve is supposed to be haunted by a *moura encantada,* an enchanted Moorish maiden who shows up once a year, in June, to wander the walls. The castle can be visited for free, and its ramparts, parts of which were built by the Phoenicians in the 8th century B.C., offer more great views over the city. Inside the walls, gardens feature jacaranda trees that bloom purple every spring. The castle opens in summer Monday to Friday 8:30am to 7pm, and Saturday to Sunday 10am to 7pm; in winter Monday to Friday 8:30am to 5pm, and 9am to 5pm at weekends. After all that sightseeing, head down to the riverside **Jardim do Coreto** ★ gardens to relax beneath the palms and enjoy an ice-cream, homemade from local products (fig-and-almond and orange-tart are among our preferred flavors), at the **Muxa Gata** ★★ (✆ **96/552-53-87**) kiosk.

OUTDOOR ACTIVITIES Beyond the salt pans and wildfowl-filled waters of the Ria Formosa lagoon, two barrier islands lay between Tavira and the Atlantic. Together **Ilha de Tavira** ★★★ and **Ilha de Cabanas** ★★★ offer 18km (11miles) of unbroken pale sand. They have some of the best beaches in the Algarve, ideal for families, with a gentle slope into calm waters, which tend to be warmer than on the western coast. Ilha de Tavira can be reached by boat from downtown, from the quay at Quatro Águas on the edge of the lagoon, or from the octopus-fishing village of Santa Luzia. There is also a little train that runs from the **Pedras d'el Rei** (www.pedrasdelrei.com; ✆ **28/138-06-00**) resort over a bridge to a stretch of the beach called **Praia do Barril.** Here, the dunes are dotted with rusting anchors, remnants of the tuna boats that once sailed from here. The train costs 1.50€ each way for non-residents, but you can also cross the bridge on foot for free. The sand can get crowded in summer near the train and boat drop-off points, where there are bar/restaurants, lifeguards, and beds and parasols to rent. But if you walk a bit you can find empty spaces of sand. Toward the southeastern end of Ilha de Tavira, the beach is officially for naturalists. Although it's called **Praia de Homem Nu** (Naked Man's Beach), all genders are welcome. The beaches on Ilha de Cabanas can be reached by taking one of the little boats that ferry passengers across the lagoon from the village of Cabanas.

SHOPPING There are sophisticated shopping choices in the tightly packed streets on both sides of the old bridge. At locations on either bank, **Kozii** (www.koziishop.com; ✆ **28/102-73-06**) is run by a pair of local designers taking inspiration from travels in India and Africa to craft elegant, summery fashion from sustainable natural fabrics. It's open daily 10am 'til midnight at 2 Rua Dr. Augusto da Silva Carvalho and 8 Travessa Dona Brites. To make sure junior is just as stylish, head to **Rosa Amor** (www.rosamor.pt; ✆ **96/625-61-34**) a gift store and workshop specializing in hand-crafting cute stuff for babies, kids, and parents. It's at 18 Praça da República, open Monday to Saturday 10:30am to 7pm. At the other end of the bridge, **Casa das Portas** (www.casadasportas.com; ✆ **28/132-10-25**) is an Aladdin's cave of art, books, and handicrafts from Portugal and beyond located in an old cobbler's shop: 1 Rua 5 de Outubro, open 10:30am to 6:30pm. Left bank art galleries include **Tavira d'Artes** (www.taviradartes.com; ✆ **28/102-36-81**) with a colorful collection inspired by Algarve landscapes, at 8 Travessa Jacques Pessoa, open Tuesday to Friday 10am to 1pm and 3 to 6pm, Saturday 10am to 2pm; and avant-garde **Casa das Artes de Tavira** (www.acasadasartes.org; ✆ **21/346-34-26**), Rua João Vaz Corte Real 96, open daily 9:30pm to 12:30am. Tavira's old riverside 1887 **market hall** lost its soul when traders were moved out to a modern out-of-town site in the 1990s. It has cafes, restaurants, and tourist-orientated stores (Largo Dr. José Pires Padinha 60; open Thurs–Tues 10am–10pm).

Where to Stay

MODERATE

Pensão Agrícola ★★★ Escape to the country in this restored 1920s farmstead surrounded by orange, fig, olive, almond, and carob trees. The "agricultural guesthouse" has three suites in the old building (it was built as a wedding gift for an only daughter and was a working farm up to the 1970s) and three more in modernist cubes out back. Most come with private patios. It manages to be both rustically comfy and hyper-trendy (hipster mags *Wallpaper* and *Monocle* have raved). Optional activities include helping wash Ernesto the mule or renting Vespas for a spin down to the beach. White predominates in the rooms with features in raw wood, cane, cotton, and wool, plus a sprinkling of modern art. Luxuries include king-size beds, Bluetooth speakers, and Nova Saboaria toiletries. Alfresco dinners are available with booking, and it's a 10-minute drive to town. Closed November to February (although they will open if you rent the whole place for at least 3 nights.)

Sítio do Valongo, Conceição de Tavira. www.pensaoagricola.com. ✆ **91/778-21-89.** 6 units. 150€–350€ suite. Free parking. **Amenities:** Garden; terrace; free bikes; outdoor pool; massage services; restaurant; bar; free Wi-Fi.

Pousada Convento de Tavira ★★ The mustard-colored walls were built to hold a convent 5 centuries before it was converted this luxury inn. You still get a feeling of ethereal tranquility as you tuck into breakfast under the arches of a Renaissance cloister or take a cooling plunge into the pool nestled under the medieval city walls. Plans to install an indoor pool had to be abandoned when construction work in the early 2000s unearthed a street of Muslim homes dating back to the years before the Portuguese conquest in 1242. Instead of the pool, there's a little museum under the bar, where you see the cobbles and examine medieval household items. Upstairs, the rooms are furnished in marble and hardwood and decked with unobtrusive modern art.

Rua Dom Paio Peres Correia. www.pousadas.com. ✆ **28/132-90-40.** 36 units. 130€–340€ double; 240€–410€ suite. Free parking. **Amenities:** Garden; outdoor pool; massage services; restaurant; bar; free Wi-Fi.

INEXPENSIVE

Casa Beleza do Sul ★★ Back in the early 2000s, when Tavira was still largely undiscovered, Italian architect Paola Boragine transformed a 19th-century merchant's house into this classy town-center B&B. The patio is packed with tropical vegetation and the rooftop terrace offers views over Tavira's russet-tiled rooftops and the river below. There are three spacious suites and a pair of cozy rooms. They all have coffee- and tea-making facilities, and breakfast can be ordered in the room. Many of the house's original features have been retained, like a traditional cane ceiling and mosaic floor tiles, enhanced with pastel shades, natural fabrics, and subtle lighting. A delightful hippy-chic place in a great (although busy at night) location.

Rua Dr. Parreira 43. www.casabelezadosul.com. ✆ **96/006-09-06.** 5 units. 40€–99€ double; 66€–121€ suite, breakfast 7.50€ extra per person. **Amenities:** Sun terrace; free Wi-Fi.

Where to Eat

Álvaro de Campos ★★ PORTUGUESE/INTERNATIONAL This restaurant is named for a Tavira-born poet whose verses decorate the walls, but who never existed. Álvaro de Campos was one of the many alter-egos created by Fernando Pessoa (p. 33) to author his poems. The little restaurant on the cobbled street leading up from the river serves a tasty mix of Algarve and international flavors in an unassuming dining room and its sidewalk terrace, with dishes like goat's cheese pie with figs, or octopus with sweet potato. Lunchtime daily specials are a real bargain.

Rua da Liberdade 47. ✆ **28/102-34-96.** Mains 8€–17€. Mon–Sat noon–10pm.

Noélia ★★ PORTUGUESE Over the years this little waterfront restaurant in a nondescript modern apartment block has become one of the country's most sought after culinary experiences. Lisbon critics and star chefs gush. One globetrotting commentator repeatedly proclaims it the best restaurant in the world and calls Chef Noélia the Picasso of Portuguese cooking. The food is exceptional. She takes the freshest Algarve ingredients to craft dishes that blend tradition with invention, like seared tuna with mango-and-ginger rice, or *xerém* (cornmeal porridge) with codfish tongues. In summer, however, it becomes a victim of its own success. There are lines around the block waiting for tables and the service struggles to cope. If you're here out of season, or are patient, it's definitely worth it.

Avenida Ria Formosa 2, Cabanas de Tavira. ✆ **28/137-06-49.** Mains 18€–28€. Thurs–Tues 12:30–3pm, 6:30–10pm.

VILA REAL DE SANTO ANTÓNIO ★★

327km (203 miles) SE of Lisbon; 60km (38 miles) E of Faro; 3km (2 miles) W of Ayamonte, Spain

If you've spend time exploring the labyrinthine, medina-like cores of Algarve and Alentejo towns, this frontier post on the mouth of the Guadiana River will come as a shock. There are no winding lanes or hilltop castles here. It's dead flat, and its old, 18th-century urbanization scheme is made up of rectangular blocks of one- and two-story buildings. It was thrown up in 1776 on the orders of the Marquês de Pombal, Portugal's prime minister, on the site of a fishing village destroyed by a tsunami 20 years earlier, to affirm Portugal's presence on the border. The plan will be familiar to anybody who's visited Lisbon's downtown Baixa district in the same Pombaline style.

It is a curious, harmonious place, lively with visitors from across the border. Vila Real enjoys a fabulous location facing its Andalusian neighbor Ayamonte across the wide river (there's a highway bridge inland and a ferry from downtown). Beaches stretch from the river's mouth for over 16km (10 miles) west toward Tavira in an unbroke arc of sand. There's a rather brash modern resort suburb at Monte Gordo, but beyond that, much of the beach is backed by little more than dunes and umbrella pines, making them great places to escape the crowds. The city is the starting point for cruises up the river, while the nearby fortress town of Castro Marim and the picture-perfect hamlet of Cacela Velha provide a contrast from Vila Real's straight lines.

Essentials

ARRIVING

BY TRAIN From Faro it takes about 1 hour and costs 5.25€. From Lisbon you change in Faro and take one of the dozen eastbound trains. It's a 10-minute walk from the station to downtown and the Ayamonte ferry.

BY BUS There are over a dozen buses from Lisbon most days by the **Rede Expressos** network (www.rede-expressos.pt); the fastest ones take 4½ hours, with fares from 20€. They also have at least one bus from Seville, taking 2 hours and costing at least 18€. EVA operates about 10 buses daily from Faro, making the trip in 1 hour 40 minutes for 5.75€ (www.eva-bus.com). For direct **shuttle buses** from Faro airport, check www.faroshuttlebus.com or www.hoppa.com. Fares start from 16€ per person.

BY CAR It's 3 hours from Lisbon on the A2 and A22 highways.

BY FERRY Ferries from Ayamonte carrying cars and foot passengers run hourly from 9:30am to 7pm in winter, increasing to every 30 minutes in summer when they run later. There's a reduced service on Sundays and holidays. The crossing takes about 20 minutes and costs 1.90€ for pedestrians, 5.50€ for automobiles (www.rioguadiana.net).

VISITOR INFORMATION

The **tourist office** is in the Centro Cultural António Aleixo, Rua 5 de Outubro 16 (© **28/151-00-00**). Open Monday to Friday 9am to 1pm and 2 to 5pm.

Exploring the Town

Vila Real is a unique example of a wholly planned community from the 18th century. It was built quickly, in just 2 years, using buildings that were prefabricated elsewhere and erected in record time. Although the town is worth visiting in the whole (with almost 200 original buildings from 1775), there aren't a great many individual landmarks to visit downtown. The **riverside esplanade ★** is a pleasant walk with views across to Spain and, beyond the Pombaline core, some grand early-20th-century buildings recall the time when the city grew rich on tuna fishing and fish canning. As you near the Atlantic, a **lighthouse** built in 1923 soars over the pines. The main square is **Praça Marquês do Pombal ★**, decorated with strips of black-and-white paving radiating from a central obelisk. It's lined with orange trees, sidewalk cafes, and stores popular with Spanish visitors. The main church, **Igreja Matriz ★**, features a statue by Joaquim Machado de Castro, Portugal's greatest baroque sculptor. The former market with its four corner turrets now houses the **Centro Cultural António Aleixo ★**, which hosts exhibitions and concerts.

A 5km (3-mile) drive north leads to the fortress town of **Castro Marim ★★**, whose original medieval castle was enlarged and adapted over the centuries into a star-shaped bulwark to guard the frontier with Spain. It's an agreeable town with white-domed churches and narrow lanes overlooking a nature reserve where flamingos and storks wade through the shallows. Shimmering salt pans yield artisanal products, particularly *flor de sal* (the first layer to be skimmed after evaporation), much prized by gastronomes. To the west of Vila Real, a 20-minute drive will take you to **Cacela Velha ★★**, arguably the most beautiful village in the Algarve. It's a tiny hamlet of traditional single-story Algarve houses, white with blue trim and fretwork chimneys pointing upward like minarets. They cluster within the walls of a fortress overseeing the easternmost edge of the Ria Formosa lagoon and beaches stretching as far as the eye can see.

OUTDOOR ACTIVITIES From Vila Real, a number of boat companies offer **cruises up the Guadiana ★★**, passing through wetland bird reserves and the forested banks of the river forming the frontier between Portugal and Spain. There's usually lunch on board or in a typical riverside restaurant and a chance to bathe in a secluded beauty spot. **Rio Sul Travel** (www.riosultravel.com; ✆ **28/151-02-00**) and **TransGuadiana** (www.transguadiana.com; ✆ **96/608-93-41**) have day-long trips for 48€ per adult. Among the beaches running west from Vila Real, our favorite is **Praia Verde ★★★**, a horizon-stretching expanse of sand sloping from pine-covered dunes to gently lapping waters. Golfers will want to head to the **Monte Rei Golf and Country Club** (www.monte-rei.com; ✆ **28/195-09-50**), where a Jack Nicklaus–designed course snuggles in the foothills of the Serra do Caldeirão. It's frequently judged Portugal's best, and the greens are matched by deluxe accommodations, dining, and pampering on offer in the resort. Work started on a second Golden Bear–designed course in 2019. The eastern Algarve came late to golf

RESORT row

Between Faro and Praia da Rocha, much of the coast is taken up by resort developments that have grown since the 1970s to meet demand for vacation homes and sunny second homes. They offer little in the way of local culture or tradition, but often boast high levels of comfort with luxury villas, plush hotels, first-rate golf, gourmet dining, and access to some of Europe's best beaches.

One of the biggest and poshest resorts is **Quinta do Lago** (www.quintadolago.com; ✆ **28/939-07-00**), just west of Faro Airport (although the flight approaches don't disturb the manicured lawns and millionaire mansions). Villas here can easily sell for over 10 million€, but you can grab a taste of the highlife by renting a holiday home or taking a room in hotels like the Miami Beach–inspired **Magnolia** (www.themagnoliahotelqdl.com; ✆ **28/900-53-00;** doubles 98€–230€); palatial **Conrad Algarve** (www.hilton.com/en/conrad; ✆ **28/935-07-00;** doubles 153€–450€; or **Hotel Quinta do Lago** (www.quintadolagohotel.com; ✆ **28/935-03-50;** doubles 216€–675€) boasting the best sea views. Non-residents can access the lovely beach (reached by a wooden causeway over the lagoon); a handful of golf courses (although **San Lorenzo** [www.sanlorenzogolfcourse.com; ✆ **28/939-65-22**] ranked among the best in continental Europe, is exclusively for members and guests at associated hotels); birdwatching on the Ria Formosa nature resort; or dining at Michelin-starred restaurants like **Gusto** in the Conrad or **São Gabriel** (www.sao-gabriel.com; ✆ **28/939-45-21**), although our favorite QdL eatery is **Gigi's** (✆ **28/939-44-81**), an upscale beach shack.

Next door, **Vale do Lobo** (www.valedolobo.com; ✆ **28/935-30-00**) is the Algarve's oldest resort, founded in the 1960s and just slightly less tony than its neighbor. It has a similar mix of beach, villas with private pools, and golf greens (the cliff-skimming 16th hole on the **Royal Course** is one of the region's iconic spots). Here too you may spot a soccer star or showbiz celeb on the way

but boasts several highly rated clubs, also including two at **Quinta da Ria** (www.quintadaria.com; ✆ **28/195-05-80**) near Cacela Velha; and **Castro Marim Golfe & Country Club** (www.castromarimresort.com; ✆ **28/153-17-74**) whose 4th hole on the Atlantic course was included in the book *1001 Golf Holes You Must Play Before You Die*.

Where to Stay

Grand House ★★★ If you've got the cash, this is really something special, opened with great fanfare in 2019 after a 2 million€ restoration brought this majestic 1920s palace hotel back to its glamorous best. The four-story Art Nouveau block was first built by tuna-canning tycoon Manuel Ramirez, who thought the city needed a prestigious resting place for visiting business types. The refurbishment has brought the Jazz Age back to the banks of the Guadiana. Light-flooded rooms come in cream, dove grey, and fawn with polished timber floors, lofty windows, and (in many cases) balconies opening onto the river. Chandeliers, vintage prints, and a scattering of antiques add to the style. There's a Gatsby-esque cocktail bar, gourmet riverside dining room, and a to the beach or clubhouse. The main hotel is the **Dona Filipa** (www.jjwhotels.com; ✆ **28/935-72-00;** doubles 173€–687€). Dining options include beachside **Breeze Papagaio** (✆ **28/935-33-57**) and **Antonio Tá Certo** (✆ **28/939-64-56**).

At **Vilamoura** (www.vilamouraworld.com; ✆ **28/931-09-00**), a whole new town has been created around Portugal's biggest marina (www.marinadevilamoura.com; ✆ **28/931-05-60**). It has mega-hotels; a casino; and a selection of golf courses, including the **Old Course** and the Arnold Palmer–designed **Victoria** (www.dompedrogolf.com; ✆ **28/931-03-33**) which are among the Algarve's best. Vilamoura has built a reputation for fine-dining and nightlife. **Willie's Restaurant** (www.willies-restaurante.com; ✆ **28/938-08-49**) has a German chef and a star from a French tire-maker; and **Thai Vilamoura** (www.thai.pt; ✆ **28/930-23-70**) is one of the country's best Asian restaurants. In summer, Lisbon's partygoers decamp to seasonal discotheques like **Bliss** (✆ **96/320-83-52**) and **Lick** (✆ **91/222-00-02**).

West of Albufeira, there's a cluster of smaller resorts around the villages of Alporchinos and Carvoeiro. Among the most luxurious are **Vila Vita Parc** (www.vilavitaparc.com; ✆ **28/231-01-00**) with its two-Michelin-star **Ocean** restaurant, and **Tivoli Carvoeiro** (www.tivolihotels.com; ✆ **28/235-11-00**), whose **Sky Bar** is one of the region's coolest cocktail spots.

Among the resorts are some hidden treasures: **Praia da Marinha ★★★** beach is loaded with honeyed sandstone rock formations, making it one of the prettiest in Portugal (if not the world); take a boat (or standup board) from Carvoeiro to discover the **Algar de Benagil ★★★**, a sea cave that opens up into natural sandstone dome pierced by sunlight; just north of Quinta do Lago, the little **Igreja de São Lourenço ★★★** church in Almancil contains a jaw-dropping interior fusing blue ceramic tiles and gold-covered wood carvings. Open Tuesday to Saturday 10am to 1 pm and 3 to 6pm; Monday 3 to 6pm.

beach club with an infinity pool and a ceviche-serving restaurant. And it's a work in progress: Plans are afoot for a spa, cafe, and concept store.

Avenida da República 171. www.grandhousealgarve.com. ✆ **28/153-02-90.** 30 units. 251€–625€ double, 502€–1,053€ suite. Parking 10€ daily. **Amenities:** Terrace; bike hire; beach club with outdoor pool; spa; massage services; 2 restaurants; 2 bars; free Wi-Fi.

Where to Eat

Casa Velha ★★ PORTUGUESE In lovely Cacela Velha is this former *tasca* now converted into a spacious restaurant with tables spilling out into a charming patio. Oysters from the Ria Formosa are the thing to start with here, before moving on to a soupy rice with razor clams. It attracts Portuguese vacationers and Spaniards from across the border, so go early to get a seat in summer (they don't take reservations June–Aug). If you're tired of fish and shellfish by now, the grilled pork or steak in cream sauce with freshly made French fries should hit the spot. Finish with a slice of almond or carob cake.

Rua Sophia de Mello Bryener, Cacela Velha. ✆ **28/195-22-97.** 9€–20€.Tues–Sun 12–3pm and 7–10pm.

ALBUFEIRA ★

256 (160 miles) S of Lisbon;46km (29 miles) W of Faro

In 1963, thriller writer Len Deighton set a spy story in Albufeira involving British agents, a sunken U-boat, and hidden Nazis. He paints a picture of a sleepy fishing village where his hero is woken only by bells tinkling on the bridles of mules and the distant songs of fisherfolk hauling home sardine nets. There are "two or three cafes—houses with a public front room." Things have changed. Shortly after Deighton's book, tourism took off big time and Albufeira today is the sprawling hub of the Algarve's vacation industry boom. Although a triangle of that village still sits pretty in white on the ochre cliff above Praia dos Pescadores beach, the streets are now filled with bars and souvenir shops. Beyond is a city of 40,000, swelled each year by millions of tourists who make this the country's second-most-visited destination after Lisbon.

Essentials

ARRIVING

BY TRAIN There are five daily direct trains from Lisbon. The fastest take 2½ hours and cost 22€. Giro buses make the 6km (4-mile) run from the station to city center every 30 minutes and the fare is 3.50€ one-way. There are about a dozen trains from Faro. Fares start at 3.35€ and the trip takes up to 37 minutes. For schedules: www.cp.pt.

BY BUS **Eva** (www.eva-bus.com) has seven *transrapido* buses making the run from Faro in 55 minutes and many more on the stopping route that takes 1 hour 25 minutes. Either way it costs 4.90€. For direct shuttle buses from Faro airport there are a number of operators. Check www.faroshuttlebus.com, www.hoppa.com, or www.terravision.eu. Fares start from 6.50€. There are buses roughly once an hour from Lisbon with Rede Expressos. Fares from 19€ for the around 3-hour trip.

BY CAR It takes 2½ hours from Lisbon straight down the A2.

VISITOR INFORMATION

The **Tourist Information Office** is at Rua do 5 de Outubro (www.visitalgarve.com; ✆ **28/958-52-79;** daily from 9am–1pm and 2–6pm).

Exploring the Town

The old whitewashed town center has a couple of pretty churches with colored trim and a brace of little museums focused on religious art and archaeology, but the big attractions here are outdoors. Besides the beaches, families beat a path to **Zoomarine** ★ (www.zoomarine.pt; ✆ **28/956-03-00**), a hugely popular water park with rides, swimming pools, a zoo and aquarium, plus dolphin shows. A one-day pass costs 26€, 19€ for over 65s and under 10s. It's 6.5km (4 miles) northwest of the center on the EN125 road. It's open daily from 10am to 7:30pm from late June to early September and it closes December to February. Beyond that, times vary and it's best to check the website.

Outdoor Activities

BEACHES The sheltered beaches and over 300 days of sunshine are why millions come each year to Albufeira. On either side of the city are some of the Algarve's best. There are dozens to pick from: tiny golden coves scalloped out of the sandstone to broad stretches of flax-colored sand. Among the most fashionable are **Praia da Galé ★★★** and **Praia de São Rafael ★★** to the west, and **Praia da Falésia ★★** and **Praia de Santa Eulália ★★** to the east. Escaping the crowds can be hard in July and August, but the dunes at **Praia dos Salgados ★★** near a nature reserve 20 minutes' drive from downtown, or the hidden inlet of **Praia da Coelha ★★★** (doe rabbit beach—don't ask us why) may be among the best bets.

Shopping

If you are unlucky enough to catch one of the Algarve's rare rainy days, **Algarve Shopping ★** (www.algarveshopping.pt; ✆ **28/910-55-00**) is where you take bored kids. The mall has 107 stores, 23 restaurants, and a multiscreen cinema all in an idiosyncratic complex that mixes indoor spaces with external walkways in a massive mockup of traditional brightly colored Algarve architecture. Brands range from posh Portuguese porcelain at Vista Alegre to Triumph lingerie and French book-and-tech emporium FNAC. Most shops open daily 10am to midnight, some open a bit earlier.

Where to Stay

EXPENSIVE

Vila Joya ★★★ At the heart of this elegant and intimate beachfront inn is the restaurant of the same name, which Austrian chef Dieter Koschina has taken to two Michelin-star status (menus start at 120€ without drinks). The place is a true hideaway, surrounded by lush gardens filled with palm and pine. All but one of the rooms have sea views and private balconies. They are furnished with understated European style in soft greys, beige and cream, with strategically positioned Asian artifacts and oriental tiles. If you work up the accommodation pecking order, you find suites with private pools, stand-alone baths, four-poster beds, and acres of floor-space.

Estrada da Galé. www.vilajoya.com. ✆ **28/959-17-95.** 21 units. 350€–990€ double; 705€–2,560 suite. Free parking. **Amenities:** Garden; terrace; tennis; free bikes; outdoor pool; spa; gym; sauna, hammam; Jacuzzi; massage services; restaurant; bar; babysitting; free Wi-Fi.

MODERATE

Grande Real Santa Eulália Resort & Hotel Spa ★ This big, family-oriented hotel sits above one of the area's nicest beaches, the tropical-looking Praia de Santa Eulália. There's a choice of regular rooms or suites and apartments with living room and kitchenette. They also do all-inclusive deals. Decor in the family-style accommodations is in bright sunny tones, but the colors are toned down a bit in the more romantic units, some of which include draped king-size beds. Accommodations open out either onto gardens or to an ocean view. The spa specializes in seawater thalassotherapy treatments. A choice of restaurants serve Portuguese and Mediterranean cuisine, and a kiddie center with trained professionals and small pools is just for the little ones.

Praia de Santa Eulália. www.granderealsantaeulaliahotel.com. ✆ **28/959-80-00.** 344 units. 75€–285€ double; 80€–490€ suite. Free parking. **Amenities:** Garden; terrace; tennis; 4 outdoor pools; spa; gym; sauna, hammam; Jacuzzi; massage services; 3 restaurants; 2 bars; nightclub; children's play area; babysitting; free Wi-Fi.

São Rafael Atlântico ★★ Lots of Algarve resort hotels have gardens. Few have one like this. A phalanx of tall, straight palms border the three circular pools. Paths leading down to São Rafael beach are lined with olive and pine trees and are especially lovely at sunset when light filters through the trees. Rooms are spacious and modern with soft textiles, natural timber, and coffee-and-cream colors. The spa is one of the plushest around, complete with a spacious hydro-massage pool. Restaurant options range from sushi to gourmet Mediterranean. It's a bargain out of season.

Rua dos Corais, Sesmarias. www.saorafaelatlantico.com. ✆ **28/259-94-20.** 149 units. 86€–464€ double, 164€–589€ suites. **Amenities:** Garden; terrace; indoor and outdoor pools; spa; gym; sauna, hammam; Jacuzzi; massage services; 3 restaurants; 2 bars; free Wi-Fi in lobby.

INEXPENSIVE

Casa dos Arcos – Boutique Hostel & Suites ★ This may be the oddest hostel in the region, set in an almost 300-year-old mansion that looks like it was inhabited by out-of-pocket aristocrats with very odd taste in art. Walls are filled with cheap old-master reproductions in gilt frames, garish tiles, chintz wallpaper, and kitsch 1950s portraits. The ensemble has a definite charm. The place is aimed at a youthful clientele and is located in the middle of downtown, so don't go expecting a quiet time. Still, there is a lovely bougainvillea-shaded patio out back for chilling. Room and dorm sizes vary; some have really limited space. No air-conditioning. Short walk to the beach. Closed November through March.

Rua 5 de Outubro 61. www.rocamarhotels.com. ✆ **93/409-18-85.** 8 units. 59€–149€ double; 19€–29€ dorm bed. **Amenities:** Garden; terrace; free Wi-Fi.

Flor de Laranja ★ Out of the bustle of town and surrounded by orange trees (plus the occasional pomegranate, lemon, and banana tree), this friendly little villa complex provides self-catering apartments, complete with kitchenette. They have a variety of units, from studios to family-size dwellings with two queen-size beds and a separate living room/kitchen, but all share the same homey, family feel. It's far from fancy, but the owners care a lot and keep the property immaculate, add cozy touches, and are full of tips on how to get the most of the area. Around the two pools are barbecue grills for guest use. It's an 8km (5-mile) drive to downtown, but just 3km (less than 2 miles) to the beach.

Estrada de Vale de Carro. ✆ **91/979-80-58.** 8 units. 36€–95€ apartment for double; 57€–119€ apartment for four. Free parking. **Amenities:** Garden; terrace; barbecue; 2 outdoor pools; children's play area; babysitting; free Wi-Fi.

Where to Eat

Pedras Amarelas ★★ PORTUGUESE/INTERNATIONAL The name means "yellow stones," and this beach bar/restaurant looks out over the sulfur-colored rocks scattered around the eastern end of Praia de Galé beach (at sunset, the rocks turn flame and copper color as part of a kaleidoscopic blaze over the bay). The building has glass walls and a broad deck for admiring the view. Seafood is the most tempting section of the menu, with Asian and Mediterranean touches spicing up trad Portuguese fare like monkfish and prawns with saffron-seafood cream or shrimp "à la plancha" with whiskey sauce. Fried smelt or calamari with tartar sauce are tasty finger-food appetizers. Out of eating hours, it operates as a cafe, cocktail bar, and late-night party place.

Praia de Galé. www.pedrasamarelas.pt. ✆ **28/959-19-51.** Mains 11€–25€. Daily noon–11pm.

Ramires ★★ CHICKEN Where you take the Albufeira turning off the EN125 road running east-west through the Algarve, the rather plain town of Guia is Portugal's capital of grilled chicken. You'll see eateries offering *franguinho* (little chicken) *à Guia* all over Portugal, because birds raised here are supposed to be especially tender and flavorsome. The technique of basting a spatchcock chicken in spicy *piri-piri* sauce before grilling over charcoal originated in Africa, but has become one of Portugal's favorite meals (specify if you want it mild or *picante*). Of the dozens of *frango* joints in Guia, this is our favorite: big, boisterous and full of greasy-lipped families. In summer they don't take reservations and you'll have to get in line for a table.

R. 25 de Abril 14, Guia. www.restauranteramires.com. ✆ **28/956-12-32.** Mains 6.50€–12€. Daily noon–11pm.

Albufeira Entertainment & Nightlife

Albufeira is a serious party town. Portuguese spring breakers and bachelor(ette) partiers from around Europe are lured by its hard-drinking, fun-in-the-sun reputation. Nightlife epicenters include the old town (*zona antiga*) especially around Largo Duarte Pacheco and Praça dos Pescadores; and the néon-lit strip known as Rua de Ouro (Av. Sá Carneiro) east of downtown. Among more laidback options, **Sal Rosa** (✆ **28/951-30-89**) has an *azulejo*-lined terrace, sunset views over Praia do Peneco beach, and award-winning cocktails. It's on Praça Miguel Bombarda 2, open daily noon to midnight. Over to the west, **Liquid Lounge** (✆ **91/452-00-69**) overlooks Praia dos Salgados, where the setting sun can be relied upon to do its thing over the beach, bay, and lagoon as you suck on a mix of rum, peppermint,

LOVING loulé

Every Portuguese schoolchild knows **Loulé ★** thanks to a folksong with a catchy chorus that goes: "*Olé, olá, Esta vida não está má; Olá, olé, Tia Anica de Loulé*" (roughly, "This life isn't so bad, Aunty Anica from Loule). And indeed life isn't so bad in the Algarve's largest inland town. After all, it's only a 20-minute drive to the coast, and the long central boulevard running down from the castle and medieval old town is lined with shady trees, cute stores, and brightly painted Art Nouveau townhouses.

The **market hall ★**, dating from 1908 and built in neo-Moorish style, is one of the Algarve's most handsome. It fills every morning from Monday to Saturday with bright stalls selling local produce and handicrafts. It's best on a Saturday, when farmers set up stalls on the sidewalk to sell the seasonal crop. Down the road on Saturday mornings, there's a separate **open-air market ★** that's a popular local gathering, offering a mishmash of clothes, shoes, linen, household goods, and handicrafts. **Café Calcinha ★** (✆ **96/406-68-42**) is a gem of a 1920s cafe, ideal for people watching and open daily from 8am to 11pm on Praça da República. From the same period is the **Cine-Teatro Louletano ★** (http://cineteatro.cm-loule.pt; ✆ **28/941-46-04**), a lively cultural hub that draws big-name national (and occasionally international) musicians. Every February, Loulé holds one of Portugal's biggest **carnival ★** celebrations with decorated floats, Rio-style dancers, and the curious custom of banging passersby on the head with squeaky plastic hammers.

Restaurant choices range from **Bocage** (www.restaurantebocage.com; ✆ **28/941-24-16**) serving traditional fare like chicken in beer or salt-cod with chickpeas in town on Rua Bocage 14; to **Henrique Leis** (www.henriqueleis.com; ✆ **28/939-34-38**) where the Michelin-starred dishes are as pretty as the balcony views, an 8-minute drive south in the village of Vale Formoso. The **Loulé Coreto Guesthouse ★** (www.loulecoretoguesthouse.com; ✆ **96/666-09-43;** doubles 45€–50€) has a friendly, youthful team, stylish and clean rooms, and prices much lower than on the coast. They also run a hostel next door that's even cheaper.

Just to the north, **Alte ★** is a well-preserved Algarve village composed of whitewashed homes with doors and windows framed in bold colors; and roofs pierced with lacy pointed chimneys. There are also freshwater pools for bathing. Its "most-typical-village" tag means Alte draws coach trips from the coast who are well catered for in cafes and handicraft stores. Another attractive hill village is **Salir ★**. Both have traditions of blanket- and basket-weaving, so look out for authentic gifts. The two villages are also stops on the **Via Algarviana ★★** (www.viaalgarviana.org; ✆ **28/941-29-59**), a long-distance hiking track. The whole thing runs for 300km (186 miles) from Alcoutim, up on the Guadiana River where it forms the border with Spain, to Cape St. Vincent on the southwestern tip of Europe. Fortunately, the path is divided into stages between 14km (9 miles) and 30km (19 miles). Mostly it runs through wild hill forests, but there are regular stops in villages and small towns. The Loulé-based administrators don't recommend walking the track in June through September when temperatures are high.

and hibiscus tea, or some other concoction by famed Italian mixologist Kiko Pericoli. It's atop the Hotel Nau on Rua da boca da Alagoa, Herdade dos Salgados. Daily 8pm to 2am.

SILVES ★

250km (155miles) south of Lisbon; 16km (10 miles) NE of Portimão

Silves is the Algarve's most visited inland city and, unlike the beach towns of the coast, heritage is the main attraction. The skyline is dominated by the outline of its mighty medieval castle, a reminder of the time when Silves was an important Arab city. During 5 centuries of Muslim rule, the city then known as Xilb was a major provincial town in empires ruled from Andalusia or North Africa and, at times, capital of an independent kingdom. After several attempts, the Portuguese captured it in 1242 in an attack led by Paio Peres Correia, grand master of the Knights of Santiago.

In the centuries that followed, the Arade river silted up. Silves lost its role as a port city to be eclipsed by Faro and Portimão, but survived as a center for cork production and dried fruits. Today, it's a sleepy town, its ancient medina reflected in the slow waters of the Arade. The land around it is surrounded by orange and lemon orchards, and almond and fig trees, which add to its Mediterranean air.

Essentials

ARRIVING

BY TRAIN From Lisbon, trains take about 3 hours, with a change at Tunes. There are four a day from 22€. The around 10 direct trains from Faro take just over 1 hour with a 5.20€ fare. There are about 10 a day (www.cp.pt).

BY BUS From Sete Rios station in Lisbon, **Rede Expressos** (www.rede-expressos.pt) has four daily buses making the 3-hour trip for 19€. There are seven buses a day from Albufeira, taking about 40 minutes and costing 4.50€, run by **Eva Transportes** (www.eva-bus.com; ✆ **28/958-06-11**).

BY CAR It should take around 2½ hours from Lisbon. Take Exit 14 from the A2 toll highway and follow the EN124 into town. From Portimão, it's about 20 minutes via the EN125 and EN124-1.

VISITOR INFORMATION

The **tourist office** (www.cm-silves.pt; ✆ **28/209-89-27**) is on Estrada Nacional 124. Open April to October: daily 9:30am to 1pm and 2 to 5:30pm; November to March: daily 9am to 1pm and 2 to 5pm. There's also a Visitor Center dedicated to Silves' Islamic Heritage (✆ **28/244-08-00**) near City Hall on Praça do Município.

Exploring Silves

Silves Castle ★★ is one of the best-preserved medieval fortresses in the country. It's commonly called the Moor's Castle and its ring of red sandstone ramparts give a good impression of the stronghold built by Moroccan-based empires in the 12th and 13th centuries, although it was battered by the 1755 earthquake and heavily restored in the 1940s. A walk around the walls offers views over the russet roofs of Silves, where you'll likely spot several storks' nests on the chimneys and ridges. To the north, densely forested hills ripple into the distance. Take strong shoes because the walls are uneven and it's quite a hike to walk around to all 11 towers. Inside the battlements you'll see the excavated foundations of the Arab governors' palace and vast underground cisterns and grain stores designed to supply the castle during sieges. There are palm trees, flower beds, and a good cafe. Admission is 2.80€, 1.40€ for over 65s and students. You can also buy a combined ticket for the castle and the archaeological museum for 3.90€. It's open July to mid-October 9am to 7:30pm; June 9am to 6:30pm; mid-October to May 9am to 5pm.

The castle comes alive for 10 days in August for the **Silves Medieval Fair ★★**, featuring re-enactments of historical events, banquets, war games, street markets, and all manner of Middle Ages merriment. The 2019 edition was themed on Islamic Silves' 9th-century relations with the Vikings, based on real events including a romance between a local poet and a Nordic queen and a battle with longboats on the Arade.

Just outside the castle gate, **Silves Cathedral ★★** (✆ **28/244-08-00**) is the most-impressive medieval church in the Algarve. It was built over the main mosque shortly after the Portuguese conquest, using local sandstone in the Gothic style. The baroque flourishes on the main facade were added later, giving it coats of magenta-and-white paint to offset the reddish stone. The interior is simple and harmonious. Under the towering arched nave are several tombs dating back to the Middle Ages. The most impressive is empty. King João II died in the Algarve in 1495, shortly after concluding the deal with Spain that divided the newly discovered Americas between the Iberian powers. He was known to the Portuguese as The Perfect Prince, and to his rival Isabella of Castile simple as *El Hombre* (The Man). His cousin and successor King Manuel I decided Silves wasn't grand enough, so he had the body transported to Batalha Monastery (p. 209). The church is open Monday to Friday 9am to 5pm with a fee of 1.50€, free for under 12s.

Using part of the city walls and a 9m-deep (30-ft.) Islamic-era well as its anchor, the **Museu Municipal de Arqueologia ★** on Rua Porta de Loulé (✆ **28/244-08-38**) is a short walk from the Cathedral. The museum has artifacts from the Roman and Visigoth times, but mostly contains pottery and other vestiges from Silves' Arab past. Admission is 2.10€, 1.05€ for students and over 65s. Open daily from 10am to 5:30pm. On the edge of the old town, an artfully restored (and bright red) building from 1914 in neo-Moorish style houses the **House of Islamic and Mediterranean Culture ★** (✆ **28/2 44-08-95**) which organizes temporary exhibitions and conferences.

Other monuments to see in Silves include the **Cruz de Portugal ★**, a white stone cross beside the road heading east out of town. In lacy Gothic carving it depicts the Crucifixion of Jesus on one side and a *pietà* on the other. The Ponte Velha bridge over the Arade has Roman origins, but the current five arches in red sandstone date from the early years of Christian rule.

Where to Stay

Colina dos Mouros Hotel ★ With so much choice on the coast, there are not many accommodations in Silves. This place, fronted by a kitschy Arabesque exterior, is pretty much the only show in town. Inside, it definitely feels like you've stepped back in time, but to a 1970s motel rather than a Moorish palace. In its favor are marvelous views across the river to Silves' medieval skyline, magical at night when the castle and cathedral light up. The large circular pool, gardens, and free parking a 10-minute walk from town are all pluses. It's also cheaper than most places on the coast.

Pocinho Santo. www.colinahotels.com. ✆ **28/201-26-51.** 57 units. 38€–82€ double. Free parking. **Amenities:** Garden; terrace; bike hire; outdoor pool; restaurant; bar; free Wi-Fi in public areas.

Where to Eat

Marisqueira Rui ★★ PORTUGUESE/SEAFOOD This inland city boasts one of the Algarve's most sought-after seafood joints. In summer and on the weekend you'll have to join the lines waiting to get in to the cozy, cork-lined interior or grab a sidewalk table. While you're waiting, the constant hammering may make you think the builders are on duty; it's actually diners smashing crab claws with wooden mallets. Order a mix of freshy prepared shellfish: crab, shrimp, garlic and cilantro clams, oysters, lobster if you're feeling flush, and wash it down with a succession of *imperiais* (small, chilled beers). An alternative is the *arroz de marisco,* a soupy kettle of seafood and rice—Rui's is one of the best in the land.

Rua Comendador Vilarinho 27. www.marisqueirarui.pt. ✆ **28/244-26-82.** Mains 10€–30€. Wed–Mon noon–midnight.

PORTIMÃO ★

282km (175 miles) S of Lisbon; 23km (14 miles) E of Lagos

The Algarve's second city has a split personality. Although its fish canning industry is now a museum piece, the city center remains a workaday place, albeit with pleasant squares and riverside promenades. Much of the action however has shifted to the seaside suburb of Praia da Rocha, which retains a magnificent 2km (1.2-mile) expanse of golden beach, but has seen much of its clifftop strip tarnished by ugly high-rises, rowdy bars, and greasy fast-food joints. The urban sprawl spreads west toward the one-time fishing village of Alvor, but the area retains some beautiful beaches, great seafood restaurants, and unspoiled nature at the Ria de Alvor lagoon.

Essentials

ARRIVING

BY TRAIN From Lisbon, take the Faro-bound train until Tunes, where you change to the westward line heading to Lagos. There are four a day, taking around 3½ hours, from 22€. Direct trains from Faro take just under 1½ hours and cost from 6€. There are about 10 a day. Information and schedules at www.cp.pt.

BY BUS There are around two-dozen direct buses from Sete Rios station in summer (fewer in winter) run by the **Rede Expressos** network (www.rede-expressos.pt; ✆ **70/722-33-44**). The journey takes around 3½ hours and fares start at 19€. From Faro airport, private shuttle operators will make the around 1-hour trip for a little as 12€, although prices vary depending on passenger numbers and stops. Check with www.faroshuttlebus.com or www.hoppa.com.

BY CAR From Lisbon, it's about 2½ hours on the A2 and A22 toll roads.

VISITOR INFORMATION

The **tourist office** (www.visitportimao.com; ✆ **28/240-24-87**) is at Largo 1 Dezembro in the city theater. There's another in Praia da Rocha (✆ **28/241-91-32**) on Avenida Tomás Cabreira. Daily 9am to 1pm and 2 to 5pm.

Exploring the Town

The heart of downtown Portimão is **Praça Manuel Teixeira Gomes ★**, a riverside plaza with trees and fountains looking across to the wide Arade River. It blends into a leafy garden, part of a long promenade along the quays where dozens of boats would unload their daily catches of sardines up to the late 20th century. Among the cafes whose terraces spill onto the sidewalk, the one with history and atmosphere is **Casa Inglesa ★** (✆ **28/241-62-90**), a city meeting point since 1922. The neon-lit emblem of soccer club Portimonense is a local icon. Open daily 8am to 11pm. Try one of their sticky, cinnamon-laden "Dom Rodrigo" cakes with your coffee and you'll have all the energy needed to visit the city. The square is named for a local writer who served as Portugal's president in the 1920s. His house just around the corner holds a little museum, the **Casa Manuel Teixeira Gomes** (✆ **28/248-04-92**), but unless there's an interesting temporary exhibit, it's really for specialists.

There's a much more interesting museum a 10-minute stroll south along the river. When I tell you that it is focused on sardine canning, you may not be convinced, but in focusing on the industry that was once the town's mainstay, the **Museu de Portimão ★★** (www.museudeportimao.pt; ✆ **28/240-52-61**) manages to tell an enthralling tale of social history through the lives of its working men and women. It opened in 2008 in a restored cannery. It has netted several international awards and is a must for John Steinbeck fans. Beyond the fishing industry it reaches back into the city's story to Roman times. A series of aquariums in old salting tanks shows underwater life in the Arade and nearby coast. It's on Rua Dom Carlos I. Open in August from Wednesday to Sunday 3pm to 11pm; Tuesday 7:30 to 11pm; for the rest of the year Wednesday to Sunday 10am to 6pm and Tuesday 2:30 to 6pm. Admission is 3€, 1.50€ seniors and youngsters 16 to 25, free for under 16s.

Portimão has a couple of interesting churches. The **Igreja Matriz ★** dates from the 15th century, with an imposing facade in mustard and white that mixes the Gothic and baroque (Mon–Fri 10am–12:30pm and 3–7pm; Sat

5–7pm and Sun 10:30am–1pm and 5–7 pm). With a similar color scheme, the hulking **Igreja do Colégio dos Jesuitas** was built in the 17th century as a Jesuit college (Mon–Fri 8am–12:30pm and 3–6pm). Don't leave town without paying a visit to **A Casa da Isabel ★★** (✆ **28/248-43-150**), a gem of a tearoom specializing in traditional Algarve pastries. Many of their recipes were gathered from convents around the region and are sinfully delicious. Open at Rua Direita 61, daily 9am to 11pm (9pm in winter).

In Praia da Rocha, if you want a break from soaking up the rays on the beach, climb the cliff stairs to the **Fortaleza de Santa Catarina de Ribamar ★**, a fortress built by Spain's King Felipe III to deter English pirates from attacking his Portuguese holdings. There's a cafe in the courtyard and entry is free. Also worth a visit is the nearby village of **Alvor ★**, which aside from great beaches and seafood has a pretty white core and is the starting point for **nature trails ★★** (www.algarvewildlife.com) through the dunes and around the lagoon. Among the excellent Alvor restaurants, we heartily recommend **Ábabuja ★★** (www.ababuja.com; ✆ **28/245-89-79**) the champions in a crowded market for grilled fish on the village quayside; and **Restinga ★★★** (www.restinga.pt; ✆ **28/245-94-34**) where the fabulous beach setting is matched by the quality of the seafood.

On the other side of the Arade, **Ferragudo ★★** is a perfect picture of terracotta-roofed houses piled on a low hill beneath another 17th-century fortress. It's long been an artists' retreat. Among its many places to eat fish well are: **Rei das Praias ★★** (www.restaurantereidaspraias.com; ✆ **28/246-10-06**) overlooking the beach at secluded Praia dos Caneiros, and **Sueste ★** (www.restaurantesueste.com; ✆ **28/246-15-92**) on the village waterfront.

Outdoor Activities

BEACHES Despite the overgrown construction on top of the cliff, **Praia da Rocha ★★** remains a glorious broad, long stretch with compact sand inclining smoothly to calm, lapping waters. Sandstone stacks and rocky outcrops add to the Instagram-able nature of the place. It draws crowds in summer, but the size means you can usually find space. To the west there are a series of smaller cove-like beaches that replicate the mix of golden sand, honeycomb cliff, and limpid waters, but with less intrusive development behind them. **Praia do Vau ★★** is lovely; **Praia do Alemão ★★** retains a natural feel with trains of scrub and umbrella pine running through the cliffs above. Although there's a degree of resort development as you approach Alvor, the beaches of **Prainha ★★★** and **Praia dos Três Irmãos ★★** are among the prettiest around. Beyond, **Praia de Alvor ★★★** is the mirror image of Meia Praia on the other side of the lagoon: a long strip of dune-backed sand separating the sea from the marshes and still waters of the Ria de Alvor.

ON THE WATER On river, sea, or lagoon, Portimão presents a number of nautical options. One of the most original is to sail up the Arade river from Portimão to the medieval city of Silves using a silent, emissions-free solar-powered boat. **Algarve Sun Boat** (www.algarvesunboat.com; ✆ **91/991-94-50**) offers the 4½-hour trip for 25€ per adult as part of their portfolio of solar boat trips. You can also make the trip in a traditional fishing skiff with **Ferragudo Boat Trips** (www.ferragudoboattrips.com; ✆ **91/684-64-25**). Boat operators heading out from Alvor across the lagoon and into the Atlantic include **Trigana Boat Trips** (www.triganaboattrips.com; ✆ **91/210-57-57**) using vintage Tagus River sailing boats; and **Alvor Boat Trips** (www.alvorboattrips.com; ✆ **96/209-15-51**), who also have a solar-powered boat in their fleet and offer a range of trips from dolphin-watching to exploring the beautiful sea caves at Benagil.

GOLF **Penina** (www.penina.com; ✆ **28/242-02-00**) is where golf began in the Algarve. The championship course was laid down in 1966 by Sir Henry Cotton. The three-time Open winner crafted his masterpiece by planting 350,000 trees and trucking in soil to cover a network of marshy rice paddies. It's still regarded as one of the best, overlooked by the grand old Penina hotel (were McCartney once jammed). It also has more forgiving 9-hole courses for beginners and intermediate golfers. Cotton loved the place and spent his final years there. His grave overlooks the course that today bears his name, as does the cozy, wood-paneled hotel bar, chockablock with golfing memorabilia.

Shopping

The main downtown shopping area is around **Praça da República**, notably on **Rua do Comércio, Rua Direita,** and **Rua Vasco da Gama,** where you can find a mix of traditional shops and international brands. For an original gift, head to the **Studio Bongard** ★★ (www.studiobongard.com; ✆ **96/836-29-30**) in Ferragudo, where sculptors Tara and Sylvain have created a Neptune's cave of ceramic art, much of it inspired by the ocean. It's a delight to browse, on Rua Infante D. Henrique 62, open Monday to Friday 10am to 5:30pm, Saturday 10am to 2:30pm. A little farther to the east, the village of Porches is renowned for its pottery. **Porches Pottery** ★ (www.porchespottery.com; ✆ **28/235-28-58**) has a vast selection of handpainted works in Algarve colors (and a shaded garden cafe). Open Monday to Friday 9am to 6pm, Saturday 10am to 4pm. The reputation of Algarve wine has been turned around in recent year thanks to producers like **Quinta dos Vales** (www.quintadosvales.eu; ✆ **28/243-10-36**). The estate is filled with artworks, many of which, like the wines, can be bought from the store. It's at Sítio dos Vales, Estombar, a 10-minute drive east from Portimão. Open Monday to Saturday 9am to 6pm.

Where to Stay

EXPENSIVE

Bela Vista Hotel and Spa ★★★ This was the first hotel on Praia da Rocha and amid its palm-shaded gardens and lounges lined with *azulejos* and mahogany paneling, it still feels like it has the clifftop and the wonderful beach to itself. This Moorish fantasy was built as a private palace in 1918 and opened as a hotel in the 1930s, serving as a refuge for deposed politicians and sun-loving celebrities. It underwent a major facelift in the 2010s when designer Graça Viterbo accentuated the glamor factor with her bouncy blends of textures and colors (check the stained-glass-and-mosaic-filled bathrooms and technicolor grand piano). Rooms are divided between the main building, a white-cube garden wing, and an *azulejo*-clad "blue house" annex. The spa is by French group L'Occitane, and the artistic dishes served in the Michelin-starred **Vista** restaurant are as easy on the eye as the views over the beach. Adults only.

Avenida Tomas Cabreira, Praia da Rocha. www.hotelbelavista.net. ✆ **28/246-02-80.** 38 units. 188€–700€ double; 344€–1,000€ suite. Parking 15€ daily. **Amenities:** Garden; terrace; bike hire; outdoor pool; spa; gym; sauna; hammam; massage service; restaurant; bar; free Wi-Fi.

MODERATE

Pestana Alvor Praia ★★ Direct access onto lovely Praia dos Três Irmãos beach (the hotel has an elevator down the cliff) is the No. 1 attraction of this resort-style hotel that opened in 1967. A recent renovation brought the rooms elegantly up to date. Their gentle color schemes reflect the sandy tones and azure waters (most) guests view from their balconies. The reception, bars, and restaurants now have a contemporary feel that blends well with retro artwork survivors from the sixties. For those who don't want sand between their toes, the expansive sundeck, lawns, and clifftop pool all offer views over the beach and bay below. Family friendly.

Praia dos Três Irmãos, Alvor. www.pestana.com. ✆ **28/240-09-00.** 202 units. 71€–350€ double; 147€–450€ suite. Free parking. **Amenities:** Garden; terrace; tennis; mini-golf; bike hire; indoor, outdoor pools; spa; gym; sauna; hammam; Jacuzzi; massage service; 2 restaurants; 2 bars; kid's play area; babysitting; free Wi-Fi.

INEXPENSIVE

NDS Prestige Guesthouse and Suites ★ Located in a saffron-painted two-story Algarve home in an old-town alley leading down to the river, this tiny but well-groomed guesthouse opened in 2017. Some of the rooms are seriously small: The Praia da Rocha "suite" is just 10 square meters (107 sq. ft.). Others have more than double that area. All of them are decorated with modern furniture, soft natural colored drapes, and big black-and-white pictures of old Portimão (nostalgists will appreciated one showing Praia da Rocha before the building boom). There's a rooftop terrace with a brightly painted Algarve chimney.

Rua de Santa Isabel 77 and 79. www.ndsturismo.com. ✆ **28/210-90-33.** 5 units. 40€–120€ double. **Amenities:** Terrace; bike hire; free Wi-Fi.

Where to Eat

Adega Vila Lisa ★★★ PORTUGUESE An Algarve institution since 1981, presidents, tycoons, and movie stars trek out to this rustic blue-white-and-yellow cottage in the village of Mexilhoeira Grande for very special dinners (owners recount how James Gandolfini fell asleep on one of the bench tables after a long night here with Robert De Niro). There's no menu. You eat a succession of six plates, each deeply rooted in regional traditions. One may contain cornmeal with razor clams, peppery baked octopus, and roast ham

MONCHIQUE: ESCAPE TO THE mountains

The **Serra de Monchique ★★** hills form the highest and coolest part of the Algarve. The bare summit **Fóia ★★** stands at just over 900m (2,953 ft.), with imperious views over the region from the palette of greens covering the wooded slopes and valleys below to vast Atlantic horizons. The peak is a scenic 50-minute drive from Portimão, winding up through forests of pine, chestnut, cork oak, oleander, and mimosa, which bursts into canary-yellow flower in January and February. Also planted thick on the slopes are eucalyptus trees, which may be good for the sinuses but are highly combustible—the forest was ravaged by wildfires in the summer of 2018.

The market town of **Monchique ★** is an agreeable place to stroll among colorful houses and gardens filled with citrus trees, camellias, and hydrangeas. Every street corner seems to offer a fresh vista over the hills. The Manueline-style **Igreja Matriz ★** church sports a famed 16th-century doorway topped with five twisted pinnacles. Colorful tiles and carved woodwork grace the interior, along with a statue of the Virgin Mary attributed to 18th-century sculptor Joaquim Machado de Castro. Up the hill, the convent of **Nossa Senhora do Desterro ★** is in ruins, but you can look at the curious tiled fountain and the impressive old magnolia tree on its grounds.

The town is renowned for handicrafts, notably blankets, basketry, and woodwork, particularly its scissor-folding wooden chairs. There are a number of stores and workshops on **Rua da Estrada Velha.** Honey, hams, and sausages made from local acorn-fed pigs are also a major draw; the **Duarte family store ★** (www.saboresdemonchique.com; ✆ **28/291-20-11**) at 18 Rua Serpa Pinto has a selection of authentic products. Then there is *medronho*, a powerful schnapps made from the little red fruits of *arbutus unedo*, a shrub that's sometimes called strawberry tree. Distilled by micro-producers around the *serra*, it can be bought at **Loja do Mel e do Medronho ★** (✆ **96/773-57-83**) in the main square. Open daily 10am to 7pm.

Just down the hill is the spa village of **Caldas de Monchique ★** (www.monchiquetermalresort.com; [tel: **28/291-09-10**). Roman bathers are believed to have launched the thermal resort, and in 1636, the bishop of the Algarve built bath houses here as the local clergy took to the health-giving volcanic spring waters. By the time King Carlos dropped by in 1897, Caldas was a smart-set resort, complete with hotels, restaurants, and a casino built in the fashionable Moorish-revival style. It was all restored in the 2000s and forms a delightful getaway surrounded by over 1,000 plant species. Staying in one of the four resort hotels or soaking in the spa makes a cool alternative to the coast.

Our preferred place to sample hearty highland cuisine is **A Charrette ★★** (✆ **28/291-21-42**) at Rua Dr. Samora Gil 30, Monchique. Go for the pork stew with chestnuts or fava beans with local sausage. Mains 10€ to 14€.

hock. After the meat course comes oxtail-and-chickpea soup scented with fresh mint. Then come anise-infused cookies and sticky fig cakes accompanied by liqueurs, firewater, and old-style coffee. Drinks are all included in the price. Don't miss it.

Rua Francisco Bivar, Mexilhoeira Grande. www.adegavilalisa.com. ✆ **28/296-84-78.** Tasting menu 35€. July–Sept: daily 7:30–10pm; Oct–Jun: Fri–Sat 7:30–10pm.

Forte e Feio ★★ PORTUGUESE On balmy summer evenings, there's a great atmosphere around the old fisherman's neighborhood beneath the bridge over the Arade. In the square and lanes, long tables set out under strings of yellow light fill with diners tucking into grilled sardines and other fishy treats. This is our pick among the array of good, simple restaurants. Don't be put off by the name (it means "strong and ugly"); the food is good and the service efficient, if brusque. Beside the grills, it does traditional Algarve treats like cornmeal with cockles, or razor-clam rice.

Largo da Barca 1. ✆ **28/241-38-09.** Mains 10€–18€. Daily noon–11:30pm.

Portimão Entertainment & Nightlife

If your dream night out involves watching English soccer on a big screen surrounded by fervent fans fired up by cheap ale; drinking an excess of technicolor cocktails; or games involving quickfire consumption of vodka shots, the strip at Praia da Rocha has a bar for you.

There's generally a more sophisticated vibe at the eastern, marina end of the beach, where **No Solo Agua** (www.nosoloagua.com; ✆ **28/249-81-80**) and **Blanco Beach** (www.blancobeach.com; ✆ **92/719-16-55**) are renowned for sunset and late-night parties, often with big name DJs.

Portimão's biggest party, however, takes place every August with the 5-day **Sardine Festival** ★, which turns the riverfront into a giant restaurant where millions of the little blue fish will be thrown onto barbecues. It's often carried live on national TV, and some of the biggest names in Portuguese music come down to play. There'll be a fairground, big wheel, and other amusements.

The city has a couple of movie theaters: **Algarcine** (✆ **28/241-18-88**) on Avenida Miguel Bombarda; and **Cineplace** (✆ **28/249-08-40**) in the Continente shopping mall. The **Hotel Algarve Casino** (www.solverde.pt; ✆ **28/240-20-00**) on the main clifftop street in Praia da Rocha has a wide range of slots and table games, plus dance and cabaret shows.

LAGOS ★★

306km (190 miles) S of Lisbon; 140km (87 miles) W of Vila Real de Santo António

Lagos is a pretty town, lively in summer thanks to the youthful crowd that flocks there both for its gentle beaches and to use it as a jumping-off point for the surfer strands to the west. Its little station is end of the line for the European railway network, which adds to its backpacker allure. Lagos also has history. It was a Roman and Arab port long before Henry the Navigator made it the launchpad of the Portuguese Voyages of Discovery. Local sailor Gil Eanes kicked off the whole enterprise when his 1433 expedition rounded Cape Bojador on the coast of Western Sahara, which Europeans had previously judged unpassable. Lagos' sandstone city walls and gold-filled churches testify to its historical importance during the Discovery Era, even if much was destroyed in the 1755 earthquake that also wrecked Lisbon. Lagos' history also casts a grim shadow. Its main riverside square is where the Atlantic slave trade began. Henry the Navigator was among the buyers in 1444 at the sale of 235 men, women, and children dragged from the coast of Mauritania. They were the first of 5.8 million Africans that Portuguese ships carried into slavery over 4 centuries.

Essentials

ARRIVING

BY TRAIN From Lisbon, take the Faro-bound train to the junction at Tunes, where you change to one that will chug westward along the coast to Lagos. There are four a day making the 4-hour trip. It costs at least 24€ one-way. From Faro, direct trains take just over 1½ hours and cost 7.40€. There are about 10 a day. Information and schedules are at www.cp.pt.

BY BUS Buses are usually a better option from Lisbon. There are around two-dozen direct buses from **Sete Rios** station between 6 and 1am in summer (fewer in winter) run by the **Rede Expressos** network (www.rede-expressos.pt; ✆ **70/722-33-44**). The journey takes around 4 hours and fares start at 19€. If you're flying to Faro airport, there are a number of private shuttle operators that will take you direct to your accommodation for as little as 15€, although prices vary depending on the number of passengers and stops. Check www.terravision.eu, www.lagos-shuttle.com, or www.faroshuttlebus.com.

BY CAR From Lisbon, it should take you a little less than 3 hours on the A2 and A22 toll highways.

VISITOR INFORMATION

The **Lagos Tourist Office** is in the former city hall on Praça Gil Eanes (✆ **28/276-30-31**). Open daily summer 9:30am to 5:30pm, winter 9am to 5pm.

Exploring Lagos

A good place to get to know the city is the **Mercado Municipal ★★**, a two-story 1920s building just across the river from the fishing port, with displays of the best the region has to offer in terms of fresh seafood and meat at street level; fruit, vegetables, bread, and spices upstairs. Open Monday to Saturday 8am to 2 pm. From the roof of the market you can walk through to the Centro **Ciência Viva de Lagos ★** (www.lagos.cienciaviva.pt; ✆ **28/277-00-00**), an interactive science museum that kids will enjoy. There's a multilingual focus on the science behind the voyages of discovery: from 15th-century ocean navigation to life in the oceans, done through hands-on games and exhibits. Admission is 5€, 2.50€ for youngsters 6 to 17, 3€ students and seniors; free for under 6s. Open Tuesday to Sunday 10am to 6pm. Just next door is the **Igreja de São Sebastião ★**, a church with a plain 17th-century facade in white and dove grey. Inside there are some pleasing baroque sculptures and marble columns, but the main attraction is the **Capela dos Ossos ★**, a tiny chapel built from human bones, a miniature version of the macabre skeletal church at Évora.

From the church, it's a short walk downhill to **Largo Gil Eanes ★**, the main city center square. In the center, the modern marble statue that looks like an astronaut actually represents King Sebastião, the reckless king who at the age of 24 set sail from Lagos with an army to conquer Morocco. He and much of the Portuguese nobility were wiped out at the Battle of Alcácer Quibir in 1578, and Spain marched in to rule Portugal for 60 years. Still, King Seb has always been viewed by some as a romantic hero and there's a legend that he will one day return to save the country. There are a couple of good cafes nearby. **Taquelim Gonçalves ★★** (www.taquelimgoncalves.pt; ✆ **28/276-28-82**) has been around since 1935 and is still the best place in town for delicious Algarvian pastries rich with almond, fig, carob, and other delights. The homemade ice cream is not bad either. Open daily 8:30am to 11:30pm. **Café Gil Eanes ★** (✆ **28/276-28-86**) is a relative newcomer founded in 1954, and its terrace is the place for Lagos people-watching; Monday to Saturday 10am to midnight.

Streets leading off the square south and west from here are the city's commercial heart. Pedestrianized Rua 25 de Abril is the busiest, lined with restaurants, bars, and stores. It leads down to **Praça Infante dom Henrique ★**, a broad plaza open on one side to the waterfront and surrounded on the other three by handsome, mostly 18th-century buildings. There's a modern fountain and a statue of Prince Henry the Navigator. In the western corner is a two-story rectangular building with a four-arched porch, known as the **Mercado de Escravos ★** (✆ **28/277-00-20**), the Slave Market. It is believed to be built on or near the site of that first 15th-century sale of people seized from West Africa. Prince Henry's chronicler, Gomes Eanes de Zurara, was on hand to record the scene as Portuguese sailors divided their haul. "Children, seeing themselves removed from their parents, ran hastily toward them; mothers clasped their children in their arms, and holding them, cast themselves upon the ground, covering them with their bodies, without heeding the blows which they were given," he wrote. The present building dates from the 17th century, and it's not certain it was ever used as a slave market. That first trade was done in the open on the quayside, although many more followed. A small, poorly equipped museum opened in 2016 but is inadequate to the task of explaining the enormity of what started here. Admission 3€, 1.50€ over 65s and youngsters 12 to 18, free under 12s. Open Tuesday to Sunday 10am to 12:30pm and 2 to 5:30pm.

Across the square, on Rua Gen. Alberto Carlos Silveira, is Lagos' greatest treasure: the **Igreja de Santo António ★★★**, an 18th-century church whose interior gleams with gold. Its gilded baroque fittings are one of the finest examples of the *talha dourada* artform that draped wood carvings with gold leaf from Brazil. The church is part of the **Museu Municipal Dr. José Formosinho ★**, a museum cluttered with a bewildering hodgepodge that includes replicas of Algarve chimneys, cork carvings, Roman mosaics, and an eight-legged calf. The museum was due to reopen at the end of 2019 after a 2-year makeover (we're curious to see if the calf is still there). The golden church remained open through the works. Admission 3€, 1.50€ over 65s and youngsters 12 to 18, free under 12s. Open Tuesday to Sunday 10am to 12:30pm and 2 to 5:30pm.

Around the corner, riverside gardens with palm trees lie beneath the impressive **city walls ★** dating back to the 15th century. On the other side of road, the 17th-century **Forte da Ponta da Bandeira ★** guards the entry to the harbor. It's used to house temporary exhibitions, and there are splendid ocean views from the bulwarks. Just outside of town, **Zoo Lagos ★** (www.zoolagos.com; ✆ **28/268-01-00**), with over 140 animal species, makes an alternative to the beach for wildlife loving youngsters. Admission 18€, 14€ for kids 4 to 11; open daily April to September 10am to 7pm, October to March 10am to 5pm.

Outdoor Activities

BEACHES Some of the region's most photographed beaches nestle beneath the amber-hued sandstone cliffs that run south from Lagos. **Praia de Dona Ana ★** is the best known, but gets very crowded in summer and has been disfigured by a 2015 artificial extension. The next up, **Praia do Camilo ★★**, retains its natural beauty looking out at chunks of honeycomb rock protruding from the still waters. They are reachable on food from downtown, but it's a bit of a walk. Sunbathers are advised not to lay too close to the crumbly cliffs. Just beyond is **Ponta da Piedade ★★★**, where the cliffs splinter in a multitude of coves, grottos, and rock formations up to 20 meters (65 ft.) high. It's fun to visit by boat (see below) but spectacular at sunset from the viewpoints next to the lighthouse. Walkways heading west along the clifftops will take you to **Praia de Porto de Mós ★★**, a much longer fine-sand beach in a sheltered bay with a couple of good restaurants. On the other side of Lagos is our favorite, **Meia Praia ★★★**, a 5km (over 3-mile) sliver of white sand curving around the bay from the city to a sapphire blue lagoon. It can get a little crowded at the city end, but at the other end you'll have acres to yourselves, bar the occasional nudist. Keep your eyes open for anything glittering in the sand: According to local legend, Spanish galleons loaded with Aztec gold lay wrecked under the bay. You can reach it by a little rowboat ferry across the river.

BOATS Walk along Lagos' palm-lined riverside promenade and you'll pass countless stands offering boat trips that range from row-your-own kayaks and fishing skiffs to explore the Ponta da Piedade caves, to highspeed dolphin-watching dinghies, game fishing, scuba-diving trips, and sunset wine cruises. Many of the operators have stores on the quayside at the **Lagos Marina,** where boats usually depart from. **Discover Tours** (www.discover.pt) and **Bom Dia Boat Trips** (www.bomdia-boattrips.com) are among the long-established operators.

GOLF **Palmares Golf** (www.onyriapalmares.com; ✆ **28/279-05-00**) is the best course in Lagos and among the best in the country. Enjoying wonderful views over Meia Praia and the Alvor lagoon, it was redesigned in 2011 by Robert Trent Jones, who turned one of the Algarve's oldest courses into a three 9-hole combo mixing parkland and links. The railroad into Lagos runs through the greens, adding a whimsical touch. A luxury hotel was added at the time of the makeover. Also highly-rated is **Espiche Golf** (www.espichegolf.pt; ✆ **28/268-82-50**), which opened in 2012 in forested land north of Lagos and boasts an award-winning clubhouse restaurant.

Shopping

Strolling among the shop-lined streets of Lagos' old town is one of the town's pleasures. In summer, stores stay open into the night to catch post-beach customers. Our top choice is **Mar d'Estórias ★★** (www.mardestorias.com; ✆ **28/279-21-65**) a maze of marvels spread over three stories of a building that once housed the fire brigade. It sells classy Portuguese products from wines to soap and ceramics in the ground-floor store, but spreads upward into homeware, books, and music, plus an excellent restaurant and rooftop bar. It's on Rua Silva Lopes, 30. Open daily 10am to midnight. On the corner of Praça Gil Eanes, it's hard to miss the brash storefront of **Força Portugal ★** (www.forcaportugal.com) decked out in the red, green, and yellow colors of the national flag and frequently featuring outsize photos of soccer players in their underwear. This is part of an Algarve chain dedicated to merchandise related to Portugal's successful teams and in particular its biggest star, Cristiano Ronaldo. Open Monday to Saturday 8am to midnight, closes 5pm Sunday. Bookworms can find solace at **The Owl Story ★** (✆ **91/741-43-86**), with new and secondhand editions in English at Rua Marreiros Netto 67. Monday to Saturday 10am to 5:30pm. Aside from the daily produce market (see above), there's a fun **farmers' market ★★** on Saturday mornings in the bus station on Rua Mercado do Levante, where small holders bring in their produce, from fresh fruit and vegetables to homemade bread, almond pastries, honey, cheese, and live chickens. In July, the 4-day **Arte Doce ★★** festival celebrates regional pastry making, a chance to buy almond paste confections that make an ideal edible souvenir.

Where to Stay

Casa Mae ★★★ In many ways, this is what a new hotel in the Algarve should be. It has beautifully restored a historic city-center mansion and installed discreet, low-rise cabins, rooms, and a pool in the delightful palm-lined back garden. They grow the food for the excellent restaurant themselves or buy from local producers. It enriches the urban landscape, plus it's a great place to stay. Rooms are cool and white with terracotta floors, blanched wood or wicker furniture, and splashes of color from natural textiles. You can take a yoga, cooking, or ceramics course, listen to a gentle *bossa nova* guitar performance, or take a fishing trip (they'll cook your catch for dinner when you get back.)

Rua do Jogo do Bolo 41. www.casa-mae.com. ✆ **96/836-97-32.** 31 units. 95€–230€ double; 210€–290€ suite. Free parking. **Amenities:** Garden; terrace; bike hire; outdoor pool; massage service; restaurant; bar; babysitting; free Wi-Fi.

Tivoli Lagos ★ As solid as a castle from the exterior, Tivoli Lagos lies within its own ramparts and moats—okay, a swimming pool and a paddling pool. It spreads over 1.2 hectares (3 acres) up a slight hill overlooking Lagos. Its lobby/lounge has a hacienda atmosphere, with white-plaster walls enlivened by sunny colors. It's one of the town's oldest hotels, but a recent renovation has given rooms a modern, if uninspiring, look with lots of grey, cream, and beige. The new Spanish owners may be preparing to take the upgrade further with price hikes planned for 2020. The big attraction is its beach club with pool and bar by the sands of Meia Praia, reached by a free 10-minute shuttle bus.

Rua António Crisógono dos Santos. www.tivolihotels.com. ✆ **28/279-00-79.** 296 units. 79€–426€ double; 124€–450€ suite. Free parking. **Amenities:** Garden; terrace; bike hire; indoor and outdoor pools; spa; gym; sauna; hammam; Jacuzzi; massage service; 3 restaurants; 3 bars; babysitting; free Wi-Fi.

Vila Galé Lagos ★★ The best of the beachfront options, this two-floor quadrangle has a south side open to Meia Praia and the blue of Lagos bay. Rooms are airy, colored cream and slate, with balconies and sea views. The hotel's arms wrap around one of the region's biggest pools (for those who can't be bothered to cross the road onto the beach). It covers 1,200 square meters (13,000 square ft.). That's almost Olympic size, although Michael Phelps and Co. never had to contend with wooden decks shaded by olive trees jutting into the water. At high season the place can seem congested, with the restaurant working on a production-line scale, but it ticks most boxes if you're looking for a family unwind by the ocean. Decor is inspired by Portuguese fashion designers, featuring lots of catwalk photos.

Rua Sophia de Mello Breyner Andresen, Meia Praia. www.vilagale.com. ✆ **28/277-14-00.** 130 units. 75€–236€ double, 112€–432€ suite. Free parking. **Amenities:** Garden; terrace; tennis; indoor and outdoor pool; spa; gym; sauna; hammam; Jacuzzi; massage service; restaurant; bar; children's play area; free Wi-Fi.

Where to Eat

Comidinha ★★★ PORTUGUESE Escape the old-town crowds and head to a rather inauspicious-looking row of apartment blocks on the way to Porto de Mós beach. This little eatery is the best in town, dedicated to preserving the traditions of Algarve cooking (although there may be a couple of Brazilian- or Mozambican-influenced dishes tossed into the mix). There's a daily, hand-written menu heavily dependent on what the fishermen have brought in. Dishes can include bean stew with whelks, oxtail slow cooked in red wine or—and this is our favorite—grouper simmered in a rich broth with rice. Be sure to finish with the fig cake flambéed in *medronho,* a fiery local liquor. Let the extravagantly mustachioed host guide you through their encyclopedic wine list.

Praça do Poder Local 5. ✆ **28/278-28-57.** Mains 15€–25€. Tues–Sun 7–10pm.

São Roque ★★★ PORTUGUESE/SEAFOOD Here's what you do. Walk or drive (there's parking outside) to this curved wood and glass structure at the city end of Meia Praia beach; don't ask for the menu, instead head to the ice box with Olga or one of the other staff members, choose a fish, and accept her suggestion for starters (e.g., clams, tuna-and-tomato salad, fried octopus, etc.); ask for a table on the city side to admire the sunset; order the house white (especially made by an illustrious Alentejo oenologist); tuck into your fish served with heavy-on-the-garlic-olive oil-and-oregano potatoes and salad; finish up with a dessert that combines an Algarvian trilogy of fig, almond, and carob; pay up and head home satisfied.

Estrada de São Roque, Meia Praia. ✆ **28/279-21-01.** Mains 12€–22€. Tues–Sun 10am–10pm.

Lagos Entertainment & Nightlife

Lagos buzzes on summer nights, thanks to the youthful international crowd that flocks here (it's particularly popular with young Aussies who find a laid-back echo of home here during their European tours). Rua Cândido dos Reis and Rua Silva Lopes are particularly hectic, but in summer pretty much the whole of the old town is filled after 10pm with bar crawlers. For a quieter night out, we recommend the rooftop at **Mar d'Estórias** (see p. 253) or the **Centro Cultural de Lagos** (✆ **28/277-04-53**), which has regular concerts of classical, fado, and other musical genres. It's at Rua Lançarote de Freitas 7; check with the tourist office for the program.

SAGRES ★★

327km (203 miles) S of Lisbon; 33km (20 miles) W of Lagos

At the extreme southwestern tip of Europe, this barren, windswept promontory can feel like the edge of the world. That's just what ancient peoples believed it to be. Yet, this may have been the Cape Canaveral of the 15th century. It was from around here that Prince Henry the Navigator plotted Portugal's first Voyages of Discovery that led to the opening up of the world to European trade and conquest. In Portuguese, Henry is known as the *Infante de Sagres.* He gathered sailors, cartographers, and scholars to pool knowledge on what lay beyond the waves before Portugal's little sailing boats started edging south.

Modern historians tend to pooh-pooh the old idea of a "school of navigation" in Sagres and point out that nearby Lagos was the real center of the early discoveries. But the prince certainly had a home out near the point where he spent much time, and eventually died here in 1460 at the age of 66.

Ships traveling from the Mediterranean to Northern Europe still have to round Sagres Point and its mirror image, Cape St. Vincent, 6km (4 miles) to the northwest. The pair of rocky headlands have a history of shipwreck and naval battles. A notable 1797 encounter saw youthful British naval hero Horatio Nelson famously disobey his admiral's orders to engage and capture two Spanish warships.

Today visitors come to Sagres to admire the austere beauty of the landscape, wander the historical sites, tan on the beaches (or surf their waves), eat freshly caught seafood, or to watch for birds, particularly in fall when hundreds of vultures, eagles, and other raptors pass overhead on their annual migration from Europe to Africa.

Essentials

ARRIVING

BY BUS The regional bus company **EVA** (www.eva-bus.com; ✆ **28/958-90-55**) runs six to nine daily buses from Lagos (where the nearest railway station is located). The trip takes about an hour and costs 4.05€ one-way. **Rede Expressos** (www.rede-expressos.pt; ✆ **70/722-33-44**) runs up to four daily buses from Lisbon in the summer for 20€.

BY CAR From Lagos, drive west on Route 125 to Vila do Bispo, and then head south along Route 268 to Sagres. From Lisbon, the quickest way is on the main A2 toll highway to the Algarve and the A22 to Lagos that takes just over 3 hours. Be aware that the A22 involves electronic tolls; check if your rental car has the automated payment mechanism (p. 468). A slower route takes you down the Alentejo coast: Leave the A2 at exit 9 and stay on the A22 until Sines, then take the N120 and N268 into Sagres. It takes 3 hours 40 minutes.

VISITOR INFORMATION

The **Tourist Office** is on Avenida Comandante Matoso (✆ **28/262-48-73;** Mon–Fri 9:30am–1pm and 2–5:30pm).

Exploring Sagres

There's always an element of drama about the drive to Sagres. After the little town of Vila do Bispo, the landscape suddenly changes and you find yourself on a flat, rock-strewn plateau with minimal vegetation. A near-constant wind blows hard from the Atlantic, which splashes up to the cliffs on either side.

Given the rugged approaches, it's something of a surprise to find the town a cheery, laidback place. The squat, mostly modern white houses contain guesthouses and cafes catering to the surfer crowd, who've largely replaced the hippies who converged here in the 1960s. There's a fishing harbor down the hill to the east, but unless you've come to eat, tan, or admire the views, there's not much to do in the town itself.

Instead, walk over to the headland and the **Fortaleza de Sagres** ★★ (www.monumentosdoalgarve.pt; ✆ **28/262-01-42**). This is a fortress with just one wall that juts inland, cutting off the tip of the peninsula. Its other defenses are the cliffs that fall vertically down to the ocean. You can see why visitors have been awestruck by the location since ancient times. Greek and Roman writers called it the "sacred promontory" and believed it to be the end of the inhabited world. The Atlantic roils up all around. Over the shrieks of gulls you can admire the view knowing there's nothing but saltwater between here and the U.S. east coast. The rampart you see was built in the 16th and 17th century to deter pirates like Sir Francis Drake (who tore through Sagres in 1587).

To visit the fort, admission costs 3€ (1.50€ for over 65s and youngsters 15–25, free for under 12s) and it's open May to September daily 9:30am to 7:30pm; October to April 9:30am to 5pm. Inside there's a small 16th-century chapel believed to have been built on the site of the one constructed by Henry the Navigator, where sailors prayed before setting out on their voyages into the unknown. Laid out on the ground is a compass rose 43 meters (140 ft.) across; it's believed to have had some navigational use in the 16th century but its exact purpose is unclear. The main reason to visit is just to absorb the immensity of the vistas from the clifftop walk (be careful—there's no guardrail) and listen to the ear-splitting roar of the ocean hitting the rock.

There's more information about Henry at the **Ermida de Nossa Senhora de Guadalupe ★** (✆ **28/263-90-42**) a tiny church just inland from here, near the village of Raposeira, that's believed to have been built by the Knights Templar in the 13th century. Henry is thought to have prayed in this simple chapel, and a modern visitor center focuses on his story. Admission 2€ (1€ for over 65s and youngsters 15–25, free for under 12s). Open May to September daily 10am to 12:30pm and 2 to 5:30pm; October to April 9am to 12:30pm and 2 to 4:30pm.

About 6km (4 miles) away is the promontory of **Cabo de São Vicente ★★**. It got its name because, according to legend, the body of St. Vincent arrived mysteriously here on a boat guided by ravens. There's a clifftop **lighthouse ★** (www.faros.pt; ✆ **28/262-46-06**) with a small museum, shop, and cafe that closes at sunset—so there's just enough time to grab a drink as you join the crowds watching the technicolor display as the rays sink into the ocean (remember to bring a warm sweater even in summer). In the parking lot outside is a much-cherished Algarve curiosity: a German hotdog stand proudly calling itself **Letzte Bratwurst vor Amerika** (Last Bratwurst Before America) where a couple from Nuremburg serve up a tasty selection of grilled sausages (www.letztebratwurst.com).

Outdoor Activities

BEACHES Beaches fringe the Sagres peninsula. Among our favorites: **Praia do Martinhal** curves around a broad bay, rarely rough but frequently blustery; **Praia do Beliche**, clawed out of the cliffs between Sagres and Cape St. Vincent, is sheltered from wind and wave and has cool caves to explore at low tide; **Praia do Castelejo** is exposed to the western waves making this hideaway a magnet for surfers; **Praia da Mareta** is easiest to get to at just a short downhill walk from town.

BOATS & BIRDS Whether you want to watch dolphins leap through the surf or hook a golden bream for dinner, there are boat operators in Sagres with all number of nautical options. **Cape Cruiser** (www.capecruiser.org; ✆ **91/975-11-75**) offers a 4-hour fishing cruise for 50€ per person; **SeaXplorer Sagres** (www.seaxplorersagres.com; ✆ **91/894-01-28**) charges 35€ per adult for dolphin (plus occasionally whale and shark) spotting; and **Mar Ilimitado** (www.marilimitado.com; ✆ **91/683-26-26**) will take you on a birdwatching boat trip for 45€ per adult. Birdwatching on land reaches a peak in October when the great migration provides one of Europe's foremost ornithological events. The **Monte da Cabranosa** ridge near Praia do Beliche is reckoned to be the best spot to watch mass raptor gatherings. Birders flock to an autumn **birdwatching festival** (www.birdwatchingsagres.com).

THE wild, wild WEST

In complete contrast to the calm beaches and tourism excesses in much of the Algarve, the region's west coast is wild. Exposed to the full force of the Atlantic on the southwestern extremity of the Eurasian landmass, it's an isolated mix of scrubby hills, surf-pounded beaches, and occasional whitewashed villages. Surfers, nature lovers, and seekers of solitude will love it. The whole coast, running into the Alentejo region to the north, is protected by the **Sudoeste Alentejano e Costa Vicentina Nature Park ★★** (www.natural.pt; ✆ **28/332-27-35**).

Coming from the north, the first Algarve beach is **Praia de Odeceixe ★★★**, which happens to be one of the region's best. It's open on one side to the surf, but has a broad stream winding around it with calm waters. The straw-colored sands are overlooked by black cliffs to the north and a chalky village on its southern flank. Next-door, little **Praia das Adegas ★★** is for nudists. The biggest town in the west is **Aljezur ★** (pop. 3,000), a laidback jumble of white-washed cottages with hills topped by a Berber castle and some squat windmills. Excellent restaurants (it's the nation's capital of sweet potato) and proximity to beaches like **Praia da Arrifana ★★**, **Praia da Amoreira ★★**, and **Praia de Monte Clérigo ★** mean it's become a major surfer base. The area is not just for beach bums though—Britain's former Prime Minister David Cameron was a repeat vacationer here while in office.

A little farther south, **Praia da Bordeira ★★★** is our top west-coast choice, even if you have to wade through a stream to reach it. It's a diamond of soft, pale sand backed by cliffs and dunes. That stream can provide an alternative when the lifeguards' red flag means the waves are too rough for ocean swimming. Near the cute hamlet of **Carrapateira,** it's long and wide enough to mean you can always find plenty of space on the sand, even at the height of summer.

Among chilled places to stay in the west, try **Casas do Moinho** (www.casasdomoinho.com; ✆ **28/294-92-66**), a cluster of tastefully restored cottages by a windmill in Odeceixe with doubles from 110€; or **Aldeia da Pedralva** (www.aldeiadapedralva.com; ✆ **28/263-93-42**), where a whole abandoned hamlet was transformed into a rustic retreat close to Praia do Amado beach; cottages from 83€. Eating options include **O Sitio do Rio** (✆ **28/297-31-19**) barbecuing fish and meat by the river running down to Praia da Bordeira; and **Cervejaria Mar** (✆ **92/793-54-18**), a storied Aljezur seafood joint.

Where to Stay

EXPENSIVE

Martinhal Beach Resort & Hotel ★★★ This is a paradise for kids (and parents who can afford it). The crown jewel of the group that also has family-based hotels in Lisbon and Cascais, this low-rise resort sits plum on the gently sloping sands of Martinhal bay. There are kids clubs with activities for age groups ranging from creche for babies to surf school and soccer academy for teens. The on-site store is well stocked with diapers, lotions, and toys. Parents are free to choose how much they want to join in the fun with junior, and how much they want to hand their kids over to the legion of teachers and animators in order to take advantage of the luxury spa, gourmet restaurant, romantic strolls on the beach, etc. Rooms are big, bright, and child-safe, complemented by a selection of self-catering units to live *en-famile.* If there's a downside, it's the frequents winds that cut across the bay.

Quinta do Martinhal. www.martinhal.com. ✆ **28/224-02-00.** 194 units. 204€–512€ double; 210€–695€ apartments and villas. Free parking. **Amenities:** Garden; terrace; tennis; bike hire; 1 indoor and 4 outdoor pools; spa; sauna; hammam; Jacuzzi; gym; massage service; 4 restaurants; bar; games room; beautician; barber; stores; 5 kids' clubs; babysitting; free Wi-Fi.

MODERATE

Memmo Baleeira Hotel ★★ This hotel of white modern lines is set on extensive lawns and provides horizon-stretching views over Baleeira fishing port, Praia do Martinhal beach, and a couple of tiny islands in the bay. It's just 50m (164 ft.) from the beach, although you may prefer the expansive wooden deck around the pool. Sun-flooded, mostly white interiors have a calculated simplicity. Most rooms come with balconies and ocean views (although the cheapest look inland). Striped headboards and plaid throws break up the rooms' whiteness. The heated indoor pool and spa are a boon on gray or windy days. The restaurant's wood oven turns out renowned pizza, and there are eggs made to order and *pastéis de nata* at breakfast.

Sítio da Baleeira. www.memmohotels.com. ✆ **28/262-42-12.** 144 units. 78€–235€ double; 175€–303€ suite. Free parking. **Amenities:** Garden; bike hire; indoor and outdoor pools; spa; sauna; gym; massage service; restaurant; bar; babysitting; free Wi-Fi.

Pousada de Sagres ★ Location is the lure here: Built in the distinctive retro style favored by Portugal in 1960 (you can find similar places in its former African colonies), this inn spreads along the edge of a cliff that projects daringly over the sea. Guests are charmed by the rugged beauty of the setting, the pounding surf, and the sense of ocean infinity. The hotel boasts a long colonnade of arches with an extended stone terrace and a lawn overlooking Sagres Fortress and Mareta beach, both a short walk away. Guest rooms are not as impressive, generally on the small side and many could use a touch-up. Still they are generally light and airy with wicker furnishings, balconies, and (in most cases) excellent views, especially if you get a west-facing room to enjoy the sunset.

Ponta da Atalaia. www.pousadas.pt. ✆ **28/262-02-40.** 39 units. 90€–325€ double. Free parking. **Amenities:** Garden; terrace; tennis; outdoor pool; massage service; restaurant; bar; free Wi-Fi.

INEXPENSIVE

The Lighthouse Hostel ★ They don't actually ban grown-ups, but politely point out that people over 40 "not familiar with this kind of housing and atmosphere" might want to look elsewhere. This is a party place aimed at youthful backpackers and surfers. They've taken over a '70s-style villa with a pool, ping-pong table, bar, and hammocks in the garden. There's a trio of wood cabin bungalows housing up to four in the garden. They do yoga classes and barbecues and offer a shuttle to the beaches.

Rua do Poente. www.thelighthousehostel.com. ✆ **28/262-53-41.** 10 units. 55€–90€; 22€–29€ bed in dorm; 75€–130€ bungalow. Free parking. **Amenities:** Garden; terrace; bike hire; outdoor pool; games room; free Wi-Fi.

Where to Eat

A Eira do Mel ★★ PORTUGUESE Inland, in the little town of Vila do Bispo, this rustic blue-and-white house is part of the Slow Food movement dedicated to taking their time in preparing traditional regional dishes. Inside, antique ceramics and agricultural implements decorate bright blue walls, and a rustic chandelier hangs from exposed roof beams. The food is old-style Algarvian. You may start with carrots pickled with cumin or anchovy filets in olive oil; move on to a mix of shrimp, acorn-fed pork, and *chouriço* cooked in *cataplana* (a copper pot that's part wok, part pressure-cooker); or rabbit stewed in red wine. Finish up with one of their famed fig "cheese" desserts (washed down with a glass of *medronho* firewater, if you're not driving).

Estrada do Castelejo, Vila do Bispo. ✆ **28/263-90-16.** Reservations recommended. Mains 15€–20€. Tues–Sat 12:30–3pm, 7:30–10pm.

Retiro do Pescador ★ SEAFOOD Informal, friendly, and simple looking, the food here is as good, if not better, as what you'll get in the town's fancier joints. As the name says, this is a "Fishermen Shelter," meaning it leads with perfectly grilled fish (and some charcoal-grilled meat for those who don't like the fruit of the sea). Our advice: Ask for the daily specials because what is freshest will change depending on the catch. You also can't go wrong with seafood cooked in a *cataplana*. Don't be afraid to try *percebes* (gooseneck barnacles), likely caught just hours before in the rocky waters near Sagres.

Rua dos Murtórios 4. ✆ **28/262-44-38.** Mains 10€–18€. Tues–Sun noon–3:30pm and 7–10pm.

Sagres Entertainment & Nightlife

The once sleepy fishing village of Sagres is now crammed with bars that draw the surfer and backpacker crowd. The nightlife focus is Rua Comandante Matoso, where youngsters from all over Europe and beyond come to relax over beer, wine, sangria, and cocktails (Brazilian *caipirinhas* are popular) after a hard day on the waves. Among the buzzy nightspots on the strip are **Bar Dromedário** (✆ **28/262-42-19**) and **Pau de Pita** (✆ **28/262-49-03**).

ALENTEJO & RIBATEJO

11

The Alentejo is a world apart. Its undulating grasslands often look more like African savannah than Western Europe. Its whitewashed medieval towns and village are the country's best-preserved, its beaches pristine and its cuisine second to none. Along much of its northern edge it blends into the Ribatejo, a region dominated by the broad valley cut by the River Tagus as it winds slowly to Lisbon and the sea.

The name Alentejo comes from "beyond the Tagus," and the river marks a distinct difference in the nature of the country. To the north, land was traditionally broken up into smallholdings; in the Alentejo vast *latifundia* estates hold sway. North of the river, towns and villages tend to be hewn from raw, uncovered granite, to the south they are painted a dazzling white. While the north is frequently hilly, the Alentejo is made up of rolling plains, dotted with olive trees, cork oak, and umbrella pines. Arab rule lasted longer here than in the north and had a greater influence over the architecture and culture. Even the politics is different: the Alentejo is traditionally a stronghold of the left in contrast to the conservative, Catholic north.

The region covers one-third of Portugal, an area the size of Belgium. Its capital **Évora ★★★** is a dazzling white city, a UNESCO World Heritage Site spreading out from the Roman temple, Gothic cathedral and arcaded Renaissance plaza at its heart. There are dozens of beautifully preserved historic towns looming with chalky brilliance out of the green plain, but among those that stand out are **Beja ★★**, the main town in the south dating back to Roman times; **Mértola ★★★**, once the capital of an emirate whose medina-like silhouette reflects perfectly in the waters of the River Guadiana; **Marvão ★★★**, a citadel atop one of the region's rare highlands guarding the Spanish approaches; and **Estremoz ★★★**, a city made of marble.

Stretching from **Troia** (p. 175) in the north down to the Algarve, the **Alentejo coast ★★★** is largely undeveloped, a chain of sandy coves and fishing ports between lengths of wild cliffs (leaving aside the major port and refinery complex outside Vasco da Gama's hometown of **Sines ★**). In 2002 an inland sea was created by building the **Alqueva ★** dam, creating one of Western Europe's largest artificial lakes, which has given a boost to the region's agriculture and added watersports to the attractions of villages like **Monsaraz ★★** and **Mourão ★** . Traditions run deep in the farm land. Alentejo men in winter will wear long fox-collared capes (in fact they are becoming fashionable for both sexes, way beyond the region). If you get the chance you should listen to the powerful singing of the region's **male-voice choirs,** or at least download some *cante Alentejano*.

The Ribatejo is characterized by the flat lands bordering the Tagus (its name means "Tagus bank"). The river's flood plain includes vast fields of rice on the south bank northeast of Lisbon, and cattle ranches: Nowhere in Portugal are bullfighting traditions stronger. These days, *campinos*—Ribatejo cowboys with distinctive scarlet vests and tasseled stocking caps—are a rare sight outside of festivals, but the region's dedication to horsemanship continues, as a visit to **Golegã ★** during the November **horse fair ★★** will show.

Santarém ★★, the regional capital, is a handsome white city on a cliff that dominates the valley with a plethora of Gothic churches. But the region's gem is **Tomar ★★★**, whose fortified convent was once a stronghold of the Templar Knights and is now one Portugal's great UNESCO-protected monuments.

Both regions are renowned for their wines (particularly robust reds) and olive oils. Ribatejo cuisine features Tagus river fish and a hearty main-course meat-and-veg soup known as *sopa da pedra* (stone soup). Alentejo lamb and beef are renowned, but above all its cuisine is based on *porco preto* (black pork) from the dark pigs that root around semi-wild, living off acorns fallen from forests of cork oak (the region is the world's biggest producer of cork). The fields of both regions have also been fertile in sprouting hotels, with excellent rural accommodation to be found in wine estates, converted convents, farmworkers' cottages, and innovative modern architecture. The climate can be harsh in the interior, with chilly winters and blistering summers. Go in spring and you'll see the Alentejo plain carpeted in wildflowers.

TOMAR ★★★

140km (86 miles) NE of Lisbon

The extraordinary architectural pile that forms the **Convento de Cristo** makes Tomar one of Portugal's must-see towns, but beyond its A-list attraction this is a very enjoyable town to visit. The downtown is a pleasing mix of leafy avenues, broad plazas and pedestrianized cobbled streets laid out beside the verdant banks of the **River Nabão.** Medieval religious sites neighbor historic cafés and independent stores.

Although there are Roman remains below the city, Tomar's founding is attributed to Gualdim Pais, a crusading warrior and grand master of the Templar Knights in Portugal. The Templars were given the land around here in 1159 after helping conquer it from the Moors, but had to fight a bloody battle to defend it from a Moroccan counterattack in 1190. The Templars were a

0
30 mi
0
30 km
Castelo Branco
Tomar
A1
A13
A23
N18
N118
Castelo de Vide
Abrantes
Marvão
A1
Portalegre
Chouto
Ponte de Sor
A15
Santarém
A1
Almeirim
Cartaxo
E01
Rio Tejo (Tagus River)
Montargil
A13
A10
To Elvas
Estremoz
Vila Franca de Xira
Coruche
E90
Borba
Vila Viçosa
A13
Vendas Novas
Arraiolos
N18
N4
A6
Rio Guadiana
A12
A6
Évora
A2
Setúbal
Reguengos de Monsaraz
Alcácer do Sal
Alcáçovas
Comporta
Viana do Alentejo
Rio Sado
Vidigueira
ATLANTIC OCEAN
Grândola
N18
Moura
A2
Beja
Santiago do Cacém
Serpa
Sines
To Mértola
FRANCE
PORTUGAL
SPAIN
Lisbon
area of detail

fighting religious order formed to protect Christian pilgrims in the Middle East. They became one of the richest and most powerful forces in medieval Europe until the king of France, in the early 14th century, decided they'd become too big for their chainmail boots, leading to the bloody suppression of the Templars across Europe, except in Portugal. Here, King Dinis simply changed their name to the Order of Christ, which continued to thrive from its base in Tomar until the 19th century. Henry the Navigator was a noted grand master, who used its resources to back the Voyages of Discovery and repaid it by embellishing the convent. Legends swirl around the Templars: There are supposed to be clues among the convent architecture indicating the location of hidden treasures, even the Holy Grail.

Tomar's importance as the Templar headquarters is reflected in the proliferation of imposing medieval churches. The town also had a thriving Jewish community in the Middle Ages, until the order of expulsion in 1496 and the arrival of the Inquisition.

Today, most visitors rush up the hill to the Templar stronghold, but it's worth taking a stroll downtown along the riverbank and around the downtown grid of streets laid out by Henry the Navigator, especially around **Praça da República** and **Rua Serpa Pinto,** where you can refuel at **Café Paraiso,** founded in 1911, or **Pastelaria Estrelas de Tomar** (www.estrelasdetomar.pt), turning out traditional pastries since 1949. The beaches of **Castelo de Bode** reservoir make a cooling break just 30 minutes' drive to the east.

Every 4 years, Tomar holds one of Portugal's biggest and most impressive festivals, the ***Festa dos Tabuleiros,*** which dates back to the Middle Ages. Its centerpiece is a parade through the city of local girls in white costumes and colored sashes carrying trays (*tabuleiros*) piled high with 30 loaves of bread together with flowers and wheat sprigs, topped with a crown to represent the Holy Spirit. Garlands of paper flowers decorate the city. The next one is scheduled for the spring of 2023.

Essentials

ARRIVING

BY TRAIN Tomar is easily reached by train from Lisbon's Santa Apolónia or Oriente stations with several daily departures. Direct regional trains take around 2 hours with tickets at 10€. Info: www.cp.pt.

BY BUS **Rede Expressos** (www.rede-expressos.pt) has three direct buses daily for 10€ from Lisbon's Sete Rios Terminal. It takes 1 hour, 45 minutes.

BY CAR From Lisbon, take the A1 north for 93km (58 miles), then take the turning east on the A32 for 16km (10 miles) before heading north again on the A13 for 14km (9 miles). The trip should take about 1½ hours.

VISITOR INFORMATION

The **Tomar Tourist Office** is on Avenida Dr. Cândido Madureira (✆ **24/932-98-23**) in a pretty yellow building on the main avenue heading up to the convent (open daily Apr–Sept: 9:30am–6pm; Oct–Mar:10am–5pm).

Exploring Tomar

Convento de Cristo ★★★ RELIGIOUS SITE The Templars' stronghold was both fortress and religious retreat. When you approach today from the parking lot, the **castle walls ★★** are the first thing you'll see. The rings of hilltop ramparts were built by the Templars using innovative defensive techniques learned in the Holy Land; it enabled them to resist a siege by a much larger force led by Caliph Yaqub Al-Mansur in 1190. Inside the walls are now peaceful formal gardens with neatly trimmed hedges and shady trees.

Once through the main entrance, you'll see one of Portugal's most brilliant architectural accomplishments, showcasing differing styles from Romanesque to Renaissance.

The highlight is an **octagonal church ★★★** built by the Templars in 12th century, inspired by the Church of the Holy Sepulcher that they had defended in Jerusalem. Its mix of Romanesque and Byzantine styles is startlingly exotic. Much of the painting and sculpture was added 300 years later, during the reign of Manuel I, but the intensity of the decoration in gold, blues, and crimson presents a harmonious whole. Squeezed into a confined space, the effect is overwhelming. Behind is a **nave ★** in typically Manueline decorations on the doorway and ceiling.

Step out into the first of the eight sets of **cloisters ★★★** built in the 15th and 16th centuries that are formed by Gothic or Renaissance arches surrounding square gardens. The earliest were built by Henry the Navigator when he was grand master of the Order of Christ. They are decorated with blue-and-white *azulejo* tiles. The grandest, with its central fountain and spiraling corner staircases, was finished by Italian architect Filippo Terzi in 1591 and is one of the greatest Renaissance works in Portugal. From the little Cloister of Santa Barbara you can gaze on the Manueline splendor of the church's west facade, dominated by the monumental **chapterhouse window ★★★**, with framed carvings of twisted ropes, coral-encrusted columns, and other maritime motifs that make it a masterpiece of the Discoveries-inspired style. From there, the building is a maze of wonders from the Spanish Renaissance–style sacristy, to *azulejo*-lined chapels, cell-lined corridors, and a barrel-vaulted refectory. Covering the hillside surrounding the convent is **the Mata Nacional dos Sete Montes ★**, forested parkland in which the **Capela de Nossa Senhora da Conceição ★** is a Renaissance gem of a chapel.

Estrada do Convento. www.conventocristo.gov.pt. ✆ **24/931-50-89.** 6€, 3€ students and over 65s, free under 12s. Daily June–Sept 9am–6pm; Oct–May 9am–5pm.

Igreja de Santa Maria do Olival ★ CHURCH In town, on the east bank of the Nabão, this little Gothic church was built in the 12th century as a burial place for the Templars. Its facade is adorned with a rose window, and there's a separate bell tower. The remains of Gualdim Pais and other grand masters lay amid the austere interior.

Rua Aquilles da Mota Lima. ✆ **24/932-98-23.** Free. Tues–Sun: Apr–Sept 10am–1pm, 2–6pm; Oct–Mar 10am–noon, 2–5pm.

RIBATEJO: a river RUNS THROUGH IT

Take a trip along the Tagus to make some beautiful and fascinating off-the-beaten-track discoveries. From Lisbon, cross the river on **Ponte Vasco da Gama ★★★**, a 17km (11-mile) stretch that is the longest bridge in Europe west of Crimea. Turn north off the highway as soon as you're over, and follow the N118 through a flat landscape of scrubby forest and pastures where black bulls graze. Pause in **Salvaterra de Magos** to watch hunting birds in action at the **Falcoaria Real ★** (www.falcoariareal.pt; ✆ **26/350-95-22**), an 18th-century complex where the royal family used to practice falconry. It's now a museum with regular displays of a variety of birds of prey. Nearby, the hamlet of **Escaroupim** has colorful fishing canoes bobbing in the river and an excellent **restaurant ★★** of the same name (✆ **26/310-73-32**), serving game, eels, and seasonal river fish.

Continue north and east. You'll start hitting more and more vineyards. Among the best to visit is the **Quinta de Lagoalva ★** (www.lagoalva.pt; ✆ **24/355-90-70**) near Alpiarça, where you can tour the estate's vineyard and ranch in a horse-and-trap before sampling reds and whites beside the lemon-yellow manor house. Cross the river at the horse-rearing center of **Golegã,** whose early **November Horse Fair ★★** is one of the biggest in Europe, dedicated to the Lusitania breed with performances of Ribatejo horsemanship. At the garrison town of Tancos, drive down to the river bank to appreciate the castle of **Almourol ★★** (✆ **91/508-17-37**). Perhaps the country's most romantic, it was built by the Templars on a river island. Boats leave hourly from the north bank, and the crossing is included in a 4€ entry fee (open daily May–Sept; Tues–Sun

Igreja de São João Baptista ★ CHURCH In the heart of town is this 15th-century church, built by Manuel I. It contains black-and-white diamond mosaics and a white-and-gold baroque altar; a chapel to the right is faced with antique tiles. Its pointed bell tower, white façade, and ornamental Gothic doorway make it the principal downtown landmark dominating the main square, where it faces city hall.

Praça da República. ✆ **24/932-24-27.** Free. Mon–Thurs 9am–6pm; Tues–Wed, Fri–Sat 9am–1pm, 2–6pm; Sun 9am–12:30pm, 3–6pm.

Museu dos Fósforos ★ MUSEUM A real curiosity. Europe's largest collection of matchboxes, with 60,000 examples from over 100 countries, decorated with everything from 1960s French pinups, to German trains and Soviet folk costumes. Local man Aquiles da Mota Lima got the collecting bug on a trip to London in 1953 when he picked up a box commemorating the coronation of Queen Elizabeth II. It's housed in a splendid 17th-century convent.

Avenida Gen. Bernardo Faria. ✆ **24/932-98-14.** Free. Tues–Sun: Apr–Sept 10am–1pm, 2–6pm; Oct–Mar 10am–noon, 3–6pm.

Sinagoga de Tomar ★★ RELIGIOUS SITE Portugal's best-preserved synagogue was built in the mid-1400s but served its original purpose only for a few decades before King Manuel ordered the expulsion or conversion of

Oct–Apr). Don't miss the last boat back—the castle is said to be haunted by a lovelorn princess.

Whitewashed **Constância ★** is the prettiest little town on this stretch of the river with a fine beach; and **Abrantes ★** has yet another medieval castle and very good restaurants, like **Cascata ★★** (www.cascata.pt; ✆ **24/136-10-11**). However, if the wind blows wrong, this area is vulnerable to smelly emissions from nearby paper mills. Our favorite spot is farther upstream where the river narrows beside the picture-postcard village of **Belver ★★**. Yep, it too has a 12th-century fortress, but this one belonged to the Templars' rivals, the Knights Hospitaller. A bridge over the Tagus takes you to a scenic riverbank walkway leading to a sandy beach looking across to the castle.

We're getting close to Spain now, but here comes the most spectacular spot on the river: the **Portas de Ródão ★★★**, where the Tagus cuts a canyon between cliffs 170m (560 ft.) high. Making the sight even more dramatic is Portugal's biggest colony of griffon vultures, which you can watch gliding over the crags. There's more birdlife farther east where the Tagus forms the border between Portugal and Spain with a wilderness reserve, the **Parque Natural do Tejo Internacional ★★**, on the north bank.

The Tagus trip can also be done by **train. CP** has a line hugging the north bank of the river. There are several daily departures from Lisbon to **Vila Velha do Ródão.** It takes just over 2 hours, or more than 3 hours depending on stops and train types. Tickets start at 13€. The rail company also organizes day-long **excursion packages** to Ródão, Belver, and other stop with return trains, lunch, sightseeing, and boat trips (www.cp.pt).

Portugal's Jews. The building was used as a jail, warehouse, and wine cellar before the 1920s when it was discovered, purchased, and restored by Samuel Schwartz, a mining engineer and Jewish scholar from Poland, who later escaped the Holocaust in Portugal. The square white interior features Gothic vaults supported by four slender pillars representing the Matriarchs: Sarah, Rebekah, Rachel, and Leah. There's a small exhibition or artifacts linked to Portuguese-Jewish life.

Rua Dr. Joaquim Jacinto 73. ✆ **24/932-98-23.** Free. Tues–Sun: Apr–Sept 10am–1pm, 2–6pm; Oct–Mar 10am–noon, 2–5pm.

Outlying Attractions

A half-hour drive east from Tomar, the **Castelo de Bode ★★** reservoir is ringed by forest and lined with bathing spots, notably at **Praia Fluvial dos Montes** and **Praia Fluvial da Castanheira,** the latter also known as **Lago Azul.** The hamlet of **Dormes ★**, which has Templar remains on a narrow peninsula, is one of the most photogenic in Portugal. The lake is popular for canoeing and other watersports. If you fancy **wakeboarding** on your Portuguese vacation, this is the place (www.wakeboardportugal.com; ✆ **91/584-44-43**). For accommodation, **Estalagem Lago Azul ★** (www.estalagemlagoazul.com; ✆ **24/936-14-45**) has an idyllic location for its lakeside pool. Doubles 60€ to 120€.

Shopping

The old town area between the river and Sete Montes park makes a pleasant window-shopping stroll, particularly around **Rua Serpa Pinto.** You can find local souvenirs among the home decor on sale at **Pinheiro Bravo,** with two shops on Rua Infantaria 15. For local handicrafts, Templar swords and model knights, check out **Loja do Ribatejo Norte** (www.lojadoribatejonorte.pt) at Rua Jacome Ratton 2 just across the river. There are also a couple of shops selling porcelain and other handicrafts at the Convento de Cristo.

Where to Stay

MODERATE

Hotel dos Templários ★★ This was state of the art when it was opened by Portugal's president in 1967, and a recent facelift ensures it meets contemporary guests' requirements while maintaining cute '60s design touches. The vast lobby/bar area is filled with light and blends onto a terrace by the lagoon-style riverside pool. There's lots of Templar imagery, down to the charging knight stamped on the pewter tea service. Rooms feature perky decor with aqua, orange, and grey coverlets, deep soaking tubs, and comfortable beds. Many have balcony views up to the convent or down to the river. There's a modern spa and health club, and it's all a short riverside walk into the historic center.

Largo Cândido dos Reis 1. www.hoteldostemplarios.pt. ✆ **24/931-01-00.** 177 units. 84€–160€ double; 150€–200€ suite. Free parking. **Amenities:** Garden; terrace; tennis; games room; indoor and outdoor pools; restaurant; bar; spa; fitness center; sauna; massage services; babysitting; children's play area; babysitting; free Wi-Fi.

INEXPENSIVE

Thomar Boutique Hotel★ It may only have opened in 2018, but this restored three-story townhouse makes the most of Tomar's history. Rooms are themed along Roman, Templar, Discoveries, and Industrial lines. We like the jungle wall designs in the Discoveries rooms and metallic Industrial finishes. Streamlined modern comfort is a common theme. Rooms come equipped with clawfoot baths, queen- or king-size beds, and Rituals bath products. It's just over the medieval bridge from downtown, and the rooftop terrace bar offers views across the river to the convent. Rooms are on the small side, but there are much larger duplex suites and an apartment.

Rua de Sta. Iria, 14. www.thomarboutiquehotel.com. ✆ **24/932-32-10.** 24 units. 68€–175€ double; 95€–195€ suite. Free parking nearby. **Amenities:** Terrace; free bikes; bar; free Wi-Fi.

Where to Eat

Chico Elias ★★★ PORTUGUESE In the land of Templars lies this temple of gastronomic tradition. Now in her eighties, Chef Maria do Céu turns out slow-roasted dishes that have made her rustic abode one of the most famed eateries in the country. Because of the time needed to marinate and cook her best-known dishes, you should call at least 24 hours in advance to order. That may sound like a hassle, but it's worth it to tuck into her rabbit cooked in pumpkin, baked codfish with acorn-sweetened pork, or duck in a cornbread crust. If you haven't booked, they'll usually find something that's available. Among the starters, baked *petinga* (a small sardine-like fish) with onions is divine. For dessert, "drunken pears" or *fatias de Tomar*—sweet, syrupy sponge slices. The decor is retro rustic, but as the celebrity photos on the walls show, this is where the great and the good of Portugal and beyond want to eat. Rua Principal 70, Algarvias. ✆ **24/931-10-67.** Reservations required. Main courses 16€–32€. No credit cards. Wed–Mon noon–3:30pm and 6–10pm.

SANTARÉM ★★

80km (50 miles) NE of Lisbon

It takes just a few seconds looking from the viewpoint in Santarém's **Portas do Sol** gardens to see why all the peoples who have passed through Portugal, from the ancient Lusitani onwards, have coveted this strategic spot. The clifftop location dominates the Tagus valley and the approaches to Lisbon. King Afonso I was so pleased to capture it in 1147 that he ordered the building of Alcobaça monastery to celebrate. Despite ruling vast territories across Spain and Africa, his rival Emir Abu Yaqub Yusuf was desperate to get it back, dying in an unsuccessful 1184 siege. On its high plateau, Santarém's compact historic center is easy to explore on foot. A profusion of medieval churches means the city is Portugal's "capital of Gothic." It's also the historic capital of the Ribatejo and guardian of the region's traditions. The **Feira do Ribatejo,** every June, is Portugal's biggest agricultural fair, luring fans of horsemanship and good food; the **bullring** is the country's biggest, holding 13,000 spectators.

Essentials

ARRIVING

BY TRAIN There are up to three trains an hour from Lisbon between 5:58am to 12:25am. The fastest expresses do it in just over 30 minutes; regional stopping trains take around 1 hour. Fares start at 6.20€: www.cp.pt.

BY BUS The **Rede Expressos** bus (www.rede-expressos.pt) will get you there in just over 1 hour leaving from Sete Rios, Lisbon. There are eight daily departures and it costs 8€.

BY CAR The A1 highway takes you right there in 1 hour. Leave at exit 6.

VISITOR INFORMATION

Find the **Tourist Office** at Rua Capelo e Ivens 63 (✆ **24/330-44-37;** May–Sept: Mon–Fri 9am–6pm; Sat–Sun 9:30am–1pm, 2–5:30pm; Oct–Apr: 10am–4:30pm).

Exploring Santarém

The **Portas do Sol gardens** ★ make a good place to start. The gardens perch right on the clifftop, surrounded by the fortifications that Afonso's men stormed in the surprise night attack that took the city almost 900 years ago. There is an archaeological museum showing remains from the Roman and

Muslim periods. The gardens are open from 9am until sunset (which is the best time to go, when the light turns the Tagus into shades of pink and orange). As you walk into town, the white-painted **Torre das Cabaças** is a 15th-century clock tower that now holds a **museum of timepieces.** Across the road, the Igreja de **São João de Alporão ★** was built shortly after the Christian conquest of the city and belonged to the Hospitaller Knights. It shows traces of Moorish influences among its mix of Romanesque and Gothic architecture. It houses a small archaeological museum.

Of wider interest is the **Igreja de Santa Maria de Marvila ★★**, a Templar church probably converted from a mosque, whose willowy columns are surrounded by 65,000 17th-century *azulejo* tiles. The church's main entrance is an impressive Manueline doorway. It's open Wednesday to Sunday 10am to noon and 2 to 5pm, free admission. A short walk downhill and we come to Santarém's most visited church: the **Igreja da Graça ★★** (**✆ 24/330-40-60**). It's the city's most beautiful Gothic church with a spectacular doorway and flamboyant rose window that scatters colored light into the plain interior. What draws the crowds, however, is the tomb of Pedro Álvares Cabral, the explorer who led the first European expedition to Brazil in 1500. The site lures a steady stream of travelers from the South American nation. In summer it's open 10am to 1pm and 2 to 6pm; winter 9:15am to 12:30pm and 2 to 5:15pm. Free admission.

Narrow **Rua Serpa Pinto** is one of the city's most charming pedestrianized alleys, leading to the central square **Praça Sá da Bandeira** overlooked by the Cathedral **Nossa Senhora da Conceição ★** which, ironically for the "capital of Gothic," is in a proudly Renaissance style, built for the Jesuits in 1711 and richly decorated with marble inside and out. Santarém's emblematic meeting place is the **Café Central ★**, dating from 1937, which reopened in 2018 after a hiatus. It's open daily 8am to midnight on Rua Guilherme de Azevedo 16. Dating from the same period is the Municipal Market, but although its ***azulejos*** **★** are as magnificent, the stalls have fallen on hard times. It closed for restoration work in the summer of 2019, with hopes of a revival when it reopens.

Where to Stay

Casa da Alcáçova ★★ This aristocratic abode has the perfect location, with the castle walls run around the bottom of the garden and stunning views over the Tagus. The canary-colored mansion dates from the 17th century, and Roman- and Arab-era artifacts have been found on the grounds. Immaculately furnished with artworks and antiques, some of the rooms feature four-poster beds and fireplaces. One named for writer Almeida Garrett has a private Jacuzzi built for two. Did we mention it's romantic? The Bocage room is named after the poet who composed erotic sonnets while staying in the house. Owners Claudia and Sergio offer Ribatejo cooking classes in the kitchen and arrange vineyard wine tastings. There's a splendid breakfast and a hidden garden pool.

Largo da Alcáçova 3. www.alcacova.com. ✆ **24/330-40-30.** 8 units. 109€–175€ double. Free parking. **Amenities:** Garden; terrace; library; outdoor pool; free Wi-Fi.

Where to Eat

Taberna Ó Balcão ★★ PORTUGUESE Traffic on the A1 highway must have increased significantly since Lisbon foodies began beating a path to this hip tavern. Chef Rodrigo Castelo digs deep into the roots of Ribatejo cuisine for his constantly changing menu that's strong on fish from the Tagus and the best local beef. Behind a bright yellow facade, there's typical tavern decor: bullfight posters, mismatched tiles, a marble-topped bar. There are *petiscos* (snacks), plates to share, and tasting menus of five or seven dishes chosen from the blackboard display. It could include river-fish soup with roe, quail stew, or oxtail with fava beans.

R. Pedro de Santarém 73. ✆ **24/305-58-83.** Mains 9€–18€; tasting menus 29€–35€. Mon–Thurs noon–3:30pm, 7–10:30pm; Fri–Sat noon–3:30pm, 7–11pm.

ÉVORA ★★★

135km (83 miles) E of Lisbon; 224km (140 miles) N of Faro.

Drive into Évora in high summer and the shimmering white outline of the walled city rises from the landscape like a cruise liner sailing on a sea of parched grassland. From the patrician houses of Praça do Giraldo, to farmhands' cottages and baroque chapels, Évora's building are kept pristine white. Only the rose-granite cathedral and the columns of its Roman temple break the monochrome magnificence. From Corinthian columns to Gothic towers, Renaissance palaces to mudéjar patios, Évora's architectural ensemble has been perfectly preserved by centuries of rural isolation. The city of 60,000 is one of Portugal's most beautiful and a UNESCO World Heritage Site.

It's also the proud capital of the Alentejo. Although the old provinces lost their administrative role decades ago, Évora hosts several institutions of regional significance, including the University of Évora, the country's second-oldest, founded in 1559. The opening of a fast highway to Lisbon in 1998 and improved rail links have helped revive and diversify the economy. Agriculture and tourism remain important, but the city has an important services sector and growing aeronautical industry thanks to out-of-town factories built by Brazilian plane-maker Embraer.

Alentejo traditions run deep, with handicrafts, unique cuisine, and the male choral singing forged among miners and farmworkers. In the rest of Portugal, you'll occasionally here jokes about *Alentejanos* being slow or uneducated, but they are also respected for their resilience. The plains—sunbaked in summer, freezing in winter—have known tough times. *Raised from the Ground*, an early novel by Nobel-prize winner José Saramago, describes the hardship of landless peasants. During the Salazar dictatorship the region was a center of resistance and suffered harsh repression. The Alentejo became a stronghold of the Portuguese Communist Party and workers seized farms after the 1974 revolution. The experiment in collective agriculture fizzled and the party no longer dominates local politics, but you'll see PCP graffiti and occasional hammer-and-sickle flags.

Special Events

Évora's major festival is the **Feira de São João ★★**, an annual fair held since at least 1569. Over the last 10 days of June, Rossio de São Brás square is the focus of this extravaganza, which draws crowds from across the region with a fun fair; big-name concerts; stands serving local wine and food; regional music and dance; and stalls selling pottery, blankets, painted furniture, and other Alentejo handicrafts.

Although it's the Alentejo's biggest city, Évora's historic center is easily explored on foot. You can do it in a rushed daytrip from Lisbon, but it would be a shame not to spend more time enjoying its relaxed delights, chill in a historic hotel, and enjoy a hearty Alentejo dinner.

Essentials

ARRIVING

BY TRAIN There are four trains a day from Lisbon (three on weekends); two in the morning and two late afternoon. You can board at Oriente, Entrecampos, or Sete Rios stations. The ride takes around 1½ hours. Second-class tickets are 12.40€: www.cp.pt.

BY BUS **Rede Expressos** (www.rede-expressos.pt) buses leave Lisbon's Sete Rios station once or twice an hour between 7am and 10pm for a trip of just over 1½ hours. Fares from 12€. From Faro there are four daily departures, with stops at Albufeira, Beja, and other spots along the way. It takes around 4½ hours and costs 17€.

BY CAR From Lisbon, take Ponte 25 de Abril on to the A2 highway heading south. After 56km (35 miles), at the fork take the A6 east for Spain until Exit 5 for Évora. The drive should take about 1½ hours. Alternatively, take Ponte Vasco da Gama and the A12 until it links up to the A2. Coming from Faro, the trip should take about 2½ hours via the A22 and A2 *autostradas*, and then the IP2 through Beja.

VISITOR INFORMATION

The Évora Tourist Information Office is at Praça do Giraldo 73 (✆ **26/677-70-71;** Apr–Oct: daily 9am–7pm; Nov–Mar: Mon–Fri 9am–6pm; Sat–Sun: 10am–2pm, 3–6pm). City Hall tourism info: www.cm-evora.pt.

Exploring the Town

Évora is a great city for wandering aimlessly among its narrow, white streets, discovering a hidden chapel or patio within a Renaissance palace. Listed below are highlights among its many treasures.

Centro de Arte e Cultura da Fundação Eugénio de Almeida ★ ARTS CENTER To show that Évora is no frozen-in-time medieval throwback, this arts center opened in 2013 to showcase contemporary art. There are regular temporary exhibitions with a focus on artists from the Alentejo and elsewhere in Portugal. The building has a sinister past: from 1536 to 1821, it housed the enthusiastic local branch of the Inquisition. A plaque commemorating its victims—most of whom were accused of practicing Judaism—was unveiled in 2016 on the Praça do Giraldo close to where executions took place.

Largo do Conde de Vila Flor. www.fea.pt. ✆ **26/674-83-50.** 2€, 1€ students and over 65s, free under 12s. Tues–Sun 10am–6pm.

Cromeleque dos Almendres ★★ HISTORIC SITE The layers of history in this city are full of surprises. Hidden amid cork oak woodland 9km (5½ miles) west of Évora is one of Europe's most important prehistoric sites: rings of 95 standing stones pointing out of the sandy soil. It's naturally called the "Portuguese Stonehenge." Although the stones at this megalithic site are generally smaller than those in England, they were erected 2,000 years earlier, starting around 6,000 B.C. This is the largest of several such sites in the area. It was only discovered in 1963. The role the circles served for the people who raised them is uncertain, although one large menhir standing apart points to the rising sun at summer solstice. The stones stand up to 3m (almost 10 ft.) high and some have indentations and carvings.

Rua do Cromeleque, Guadalupe (then take the dirt track). Free. Daily, open 24 hr.

Igreja de São João Evangelista ★★ / Palácio Cadaval ★ CHURCH/PALACE Semi-detached from the old convent which now houses the Pousada (see below) is this little gem of a church filled with *azulejo* panels painted in 1711, a Gothic vaulted ceiling, and a carved altar covered in gold leaf. It is the private chapel and mausoleum of the Dukes of Cadaval, one of Portugal's oldest noble families. Their palace lies next door, linked directly to the gilded baroque family box hanging on the church wall. The family still lives in the palace, which incorporates parts of Évora's old Moorish walls, but you can cross the grassy patio to visit some rooms where interesting art exhibitions are sometimes held.

Largo do Conde de Vila Flor. www.palaciocadaval.com. ✆ **26/670-47-14.** 4€ for the church, 8€ church and palace combined. Daily 10am–6pm.

Igreja e Colégio do Espírito Santo ★ CHURCH/HISTORIC BUILDING Colégio Espírito Santo and its neighboring church were the focal point of the university founded in 1559—the country's second oldest after Coimbra (p. 299). That long history was interrupted in 1779 when the Marquês de Pombal, Portugal's post-earthquake strongman, ordered it shut down as part of his crackdown on the Jesuits who were running the place. It didn't reopen until 1973. Now part of the working university, the double-tiered baroque main building surrounds a large quadrangle. Marble pillars support the arches, and brazilwood makes up the ceilings. Blue-and-white tiles line the inner courtyard.

Largo dos Colegiais, 2. www.uevora.pt. ✆ **26/674-08-00.** 3€, free for under 12s. Mon–Sat 9am–8pm.

Igreja Real de São Francisco ★★ CHURCH It's one of the biggest and most architecturally complex churches in town, but nobody comes here to admire the arcaded narthex, Flemish paintings, or gilded baroque carvings: They come here for the skeletons! Just beside the entrance is the **Capela dos Ossos** ★★★ (Chapel of Bones) with walls and pillars made from human skulls and bones. The ghoulish sight was created by a 16th-century friar aiming to remind sinners of life's transitory nature, as the "We bones that are here, await for yours" sign above the door cheerfully declares. About 5,000 bodies are believed to be built into the chapel, said to have been dug up from overcrowded monastic graveyards.

Praça 1 de Maio. www.igrejadesaofrancisco.pt. ✆ **26/670-45-21.** 5€, 3.50€ under 25s and over 65s. Daily 9am–6:30pm summer, 9am–7pm winter.

Praça do Giraldo ★★★ PLAZA The heart of old Évora is this cigar-shaped plaza laid out in the 1570s and named for Geraldo the Fearless, who grabbed Évora from the Moors in 1167. It's bookended by the Renaissance Church of Santo Antão and a marble-fronted bank. Along the sides are handsome, white four-story houses. On the north side they are fronted by an arcade lined with shops and cafes, whose tables spill out onto the paved square. Water trickles from a monumental marble fountain with eight spouts representing the eight streets running into the square. It's the social center of the city, where folks come to stroll, chat, or read the paper over a coffee. **Café Arcada** ★★ is the most atmospheric watering hole since 1942, open daily 8am to 10pm. A few doors away, the **Livraria Nazareth** ★ started selling books in 1897 (daily 10am–7pm).

Roman Temple ★★ HISTORIC SITE Everybody calls it the *Templo de Diana,* but experts now believe Évora's 1st-century temple was actually dedicated to the Emperor Augustus, who was revered as a god even during his lifetime. The marble-and-granite structure stood in the forum when this was an important Roman town, but was wrecked when Germanic invaders swept in, in the 5th century. The ruin was incorporated into a medieval fortification and later used as a butcher shop. In the 1860s, an Italian architect was brought in to disengage the 14 Corinthian columns and other surviving bits of the temple, revealing it in the form we see today. There's no admission to the temple, but you can admire it from close up. It's particularly impressive when lit at night.

Largo do Conde de Vila Flor.

Sé (Cathedral) ★★ CHURCH Built on the highest point of the city, the 13th-century cathedral with its three asymmetrical cone-topped towers dominates the skyline. It's built from pink-tinged granite in the fortress-like style that characterized Portugal's medieval cathedrals. The main doorway is flanked by marble columns topped with **statues of the apostles** ★★★ sculptured in the 1330s; they are Gothic masterpieces.

Inside the stone walls, it can seem a little gloomy, despite the abundance of gold-coated chapels. That changes when you reach the **main altar** ★★★

THE carpet CAPITAL

Arraiolos ★★ is a typical comely Alentejo town: hilltop castle; warren of white streets; 16th-century convent converted into a **Pousada** inn **★★** (www.pousadas.pt; ✆ **26/641-93-40**). However, Arraiolos has something special that sets it apart: Since the 15th century, its women have woven beautiful woolen **carpets ★★★** of clear Middle Eastern inspiration. The origins of this are uncertain. Some say they lie with Muslim-origin families who stayed in Portugal after the *Reconquista,* others that the rugs were originally made by nuns imitating oriental carpets brought back by Discovery Era traders. It's rare these days to see women sitting on their doorsteps working on rugs, but the skills are very much alive, despite competition from Asian imitations. Using wool from the flocks that roam the Alentejo landscape, the carpets are woven into intricate designs using motifs from the countryside: flowers mostly, but also birds and animals. A 120cm by 180cm rug (about 4×6 feet) costs around 600€. You can find out more at the **Centro Interpretativo do Tapete de Arraiolos** (CITA) museum (www.tapetedearraiolos.pt; ✆ **26/649-02-54**) or make a purchase at **Casa dos Tapetes ★★**, Rua Lima e Brito 8 (www.casatapetesarraiolos.com; ✆ **26/641-95-26**).

covered in soaring sheets of marble in pink, grey, and white, designed in the 18th century by German baroque architect Johann Friedrich Ludwig, who built the convent/palace at Mafra (p. 171). In one of the gilded side chapels is a brightly painted wooden statue of a heavily pregnant Virgin Mary, the **Senhora de Ó ★★** to whom women pray for fertility.

The 14th-century **cloisters ★★** are in a pure Gothic style, the austerity of the vaulted arches lightened by the orange trees in the gardens. One of the highlights is to climb up to the **roof ★★** where, beside the views over the city and Alentejo plains, you can see close up the cones topping the towers with their turrets and shiny *azulejos.* For an extra cost, you can visit the **museum ★** holding religious treasures, including a 13th-century ivory carving of the Virgin and a reliquary studded with sapphires, rubies, diamonds, and emeralds.

Largo Marquês de Marialva. www.evoracathedral.com. ✆ **26/675-93-30.** Cathedral and cloister 2.50€, 3.50€ to include roof. Daily 9am–4:30pm.

Shopping

Streets around Praça do Giraldo are lined with shops selling handicrafts from around the Alentejo and beyond. Much of the region's famed output comes from smaller towns (pottery from Redondo, clay figures from Estremoz, carpets from Arraiolos, etc.), but you can find just about anything in the regional capital. **Rua 5 de Outubro** is the busiest shopping street. Quality varies, but a couple of reliable places are: **O Cesto** (www.ocesto.pt) at No. 57 and No. 77; and **Gente da Minha Terra** at No. 39. Our favorite Evora shop is **Capote's Emotion** (www.capotes.pt), which makes traditional Alentejo capes and coats, plus snazzy variations of them, for men, women, and children. The store is just off Giraldo on Miguel Bombarda 16. Check out **Aldeia da Terra** (www.aldeiadaterra.pt) for fun modern clay figures, at Rua de São Manços 15 and 19.

Évora's lively produce market is on Praça 1 de Maio. If the fresh fruit and vegetables are too hard to take home, posh **Divinus Gourmet** (www.divinus.pt) has over 500 transportable edibles from the Alentejo and beyond: from Sharish gin to sweet-potato-and-chestnut compote and Serpa ewe's cheese. To get regional olive oil, head to **Tou c'os Azeites** at Rua da Alcárcova de Baixo 51, which has a fine selection of oils, plus soaps, pâtés, and other olive-based options. Wine buying (and tasting) can be had at the **Rota dos Vinhos** visitor center dedicated to all Alentejo wines (www.vinhosdoalentejo.pt; ✆ **26/674-64-98**) at Praça Joaquim António de Aguiar 20. Or try the city outlets of some of the region's quality producers: **Enoteca Cartuxa** (www.cartuxa.pt; ✆ **26/674-83-48**) on Rua de Vasco da Gama, has a restaurant, wine bar, and store promoting an excellent out-of-town winery; at **Wine Shop Ervideira** (www.ervideira.pt; ✆ **26/670-04-02**) on Rua 5 de Outubro, you can sample more distinguished tipples from an estate in nearby Reguengos de Monsaraz.

Where to Stay

EXPENSIVE

Convento do Espinheiro ★★★ Even if you don't have the pleasure of staying here, it's worth taking the 8€ taxi drive out to this magnificent 15th-century convent surrounded by vineyards and an enormous garden scented with lavender, honeysuckle, and rosemary. Kings would bed down here when they visited Évora: It's said Manuel I heard Vasco da Gama had reached India while he was lodged here. The convent church has a fabulous painted ceiling, loads of gold carvings, and *azulejo* panels. It's popular for weddings. Spacious rooms (33 sq. m/345 sq. ft minimum) are divided between the convent and a new design wing, and are decorated accordingly. Bathrooms gleam with local marble. A famed gourmet restaurant, bars in historic surroundings, a large pool in the garden, and an award-winning spa round out the amenities.

CM1089-1, Canaviais. www.conventodoespinheiro.com. ✆ **26/678-82-00.** 92 units. 129€–420€ double; 308€–1,180€ suite. Free parking. **Amenities:** Garden; terrace; bike hire; indoor and outdoor pools; spa; sauna; hammam; Jacuzzi; gym; massage service; 2 restaurants; 3 bars; library; bike rentals; kid's play area; babysitting; free Wi-Fi.

MODERATE

Pousada Convento de Évora ★★★ What do you know, another convent. This one is slap in the middle of town (be careful not to bump the Roman Temple when you pull out of the drive) and is one of the jewels of the Pousada chain. Guest rooms are furnished in traditional style, with antique reproductions. Because they used to be monks' cells, rooms are rather small, but they come equipped with modern comforts. Family rooms are a little bigger and can accommodate an extra bed. The building is bright, painted white-and-yellow, with a kidney-shaped pool and loungers in the sunny garden. Take breakfast in the mudéjar-style cloisters and dine in style under the vaulted ceiling of the monks' refectory.

Largo Conde de Vila Flor. www.pousadas.pt. ✆ **26/673-00-70.** 32 units. 109€–250€ double; 260€–500€ suite. Free parking. **Amenities:** Garden; terrace; restaurant; bar; outdoor pool; free Wi-Fi.

INEXPENSIVE

Albergaria do Calvário ★★ This modest hotel is in a former olive-oil press on the edge of the old city, a 10-minute walk to the Roman Temple. It's of typical white-and-yellow Alentejo architecture, with some of the raw brick walls exposed inside. Rooms have bright colored fabrics and marble bath fittings. They pride themselves on the organic breakfast (fresh fruit and home-made pancakes feature), which you can take in your room or under the shade of olive trees in the patio. That patio is also an excellent place to enjoy a complementary welcome drink of local wine or juice where the friendly and helpful staff share tips on what to explore in town.

Travessa dos Lagares 3. www.adcevora.com. ✆ **26/674-59-30.** 22 units. 88€–155€ double. Free parking. **Amenities:** Terrace; garden; bike hire; bar; babysitting; free Wi-Fi.

The Noble House ★★ It's difficult to remember what hits you first: the light, the colors, or the history. Once a 16th-century count's mansion, this became Évora oldest hotel back in the 1920s: the Pensão Policarpo. Thoroughly updated, the decor still reflects its heritage, from the medieval battlements running through the kitchen to the pension's vintage telephone box. Natural light floods into the rooms, and several have balconies or even a private garden. Our fave is No. 18, which used to be the manager's lodgings because the owners thought guests wouldn't like those old wall tiles. The yellow-and-blue 16th-century *azulejos* run into the corridors and bar (you can buy hand-painted copies and other tasteful regional souvenirs in the little store). More color comes from the bougainvillea by the entrance and traditional blankets thrown on the bed (you can buy them too). Breakfast and snacks on the terrace include wonderfully chewy Alentejo bread paired with regional cheese and cold cuts. Friendly staff are happy to share local knowledge or book activities from wine-estate visits to balloon trips.

Rua da Freiria de Baixo 16 (the back parking lot is on Rua do Conde da Tourega 9). www.thenoblehouse.pt. ✆ **26/624-72-90.** 24 units. 68€–150€ double; 107€–191€ suite. Parking 12.50€ daily. **Amenities:** Terrace; bar/restaurant; free Wi-Fi.

Where to Eat

Botequim da Mouraria ★★ PORTUGUESE Once a locals' well-kept secret, this tiny restaurant tucked away in the old Arab quarter is now globally reputed. It's run by a culinary wonder-couple: Domingos serves at the counter and chats warmly with guests while Florbela cooks inspired Alentejo food. Daily specials could include lamb chops or roast black pork, but be sure to try starters like ham with figs or baked Serpa cheese with oregano. In a city with so many great restaurants, this one sits near the top of the heap. There are no reservations and only nine seats, so go early to get a place.

Rua da Mouraria 16. ✆ **26/674-67-75.** Mains 11€–30€. Mon–Fri 12:30–3pm and 7–9:30pm.

Fialho ★★★ PORTUGUESE Defending the best traditions of Alentejo cuisine since 1945, the winner of just about every gastronomic award in the country and now run by the third generation of the Fialho family, this should be everybody's first choice. Over the years, Hollywood stars, political leaders, and crowned heads have dined in the rustic space (they say the old king of Spain used to regularly nip across the border). There's a sumptuous array of appetizers to choose from (we'd always include the game pies; scrambled eggs with wild asparagus; and local cured ham among any selection), before moving on to a main like roast Alentejo lamb, rice with wild pigeon, or dogfish with cilantro. The famed wine list has all the region's vintages, and dessert has to be one of the eggy local temptations like *pão de rala.*

Travessa dos Mascarenhas 14. www.restaurantefialho.pt. ✆ **26/670-30-79.** Reservations recommended. Main courses 13€–23€. Tues–Sun 12:30–3pm, 7:30–10pm.

Taberna Típica Quarta-Feira ★★ PORTUGUESE Here's another backstreet classic in the old city. Amid a typical Alentejo tavern setting, this family-run place serves up a renowned slow-roasted pork and ribs with cauliflower *migas* (a local mash). There's no menu, so just go with the recommendations. Local smoked sausage, cheese with pumpkin jam, or fresh tuna salad with pomegranate can feature among the range of appetizers. Book ahead or go early, because the "Wednesday Tavern" usually fills up any day of the week.

Rua do Inverno 161. ✆ **26/670-75-30.** Reservations recomended. Main courses 11€–16€. Tues–Sat 12:30–2:30pm, 7:30–9:30pm; Mon 7:30–9:30pm.

Évora Entertainment & Nightlife

As a university town, Évora has a lively nightlife. A night out might start on a **Praça do Giraldo** terrace, or a patio bar like **Art Café** on Rua de Serpa Pinto. As the night warms up, an old-town pub crawl could take in **Bar O Tunnel** with regular live music on Rua Alcárcova de Baixo or **Culpa Tua,** renowned for its gins, on Praça Joaquim António de Aguiar. **Bar Capítulo 8** on Rua do Raimundo is where international students come to dance into the night; **Molhóbico** at Rua de Aviz, 91 is another live music dive; and **Praxis** is the best disco in town (open 11pm–6am, Tues–Sat) at Rua de Valdevinos 21.

There's a fine 19th-century theater, the **Teatro Garcia de Resende.** Its plays and comedy shows will be challenging for non-Portuguese speakers, but there are also regular concerts. For the program check www.cendrev.com or call ✆ **26/674-11-81.** The only movie house is **Cinemas Nos Évora Plaza,** in a suburban mall (www.cinemas.nos.pt), showing Hollywood and European new releases.

ESTREMOZ ★★★

170km (106 miles) E of Lisbon and 47km (30 miles) NE of Évora.

In a region where all the cities are white, Estremoz is known as "the white city." The reason is **marble.** Mines around here produce one of Europe's purest, second only to Carrara in Tuscany. It comes in pinks, greys, creams, and blacks, as well as white. There's so much they use it as paving stones and even grind it up in whitewash that gives the houses a special sheen.

The walled city occupies a low hill, its skyline dominated by the 13th-century tower of a **castle** associated with St. Isabel the Peacemaker, queen of Portugal who died there in 1336 after riding out to negotiate a truce between the armies of her son King Afonso IV of Portugal and her grandson King Alfonso XI of Castile. Estremoz' strategic location overlooking the road from Spain to Lisbon meant it was often in the frontline; decisive battles were fought here in the 17th-century war that restored Portuguese independence after 60 years of Spanish rule.

The old town tumbles down a hillside from the castle and spreads around **Rossio Marquês de Pombal,** one of the biggest town squares in the country, surrounded by churches, stores, and cafes. It is the site of one of the region's biggest **markets** every Saturday. Estremoz is also famed for its **painted clay figures,** its wines, and olive oil.

Essentials

ARRIVING

BY BUS **Rede-expressos** has seven direct buses daily from Lisbon's Sete Rios station, taking between 2 to 2½ hours. It costs 15€. From Évora, the firm's four buses take around 40 minutes, but only leave in the afternoon and cost 8€. Details at www.rede-expresso.pt. Regional bus company **Rodoviária do Alentejo** has a number of lines that crawl through the countryside, taking over an hour from Évora. For timetables: www.rodalentejo.pt or call the Estremoz bus station at ✆ **93/887-63-33.**

BY CAR From Évora take the IP2 until it merges with the A6 from Lisbon. Once on the highway it's 15 minutes until you hit exit 7 into Estremoz. Coming directly from Lisbon it takes about 1 hour 45 minutes on the A2 and A6.

VISITOR INFORMATION

The **Tourist Office** is on Rossio Marquês de Pombal (✆ **26/833-92-27;** daily 9am–12:30pm, 2–5:30pm).

Exploring Estremoz

Start out at the top of the hill on the square that's named after King Dinis **(Largo Dom Dinis)** ★ but dominated by the white marble **statue** of his wife St. Isabel. She's holding a bunch of roses. A much-loved legend has it that the king was peeved his saintly spouse kept wandering off to distribute alms to the poor. One winter's day he caught her heading out of the palace with bread rolls hidden under her skirts. "They're roses," she told hubby when challenged and, sure enough, when the king looked, the loaves had been miraculously transformed into flowers. The square has a sweeping **view ★** over the plains on one side and is surrounded by historic buildings including the medieval former **City hall,** which sometimes hosts handicraft and art exhibitions, and the 16th-century **Church of Santa Maria,** which is only occasionally opened.

What is open is the **Castle ★★**, which Dinis turned into a royal palace for his wife and where Isabel eventually died. Although the palace is occupied by a hotel (see below), visitors can explore the medieval and 18th-century salons and climb the 27m (89-ft.) **Torre das Três Coroas ★★**, a defensive tower in rosy-hued marble, for incredible views over the city and countryside across to the **Serra de Ossa** hills. Free admission (open Tues–Sun 9am–12:30pm, 2–5:30pm). Head down Rua Rainha Santa Isabel, a narrow, cobbled alley, and take a peek on the right in the **15th-century jail ★** (now a restaurant and wine bar; ✆ **26/832-34-00**). Carry on down and you descend marble stairs and pass through various layers of city wall before reaching downtown.

Rossio Marquês de Pombal ★ is the social and commercial heart of the town. Among several ecclesiastical buildings facing the broad plaza is **Convento dos Congregados ★**, with twin bell towers and a curved baroque facade. It now houses the Town Hall and a small museum, which are worth a look to admire antique blue-and-white tiles depicting hunting, pastoral, and historical scenes. The square is particularly pretty in spring when the jacaranda trees bloom. On the eastern side, the **Convento das Maltezas ★** is a Renaissance convent converted into a science museum that might appeal to budding geologists. Wrapping up the square's churches, **Igreja de São Francisco ★** is the most interesting, with an 18th-century marble facade and several medieval marble tombs inside. Standing out on the square's western edge is the startling Art Nouveau frontage of the **Café Águias D'Ouro ★**, with red tiles, stained glass, and wrought-iron balconies. It's been a social hub since 1908, rivaled just a bit by its neighbor the **Café Alentejano ★** which is dowdier and a few decades younger but still a local favorite. A photo op, just off the square is the **Lago do Gadanha ★**, an expansive marble-lined water tank produces pleasing reflections of the surrounding white houses and the hilltop castle. Go around sunset for the best pics.

If you've got wheels, pop out to one of the **wineries** around Estremoz. Less than 10 minutes to the west, **Adega Vila Santa ★★** is the headquarters of João Portugal Ramos, one of Portugal's most renowned winemakers. It offers tours, tastings, excellent lunches, and at harvest time, the chance to help pick the grapes (www.jportugalramos.com; ✆ **26/833-99-10**). There's a similar service at **Herdade das Servas ★★** (www.herdadedasservas.com; ✆ **26/832-29-49**), a typical Alentejo estate nearby which also has an excellent restaurant.

Farther afield, the hilltop village of **Evoramonte ★** has a bunker-like 12th-century castle where a treaty was signed in 1834 to end Portugal's 6-year civil war. The main street has a couple of cute stores selling handicrafts and olive oil and there's an excellent B&B, **The Place ★** (www.evoramonte.com; ✆ **92/760-38-84**), with doubles from 85€ to 120€.

PORTUGAL'S great LAKE

In 2002, floodgates closed on a dam crossing the River Guadiana close to Portugal's border with Spain. That created one of Europe's biggest artificial lakes, a flooded area of 250 square km (97 sq. miles). The creation of **Alqueva Lake ★★** was controversial: Villages and habitats were flooded, but it brought power and valuable irrigation to the region. It also created an inland sea that's become an important attraction for lovers of the outdoors. At the **Marina de Amieira ★★** (www.amieiramarina.com; ✆ **26/661-11-73**) you can rent houseboats for a stay afloat, take a tour on the water, or indulge in watersports from wake-boarding to kayaking and fishing. There are also sandy beaches ideal for cooling off in the Alentejo summer. The village of **Monsaraz ★★★** was already one of Portugal's most beautiful even before its castle walls and white cottages got added lake views. Stay there at the rustic-chic **Monte Alerta ★★** B&B (www.montealerta.pt; ✆ **96/875-67-85**) or the luxurious **São Lourenço do Barrocal ★★★** (www.barrocal.pt; ✆ **26/624-71-40**) spa retreat. The lake is surrounded by wine estates. Among the best for visits and tastings is **Herdade do Esporão ★★** (www.esporao.com; ✆ **26/650-92-80**) for both its fabulous tipples and audacious architecture. Alqueva's distance from urban centers means it's one of the best places in Europe to observe the **night sky ★★**. **Dark Sky Alqueva** (www.darkskyalqueva.com; ✆ **91/310-35-40**) operates an observatory and organizes tours that combine stargazing with other activities, from nocturnal canoeing to astrophotography workshops.

Vila Viçosa ★★, 20 minutes to the east of Estremoz, is another pretty marble town. It is home to one of Portugal's most grandiose stately homes, the **Paço Ducal de Vila Viçosa ★★**, ancestral seat of the Braganza dynasty that ruled Portugal from 1640 to 1910. The palace dates to the early 1500s and the regal family continued to use it as a vacation home after they moved to Lisbon. Its 110m (360-ft.) facade is covered in pink marble. Inside, the palace is filled with tapestries, porcelain, and paintings. The frescoes depicting a 16th-century North African battle are particularly impressive (www.fcbraganca.pt; ✆ **26/898-06-59;** June–Sept: Wed–Sun 10am–noon, 2–5pm, Tues 2–5pm; Oct–May: Wed–Sun 10am–noon, 2–4pm, Tues 2–4pm). Admission 7€, free for under 12s.

Shopping

Every Saturday morning, the Rossio fills up with a **farmers' and flea market ★★**. It's one of the region's biggest with vendors hawking everything from lemons and pumpkins to accordions and leather belts; chouriço sausage to painted furniture to secondhand CDs. It's lots of fun and there are bargains to be had. The town's best buy, however, are ***Bonecos de Estremoz* ★★★**. The painted clay figures are traditionally dated to at least the 18th century and now have UNESCO World Heritage status. Local artists produce nativity scenes and other Bible images, portraits in local costumes or allegorical figures (Blind Love is a favorite). They are unique and delightful. Among the best workshops are the **Flores sisters** on Largo da República 31 (✆ **26/832-42-39**) and **Afonso Ginja** on Rua Direita 5 (✆ **26/808-16-18**). For leather goods, traditional clothing, and handicrafts (including Alentejo cow bells, another recent addition to UNESCO's heritage list) visit **Casa Galileu ★★** on Rua Vítor Cordon 16 (www.casagalileu.pt; ✆ **26/832-31-30**).

Where to Stay

EXPENSIVE

Dá Licença ★★★ This simply extraordinary labor of love was realized by Vitor Borges and Franck Laigneau, who left the Parisian fashion and art world to transform this farm dating back to the 1830s into a uniquely stylish guest-house which opened in 2018. It's a short drive out of town and sits peacefully alone surrounded by 13,000 olive trees. Each of the enormous suites and rooms are decorated individually with airy sophistication. Local marble and Franck's world-class collection of Arts and Crafts and Jugendstil furniture take center stage. Two of the suites have private marble pools. Rooms open out onto amazing rooftop views or intimate citrus groves. There are Claus Porto soaps in the all-marble bathrooms, huge handmade Italian beds, and artworks you'd pay to see in a museum. Plank pathways wiggle around the aromatic gardens, scattered with chunks of raw marble, to the selection of swimming pools. In the main house you can lounge among the amazing art, or order dinner in one of three private dining rooms. No children. Minimum 2 nights.

Outeiro das Freiras – Santo Estêvão. www.dalicenca.pt. ✆ **96/295-05-40.** 8 units. 300€ double; 400€–500€ suite. Free parking. **Amenities**: Garden; terrace; 4 outdoor swimming pools; 3 dining rooms; massage service; free Wi-Fi.

MODERATE

Pousada Castelo Estremoz ★★★ Live like medieval royalty in this delightfully restored building that's part palace, part fortress. These regal digs overlook the town and the Alentejo plains. Gold leaf, marble, velvet, and satin mingle with 17th- and 18th-century style furniture in the guest rooms and grand salons. Size varies: Some standards are just 20 square meters (215 sq. ft.) while others are more than double that, spaciously bedecked with canopied beds, gilt fittings, and aristocratic portraits. There's a pool in the garden, an excellent restaurant, and a bar with velvety armchairs ideal for dozing into history over a post-dinner *aguardente.* Round the back, discover a hidden treasure: a baroque chapel gleaming with gold and azulejos dedicated to St. Isabel and built by one of her successors as Portugal's queen.

Largo Dom Dinis. www.pousadas.pt. ✆ **26/833-20-75.** 29 units. 91€–190€ double; 190€–290€ suite. Free parking. **Amenities:** Garden; terrace; outdoor pool; restaurant; bar; game room; free Wi-Fi.

INEXPENSIVE

Páteo dos Solares ★ This simple, cozy hotel gives a taste of Portuguese country life. It opened in 2002 in a restored mansion that incorporates parts of the old city walls. From the tree-filled garden, you can climb up onto the ramparts to admire the view. There's a cozy lounge with a clay brick floor, a fireplace for winter, antique cabinets, and comfortable if slightly dated furniture. The restaurant is one of the best in town for regional food (in season, try the rice with partridge). Rooms are not supersized, but are far from cramped. They are neatly decorated in cream, beige, and taupe, with such contemporary twists as hydromassage tubs in some rooms. A couple have fireplaces. There's marble everywhere; even the elevator is lined with the stuff.

Rua Brito Capelo. www.pateosolares.com. ✆ **26/833-84-00.** 41 units. 81€–145€ double. Free parking. **Amenities:** Garden; terrace; outdoor pool; spa; sauna; hammam; Jacuzzi; gym; restaurant; bar; babysitting; free Wi-Fi.

Where to Eat

Gadanha Mercearia e Restaurante ★★ PORTUGUESE When you give an Italian-trained Brazilian chef access to the Alentejo's wealth of natural ingredients, this is the result. Michelle Marques from Petrópolis fell in love with the cuisine of her adopted region, but renovates traditional dishes to create artistically plated delights that have wowed Lisbon food critics. The layered *mille-feuille* of codfish and cured ham rivals pork cheeks slow braised in red wine for title of signature dish. Michelle looks homeward for the temptingly tropical mango and passionfruit dessert. It's relaxed and friendly, with a fine selection of local wines. *Mercearia* means grocery shop and there's one out front where you can grab wine and other goodies to go.

Largo Dragões de Olivença, 84A. www.merceariagadanha.pt. ✆ **26/833-32-62.** Reservations recommended. Mains 15€–24€. Tues–Sat 12:30–3pm, 7:30–10:30pm; Sun 12:30–3pm.

ELVAS ★★

215km (132 miles) E of Lisbon; 85km (53 miles) NW of Évora

Elvas and its neighbor Badajoz get along very well. Frontier controls are long gone. Spaniards pop over for lunch or to stock up on Alentejo wine; Portuguese go the other way to fill up on low-tax gasoline or shop in the swanky El Corte Inglés department store. It wasn't always so. Elvas is a UNESCO World Heritage Site because of its mighty fortresses designed to keep the Spanish out. The city known as the "key to the kingdom" has been in the vanguard of military struggle from the time of Roman legionaries, up to battles between British redcoats and Napoleonic invaders. If Elvas hadn't resisted a siege during the war to restore Portuguese independence in 1659, you'd probably be reading this in a chapter of the *Frommer's Guide to Spain.*

The city has an impressive medieval castle, but its main claim to fame are the star-shaped fortresses built in the 17th and 18th centuries, the biggest of their type in the world. Between them, Elvas' walled old town is a hilly maze of alleys with the usual whitewashed Alentejo mix of high-chimneyed cottages, baroque churches, and marble-adorned mansions. The city's main non-military monument is a 16th-century aqueduct whose high arches stride for almost 8km (5 miles) into the countryside.

Essentials

ARRIVING

BY TRAIN There are three slow trains leaving Lisbon daily between 7 and 9am, with changes in Entroncamento or Abrantes. The trip takes at least 4½ hours. Tickets from 16€, www.cp.pt.

BY BUS The bus from Lisbon takes about 3 hours from Sete Rios station. **Rede-expressos** runs eight a day with tickets at 18€. Regional operator **Rodoviária do Alentejo** has buses from Évora and other Alentejo cities. For timetables, see www.rodalentejo.pt.

BY CAR From Évora take the IP2, then the A6 highway heading east. It's a 1-hour drive. From Lisbon, take either bridge over the Tagus to join the A6, the main road to Madrid. It will take you just over 2 hours to reach Elvas.

VISITOR INFORMATION

The **Elvas Tourist Office** is on Praça da República (✆ **26/862-22-36;** Mon–Fri 9am–7pm [6pm in winter], Sat–Sun 9am–12:30pm, 2–5:30pm).

Exploring the Town

Aqueduto da Amoreira ★★ MONUMENT This engineering marvel was built to ensure the city and its garrison would have a steady supply of water in wartime. Built between 1537 and 1622, its 833 arches loop out of the city into nearby hills where they link to subterranean springs. Almost 1.4 km (1,500 yards) of the structure runs underground. The work was overseen by Francisco de Arruda, architect of the Torre de Belém in Lisbon (p. 112). In places, particularly as it gets close to the city walls, the aqueduct is over 30m (almost 100-ft.) high and stamped with a marble-and-azulejo coat of arms. Unlike Lisbon's aqueduct (p. 114), you can't walk along this one, but it is a spectacular sight from the sloping public gardens beneath where it enters the town.

Castelo de Elvas ★ CASTLE One of Portugal's most imposing and best-preserved medieval castles. Celts, Romans, and Visigoths had defenses on this hilltop before it was taken by Moors, who took it in the 8th century to form the core of today's castle. It changed hands several times during the Reconquista, until King Sancho II seized it for Portugal in the 1220s. Over the centuries, various monarchs raised and extended the walls, which you can walk to admire the view. There's a garden inside with a bar. Just behind the castle, the **Cemitério dos Ingleses ★** cemetery holds the remains of hundreds of British soldiers who died here defending Portugal from Napoléon.

Rua da Parada do Castelo 4-8. www.cm-elvas.pt. ✆ **26/862-64-03.** 2€. Tues–Sat 9am–6pm.

Forte da Graça ★★★ CASTLE This most-impressive of Elvas' fortifications is one of the biggest bulwarks in Europe. Abandoned for years after the army pulled out, it was restored and reopened as a museum in 2014. Exploring its massive earthworks is a delight for history buffs, but the scale of the place will impress anybody. Paths around the 10 pointed bastions offer infinite views across the plains. They alternate with endless subterranean corridors and barracks marked by curious military graffiti. It's all topped by a surprisingly dainty yellow-and-white chapel and governor's house. The huge structure was built over 30 years, starting in 1763, by a German General, Count William of Schaumburg-Lippe, who was sent to modernize the Portuguese armed forces during the Seven Year War. It resisted attacks by Spanish, French, and British troops in the early 19th century, and was used to incarcerate political prisoners during the Salazar dictatorship.

Monte da Senhora da Graça. ✆ **26/862-52-28.** 5€ 2.50€ youngsters 12–18 and over 65s, free under 12s. Tues–Sun: May–Sept 10am–6pm; Oct–Apr 10am–5pm.

Forte de Santa Luzia ★★ CASTLE This is a mirror image of Forte da Graça to the south of the city. It is smaller and older, built in 1648, and played a key role in the war to restore Portugal's independence a decade later, holding off a Spanish siege. You can visit the four bulwarks, a church, the canary-yellow governor's house, and bomb-proof vaults, together with water tanks designed to sustain a garrison of up to 400 for 3 months. There's also a small **military museum** with weapons and uniforms.

Monte da Santa Luzia. ✆ **26/862-83-57.** 2€ adults, 1€ youngsters 12–18 and over 65s, free under 12s. Tues–Sun: May–Sept 10am–6pm; Oct–Apr 10am–5pm.

Igreja de Nossa Senhora da Assunção ★ CHURCH The marble-embellished former cathedral is something of a mishmash of styles, built in the early 16th century by Francisco de Arruda. It has a pretty Manueline side door, together with Renaissance and baroque touches, as well as Gothic gargoyles grinning out along the upper walls. Inside, the painted ceiling, marble altar, and gilded organ are highlights. The church stands on **Praça da República ★**, the main square in the old town, with its attractive paving, open-air cafes, and fetching white houses. Round the back, there's a much-photographed plaza with a marble pillory; a **graceful arch** connecting a medieval tower to a Renaissance palace; and a tiny, octagonal church, **Igreja das Domínicas ★**, which, if you catch it open (hours are irregular) is a jewel box of blue-and-yellow ceramics.

Praça da República. ✆ **26/862-59-97.** Free. Daily: summer 10am–noon, 3–6pm; winter 10am–12:30pm, 2:30–5pm.

SHOPPING Narrow streets running south from Praça da República are filled with small shops were you can buy local food products, wine, and handicrafts. **Casa da Joana,** Rua de Alcamim 18A, is a quirky store run by an artisan out of her house. Nearby, at **Casa Mimosa** at 6 Rua de Cadeia, you can buy the towns' best-known treat, **Ameixas de Elvas.** These are super-sweet preserved plums, made from greengages picked in early summer then soaked in a sugar-bath for 6 weeks. They are much sought after by the British upper set (it's said Queen Elizabeth is a big fan) who've been importing them since the days when they were over here fighting Napoléon. The plums go well with cheese or *sericaia,* an Alentejo milk, egg, and cinnamon dessert. You can also find them at the municipal market. It has seen better days, but remains a good place to stock up on cheese, olives, and charcuterie.

RIDING THE alentejo WAVE

Familiar Alentejo images involve rolling plains, forests of cork oak and olive, and white inland cities. Yet the region boasts 130km (86 miles) of coast from the tip of Troia's peninsula (p. 175) to the Algarve. Until recently, its beaches were largely unknown. Many still offer pristine sands where you can find wide open spaces to spread your towel. There are also some great places to stay and eat. Here's our guide to the best of the Alentejo shore:

THE BEST BEACHES

Paia da Galé ★★★ An unbounded strand of soft, pale sand, backed by mango-colored cliffs and calm waters, make this the pick among several great beaches south of Comporta (p. 190) near the town of Melides.

Praia de Santo André ★★★ Atlantic rollers can give Alentejo bathing a washing-machine feel, but not here. A cobalt-blue lagoon provides calm, shallow waters surrounded by Saharan expanses of white sand. Kids will also love the **Badoca Safari Park ★** (www.badoca.com), a short drive inland.

Praia da Samouqueira ★★ Between Vasco da Gama's birthplace of Sines and the pretty white fishing harbor at Porto Covo, this beach features crescent coves of fine sand between grass-topped cliffs. The crystalline waters look tropical, but are usually chilly.

Praia das Furnas ★★ Vila Nova de Milfontes is the busiest resort on the Alentejo coast, a cheerful little town that can get a little crowded in high season. This beach curls round the mouth of the River Mira, which joins the ocean here, so bathers can choose between calm or surf.

Praia da Zambujeira do Mar ★★ Nestled below the fishing port of the same name, this broad swath of sand is in a sheltered bay with a gentle slope into the waves. It fills up fast for 5 days in

Where to Stay

EXPENSIVE

Torre de Palma Wine Hotel ★★★ It's worth the 30-minute drive out of town to stay at this country estate surrounded by vines and olive trees. Central to the estate is a turreted white tower built in 14th century, but the history dates back to a Roman villa uncovered nearby. There's a tradition of guests taking a glass of the estate's (excellent) wines atop the tower as the sun goes down. Rooms and shared spaces overflow from the tower into the white-with-apricot-trim manor house and rows of farm cottages around the courtyard. Some standard rooms are small (go for a superior room if you can afford it), but designer Rosarinho Gabriel fills them all with a comfy sophistication using idiosyncratic details: piles of antique French novels, blowup photos of Balinese dancers, fishing nets, oversize rag dolls. There's a lovely spa, an amazing restaurant serving modern-Alentejo cooking, and the chance to ride Lusitano horses. Did we mention they make great wine?

Herdade de Torre de Palma, Monforte. www.torredepalma.com. ✆ **24/503-88-90.** 18 units. 136€–340€ double; 255€–480€ suite. Free parking. **Amenities:** Garden; terrace; free bikes; horse riding; indoor and outdoor pools; spa; sauna; hammam; Jacuzzi; massage service; restaurant; bar; babysitting; free Wi-Fi.

August when the village is invaded by the MEO Sudoeste music festival.

THE BEST HOTELS ON THE COAST

A Serenada Enoturismo ★★ With just six rooms, this cozy restored farmhouse producing its own wine is an oasis of tranquility in the hills near Grândola. There are glorious views over cork oak forests to the beaches of Melides, a 20-minute drive away (www.serenada.pt; ✆ **26/949-80-14;** doubles 80€–120€, suites 125€–170€).

O Lugar ★★ A bijou B&B in the heart of the Porto Covo fishing village a few steps from the beach, rooms here are a rhapsody in navy blue and white, with lots of basketwork features. You're guaranteed a warm Alentejo welcome (www.quietude.pt; ✆ **96/580-05-57;** doubles and suites 70€–90€; minimum 2-night stay).

HS Milfontes Beach ★ Enjoy a hammock with a view from your balcony at this well-equipped hotel on the waterfront in the center of Vila Nova de Milfontes. Decor needs refreshing, but the location is great (www.hsmilfontesbeach.com; ✆ **28/399-00-70;** doubles 65€–149€).

Herdade de Touril ★★★ This traditional blue-and-white *monte* (farm) surrounded by sunflower fields near Zambujeira is a short walk or bike ride to the ocean. The pool makes it a lovely place to stop for walkers on the Rota Vincentina hiking route (www.herdadedotouril.com; ✆ **28/395-00-80;** doubles 90€–221€, suites 144€–257€).

Paraíso Escondido ★★ Lost in the forest hills behind Zambujeira is this "hidden paradise," a mix of renovated Alentejo farmstead and treehouse bungalows. Glampers will love its luxurious style and Asian decor touches (www.paraisoescondido.pt; ✆ **91/247-02-26;** doubles 140€–195€, suites 220€–250€, bungalows 250€–300€).

MODERATE

SL Hotel Santa Luzia ★ Built in 1942 this was the first of the then-state-owned Pousadas, but at some point parted company with the chain and is now independently run. Although it's packed with thoroughly modern comforts, the architecture reflects a typical mid-20th-century Portuguese style. It's very popular with Spanish visitors, not least as the supposed birthplace (in 1947) of *bacalhau dorado,* a codfish dish that's become popular across the border. Rooms are bright in cream, lemon, or azure shades with white-painted wooden headboards reflecting the floral designs of traditional Alentejo furniture.

Avenida de Badajoz. www.slhotel-elvas.pt. ✆ **26/863-74-70.** 25 units. 74€–204€ double. Free parking. **Amenities:** Garden; terrace; bike hire; tennis court; outdoor swimming pool; restaurant; bar; free Wi-Fi.

Where to Eat

Taberna do Adro ★★ PORTUGUESE It's time to discover *migas.* This most *Alentejano* side is a mush of old bread that's soaked, then fried with olive oil or pork fat. Garlic and maybe other ingredients will be thrown in. Here they will serve three variations: with cauliflower, potato, and tomato. It doesn't translate well, but is seriously satisfying, especially served with fried black pork, roast pork neck, or pigs' feet in cilantro, as they do it in this rustic village restaurant 15 minutes from Elvas. You go with the flow in this dining room crammed with Redondo clay pottery. They'll sit you down on long benches, you'll order some roast red peppers, smoked sausage, or other appetizer, then *migas* and some of that meaty stuff to share. Save space for at least one of the quartet of only-in-Alentejo desserts (and the glass of complementary homemade cherry liqueur). Largo João Dias de Deus 1, Vila Fernando. ✆ **26/866-11-94.** Mains 9€–13€. Thurs–Sat, Mon–Tues 12:30–3pm, 7:30–10pm; Sun 12:30–3pm.

BEJA ★

180km (112 miles) SE of Lisbon; 80km (50 miles) S of Évora

Beja is old. It was founded in 48 B.C. by Julius Caesar, who spent years in Hispania Ulterior (modern-day southern Spain and Portugal) battling the Lusitanians and his Roman rivals. The city was once a center for Visigoth culture and the capital of an Arab principality. Today it's the biggest city in the southern Alentejo. Like other Alentejo burgs, Beja can be seen from afar. Its granite-and-white skyline crests a low hill amid fields of olive, vines, and wheat (although the region is no longer the bread basket of a country that now imports most of its flour from Spain). The city lives a little in Évora's shadow, but although it lacks the monumental scale of its neighbor to the north, Beja has Portugal's tallest castle keep and the region's most interesting art museum. It's also a charming (and relatively tourist-free) place to wander. There's a North African feel to its labyrinthine streets; squares verdant with orange- and palm trees; and sun-blanched facades. It's also proud of its heritage, a stronghold of traditional cooking, handicrafts, and *cante Alentejano* male-voice choirs. Summer here gets very hot with average highs in the low 30s C (90s F). Spring is cooler and the meadows around will be blooming. For a top Alentejo experience, come in April during **Ovibeja,** the region's biggest agricultural fair with 5 days of music, folk art, livestock displays, and other activities linked to the land, its preservation, and its traditions.

Essentials

ARRIVING

BY TRAIN There are four trains a day from Lisbon (three on weekends); two in the morning and two late afternoon, with a change in Évora. You can board at Oriente, Entrecampos, or Sete Rios stations. The ride takes around 2½ hours. Second-class tickets cost 14€. See www.cp.pt.

BY BUS Busses from Rede Expressos leave Lisbon Sete Rios about once an hour between 7:30am and 9:30pm for the roughly 3-hour ride. The one-way fare is 13:30€. From Faro the trip takes slightly less than 3 hours and there are three a day for 14.20€.

BY CAR From Lisbon stay on the A2 toward the Algarve until exit 10, then follow the IP8 eastbound; that will take you into Beja. The drive takes about 2 hours. If you are coming from Évora, it's an hour's drive on the IP2.

A nun's TALE

A tale of forbidden passion and caddish betrayal made Beja the center of a literary scandal in the 17th century that continues to echo today, particularly in France. At its center was a young nun named Mariana Alcoforado, who entered the Convento da Conceição at the age of 11. When she was 25, Mariana was seduced by a French officer helping Portugal fight for its independence from Spain. Their affair lasted several months until he abandoned her and trotted back to Paris. The young woman wrote a series of impassioned (and, for the time, rather racy) letters recalling their embraces and imploring the heartless marquis to come back for her. Not only did he never reply, but he shared the letters with his pals and eventually had them published, creating a Parisian *succès de scandale*. She died in the convent at age 83; he went on to become a top military commander. *The Letters of a Portuguese Nun* have remained in print ever since, spawning novels and movies. Debate rages over whether the sophisticated letters were really penned by a country nun or faked by Parisian literary types, but in the museum you can see the window from where Mariana is supposed to have first glimpsed the handsome Noël Bouton de Chamilly.

VISITOR INFORMATION

The **Beja Tourist Office** is at Largo Dr. Lima Faleiro 1 (✆ **28/431-19-13**) inside the castle. It's open daily 9:30am to 12:30pm and 2 to 6pm.

Exploring the Town

Beja's top attraction is the **Museu Regional** ★★ (www.museuregionaldebeja.pt; ✆ **28/432-33-51**). The most important collection of art and antiquities in the Alentejo is housed in the city's most beautiful building: the **Convento da Conceição** ★★, a 15th-century convent that's a showcase of architectural styles. Its exterior is decorated by rows of graceful Gothic arches; a latticework frieze runs along the top of the walls; there's a pointed bell tower and Manueline doorways. The convent was built on the orders of King Manuel's parents, who made it one of the richest nunneries in the country. Inside you'll find an extravagant baroque church filled with gold-covered carvings, cloisters with arabesque flourishes, and walls coated with symphonies of Portuguese and Andalusian tiles. The museum's collection contains Flemish, Spanish, and Dutch old masters as well as works from the Portuguese Primitive school, most notably the somber ***Ecce Homo*** ★, whose 15th-century painter is anonymous but produced one of his country's best-known paintings. The museum also has renowned collections of decorative arts and archaeology. The ***escudela de Pero de Faria*** ★, a bowl dating from 1541, is considered a masterpiece of Ming dynasty porcelain. The museum is on Largo da Conceição (admission 2€, 1€ for students and retirees, free under 15s; Tues–Sun 9:30am–12:30pm and 2–5:15pm). Some of its important archaeological finds are housed in the nearby **Visigoth Museum** ★, a church that dates back to the time of that Germanic people.

ALENTEJO m&m: MÉRTOLA & MARVÃO

Two of the Alentejo's most striking towns, **Marvão ★★★** and **Mértola ★★★** stand at opposite extremities of the region's eastern border with Spain.

In a region renowned for its gently rolling landscapes, **Marvão** holds a gravity-defying position atop a rocky crest that surges precipitously over 1,000 meters (3,300 ft.) above the plain. *The New York Times* named it one of the "1,000 places to see before you die." With vertical drops on either side, the walled village clings to the ridge, its cobbled streets running north-south between the castle, built on the site of a Roman watchtower at the highest point, to the little chapel by the southern rim. It's possible to walk the complete rampart circuit. Doing it at sunset or sunrise will accentuate the phenomenal spectacle. The city is believed to have been founded by a Muslim knight, Ibn Marwan, in the 9th century, although people have lived on the crag since prehistoric times. It's a great base for exploring the **Serra de São Mamede ★★** (a highland wilderness area) and nearby towns **Castelo de Vide ★★**, which has a long Jewish heritage; and **Portalegre ★**, whose tapestry tradition can be explored at the excellent **Museu de Tapeçaria Guy Fino ★★** (✆ **24/530-75-30**) and a **factory ★★** (www.mtportalegre.pt; ✆ **24/530-14-00**) where you can pick up a stylish souvenir. The **Pousada Marvão** (www.pousadas.pt; ✆ **24/599-32-01**) is the place to stay in the village, doubles 85€ to 120€. Best dining options are down in the valley at **Restaurante Mil Homens ★★** (✆ **24/599-31-22**) or **Churrasqueira Sever** (www.mtportalegre.pt; **24/5 99-31-92**)

Mértola's position is no less prominent. It sits high above a bend in the Guadiana River which reflects the white town, tightly bound within its medieval fortifications. Here too, there's an ancient heritage. It was a Phoenician trading post, Roman river port, and, for a while, capital of an independent Muslim state that broke away from the caliphate ruling in Andalusia. There's a dramatic horseback statue by the castle walls of the town's 12th-century leader Ibn Qasi. Of all the churches in Portugal, Mértola's graceful **Igreja Matriz ★★** shows its Islamic origins most clearly. The forest of slender columns, Arab-style doorways, and a mihrab reveal its past as a mosque. Every 2 years, in May, the city celebrates its heritage with an **Islamic Festival ★★** (www.festivalislamicodemertola.com) featuring visiting musicians and a souk of handicrafts from North Africa and the Middle East. To cool off in summer, there are several bathing spots on the river, and you can rent kayaks to explore them. There's also a lakeside sandy beach in the nearby former mining village of **São Domingos ★**. To stay, **Quinta do Vau ★★** (✆ **96/564-55-40**) offers fabulous views toward the town, including from the riverside pool (doubles 50€–75€). Dining options include: **Casa Amarela ★★** (✆ **28/609-41-02**), with more river views; and **O Brasileiro ★** (✆ **28/661-26-60**) for Alentejo tradition.

Head north and you pass pretty churches like the **Igreja de Santa Maria ★** with its four-towered porch and stately main square, **Praça da República ★**, where cafe terraces are overlooked by Manueline arches and *azulejo*-tiled facades. The **Castelo de Beja ★** (✆ **28/431-19-13**) castle was built in the early 14th century on the ruins of a Roman fortress. At 40 meters (130 ft.), the medieval tower is Portugal's highest, built in marble with more than a touch of moss. Rather than rushing up the 183-step spiral staircase for the glorious rooftop views, vertigo sufferers may prefer to linger in the interior chambers to admire the star-vaulted ceilings and knightly tombstones, or explore the exhibitions in the saffron-painted governor's house. The entrance is on Largo Dr. Lima Faleiro. Admission is free (the tower is open in summer Mon–Fri 9:30am–noon and 2–5:30pm, closing at 4:30pm from Nov–Mar). Other parts of the castle stay open until 6pm.

Shopping

Beja is known for handicrafts, including charming hammered copper, pottery, and woodcarvings. **Rua Capital João Francisco de Sousa** in the town center is lined with all manner of shops. You can also find the work of local craftspeople in the **Tourist Office** by the castle; the **city market** (open Mon–Sat from 6:30am–2pm) on Rua Transversal ao Largo dos Correios; or at the **Regional Association of Artists and Artisans** (ARABE) based in **Igreja da Misericórdia,** a church inspired by the Florentine Renaissance on Praça da República.

Where to Stay

Pousada Convento de Beja ★★ The long outdoor pool in a palm-shaded garden will be most welcome should you come in Beja's blazing summer. Otherwise any time of the year is good to appreciate this hotel carved out of a 13th-century Franciscan monastery. Because rooms were once monks' cells, some standards are on the small sides, but they vary: The family rooms are very spacious. All feature floral bedcovers and antique-style furnishing with wooden headboards in the "Dona Maria" style, clay-brick floors, and framed prints, as well as well-equipped marble bathrooms. Dine on gazpacho and Alentejo lamb in the splendid 15th-century dining room.

Largo Dom Nuno Álvarez Pereira. www.pousadas.pt. ✆ **28/431-35-80.** 35 units. 79€–185€ double; 135€–199€ suite. Free parking. **Amenities:** Garden; terrace; tennis; outdoor pool; massage service; games rooms; restaurant; bar; children's play area; free Wi-Fi.

Where to Eat

Adega Típica 25 de Abril ★★ PORTUGUESE This tavern, named for the date of Portugal's 1974 revolution, is woven into the fabric of the city. In a simple room decorated with wine jars and hunting trophies, families and groups of friends come to dine on classic Alentejo food at long tables. It's best known for grills featuring lamb and, mostly, the juicy pork from black pigs that live semi-wild hereabouts rooting for acorns amid forests of cork oak. *Secretos* and *lombinhos* are the tenderest cuts. Other specials include a main-course tomato soup fortified with salt-cod and poached eggs. Look for the bargain wine of the week.

Rua da Moeda 23. ✆ **28/432-59-60.** Mains 5€–10€. Tues–Sat 12:30–3pm, 7:30–10pm; Sun 12:30–3pm.

12 COIMBRA & THE BEIRAS

The three historic provinces making up the Beiras are often overlooked by travelers heading to the northern wine lands, Algarve beaches, or Lisbon's capital attractions. That is a mistake. The Beiras comprise spectacular mountain landscapes, historic cities, picturesque villages, unspoiled beaches, and restaurants serving some of the country's most enticing cuisine.

Among the urban attractions, pride of place goes to the historic university city of **Coimbra.** The region's de facto capital sits on a bend in the slow-moving River Mondego. At its heart is the 13th-century university, with its wonderful baroque library. Almost 25,000 students ensure that the city's UNESCO World Heritage old town is no sleepy antique. Narrow alleys and plazas are packed with taverns and restaurants serenaded by students' own version of fado music. Crammed with museums and monuments, Coimbra makes a great base for exploring the region. On its doorstep are the ruins of the Roman town of **Conimbriga,** the medieval riverside fortress at **Montemor-o-Velho,** and verdant **Penacova,** a jumping-off point for kayaking trips down the Mondego.

Figueira da Foz is the main resort on Portugal's **Costa da Prata** (Silver Coast), which stretches up to Porto. The town draws sun devotees to its broad wedge of pale sand—Europe's widest urban beach. In the grid of streets behind a highrise seafront are charming Art Deco buildings recalling the boom days of the 1920s and '30s. Seekers of solitude can find unspoiled beaches like the 30km (19-mile) stretch of unbroken sand stretching north from **Praia de Quiaios.** Inland from here, the **Bairrada** wine region is renowned for Portugal's best sparkling wines among an array of excellent reds and whites. It's also home to some of the country's most atmospheric old spa hotels and one of its gastronomic treasures, *leitão à Bairrada* (roast suckling pig).

The coastal city of **Aveiro** is Portugal's "Venice," crisscrossed by a network of canals leading out into its vast, mysterious, marshy lagoon. A tour in one of the colorful high-prowed *moliceiro* boats is a must.

Beyond the coastal strip, the two inland provinces of **Beira Alta** (Upper Beira) and **Beira Baixa** (Lower Beira) form a land of spartan beauty. Empty highlands are strewn with giant boulders and the

Coimbra & the Beiras

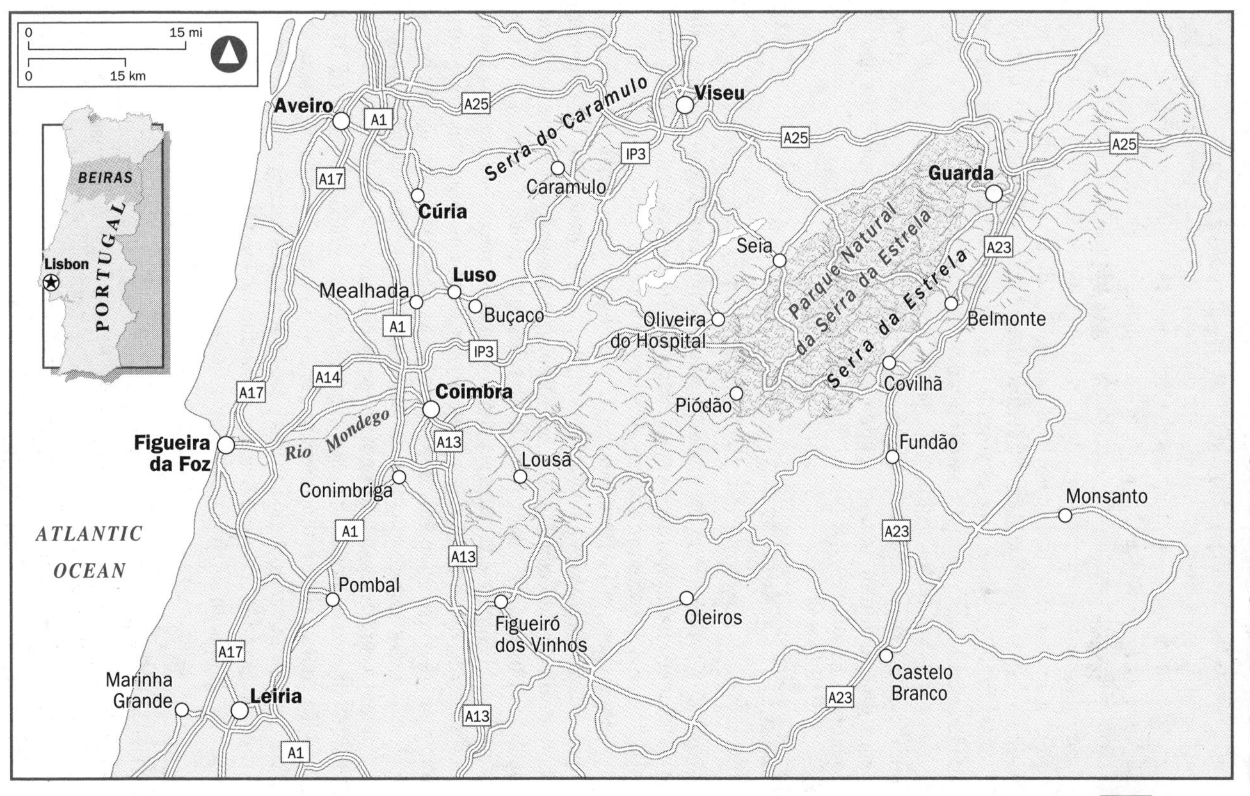

occasional rock-hewn village. They rise to peaks of almost 2,000 meters (6,562 ft.) in the **Serra da Estrela.** Mainland Portugal's highest mountain range boasts the country's only ski resort. The pistes may not be world class, but the landscapes are breathtaking, the creamy ewes'-milk cheeses crafted by local shepherds are to die for, and the indigenous Estrela mountain dog (*cão da Serra da Estrela*) is a shaggy, bear-size bundle of cuteness.

Guarda and **Viseu** are the main cities of the Beira Alta, clustered around sturdy granite-built medieval cathedrals. Along the border with Spain are a string of historic fortified towns and villages, including **Almeida,** sheltered within a vast star-shaped fortress; **Belmonte,** with its unique Jewish history; **Monsanto,** offering vast views from homes encrusted into a rocky hillside; and the Beira-Baixa capital **Castelo Branco.**

The climate of the interior can be harsh. Summers are hot and winters icy, but the Beira Baixa reveals a gentler side in spring, when the slopes of the **Serra da Gardunha** around **Fundão** are coated with the pink blossoms of countless cherry trees.

COIMBRA ★★★

118km (73 miles) S of Porto; 198km (123 miles) N of Lisbon

Coimbra is perhaps Portugal's most romantic city, thanks to its association with the tragic medieval love story of Pedro and Inês and the tradition of guitar-wielding students serenading their sweethearts with alfresco **fado** tunes.

The city is one of Portugal's oldest. It briefly served as capital in the Middle Ages, when King Afonso Henriques was pushing the borders of his kingdom southward. Its old cathedral, the **Sé Velha,** is a reminder of those turbulent times, constructed more like a fort than a place of worship, a defendable haven in case of Muslim counterattack. Coimbra's narrow streets are crammed with museums and monuments, from Roman granaries to baroque churches, most important of which is the **university,** founded in 1290. The old academic buildings surround a hilltop square, including a spectacular 18th-century **library.**

All those students make Coimbra a lively place. Male and female students traditionally wear black suits and capes decorated with the colors of their faculties: yellow ribbons for medicine, red for law, etc. In early May, the ribbons are ceremonially burned to mark the end of the academic year, the spark for one of Europe's biggest student celebrations: the **Queima das Fitas,** a week of processions, fado concerts, and booze-fueled parties.

Essentials

ARRIVING

BY TRAIN Coimbra has two train stations: **Coimbra-A,** in the city center, and **Estação Coimbra-B,** 2km (1½ miles) north of downtown. Mainline trains from Lisbon and Porto stop at Coimbra-B, where you can change to a local shuttle train for the 4-minute trip to Coimbra A. Over 20 trains run daily to Coimbra from Lisbon's Oriente station, from 6:09am to 10:09pm. On the

Coimbra

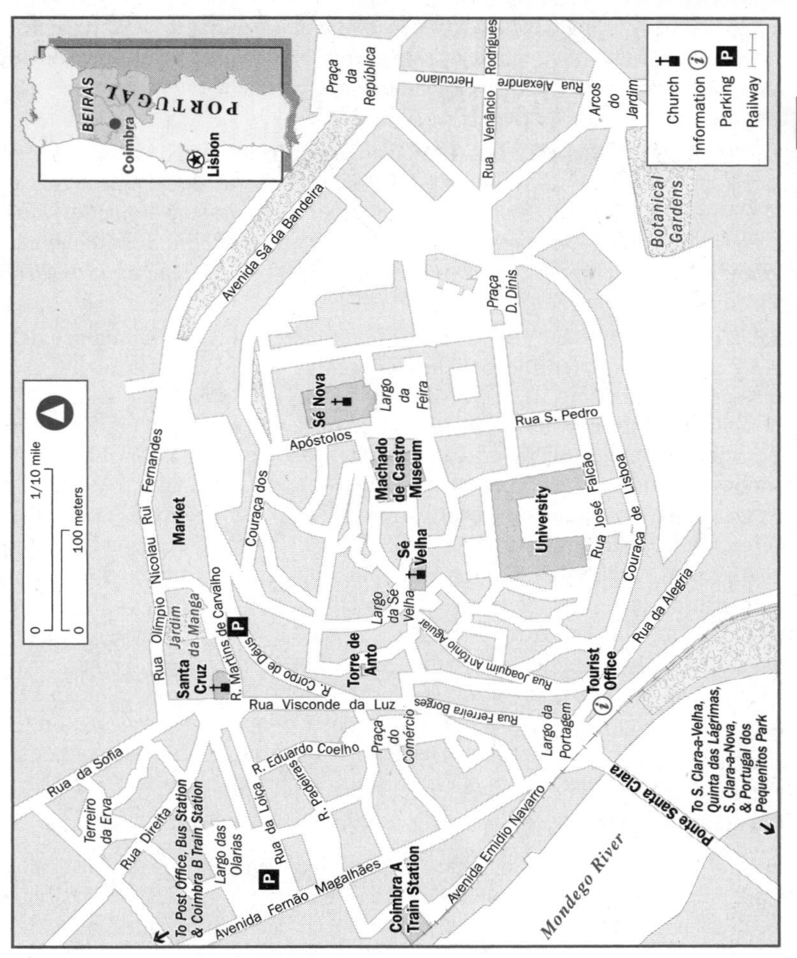

fastest Alfa-Pendular trains, the journey takes just over 1 hour 30 minutes. A second-class one-way ticket costs 24€. From Porto's Companhã station, the journey to Coimbra takes around 1 hour on the Alfa and costs 17.20€. Tickets and info from the CP rail company: www.cp.pt; ✆ **77/210-22-20.**

BY BUS Buses leave from Lisbon roughly every 30 minutes for the 2½-hour trip to Coimbra, from 6:15am to just after midnight. Tickets cost 13.80€. From Porto, it's 11.90€ for the 1½-hour journey. Coimbra's **bus station** is on Avenida Fernão de Magalhães. For tickets and information from the **Rede Expressos** national bus company: www.rede-expressos.pt; ✆ **70/722-33-44.**

BY CAR From Lisbon, it should take about 2 hours north on the A1 express highway. From Porto, it takes just over 1 hour heading south on the same road. If your hotel does not have a car park, driving and parking in the city center can be a challenge. It is sometimes possible to find free parking in side streets up by the modern part of the university. If not, there are a number of paying parking lots down by the river.

VISITOR INFORMATION The main **Coimbra Tourist Office** is on Largo da Portagem (www.cm-coimbra.pt; ✆ **23/948-81-20;** summer hours Mon–Fri 9am–8pm, Sat–Sun 9am–6pm; winter Mon–Fri 9am–6pm, Sat–Sun 9:30am–1pm and 2–5:30pm). There's a second office on Praça da República (Mon–Fri 9:30am–6pm). For more info on the city and the region: www.visit centro.com.

GETTING AROUND The narrow, often car-free streets of Coimbra's old town are best explored by foot. In fact, getting lost in a stroll around the ancient warren of lanes is one of the city's great pleasures. That being said, climbing from the downtown **Baixa** district to the university and other sites in the uphill **Alta** neighborhood can be tough on the legs. Public transport options include the safe and efficient bus network (www.smtuc.pt). As well as regular buses, it operates an **elevator** from the colorful food market up to the university from 7:30am to 9pm for 1.60€ (from 10am Sundays), and electric **buses** called *pantufinhas* that run a hop-on, hop-off service through the historic districts once or twice an hour on weekdays, mornings only on Saturday; they don't run Sunday. Tickets offering unlimited travel on all services can be bought for 3.50€ from the ticket office in front of the elevator and other sites. Single-journey tickets bought on buses are 1.60€. **Taxis** (www.politaxis.pt) are plentiful and inexpensive. A trip from the Coimbra-A railway station to the old university should cost less than 5€. The central reservation number is ✆ **23/949-90-90.** Uber started operations in Coimbra in the spring of 2019.

Exploring Coimbra

Most of Coimbra's sights are shared between the **Alta** upper town, Portugal's academic center where the country's oldest and most prestigious **university** is located; and the **Baixa,** traditionally the city's commercial heart, although the stores along the elegant **Rua Ferreira Borges** and the maze of narrow shopping streets have suffered from the opening in recent years of a couple of megamalls on the outskirts. It's also worth taking a stroll along the green banks of the **Mondego River,** which inspired countless student fado singers, and crossing the river to visit the monasteries of the **Santa Clara** district.

Arco e Torre de Almedina ★ MONUMENT The arch and tower of Almedina form the gateway into the upper town, or Alta, leading to steps and lanes that clamber up toward the university. The Gothic arch and medieval tower form an imposing entry point into what was the Arab medina before the city fell to the Portuguese in 1064. Beyond, the sharply rising **Rua Quebra Costas** is Coimbra's most emblematic street. Its name, "back break street," references the difficulty in climbing up with a heavy load and the dangers of slipping on the steep stairs. Nowadays, it's lined with bars and shops, and is one of the best places to pick up a souvenir. At the top, close to the university and the museum, is the **Sé Nova,** or New Cathedral, once the home of the Jesuit order. Its rather austere Mannerist style inspired Portuguese colonial church builders from Brazil to India. Admission is free. It's open daily 9am to 12:30pm and 2:30 to 6:30pm.

Baixa ★★ NEIGHBORHOOD This downtown district was for centuries Coimbra's commercial heart. In recent years some of the life has been sucked out due to the construction of out-of-center shopping malls, particularly the giant **Forum Coimbra.** Nevertheless, the neighborhood retains great charm. It's also fighting back thanks, in part, to the growth of tourism, with trendy new shops opening alongside traditional stores that give the narrow streets a souk-like buzz. The area's main drag is the elegant, boutique-lined **Rua Ferreira Borges,** now pedestrianized to provide a pleasant stroll between the Praça 8 de Maio and another cafe-lined plaza, the riverside Largo da Portagem. The **Café Briosa** (www.pastelariabriosa.com; ✆ **23/982-30-94**), established in 1955, is the best place to try the Coimbra region's sinfully tasty pastries, like the *pastéis de Tentúgal* (cigar-shaped filo-pastry tubes with a cinnamon-scented filling) or the *pastéis de Santa Clara* (pastries filled with almond paste). Between Ferreira Borges and the river, the Baixa fragments into a maze of narrow alleys filled with quirky stores, where you can buy everything from a jersey of the local soccer club, Académica, to agricultural implements. At **Praça do Comércio,** the lanes broaden out into an elongated plaza surrounded by the narrow white facades of townhouses reaching seven stories high. At the northern end of the plaza is the **Igreja de São Tiago,** one of the city's oldest churches, its earliest parts dating back to the 10th century. It's open daily 10am to 5pm. Its Romanesque interior is gloomy and atmospheric.

Jardim Botânico ★ GARDEN Founded by university researchers in 1772, this is a green escape in the center of the city. Just behind the university, you can roam trails through 13 hectares (32 acres) of orchards, jungles, and bamboo forests (plus greenhouses) to discover rare plants. The garden is crossed by the city's historic aqueduct.

Calçada Martim de Freitas. www.uc.pt. ✆ **23/982-52-73.** Free. Apr–Sept Daily 9am–8pm; Oct–Mar daily 9am–7:30pm.

Mosteiro de Santa Clara-a-Nova ★ CHURCH On the left bank of the Mondego, on a hill with commanding views over the city, is the New Convent of St. Clara. Its gold-covered baroque interior is one of the best examples of *talha dourada,* the Portuguese artform that involves covering intricate carved woodwork in gold leaf. It surrounds a **silver casket** holding the remains of St. Isabel of Aragon, a 13th-century queen of Portugal revered for her work helping the poor and her peacemaking efforts between Spain and

Portugal. There's a small museum dedicated to the saint and a peaceful double-decked Renaissance cloister.

Alto de Santa Clara. www.rainhasantaisabel.org. ✆ **23/944-16-74.** 3€. Daily 9am–5pm.

Mosteiro de Santa Clara-a-Velha ★ CHURCH The original Santa Clara convent was built down the hill on the riverbank by St. Isabel herself, when she lived with nuns of the Poor Clare after the death of her husband King Dinis in 1325. Unfortunately, the site is prone to flooding, and the fine Gothic structure was gradually swamped by mud, hence the building of the new convent up the hill, where the saint's remains were taken in the 17th century. The convent has undergone extensive restoration work to clear it of centuries of ooze, which, it turned out, had done an effective job of preserving much of the ruin's medieval decoration. It's also used as a site for summer concerts and outdoor theater productions.

Rua das Parreiras. www.culturacentro.gov.pt. ✆ **23/980-11-60.** 4€, 2€ students and over 65s, free under 12s. Apr to mid-Oct Tues–Sun 10am–7pm; mid-Oct to Mar 9am–5pm.

Mosteiro da Santa Cruz ★★ CHURCH The fabulous white-stone entrance of the Holy Cross Monastery looks out over **Praça 8 de Maio,** one of Coimbra's prettiest downtown plazas lined with little stores selling everything from handcrafted guitars to fine wines. The church dates back to the earliest days of the Portuguese kingdom, in the 12th century. The swirling white additions to the facade were built in 1507, a masterpiece of the Manueline, that uniquely Portuguese architectural style inspired by the age of maritime discoveries (ropes, sea plants, and ornate decorations that recall Indian temples—they're all in the mix). Inside is the **Gothic tomb** of Portugal's first king, Afonso Henriques, his feet resting on a lion. His son, Sancho I, lies nearby. The rich decoration includes a **pulpit** carved by Frenchman Jean de Rouen, and **choir stalls** that preserve, in carved configurations, the symbolism, mythology, and historic import of Portuguese exploration. With its twisted columns and 13th-century tombs, the two-tiered Gothic-Manueline **cloister** is impressive. All in all, the church is a heady architectural cocktail of Gothic, Manueline, and Renaissance styles.

St. Anthony of Padua lived in the monastery as a young Franciscan friar in the 12th century. A century later, the church was the scene of the gruesome denouement of the Inês de Castro story, when King Pedro I had the body of his murdered lover dug up and crowned queen beside him (see box p. 23).

Attached to the church is one of Portugal's nicest historic cafes. The **Café Santa Cruz**, opened in 1923, was built into an abandoned wing of the monastery in a monumental neo-Manueline style (splendid arched ceiling and stained-glass windows) that reflects its holy neighbor. It is one of the best places in town to hear **fado,** with regular free concerts at 6pm and 10pm (www.cafesantacruz.com; ✆ **23/983-36-17**).

Praça do 8 de Maio. ✆ **23/982-29-41.** 3€. Mon–Sat 9am–4:30pm; Sun 1–5:30pm.

Museu Nacional de Machado de Castro ★★★ MUSEUM Even if it were empty, this museum would be worth a visit for the stunning historic building alone. Housed in a palace that was home to the city's bishops in Renaissance times, the upper floors contain an award-winning extension completed in 2012, including a cafe offering panoramic views over the city. In the basement are the ruins of Coimbra's ancient Roman forum, where visitors can take a subterranean stroll through 1st-century warehouses and market stores. Within is one of Portugal's best art collections. The focus is on medieval painting and sculptures, with masterpieces such as the *Passion of Christ* by Flemish artist Quentin Matsys, a golden chalice dating from the 12th century, and the haunting *Last Supper,* a monumental series of saintly sculptures shaped by Philippe Hodart in the 1530s.

Largo Dr José Rodrigues. www.museumachadocastro.gov.pt. ✆ **23/985-30-70.** 6€, 3€ students & and over 65s, free for under 12s. Apr–Sept: Tues–Sun 10am–6pm; Oct–Mar Tues–Sun 10am–12:30pm & 2–6pm.

Sé Velha ★★ CHURCH Of Coimbra's two cathedrals, this is the older and more interesting. Its fortress-like construction—plain stone with crenellated battlements and arrow-slit windows—is a reminder of the days when the Mondego was a frontline in battles between Christians and Muslims for control of the Iberian Peninsula. Founded in 1170 by Portugal's founder king, Afonso Henriques, it is considered Portugal's best-preserved Romanesque cathedral. But inside, in the wide, atmospheric space beneath great barrel-arched roof, you'll see the lingering Islamic influence on Portuguese art in the plant and animal carvings at the tops of the columns and the geometric ceramic tile patterns. Look around and still *another* influence intrudes: Contrasting with the Romanesque simplicity, the main chapel is filled with a soaring flamboyant Gothic **retable** carved by Flemish artists in the 15th century with gilded sculptures telling the story of Christ. The cloister shows the transition from Romanesque to Gothic. Sé Velha is located on the way down from the university to the Baixa district and is surrounded by cafes, bars, and restaurants.

Largo Sé Velha. www.sevelha-coimbra.org. ✆ **23/982-52-73.** Free (2.50€ donation requested). Mon–Fri 10am–5:30pm; Sat 10am–6:30pm; Sun and holidays 11am–5pm.

Universidade de Coimbra ★★★ HISTORIC SITE Most visitors' first impression of the ancient university is something of a shock. Instead of buildings reflecting the medieval origins of this venerable house of learning, they are confronted with a row of very 20th-century monolithic faculty blocks constructed during the Salazar dictatorship and reflecting the Fascist-inspired architectural tastes of the time. Things change when you step through the 17th-century **Porta Férrea** (iron gate) leading to the university's inner core.

Inside is a harmonious quadrangle surrounded on three sides by the facades of buildings dating back to the 15th century, when the university was installed in what was a royal palace.

Grabbing the eye is a cloistered arcade, the **Via Latina** and the baroque clock tower, which has become a symbol of the city despite the unkind nickname, ***a cabra*** (the she-goat), given to it by generations of students called back to class by the tolling of its bell. Up the double staircase, where there may be a guitar-strumming student wrapped in the traditional black cape, you enter a series of ornate halls that for centuries have hosted grand royal and academic events. Most splendid is the **Sala Grande dos Actos** (Ceremonial Hall) decorated with red-damask walls, blue-and-white *azulejos* (tiles), and an intricately painted ceiling. Kings of Portugal once held court here. Their stern-faced portraits look down on the chamber where solemn ceremonies, such as the formal opening of the school year and the handing out of doctoral awards, are still held.

Other highlights of the university tour include the **University Chapel,** its interior a blaze of blue-and-yellow *azulejos*, gold-covered altars, marble columns, and a glorious baroque organ. In contrast is the grim **Academic Prison.** Its cells, with their thick stone walls and iron-barred doorways, were used to punish badly behaved students from 1593 until 1834. The university's star attraction is the **Biblioteca Joanina,** one of Europe's great historic libraries. Named after its founder, King João V, who used the vast riches of newly discovered Brazilian gold mines to embellish the country with baroque monuments, the early-18th-century library contains over 300,000 books. Some are over 500 years old, including early accounts of the Portuguese Discoveries. You'll find volumes of historic or artistic import, opened and put on display in glass cabinets on the library's lower floor.

There are three high-ceilinged salons walled by two-story tiers of lacquer-decorated oak bookshelves. Pale jade-and-lemon-colored marble floors complement the gilded woodwork. Chinese-inspired patterns are painted on emerald, red, and gold lacquer work. The library tables are built of ebony and lustrous rosewood, imported from the former Portuguese colonies in India and Brazil. The overall effect is sumptuous.

Tickets can be bought at the store of the university's modern library building to the right of the Porta Férrea. There is a somewhat bewildering variety of ticket options for visiting different parts of the university. To see the main sights, a combined ticket allowing unguided access to the ceremonial chambers, chapel, and library costs 12.50€, 10€ for seniors 65 and over and students under 26; it's free for children under 12. For a bit more you can customize, adding the 18th-century Physics Laboratory and Natural History collection (7€ more), or the tower (an extra 2€). Due to limited space, the library door is opened every 20 minutes to let in a maximum of 60 people at a time.

Largo Porta Férrea. www.uc.pt. ✆ **23/924-27-44.** Mar–Oct daily 9am–7:15pm; Nov–Feb daily 9am–12:40pm, 2–4:40pm. Closed Dec 24–25 and Jan 1. Closed Jan 31 at 4pm and May 8 at 1pm for the Queima das Fitas Parade to mark the end of the school year.

Especially for Kids

For some open-air fun right in the city, head to the **Parque Verde Mondego** ★ (Av. Emídio Navarro, free, open 24 hr.), a cool riverside park that opened in 2004. It contains bike paths, a skate park, playgrounds, a swimming pool, and waterfront cafes, with bikes, canoes, and paddle boats to rent. A footbridge named after the tragic lovers Pedro and Inês spans the river.

Older children will enjoy an adventurous **kayak trip** ★★ down the Mondego from the pretty upriver town of Penacova to Coimbra. The longest established company offering the service is **O Pioneiro do Mondego** (www.opioneiro domondego.com/en; ✆ **23/947-83-85**). Prices start at 22.50€ for adults, less for students and groups, transport from Coimbra included. Founded by a Belgian couple in 1988, they offer two trips from Penacova, one 18km (11 miles) lasting 3 to 4 hours to Torre de Mondego, the other a full 25km (15 miles) into Coimbra itself. For most of the trip the current pushes you through the thickly forested banks, but there are a couple of modest rapids to get the adrenalin going and a sandy beach where you can picnic or take a dip.

Museu da Ciência ★ MUSEUM Up on university hill, the charmingly eccentric Science Museum combines collections of gemstones, stuffed animals, and mockups of 18th-century chemistry labs with state-of-the-art interactive exhibits to fire up young imaginations. Nominated for a European Museum of the Year Award when it opened in 2006, it is housed in a graceful old neoclassical palace.

Largo Marquês de Pombal. www.museudaciencia.org. ✆ **23/985-43-50.** 4€, 2€ students, teachers, and over 65s, free under 5s. Tues–Sun 10am–6pm, some rooms closed weekends.

Parque Biológico da Serra da Lousã ★ ZOO A stroll through forested slopes takes you to enclosures containing animals who live, or once lived, in the Portuguese interior. There are deer, foxes, boar, lynx, wolves, and bears on show. The park also has a handicraft store and an excellent restaurant, the **Museu da Chanfana,** which rather incongruously serves some of the species you've just seen in the park (the best dish on the menu: *chanfana*, which is aged goat slow-cooked in red wine, a local specialty). It's about 30 minutes' drive southeast of Coimbra.

Parque de Lazer da Quinta da Paiva, Miranda do Corvo. ✆ **23/953-84-44.** 7€, 4.50€ children 3–15, free under-3s. June–Aug daily 10am–6pm, Apr–May & Sept 1–15 10am–5pm, Sept 15–Mar 10am–4pm.

Portugal dos Pequenitos ★ AMUSEMENT PARK "Portugal for the Little Ones" is a retro theme park built in the 1940s and dear to the heart of generations of Portuguese. Children can feel like Gulliver strolling through this Lilliputian world made up of miniature reconstructions of Portugal's main monuments and traditional homes from around the country. Since it was built in colonial times, there are also Indian temples, Chinese palaces, and African villages, surrounded by tropical vegetation. If all that wasn't sufficiently high on the kitsch quota, there's also a **Barbie Museum,** with over 300 of the diminutive beauties. As we were going to press, plans were afoot for an expansion and modernization of the park, which could entail moving the entrance to a new address.

Largo Rossio de Santa Clara. www.portugaldospequenitos.pt. ✆ **23/980-11-70.** 10€, 6€ children 3–13 & over 65s, free under 3s. June–Sept 16 daily 9am–7:30pm; Mar–May & Sept 16–Oct 15 daily 10am–6:30; Oct 16–Feb daily 10am–4:30pm.

Shopping

Along **Rua Ferreira Borges,** up the steep **Rua Quebra Costas,** and through the warren of lanes making up the **Baixa,** there's a plethora of small stores selling potential souvenirs, from CDs of Coimbra fado to handmade preserves, colored wool blankets from the hills, or hammered copper work. The most authentic buy in Coimbra is **pottery,** hand-painted in colorful, centuries-old designs (clay plates, pitchers, vases, boxes, and much more). Traditional patterns feature birds, animals, and flowers, which clearly show the Arabic influence on Portuguese artwork of the time. **Malabar,** Arco de Almedina, 25 (www.malabarcoimbra.com; ✆ **23/983-61-19**) has a quality ceramic selection.

Where to Stay

EXPENSIVE

Hotel Quinta das Lágrimas ★★★ The most luxurious place in town, the "Estate of Tears" gets its name from the medieval love story of Pedro and Inês de Castro. She was murdered on the *Quinta's* grounds and it's said her tears were transformed into a pure, fresh stream of water that still bubbles forth in the garden. The red color of the rocks is reputedly from her spilled blood. The building traces its roots back almost 700 years; guests have included the Duke of Wellington, an emperor of Brazil, and various kings of Portugal. Today's visitors can choose between romantic rooms in the old building reflecting the palatial 18th-century style, or the cool, contemporary new spa wing, which offers individual Jacuzzis and views over the lush tropical gardens. It's a 15-minute walk to the city center.

Rua António Augusto Gonçalves. www.quintadaslagrimas.pt. ✆ **23/980-23-80.** 57 units. 135€–230€ double, 207€–400€ suite. Free parking. **Amenities:** Garden; terrace; golf; indoor & outdoor pools; fitness center; spa; sauna; hammam; Jacuzzi; massage service; 2 restaurants; bar; babysitting; free Wi-Fi.

MODERATE

Hotel Oslo ★ It might not look much from the outside, but beyond the drab exterior, this friendly, family-run place is a good value downtown option. The quirky, 1960s decor mixes Nordic-style design with lots of pale pine with traditional Portuguese textiles and Coimbra ceramics. Rooms were renovated in 2014. Standards are smallish, but neatly furnished with white walls, fresh linen, and soft woolen throw blankets. The rooftop bar—and several of the upper-floor rooms—offer some of the best views of the city, lovely in the twilight. Superior rooms have floor-to-ceiling windows and private verandas. Free valet parking is a plus.

Av. Fernão de Magalhães 25. www.hoteloslo-coimbra.pt. ✆ **23/982-90-71.** 36 units. 65€–165€ double, including breakfast. Free parking. **Amenities:** Sun terrace; free bikes; bar; free Wi-Fi.

Palácio da Lousã ★★ This beautifully restored aristocratic 18th-century residence is in Lousã, a small town up in the hills about a half-hour drive from Coimbra. Its soft pastel furnishings recall the time of its construction by one of the region's grandest families. Rooms are divided between the palace and a modern new wing. During the Napoleonic wars, the palace was the scene of a famous incident, when the French general occupying the palace fled so fast from a surprise British attack that the Duke of Wellington was able to sit in the dining room and enjoy the meal prepared for his foe. The restaurant today retains great period charm and serves such delights as "pork Wellington" with chestnuts.

Rua Viscondessa do Espinhal, Lousã. www.palaciodalousa.com. ✆ **23/999-08-00.** 46 units. 75€–117€ double, 109€–169€. Free parking. **Amenities:** Garden; terrace; bike hire; outdoor pool; restaurant; bar; games room; children's play area; free Wi-Fi.

Pousada de Condeixa ★★ Part of the Pousada chain of luxury inns, this hotel in the small town of Condeixa, 16km (10 miles) southwest of Coimbra, is a perfect base for visiting the nearby Roman ruins of **Conímbriga.** It's housed in a noble manor house with red roof tiles dating back to the 16th century, although much restored prior to its opening in 1993. The furnishings feature many antiques, and rooms are spacious with tiled bathrooms. There are extensive gardens and an outdoor pool that's perfect for cooling off after a day of sightseeing.

Rua Francisco Lemos, 3–5, Condeixa-a-Nova. www.pousadadecondeixa-coimbra.com. ✆ **23/994-40-25.** 43 units. 75€–144€ double; 135€–150€ suite. Free parking. **Amenities:** Garden; terrace; bike hire; outdoor pool; sauna; massage service; restaurant; bar; children's play area; babysitting; free Wi-Fi.

Sapientia Boutique Hotel ★★ This spanking new hotel filled a gap for stylish accommodation in the uptown university district. The restored cluster of buildings was once part of a Jesuit college. The rooftop bar feels like an extension of the university courtyard. Decor is white minimalist mixed with raw wood, rustic wool blankets, and exposed stone walls. Up the monumental staircase, rooms reference great Portuguese writers who passed through Coimbra. Excellent home-baked breakfast can be taken in the patio beneath a 100-year-old walnut tree surrounded by ivy, rosemary, and lavender. Later on, try a glass of the draft local craft beer.

Rua José Falcão 4. www.sapientiahotel.com. ✆ **23/915-18-03.** 22 units. 91€–139€ double, 109€–205€ suites and apartments. **Amenities:** Terrace; bike hire; restaurant; bar; free Wi-Fi.

Vila Galé Coimbra ★★ Portugal's Vila Galé group is best known for its seaside hotels, and this ultra-modern hotel has the air of a beach resort in the city center. The L-shaped, white-stone-and-glass four-story building is wrapped around the wide, riverside outdoor pool. When the weather is cooler, there's an indoor pool, spa, and fitness center. The lobby is decorated with costumes from the national ballet company. Rooms are spacious, with about half offering views over the pool and the Mondego, although some guests complain that the railway line running between the pool and the river spoils the vista. It's a 10-minute walk to downtown.

Rua Abel Dias Urbano, 20. www.vilagale.com. ✆ **23/924-00-00.** 229 units. 98€–127€ double, 147€–193€ suite. Parking 7.50€ per day. **Amenities:** Garden; terrace; indoor & outdoor pools; spa; gym; sauna; hammam; massage service; restaurant; bar; free Wi-Fi.

INEXPENSIVE

Casa Pombal ★ Tucked away in a winding hillside alley close to the university, Casa Pombal is a no-frills guesthouse that was once a *república*, a traditional university frat house. Plaques on the wall outside tell of the medical pioneers who spent their student years there. The place is being renovated room by room, so some have newish furniture and pleasing wallpaper, others need a facelift. Some have shared bathrooms. Still, it's clean and friendly, you can enjoy a homemade breakfast in a room with azulejos, and there's a little terrace with views over the city.

Rua das Flores 18. www.casapombal.com. ✆ **23/983-51-75.** 9 units. 43€–52€ double. **Amenities:** Terraces; free Wi-Fi.

Hotel Astória ★ A Coimbra landmark dating back to the 1920s, in a mixture of Belle Epoque, Art Nouveau, and Art Deco styles, the wedge-shaped building is an exuberant collection of cupolas, balconies, and wrought-iron balustrade arches. The location is swell, in the heart of the city looking out over the river. "Faded grandeur" are the words that come to mind. The Astoria may not have all mod cons, but the rooms are comfortable, with high ceilings, windows looking out over the Mondego or the old city, and period furnishings. The reception and bar are a step back to the Jazz Age. It's perfect for those seeking old-world elegance, even if it's a bit creaky.

Avenida Emídio Navarro 21. www.almeidahotels.pt. ✆ **23/985-30-20.** 62 units. 66€–118€ double. No parking. **Amenities:** Bike hire; bar; babysitting; free Wi-Fi in public areas.

Serenata Hostel ★★ Taking its name from the moonlight serenades sung by Coimbra's wandering fado singers, this is the city's premier hostel. Located in an early-20th-century townhouse that once served as a maternity hospital and a music school, today it's a vibrant meeting place for travelers, offering both private rooms and dorms for up to 10 people, with bunk beds and private lockers. The private rooms and suites are of the standard of a good boutique hotel, although some have shared bathrooms. The location couldn't be more central, right next to the medieval Sé Velha cathedral. Decor is stylishly shabby chic, with many of the building's original features maintained.

Walls are decorated with large-scale line drawings of Portuguese cultural figures and handwritten poetry quotations. This place can be noisy, and not just from serenading singers.

Largo da Sé Velha, 21/23. www.serenatahostel.com. ✆ **23/985-31-30.** 18 units. 38€–84€ double; 15€–22€ dormitory bed. **Amenities:** Terrace; bar; kitchen; games room; free Wi-Fi.

Where to Eat

Arcadas ★★★ MODERN PORTUGUESE Coimbra isn't overflowing with fine dining options, but the swish restaurant at the Hotel Quinta das Lágrimas is one of Portugal's foremost gourmet experiences. Chef Vítor Dias uses fresh, seasonal produce, with many of his fruits, vegetables, and herbs grown organically in the hotel garden. The menu changes with the seasons, but typical delights could include mixed fish in lobster sauce with samphire or veal loin with turnip greens and bone-marrow *jus*. Dias's dishes are a visual delight, combining forms, textures, and colors to make each plate a work of art. The restaurant is located in the old palace stables, its arched windows overlooking a lush, tropical garden. There's a terrific selection of wines, with a focus on the Dão and Bairrada regions just north of Coimbra.

Rua António Augusto Gonçalves. www.quintadaslagrimas.pt. ✆ **23/980-23-80.** Mains 24€–34€; tasting menus 60€–120€. Daily 7:30–10pm.

Casas do Bragal ★★ PORTUGUESE A refined yet relaxed place serving traditional Portuguese food with a modern touch. The dining room is decorated with striking paintings by the owner, featuring portraits of Portuguese divas like *fadista* Mariza or *Pulp Fiction* star Maria de Medeiros. There are always seasonal variations, but roast kid is the signature dish, served with roast potatoes, rice cooked with the goat's offal, and broccoli rabe. Fish options include salt cod cooked with onions and vintage port. Located east of the city center in a leafy residential suburb, it's well worth making the trip out, especially for those with a sweet tooth—the buffet of traditional desserts is legendary.

Urbanização de Tamonte – Rua Damião de Gois. ✆ **91/810-39-88.** Mains 12€–30€. Fri–Sat 1–3pm & 8–11pm, Sun 1–3pm, Tues 8–10pm, Wed–Thurs 1–3pm, & 8–10pm.

Fangas Mercearia & Bar ★ PETISCOS The Portuguese equivalent of Spain's tapas are *petiscos,* and this friendly, trendy place amid the narrow streets leading up the university is the place to sample them. Bright colors dominate, with a stylized cityscape painting on one wall, bold stripes on another. There's a vast range of snacks and light meals to share—tinned tuna in olive oil, baked mussels, blood sausage with turnip greens, duck breast with figs—best washed down with a glass of sangria or something from the extensive Portuguese wine list. You can also drop in for a coffee or tea with one of their delicious sweets, like roast apple with *moscatel wine*.

Rua Fernandes Tomás 45/9. ✆ **93/409-36-36.** Snacks from 6€–15€. Mon–Thurs noon–3:30 & 7pm–11:30pm; Fri–Sat noon–3:30 & 7pm–midnight; Sun noon–4 & 7pm–11:30pm.

Nacional ★★ PORTUGUESE Off the beaten track, on a side street on the northern edge of the Baixa, this place was a renowned billiards hall before it was turned into a spacious, second-floor restaurant in 1977. Now it's an institution where generations of families, office workers, and groups of friends come to enjoy homestyle Portuguese comfort food. There's modern art on the bare stone walls, but also a feeling that little has changed here for years. A selection of regular specials is offered each day of the week. Friday, for example, offers *cozido à Portuguesa* (mixed boiled meats, traditional smoked sausages, boiled vegetables, and rice); *pato assado à Ribatejana* (roast duck, giblets in rice, and smoked sausages); or *bacalhau à Vila Nova* (fried salt-cod with mayonnaise and mashed potatoes). It's old school, but delicious. A half-portion (*meia dose*) will satisfy all but the most gargantuan appetites.

Rua Mário Pais, 12. www.restaurantenacional.pt. ✆ **23/982-94-20.** Mains 9€–16€. Mon–Sat noon–3pm and 7–midnight.

O Trovador ★ PORTUGUESE A romantic place in the city's heart, just in front of the old cathedral, "the Troubadour" offers the chance to eat traditional Portuguese food in refined surroundings and listen to some of Coimbra's best guitarists and fado singers. There are azulejos, vintage photos of the city and its illustrious inhabitants on the walls, and white-shirted waiters providing old-fashioned good service. *Chanfana,* an emblematic dish from the hills above Coimbra involving goat slow-cooked in red wine, is excellent here.

Largo Sé Velha, 15. www.restaurantetrovador.com. ✆ **96/692-32-78.** Mains 11€–18€. Mon–Sat noon–3pm and 7–10pm.

Zé Manuel dos Ossos ★★ PORTUGUESE As a student town for centuries, Coimbra is filled with backstreet taverns serving hearty, cut-price cooking. This is the most famous, serving up the likes of roast baby goat (*cabrito assado no forno*), bean stew with wild boar (*feijoada de javali*), or ribs with beans and rice (*ossos com arroz de feijão*). It's tiny, cramped, and you'll probably have to stand in line to get in because they don't take reservations. But a meal squashed in beneath the hundreds of messages of appreciation stuck to the walls by grateful students—along with other oddities like a bespectacled stuffed boar's head and an alligator hanging from the ceiling—will undoubtedly be a memorable occasion. A half-portion (*meia dose*) will normally more than suffice for one hungry person.

Beco do Forno, 12. ✆ **23/982-37-90.** Mains 6€–9€. Mon–Sat 12:30–3pm & 7:30–10pm.

Coimbra Entertainment & Nightlife

The city's large student population guarantees an active, sometimes raucous nightlife. You'll find plenty of **bars** around **Largo Sé Velha,** packed with students, professors, and locals who drink, gossip, and discuss politics. **Bar Quebra Costas,** on Escadas de Quebra Costas, 45/49 (✆ **23/984-11-74**) is one of the oldest and most popular spots. There are also several late-night hangouts around Praça da República that are popular with students, like **Café Tropical**, open 'til 3am at No. 34. Quirky **Aqui Base Tango** (Rua Venâncio

Rodrigues 8; ✆ **91/688-27-31;** Mon–Sat 3pm–4am) may be the most interesting. Housed in a pink-painted former police station, it has fab cocktails and eclectic music ranging from bossa nova to indie rock that spills over from the retro interior into a cool garden.

For late-night **fado,** head for **À Capella,** Rua Corpo de Deus (www.acapella.com.pt; ✆ **23/983-39-85**), which was turned into a cafe from a chapel constructed back in 1364. Open daily 6pm to 2am, it offers nightly performances starting from 9:30pm. An earlier alternative is **Fado ao Centro,** Rua de Quebra Costas 7 (www.fadoaocentro.com; ✆ **91/323-67-25**). It provides a great introduction to the music, with daily 6pm performances from top-class musicians lasting 50 minutes. They'll also explain the often-mysterious world of fado and are happy to chat after the show over a glass of port that's included in 10€ entry fee.

Movie fans can visit the multiple screens in the **Alma** shopping mall, Rua General Humberto Delgado (✆ **23/979-80-90**) or the **Fórum Coimbra** mall (✆ **70/724-63-62**). For a more intimate experience, try the University theater at **Teatro Académico de Gil Vicente,** Praça da República (www.tagv.pt; ✆ **23/985-56-36**), which also hosts regular concerts and plays as well as movies. A major new cultural center: the **Convento São Francisco** (www.coimbraconvento.pt; ✆ **23/985-71-91**) opened in 2016 in a 17th-century former convent. The music and dance program ranges from jazz and classical to fado and pop.

Side Trips Around Coimbra

One of Europe's great Roman archaeological finds, **Conímbriga ★★**, is 16km (10 miles) southwest of Coimbra. A stroll around the ruins will give you a taste of everyday life in Rome's Lusitania province from the time of Emperor Augustus, in the 1st century A.D. There's a forum, a theater, thermal baths, and the later addition of a Christian basilica, but the private houses are the most fascinating, giving a real insight into domestic life from the 1st to 3rd centuries. The homes have colonnaded courtyards, fountain-filled gardens, and magnificent mosaics showing scenes of hunting and mythology, or geometric patterns in blood red, mustard, gray, sienna, and yellow. An on-site museum shows the development of the site from Celtic village to thriving provincial town until its destruction by Germanic invaders in the 5th century.

The ruins are open daily 10am to 7pm. Admission is 4.50€ (www.conimbriga.gov.pt; ✆ **23/994-11-77**).

If you fancy lunch, the charming main square in Condeixa has a number of restaurants specializing in roast kid (*cabrito assado*). **O Regional do Cabrito ★** is a safe bet, Praça da República, 14 (✆ **23/994-49-33**).

If you have a car, winding roads through hills to the east of Coimbra provide a chance to get in touch with a hidden side of Portugal, where culinary, cultural, and handicraft traditions run deep. In the **Serra da Lousã ★** and **Serra do Açor ★** hills, the **Aldeias do Xisto** initiative is an attempt to inject new life into highland villages that were suffering from desertification as younger people moved to the cities. Twenty-seven villages constructed from the dark local schist stones are included, many hosting shops that sell local crafts including basketwork, woolen blankets, honey, and liquors. They also organize hiking, cross-country biking, kayaking, and other outdoor activities. For more information, go to www.aldeiasdoxisto.pt (© **27/564-77-00**). The website also lists rural restaurants, and accommodations ranging from rustic home stays to luxury hotels.

One of the most imposing of the small towns in the hills is **Penela ★**, a half-hour drive south from Coimbra. Its heart is a cluster of whitewashed homes sheltering beneath the imposing medieval **castle,** another reminder of the days of *reconquista,* when it formed part of a network of defenses against Muslim counterattacks. Admission is free. It's open daily 9am to 7pm (until 9pm Apr–Sept). Sheep and goats roaming the hillsides here are used to make ***queijo de Rabaçal,*** mild cheeses tasting of wild herbs that come in hockey-puck-size rounds. Along the main street in the village of Rabaçal you can buy from cafes, stores, and private homes of small producers.

While the Mondego upriver from Coimbra winds through forested hills, once it's through the city, the river broadens out and flows gently to the Atlantic through marshes, rice paddies, and salt flats. Dominating the landscape is the imposing **castle** of **Montemor-o-Velho ★**, 28km (17 miles) west of Coimbra on the road to the ocean. This was a bastion in the medieval fight for control of Portugal, captured from the Moors in 1064. The fortress was expanded over the years, and its current form dates mostly from the 14th century. There's a gem of a Romanesque church within its walls, and a modern teahouse (*casa de chá*) built into the ruins of the *Paço das Infantas* (Princesses' Palace).

A prized specialty in the watery lands around Montemor is duck served roasted (*pato assado*) or with rice (*arroz de pato*). One of the best places to try such delights is **Casa Arménio ★★** in the village of **Tentúgal,** on Rua Mourão between Coimbra and Montemor (meals around 17€ but enough for two; © **23/995-11-75**). This rustic restaurant located in an old aristocratic manor house is a temple to regional cuisine. This is very much a local favorite with little preparation for international visitors, but the staff is friendly and the food is divine. Finish off with some of the almond-egg-cinnamon confections that have their origins in the nearby convent and are now favorite sweet treats around the country. There are also a number of good cafes serving *pastéis de Tentúgal* and other wonderful regional pastries: Bustling **Pousadinha ★★**, Estrada Nacional 111 (www.apousadinha.pt; © **23/995-11-58**), is the best.

FIGUEIRA DA FOZ ★

140km (90 miles) S of Porto; 200km (125 miles) N of Lisbon; 50km (30 miles) W of Coimbra

With one of Europe's largest urban **beaches,** 2.5km (1.6 miles) long and 600m (2,000 ft.) at its widest, Figueira has been attracting sunseekers since the 19th century, and remains a popular vacation destination of Portuguese families and Spaniards, who race down the highway to hit the sand here every summer.

These days, the beach is backed by a jumble of steel, glass, and concrete high-rises, which give it something of mini Copacabana feel. However, some remnants of the more elegant Belle Epoque and Art Deco constructions of the resort's golden age can be found in streets behind the waterfront, particularly in the **Bairro Novo** district, just inland from the Mondego.

Figueira in summer is a busy, happening place, with its **casino** hosting big-name concerts. The size of the beach means there's always space for the colorful, candy-striped beach huts and tents. Sunsets are amazing.

Anyone seeking a quieter time can head over the **Serra da Boa Viagem,** a mountainous, forest-covered headland; to the wild and wonderful **Praia de Quiaios** beach; or a string of popular surfing spots south of the Mondego River.

Essentials

ARRIVING

BY TRAIN Trains leave hourly from Coimbra to the station at Largo da Estação near the river. The trip lasts around 1 hour. One-way tickets 2.80€.

BY BUS The bus station, **Terminal Rodoviário,** is next door at Avenida Saraiva de Carvalho. Five buses a day arrive from Lisbon; the trip takes around 3 hours and costs 15.20€ one-way. The Moises bus company (www.moises-transportes.pt; © **23/982-82-63**) runs buses around once an hour from Coimbra to Figueira for 4.30€. The journey takes around 1 hour and 30 minutes one-way.

BY CAR From Lisbon, it's a 2-hour drive up the A8 and A17 toll highways, and from Coimbra 40 minutes on the A14.

VISITOR INFORMATION

The **Figueira da Foz Tourist Office** is on Avenida do 25 de Abril (© **23/342-26-10**) and is open daily 9:30am to 1pm and 2 to 5:30pm.

Exploring Figueira da Foz

Figueira is easily explored on foot. A good place to start is the **Forte de Santa Catarina** fortress, perched at the mouth of the Mondego. Built in the 17th century to ward off pirates, it now houses a seafood restaurant and offers a fine view over the beach and the curving, cafe-laden **Av. 25 de Abril** running along the waterfront. A good place for a break is the **Geladaria Emanha ★**, Av. 25 de Abril, © **23/342-65-67,** which has been serving handmade ice cream for generations. Open in summer from 10:30am to 2am, in winter 1pm to midnight.

Most visitors don't come to Figueira to look at museums, but there are a couple of good ones. In a country famed for its own ceramic tiles, the **Casa do Paço ★**, Largo Prof. Vítor Guerra 4 (www.cm-figfoz.pt; © **23/343-01-03;** Tues–Sat 10am–5pm, admission 2.45€ adult, 1.20€ children and seniors) contains one of the world's greatest collections of 18th-century **Delft tiles** from the Netherlands, numbering almost 7,000, depicting landscapes, ships, and warriors with gaudy plumage, among other things. Nobody is quite sure how they got here, but local legend has it they were recovered from a Dutch frigate wrecked off the beach in 1706. The collection is housed in a neoclassical palace fronted by a bougainvillea-rich garden. It was the center of Figueira's social life in the 19th century when royalty attended balls there.

Up the hill, the **Museu Municipal Santos Rocha ★**, Rua Calouste Gulbenkian (✆ **23/340-28-40**) is a modern building housing an eclectic collection ranging from medieval sculpture to historic firearms, the most interesting of which relate to Portugal's colonial past, with artifacts from Africa, South America, and Asia. There's an abundance of Indo-Portuguese furniture resulting from a fusion of styles in the colonial days of the 17th century. In summer it's open Tuesday to Friday, 9:30am to 6pm; weekends 2 to 7pm. In winter it's closed all day Sunday and weekdays from 5pm. Admission is 2€ for adults.

OUTDOOR ACTIVITIES Figueira's main attraction is the beach. The main urban beach, known as **Praia da Claridade ★★**, has a Sahara-like vastness. It can take 5 minutes to reach the ocean along the wooden boardwalks that run toward it from the promenade. The beach has soccer fields, volleyball pitches, and cycle paths. At the northern end, the beach narrows as it approaches the **Buarcos ★** neighborhood, once a fishing village, which has many cafes and restaurants and a cozier feel than the main Figueira strip. The strand here has some rocky coves and is popular with windsurfers.

For solitude, take a ride over the towering **Serra da Boa Viagem ★** hills that reach the Atlantic at the **Cabo Mondego** promontory. The views over the city and the wilder coast to the north are spectacular, especially at sunset. Unfortunately, the site is scarred by an abandoned cement works; however, it is not visible from many of the viewpoints and there are plans to recover the land. Beyond the cape, the great **Praia de Quiaios ★★★** stretches away to the horizon, backed by dunes and pine forest. There is a small settlement with a couple of restaurants and a small hotel, but for mile after mile, there is just beach. It is one of Portugal's best beaches, but tides and waves on the west coast can be dangerous. Don't swim if there's a red flag flying. If in doubt, ask the lifeguard stationed near the beach restaurant through the summer season.

South of the Mondego, there's a string of excellent beaches, too, which are very popular with surfers from around Europe. Fine white sand and regular waves make **Praia do Cabedelo ★★** a particular favorite.

Where to Stay

MODERATE

Eurostars Oasis Plaza ★★★ Opened in 2014, the futuristic 15-story building was inspired by the curving forms of a classic cruise liner, its prow pointing toward the ocean. A flagship of the Spanish Eurostars group, it provides state-of-the-art comfort. The suites are a spacious 50 square meters (540 sq. ft.) with balconies and sea views. Furnishings are in soft earth colors. The beach is just across the avenue, but you may not want to tear yourself from the top floor indoor pool with its wide Atlantic views.

Avenida do Brasil. www.eurostarshotels.com.pt. ✆ **23/320-00-10.** 160 units. 75€–133€ double, 95€–213€ suite. Parking 10€ per day. **Amenities:** Terrace; indoor pool; gym; spa; hammam; massage service; restaurant; bar; babysitting; free Wi-Fi.

Mercure Figueira da Foz ★★ On the seafront promenade overlooking the ocean, this renovated 1950s-era hotel has an undeniable retro charm. An architectural landmark, it could do with a bit of freshening up. But it has a prime seafront location, close to the casino and next door to the Figueira Beach Club pool complex. The interior is a world of marble and glass, with some cute vintage Portuguese tapestries in the lobby. Most rooms have ocean views and balconies.

Av. do 25 de Abril 22. www.accorhotels.com. ✆ **23/340-39-00.** 102 units. 64€–175€ double. **Amenities:** Terrace; restaurant; bar; free Wi-Fi.

Quinta da Anta – Hotel Rural ★★★ A rice farm turned into a super-relaxed and super-chic retreat for upscale beach bums. It's actually 16km (8 mile) from the beach, but they'll bus you out there for a surf lesson, or you can grab one of the handy VTT bikes and peddle through the paddy fields. (Or just chill by the pool and pretend you're at the beach.) Digs are in modernist, single-story white cubes. Most have private terraces. Decor features raw wood paneling, natural fabrics, vintage surf boards, and a patio with vertical garden. The (optional) activity program means you could surf in the morning and take a yoga class in the afternoon. The chef will slow cook dinner in their wood-fired oven or rustle up a typical dish with local rice.

Rua Poeta João de Lemos, 32, Maiorca. www.quintadanta.pt. ✆ **96/499-45-15.** 18 units. 59€–150€ double. Free parking. **Amenities:** Garden; terrace; barbecue; tennis; bike hire; outdoor pool; gym; massage service; games room; restaurant; bar; children's play area; babysitting; free Wi-Fi.

Universal Boutique Hotel ★★ A salmon-colored four-story town house in the quaint Bairro Novo neighborhood on a side street, a block from the beach, Universal was recently renovated and oozes lowkey glamour. Its style is softly contemporary with antique touches, like the patrician portraits in the stylish first-floor bar. Some rooms are on the small side, and those under the sloping attic roof mean guests have to watch bumping their heads, but they are romantic, with pastel colors and soft lights. This is a cozy contrast to the big beachfront options.

Rua Miguel Bombarda 50. ✆ **23/309-01-10.** 29 units. 72€–130€ double. **Amenities:** Bike hire; bar; babysitting; free Wi-Fi.

INEXPENSIVE

Paintshop Hostel ★ Probably not the place to go if you want a quiet break, this is a hip, fun place for the surf-and-party crowd. We're talking budget accommodations and a cool vibe, plus bike, board, and wetsuit hire. There are funky private rooms for couples and discount dorms for groups. The English owners organize regular BBQ and pizza nights, and there's a hip bar and

LITTLE piggies

Strung out along the old Lisbon to Porto highway, **Mealhada** is not one of Portugal's most beautiful towns. It is, however, the center of one of the country's gastronomic treasures: ***leitão da Bairrada*** ★★★. Vegetarians should look away now. *Leitão* is suckling pig, a piglet in the first weeks of life still fed on its mother's milk. Here they are dispatched on an industrial scale. It's estimated 3,000 are eaten every day in the restaurants of Mealhada and the surrounding Bairrada region. Many of the factory-size eateries in the town raise and slaughter their own animals. They are basted in a garlic-and-black-pepper sauce, then spit-roasted in wood-fired ovens until the skin is crisp and golden, the flesh pink and oh-so-tender. It's usually served with freshly fried potato chips, salad, and slices of orange, and washed down with excellent **Bairrada wines.** Some prefer to serve either white or red sparkling wine (*espumante*); others insist a hearty red is best. Locals are passionate defenders of their favorite among the over 30 *leitão* restaurants along the N1 road. **Pedro dos Leitões** (✆ **23/120-99-50**), set up in 1949, is best known, with space for 430 diners. Its neighbor and competitor, **A Meta dos Leitões** (✆ **23/120-95-40**) is of similar dimensions. Across the road, **Rei dos Leitões** (✆ **96/812-30-84**) is more upmarket. There are those, however, who say the very best *leitão* can be had a few miles to the north at **Casa Vidal** (✆ **23/466-63-53**) in the village of Águeda de Cima.

patio out back for hanging out and making friends. It's closed from mid-October through April. It's located in a typical Figueira town house down a side street a short walk from the beach and the station.

Rua da Clemencia, 9. www.paintshophostel.com. ✆ **91/667-82-02.** 8 units. 40€–50€ double, 18€–20€ dormitory beds. Free parking. **Amenities:** Bike hire; games room; bar; free Wi-Fi.

Where to Eat

Casa Havanesa ★ PETISCOS Open since 1885, this place has been a cigar store (hence the name—"house of Havana"), grocery, drugstore, bookshop, and photographer's studio. It's always been a meeting place, part of the city's fabric in the heart of the Bairro Novo. Today, Casa Havanesa overflows with a jumble of books, wine crates, sardine cans, and artifacts that recall past days. You can pop in for coffee, a drink (their gin selection is legendary), *petiscos* (Portugal's answer to tapas), or a full meal, attend a book launch, or dance the night away. Food choices range from scrambled eggs with spiced sausage to dogfish stew or salt-cod hamburgers. There's a fine outdoor terrace overlooking a pedestrian street. Opening hours are flexible: Officially they don't open for lunch, but sometimes they just are.

Rua Cândido dos Reis 89. www.casahavanesa.com. ✆ **96/455-54-61.** Mains 15€–25€, *petiscos* from 1.95€. Sun–Thurs 6pm–1am; Fri–Sat 6pm–4am.

Marégrafo ★★ PORTUGUESE/SEAFOOD They actually do a range of steaks, but seafood is the main attraction of this simple and relaxed old house in the fishermen's district of Buarcos. The fish dishes vary depending on the catch, but can include fried anchovies, grilled tuna belly, and cod-tongue rice. You can also choose seafood *petiscos* from a vast selection that includes fried eels or roe salad. The interior is decorated with blue-and-white tiles, wine bottles, and vintage newspaper cuttings, but you may prefer to sit outside in a sunny square overlooking the Atlantic.

Largo Maria Jarra, 2. ✆ **23/343-31-50.** Mains 8€–15€. Wed–Mon noon–2am.

O Peleiro ★★ PORTUGUESE Perhaps because their restaurants are so dependent on the tourist trade, Figueira locals tend to be a bit sniffy about eateries in town. However, they flock to this place in the village of Paião, 10km (6¼ miles) south over the Mondego bridge. It's a classic rustic Portuguese place: terracotta floors, *azulejos* on the wall, dark-wood furnishings in a barnlike building that used to be a tannery—the leopard skin on the wall is a clue to its former use. Specialties include *sopa da pedra* (a rich soup of beans, smoked sausage, and vegetables), *cabrito assado* (roast kid), and *espetadas* (grilled skewers of meat or fish).

Largo Alvideiro 5, Paião. ✆ **23/394-01-59.** Mains 14€–23€. Mon–Sat noon–4pm and 7pm–midnight.

Shopping & Nightlife

The Mondego estuary south and east of Figueira is a strange, watery landscape made up of salt pans—shallow rectangular pools where the summer sun evaporates seawater, leaving behind pure, white **sea salt.** Bags of the stuff are sold around town in various grades that can make a taste-enhancing souvenir. The best is *flor de sal*, the first layer taken from the surface, great on salads. Others include salts flavored with herbs and spices. A number of stores in town sell it, including at the **Mercado Municipal,** Passeio Infante Dom Henrique, Figueira's handsome covered market where locals have been going to stock up on food since 1892. Recently renovated, it's a wonderful place to buy fresh fish or fruit and vegetables or to just soak up the bustling atmosphere. The market is open in summer daily from 7am to 7pm and in winter from Monday to Saturday, 7am to 4pm. Some of the salt producers also sell their products directly to visitors. Head out to the little salt museum **Núcleo Museológico do Sal,** Armazéns de Lavos, Salina Municipal do Corredor da Cobra (✆ **23/340-28-40;** summer Wed–Sun 10:30am–12:30pm, 2:30–6:30pm, in winter from Thurs–Sun, 10:30am–12:30pm, 2:30–4:30pm; 1€ adults, children and seniors free); or hike the salt pans walking route, where you might spot pink flamingos among the pyramids of fresh salt.

From the outside, **Casino Figueira,** Rua Dr. Calado 1 (www.casinofigueira.pt; ✆ **23/340-84-00;** free admission; daily 4pm–4am, 4pm–3am Sun–Thurs in winter) is a city-block-size cube of glass. Inside, the gilt-painted domed ceiling of its grand salon recalls a colorful history dating back to the 1880s. The casino is the focus of Figueira nightlife, featuring nightly shows, dancing, a nightclub, and gambling salons, and hosts regular big-name concerts. Games of chance include blackjack, roulette, poker, and slot machines. The live show begins at 11pm.

BUÇACO ★★

30km (29 miles) N of Coimbra; 230km (145 miles) N of Lisbon

The **Mata Nacional do Buçaco** is a magical place of tranquil beauty: a small range of hills covered with exotic forest planted by monks in the 17th century using seeds and saplings sent by far-flung missionary brothers. Amid the lush greenery is the **Bussaco Palace Hotel,** a fairytale fantasy built as a royal retreat in the dying days of the Portuguese monarchy, now an atmospheric hotel. The nearest town is the quaint spa center of **Luso,** which together with its nearby rival **Curia** provides an excellent opportunity to relax amid the hot springs and old-world atmosphere.

Essentials

ARRIVING

There are five **buses** a day from Coimbra to Buçaco on weekdays, two on Saturdays. One-way tickets cost 3.85€. **Trains** from Coimbra to Luso run three times a day and cost 2.65€. A taxi from Coimbra should cost around 30€, and from Luso around 5€. By car it takes about 40 minutes from Coimbra.

VISITOR INFORMATION

Luso Tourist Office is on Rua Emídio Navarro 136 (✆ **23/193-01-22;** summer 9:30am–1pm, 2:30–6pm; winter 9am–12:30pm, 2–5:30pm).

Exploring the Area

The Buçaco (you may also see it spelled Bussaco) hills have been a hideaway for hermits and monks since at least the 7th century. In 1628, the humble order of barefoot Carmelites embarked on their program of forestation around their isolated monastery. To native species they added eucalyptus, Chilean pine, Mexican cedars, monkey puzzle trees, and giant ferns. The natural beauty of the place earned such renown that the pope threatened to excommunicate anyone caught destroying trees.

There are trails through the **Mata Nacional ★★** (national forest), leading to panoramic viewpoints, ruined chapels, and springs bubbling with cool water.

The climb up to the 550m (1,804-ft.) high point at **Cruz Alta** is one of the best ways to savor Buçaco. Pass through the vegetation and hermitages and you are rewarded with a fabulous view from the summit.

Entry is free if you walk or bike up from Luso, although you will be charged 7€ for bringing a car into the park. A foundation runs the park and its office next to the hotel can provide information on trails and organized guided visits (www.fmb.pt; ✆ **23/193-70-00**). The toll gates on the road into the park are open 9am to 5pm.

Near the Palace Hotel (see below) are the remains of the **Santa Cruz do Buçaco** convent, which houses some intriguing religious paintings and venerated statues. There's also a **small military museum** (✆ **23/193-93-10;** Tues–Sun 10am–12:30pm and 2–5pm; admission 2€) recalling the events of 1810, when the peace of the forest was shaken by a major battle between

ART WITH wine

The **Aliança Underground Museum ★★** (www.bacalhoa.pt; ✆ **23/473-20-45**) is an extraordinary fusion of winery and art museum in the small town of **Sangalhos,** in the heart of the Bairrada wine region between Coimbra and Aveiro. In its cool, dark, subterranean caverns you file past great wooden barrels filled with ripening brandy or countless thousands of backlit bottles of maturing sparkling wine. In amongst them are wonderfully diverse collections of **African art,** ranging from 500-year-old Nigerian phalluses to contemporary works by Zimbabwe's leading sculptors. There are glistening Brazilian mineral samples, fossils dating back 20 million years, and a definitive selection of Portuguese ceramic art over the centuries. It's all the brainchild of self-made millionaire and art connoisseur **Joe Berardo,** whose magnificent modern art acquisitions form the heart of one of Lisbon's most sought-after museums (p. 110). Berardo invested in the venerable Aliança vineyards and used its vast cellars to showcase his collections. Visits are by guided tour only and can be booked on the website or by phone. Tours last 1 hour and 30 minutes, and run daily at 10am, 11:30am, 2:30pm, and 4pm. The price is 3€. Wine tastings are also available.

Many of the other wineries in the Bairrada region offer visits, where you can follow the production process, sample and buy wines, and sometimes enjoy a meal. **Quinta do Encontro ★**, Rua de São Lourencinho, São Lourenço do Bairro, Anadia (www.quintadoencontro.pt; ✆ **23/152-71-55**) is one of the most striking. Its curved wooden facade resembles a giant barrel emerging from the vine-covered fields. As well as tastings and tours, there is an excellent restaurant that serves modernized regional cuisine.

Anglo-Portuguese forces led by Duke of Wellington and a French army commanded by Marshal André Massena, one of Napoleon's most trusted generals. Wellington slept in the convent the night after his victory.

At the beginning of the 20th century, King Carlos I built a hunting lodge over the ruins of the convent. It's a palatial structure, now the **Bussaco Palace Hotel ★★★,** with twisted columns and towers topped by navigational spheres—an exuberant architectural tribute to the Age of Discoveries (in the style known as neo-Manueline). It's also heavily influenced by the medieval romanticism of Carlos's German grandfather, recalling the fairytale mountaintop castles of Bavaria. The king didn't have long to enjoy it. He was assassinated, along with his son, Crown Prince Filipe, in 1908. After the fall of the monarchy 2 years later, it was turned into a very special place to stay (see below). Even if you are not staying overnight, pop in for a peek at the amazing decor.

Just outside the walls of the forest park is the little spa town of **Luso ★.** Bottled water bearing the Luso brand is sold all over Portugal, and visitors come here to stroll the shady avenues, admire the turn-of-the-century villas, and fill up bottles from the springs.

For a more serious taking of the water, the spa center **Termas do Luso ★,** Rua Álvaro Castelões 9 (www.termasdoluso.com; ✆ **23/193-79-10;** July–Sept Sun–Fri 9am–1pm and 2–7pm; Sat 10am–1pm and 2–8pm; Oct–Jun Mon–Fri

10am–1pm, 2–6pm, Sat 10am–1pm, and 2–7pm) offers treatments from everything from skin conditions to kidney stones. You can go just for pampering, with the full range of massages, facials, and body treatments. A 2-hour detox wrap and massage costs 145€. There's a splendid 1930s hotel linked to the spa, with an Olympic-size pool (see below).

Down the hill, about 20 minutes' drive to the northwest, is a rival spa town, **Cúria ★**, which maintains a decidedly 1920s feel with its gardens, lakes, and grand old hotels. The lemon-and-white late-19th-century building of the **Termas da Cúria ★** spa center (www.termasdacuria.com; ✆ **23/151-98-00**) also offers a range of wellness and medicinal treatments.

Where to Stay

EXPENSIVE

Bussaco Palace Hotel ★★★ A national treasure, in 2017, the Bussaco palace celebrated 100 years since the former royal retreat was turned into one of the country's foremost hotels. It may be showing its age in places, and service and furnishing can be a tad creaky, but the shortfalls will be forgotten among the splendor of the architecture, decoration that includes splendid *azulejos*, paintings by some of Portugal's best 19th-century artists, colonnaded verandas, monumental staircases, a gloriously lit dining room, a regal bar and more. Outside there are formal gardens and pools where swans glide by, all surrounded by the tropical majesty of the Buçaco forest. For a really special occasion, try the royal suite decked out in a sumptuous Louis XVI style, complete with 1920s marble bathroom.

Mata do Buçaco. www.almeidahotels.pt. ✆ **23/193-79-70.** 64 units. 115€–195€ double; 243€–710€. Free parking. **Amenities:** Garden; terrace; restaurant; bar; babysitting; Wi-Fi free in public areas.

MODERATE

Cúria Palace ★★ There's a definite "Grand Budapest" air about this splendid palace, recently restored to its original 1920s glory. The Art Deco gem is under the same management as the Bussaco Palace (above) and it exudes glamour. You expect to see flappers dancing the Charleston here. Spacious rooms with a mix of understated modern and antique furnishings look out on swans gliding by on ornamental ponds and a swimming pool inspired by the Golden Age of ocean liners (alas, it needs freshening up). Everywhere, there's marble, wrought-iron work, and dark polished woodwork. A trip back to an age of elegance. There's a fine spa and a golf course nearby.

Avenida dos Plátanos, Cúria. www.almeidahotels.pt. ✆ **23/151-03-00.** 100 units. 68€–135€ double. Free parking. **Amenities:** Garden; terrace; bike hire; tennis; indoor and outdoor pools; spa; hammam; sauna; Jacuzzi; massage service; restaurant; bar; children's play area; babysitting; Wi-Fi free in public areas.

Grande Hotel de Luso ★★ Built in 1940, the Grande Hotel is a prime example of Portugal's take on the Art Deco style. Its lemon-yellow exterior makes a pretty counterpoint to the glistening blue of its Olympic-size outdoor pool, the green forest surrounds, and purple bougainvillea in the gardens.

There's also an indoor pool and a private tunnel, which means guests have an easy stroll to the next-door thermal center. While the lobby maintains a vintage air with its flowing Art Deco curves, the rooms have been modernized and decorated in a familiar beige-and-dove-gray contemporary style.

Rua Dr. José Cid de Oliveira. www.hoteluso.com. ✆ **23/193-79-37.** 132 units. 72€–132€ double. Free parking. **Amenities:** Garden; terrace; bike hire; tennis; squash; indoor & outdoor pools; spa; sauna; gym; restaurant; bar; free Wi-Fi.

INEXPENSIVE

Quinta de Lograssol ★ An alternative to all the grand old hotels, this boutique, family-run establishment opened in 2012 in a converted 19th-century farmhouse. It's 5km (3 miles) from Buçaco. There are six spacious rooms located in the pastel yellow main building and a modern extension. Simple decor makes the most of the house's original wood floors, ceilings, and other features. There's a shaded porch looking out over the gardens and pool. The cozy lounge decorated with family artifacts around an old-fashioned fireplace is a big favorite with guests.

Rua Joaquim Luís Alves de Melo, Lograssol. www.quintadelogressol.com. ✆ **23/193-91-45.** 6 units. 70€–90€ double, 110€–140€ suite. No credit cards. Free parking. **Amenities:** Garden; terrace; outdoor pool; Wi-Fi free in public areas.

Where to Eat

Mesa Real ★★ FRENCH/PORTUGUESE The restaurant of the Bussaco Palace Hotel was once a royal dining room, and it is a glorious setting for any meal. The Moorish-inspired ceiling glistens with countless small lights, ornate horseshoe-shaped windows look out on a romantic terrace and the forest beyond, and walls are lined with epic paintings by João Vaz, a 19th-century artist. The cooking is rooted in classic French and regional Portuguese cuisine. Notable dishes include salt cod slow-cooked in local olive oil with celery purée and sautéed cabbage, or venison in red wine with squash and cranberries. The wine cellar is legendary, with vintages dating back to the 1940s. This is a unique fine-dining experience.

Mata do Buçaco. www.almeidahotels.pt. ✆ **23/193-79-70.** Main courses 23€–30€. Daily 1–3pm and 8–10pm.

AVEIRO ★★

250km (160 miles) N of Lisbon; 80km (50 miles) S of Porto

Inevitably, Aveiro gets called the "**Venice of Portugal.**" The city is crisscrossed with canals, flowing between colorful, high-gabled houses and traversed by humpbacked bridges. Narrow boats called ***moliceiros*** glide along the waterways, their high bows brightly painted with images ranging from the religious to the risqué.

Although its roots are ancient, Aveiro boomed in the 19th and 20th centuries, thanks in part to its role in the cod trade. Its rich architectural heritage of **Belle Epoque** and **Art Nouveau buildings** bear witness to this prosperous age.

The center can easily be explored on foot (or from a tour in a *moliceiro*), but it's worth getting out of town to explore its vast and mysterious lagoon, the **Ria de Aveiro ★★**, now mostly a nature reserve; its fine beaches, particularly the resort suburb of **Costa Nova ★** with its distinctive candy-striped houses; and the historic **Vista Alegre ★** fine porcelain factory in Ílhavo.

Aveiro cuisine is centered on eels from the lagoon, the salt cod its ships once brought to its harbor from Norway and Greenland, and sweet eggy treats called *oves moles*.

Essentials

ARRIVING

BY TRAIN Fast Alfa Pendular trains run 10 times a day from Lisbon, making the trip in just over 2 hours. Tickets cost 27.10€. From Porto, the trip takes 30 minutes and costs 14.70€.

BY BUS **Rede Expressos** (www.rede-expressos.pt; ✆ **70/722-33-44**) runs between 6 and 14 buses a day from Lisbon to Aveiro. The trip takes 3 to 4 hours and costs 15.70€.

BY CAR The drive north from Lisbon takes about 2 hours and 30 minutes either along the A1 toll highway via Coimbra, or the more westerly route along the A8 and A17 highways, which tend to have less traffic.

VISITOR INFORMATION

The **Aveiro Tourist Office,** Rua João Mendonça 8 (✆ **23/442-07-60;** open summer Mon–Fri 9am to 7pm, weekends 9am–6pm; winter Mon–Fri 9am–6pm, weekends 9:30am–1pm and 2–5:30pm). The site www.turismoinaveiro.com also has lots of information on the city.

Exploring Aveiro

The best introduction to Aveiro is a ***moliceiro*** **boat tour ★★** along the canals. Looking a bit like mini-Viking long boats or pimped gondolas, the *moliceiros'* high, pointed bows and sterns are painted with colorful design themes, ranging from saints to soccer stars to lewd jokes. The boats were originally used to collect seaweed from the lagoon, which was used for fertilizer. Nowadays, they ferry tourists around town, past wharfs lined with brightly painted fishermen's cottages or Art Nouveau mansions covered in shining *azulejos*. You can book an excursion at the tourist office or online from a number of companies like **Viva a Ria** (www.vivaaria.com; ✆ **96/900-86-87**) or **Aveitour** (www.aveitour.com; ✆ **23/409-75-73**). Tours start from 10€ per person for trips of up to 40 minutes around the city; you also have the option of spending a whole day exploring the wide, watery spaces of the lagoon.

A short walk from the double bridge over the main canal is the **Museu de Aveiro ★★**, Avenida Santa Joana (✆ **23/442-32-97;** Tues–Sun 10am–12:30pm and 1:30–6pm; 4€, free for under 12s and over 65s), housed in a 15th-century convent. The museum centerpiece is the **Igreja de Jesus** church decorated with golden woodwork and blue *azulejos*, it's an exquisite example of the Portuguese baroque style. Amid it all is a masterpiece, the **tomb of St. Joana,** a Portuguese princess who retired to the convent in 1472. Her remains are housed in a grand confection of multicolored Italian marble. An enigmatic **portrait** of the rosy-cheeked young princess by an unknown 15th-century artist is one of Portugal's most cherished artworks.

Some of Aveiro's prettiest **Art Nouveau** buildings are around the canal-side **Rossio** gardens; one splendid sky-blue town house fronted with white-stone carvings of eagles and floral columns was recently converted into a little museum dedicated to the style. The **Museu Arte Nova ★**, Rua Barbosa de Magalhães, 9–11 (✆ **23/440-64-85;** Tues–Sun 10am–12:30pm and 1:30–6pm; admission 2€ adults, free for under 12s and over 65s, includes entry to another small museums on the city's history) also contains a charming period **teahouse** that makes a hip alternative to the more traditional cafes serving the artery-clogging local specialty: *oves moles.* It turns into a cocktail-fueled bar and cultural space in the evenings. The tearoom opens at 9:30am and stays open until 2am (3am on Fridays and Saturdays).

About 6km (4 miles) south of central Aveiro, the town of Ílhavo has a pair of worthwhile museums bearing witness to the area's industrial heritage. The **Museu Marítimo de Ílhavo ★★**, Avenida Dr. Rocha Madahíl (www.museumaritimo.cm-ilhavo.pt; ✆ **23/432-99-90;** Tues–Sat 10am–5:15pm, Sun 2–5:15pm; Admission 6€, 3€ youngsters 6–17 and over 65s) focuses on cod fishing. It gives an insight into the centrality of *bacalhau* to the Portuguese psyche and to the tough life of the fishermen who sailed out for months at a time to the coasts of Canada and Greenland, braving north Atlantic storms to bring back the salt fish that became a national stable. There's even an **aquarium** filled with live cod and a 1940s trawler that can be visited separately for an extra 2€.

Nearby is the factory settlement of **Vista Alegre ★★**, which has been producing fine porcelain for almost 200 years, gathering past and present European royalty among its fans. Britain's Elizabeth II has a personalized set of tableware. By the standards of the time, the early-19th-century Vista Alegre factory was known as an enlightened place, providing decent housing, a school, a chapel, and a theater for its workers. They can be visited today, along with the working factory, a **museum** tracing the history of the brand and a factory outlet shop to pick up a bargain souvenir. You can even attend a pottery or painting workshop to try your hand at producing some of the delicate porcelain, although you may struggle to match some of the top modern artists the factory now contracts to produce special pieces. The **Vista Alegre Museum** (www.vistaalegre.com; ✆ **23/432-06-00**), is open daily May to September 10am to 6:45pm; October to April 10am to 6:15pm. Admission 6€ adults; 3€ youngsters 6 to 17, over 65s, and students; free for under 6s.

OUTDOOR ACTIVITIES

The **Ria de Aveiro ★★** lagoon is one of Europe's largest coastal marshlands and a magnet for birdwatchers. A number of the companies organizing *moliceiro* boat tours in the city also offer longer trips into the lagoon. Half-day or full day tours by **Sentir Aveiro** (www.sentiraveiro.com; ✆ **91/008-59-37**) can include visits to boat builders and an eel cannery; from 45€. A new lagoon attraction is a chance to bathe in **salt pans,** which give a "Dead Sea"–like floating experience in the heavily salted water. Visitors can also enjoy the health benefits of a salt-infused mud bath (www.salinasaveiro.com; ✆ **23/405-61-49** or www.caledooiro.com; ✆ **91/566-14-80**). Daily 10am to 7pm.

Beyond the lagoon, there are some excellent beaches north and south of Aveiro. **Costa Nova ★** is a family spot best known for its beach shacks painted in bold stripes of white with red, blue, or yellow. Much wilder is **Praia de São Jacinto ★★** in a protected nature reserve; its dunes are beloved by seekers of seclusion, its waves favored by surfers. The **A Peixaria ★** restaurant (Rua Mestre Jorge Pestana; ✆ **23/433-11-65**) in the nearby lagoon town of São Jacinto is famed for fish, fried or grilled. Farther south, **Praia de Mira ★** is another surfers' favorite, where fishermen have only recently swapped oxen for tractors to haul their nets ashore.

Where to Stay

MODERATE

Hotel Moliceiro ★ Graced with a central location overlooking the canal-side Rossio gardens, the exterior is a cubist block partly covered with modern *azulejos*. Inside is more attractive. Superior and deluxe rooms enjoy views over the canal or lagoon, and individual designs that range from Chinese- or Moroccan-style exotica to bold black-and-white motifs inspired by Coco Chanel's Paris, to soft, summery mint-green pastel shades. The standard rooms are more modest but feature original artworks and a restrained modern design where dark-wood hues predominate. This is a sophisticated downtown choice.

Rua Barbosa de Magalhães. www.hotelmoliceiro.pt. ✆ **23/437-74-00.** 49 units. 114€–230€ double, 341€–445€ suite. **Amenities:** Bike hire; bar; free Wi-Fi.

Montebelo Vista Alegre Ílhavo Hotel ★★★ Opened in 2015, this is the first five-star hotel around the lagoon, a spectacular fusion of old and new that incorporates the palatial former home of the Vista Alegre factory owners and a low-rise modern block filled with white light. In the new wing, the rigorous modernism of the rooms is softened by whimsical touches that reflect the links with the porcelain manufacture: painted plates on the walls and cobalt-blue flowers painted on the sink in the state-of-the-art bathrooms. A sweeping spiral staircase leads to the palace wing, where the decor reflects its patrician heritage. The restaurant is first-class, focused on bacalhau dishes. There's a big outdoor pool and a fine spa center. The hotel looks out over the lagoon and offers tours and workshops to expand guests' understanding of Vista Alegre's world-renowned porcelain.

Lugar da Vista Alegre Ílhavo. www.montebelohotels.com. ✆ **23/424-16-30.** 95 units. 91€–172€ double, 131€–577€ suite. Free parking. **Amenities:** Garden; sun terrace; bike hire; indoor and outdoor pools; spa; sauna; hammam; Jacuzzi; fitness center; massage service; restaurant; bar; babysitting; free Wi-Fi.

Pousada Ria ★★ It's hard to get any closer to the immensity of the Aveiro lagoon than a stay here. Built in the 1960s, right on the shore, it can seem from the balcony rooms or the panoramic bar that the hotel is floating over the waters. The Pousada chain is a guarantee of quality, although sometimes things do need a little refreshing. The public rooms have a delightful retro feel, with many original features and furnishings. Sunny pastel colors in the rooms are enhanced by the natural light that floods in. This is a great location for exploring the lagoon or visiting the beaches. Downtown Aveiro is a 30-minute drive around the lagoon, but a ferry cuts the journey in half and is more fun. The lagoon-side pool is a plus.

Bico do Muranzel, Torreira-Murtosa. www.pousadas.pt. ✆ **23/486-01-80.** 24 units. 76€–169€ double. Free parking. **Amenities:** Garden; terrace; free bikes; private beach; outdoor pool; restaurant; bar; free Wi-Fi.

INEXPENSIVE

Hotel Aveiro Palace ★ With its rows of arches and monumental facade, this has been a landmark in the heart of the city since it opened in 1937. Recently extensively remodeled, it practically has the waters of the main canal lapping against its front door. The modernization work has left the rooms without any historical charm, but they are light and comfortable. Most have canal views, but the downside of its central location means nights can be noisy on the streets outside. There's a treat in the breakfast room, with walls covered with 1930s painted tiles uncovered during the restoration work. The collection of black-and-white photos also point to the hotel's status as part of the fabric of the city.

Rua de Viana do Castelo, 4. www.hotelaveiropalace.com. ✆ **23/442-18-85.** 48 units. 73€–108€ double,108€–156€ suite. Parking 8€ per day. **Amenities:** Bar; laundry; free Wi-Fi.

Where to Eat

Mercado do Peixe ★ SEAFOOD The fish can hardly be fresher at this restaurant on the second floor of Aveiro's covered market, where the catch of the day is shipped in for sale on the stalls downstairs. The dining area is a glass-fronted space incorporated into the iron frame of the 19th-century building. It looks out onto the canal and down into the market. The menu varies daily with the catch, but there's usually expertly grilled bass (*robalo*), brill (*rodovalho*), and a shoal of other creatures that were swimming in the Atlantic a couple of hours before landing on your plate. There's also the typical Aveiro selection of eel (*enguia*) and salt-cod (*bacalhau*) dishes, along with steaks for confirmed carnivores.

Largo da Praça do Peixe 1. www.restaurantemercadodopeixeaveiro.pt. ✆ **23/435-13-03.** Mains 12€–20€. Tues–Sat noon–3pm and 7:30–11pm; Sun noon–3pm.

O Telheiro ★ PORTUGUESE For more than 30 years this no-nonsense place has been serving excellent regional cuisine to crowds of appreciative locals and visitors. The layout is labyrinthine with a succession of noisy rooms filled with families tucking in. Specialties include *caldeirada de*

A WALK ON THE wild side

The **Passadiços do Paiva ★★** are a series of walkways winding for 8.7km (5.5 miles) through the wild, untouched hills of the **Paiva river valley**—a UNESCO-recognized geo-park. This is a bracing outdoor adventure. The paths run along wooden walkways that include steep climbs, plunging descents, and a narrow rope bridge stretched over a gorge. A hike back and forward along the full length of the walk is not for the faint-hearted, but it is possible to walk just a part of it or to catch one of the waiting taxis back to the start (about 15€). There are picnic spots along the route. You can start at either end. Setting out from the Areinho end means you get the hardest climb over early but ending there means you can cool off with a plunge from one of the **river beaches.** Tickets cost just 2€, but you need to book in advance: online (www.passadicosdopaiva.pt), by phone (✆ **25/694-02-58**), or at the tourism office at Rua Abel Botelho, 4, in **Arouca,** the nearest town to the walkways, an hour's drive northeast from Aveiro. (Open daily May–Sept 8am–8pm; Apr Mon–Fri 9am–6pm, Sat–Sun 9am–7pm; Oct–Mar 9am–5pm.)

enguias (eel stew), *polvo à lagareiro* (roast octopus), and *cabrito assado* (roast kid). They'll bring a vast selection of appetizers, which is good because when it's busy, the mains may take a while.

Largo da Praça do Peixe 20-21. ✆ **23/442-94-73.** Mains 7€–19€. Tues–Sun noon–3:30pm and 7:30–11:15pm.

Salpoente ★★ MODERN PORTUGUESE Behind the bright-red wooden boards of an old salt warehouse is this exciting restaurant, run by young chef Duarte Eira. His kitchen team builds on Aveiro's history as a center of the cod and salt trade with the aim of producing the best *bacalhau* in the world. Their "Discovery" menu of regional products starts with oysters and ends with *ovos moles,* passing by seafood soup; salt cod with clams and samphire; and Marinhoa beef.

Canal de São Roque, 82. www.salpoente.pt. ✆ **23/438-26-74.** Mains 18€–30€. Daily 12:30–3pm and 7:30–10:30pm.

VISEU ★★

290km (180 miles) NE of Lisbon, 128km (79 miles) SE of Porto

Handsome granite houses, cobbled streets, graceful churches, leafy public gardens, and a collection of some of the country's best Renaissance art make this provincial capital a great base for exploring the rugged highlands of the Beira Alta region.

Viseu is full of history. A cave nearby was the hideout of Viriato, legendary leader of the Lusitanian resistance to the Romans. It's also a lively place, perfect for sampling hearty highland cuisine and wines produced in the valleys of the Dão region to the east. The city is also renowned for handicrafts, most notably its distinctive black clay pottery.

Essentials

GETTING THERE

BY TRAIN Trains don't run to Viseu. The nearest station is **Nelas,** about 20km (15 miles) south. There are three direct trains from Lisbon. The journey lasts just over 3 hours, and second-class tickets cost 20.30€.

BY BUS is much easier. **Rede Expressos** has over 20 daily departures from Lisbon. The journey lasts 3 to 4 hours and costs 18.12€ (www.rede-expressos.pt).

BY CAR Take the A1 highway to Coimbra then the IP3 expressway, where some care should be taken as it twists through the hills. The drive takes around 3 hours.

VISITOR INFORMATION

The tourist office is at Rua Formosa 17 (www.visitviseu.pt; ✆ **23/242-74-27**). Daily 10am to 6pm.

Exploring Viseu

The place to start is **Adro da Sé,** one of the most harmonious squares in Portugal, where the severe bare-stone facade of this cathedral faces the airy white baroque front of the Igreja da Misericórdia.

The hilltop **Sé** ★, or Cathedral, at Largo da Sé (Mon–Sat 9am–noon and 2–6pm, Sun 9:30am–noon and 2–6pm; free admission, 2€ to visit the museum) dates back to the 12th century, but has been much modified over the centuries. The fabulous interior features just about every architectural style, from Romanesque columns to a splendid Manueline ceiling made of knotted stone ropes and a cloister that is one of the earliest Renaissance buildings in Portugal.

Between the Sé and the Misericórdia church is the **Museu Grão Vasco** ★★, Adro da Sé (www.museunacionalgraovasco.gov.pt; ✆ **23/242-20-49;** Tues 2–5:30pm and Wed–Sun 10am–5:30pm; admission 4€, free for children under 12), housed in the severe gray stone former bishop's palace. This houses one of Portugal's best art collections, showcasing the work of Vasco Fernandes, known as "Grão" (great) Vasco, who was born here in 1475 and became the country's finest Renaissance painter. His hometown museum has the most complete collection of his work, including the masterly *St. Peter Enthroned.* There's also an intriguing collection of sculpture from the 13th to the 18th centuries, with a stunning **Throne of Grace** from the 1300s. The rest of the collection ranges from 14-century religious regalia to Portuguese modern art.

A walk **through the old city** ★★ of Viseu reveals ancient walls, handsome mansions, and quirky traditional stores. Just south of the cathedral, **Praça Dom Duarte** is surrounded by fine stone houses and overlooked by the **Passeio dos Cônegos,** or cannons' walk, a covered passage along old defensive walls. **Rua Direita** and Rua Formosa are long pedestrian streets lined with shops and restaurants.

The narrow lanes of the old town eventually open up to the east to a broad tree-shaded plaza officially called **Praça da República** but known to the locals, who come to stroll or sit out at the sidewalk cafes, as Rossio. If you can't find that ideal Viseu souvenir amid the old town stores, take a short walk to the **Casa da Ribeira,** Largo Nossa Senhora da Conceição (✆ **23/242-74-28**), a restored water mill on the banks of the River Paiva which serves as an exhibition space and sales point for many of the region's best artisans.

Where to Stay

MODERATE

Pousada de Viseu ★★ This former hospital from 1842 is a lovely first-class hotel designed by architect Gonçalo Byrne. Rooms are furnished with sleek, contemporary pieces. Guests seeking more luxury can book one of the spacious suites with great views. The splendid neoclassical facade is topped by statues representing faith, hope, and charity. There's a spacious atrium bar, a huge swimming pool in the garden, and a soothing spa. The *pousada* also has a fine, first-rate restaurant specializing in local products, like tender veal from the nearby Lafões region.

Rua do Hospital. www.pousadas.pt. ✆ **23/245-73-20.** 84 units. 64€–126€ double, 125€–160€ suite. Free parking. **Amenities:** Garden; terrace; indoor and outdoor pools; spa; hammam; sauna; Jacuzzi; gym; massage service; restaurant; bar; games room; babysitting; free Wi-Fi.

INEXPENSIVE

Casa da Sé ★ This boutique option overlooks one of Viseu's most atmospheric squares, right beside the cathedral. The owners aim to blend 21st-century comfort with 18th-century charm. The building is filled with antiques and period furnishings. Rooms are named after historical Viseu characters and are individually decorated. There are guitars in the room bearing the name of renowned fado player Augusto Hilário and regal velvet drapes in the King Duarte suite. The bonus is that if you like the furnishings, you can take them home: Many of the antiques are for sale.

Rua Augusta Cruz, 12. www.site.casadase.net. ✆ **23/246-80-32.** 12 units. 76€–110€ double, 131€–145€. **Amenities:** Terrace, bar; gourmet store; free Wi-Fi.

Palácio dos Melos ★★ Nestled among the monuments of the old town, this former palace has been modernized into a boutique hotel full of charm and grace. It's built into the city walls, next to one of the ancient seven gateways that lead into the city's heart. Spacious, well-designed guest rooms are either in the main building or in a wing alongside. Those in the older building are more atmospheric, with warm navy or crimson fabrics. The esplanade makes a great spot for drinks with a view. Lack of parking can be a problem.

Rua Chão Mestre 4. www.montebelohotels.com. ✆ **23/243-92-90.** 27 units. 62€–100€ double. **Amenities:** Garden; terrace; restaurant; bar; free Wi-Fi.

Where to Eat

Muralha da Sé ★ PORTUGUESE There's an upmarket take on regional cooking in this noble house hewn from local stone in the cathedral square. The dining room is spacious and classically stylish with white linen table covers.

PORTUGAL'S mother ROAD

An original way of discovering Portugal's interior is to take a drive on Estrada Nacional 2 that snakes for 725km (450 miles) through the heartlands, from the Roman city of **Chaves** (p. 403), on the Spanish border in the north, down to the balmy southern beaches of the **Algarve coast.** The road cuts through rugged and little-visited scenery, passing the **Douro Valley** (p. 372) vineyards, wild highlands, pristine lakes and a string of historic towns, including **Viseu,** and photogenic villages. More and more Portuguese have been taking the iconic road trip since deadly 2017 bush fires led to a upswell of interest in the often-neglected interior. Taking the slow road allows you to linger in some of the fabulous accommodations along the way, such as the **Montebello Aguieira Lake Resort & Spa** (www.montebelohotels.com), where you can unwind by a forested waterside; the **Convento da Sertã** (www.conventodasertahotel.pt) a 17th-century convent turned boutique hotel that's a hub for hikers, bikers and kayakers; and **L'and Vinyards** (www.l-and.com), an ultramodern Alentejo winery complete with Michelin-starred restaurant.

Dishes are attractively presented on fine porcelain crockery. Grilled local veal, slow-cooked goat, and salt cod baked with olive oil and skin-on potatoes are among the specialties. On summer evenings, the outdoor terrace offers a romantic view of the cathedral. Prices are above average, but you can ask for a *meia-dose* (half-portion) that will satisfy most appetites.

Adro da Sé. www.muralhadase.pt. ✆ **23/243-77-77.** Mains 13€–20€. Wed–Sat & Mon noon–10pm, Sun noon–3pm.

O Cortiço ★★ PORTUGUESE Open since the 1960s, this is a place of pilgrimage for lovers of Portugal's traditional cooking. A plain stone house in the heart of the old town, with bare granite walls and rustic furnishing, it is uncompromisingly dedicated to preserving the cuisine of Viseu and its surrounding villages. Signature dishes include duck baked in rice and butter-fried octopus. A selection of smoked sausage and blood sausage fried up as an appetizer is most recommended. There's an excellent selection of local Dão wines. Game dishes are served in season.

Rua de Augusto Hilário, 45. www.corticogastronomiatradicional.pt. ✆ **23/241-61-27.** Mains 10€–26€. Tues–Sat noon–3pm and 7–10pm, Sun noon–3pm.

GUARDA ★

325km (200 miles) NE of Lisbon; 200km (125 miles) SE of Porto

Squatting on a hilltop guarding the main road into Portugal from northern Europe, Guarda is known as the city of five "f's." While everybody can agree with "fria" (cold), "forte" (strong), "farta" (well-fed), and "fiel" (loyal—thanks to its resistance to Spanish invaders), there is some dispute if the final adjective is "formosa" (beautiful) or "feia" (ugly). The answer is in the eye of

THE high mountains OF PORTUGAL

The **Serra da Estrella ★★★** is Portugal's highest, wildest, and most spectacular mountain range. Over 1,000 square kilometers (380 sq. miles), it is protected as a nature park filled with bald, rounded summits; crystalline lakes; craggy peaks; plunging waterfalls; and boulder-strewn plateaus. At just under 2,000m (6,600 ft.), the mountain of **Torre** is the highest point of mainland Portugal, although Pico in the Azores is higher. With its marvelous scenery and wealth of traditional culture, a trip to the high Serra can be an invigorating counterpoint to the beaches or historic cities.

The climate here can be bracing. In summer it can get hot, although at times visitors driving up from the heat of the lowlands are caught by icy winds on the summits. Spring provides a carpet of wildflowers, while turning leaves can make fall a delight. Winter snowfall can mean crowds heading for the modest ski slopes—the only ones in Portugal.

Heading up from Coimbra, the gateway to the park is the town of **Seia,** which has a visitor center providing a good introduction to the mountains and tips on hiking trails, the **Centro de Interpretação da Serra da Estrela,** Rua Visconde de Molelos (✆ **23/832-03-00**), and a quirky museum dedicated to bread production housed in traditional stone buildings. The **Museu do Pão** (www.museudopao.pt) complex also contains a shop selling local products, a cafe with great views, and a popular buffet restaurant serving local dishes. Heading up towards Torre, the road winds into **Sabugueiro,** a picturesque place of rough-hewn stone houses, that is Portugal's highest village. It's a good place to see the unique **Estrela mountain dog,** a gentle giant of a canine traditionally used to deter wolves from getting too close to the flocks of sheep kept on the high pastures. The puppies are irresistibly cute. Sabugueiro is also packed with stores selling mountain treats like bread baked in the communal oven, smoked ham, juniper firewater (*zimbro*), and most of all, the soft, creamy ***Queijo da Serra,*** the king of Portuguese cheeses, made from local ewes' milk. Local aficionados will tell you it's best when runny enough to be served with a spoon.

the beholder. Guarda today is surrounded by modern, high-rise suburbs, but its medieval core, clustered around the chunky **Gothic cathedral,** is certainly worth a visit.

Essentials

GETTING THERE

BY TRAIN There are four direct **trains** from Lisbon to Guarda with journey times of just over 4 hours, with more involving a change at Coimbra. One-way tickets start at 21.10€. The evening international train heading on to Madrid is more expensive.

BY BUS There are six daily **buses** run by Rede Expressos from Lisbon; journey times are about 4½ hours and the cost is 17.10€.

BY CAR The trip from Lisbon takes just over 3 hours along the A1 and A23 toll highways. Porto is 2 hours away on the A1 and A25. For travelers heading

Torre itself can be bit of a disappointment, with its crowded ski slopes in season and some bland souvenir shops, although the views are rewarding, and the white spheres of abandoned NATO radar posts add a surreal touch.

Down the slope heading north, **Manteigas** is the main town in the park and makes a fine base for visiting some of the Serra's best attractions, like the rocky, unspoiled peaks at **Penhas Douradas,** the wild beauty of the **Zêzere Glacial Valley,** or **Vale do Rossim,** where the lake has one of the best inland beaches in Portugal. Soft wool blankets and sweaters are sold all over the serra, but the **Burel Factory** (www.burelfactory.com; ✆ **92/654-20-95**) in Amieiros Verdes, Manteigas, has given the handicraft a modern take, making fashionable clothes, furnishings, and accessories from the wool as well as more traditional items.

Farther north, the serra is even less populated. Watch out for golden eagles, peregrine falcons, and other birds of prey enjoying the solitude. There is, however, a scattering of pretty villages, like **Linhares da Beira,** clustered around its castle. To the south are the bigger towns of **Covilhã** and **Fundão,** where in spring the hillsides are covered in pink cherry blossoms.

The mountains are dotted with some excellent hotels for a get-away-from-it-all stay. Among the best is **Casa das Penhas Douradas ★★** (www.casadaspenhas douradas.pt; ✆ **96/338-40-26;** doubles 123€–175€), which combines a remote highland location with cool 1950s furnishings, mountain views, a warming spa, and a roaring fire in the restaurant serving modern Portuguese cooking based on seasonal local products. Another sure choice is the **Pousada da Serra da Estrela ★★** (www.pousadas.pt; ✆ **21/040-76-60;** doubles 75€–150€), located 1,200m (4,000 ft.) up in an imposing former sanatorium, complete with spectacular views, spa, and restaurant serving a choice of traditional and contemporary cuisine. The five-star spa resort, **Aqua Village ★★** in Caldas de São Paulo (www.aquavillage.pt; ✆ **23/824-90-40;** rooms and apartments 94€-495€), brings an advanced level of pampering to the western slopes of the serra.

to Lisbon from Northern Europe on the E80 international road through Spain, Guarda will be the first Portuguese city they meet.

VISITOR INFORMATION

Guarda's **Welcome Center** is on Praça Luís de Camões (✆ **27/120-55-30;** Mon–Fri 9am–5:30pm; Sat–Sun 9am–1pm and 2–5pm) in the historic center and also sells local handicrafts and food products.

Exploring Guarda

Guarda has its detractors, but there is no doubt that the heart of this hilltop city founded in 1190 has a robust, if austere, charm. The high point of Portugal's highest city is the **Sé** (cathedral), Praça Luís de Camões (✆ **96/933-09-10;** open Apr–Oct 10am–1pm and 2–5:30pm; Nov–Mar 9:30am–10pm and 2–5pm; admission 1€, 2€ to visit roof terrace). The roof offers a viewpoint for looking down on the white-painted, red-roofed granite houses on the town and the surrounding rocky landscape. Built in bare local stone in 1390, its rugged,

VILLAGES OF THE beira interior

The rocky inland highlands of the Beira region are peppered with **historic small towns and villages ★★★**. Constructed with blocks of naked local stones, they often appear to grow organically out of the landscape. With their stark beauty, fascinating stories, and glimpses of unique rural lifestyles, the villages have a timeless attraction. Lately, the opening of several excellent hotels in restored buildings has given new life to remote areas and ensures travelers can visit in comfort. There's an excellent online guide to many of the villages at www.aldeiashistoricasdeportugal.com.

One of the most intriguing places is **Belmonte ★★**, where a Jewish community survived by pretending to be Catholic through the dark years of the Inquisition. It continued to practice in secret until the 1990s, when contacts with the Israeli embassy and Jewish community in Lisbon led them to come out. Today, there's a synagogue and a **Jewish Museum** (open Tues–Fri 9:30am–1pm and 2:30–6pm; 9am–12:30pm and 2–5:30pm in winter). The stone village sheltering beneath its medieval castle also holds special attraction for visitors from Brazil. Pedro Álvares Cabral, the first European to land there, was born in Belmonte in 1467. **The Pousada Convento de Belmonte ★★** (www.conventodebelmonte.pt; ✆ **27/591-03-00**) offers luxurious accommodations in a 16th-century convent overlooking the village, with award-winning cuisine produced by its Brazilian-born chef. Rates are 81€ to 150€ double.

Farther south, **Monsanto ★★** has been known since the 1930s as the "most Portuguese" village. It is a stunning location, with cobbled streets and houses fused with the boulders clinging to its hillside site. Climb the winding paths above it for stunning **views** of the sand-colored village and the endless plain stretching away toward Spain to the east. There are several cozy homestay options in the village; among the best are **Casa Tia Piedade** (www.casadatiapiedade.com; ✆ **96/691-05-99**) and **Taverna Lusitana** (www.tavernalusitana.com; ✆ **27/731-40-09**).

Arrive at dusk and the lights of **Piodão ★★**, glittering on the forested slope, look for all the world like a real, life-size Neapolitan crèche. Cut off from major routes, Piodão has a story linked to bandits and fugitives. Its cluster of homes is made from black-and-rust schist rock, their dark forms offset by the wedding-cake fantasy of the white painted parish church. Come in summer and there's a cooling pool built into the village stream, as well as Alpine-style, good value accommodations at the **Inatel Piodão** hotel (https://hoteis.inatel.pt; ✆ **23/573-01-00**) on the opposite slope.

Other wonderful Beira village locations include **Almeida ★★,** behind the mighty walls of its star-shaped fortress; **Idanha-a-Velha ★,** with roots dating back to Roman and Visigoth times; and **Sortelha ★,** which contains mysterious rock-carved tombs and a restaurant, **Dom Sancho** (✆ **27/138-82-67**), renowned for game, within its medieval battlements. **Castelo Branco ★** is not a village, but the often-overlooked capital of the Beira Baixa. It has as splendid renaissance gardens, fine restaurants and excellent **museum ★★** dedicated to both local embroidery traditions and modern artist Manuel Cargaleiro.

fortress-like outline is an appropriate symbol for this border city. The soaring interior combines Gothic and Manueline styles in a nave leading up to a magnificent altarpiece carved in limestone by the Renaissance master Jean de Rouen.

The cathedral opens onto the old town's central plaza, the triangular **Praça Luís de Camões,** which is surrounded by sturdy stone houses, some featuring arcades and balconies that show the Castilian influence on the local architecture. Within the old city walls is an atmospheric warren of narrow stone lanes winding between traditional stores, cafes, and restaurants.

One area of special interest is the **Judaria,** or Jewish quarter, a thriving area until Jews were forced to convert or flee in 1497. Some of the houses still bear crosses scratched into doorways as a sign of the inhabitants' (at least outward) conversion to Christianity. It's located behind the **Igreja São Vicente,** which together with the **Igreja de Misericórdia,** represents the best of baroque church architecture in the city.

More of the city's history is told in the **Museu da Guarda,** Rua General Alves Roçadas, 30 (www.museudaguarda.pt; ✆ **27/121-34-60;** Tues–Sun 9am–12:30pm and 4–5:30pm; admission 3€, 1.50 students and over 65s, free for under 12s). Housed in a 17th-century bishop's palace, its exhibits range from prehistoric archaeological finds to contemporary art.

Where to Stay

Hotel Santos ★ A clean, simple, low-cost option, this granite-hewn hotel is built into the medieval walls, next to the Torre dos Ferreiros defensive tower. The massive stone fortifications are a feature in the lobby. The rooms are dated, but comfortable; some on the upper floors offer a view over the rooftops to the cathedral, which is particularly atmospheric at night. There's a hearty breakfast.

Rua Tenente Valadim, 14. www.hotelsantos.pt. ✆ **27/120-54-00.** 25 units. 50€ double. Free parking nearby. **Amenities:** Terrace; bar; babysitting; free Wi-Fi.

Solar de Alarcão ★ In a city not overflowing with accommodations, this guesthouse, located in a noble stone mansion built in 1686, is the best old-town option. The location next to the cathedral is perfect, and the guesthouse has a covered arcade, patio, and magnolia-shaded garden. Inside there are period furnishings that tread a thin line between charmingly antique and old-fashioned kitsch, but the welcome is warm. It's not the place for travelers expecting "mod cons" and luxurious fittings, but parking is easy, there's a hearty fire in the hearth to keep out the winter cold, and a fine breakfast is served in the tearoom.

Rua Dom Miguel de Alarcão, 25. www.solardealarcao.pt. ✆ **96/232-71-77.** 13 units. 65€–85€ double. Free parking. **Amenities:** Garden; terrace; games room; bar; free Wi-Fi in public areas.

Where to Eat

Belo Horizonte ★★ PORTUGUESE Serving up muscular Beira Alta cuisine since 1963, this is an old-town institution—dark-wood furnishings, white linen table coverings, bare granite walls. Specialties include a creamy, garlicy salt-cod dish inspired by the Count of Guarda, and mixed grilled meats served with rice and beans. There's an excellent selection of local smoked sausages and Portuguese wines. In the hunting season through fall and winter, the rice with hare (*arroz de lebre*) and stewed boar (*guisado de javali*) attract fans from across the border in Spain.

Largo São Vicente 2. www.restaurantebelohorizonte.com. ✆ **27/121-14-54.** Mains 8.50€–18€. Tues–Sat noon–3pm & 7–10pm, Sun noon–3pm.

Restaurante DonGarfo ★ MODERN PORTUGUESE This island of fine dining is a surprise in a modern neighborhood down the hill from the old city. Chef Dona Olímpia has divided her menu between modern takes on regional dishes and her own creative inventions, which include dishes like salt-cod and shrimp "strudel"; and foie-gras with apple, chestnuts, and balsamic. The three dining rooms share a sophisticated modern design, with bold colors and outsize vintage photos of cute kids and Jazz Age lovers.

Rua Bairro 25 de Abril, 10. https://restaurante-dongarfo.business.site. ✆ **27/121-10-77.** Mains 12€–28€. Mon–Sat noon–11:30pm, Sun noon–10pm.

PORTO & THE DOURO

Roughly translated, Rio Douro means "river of gold." The name is appropriate—when the setting sun catches its waters, they glow with the color of burnished bullion. The name may also refer to the riches that the river's banks have brought to Portugal through the wine trade; in particular, the export of its legendary fortified ports.

13

From its source deep in the Spanish heartlands, the Douro winds westward 900km (560 miles) toward its meeting with Atlantic just beyond the city of Porto. For a while, it serves as the border between Spain and Portugal, carving a deep canyon through wild and remote country. For the 322km (200 miles) when it's exclusively Portuguese, the Douro Valley provides some of the country's most beautiful scenery. It contains three very different UNESCO World Heritage Sites: the historic but vibrant city of Porto, mysterious prehistoric artworks at Foz Côa, and vine-covered slopes that form what many view as the world's most-beautiful wine region.

PORTO ★★★

320km (200 miles) N of Lisbon; 566km (350 miles) W of Madrid, Spain

Porto is Portugal's second city, a major commercial center and capital of the industrious northern region. Its inhabitants like to repeat an old saying: "Braga prays, Coimbra sings, Lisbon has fun, and Porto works." Yet like other energetic second cities—from Manchester to Milan, Mumbai to Shanghai—Porto has developed a reputation for playing as hard as it works.

In recent years, the city has taken off as a center of the arts, fashion and nightlife. The expansion of its airport to take direct flights from North America and low-cost hops from dozens of European cities has opened it up to tourism. Atmospheric but rundown old neighborhoods have been getting facelifts. Swish accommodation options have sprung up across the city, while its hip restaurants and bars rival those in the capital. Modern architectural landmarks and cultural hubs like Rem Koolhaas' Casa da Música, the Serralves art center designed by hometown boy Álvaro Siza Vieira or the Leixões Cruise Terminal are internationally renowned.

The rapid growth of tourism, and in particular the spread of vacation apartment rentals which now occupy up to half the housing in some historic parts of the city, have some worried. But Porto manages to keep its timeless charm. The windows overlooking narrow streets of the riverside Ribeira district are still hung with washing out to dry; restaurants serve gargantuan plates of beans and tripe; and across the river, in the wine lodges of Vila Nova de Gaia, countless oak barrels still hold their hoard of silently maturing port wine.

Essentials

ARRIVING

BY PLANE Portugal's **TAP** (www.flytap.com) airline runs direct daily flights from Newark Airport to Porto's **Aeroporto Francisco de Sá Carneiro.** Canada's **Air Transat** (www.airtransat.com) also runs six weekly flights from Toronto, plus additional seasonal flights from Montreal. In high season, there are more flights from Toronto with Air Canada Rouge and from Newark with United.

Porto has direct flights from Brazil, Africa and the Middle East, and is connected to dozens of European destinations, from Alicante to Wroclaw, mostly by low-cost airlines. Ireland's **Ryanair** (www.ryanair.com) offers the most choice. TAP offers a hassle-free hourly shuttle between Lisbon and Porto between 6am and 11:20pm. Tickets can cost as little as 30€ each way for the 55-minute flight.

It's easy to get from the airport into town. The clean, efficient subway system, the **Metro,** covers the 11km (7 miles) to the Bolhão station in the center in less than 30 minutes. Take the E line with the violet color code. You can buy an Andante ticket (see below) from machines at the airport. A one-way ticket is 2€. Buses 601, 602, or the 3M night bus run from the arrivals lounge into town. You can buy tickets on board. It costs the same as the metro but takes longer. Taxis normally cost 25€ to 30€ from the airport to the city center. Several ride hailing services operate in Porto, including Uber, Bolt, Kapten, and Cabify.

BY TRAIN Coming from Lisbon, the train is a quick, comfortable alternative to flying. The journey on the fastest **Alfa Pendular** express trains takes 2 hours and 35 minutes from Lisbon's Oriente station to Porto's **Campanhã** station, and costs 31.20€ for a second-class one-way ticket. If you choose to take the 4-minute shuttle train from Campanhã into the more central **São Bento** station, the price is included in the ticket. You can also take the metro from Campanhã. The **CP** railway company (www.cp.pt; ✆ **70/721-02-20**) runs a dozen Alfa Pendular trains daily from Lisbon to Porto, stopping at Coimbra and Aveiro. There are also slower Intercity (IC) trains.

BY BUS The **Rede Expressos** bus company (www.rede-expressos.pt; ✆ **70/722-33-44**) runs trips from Lisbon to Porto at least once an hour between 6am and midnight. The trip takes around 3½ hours and costs 19€ one-way. The **bus station** is central, at Rua Alexandre Herculano, 366. If you're coming from outside Portugal, the **Eurolines** (www.eurolines.eu) bus

Porto

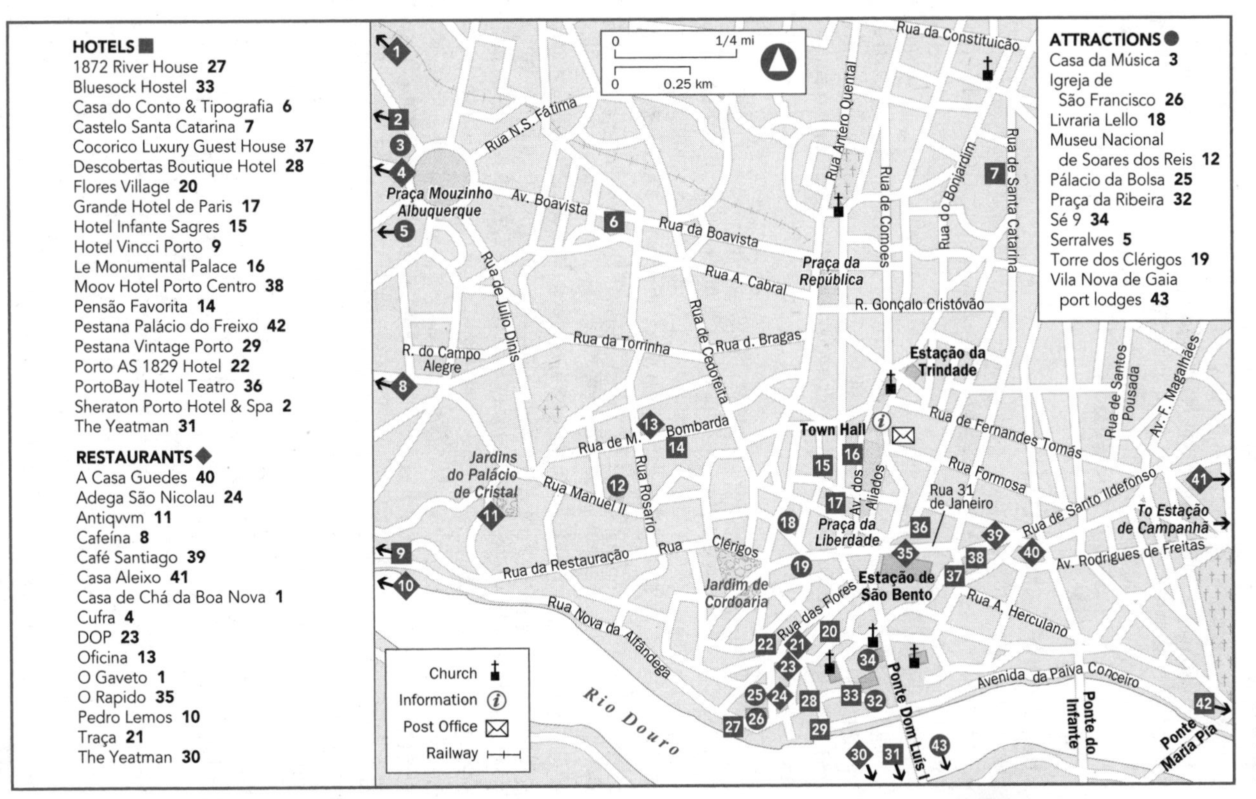
HOTELS
1872 River House 27
Bluesock Hostel 33
Casa do Conto & Tipografia 6
Castelo Santa Catarina 7
Cocorico Luxury Guest House 37
Descobertas Boutique Hotel 28
Flores Village 20
Grande Hotel de Paris 17
Hotel Infante Sagres 15
Hotel Vincci Porto 9
Le Monumental Palace 16
Moov Hotel Porto Centro 38
Pensão Favorita 14
Pestana Palácio do Freixo 42
Pestana Vintage Porto 29
Porto AS 1829 Hotel 22
PortoBay Hotel Teatro 36
Sheraton Porto Hotel & Spa 2
The Yeatman 31
RESTAURANTS
A Casa Guedes 40
Adega São Nicolau 24
Antiqvvm 11
Cafeína 8
Café Santiago 39
Casa Aleixo 41
Casa de Chá da Boa Nova 1
Cufra 4
DOP 23
Oficina 13
O Gaveto 1
O Rapido 35
Pedro Lemos 10
Traça 21
The Yeatman 30
ATTRACTIONS
Casa da Música 3
Igreja de São Francisco 26
Livraria Lello 18
Museu Nacional de Soares dos Reis 12
Pálacio da Bolsa 25
Praça da Ribeira 32
Sé 9 34
Serralves 5
Torre dos Clérigos 19
Vila Nova de Gaia port lodges 43
0 1/4 mi
0 0.25 km
Church
Information
Post Office
Railway
Rua da Constituicão
Rua N.S. Fátima
Praça Mouzinho Albuquerque
Av. Boavista
Rua da Boavista
Rua Antero Quental
Rua de Comoes
Rua do Bonjardim
Rua de Santa Catarina
Praça da República
Rua A. Cabral
R. Gonçalo Cristóvão
Rua de Julio Dinis
R. do Campo Alegre
Rua da Torrinha
Rua de Cedofeita
Rua d. Bragas
Estação da Trindade
Rua de Santos Pousada
Av. F. Magalhães
Rua de M. Bombarda
Town Hall
Rua de Fernandes Tomás
Jardins do Palácio de Cristal
Rua Manuel II
Rua Rosario
Av. dos Aliados
Rua Formosa
Rua 31 de Janeiro
Praça da Liberdade
Rua de Santo Ildefonso
To Estação de Campanhã
Rua da Restauração
Rua Clérigos
Jardim de Cordoaria
Estação de São Bento
Av. Rodrigues de Freitas
Rua A. Herculano
Rua das Flores
Rua Nova da Alfândega
Rio Douro
Avenida da Paiva Conceiro
Ponte Dom Luís I
Ponte do Infante
Ponte Maria Pia

company operates routes to Porto from several destinations. From Paris the trip takes just over 20 hours and costs around 74€.

BY CAR The trip up the A1 toll highway from Lisbon takes around 3 hours. If you are driving from elsewhere in Europe, it is just over 7 hours from the Spanish-French border crossing at Irun. Take the E80/AP-1 highway to Burgos, then the A-231 to León. From there, turn south on the A-66 to Benavente, then west on A-52 to Verín, before crossing into Portugal at Chaves and driving into Porto on the A27 and A7.

VISITOR INFORMATION

The main **tourist office** is close to city hall in Rua Clube dos Fenianos 25 (✆ **30/050-19-20;** open Aug 9am–9pm; May–July and Sept–Oct 9am–8pm; Nov–Apr 9am–7pm). There are smaller tourist offices and stands near the cathedral, in the Ribeira neighborhood, the airport, and Campanhã station. The tourist board runs a good website with information in English: **www.visitporto.travel**. Other useful sites include that of the northern region tourist board: **www.visitportoandnorth.travel**; and **www.introducingporto.com**.

Getting Around

Porto's historic center is compact, and **walking** around the winding alleys of Ribeira or bustling thoroughfares of the Baixa is one on the city's great pleasures. Be warned, however, that the steepness of the streets leading up from the riverside can be hard on the calves. An alternative is the **Guindais funicular,** dating back to 1891, which hauls passengers from Ribeira to the uptown Batalha district in 2 minutes, offering great views of the Dom Luís I bridge along the way. It runs daily from 8am to 8pm, later during the summer and at weekends. Tickets can be bought on-site for 2.50€. Offering even better views is the **Teleférico de Gaia** (www.gaiacablecar.com; ✆ **22/374-14-40**), a cable car linking the port wine lodges of Vila Nova de Gaia to the clifftop upper deck of the Dom Luís I bridge. Opened in 2011, it's become a major attraction in its own right (as well as a way to save on shoe leather). It runs from 10am to 6pm, although that's extended to 8pm from late April to late September. One-way tickets are 6€ adults, half-price for children.

For traveling farther afield, Porto's subway system, the **Metro,** is quick, clean, and efficient. There are five lines designated by letter and color. For example, line E is the purple line, running from the airport to the Estádio do Dragão, soccer stadium, home of two-time European champion FC Porto. As well as serving the city center, lines run up the coast to the seaport of Matosinhos and as far as the beaches at Vila do Conde and Póvoa de Varzim. To get the most from a short stay, buy an **Andante Tour** ticket, which allows unlimited travel on all metro lines, city buses, and suburban trains. A 24-hour ticket costs 7€, 72 hours costs 15€. Alternatively, you can buy an **Andante Azul** ticket, which costs 60 cents, but then needs to be charged up with the number of rides you want to make. The zoning system controlling the prices is rather complicated. You can buy a Z2 version limited to the city center where each trip costs 1.25€, but if you charge 10 to your ticket, you get one free. Tickets with a wider range, such as the Z4, include the airport for 2€ a trip. The metro operates from 6am to 1am. You can buy the tickets at machines in metro stations, at the airport and at selected locations around town.

Whatever type of ticket you buy, you'll need to validate it each time you travel by swiping it against one of the electronic machines on the way to the platforms. For more information, **Metro de Porto** has a well-explained English-language website: www.metrodoporto.pt.

Andante tickets are valid on the extensive **bus** network. You can also buy individual tickets on buses for 2€. Porto's buses offer free onboard Wi-Fi. There are also three **historic streetcar** (*eléctrico*) lines. Line 1 runs along the north bank of the Douro from Praça São Francisco, in the heart of the old city, to the Passeio Alegre in the seaside suburb of Foz; Line 18 runs from the riverside **Museu do Carro Eléctrico** to the *azulejo*-covered Carmo church; and Line 22 takes a circular route around the city center, connecting with the funicular stop in Batalha. Tickets can be bought from the streetcar drivers for 3€. The **STCP** bus company has an English website on www.stcp.pt.

Another transport option is to buy a **Porto Card** from one of the city tourist offices or online (www.visitporto.travel). It offers free access to six museums and discounts on many of others, plus restaurants, wine cellars, stores, and more. You can get one with free public transport included, or a pedestrian version. Those with free transport range from 13€ for 24 hours to 33€ for 4 days.

Taxis are available 24 hours a day; they are plentiful and relatively cheap. It's usually easy to hail one on the street or from stands around the city. You can also phone or book online from centrals such as **Táxis Invicta** (www.taxisinvicta.com; ✆ **22/507-64-00**) or **Radiotáxis** (www.radiotaxis.pt; ✆ **22/507-39-00**). The around 5km (3-mile) trip from Campanhã station to Praça da Batalha should cost less than 6€. Despite early resistance from cab drivers, app-based **ride hailing operators** including **Uber**, **Bolt**, **Kapten,** and **Cabify** are available in the city.

Electric **tuk tuks,** a Southeast Asian import, have taken off in the narrow streets of Portuguese cities. They can be hired in the street or through companies such as **Tuktour Porto** (www.tuktourporto.com; ✆ **91/509-44-43**), which offers several tour options. They are a fun but pricey way to get around.

With its steep hills and cobbled streets, Porto is challenging for **cyclists.** But there are a number of bike paths, notably the 5km (3-mile) ride along the river and Atlantic coast at Foz. There are several companies where you can rent bikes and get info on routes, such as **Porto Rent a Bike** (www.portorentabike.com; ✆ **22/202-23-75**), whose prices start at 6€ for 2 hours.

City Layout

The best place to grasp the lay of the land in Porto is from the **Miradouro do Mosteiro da Serra do Pilar** on the south bank of the **River Douro.** The broad, clifftop terrace gives a panoramic view over the city. Technically it isn't in Porto. This side of the river is **Vila Nova de Gaia,** a separate city, but effectively a suburb of Porto. To the west, you see the overlapping jumble of red-tiled roofs over the **port wine lodges** that are Gaia's main attraction.

The way back to Porto proper lies across the vertigo-inducing upper span of **Dom Luís I bridge.** Below is the tightly packed **Ribeira** district, Porto's most characteristic neighborhood. Behind the colorful facades of riverside merchant houses is a maze of narrow streets where kids kick soccer balls while their grandmas string out the washing from window to window on the upper floors, although the booming vacation rental business has squeezed out many locals. Beyond Ribeira, other medieval neighborhoods cling to hillsides rising up from the river, like **Sé, Miragaia, Barredo,** and **São Nicolau,** where among the tangle of lanes you'll find hip bars, timeless old stores, and churches filled with gold-covered wood carvings.

At the top of the hill is Porto's commercial center, oddly called the **Baixa,** which means "low." The main drag is **Avenida dos Aliados,** a stately avenue laid out in 1916, lined with grandiose hotels and banks and topped by the imposing **City Hall.** The area's main shopping street is the pedestrianized **Rua de Santa Catarina.** The whole area is a dynamic mix of wonderful old cafes, historic shops, and trendy new boutiques. Landmarks include the soaring baroque tower of the **Clérigos** church, the tile-covered **São Bento** railway station, and the **Bolhão** covered market, expected to reopen in 2021 after a 22€-million makeover (until the work is finished, there's considerable disruption in this part of the city).

Outside the center, the posh western district of **Boavista** has leafy boulevards, modernist villas, spacious parks, and two top cultural attractions: the **Serralves** art center and the **Casa da Música** concert hall, both icons of modern architecture. Beyond Boavista is the seaside suburb of **Foz,** boasting some of Portugal's best urban beaches. Up the coast, **Matosinhos** and **Leça da Palmeira** are no-nonsense seaports, renowned for their fish restaurants. At the northern end of the Porto metro system are the coastal towns of **Vila do Conde** and **Póvoa de Varzim,** where historic centers lay beside fine sandy beaches.

[FastFACTS] PORTO

ATMS/Banks Approximately 2,000 ATMs are scattered around the Porto metropolitan area; most offer multilingual services. There's a concentration of banks around the Avenida dos Aliados in the Baixa area and the Rotunda da Boavista to the west. Banks are open usually open from 8:30am to 3:30pm, although smaller branches may shut down for lunch. There are currency-exchange counters in Porto airport, but you'll generally get a better rate at an ATM (there are also several ATMs at the airport).

Consulates Neither the United States, UK, nor Canada maintains consulates in Porto. In emergencies, contact the embassies in Lisbon (see "Fast Facts" in chapter 16). Several countries, from Brazil to Sweden, do maintain full or honorary consulates in the city; a full list with contacts can be found on the website of the tourism board: www.visitporto.travel.

Drugstores Pharmacies are normally open Monday to Friday 9am to 7pm, and

Saturdays 9am to 1pm. However, they take turns staying open later and on Sundays, serving as *farmácias de serviço*. They will be listed on a notice posted in the windows of all pharmacies and on the website: www.farmaciasdeservico.net, which is in Portuguese only, but quite straightforward since you only have to click on the name of towns and districts to get a list. There's a limited number of pharmacies open 24/7, including **Farmácia Barreiros,** Rua Serpa Pinto, 12 (www.farmaciabarreiros.com; ✆ **22/834-91-50**), and **Farmácia Avenida,** Rua Primeiro de Janeiro, 20, close to the big hotels in Boavista (www.farmacia-avenida.com; ✆ **22/600-88-88**).

Emergencies Use the **112** European emergency number for police, firefighters, and ambulances. Porto's **Tourism Police,** with English-speaking officers, are based next to the tourist office at Rua Clube dos Fenianos 11 (✆ **22/208-18-33**), open daily 8am to midnight. The regular police, known as the **PSP,** are based at Largo 1 de Dezembro (✆ **22/209-20-00**).

Hospital The two major state health service hospitals are **Hospital de Santo António,** Largo Prof. Abel Salazar (✆ **22/207-75-00**), in the city center, and **Centro Hospitalar de São João**, north of downtown in Alameda Prof. Hernâni Monteiro (✆ **22/551-21-00**). Although both have English-speaking staff, there are a number of private hospitals that are better prepared for handling international patients, including **CUF Porto,** Estrada da Circunvalação, 14341, toward Foz (www.saudecuf.pt; ✆ **22/003-90-00**), and **Lusíadas Porto,** Avenida da Boavista 171 (www.lusiadas.pt; ✆ **22/605-64-50**). The **Prelada** clinic, Rua João Andresen 76 (www.dentista.com.pt; ✆ **22/832-80-31**) offers 24-hour emergency dental treatment and has an English-speaking staff.

Internet Access Porto is a wired-up city. You'll get free Wi-Fi in most hotels, on buses and taxis, at free hotspots around the city in places like the Casa da Música or public libraries, and in many restaurants and cafes.

Post Office The postal company is called **CTT.** Its most central office is at Rua Entreparedes near Praça Batalha (open Mon–Fri 9am–6pm). There is a post office at the airport (open Mon–Fri 8:30am–9pm, weekends 9am–12:30pm and 2–5pm).

Safety Porto is generally a safe city. Violent crime against strangers is rare. However, pickpocketing is a problem, particularly in crowded tourist areas and on public transport, so keep an eye on your wallets, cameras, and purses.

Exploring the City

RIBEIRA

Igreja de São Francisco ★★★ CHURCH From the outside, this church, built between 1383 and 1410, looks like a rather plain and ungainly appendix to the adjoining Stock Exchange. Inside, it's astonishing, like a cave lined with gold. That's because the baroque woodwork, installed in the 17th and 18th centuries, is dripping with some 100kg to 600kg (220 to 1,300 lb.) of the stuff, which is used to gild cherubs, rose garlands, fruit cornucopia, and frenzied animals. Soaring overhead are wide-ribbed marble arches that seem to fade and blend mysteriously with the gray granite columns and floors. The church is considered the high point of ***talha dourada,*** Portugal's unique style of wood carvings gilded by the product of an 18th-century Brazilian gold rush. Amongst it all is the towering **Tree of Jesse,** an impossibly ornate carving purporting to show Christ's descent from the kings of Judah. In complete

PERUSING the port

Port is one of the world's great wines. But unlike Burgundy, Bordeaux or Chianti, it isn't a table wine meant to be quaffed over a meal. Port is made by fortifying regular wine (mostly red, sometimes white) with *aguardente*, or brandy. The result is a warm, silkily intense sweet wine. Traditionally, ports are taken after dinner with cheese, chocolatey desserts, or a good cigar.

The variety of port types can be confusing; they range from cheap and cheerful whites often used as mixers to wonderfully complex vintages that can be stored for generations and cost a fortune.

TYPES

Dry whites are the lightest ports, made with white grapes. They are usually served as an aperitif—great with toasted almonds or smoked ham—and are also used to make cocktails. They are popular in Portugal as a summer refresher mixed with tonic, on ice with a slice of lemon.

Beside the grape types, it's the aging process that makes the different styles of port. They break down into those aged in wooden barrels and those that age mostly in the bottle. **Ruby** is the entry-level of red ports. As the name indicates, it has a gemlike reddish hue, fruity flavor, and is usually drunk young, after just a couple of years of barrel aging. Ruby goes well with blue cheese and red-fruit desserts.

Tawny ports are darker, richer blends. Kept longer under oak, sometimes for decades, they develop the sticky sweetness of dried figs or dates. They are great with caramelized fruits, chocolate or mature hard cheeses. **Colheitas** are tawny ports made from grapes harvested in a single year and matured at least 7 years in the barrel.

Vintage ports are the top of the range. They are only made in particularly good years and spend just 2 years in the barrel before being left to age for at least 10 years in their bottles. The best are left for several decades, even centuries, and can cost thousands of dollars. They are sipped on their own like a fine cognac, or sublime with dark chocolate or Stilton cheese. **Single quinta vintages** are produced with grapes from a single estate, or *quinta*, rather than the traditional blending of several made in the port lodges by the riverside in Vila Nova de Gaia. **Late-bottled vintage,** or LBV, is a style developed since the 1970s. It uses grapes from a single exceptional year's harvest like a vintage, but the wine is kept in barrels longer, for 4 or 5 years, and is usually ready to drink rather than be kept in the bottle. Unlike true vintages, LBV can also be poured straight from the bottle, rather than needing to be decanted to remove the natural sediment and allow the wine to "breathe."

HISTORY

Legend has it that port wine took off due to a 17th-century war between England and France. Cut off from their traditional supplies of claret, the Brits increased imports from Portugal and found that adding small amounts of brandy helped the wines weather the long sea journey from Porto. From there, the technique of fortifying the wine developed, leading to port's special character. Rules over where and how true port wine should be produced were first laid down in 1757 by the Marquis of Pombal, the statesman who oversaw the rebuilding of Lisbon after the great earthquake of 1755. The historic role played by the British producing and shipping port is still reflected in leading names today, like Croft, Cockburn's, and Taylor's, although shippers from Germany and the Low Countries also took up the trade.

TASTING

The best way to plunge into the flavors and history of port is to visit one of the **historic port lodges ★★★** on the south bank of the Douro, in **Vila Nova de Gaia.** Over a dozen of these old red-tiled warehouses spread back from the quayside, offering tours and tastings. They also keep a few of the narrow, flat-bottomed sailing boats known as ***barcos rabelos,*** moored in the river, although they are no longer used to ship barrels of wine down from the vineyards of the upper Douro.

Among the best port lodge experiences, **Graham's** 1890 lodge up the hill in Rua Rei Ramiro (www.grahams-port.com; ✆ **22/377-64-92**) holds over 2,000 *pipas* (oak casks) within its cool granite caves. Its tasting rooms and award-winning restaurant offer wonderful views over the Douro and the river beyond. The basic tour and a tasting of three wines starts at 17€, but there are significantly more expensive options where you can sip rare vintages in the clublike private tasting room. Visits only with advance booking (open Apr–Oct 9:30am–5:30pm; Nov–Mar 9:30–4:45pm).

A visit to the **Caves Ferreira,** Av. Ramos Pinto, 70 (https://winetourism.sogrape.com; ✆ **22/374-61-06**) is a chance to discover a Portuguese-run port house dating back to 1751. As well as the cellars and tasting rooms, there's a museum behind the whitewashed walls of the warehouses. It's dominated by the story of **Dona Antónia Ferreira,** a legendary figure who battled to preserve the quality of the wines at a time when the region was hit by an attack of the vine-destroying phylloxera blight. Among the vintage bottles stored here are some from 1815. Tastings are held under a splendid wooden ceiling in the lodge shop, or the tile-decorated *sala dos azulejos.* Tours start from 13€, with a tasting of two wines.

Not a port lodge, but one of the most enjoyable places along the quay to try port is the **Espaço Porto Cruz,** Largo Miguel Bombarda, 23 (www.myportocruz.com; ✆ **22/092-53-40**) an exhibition, multimedia, and leisure space from the French-owned Cruz label. Occupying an 18th-century riverside building, it's a flashy combination of old and new, with neon mixing with *azulejos* to brighten up the nighttime facade. Inside there are art shows, films, and digital displays tracing the story of port; a tasting room; restaurant run by star chef Miguel Castro e Silva; and a rooftop bar ideal for sipping cocktails while gazing over the river at the twinkling lights of Porto on the far bank. Tasting options include port pairings with cheese or chocolate, and prices range from 9.50€ to 55€ depending on the number and quality of the wines you sip on. (The wine shop is open from Tues–Sun 11am–7pm.)

Be aware that while most of the port lodges have shops where you can buy the wines you've tried, the prices are not necessarily cheaper than in stores in town.

contrast are the spooky **catacombs** below, which contain sober, barrel-arched cellars lined with family burial vaults and a mass grave filled with thousands of skeletons into which you can peer, if you dare.

Rua do Infante Dom Henrique. ✆ **22/206-21-25.** Church and museum 7€. Daily Nov–Feb 9am–7:30pm; Mar–June and Oct 9am–7pm; Jul–Sept 9am–8pm. Metro: São Bento.

Palácio da Bolsa ★★ MONUMENT In the mid-19th century, Porto business leaders decided to build a stock exchange so ornate it would earn the instant credibility of investors throughout Europe. This grand building is the result. Although the long neoclassical facade may look a little dull, the interior is an extravaganza of marble, crystal, and tropical woodwork. The grand chambers and reception rooms borrow decorative elements from ancient Rome, Renaissance Italy and the court of Versailles. The most extraordinary of its architectural artifices is the **Salão Árabe ★★★** (Arabian salon), a glittering, gold-covered Moorish confection that looks like a Hollywood set for *One Thousand and One Nights*. Oval in shape, it is adorned with arabesques, carved woodwork and stained-glass windows, all evocative of the Alhambra in Grenada. It's used for formal civic events and the occasional free classical music concert—catch one if you can. Other highlights include the domed **Hall of Nations,** which once housed the trading floor, and a clubby, upmarket restaurant called O Comercial.

Rua Ferreira Borges. www.palaciodabolsa.pt. ✆ **22/339-90-90.** Admission by guided tour only. Tour lasts around 45 min. and is available in English. 10€ adults, 6.50€ students and seniors, free for children under 12. Daily Nov–Mar 9am–12:30pm and 2–5:30pm; Apr–Oct 9am–6:30pm. Metro: São Bento.

Praça da Ribeira ★★ PLAZA Porto's riverside district opens out onto the Douro here, looking across to the wine lodges of Gaia and the curving double-decker ironwork of the Dom Luis I bridge. To the east, the lanes of the Ribeira neighborhood run behind the row of narrow-fronted medieval town houses. To the west are gray stone arches of grander buildings constructed during an 18th-century remodeling. Everywhere, the facades are enlivened with yellow, red, and white paintwork or blue *azulejos*. The northern side is occupied by a three-story-high fountain built in the 1780s. Today, the square is filled with cafe terraces and is a hub of Porto's tourism, but it's not hard to imagine the noisy fish trading and bustling quayside commerce that for centuries took place here.

Metro: São Bento.

Sé ★★ CHURCH Porto's cathedral dates to the 12th century, and much of its form is in the original Romanesque style of the early Middle Ages. Fronted by two towers and a rose window, its squat outline in pale gray stone cuts a brooding figure on the city skyline. Inside there is a purity in its curved barrel-arched nave. Many of the chapels have baroque additions, notably the altarpiece fashioned entirely of silver in the **Chapel of the Holy Sacrament** (the work is so elaborate that the whole piece gives the illusion of constant movement). King João I married the English princess Philippa of Lancaster here in 1387, sealing the world's oldest diplomatic alliance. The cathedral is at its most charming in the **cloister,** where giant panels of *azulejos* depicting biblical scenes coat the walls between vaulted Gothic arches. Also notable is the **Casa do Cabido,** above the cloister, which features more *azulejos* and a sumptuous painted ceiling.

Terreiro da Sé. ✆ **22/205-90-28.** Cathedral free; cloister 3€. Apr–Oct: Mon–Sat 9am–6pm, Sun 9am–12:30pm & 2:30–5:30pm. Nov–Mar: Mon–Sat 9am–6pm, Sun 2:30–6:30pm. Metro: São Bento.

BAIXA

Avenida dos Aliados ★★ STREET Porto's grandest avenue celebrated its centenary in 2016. Named in honor of Portugal's World War I allies, the Avenida dos Aliados is Porto's living room, the place where locals come for a Sunday stroll, or to celebrate—on New Year's, during the Saint John's day parties in mid-June, or when FC Porto secures a soccer success. The boulevard runs from the dashing horseback statue of **King Pedro IV** (aka Emperor Pedro I of Brazil) uphill for 300 meters (330 yards) to the great tower of the mid-20th-century **City Hall.** Along the way it's lined with grand Belle Epoque buildings housing banks, insurance companies, fancy stores and ever more hotels as the tourist boom leads to a wave of renovation and conversion projects. The little **statue** of a flat-capped fellow shouting the Portuguese equivalent of "read all about it" is a reminder that in years gone by newspapers once had their offices here. Another cherished statue is ***Juventude*** (Youth) made by local sculptor Henrique Moreira in 1929 and known affectionately as *a menina nua* (the naked girl). Opinion is divided over the city council's decision not to replant the gardens that ran down the center of the thoroughfare and were ripped up during work on the city subway in the early 2000s. Instead, Porto's two Pritzker Prize–winning architects, **Álvaro Siza Vieira** and **Eduardo Souto de Moura,** joined forces to design an open space of granite flagstones flanking a rectangular **pool** that reflects the surrounding buildings. Two places worth visiting along the Avenida are the **Guarany Café,** dating back to 1933 at No. 85/89 (www.cafeguarany.com; ✆ **22/332-12-72**; open daily 9am–midnight), and the Art Deco **Culturgest** art center (www.culturgest.pt; ✆ **22/209-81-16;** open Wed–Sun 10am–4pm & 3–6:30pm) on the other side at No. 104.

Metro: Aliados.

Livraria Lello ★★ HISTORIC STORE A contender for the world's most beautiful bookshop, this store, opened in 1906, is simply amazing. A slender Gothic Revival front decorated with Art Nouveau paintings representing art and science adorns the outside. Inside are twisting, interlocking wooden staircases, carved balconies and balustrades, stained-glass skylights, richly painted ceilings, and layer upon layer of dark wood bookshelves. It's more a temple to literature than a mere store. Lello is no frozen museum piece, however—it remains a dynamic cultural hub, hosting readings, book launches, and art events. Unfortunately, the store is a victim of its own success. Crowds wanting to get in mean there are often long lines. To limit numbers, the owners have introduced a 5€ voucher system for entry, which you can reclaim against purchases.

Rua das Carmelitas 144. www.livrarialello.pt. ✆ **22/200-20-37.** Daily 9:30am–8pm. Metro: São Bento.

Museu Nacional de Soares dos Reis ★ MUSEUM Recently renovated, Portugal's oldest public art museum (founded in 1833) retains a pleasingly old-fashioned feel. Housed in a grand 18th-century palace, it was once the residence of the royal family when they sojourned in the north. Its eclectic collection contains artifacts ranging from Visigoth jewelry to Japanese screen paintings depicting the disembarkation of Portuguese merchants in the 1600s. The museum is best known for housing the north's widest collection of Portuguese painting and sculpture. The naturalist portrayals of Portuguese life by painters Henrique Pousão (1859–87) and António Silva Porto (1850–93) are particularly striking. Pride of place, however, goes to sculptor António Soares dos Reis (1847–89) for whom this museum is named. His statue in pure white Carrara marble, ***O Desterrado*** ★★ (The Exile), is a melancholic masterpiece. There's a charming formal garden in the back.

Rua de Dom Manuel II. www.museusoaresdosreis.gov.pt. ✆ **22/339-37-70.** 5€, 2.50€ seniors and students, free for children under 12. Wed–Sun 10am–6pm, Tues 2–6pm. Metro: Aliados.

Rua de Santa Catarina ★★ STREET Porto's main shopping drag is a bustling 1.5km (almost 1 mile) long. Most of it is pedestrian-only and covered with artful black-and-white paving stones. Shopaholics can find almost anything along Santa Catarina or the side streets running off it. There are big-name European brands like Zara, H&M, or FNAC alongside venerable family stores selling everything from freshly baked bread to upmarket leather goods. Among the landmarks are the **Majestic Café** at No. 112 (www.cafemajestic.com; ✆ **22/200-38-87**), the chicest place for a *cimbalino* (as the people of Porto call a shot of espresso) since 1921. It's filled with gilt-framed mirrors, marble-topped tables, and smiling plasterwork cherubs, and serves divine *rabanadas*—Porto's take on French toast. Continuing the Old World charm is the **Grande Hotel do Porto** at No. 197. There are two stylish **Art Nouveau corner shops** guarding the southern entrance to the street beneath the *azulejo*-clad **Church of Saint Ildefonso,** and a modern shopping mall with a colorful facade at No. 312 (behind which the **city market** is temporarily housed while work continues to restore the emblematic Mercado do Bolhão). The greatest gem on the street, however, is the **Capela das Almas,** at No. 428, a tiny church covered with tiles with such an intensity of blue they rival the summer sky. The church is from the 18th century, but although painted in the baroque style of that time, the tiles were actually added in 1929.

Metro: Bolhão.

potter IN PORTO

Was **Harry Potter** made in Porto? The answer is a mystery, but it is certain that Scottish author **J. K. Rowling,** creator of the world's most famous boy wizard, spent almost 2 years living in the city in the early 1990s while she was working on the manuscript of what would become the first Potter novel.

She taught English and was briefly married to a Portuguese journalist. They say Rowling jotted down key chapters of *Harry Potter and the Philosopher's Stone* while sipping coffee at the marble tables of the 1920s **Café Majestic,** where she was a regular customer. The marvelous **Lello bookshop** is said to have inspired Flourish and Blotts, the fictional store where junior sorcerers browsed for volumes of spells. Lello's seemingly endless staircase is supposedly the model for the moving stairs of Hogwarts School.

The school uniforms of Hogwarts bear an uncanny resemblance to the traditional black suits and capes worn by Portuguese university students. One story says that Rowling got the idea for Gryffindor house from the **Fonte dos Leões** fountain, featuring four winged lions cast in bronze, just up the hill from Lello.

Some say the broomsticks used in the game of Quidditch may just have entered the writer's imagination at the **Escovaria de Belomonte,** a 90-year-old store selling a baffling array of handmade brooms and brushes. The sinister wizard Salazar Slytherin could have been named for Portugal's long-lasting dictator, **António de Oliveira Salazar.**

How much of this is urban legend is not clear. Rowling certainly frequented the Majestic and the Lello, but doesn't talk much about her years in Porto, which were economically and emotionally tough. Potter, however, has been good for the city, as fans seek out the sorcerer's roots. Thousands besieged Lello when the bookshop organized a late-night launch of the latest volume, *Harry Potter and The Cursed Child.* Enterprising guides offer tours of Harry-related haunts around the city; for details: www.potterheadsportotours.com and visit www.withlocals.com.

Torre dos Clérigos ★★ LANDMARK What the Eiffel Tower is to Paris or the Empire State Building is to New York, this is to Porto: a 76m (250-ft.) church tower looming over the city center that's a cherished icon to the people of Porto. It was designed in 1754 by Italian architect Nicolau Nasoni, who left his baroque mark all over Porto and is buried in the handsome church attached to the tower. The richly decorated granite landmark was the tallest building in Portugal when it was built and still dominates the skyline. Views from the top are breathtaking—if you have any breath left after climbing the 225 steps spiraling up to the top.

Rua São Filipe De Nery. www.torredosclerigos.pt. ✆ **22/014-54-89.** Admission including the tower and exhibitions in the church 5€, free for children under 10. Daily 9am–7pm. At times, it is possible to climb the tower at night with pre-arranged visits that can also include wine and chocolate tasting in the church. Metro: São Bento.

BOAVISTA

Serralves ★★★ MUSEUM You get three attractions in one with a visit to Porto's premier modern art venue out in the leafy Boavista district. On-site is a splendid 1930s **villa** in blushing pink, the best Art Deco home in Portugal. Behind it is an 18-hectare (44-acre) handsomely landscaped **park** featuring over 200 species of native and exotic plants. The centerpiece, the **Museum of Contemporary Art**, which opened in 1999, is a masterpiece of modern architecture by native son Álvaro Siza Vieira. His use of diagonal white planes rising and falling at odd angles creates startling and constantly changing contrasts between sunlight and shadow, open sky, and the surrounding lawns.

Serralves has become the most dynamic cultural hub in the north, perhaps in the whole country. As well as a permanent collection of over 4,000 works by Portuguese and international artists, it hosts regular temporary exhibitions, concerts, and a 4-day arts festival, **Serralves em Festa,** every June. In 2016, the museum received 84 works by the Spanish artist Joan Miró, which are now a central part of the permanent collection and in 2019 added a **cinema museum** dedicated to local director Manoel de Oliveira (1908–2015). There is a restaurant and teahouse with a verdant terrace, plus shops selling art books and Portuguese design items.

Rua Don João de Castro 210. www.serralves.pt. ✆ **80/820-05-43.** Admission to the museum, house and park 18€, 9€ students and seniors, children under 12 free. Museum only 12€ adults. Apr–Sept: Mon–Fri 10am–7pm, Sat–Sun 10am–8pm; Oct–Mar: Mon–Fri 10am–6pm; Sat–Sun 10am–7pm. Bus: 201, 203, 502, or 504.

WALKING TOUR: THE HEART OF PORTO

START: **Cais da Ribeira.**

FINISH: **Mosteiro da Serra do Pilar.**

TIME: **2 hours.**

BEST TIMES: **Afternoon (or morning, heading in the other direction).**

WORST TIME: **After dark.**

Begin your tour in the heart of the old town, at:

1 Cais da Ribeira

If you've lunched on Porto's signature dish of tripe and beans in one of the riverside neighborhood's restaurants—**Adega São Nicolau** would be a good choice—you'll now be ready to walk off the calories. Start by admiring the view along the river, then set to the round, whitewashed church high on a cliff on the opposite bank as your eventual target.

Head along the river to Praça da Ribeira, then carry on along Cais da Estiva, admiring the facades of the high merchant houses behind the granite wall to your right, onto Largo do Terreiro. Then carry on up the pedestrianized Rua Alfândega.

2 Casa do Infante

At No. 10 is this solid stone house built in the 14th century and supposedly the place where Henry the Navigator was born in 1394. It was once the customs house and now holds exhibitions about the Portuguese Discoveries and the history of Porto (✆ **22/206-04-00;** admission 2.20€; Tues–Sun 10am–5:30pm).

Walking Tour: The Heart of Porto

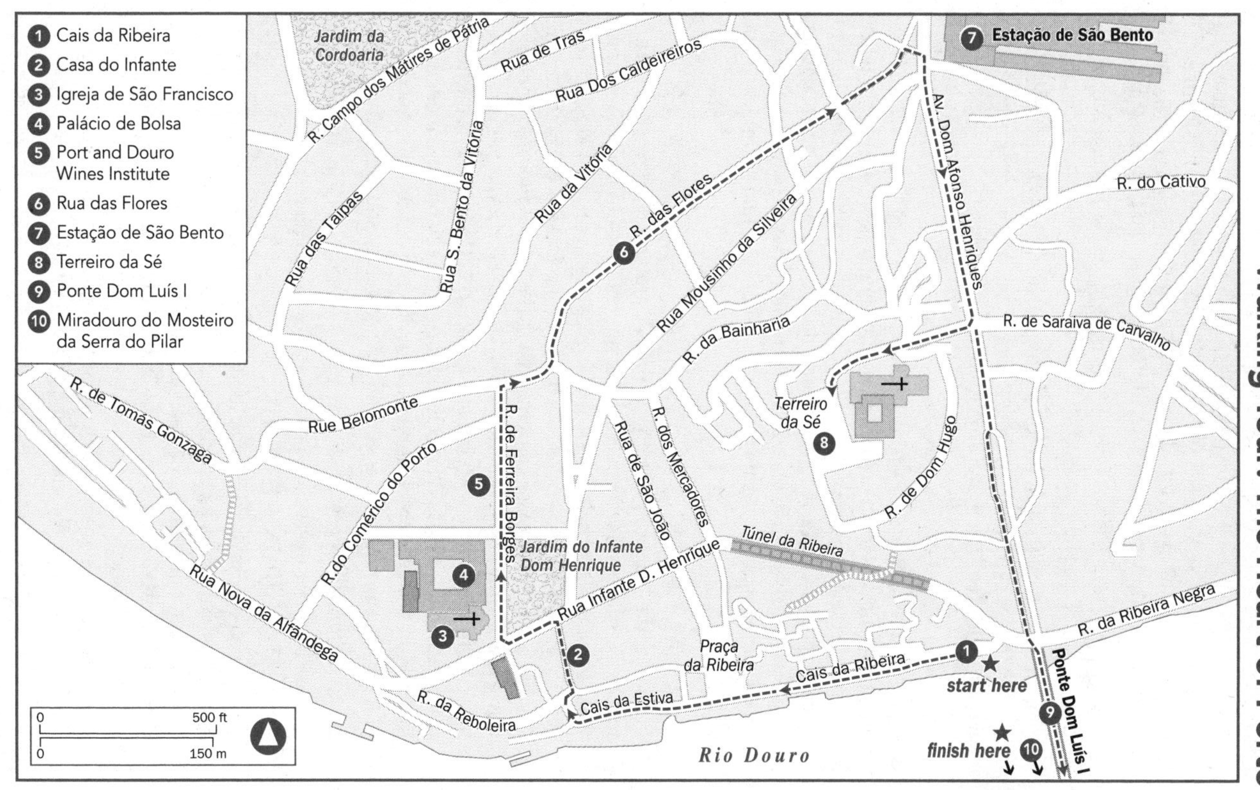

At the top of the road you'll find the gently sloping lawns of the Jardim do Infante. Your next destinations are on the left.

3 Igreja de São Francisco

The plain stone Gothic rear of the church that you see from the gardens will not prepare you for the glittering interior of Porto's "**golden church.**" If you visit one church in Porto, this is the one (see p. 337).

Just next door.

4 Palácio de Bolsa

This massive neoclassical building with its sober gray stone facade once housed the Stock Exchange. Grab a tour of its opulent interior, especially the fairytale **Arabian Salon** (see p. 340).

Continue up Rua de Ferreira Borges until you reach No. 27.

5 Port and Douro Wines Institute

The understated, cream-colored two-story building facing you is where the port wine trade—recently valued at a cool 380€ million—is regulated. Inside you can get a guided tour, do some tasting of your own, and discover more about how this nectar is produced (www.ivdp.pt; ✆ **22/207-16-69;** admission free, tasting from 1€; Mon–Fri 11am–7pm).

At the top of the hill, turn right onto Largo São Domingos.

6 Rua das Flores

For some, the "street of flowers" is Porto's prettiest. Cars are banned and it rises in a lazy curve between rows of centuries-old houses decorated with wrought-iron balconies. You'll pass monuments like the 16th-century **Igreja da Misericórdia** church or the **Casa dos Maias,** a long-derelict aristocratic mansion reborn in 2019 as the five-star **PortoBay Flores** (www.portobay.com; ✆ **22/004-70-00**) hotel. Another new arrival is the **ViniPortugal** (www.viniportugal.pt; ✆ **22/332-30-72**) wine tasting center at Nos 8–12. It is the eclectic mix of stores old and modern that make Flores such a fascinating thoroughfare, from artisan chocolatiers and trendy restaurants to Art Nouveau jewelers and the purveyors of Porto's famed luxury soaps.

When you reach the top of the street, look straight ahead across the little square.

7 Estação de São Bento

Facing you across the square at the top of Rua das Flores, this is Portugal's grandest railroad station. It was built at the beginning of the 20th century in imitation of the Parisian Beaux-Arts style. Inside, however, the decor is purely Portuguese, with **20,000 tiles** painted by artist **Jorge Colaço** and formed into monumental wall panels depicting the history of transport and scenes of medieval daring-do. As we were going to press the future of a gourmet market in the station was in doubt.

Now you have a steep climb up Av. Dom Afonso Henriques toward the cathedral.

8 Terreiro da Sé

This broad square almost surrounding the **cathedral** provides a great view over the rooftops of Porto's old neighborhoods and offers a chance to admire the stone Romanesque facade of the Sé and the adjoining white **Episcopal Palace** designed by Italian baroque master Nicolau Nasoni. The impressive-looking pillory in the square is actually a fake, built in the 1940s to 18th-century plans.

Behind the cathedral, take Av. Vimara Peres north toward the river.

9 Ponte Dom Luís I

After a short walk you'll find yourself high on the upper deck of this mighty iron bridge with the Douro below and the city at your feet. When it was built in 1886, it was the longest bridge of its type in the world. The engineer behind it was Frenchman **Théophile Seyrig,** an associate of **Gustave Eiffel** of tower fame. Eiffel himself built the **Maria Pia Bridge** just a bit farther upstream, in 1877, which was also a world record-breaker at the time.

Once you cross the bridge, follow the streetcar tracks past the Jardim do Morro gardens, then take a sharp right up the Rampa do Infante Santo.

10 Miradouro do Mosteiro da Serra do Pilar

You have now reached your destination. The unusual round church behind you is worth a visit for its cloister, dome and exhibitions on northern Portuguese heritage. There is history here, too. During the Portuguese Civil War in the 1830s, Liberal forces fought a heroic defense to prevent Conservative troops from taking Porto. The real reason for the climb, however, is the breathtaking **view** over the Douro and the city beyond. If you've timed it right, you'll arrive as the sun goes down and the lights of Porto start to twinkle against the purple sky. After that, head back down to Ribeira's bars or the wine lodges of Gaia for a well-deserved thirst-quencher.

Where to Stay

EXPENSIVE

1872 River House ★★ A pink-painted townhouse perched over the Douro on the old quayside where sailing ships used to moor to unload their cargoes of salt cod, this is now a fancy boutique B&B in the atmospheric Ribeira district. It is cozy, family-run, and best for guests seeking an up-close immersion into Porto life, rather than an amenity-heavy hotel experience. Half of the eight rooms look out right onto the Douro (offering views over to the wine lodges), and a few have balconies. The decor is in natural stone, wood, and *azulejos*. One room has a bed emerging from a huge stone fireplace. There's a comfortable lounge for relaxing and gazing out along the river.

Breakfasts are a copious blend of fresh orange juice, cappuccinos, breads, pastries, fruit, and eggs made to order. It's served as late as you like it.

Rua do Infante D. Henrique, 133. www.1872riverhouse.com. ✆ **96/117-28-05.** 8 units. 169€–264€ double. Parking nearby 24€ per day. **Amenities:** Bike rental; bar; babysitting; free Wi-Fi.

Flores Village ★★ Behind the *azulejo*-covered facade of an 18th-century, five-story building (on the delightful Rua das Flores, see. p. 346) lies a different type of accommodation. Besides regular rooms, the hotel has suites and self-catering apartments for up to eight people, making it ideal for families. Rooms cluster around a sunny urban garden, and many have huge windows and balconies that look across to the towers of the cathedral on the opposite hilltop. Common areas include salons with baroque ceiling paintings and tasteful furnishings, and an exceptional spa with a Roman-style bath sunk among the foundations. Recent renovations have highlighted the painted ceilings of the Noble Salon and installed a classy jeweler's shop next to the lobby.

Rua das Flores, 139. www.floresvillage.com. ✆ **22/201-34-78.** 35 units. 130€–244€ double; 130€–460€ studios & apartments. Parking nearby 24€ per day. **Amenities:** Garden; terrace; indoor pool; spa; hammam; sauna; Jacuzzi; gym; massage services; free Wi-Fi.

Hotel Infante Sagres ★★ For decades this was the default option for downtown luxury in Porto, built in 1951 as the domain of cigar-chomping, port-swilling stalwarts of the wine trade and barons of northern Portugal's textile and furniture trade. Guests have included Bob Dylan, the Dali Lama, and British royalty. It reopened in 2018 after a major renovation that has revitalized its Old World elegance, giving a new shine to the wrought-iron balconies, silk wall hangings, stained-glass windows, and genuine antique furnishings. Rooms retain their charm with heavy drapes, vintage prints, and marble-sheathed bathrooms, but now come with sound-proof windows, tech connections and other mod cons. Europe's only Vogue cafe provide chic eating options on the ground floor. Although there's a small plunge pool, plans to install a spa have been delayed by a dispute with the neighbors.

Praça Filipa de Lencastre 62. www.infantesagres.com. ✆ **22/339-85-00.** 85 units. 142€–324€ double, 246€–674€ suite. Nearby parking 29€ daily. **Amenities:** Sun terrace; restaurant; bar; babysitting; free Wi-Fi.

Le Monumental Palace ★★★ The opening of this five-star option in 2018 confirmed two trends: Porto is exciting as much interest from French investors as it is from French tourists; and luxury hotels are fast reclaiming the grand Avenida dos Aliados running through the heart of Porto. This splendid 1920s building once held Porto's grandest cafe, but long ago fell on hard times until the Paris-based Albar group renovated its majestic mix of Belle Epoque, Art Nouveau, and Art Deco with great sensitivity and *savoir-faire*. The sidewalk cafe has been restored to its former glory, serving bistro-style meals at lunch time (there's also a fancy gastronomic restaurant and a *Bar Américain* for cocktails and port). The spa features a grey-marble and blue-tile pool and

PORTO by the sea

As if all the history, wine, and culture were not enough, Porto boasts some of Portugal's best urban beaches. If the traffic's moving, a little over 20 minutes by bus will whisk you from Avenida das Aliados to the soft sand and rolling Atlantic surf of the beach resort of **Foz do Douro.** Foz features fine seaside promenades; a string of beaches broken up by rocky outcrops; and plenty of good shops, cafes, and restaurants amid Porto's most sought-after real estate.

We particularly like **Bonaparte,** Av do Brasil, 130 (✆ **22/618-84-04;** open daily 5pm–2am or 3am Fri-Sat), a delightfully cluttered seafront bar serving snacks and a range of beers since 1975. Among the beaches, **Praia Homem do Leme** is many people's favorite, with shaded lawns and a couple of good beach bars.

Follow the coast a bit farther up and you reach **Matosinhos,** a fishing port that draws crowds from Porto, just 30 minutes away by metro, to its cluster of ***marisqueiras*** (seafood restaurants) around Rua Roberto Ivens. Matosinhos and neighboring **Leça da Palmeira** are also a draw for modern architecture enthusiasts, featuring works by hometown boy **Álvaro Siza Vieira** (b. 1933), including the **Piscinas das Marés** swimming complex on Leça beach (currently being renovated) and the **Casa de Chá** (teahouse) rising out of the rocks on **Boa Nova beach,** now a fancy restaurant.

A new architectural landmark sprung up on the Matosinhos harborfront in 2015, the spiraling white **Leixões cruise terminal,** and a major new exhibition space, the **Casa da Arquitectura** (www.casadaarquitectura.pt; ✆ **22/240-46-63**), opened in 2018 on a former industrial site to showcase architecture and modern art.

Farther north, the Porto metro's red line extends up to the historic seaside town of **Vila do Conde,** which features a quaint medieval center, monumental convent overlooking the River Ave, and some of the best beaches in the north, notably **Praia de Mindelo** and **Praia de Moreiró.**

To the south, just downriver from Vila Nova de Gaia, is the pleasant fishing village of **Afurada** and a string of fine sandy beaches leading down to **Espinho.** Among the best, **Praia do Senhor da Pedra** is easily reachable by suburban train to the Miramar stop; it features a little white chapel on the rocks as a counterpoint to the vast expanse of sand. **Praia de São Pedro da Maceda,** backed by dunes and pine forest, is good for seekers of solitude, although care is needed with the rip currents.

Nuxe pampering products. Rooms are classically luxurious with a design that continues the revived "grand hotel" style of the building.

Avenida dos Aliados 151. www.maison-albar-hotels-le-monumental-palace.com. ✆ **22/766-24-10.** 76 units. 197€–494€ double, 368€–594€ junior suite. Parking 25€ daily. **Amenities:** Bike hire; indoor pool; gym; spa; sauna; hammam; Jacuzzi; massage services; 2 restaurants; 2 bars; babysitting; free Wi-Fi.

Pestana Palácio do Freixo ★★★ Only the 18th-century formal garden and its gently trickling fountain separate this magnificent baroque palace from the River Douro. The location and the main building are spectacular. It was built around 1750 by Nicolau Nasoni, the architect behind Porto's landmark Clérigos tower, and is protected as a national monument. Inside, the chapel, lounge, and restaurant are decorated with airy murals, high windows, and gilded columns. Monumental fresh flower arrangements add to the "wow factor." The spacious rooms are located next to the main building in a 19th-century flour mill that underwent a remarkable renovation ahead of the hotel's opening. Standard rooms overlook the lush garden at the back; others look out over the river. Completing the picture is an excellent restaurant serving classic Porto dishes, plus a luxurious spa, and a riverside pool. It is a bit out of the city center, but that means peace and quiet, and there is a free shuttle into town three times a day. The latest update installed charging points for electric cars.

Estrada Nacional 108. www.pestana.com. ✆ **22/531-10-00.** 87 units. 125€–487€ double, 335€–548€ suite. Free parking. **Amenities:** Garden; terrace; indoor and outdoor pools; spa; fitness center; sauna; hammam; Jacuzzi; restaurant; bar; free Wi-Fi.

Pestana Vintage Porto ★★ This hip option is smack in the center of the Ribeira district and comprises two blocks of buildings, some dating back over 400 years. The main edifice is a yellow landmark where Praça da Ribeira meets the river. Within its granite walls, the atmosphere is zesty and youthful. There's quirky art in the lobby, cool retro furniture and a riverside bar where you can down a white port with tonic and chew on ceviche. No corners are cut with comfort in the rooms, where stylish modern design complements the building's original features. The award-winning restaurant specializes in beef.

Praça de Ribeira 1. www.pestana.com. ✆ **22/340-23-00.** 103 units. 168€–499€ double, 349€–478€ suite. **Amenities:** Restaurant; bar; free Wi-Fi.

The Yeatman ★★★ This place really has it all: a Michelin-two-star restaurant serving some of the country's finest haute cuisine, a fabulous spa, super-comfortable rooms, and, most of all, views. From its hillside location above Gaia's wine lodges, the Yeatman has Porto laid before it. You can admire the skyline not just from your balcony, but also from your bathtub; not just from the restaurant and terrace bar, but also from the indoor and outdoor pools. The hotel is built in the style of a pastel-painted colonial villa. Owned by one of the old port-shipping firms, it is dedicated to wine, with the decor of each room inspired by famed vineyards. Splash out on the presidential suite with 170 square meters (1,830 sq. ft.), a private pool and a bed in a giant port cask. The spa offers Caudalie wine therapy scrubs and massages. The cellar contains over 1,000 wines, including vintage ports dating back to the 1850s.

Rua do Choupelo, Vila Nova de Gaia. www.the-yeatman-hotel.com. ✆ **22/013-31-03.** 109 units. 234€–499€ double, 443€–2,310€ suite. Parking 20€ daily. **Amenities:** Garden; terrace; bike hire; indoor and outdoor pools; fitness center; spa; hammam; sauna; Jacuzzi; massage service; 2 restaurants; 2 bars; kid's play area; babysitting; free Wi-Fi.

MODERATE

Casa do Conto & Tipografia ★★ The name of this B&B means "the house of stories," and it has quite a story of its own. In 2009, a couple of weeks before it was due to open as a meticulously restored 19th-century town house B&B, fire swept through the building, destroying the interior. The architect owners pressed ahead, but now beyond the tile-covered facade there's nothing old timey about the place. Its hip looks are minimalist and contemporary, with large rooms spun off from a raw concrete staircase. In 2019 they opened a second place, a short walk away in a converted 19th-century typography workshop, featuring a bar and patio pool. In both places, guest rooms are individually designed: white and bare grey cement are the dominant colors, enlivened by bright splashes—a gold-framed mirror, mustard leather sofa, blue sky shining through the skylight or broad bedroom windows. It can feel a bit like living in a rather austere art installation, but the welcome is warm and there's a cute garden out back. They are located close to the Casa da Música and the up-and-coming Cedofeita neighborhood.

Rua da Boavista, 703. www.casadoconto.com. ✆ **22/206-03-40.** 16 units. 103€–181€ double, 133€–224€ suite. Parking nearby 15€ daily. **Amenities:** Garden; sun terrace; bike hire; outdoor pool; bar; babysitting; free Wi-Fi.

Cocorico Luxury Guest House ★★ The little guest house's new French owners have turned it into a celebration of Franco-Portuguese friendship—or more: guest rooms are named after romantic couples (José and Joséphine, Catarina and Benoit, etc.). There's a relaxed, country house feel in rooms that have retained a colorful mix of natural finishes in wood, cork, cotton, and linen, always seeking to blend motifs from the two countries. To keep the romance going, breakfast can be served in the room for no extra charge. Most units have high French windows and some feature balconies. There are spacious family rooms. They've introduced a brasserie restaurant where Parisian chef Flora Mikula serves up *bacalhau* dishes typical of northern Portugal as well as *magret de canard* and *crêpes Suzette.* It's a short walk from São Bento station and the shops of Rua de Santa Catarina.

Rua Duque de Loulé, 97. www.cocorico-porto.pt. ✆ **22/201-39-71.** 10 units. 137€–269€ double, 211€–269€ suite. Public parking nearby 10€ daily, reservation required. **Amenities:** Garden; terrace; restaurant; bar; free Wi-Fi.

Descobertas Boutique Hotel ★★ Passersby often wander into the lobby of this hotel tucked away in a Ribeira back street, thinking it's an upscale, exotic antique shop. It's packed with Indian silk slippers, African fabrics, Chinese ceramics, cushions sown from tea or coffee sacks, and other items that recall destinations reached by Portuguese explorers. *Descobertas* means "Discoveries," and each floor is dedicated to a particular country, from Cape Verde to Macau. The building once housed a trade association, and you'll see that early-20th-century industrial heritage in the massive stone walls, iron pillars, and exposed wood beams. Guests with a sweet tooth will love breakfast.

Rua Fonte Taurina 14-22. www.descobertasboutiquehotel.com. ✆ **22/201-14-73.** 18 units. 95€–263€ double. **Amenities:** Library; babysitting; free Wi-Fi.

Hotel Vincci Porto ★★ If the thought of sleeping in a fish market doesn't sound appealing, think again. All right, this is not a *working* fish market, but traders once haggled over catches of hake and bass in this iconic 1930s building. Its cool Art Deco lines make it a lovely alternative to older-styled hotels downtown. The high-ceilinged, glass-fronted lobby, in particular, is a light-filled jewel. Sip a *porto tónico* in the bar and you can imagine yourself on a Jazz Age cruise liner. The **33 Alameda** restaurant is another Art Deco beauty, featuring onyx columns and vertical lighting, not to mention an excellent modern take on Mediterranean cooking. As for the digs: Guest rooms and baths are large and handsomely color-coordinated. Some offer river views. The historic tram line stops just outside to whisk guests downtown.

Alameda Basílio Teles, 29. www.vincciporto.com. ✆ **22/043-96-20.** 95 units. 128€–237€ double. Parking 10€ per day with reservation. **Amenities:** Terrace, restaurant; bar; free Wi-Fi.

Porto AS 1829 Hotel ★★ Overlooking the coolest square in Porto, this azulejo-clad building once held Europe's oldest stationery shop, opened in 1829 (part of it survives next door). The reception is filled with mementoes from the former business, with antique typewriters, counters polished by generations of wear and framed prints. Rooms maintain the vintage theme, with rotary dial phones, clawfoot baths, and wooden floors. They are painted in soothing shades of dove grey and café-au-lait. Blackout curtains should guarantee a good snooze. The ground-floor restaurant spills onto the square which is perfect for watching city life.

Largo São Domingos 45-55. https://as1829.luxhotels.pt. ✆ **22/340-27-40.** 41 units. 127€–309€ double. **Amenities:** Bike hire; restaurant; babysitting; free Wi-Fi.

PortoBay Teatro ★★ Unleash your inner drama queen. The Hotel Teatro was built on the site of an 1850s playhouse and its styling by designer Nini Andrade Silva is an homage to the bohemian glamour of the site's past. Lighting is low and dramatic. The decor comes in gold, copper, and chestnut tones. Racks of flamboyant theatrical costumes decorate the lobby, and guest rooms are sultry and decadent, with expansive soft beds, standalone baths and wall-to-wall mirrors. The Palco restaurant has been in the limelight for dishes like crispy pork belly or roast pineapple with vanilla and coconut. In the heart of the Baixa, it's had a little facelift since acquisition in 2018 by the Madeira-based PortoBay group, opening up the lobby and bringing in extra natural light.

Rua Sá da Bandeira, 84. www.portobay.com. ✆ **22/040-96-20.** 74 units. 109€–247€ double, 184€–345€ suite. Parking 16€ daily, reservation required. **Amenities:** Gym; restaurant; bar; babysitting; free Wi-Fi.

Sheraton Porto Hotel & Spa ★ Here rooms are spacious, light-filled, and decorated in refined chocolate and white. Furnishings are contemporary and stylish. Live music is a nightly feature in the New Yorker Bar. Guests in the club rooms enjoy a rooftop terrace with a panoramic view. The hotel spa, with its adjacent juice bar, is among the finest in the city. Located in the leafy Boavista neighborhood, it's near to the Casa da Música and Serralves park.

Rua de Tenente Valadim 146. www.sheratonporto.com. ✆ **22/040-40-00.** 266 units. 124€–214€ double, 285€–424€ suite. Parking 9€. **Amenities:** Terrace; garden; indoor pool; gym; spa; hammam; sauna; Jacuzzi; restaurant; bar; free Wi-Fi.

INEXPENSIVE

Bluesock Hostel ★ Spain's Carrís hotel chain chose Porto for its first venture into the backpacker market, with this upscale hostel that opened in 2016 (it now has more in Lisbon and Madrid). Occupying a traditional blue-tiled town house on the street leading out of Ribeira toward the Baixa, it offers a range of accommodations from cool modern suites with private bathrooms to dorms for up to 13 people with extra-wide bunks and locker space for luggage. Dorms are either mixed or women only. All can access chill-out lounges, computer rooms and a bar that's become a popular city venue with frequent live music. They feature playful furniture set among raw stone walls, wooden beams, and the great arched basement ceiling.

Rua de São João, 40. www.bluesockhostels.com. ✆ **22/766-41-71.** 27 units. 81€–164 € double, 17€–47€. dorm beds. **Amenities:** Library; games room; bar; free Wi-Fi.

Castelo Santa Catarina ★ A definite oddity. Built in 1887 as a textile baron's folly, it looks uncannily like a bling version of Lisbon's Torre de Belém, with turrets, battlements, and arched windows. The "castle" is set in a private compound surrounded by pine and palm trees. Beyond the tile-covered exterior is an eccentric Victorian labyrinth of halls and stairways filled with painted ceilings, stained glass, and rosewood furniture. The rooms are rather more restrained, although the plumbing fixtures are designed with a florid Art Nouveau flair. There's a modern wing across the courtyard garden with a more contemporary feel. It's located in a residential neighborhood about 20 minutes' walk, or a short metro trip, to the town center.

Rua de Santa Catarina 1347. www.castelosantacatarina.com.pt. ✆ **22/509-55-99.** 25 units. 72€–96€ double, 91€–129€ suite. Parking 10€ daily. **Amenities:** Garden; terrace; bar; free Wi-Fi.

Grande Hotel de Paris ★ Porto's oldest hotel was opened in 1877, a couple of steps away from the Avenida dos Aliados. Early guests in what was for years a French-owned establishment included the great novelist José Maria Eça de Queirós and artist Rafael Bordallo Pinheiro. New owners have renovation planned, but for the moment room decor is a bit fusty. Still, it's a solid budget option, oozing Old World charm and right in the city center. A real treat is the magnificent Belle Epoque salon where an equally impressive breakfast is served, including the likes of "English-style bacon" and Porto's cinnamon- and port-wine–infused French toast. In summer, breakfast is served under striped awnings in the garden, an unexpected haven of tranquility in the heart of the city. There's a small museum featuring old telephones, gramophones and newspaper clippings from the hotel's golden days.

Rua da Fábrica, 27/29. www.stayhotels.pt. ✆ **22/207-31-40.** 45 units. 86€–211€ double, including breakfast. Public parking nearby, 12€ per day, reservation needed. **Amenities:** Garden; terrace; bike rental; bar; free Wi-Fi.

Moov Hotel Porto Centro ★ Behind the emblematic Art Nouveau facade of this low-cost option was once the Cinema Águia D'Ouro, one of the oldest in the city. It opened in 1908 but closed after 80 years, leaving the building abandoned. The rooms and reception continue the theme with big movie star posters featuring prominently amid the simple modern decor where pine boards, white walls and light-colored drapes predominate. There's a big variety of room sizes to choose from. Breakfast is extra but can be taken in the pátio garden outback. The location is excellent, just a few steps from Rua Santa Catarina and the funicular down to the riverside.

Praça da Batalha 32. www.hotelmoov.com. ✆ **22/040-70-01.** 125 units. 57€–82€ double, breakfast extra. Parking 8€ daily. **Amenities:** Garden; free Wi-Fi.

Pensão Favorita ★★ This arty guesthouse is in the core of Porto's trendy gallery and design district. Rooms in the main townhouse building are large and mostly white, but with colorful Portuguese touches, like cushions covered with traditional chintz fabrics from Alcobaça. Those in the newer red-brick garden extension are smaller but have the advantage of a patio opening out into the lush, peaceful garden. There's a friendly welcome and families are catered to with roomy suites. The veranda is the perfect place to sip a glass of port or one of the Portuguese craft beers on offer.

Rua Miguel Bombarda, 267. www.pensaofavorita.pt. ✆ **22/013-41-57.** 12 units. 60€–119€ double, 115€–124€ suite. **Amenities:** Garden; terrace; bike rental; bar; games room; babysitting; free Wi-Fi.

Where to Eat

The people of Porto are known across Portugal as *tripeiros*, or "tripe eaters." The nickname comes from the city's signature dish, *tripas à moda do Porto,* a hearty stew that includes butter beans, calves' feet, pigs' ears, and paprika-spiced chouriço sausage along with tripe—the chewy white lining of a cow's stomach.

Legend has it the city became hooked on offal after its patriotic citizens handed over all their meat to Prince Henry the Navigator in the 15th century to feed his army on its way to invade Morocco, leaving just the offcuts.

Lately Porto has undergone a culinary revolution. You can still find plenty of great traditional joints serving monster portions of *tripas* and other old favorites, like deep-fried octopus or wonderful *francesinha* sandwiches, but a new generation of innovative chefs is updating traditional north-Portuguese cooking to make Porto a hot destination for gourmet travelers.

EXPENSIVE

Antiqvvm ★★ MODERN PORTUGUESE Take an 18th-century manor house surrounded by a romantic park with splendid views over the Douro. Add a hugely talented chef and you have Antiqvvm. Vítor Matos proposes art-on-a-plate dishes that have earned the restaurant a Michelin star. There are three tasting menus, including one for vegetarians. Dishes are crafted from sole with pink shrimp, lime, and artichoke; or veal with truffle, pecan, and tangy Azores cheese. Let the sommelier guide you through the fabulous wine list.

Rua de Entre-Quintas 220. ✆ **22/600-04-45.** Reservations required. Mains 19€–35€, tasting menus 80€–230€. Tues–Sat noon–3pm and 7:30–10:30pm. Bus: 200, 201, 207, 208, 302, 501, or 507.

Casa de Chá da Boa Nova ★★★ MODERN PORTUGUESE Here you are eating in a national monument, a low-lying concrete-and-glass building that seems to merge with the rocks tumbling down to the Atlantic. It's an early masterpiece by Porto's great modernist architect, Álvaro Siza Vieira. His "teahouse," which opened in 1963, had fallen on hard times, but reopened in 2014 in the hands of Chef Rui Paula, the man behind Porto's DOP restaurant (below) and the riverside DOC up the Douro. Amid Siza Vieira's wood-lined interior, Paulo creates menus equal to the architecture and the setting. His latest selection involves 21 verses inspired by a quote from the poem "To seas Never Before Navigated" by Luís de Camões. Looking over the surf, diners can tuck into exquisitely presented dishes like scallop with black radish; red mullet with cashew and cassava; or a Korean-inspired langoustine. There's a vegetarian option for non-piscivores. This is a truly special dining experience out in the seaside suburb of Leça da Palmeira.

Avenida da Liberdade 1681, Leça da Palmeira. www.casadechadaboanova.pt. ✆ **22/994-00-66.** Reservations recommended. Tasting menus 90€–270€. Tues–Sat 12:30–3pm and 7:30–11pm. Bus: 507 or take the metro to Mercado do Matosinhos and grab a cab.

DOP ★★ MODERN PORTUGUESE Chef Rui Paula is a star of new Portuguese cooking and this classy fine-dining option is his hometown base. The restaurant is in the stately Palácio das Artes building, which once held the Porto branch of the central bank. Four big French windows open onto pretty Largo São Domingos square. Inside, the cream and soft browns of the decor have a Nordic simplicity. Paula says he's searching for "food with history" based on traditional mainstays of Portuguese cuisine, such as shoulder of lamb with goat cheese purée or stewed salt-cod. There are two tasting menus, one of north Portuguese traditions, the other inspired by the sea.

Largo de São Domingos 18. www.doprestaurante.pt. ✆ **22/201-43-13.** Reservations required. Mains 14€–29€, tasting menus 90€–150€. Mon 7:30–10:30pm, Tues–Sat 12:30–3:30pm and 7–10:30pm. Metro: São Bento.

Pedro Lemos ★★★ MODERN PORTUGUESE Amid a tangle of narrow residential streets behind the seafront at Foz is a little stone house that once housed a British pub and which many believe holds the most extraordinary modern restaurant in Porto, if not the country. Chef Pedro Lemos won his first Michelin star here in 2014 and continues to shine with his 8- or 10-course tasting menus. What's on them depends on what the boats have brought in that morning, or what's in season in Lemos' vegetable garden, but they will include treats like sea urchin with cantaloupe, duck *foie gras* with pear, or banana and lavender. All is served in two intimate dining rooms decorated in warm gold and blue, and a rooftop terrace looking toward the mouth of the Douro.

Rua do Padre Luís Cabral 974. www.pedrolemos.net. ✆ **22/011-59-86.** Reservations required. Tasting menus 110€–210€. Tues–Sun 12:30–3pm and 7:30–11pm. Bus: 202.

The Yeatman ★★★ MODERN PORTUGUESE If they were serving soggy hotdogs, you'd want to come to this restaurant for the view alone.

MARKET forces

Hopefully, by the time you are reading this Porto's **Bolhão ★★** (www.mercado bolhao.pt) market will be back on its feet. The iconic 1850s double-deck structure was shut down in 2018 for a 22€-million renovation. It's due to reopen in 2021, but many wonder if the landmark will ever recover its old role as a window onto the soul, or at least the stomach, of Porto.

In the heart of the city, decorated with colorful vintage-tile advertising panels, the old market featured greengrocers and florists, fishmongers with a gleaming catch-of-the-day selection and rock-hard planks of salted cod, bakers selling chunky cornbread loaves, bucket-loads of olives, butchers hawking smoked pigs' heads and rings of blood sausage, snack bars, and handicraft stalls.

After decades of dithering, city hall finally moved ahead with much-needed structural repairs. Stallholders were temporarily located to a nearby shopping mall on Rua Fernandes Tomás. It's still worth a visit but lacks the special atmosphere of the old place. All true *tripeiros* will be hoping that the market reopens soon and recovers its old vim.

Elsewhere, the **Mercado do Bom Sucesso,** Praça Bom Sucesso 74-90 (www.mercadobomsucesso.pt) out toward Boavista has already had a makeover. In its 1952 building, traditional stallholders now stand alongside fancy food shops and gourmet snack bars. Show cooking, art exhibitions, and concerts are held here. The traditional part of the market is open Monday to Saturday 9am to 8pm, while the hip new part runs all week 10am to 11pm, staying open until midnight on Fridays and Saturdays.

Out on the coast, the cute little market in **Foz,** Praça Dom Luís I, 44, and the excellent covered market in a 1940s building in the fishing town of **Matosinhos** (www.matosinhoswbf.pt) Rua Álvaro Castelões, also blends old and new. The regular supply of fresh raw material has made the **sushi bar** at the Matosinhos market much sought after.

Porto also hosts a number of regular open-air markets, which can make for some offbeat browsing. Perhaps the most colorful is the **Feira dos Passarinhos,** or bird market, which sells birds and pet-related items in the streets of the riverside Fontainhas neighborhood on Sunday mornings.

Fortunately, the kitchen is run by Ricardo Costa, one of Portugal's most talented young chefs and holder of two Michelin stars since 2017. His tasting menus are a never-ending parade of superlative mini-dishes—crab ceviche with avocado and black-beer foam; suckling pig with mango and coconut; and strawberries with mascarpone ice cream can be among the delights. The wines chosen to accompany each dish come from the hotel's selection of more than 1,000 tipples, with an emphasis on port and the Douro. Service is an impeccable blend of knowledge, warmth, and efficiency. The expansive dining room is bright, light, and decorated with murals of tropical landscapes. Then there's that view. Watching the sun fade to gold over the river and the lights of Porto twinkling in the twilight is unforgettable.

Rua do Choupelo, Vila Nova de Gaia. www.the-yeatman-hotel.com. ✆ **22/013-31-00.** Reservations recommended. Tasting menus 170€–245€. Daily 7:30–10pm. Metro: General Torres.

MODERATE

Adega São Nicolau ★★ PORTUGUESE This Ribeira joint is where many of Porto's top chefs go when they want to eat good, homestyle Porto cooking. Of course, its location in a charming Ribeira alleyway makes it popular with tourists, too, but the cuisine is authentic and the service friendly. Behind an unprepossessing exterior is a low, dramatically lit dining room with a curved wood ceiling. Fried octopus (*filetes de polvo*) is a signature dish, but it's also a good stop for tripe, grilled fish, and unusual dishes like oxtail stew, or chicken slow-cooked in red wine.

Rua de São Nicolau 1. ✆ **22/200-82-32.** Reservations recommended. Mains 10€–24€. Mon–Sat noon–11pm. Metro: Tram 1 or Metro São Bento.

Cafeína ★ PORTUGUESE/FRENCH For 20 years this relaxed, cosmopolitan place has been serving good food a block from the sea out in the beach resort of Foz. Inside the tile-covered villa, there's background jazz, soft lighting, and discreet service. In 2018 it was bought up by Lisbon culinary wunderkind José Avillez, but the food continues as a mix of classic French and Portuguese, with some Italian touches. Portugal's cherished salt cod comes with *au gratin* with roasted onion purée. There's duck breast in port wine sauces and a renowned Beef Wellington. Save some space for pear-and-almond pie with tawny port ice cream.

Rua do Padrão 100. www.cafeina.pt. ✆ **22/610-80-59.** Reservations recommended. Mains 17€–22€. Daily 12:30–4pm & 7:30pm–12:30am. Bus: 200, 202, or 203.

Casa Aleixo ★ PORTUGUESE The epitome of a traditional Porto eatery, Casa Aleixo is made up of a couple of long, low, cave-like dining rooms with walls of bare stone decorated with fading photos of illustrious diners. The place echoes with the chatter of regulars and foreigners who have hiked out to the off-the-beaten-track neighborhood near Campanhã station lured by a legendary version of a Porto classic—deep-fried filets of octopus served with octopus risotto (*filetes de polvo com arroz de polvo*). If octopus isn't your thing, their *tripas* is justly famed, and there's a mean steak made from a tasty breed of north Portuguese cattle (*posta de vitela Maronesa*). The typical northern desserts include *aletria* made from pasta, milk, and cinnamon.

Rua da Estação, 216. ✆ **22/537-04-62.** Mains 12€–20€. Mon-Sat noon–2:30pm & 7:30–10pm. Metro: Campanhã.

Oficina ★★ PORTUGUESE Chef Marco Gomes is the man in charge here and he's passionate about the burly food of his home region of Trás-os-Montes up in Portugal's remote northeast. A meal in his hands could start with fava beans stewed with *chouriço* sausage and Terrincho cheese, move on to lamb with the *transmontana* version of couscous and finish up with warm walnut cake and cinnamon ice cream. This all takes place in a former auto-repair shop converted into a spacious restaurant and art gallery in the hip Cedofeita neighborhood.

Rua de Miguel Bombarda 282. www.oficinaporto.com. ✆ **96/671-23-84.** Mains 19€–45€. Mon 7:30pm–11, Tues–Thurs 12:30–3pm and 7:30pm–11, Fri–Sat 12:30–3pm and 7:30pm–midnight. Bus: 300, 603. Metro: Trindade.

O Gaveto ★★★ SEAFOOD/PORTUGUESE The cluster of *marisqueiras*, or seafood restaurants, in the center of the seaside suburb of Matosinhos is a magnet for fish-favoring foodies from around Portugal. Seemingly little-changed since it opened in the 1970s, this place features a bar—where locals snack perched on stools, hemmed in by glass tanks filled with crab and lobster—and a dining room out back that's a favorite with the Porto wine trade. The menu features a long list of ultra-fresh shellfish—from cat-size rock lobsters (*lagosta*) to gnarled goose barnacles (*perceves*)—by the kilo; catch-of-the-day fish waiting to be slapped on the grill; and regular dishes of the day from the Porto cookbook. Mondays and Saturdays, there's a formidable *tripas à moda do Porto*. Also look out for seasonal dishes like shad (*savel*). To wash it down, the excellent house white is just 12.50€ but if you feel like pushing the boat out, the list of ports includes a bottle from 1882 for 5,500€.

Rua Roberto Ivens, 826, Matosinhos. www.ogaveto.com. ✆ **22/937-87-96.** Mains 13€–20€. Daily noon–midnight. Metro: Matosinhos Sul.

Traça ★★ PORTUGUESE/GAME This corner restaurant in a former drugstore has launched Largo São Domingos' transformation into the center of Porto's culinary renovation. Design is functional, maintaining elements of the 19th-century shop, with walls divided between white tiles and dark wood panels. Antlers mounted on one wall point to a menu where game is a major factor. In season expect to find delights like wild partridge stewed with shallots and peas, or loin of venison with liver and wild mushrooms. There are fish, salad, and vegetarian options, but this is a seriously carnivorous hangout. Go in summer and you can eat on the terrace and watch the city walk by.

Largo São Domingos 88. www.restaurantetraca.com. ✆ **22/208-10-65.** Reservations recommended. Mains 15€–21€. Mon–Thurs noon–3pm & 7–11pm, Fri noon–3pm and 7pm–1am, Sat 12:30–4pm and 7pm–1am, Sun 12:30–4:30pm and 7–11pm. Metro: São Bento.

INEXPENSIVE

A Casa Guedes ★★ SANDWICHES If the *francesinha* has a rival in the hearts of Porto's snackers, then it is the roast pork sandwiches (*sandes de pernil*) produced in this retro hole-in-the-wall near the São Lázaro gardens. The meat is tender, marinated in a secret sauce and served with its roasting juice in a fist-size bread roll. There's a luxury version that comes with an added dose of creamy *queijo da serra* sheep's cheese. The accompaniment of choice is a glass of cold *vinho verde* (the crisp white wine of northwest Portugal) or a dark beer. There are a number of alternatives where the rolls are filled with smoked sausage or ham. Eat at the bar, in the street, or on the little sidewalk terrace in summer.

Praça dos Poveiros 130. ✆ **22/200-28-74.** Main courses 3€–9€. No credit cards. Mon–Thurs 10am–11:45pm, Fri–Sat 10–1am, Sun 11am–9pm. Metro: Bolhão.

Café Santiago ★★★ SANDWICHES Porto's cherished *francesinha* is one of the world's great sandwiches. Take two thick slices of white bread, fill them with mortadella, chipolata, smoked sausages, steak, ham, and cheese. After toasting, it's wrapped in more cheese, baked, and then served hot, doused in a spicy sauce that every cafe in Porto will tell you is a state secret. The line waiting outside under this unpretentious cafe's neon sign is a clue that many consider this the best place on the planet to eat one. The sauce's special flavor apparently comes from being made in the same pan every day for decades. You can get them with or without fries, and you can add a fried egg on top. They're best washed down with a cold beer. As for the name—*francesinha* translates as "little French girl"—the story goes that a Porto waiter, who returned from a spell working in France, invented the sandwich in the 1950s and named it because the sauce was as piquant as his memories of Parisian mademoiselles. They opened a second joint just down the road in 2011, but still couldn't cope with demand, so Santiago+ opened up the hill in Praça dos Poveiros in 2017.

Rua Passos Manuel, 226. www.caferestaurantesantiago.com.pt. ✆ **22/205-57-97.** Mains 5€–10€. Mon–Sat 11am–11pm. Metro: Bolhão.

Cufra ★ PORTUGUESE A Porto institution since its opening in 1974, the decor looks little changed, with wood-paneled walls, leather-wrapped bench seats, and white table covers. Serving from noon until way into the night, it's a snack bar, beer hall, seafood joint, and purveyor of traditional Porto food for generations. The *francesinhas* are renowned—they even do a special version with added shrimp—but the array of dishes is enormous, from hamburgers to boiled fish head; tripe to a famed mixed seafood grill (*parrilhada*). Steaks are a late-night favorite. It's located on a main road out in the Boavista neighborhood. Expect it to be crowded and noisy, especially when there's a soccer game on the big TV screens.

Av. da Boavista 2504. www.cufra.pt. ✆ **22/617-27-15.** Mains 7€–24€. Tues–Sun noon–2am. Bus: 201, 203, or 502.

O Rapido ★★ PORTUGUESE This unassuming little place, tucked on a side road behind São Bento station, serves up the finest *tripas à moda do Porto*. Served in steaming pots and topped with slices of sausage, it's the real deal. The place takes its name from the fast trains that once pulled into São Bento from Lisbon. Other options include T-bone steaks from cattle raised in the highlands around the little town of Arouca (*costeletas de vitela Arouquesa*), or salt cod with eggs and potatoes (*bacalhau à Gomes de Sá*). The decor features bold oversized photos of Porto scenes. There's an extensive wine list. Check the daily specials for bargain options.

Rua da Madeira, 194. ✆ **22/205-48-47.** Main courses 8€–14€. Mon–Sat noon–10pm. Metro: São Bento.

Shopping

Shopping in Porto is an exciting mix of top European brands, cutting-edge local design, and timeless stores little changed in generations, offering authentic and original souvenirs.

The most vital Porto shopping street is the pedestrianized promenade of **Rua de Santa Catarina ★★**, running north for 1.5km (almost 1 mile) from Praça da Batalha. There's a great range of shops here, from Art Nouveau jewelers to the multicolored, modern **ViaCatarina ★** shopping mall filled with international names (and in summer topped by the city's biggest rooftop bar). As examples of the diversity: **LeYa na Latina ★** at No. 2 (✆ **22/347-27-54**) is a bookstore that first opened in the 1940s; you can dress as a 1940s pinup (or a heavy-metal warrior) at **Oblivion Alternative Wear ★** (www.oblivionshop.net; ✆ **22/201-16-09**) at No. 356; or you can splash out for a top-of-the-range Swiss watch at **Marcolino ★** (www.marcolino.pt; ✆ **22/200-16-06**), jewelers since 1926, at No. 84.

Streets running off Santa Catarina are full of intriguing traditional stores, particularly those around Bolhão market. Among them are **Casa dos Linhos ★**, Rua de Fernandes Tomás, 660 (✆ **22/200-00-44**), which specializes in linen goods, like the colorful, embroidered *bordados dos namorados* typical of northern Portugal; and its big sister, the **Armazém dos Linhos ★★**, Rua de Passos Manuel 15 (www.armazemdoslinhos.myshopify.com; ✆ **22/200-47-50**), selling a dazzling array of traditional textiles since 1905; the **Pérola do Bolhão ★★★**, Rua Formosa, 279 (✆ **22/200-40-09**), a grocery founded in 1917; or its rival, the **Favorita do Bolhão ★★**, Rua de Fernandes Tomás 783 (✆ **22/200-16-24**), little changed since 1934; and the **Casa Januário ★★**, Rua do Bonjardim, 352 (www.casajanuario.pt; ✆ **22/332-01-53**), a wine shop and grocery, where you're assailed by the aroma of freshly ground coffee. Casa Januário has been in the same family since 1926. **Potteria ★** (✆ **91/343-12-14**) at Rua de Santo Ildefonso 36 has a fabulous selection of Portuguese pottery modern and traditional; and **La Portuguese Porto Market ★** (www.laportuguese.pt; ✆ **93/839-86-76**) sells all kinds of quirky stuff from around the regions of Portugal at Rua Formosa 200.

For something completely different, the **FC Porto Store,** Rua Sá da Bandeira, 270 (www.fcporto.pt; ✆ **22/508-33-53**) is packed with merchandise of the European Champions' League–winning soccer club.

Wine, of course, makes an excellent gift from Porto. Besides picking up a bottle or two after tastings in the **Gaia wine lodges,** there are some top-notch wine stores in town. One of the best is **Touriga ★**, Rua da Fábrica 32 (✆ **22/510-84-35**) just off Avenida dos Aliados, which specializes in ports and other wines from the north and central Portugal and organizes regular tastings. It ships internationally, should you buy more than you can carry on the plane.

Another quality traditional product from Porto and its surroundings is **filigree jewelry ★★★**, in which fine strands of gold or silver are stretched and twisted into delicates shapes. Hearts and crosses are typical, but a range of necklaces and earrings are also made from *filigrana*. Women in Viana do Castelo wear layer upon layer of filigree necklaces over traditional costumes on special occasions, but lately international stars from Sharon Stone to Queen Letizia of Spain have been spotted wearing them as accessories. Jewelers around Porto sell them, but quality varies. Jeweler **Machado ★★**, Rua 31 de Janeiro, 200 (www.machadojoalheiro.com; ✆ **21/154-39-40**) has been around since 1880 and has a fine selection. Bringing a contemporary touch to the tradition is **PURA Filigrana** ★ (✆ **92/917-74-87**) in the Bom Sucesso market.

For a one-stop shop for all your Portuguese traditional goods, head to the Porto branch of **Vida Portuguesa ★★★,** Rua Cândido dos Reis, 36 (www.avidaportuguesa.com; ✆ **22/202-21-05**). Located in the shadow of the Clérigos tower on the ground floor of a former textile store, this vast, light-filled space is packed with woolen blankets from the Alentejo, Algarve sea salt, tins of Azores tuna, ceramic swallows based on 100-year-old designs, and handmade scented soaps from around Porto. Its latest collection celebrates the work of modernist artist Sarah Affonso (1899–1983). Nearby are a couple of branches of Porto's **Marques Soares** department store, Rua das Carmelitas, 80–104 and 130–136 (www.marquessoares.pt; ✆ **22/204-22-00**), founded in 1964 and selling a huge range of international and Portuguese fashion brands, including must-have locally made shoes by **Fly London** (www.flylondon.com) and **Luís Onofre** (www.luisonofre.com).

Two of Porto's hippest shopping streets are **Rua do Almada** and **Rua Miguel Bombarda.** Running parallel to Avenida dos Aliados, Rua do Almada has a cool urban feel, with places like vintage furnishings and design store **Casa Almada** ★ at No. 544 (www.casaalmada.com; ✆ **22/201-00-89**); **Louie Louie,** a vintage record emporium at No. 536 (www.louielouie.biz; ✆ **22/201-03-84**); and **Chua** ★ designer kids' wear around the corner on Rua Alferes Malheiro No. 189 (www.chua.pt; ✆ **91/376-00-85**). Don't forget **Arcádia ★★**, chocolate maker since 1933 at No. 63 (www.arcadia.pt; ✆ **22/ 043-73-10**). Their port-filled chocolate bites are hard to resist. Rua Miguel Bombarda is the heart of Porto's art district, lined with galleries, designer and vintage clothes shops, and a fair sprinkling of cool cafes. Many of the most interesting stores are in the **Centro Commercial Bombarda,** a mini-shopping mall at No. 285. Try to check out one of the street's "**simultaneous opening**" nights, when the galleries all launch new exhibitions and customers stroll around to view them all. Check with the tourist board for dates.

The **Boavista** and **Aviz** neighborhoods have Porto's poshest shopping. The **Wrong Weather** store, Av. da Boavista, 754 (www.wrongweather.net; ✆ **22/605-39-29**) has an uber-trendy collection of international menswear, including Comme Des Garçons, Maison Margiela, and Kenzo. Other fashionista haunts in the neighborhood include **Ltd Edition ★**, Rua Pedro Homem de Melo, 38 (www.ltd-edition.pt; ✆ **22/616-15-79**) and **Fashion Clinic ★**, Av. da Boavista, 4167 (www.fashionclinic.com; ✆ **22/610-30-59**).

More down to earth, one of the nicest places to shop is **Rua das Flores,** which winds downhill from São Bento station. It's lined with little stores, cafes, and restaurants. Among the most interesting are **Flores Creative Concept Store** ★ at No. 270 (✆ **22/200-48-51**), selling modern and traditional Portuguese design; a hip deli, **Mercearia das Flores** ★ at No. 110 (www.merceariadasflores.com; ✆ **22/208-32-32**), offers regional food products from cheese and sausage to canned sardines; modern jeweler **Elements ★** (www.elements.com.pt; ✆ **22/319-20-31**) at No. 249; and **Livraria Chamine da Mota ★★** at No. 18 (✆ **22/200-53-80**), a bookworm's delight with a four-floor maze of rare, antiquarian, and secondhand books.

One easy-to-pack Porto gift is **soap ★★**. The city has a soap-making tradition dating back over 100 years, with classic brands like **Portus Cales, Castelbel** (www.castelbel.com), and **Ach. Brito.** The oldest, **Claus Porto ★★★** (www.clausporto.com), has a flagship store on No. 22 Rua das Flores making soaps, sweetly scented candles, perfumes, and ambient fragrances with aromas of citrus, mimosa, and other aromatic delights designed to bring back memories of Portugal.

Porto Entertainment & Nightlife

Porto is currently a hotspot on the European nightlife scene. Hipsters jet in on low-cost flights to troll its happening bars and clubs on weekends. If you want to dance until dawn, the options are unlimited. If your idea of a night out is a nightcap after a concert of top-class classic music or a couple of hours listening to cool jazz, Porto also has that covered.

One venue offers all those options under one roof. The **Casa da Música ★★★,** Av. da Boavista 604–610 (www.casadamusica.com; ✆ **22/012-02-20**) is an architectural landmark built by Dutchman Rem Koolhaas, a giant irregular rhombus in glass and white concrete that seems to balance precariously over the surrounding avenues. Its array of auditoria large and small, multimedia studios, bars, and restaurants host a huge variety of events. In a typical week you can listen to a Tchaikovsky symphony, bop to a Brazilian samba star, be serenaded by a top fado guitarist or watch a big screen showing of *An American in Paris* accompanied by a live orchestra.

Other venues include the **Rivoli theater ★★,** Praça D. João I (www.teatromunicipaldoporto.pt; ✆ **22/339-22-01**), a legendary place in the Portuguese rock world that hosts classical, jazz, and pop concerts, as well as plays and dance. The **Coliseu ★★,** Rua Passos Manuel, 137 (www.coliseu.pt; ✆ **22/339-49-40**), holds shows by big names in Portuguese and international music, like Bob Dylan, fado star Mariza, and the Chinese National Ballet. Porto's grandest theater is the **Teatro Nacional São João ★★**, Praça da Batalha (www.tnsj.pt; ✆ **22/340-19-00**). It has a dynamic repertoire of classic and modern plays, often with English subtitles, as well as regular opera performances.

Jazz fans should head for the **Sala Porta Jazz ★**, Rua de João das Regras 305 (www.portajazz.com; ✆ **91/419-99-13**), which holds regular sessions most weekend nights and also organizes open-air shows on summer evenings in the Palácio de Cristal gardens; or the intimate **Hot Five Jazz & Blues Club ★**, with locations at Largo Actor Dias, 51 and Rua de Guerra Junqueiro 495 (www.hotfive.pt; ✆ **93/432-85-83**).

Unlike most other European countries, cinemas in Portugal mostly show **movies** in the original language, with subtitles in Portuguese, which makes

Porto & the Douro

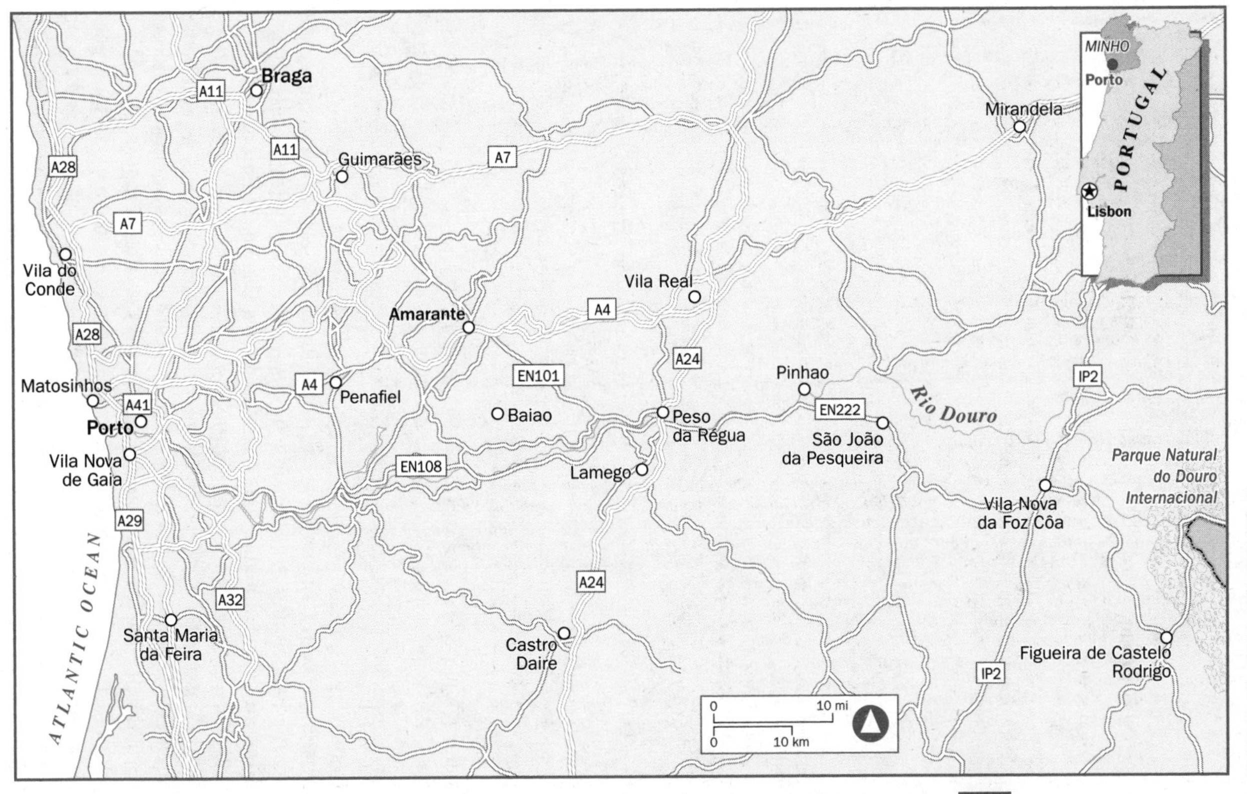

revealing THE ROMANESQUE

Portugal's northwestern corner was the nation's birthplace: first as an outpost of a Spanish mountain kingdom resisting Muslim rule, and then, after 1139, as an independent nation. Just east of Porto and south of the country's first capital in Guimarães, the valleys of the Sousa and Tâmega rivers are full of monuments from that early medieval era. Almost 60 of them are linked by the **Romanesque Route ★★** (www.rotadoromanico.com; ✆ **25/581-07-06**).

The route includes bridges arched over leafy streams and stern stone fortresses, but most of all, churches. They include the 10th-century Benedictine monastery of **Santa Maria de Pombeiro ★**, Pombeiro de Ribavizela, Felgueiras (✆ **25/581-07-06;** Wed–Sun 10am–6pm; entry 2€) and the **Salvador de Paço de Sousa ★** monastery, Largo do Mosteiro, Paço de Sousa (✆ **91/811-64-88;** open on request; admission free) outside Penafiel. Built in golden-tinged sandstone in the 13th century, it contains the tomb of an early national hero, Egas Moniz, tutor to the first king, Afonso Henriques.

Nearby is an even older monument, the **Castro de Monte Mozinho ★★**, Lugar de Vila, Oldrões, Penafiel (www.museudepenafiel.com; ✆ **25/571-27-60**) a hill fort built by Celtic people at the time of the Roman occupation. The ruins are remarkably well preserved. The visitor center is open May–Sept: Mon–Fri 9:30am–1pm & 2–5:30pm, Sat 10am–1pm & 2–6pm; Oct–Apr: Mon–Sat 9:30am–1pm & 1:30–5pm. Access to the site remains open all day and is free.

Solar Egas Moniz ★★★, Rua dos Monges Beneditinos, 158, Paço de Sousa (www.solaregasmoniz.com; ✆ **25/575-42-49;** doubles 96€–139€) is a swell base for exploring the route and the wider region. In this sweet and chic family-run hotel in a restored manor house, the charm of the individually decorated rooms is matched by the warmth of the welcome.

It's perhaps best to fast for a couple of days before dining at **O Sapo ★★★**, Lugar da Estrada, Irivo, Penafiel (✆ **25/575-23-26;** mains 11€–15€; closed Mon), a big, boisterous, belt-busting place that easily fills its 150 places on weekends with hungry locals and fans driving out from Porto to gorge on the seemingly endless plates of appetizers that land on the table—from smoked meats to fried octopus, or fresh fried eggs on cornbread—followed by roast meats or fish served with local wines. It's a classic that's not to be missed if you're in the area.

things easier for English-speaking film fans. The big movie theaters are mostly in shopping malls outside the city center. Among the closest are the **Cinemas Nos Alameda Shop e Spot,** Rua dos Campeões Europeus, 28-198 and the **Cinemas Nos GaiaShopping** (both on www.cinemas.nos.pt; ✆ **16 996**). A more intimate space that mixes Hollywood products with arthouse films is the **Cinema Trindade ★,** Rua do Almada 412 (www.cinematrindade.pt; ✆ **22/ 316-44-25**). The **Fundação Serralves ★,** Rua Serralves, 997 (www.serralves.pt; ✆ **22/615-65-00**) also has a program of alternative and independent films, with regular showings of classics on Sundays at 6pm. Updates on theater programs across Portugal can be found on the website www.cinecartaz.publico.pt. It's only in Portuguese, but you can usually work out what's on where.

Porto's **bar and club scene** spreads out around the city. There are plenty of places to have a drink down by the riverside in Ribeira and Gaia or out by the beach in Foz. The artsy **Cedofeita** district has its fair share of cool bars, like **Catraio ★★** (www.catraio.pt; ✆ **93/436-00-70**), a pioneer of the city's burgeoning craft beer scene on Rua de Cedofeita 256. The epicenter of nightlight is in the Baixa area around the parallel streets of **Rua Galeria de Paris ★★**, and **Rua Cândido dos Reis ★★**. Among the in places for a drink are **The Royal Cocktail Club ★★**, Rua da Fábrica, 105 (✆ **96/476-49-71;** Sun–Thurs 7pm–2am and Fri–Sat 7pm–4am) where star barmen serve inventive and classic mixes; and **Casa do Livro ★★**, Rua Galerias Paris, 85 (✆ **91/967-69-69**; Sun–Thurs 9pm–3am and Fri–Sat 9pm–4am), a laidback watering hole in an old bookstore. Among the rooftop bars, **17° ★** (www.decimosetimo.pt; ✆ **22/340-16-17**) atop the Hotel Dom Henrique, Rua do Bolhão 223, is a place to watch the city lights until 2am; or **Mirajazz** (✆ **91/924-90-17;** Tues–Sun 4–9pm), which has live jazz and sunset views over the Douro on Escadas do Caminho Novo 11.

When things start jumping, hot clubs include **Plano B ★**, Rua Cândido dos Reis, 30 (✆ **22/201-25-00;** Weds–Sat 10pm–6am); the funky **Café au Lait ★★**, Rua Galeria de Paris, 46 (✆ **22/208-44-86;** Tues–Sat 10pm–4am); or the discotheque-in-a-tunnel **Gare ★**, Rua da Madeira, 182 (www.gareporto.com; ✆ **22/202-60-30;** Wed–Thurs 11:45pm–6am, Fri–Sat 11:45pm–8am).

Gay Porto's favorite spots include **Café Lusitano ★★**, Rua de José Falcão 137 (www.cafelusitano.com; ✆ **22/201-10-67;** Wed–Thurs 9:30pm–2am and Fri–Sat 10–4am), serves as a cocktail bar, restaurant, and a dancehall that really heats up at weekends. Other gay nightspots include the industrial-chic **Conceição 35 ★**, Rua da Conceição 35 (✆ **22/093-80-34;** Mon–Sat 7pm–2am), which transforms from a gin and tapas bar into a dance club; and the party palace **Zoom ★**, Rua Passos Manuel, 40 (✆ **91/835-32-82;** Fri–Sat 12:30–6am).

If you happen to be in Porto in June, be aware that practically the whole city turns into a giant, wild nightspot on June 23, the **noite de São João ★★★**, when *tripeiros* celebrate their patron Saint John. There are street parties, bonfires, mass consumption of *caldo verde* (cabbage soup), and grilled sardines washed down with beer and red wine. A spectacular firework display lights up the Douro around midnight and the festivities from Ribeira to Foz carry on into the wee hours. Earlier in June, the **Nos Primavera Sound ★★** festival annually brings some of the biggest names in rock and pop to Porto for 3 nights of open-air music.

AMARANTE ★★

60m (37 miles) E of Porto; 368km (229 miles) N of Lisbon

Nestled in a willow-lined curve of the River Tâmega, Amarante's Renaissance buildings, art history, and reputation for delectable pastries make it one of the most attractive small towns in Portugal.

ARRIVING

BY BUS The **Rodonorte** company (www.rodonorte.pt; ✆ **25/934-07-10**) runs up to 12 buses a day from Porto's Rua Ateneu Comercial do Porto, 19, to Amarante. The journey lasts 50 minutes and costs 7.80€. There is no rail service.

BY CAR Amarante is a 40-minute drive from Porto on the A4 autostrada.

VISITOR INFORMATION

The **Tourist Office** is at Largo Conselheiro Antonio Candido (www.cm-amarante.pt; ✆ **25/542-02-46**). It's open June–Sept daily 9:30am–7pm and Oct–May daily 9am–6pm.

Exploring Amarante

Amarante clusters photogenically around a high arched bridge over the Tâmega, which spills down from Spain through the surrounding hills on its way to meet the Douro. There is a succession of balconied, red-tiled houses rising up from the main square dominated by the Renaissance church of **São Gonçalo ★★**, Praça da República (✆ **25/543-74-25;** Mon–Sat 8am–7pm and Sun 8am–8pm; free). Built in the soft brown local granite, the church's main facade has a distinctly un-Portuguese feel. It was mostly built during the Spanish occupation in the late-16th century and the three-tiered entrance has a Castilian grandiosity (oddly, the tiled dome and arcaded gallery carrying the statues of four kings is distinctly Italianate). Inside, the gold-covered baroque woodwork is more typically Portuguese. The church holds the tomb of Saint Gonçalo, a 12th-century monk, who has become the patron of spinsters on the lookout for a husband and the focus of fertility rituals with their roots in pagan times. Legend has it that if an unmarried woman pulls three times on the rope belt of a wooden statue of the saint in the church's sacristy, she will find a husband. To ensure that the marriage is fecund, she's also supposed to eat a larger-than-life pastry that's decidedly phallic in form, known as a *doce de São Gonçalo.*

Thankfully for those with a sweet tooth, Amarante has other confectionary delights that are much more palatable. Just across the river is the **Confeitaria da Ponte ★★★**, Rua 31 de Janeiro, 186 (www.confeitariadaponte.pt/wp/index.php; ✆ **25/543-20-34;** daily 8:30am–8pm), which is widely considered to produce some of the country's best traditional pastries. Opened in 1930, it specializes in regional cakes and those based on centuries-old recipes from nuns in the convents of northern Portugal. Rich in almonds, cinnamon, and eggs, they carry evocative names like bacon from heaven (*toucinho do céu*), angels' cheeks (*papos de anjo*), or little kisses of love (*beijinhos de amor*). There's also a tea-room with a terrace overlooking the river where you can sample them, accompanied, if you like, with a glass from their selection of port wines.

The graceful **Ponte de São Gonçalo ★** bridge that links the two halves of the town was built in 1790 after the 13th-century original was washed away in flooding. Constructed in the same golden stone as the church it leads to, the bridge has three arches and is decorated with a pair of baroque spires. The bridge also has historical significance as the site of the heroic battle in 1809 when a small Portuguese force, aided by a few British soldiers and the townsfolk, held back for 14 days a much larger contingent of Napoleon's invading army. Eventually the French broke through and pillaged the town in revenge. Signs of the battle can still be seen with the marks of shell fragments in the church and ecclesiastical robes ripped by bayonets in the church sacristy.

After Saint Gonçalo, Amarante's most famous son is Amadeo de Souza-Cardoso (1887–1918), arguably Portugal's greatest modern painter. Located in an old Dominican monastery linked to the church is the **Museu Municipal Amadeo de Souza-Cardoso ★★**, Alameda Teixeira de Pascoaes (www.amadeosouza-cardoso.pt; ✆ **25/542-02-82;** open Tues–Sun Oct–May 9:30am–noon and 2–5pm, June–Sept 10am–noon and 2–5:30pm; admission is 1€ adults, 0.50€ students and seniors, children under 15 free). Besides a collection of works by Souza-Cardoso, whose style absorbed influences from Cubism and Expressionism as well as Portuguese folk art, this small-town museum has a surprisingly wide selection of modern and contemporary works, mostly by Portuguese artists, and holds regular temporary exhibitions. Among the oddest works on show are a couple of oversize male and female demons sculptured in wood, supposedly copies of medieval originals shipped in from Indian trading posts and destroyed by the pillaging French. They, too, are linked to ancient fertility cults, as you might be able to guess from their prominent physical attributes.

Spreading out from the bridge are a number of pretty streets like **Rua 5 de Outubro** and **Rua 31 de Janeiro,** lined with centuries-old town houses where the white-painted facades contrast with naked stone window frames and corner posts. There are plenty of little stores selling woolen blankets from the hills and other handicrafts. It's also worth walking up the hill to the little round **Igreja de São Domingos** church, which has great views over the town and the river. Inside, there's a golden baroque altar and a museum of religious art. After all the sightseeing, a great place to relax is the **Café-Bar São Gonçalo ★**, Praça da República, 8 (✆ **25/543-27-07**, daily 7am–2am) a center of the town's social life since the 1930s, which retains its original decor, plus a life-size statue of local poet Teixeira de Pascoaes (1877–1952), who was a regular customer.

Where to Stay & Eat

Casa de Calçada ★★★ A member of the prestigious Relais & Chateaux group, Casa de Calçada is a five-story mansion in lemon-yellow tones dating back to the 1600s. Its location is a romantic one, beside the Tâmega looking across to the historic heart of Amarante. All but the cheapest rooms have views of the city, and several have balconies. Furnishings are plush and in a classical style, with velvet armchairs, damask drapes, soft lighting, and huge vases of fresh flowers. There's a spacious garden and outdoor swimming pool, spa, and nearby golf course. In the on-site, Michelin-starred Largo do Paço

VINHO VERDE by the douro

Although the Douro is best known for port and big red wines, the region just east of Porto and the slopes running down to the river from Amarante are cultivated to produce ***Vinho Verde,*** "green wine," Portugal's fresh, mostly white tipples that are one of the country's most distinctive products.

The region is a delight to drive, with roads that twist up and down the valleys through forests and vineyards, curving suddenly to open up to vistas of the slow-moving Douro way below, or reveal the baroque tower of a whitewashed hilltop church.

Wine estates in this verdant area are also a pleasure to visit. Most organize tours and tastings but may require booking in advance.

Among the most impressive is the **Quinta da Aveleda,** Rua da Aveleda, 2, Penafiel (www.aveleda.com; ✆ **25/571-82-42**), where you can wander through lush, tropical gardens surrounding the aristocratic family home and cellars where casks of fabulous **Adega Velha** brandy ripen, as well as tour the vineyards and taste their *vinho verdes*. Open daily 9am to 6pm, reservation needed.

At **Quinta de Covela,** São Tomé de Covelas, Baião (www.covela.pt; ✆ **91/306-56-91**), you can sample highly rated *vinhos verdes* alongside other whites and reds in a stone manor dating back to the 1500s that once belonged to film director Manoel de Oliveira (1908–2015). The views down the valley to the Douro are heavenly. Booking is required.

The **Casa de Tormes,** Caminho Particular de Tormes, Santa Cruz do Douro (www.feq.pt; ✆ **25/488-21-20;** Tues–Sun 9:30am–12:30pm and 2:30–4:30pm; admission 5€, 3.50€ students and seniors) offers the chance to mix wine with culture. The house once belonged to the writer José Maria de Eça de Queirós (1845–1900) and has been preserved as a museum. Fans like to walk up the hillside to the house from the pretty little railway station of Aregos on the banks of the Douro, a climb immortalized in his novel *The City and the Mountains*. The foundation that runs the museum and the vineyard has a restaurant (www.restaurantedetormes.com; ✆ **25/5 13-78-62;** closed Sunday evenings and Monday all day) where you can lunch or dine (except in winter) on regional cuisine.

There are plenty of other excellent places to eat and sleep in the region. Among the accommodations, the **Casas de Pousadouro,** Caminho dos Moinhos, Laranjal – Santa Cruz do Douro (www.casasdepousadouro.com; ✆ **91/329-66-04**) is a standout, offering five restored and beautifully furnished rural stone houses on the banks of the Douro, from 120€. Nearby are two luxury spa hotels also spectacularly located above the river: the **Douro Palace,** Lugar do Carrapatelo, Santa Cruz do Douro (www.douropalace.com; ✆ **25/488-00-00;** double from 88€), and the **Douro Royal Valley,** Portela do Rio Pala, Ribadouro (www.douroroyal.com; ✆ **25/507-09-00;** double from 112€).

Hearty rustic restaurants abound. Locals drive for miles to the remote highland village of Almofrela to tuck into the lamb or chunks of young beef roasted in the wood-fired ovens of the **Tasquinha de Fumo,** Rua de Almofrela (✆ **96/581-43-39**). Similar hearty cuisine can be found at the **Residencial Borges,** Rua de Camões, 4, Baião (www.residencialborges.com; ✆ **25/554-13-22**) and the **Casa do Almocreve,** Rua da Serração, Portela do Gôve (www.casadoalmocreve.pt; ✆ **25/555-12-26**). Both also have guest rooms, which might be a good idea after trying local specialties such as *bazulaque*, a rich stew made from lambs' offal.

restaurant, Chef Tiago Bonito plates food almost too pretty to eat, with creations like turbot in a smoky sauce with Algarve shrimp and celery; or Barrosã veal with artichoke, leeks, and fermented mushroom. The hotel recently opened a second restaurant serving Bonito's take on regional cooking.

Largo do Paço, 6. www.casadacalcada.com. ✆ **25/541-08-30.** 30 units. 90€–280€ double, 235€–325€ suite. Free parking. **Amenities:** Garden; terrace; bike hire; outdoor pool; 2 restaurants; bar; games room; free Wi-Fi.

Hotel Monverde ★★★ For a full-immersion experience in *vinho verde* culture, this is the place. Located in the Quinta da Lixa estate, the hotel is dedicated to all things enological. Your room will look out over the vines; you can get a massage with grape skins and leaves in the spa, or sip the estate's wines with your creamy fish and lobster rice with cilantro or rack of lamb with pumpkin and thyme in the gourmet restaurant. You can even join in the seasonal work of the vineyard, including crushing grapes by foot during the late summer harvest, or get a master class in wine tasting. It's all in a modern architectural unit that uses natural local stone and wood to produce a contemporary but cozy environment complete with cotton duvets and a blazing fireplace for cooler evenings. It's a 20-minute drive north from Amarante.

Quinta de Sanguinhedo, Castanheiro Redondo, Telões. www.monverde.pt. ✆ **25/514-31-00.** 30 units. 99€–219€ double, 212€–322€ suite. Free parking. **Amenities:** Garden; terrace; free bikes; indoor & outdoor pool; spa; sauna; hammam; Jacuzzi; massage service; fitness room; restaurant; bar; games room; children's play area; babysitting; free Wi-Fi.

LAMEGO ★★

130km (70 miles) E of Porto; 350km (220 miles) N of Lisbon

Set back from the south bank of the Douro, this is another charming small town in the heart of wine country. Highlights include a marvelous hilltop church, an exceptional museum and mouthwatering ham pies.

Essentials

ARRIVING

BY BUS **Rede Expressos** (www.rede-expressos.pt) has three to six daily buses from Lisbon. The journey lasts 5 hours and costs 19.50€. Its buses from Porto take about 3 hours, cost 10.90€, and most require changes in Vila Real or Viseu. **RodoNorte** (www.rodonorte.pt) buses from Porto cost the same and also require a change in Vila Real.

BY TRAIN There is no rail link to Lamego, but you can take the train (www.cp.pt) that runs on the **scenic route** along the Douro from Porto to Régua. From there it's a 15-minute bus trip to Lamego.

BY CAR It takes just over 3 hours to get there from Lisbon. Take the A1 autostrada north. Switch to IP3 at Coimbra, then take exit 9 in Viseu to join the A24. From Porto, the fastest way is to take the A4 east to Vila Real, then head south on the A24. It takes about 1 hour and 20 minutes.

BOATS, trains & automobiles

Between Porto and the Spanish border, the **Douro** flows through some of the world's most beautiful wine country. Hill after hill and valley after valley are covered with terraced vineyards overlooking the big river and its fast-flowing tributaries like the Côa, Tua, Sabor, and Corgo. Dotted among the scenery are the wineries. Many are located in centuries-old manor houses emerging from the greenery as specks of white paintwork and pale gray granite.

There are many options for exploring this UNESCO World Heritage landscape, but a **boat trip** ★★★ gets up close and personal with the river. They range from cheap and cheerful day trips from Porto with lunch on board and a scenic rail journey back, to romantic sailing tours or cabin-ship cruises lasting several days with side journeys to Lisbon or into Spain.

Among day-trip operators, **Rota do Douro** (www.rotadodouro.pt; ✆ **22/375-90-42**) offers a cruise popular with locals that starts at 8:45am at the quayside in Vila Nova de Gaia. You get breakfast and lunch on board, a slow trip upriver, then a couple of hours in Régua to visit the Museum do Douro (see p. 376) before heading back by train. Prices start from 67€. They also offer other trips heading farther up the Douro to **Pinhão** or **Barca D'Alva,** through some of the most dramatic scenery. Other local day-trip operators include **PortoDouro** (www.portodouro.com; ✆ **22/938-99-33**) and **Cruzeiros Douro** (www.cruzeiros-douro.pt; ✆ **22/619-10-90**).

For **longer trips,** international companies such as AmaWaterways, CroisiEurope, Scenic Cruises, Viking River Cruises, and Uniworld Boutique River Cruises offer voyages for a week or more on the Douro, including during the September grape harvest. Vessels often feature a pool on top so that passengers can take advantage of the usually sunny climate.

Cruises including trips to vineyards and towns along the route, meals, and live fado music on board start from around $1,000 a week but can run over $8,000 depending on services and season. Some companies offer add-on excursions to Lisbon or cities in Spain such as Madrid or the university city of Salamanca. The main local operator is Porto-based **Douro Azul** (www.douroazul.com; ✆ **22/340-25-00**), which has a fleet operating on a variety of routes on the river. Its unique attraction is the **Spirit of Chartwell,** a luxury barge fitted with artifacts from Pullman carriages and vintage liners. It was used to waft Britain's Queen Elizabeth II down the Thames on her Diamond Jubilee in 2011 before being sold to the Portuguese company.

Hiring your own boat is also possible. Douro Azul and a number of smaller specialized companies have crewed vessels for hire. One of the best is **Douro à Vela** (www.douroavela.pt; ✆ **91/879-37-92**),

VISITOR INFORMATION

The **tourist office** is at Rua Regimento de Infantaria, 9 (✆ **25/409-90-00**). It's open in summer 10am to 7pm; in winter 10am to 1pm and 2 to 6pm.

Exploring Lamego

However you arrive in Lamego, it's hard to avoid the **Santuário de Nossa Senhora dos Remédios** ★★, Monte de Santo Estevão (✆ **25/465-53-18;** open daily 11:30am–4pm). The twin-towered rococo church looms over the which offers trips from 2 hours to 3 days on its sailing yacht or a 60-year-old river launch. Their cruises take in some of the most beautiful stretches upstream from Régua. Among the most popular is the 4-hour sunset dinner cruise, with catering by the award-winning DOC restaurant; 290€ for two. **Pipadouro** (www.pipadouro.pt; ✆ **93/919-62-62**) seeks to create a refined 1950s ambiance with its "gentlemen's vintage boats" operating out of Pinhão. One once transported admirals in Britain's Royal Navy.

If you'd rather stay on dry land, there are **trains ★★★** along the line that dip down to the Douro soon after leaving Porto and cling to the bank for over 3 hours before terminating at Pocinho, up near the Spanish border. There are five departures a day and the trip costs 13.35€ one-way. Trains also stop at several pretty, *azulejo*-decorated stations serving the wine towns and villages along the line. The **CP** rail company (www.cp.pt; ✆ **70/721-02-20**) also runs special day trips between June and October in historic carriages pulled by a **1925 steam engine** with local musicians and port tastings on board. Prices start at 42.50€ adults, 19€ children. Then there's the **Presidential train** (www.thepresidentialtrain.com; ✆ **91/463-95-16**). Built in 1890 to carry heads of state, it's been beautifully restored and now hauls lucky passengers on spring and fall runs along the Douro line. The 9-hour trip includes wine tastings at a top-class *quinta* and lunch served on board by leading chefs. Details of the 2020 program were still being finalized as we went to press, and a new project was likely to take its place in 2021. In 2019 the trip was priced at 650€ per person.

Get a **car** and you can discover the road proved scientifically to be the world's best drive. The **N-222 ★★★** sweeping along the south bank of the Douro between Régua and Pinhão beat the likes of California's Highway 1 and Australia's Great Ocean Road in tests to evaluate the thrill factor of the world's scenic routes, organized by rental company Avis and carried out in 2015 by a race-track designer, quantum physicist, and roller-coaster builder. It is, however, just one of the dramatic drives around the Douro. The climb from Pinhão to the winery-packed village of **Provesende** is another. Given the twisting tracks, however, it's doubly important that drivers avoid the temptations on offer in vineyards along the way.

If you'd rather discover the Douro under your own steam, **We Love Small Hotels** (www.welovesmallhotels.com; ✆ **21/099-18-99**) organizes walking and cycling tours among the vineyards and historic sites, as well as self-drive trips, with overnight stops in some of the region's most charming accommodations, like the scrumptious **Vintage House** (www.vintagehousehotel.com; ✆ **25/473-02-30**) overlooking the Douro in Pinhão.

city from its hilltop perch, linked to downtown by a monumental 686-step **staircase ★★★** that zigzags up to the summit in a cascade of blue tiles, baroque spires, fountains, and statues surrounded by greenery. It is an exceptional sight. At night, it's bathed in golden light. Work on the church started in 1750 on the site of a ruined 14th-century pilgrim's chapel, but it wasn't finished until 1905. The interior is a riot of gold-covered woodwork and *azulejos* under a carved ceiling in sky-blue and white. If you can't face the walk up the stairs, there's a road that snakes up through the forested hillside

KINGS OF THE quintas

There are over 200 *quintas,* or wine estates, sprinkled around the Douro wine region. Their owners include multinational beverage industry giants and powerful dynastic producers, but many are small, family-run wineries who have been working the land for generations. Until a few decades ago, production was dominated by port, with raw wines shipped down to Porto to be blended and fortified. Since the 1990s, however, the region has become increasingly recognized for its DOC table wines, both red and white, winning international kudos for drinks that rival the best of Bordeaux or Chianti.

A **visit to a quinta ★★★** is a must. Most are open to visitors with offers that range from tastings and tours to meals and overnight accommodations, even a chance to join the harvest and press the grapes. It's usually best to call in advance to book a visit, although if they aren't too busy, wineries may welcome visitors who simply show up. Here are some offering the best visitor experiences:

Quinta do Bomfim, Pinhão (www.symington.com; ✆ **25/473-03-70**). Not only does this produce Dow's ports regularly judged to be among the world's top wines (*Wine Spectator* said its 2011 was the best in the world), but it's also just a 5-minute walk from Pinhão railway station and quayside, making it an easy visit for travelers without a car. The main lodge, with its cellars containing giant vats and barrels, dates back to 1896. There's a museum and tasting room overlooking the river. It's owned by the Anglo-Portuguese Symington family, which has been in the Douro wine business for 14 generations. Open April to October 10:30am to 6pm, November to March 9:30am to 5pm. Guided tours and tastings from 17€. Booking required. Guided tours and picnics on request.

Quinta do Pôpa, EN 222, Adorigo (www.quintadopopa.com; ✆ **91/567-84-98**). This small family winery has one of the best views and warmest welcomes of any along the Douro. It also has a heartwarming story of an emigrant returning to fulfill his father's dream of owning a vineyard in the Douro, where he'd toiled for years as a laborer on the estates of others. Today, the third generation produces wines that are a tribute to the grandfather nicknamed "Pôpa"—a crested bird. The youthful team invites visitors to taste, tour or lunch at the

to the back of the church with parking at the top. Every year in late August/early September, **pilgrimages** to the summit draw thousands to follow a procession behind sacred statues of the Virgin Mary carried on ox-drawn carts or the shoulders of devotees. One of the biggest religious festivals in Portugal, it's accompanied by 2 weeks of street parties, concerts, and fireworks.

Down in the city, many of Lamego's main sites are concentrated at the end of a broad tree-lined avenue, **Avenida Visconde Guedes Teixeira,** that leads toward the stairway. At No. 31, the **Pastelaria Scala ★** (✆ **25/461-26-99;** open Thurs–Tues 8am–8pm), makes a good place for a break. Its dark wood-lined interior conjures up a distinct 1950s feel, and it's usually packed with locals lining up to buy ***bôlas de Lamego***—thin slices of pie that can be filled with tuna, sardines, salt cod, or pork marinated in red wine, but most typically the famed local ham.

winery. Their summer picnics are particularly renowned. Tours and tastings start from 20€ per person. (Open Apr–Oct: Tues–Sat 10:30am–5pm; Nov–Mar: Tues–Fri 10:30am–5:30pm.)

Quinta das Amendoeiras, Seixo de Ansiães (www.negreiroswine.com; ✆ **91/069-62-27**). The slopes of this family-run winery run down to the banks of the Douro in one of the most-beautiful, yet least-visited stretches of valley. There is a boat which owner Mário Negreiros will use to take you for a cruise; water-skiing; or pickups from the little railway halt on the far bank, if you arrive by train from Porto. "If you want to be treated like a king or a queen, please don't come. If you want to know a real Douro quinta, where real people make real wine in a real winery, you're most welcome!" Negreiros, a former journalist, says on his website. Make no mistake though, you're not slumming it here. Rooms are furnished with great care and taste; the red wine is marvelous, and you can dine at the communal table to a home-made dinner of *alheira* sausages from the barbecue and vegetables from the garden. No public tours or tasting. Doubles from 40€.

Quinta do Portal, EN 323 Celeirós, Sabrosa (www.quintadoportal.com; ✆ **25/993-70-00**). The cellars here were built by the great Porto architect Álvaro Siza Vieira in 2008 and form one of the most striking buildings in the region: amber-colored blocks coated in places by cork and slate for natural insulation. Inside it's a vast, temperature-controlled bunker lined with silently aging port barrels. You can linger in the estate's older buildings, converted into a sophisticated boutique hotel (double rooms 100€–160€, including breakfast) and a renowned restaurant that serves dishes like baked salt cod with rosemary and olive oil, paired with the estate wines. Cellars are open from 10am to 5:30pm; guided tours with tasting are 7.50€.

For more details on quintas and Douro wine production, check out www.dourowinetourism.com, which has wide range of information. Specialists in wine tours include **Wine Tourism Portugal** (www.winetourismportugal.com; ✆ **22/610-20-75**) and **Grape Discoveries** (www.grapediscoveries.com; ✆ **93/475-32-84**), which specializes in private SUV tours into some of the most scenic and off-the-beaten track parts of the wine region.

At the northern end of the avenue is the **Museu de Lamego ★★**, Largo de Camões (www.museudelamego.gov.pt; ✆ **25/460-02-30;** daily 10am–6pm; admission 3€ adults, 1.5€ students and seniors), one of Portugal's best regional museums. Housed in the former bishops' palace built in the 1700s, it holds an array of treasures including a series of five paintings by the Renaissance master **Grão Vasco** (1475–1542) depicting Biblical scenes, including a charming depiction of the creation of animals. There's a series of huge **Flemish tapestries** from the 16th century, enchanting multicolored tiles from the 17th century, and rare medieval sculptures. It also organizes regular cultural events, from open-air movie showings to exhibitions of photography and contemporary art.

Across the square from the museum is the **Sé ★**, Lamego's cathedral, Largo da Sé (✆ **25/461-27-66;** open 9am–12:30pm, 2:30–7pm; free admission). It was founded in 1159, but of the original building, ordered by Portugal's founding king Afonso Henriques, only the stubby, square bell tower remains. Most of the church is late-medieval Gothic in style. Beyond the great granite arches of the main door is a dramatic arched ceiling coated with **brightly colored frescos** showing Old Testament scenes. They were painted in 1738 by Nicolau Nasoni, the Italian architect who put the baroque into Porto's skyline. The graceful, double-level Renaissance cloister enclosing a tranquil garden is also worth a visit.

The oldest part of the city curves uphill toward the medieval castle along streets full of charm, like **Rua de Olaria** and **Rua do Castelo.** Busy **Praça do Comércio** is lined with handsome town houses fronted by high windows and wrought-iron balconies. The **Castle ★**, Rua do Castelo (✆ **25/409-80-90;** open Tues–Sun 10am–6pm; free admission) was fought over by Muslims and Christians in the 10th and 11th centuries. On misty nights, they say, the battlements are haunted by the spirit of a Moorish princess slain by her father for eloping with a Christian knight. The walls offer great views, and a recently opened **medieval water tank** in the basement holds a multimedia exhibition on the history of the city.

If you have time, pop into the nearby church of **Santa Maria de Almacave,** Rua das Cortes (✆ **25/461-24-60;** open 7:30am–noon and 4–7:30pm; free admission). Built in the 12th century in the Romanesque style, it's one of the oldest buildings in Lamego and is where Afonso Henriques held the first *cortes,* or parliament, of Portuguese nobles in 1143 after declaring independence from Spanish overlords. The interior is modest but has some pretty *azulejos.* Visitors staying into the evening should catch a show at the **Teatro Ribeiro Conceição,** Largo Camões (http://trc.cm-lamego.pt; ✆ **25/460-00-70**), which has regular concerts and movie showings. The building was constructed as a hospital in the 1720s. After a fire destroyed the interior, it was converted into an elegant, three-tiered theater in the 1920s.

A pleasant hour-long walk from downtown (or a 10-minute drive) is the **Capela de São Pedro de Balsemão ★** on a little unnamed lane beside the stream running north out of town (www.culturanorte.pt; ✆ **25/460-02-30;** open Tues–Sun 10am–1pm and 2–8pm; free admission). This is reputed to be one of the oldest churches in Portugal, dating back to the 6th century. Although the outside was transformed in the 1700s, the interior is a fascinating mix of Visigoth and Romanesque with some unusual Islam-influenced touches. There's a splendid medieval tomb containing the remains of the bishop of Porto.

Farther afield, the pretty village of **Ucanha ★**, a 15-minute drive south of Lamego, is worth a visit for the imposing medieval tower protecting its stone bridge and the **Caves da Murganheira,** a sparkling-wine producer with its cellar carved deep into the rock (Abadia Velha, Ucanha, www.murganheira.com; ✆ **25/467-01-85;** Visits by guided tour: hourly Tues–Sat 9:30–11:30am & 2:30–4:30pm, by appointment only).

Where to Stay & Eat

Hotel options in the town center are limited. You're better off staying in one of the resorts or wine estate hotels in nearby villages and down the valley by the Douro.

Casa de Santo António de Britiande ★★ A lovingly restored 16th-century manor house, once the retreat of Franciscan friars, the hotel stands surrounded by 5 hectares (12 acres) of gardens planted with flowers, vines, and fruit trees. Beside the pool is a blaze of lavender. The owners have counted 26 species of wild birds here. Inside the thick stone walls the house is softly lit with coach lamps. Antique-style furnishings include big wooden beds with embroidered cotton covers and splashes of color provided by traditional Portuguese fabrics. You can sample wines grown on the owners' estates, accompanied by homemade delicacies: Lamego ham pies, smoked hams, and sausages, or a full meal of local treats featuring meats roasted in the wood-fired oven. It's a 5-minute drive from downtown Lamego. Minimum 2 nights.

Largo de S. Sebastião, Britiande. www.casasantoantoniobritiande.com. ✆ **25/469-93-46.** 6 units. 115€–123€ double. Adults only. Free parking. **Amenities:** Garden; terrace; bikes; barbeque; outdoor pool; restaurant (prior booking needed); shop; free Wi-Fi.

Quinta da Pacheca Wine House Hotel ★★ After driving through vineyards enclosed by a bend in the Douro, you enter though a noble stone gate and drive up to the house down an alley shaded by plane trees. Since 2019, this classy quinta offers a unique experience: sleeping in giant wine casks turned into bungalows with private decks laid out among the vines. There are 10 of them, equipped with all mod cons. If you prefer something more traditional (and cheaper), rooms in the ivy-covered 18th-century manor at the heart of the estate are spacious (smallest are 28 sq. meters/92 sq. ft.) and come decorated in an uncluttered mix of old and new, with antique prints and natural colors. Some have balconies and four-poster beds. You can taste award-winning wines and drink more over a meal in the restaurant. More expansion is underway, in 2020 a pool, spa and extra rooms are set to open.

Rua do Relógio do Sol, 261, Cambres. www.quintadapacheca.com. ✆ **25/433-12-29.** 25 units. 117€–373€ double. Free parking. **Amenities:** Garden; terrace; bike hire; restaurant; babysitting; free Wi-Fi.

Six Senses Douro Valley ★★★ In 2015, Asia's super-luxurious Six Senses group chose a 19th-century manor overlooking the Douro for its first European resort. The result is simply stunning—a vast estate where landscape gardens blend into terraced vineyards and soothing Thai spa treatments can be followed up with tastings from the range of over 750 wines. The panache of its blend of Portuguese heritage with contemporary design in the huge rooms and suites, rivals the wizardry of its chefs crafting exquisite updates of regional cuisine. The outdoor pools are set in 8 hectares (20 acres) of land. Huge rooms offer views over the river or vineyards. It's a 20-minute drive north from downtown Lamego. It regularly picks up awards and placings on "best of" lists and is set to get bigger with the addition of 10 new rooms due by the start of 2020.

Quinta de Vale Abraão, Samodães. www.sixsenses.com. ✆ **25/466-06-00.** 60 units. 296€–870€ double, 540€–1,320€ suite. Free parking. **Amenities:** Garden; terrace; bike rental; tennis; indoor and outdoor pools; spa; hammam; sauna; Jacuzzi; massage service; fitness center; 4 restaurants; 2 bars; library; games room; babysitting; free Wi-Fi.

PESO DA RÉGUA ★

120km (75 miles) E of Porto; 360km (225 miles) N of Lisbon

Peso da Régua, or simply Régua, is the main river port in the wine region, the place where raw wine used to be floated downstream in sailing boats to be turned into port. It is still a busy transport hub today, with bridges spanning the Douro. Despite a dramatic location and riverside promenades, it's not the prettiest town, but it is the center of the wine trade with a fine museum, some excellent restaurants, and wineries galore in the surrounding hills.

Essentials

ARRIVING

BY TRAIN The trip along the Douro-hugging railroad from Porto is a treat. It lasts just less than 2 hours and costs 9.75€. There are seven daily direct trains from Porto's Campanhã station. Four more are slightly longer and slightly cheaper, involving a change in Marco de Canaveses.

BY BOAT Régua is a major stop for river cruises, with many lines starting, ending, or stopping off here (see p. 370).

BY BUS **Rodonorte** (www.rodonorte.pt; ✆ **25/934-07-10**) has six daily buses from Porto, with a change in Vila Real. The trip costs 9.50€ and lasts about 2½ hours. **Rede Expresso** has 3 daily buses from Lisbon the trip lasts just over 5 hours and costs 19.50€.

BY CAR It's 3½ hours from Lisbon. Take the A1 north to Coimbra, turn onto the IP3, then take the A24 in Viseu. From Porto it's 1 hour and 15 minutes along the A4 east to Vila Real, then south on the A24.

VISITOR INFORMATION

The **tourist office** is at Rua da Ferreirinha (✆ **25/431-28-46;** open Mon–Sat 9:30am–noon and 2–6pm).

Exploring Régua

Whether you arrive by train or boat, it's a short walk to the **Museu do Douro,** Rua Marquês de Pombal (www.museudodouro.pt; ✆ **25/431-01-90;** open daily Mar–Oct: 10am–5:45pm, Nov–Feb 10am–5:15pm; admission 6€, 3€ seniors and students, free under 12s). This riverside museum is Régua's main attraction. Don't be put off by the largely Portuguese-only website, the museum itself offers a modern, multimedia explanation of wine production, history and traditions of the region. It's housed in a 19th-century building built as the headquarters of the agency that regulated the port trade and spills over into a modern extension.

STONE-AGE graffiti

The wild and beautiful **Côa River** valley was due to be drowned by a dam project in the 1980s. But before construction began, archaeologists poking around in the verdant banks where the Côa runs into the Douro made a startling discovery: rocks scattered about the valley were covered in images. Thousands of carvings of deer, goats, horses, and horned aurochs (ancestors of modern cattle) were etched into the stone. It turned out to be some of the world's oldest graffiti, dating back over 20,000 years.

After a campaign, work on the dam was abandoned and the valley is now a UNESCO World Heritage Site. Nobody really knows why prehistoric people over millennia kept coming to this spot to carve their images. Everything that is known about the engravings is explained in a striking modern museum rising out of a nearby hilltop. The **Museu do Côa ★★★**, Rua do Museu, Vila Nova de Foz Côa (www.arte-coa.pt; ✆ **27/976-82-60**) is itself an architectural treasure, with an excellent restaurant and stunning views over the Douro landscape (open June–Sept 9:30am–7pm, Mar 1–May 9:30–6pm, Oct–Feb 9am–5pm; admission 6€, seniors 4€, children 4–12 3€, free for under 4s).

The rock carvings in the **Parque Arqueológico do Vale do Côa ★★★** can be visited on a guided tour arranged by the museum. They will take you by jeep into the valley and escort you on foot to see the rocks (15€, 12€ seniors, 7.50€ youngers 4–12). There are also nighttime visits. Special arrangements can be made for disabled visitors. It is difficult not to be awed in the presence of some of humanity's earliest art, although, it must be said, some visitors are underwhelmed when they actually see the carvings. They can be hard to visualize given that the artists scratched over their own or other's work. Guides refer to one particularly contorted site of overlapping scratches as "spaghetti rock."

If you need R&R after clambering over the rocks, the **Longroiva Hotel Rural ★★**, Lugar do Rossio, Longroiva (www.hoteldelongroiva.com; ✆ **27/914-90-20;** double rooms with breakfast 70€–160€) is the place. A 10-minute drive south of the Stone Age site, this crimson tile-covered 18th-century building was constructed over hot springs used since Roman times. The hotel, which also has a striking modern wing, offers stylishly comfortable rooms, a spa featuring a heated outdoor pool, and an excellent restaurant serving regional cooking.

There are also plenty of vineyards to visit amid the vine-covered hillsides around here. The best known near Foz Côa is the **Quinta de Ervamoira** (www.ramospinto.pt; ✆ **27/975-92-29;** visits by appointment), which is located in the archaeological park and was saved from flooding by the discovery of the rock carvings. It is part of the Ramos Pinto port company and was the setting of a romantic French novel. Visits can include tastings, lunch, a tour of the estate's small museum, and a trip to the rock-carving sites.

The collection includes paintings of Douro landscapes, antique wine-making equipment, and vintage advertising posters. There are regular temporary exhibitions that can range from historic photographs of work in the vineyards to contemporary art.

There's also a wine bar overlooking the river, a restaurant serving excellent value regional dishes and a shop where you can stock up on wine or local handicrafts.

Where to Stay

Quinta do Vallado ★★ One of the oldest and most famous of the Douro's wine estates, this quinta is a 10-minute drive from the center of Régua. It produces some of the region's best wines and is still run by the descendants of Dona Antónia Ferreira, a legendary figure in the story of port. Guest rooms are in the 18th-century manor or a modern extension in local schist stone that blends into the surrounding wine terraces. The views across the vine-covered hillsides are breathtaking, although slightly marred by the highway. There's a relaxing garden containing a pool with a view. Both the 21st-century and 18th-century rooms are tastefully furnished with natural materials and understated colors. Included with the room are visits to the winery, tastings, bikes, and fishing gear—in case you fancy trying to lift a trout from the Rio Corgo, which flows past on its way to the Douro.

Vilarinho dos Freires. www.quintadovallado.com. ✆ **25/431-80-81.** 13 units. 150€–240€ double, including breakfast. Free parking. **Amenities:** Garden; terrace; free bikes; fishing; outdoor pool; sauna; hammam; Jacuzzi; massage service; restaurant; bar; games room; library; babysitting; free Wi-Fi.

Where to Eat

Castas e Pratos ★ PORTUGUESE The name means "grapes and plates," and that just about sums up this modern place in a converted railway warehouse brimming with industrial chic. There's a well-stocked wine bar and store showcasing Douro products on the ground floor, and a light-filled dining room under the rafters upstairs. The kitchen serves up prettily presented food like grilled octopus with aioli and quinoa, or guineafowl in stout.

Avenida José Vasques Osório. www.castasepratos.com. ✆ **92/720-00-10.** Mains 19€–34€. Daily 10:30am–11pm.

DOC ★★ MODERN PORTUGUESE With a fabulous location right on the south bank of the Douro, 10 minutes upstream from Régua, this upscale modern restaurant is part of the culinary empire of stellar Porto chef Rui Paula. With the river lapping up against the glass walls, sit back, relax, and let his tasting menus take you on culinary tour of the region's finest products, from mountain-raised beef to the purest Trás-os-Montes olive oil, all presented in contemporary art-on-a-plate style.

Estrada Nacional 222, Folgosa. www.docrestaurante.pt. ✆ **25/485-81-23.** Mains 15€–35€, tasting menus 90€–280€. Thurs–Mon 12:30am–3:30pm & 7:30–10:30pm, Wed 7:30–10:30pm.

O Maleiro ★ PORTUGUESE This is an archetypal local Douro restaurant: shoulder-to-shoulder diners, noisy, brightly lit, with the ambition since 1975 to fill customers with unpretentious, hearty regional cooking. There are *azulejos* on the wall, soccer on the TV, and plates filled with baked cod and roasted-in-their-skins potatoes dripping with garlic and olive oil, or slow-roasted young goat. Don't come for a romantic dinner, but for a great slice of Douro life.

Rua dos Camilos 108. ✆ **25/431-36-84.** Main courses 8€–18€. Mon–Sat 11:30am–midnight.

THE MINHO & TRÁS-OS-MONTES

14

Portugal's two northernmost provinces present a contrast. The Minho, occupying the northwest, is a lush, green region where rivers rush to the Atlantic coast through hillsides covered with trellised vines producing famed vinho verde white wines. It is a center of Portugal's fashion and footwear industries, where ancient cities like Braga, Guimarães, and Viana do Castelo have developed thriving cultural scenes. The Minho is the birthplace of the Portuguese nation, a region where Celtic hill forts, churches built by Germanic settlers after the Romans retreated, medieval fortresses, and baroque mansions bear witness to a long, rich history.

To the east, between the River Douro and the Spanish border, Trás-os-Montes is a wild, otherworldly place. Its name means "beyond the mountains," and for centuries it was remote, cut off from the rest of the country by the highland ranges to the south and west. Although fast highways have brought it within easy reach of Lisbon and Porto, the region still has a distinct identity. The landscape is a rugged mix of high plateaus and rounded peaks. Population is sparse and there are few major cities, but in rough-hewn hamlets rural traditions linger on: Villagers play Celtic bagpipe music and speak Mirandese, a language spoken only in Portugal's far northeastern corner. During winter festivals, they don masks and weird costumes rooted in pagan lore.

What both regions share is a hearty cuisine, rich handicraft heritage, spectacular natural landscapes, and a reputation for hospitality combined with some wonderful places to stay—from palaces and restored convents to country-chic home-stay cottages, even agrain-silos made into a boutique hotel.

GUIMARÃES ★★★

55km (35 miles) NE of Porto; 365km (225 miles) N of Lisbon

Guimarães is the cradle of Portugal. It was the birthplace of the country's founding father, King Afonso I Henriques, in 1109, and the country's first capital. Its fortress was the base from where Afonso Henriques led the *Reconquista,* moving south to reclaim land taken by Arab forces centuries earlier. "Guimarães is Portugal, the rest is just what we conquered," is a popular saying in the city.

Today's Guimarães is a fascinating place to visit. When it declared the city's historic center as a World Heritage Site, UNESCO called it a "well-preserved and authentic example of the evolution of a medieval settlement into a modern town." That can be seen from the ramparts of the founding king's castle through its Renaissance-era royal palace to the brightly colored, tile-covered town houses along its maze of cobbled alleys and picturesque plazas.

Guimarães is also a busy modern city. Its position as a center for the textile and shoe industries means there are plenty of fashionable shopping bargains. Its squares are lined with cafes, and its role as a leading northern arts center has been boosted since it was European Cultural Capital in 2012. Among its major events is a 10-day jazz festival that draws big international names in early November.

Essentials

ARRIVING

BY TRAIN Over a dozen daily trains make the hour-long run between Porto and Guimarães. The fare is usually 3.10€. There are a couple of express options that get you there 15 mins earlier but cost 3-times more. Most trains from Lisbon involve a change in Porto. Fares from the capital start at 26.50€.

BY BUS Several bus companies operate between Porto and Guimarães. The journey takes about an hour and costs 6€ on the **Rede Expressos** national line, which runs a dozen daily trips on weekdays. From Lisbon the trip takes about 4 hours, usually with a change in Porto, and costs 20€. **Get Bus** (www.getbus.eu; ✆ **25/326-23-71**) runs a shuttle from Porto airport with eight daily departures for 8€ for adults, 4€ for children 4 to 14, and free for younger kids.

BY CAR From Porto, the journey takes about 45 minutes on the A3 and A7 toll roads.

VISITOR INFORMATION

The **Tourist Office** is at Praça de São Tiago in the center of the old town (www.guimaraesturismo.com; ✆ **25/342-12-21;** open June 1–Sept 15 Mon–Fri 9:30am–7pm, Sat 10am–1pm and 2–7pm, Sun 10am–1pm; Sept 16–May 31 Mon–Fri 9:30am–6pm, Sat 10am–1pm, 2–6pm, Sun 10am–1pm).

Minho & Trás-os-Montes

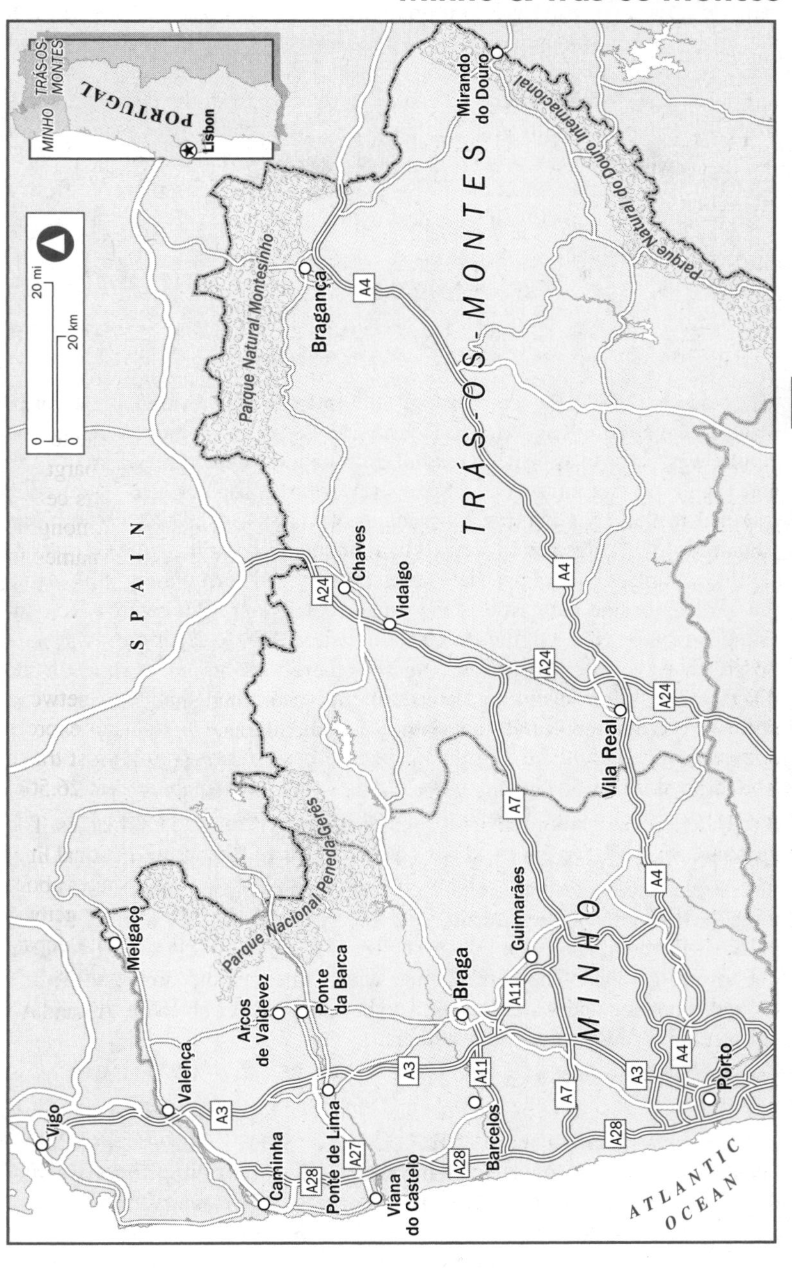

Exploring Guimarães

Alto da Penha ★ PARK Looming over the city, 620m (2,000 ft.) up at the top of a mini-mountain range is this forested park, a favorite summer getaway for the citizens of Guimarães, particularly on summer days when the hilltop air stays cooler. There's a cable car running from the city. The views from the top are magnificent. The park is a great place for a picnic or for wandering the woods, clambering around boulders, and exploring grottos. Above it is a church built in the 1940s that looks like it's been carved from a solid block of local granite. It's the destination of a pilgrimage held the second Sunday of September.

Santuário da Penha, Penha-Costa. www.penhaguimaraes.com. ✆ **25/341-41-14.** Mon–Fri 10am–6:30pm, Sat–Sun 9am–8pm. Free. For the cable car: Rua Aristides Sousa Mendes, 37. www.turipenha.pt. ✆ **25/351-82-39.** Round trip 7.50€ adults, 2.5€ children 6–11, free under 6s. Daily 10am–6:30pm, later at weekend and in summer.

Castelo ★ CASTLE This striking hilltop fortress is revered as the birthplace of the nation. King Afonso Henriques was reputedly born here and the citadel was his base as he declared his lands an independent kingdom in 1139 and fought off the advances of Spanish overlords. The castle is even older, founded in 958 by Countess Mumadona of Galicia to protect her subjects from raids by Vikings and Moors. Its battlements still dominate the Guimarães skyline and offer panoramic views over the city and surrounding hills. Amid the gardens beside the castle is the squat, rectangular 12th-century Romanesque **Igreja de São Miguel de Castelo,** where Afonso Henriques was supposed to have been baptized. Nearby there's a heroic **statue** of the mustachioed, armor-clad king, helmeted with sword and shield in hand—an obligatory selfie opportunity for visiting schoolchildren.

Rua Conde Dom Henrique. www.pacodosduques.gov.pt. ✆ **25/341-22-73.** Admission 2€, 1€ over 65s and students, free under 12s. Combo tickets include Alberto Sampaio Museum and the Paço dos Duques de Bragança for 8€. Daily 10am–5:30pm.

Centro Cultural Vila Flor ★ ARTS CENTER This ultra-modern cultural center incorporating a renovated 18th-century palace spearheaded Guimarães' re-emergence as a center for the arts. One outside wall of the old palace is lined with baroque granite statues of Portugal's early kings overlooking formal gardens. They are planted with camellias and boxwood hedges around fountains and water basins. The building holds exhibition spaces and concert halls, plus a cafe and restaurant.

Avenida D. Afonso Henriques, 701. www.ccvf.pt. ✆ **25/342-47-00.** Admission prices depend on events. Tues–Sun 10am–1pm, 2–9pm.

Citânia de Briteiros ★ HISTORICAL SITE Before the Romans invaded the Iberian Peninsula, Celtic peoples lived in hilltop fortress settlements across the northwest of Spain and Portugal. A half-hour's drive north of downtown, this is a remarkably well-preserved example. The cluster of ruined, round, and rectangular dwellings shows a well-organized civilization with a network of streets, protective walls, barns for cattle and a ceremonial crematorium. Some of the buildings have been reconstructed to give visitors an idea of what they were like at the settlement's Iron Age peak. The site is located on a hillside giving striking views over the valley of the River Ave. Back in the city, the **Museu Martins Sarmento,** Rua Paio Galvão, has a collection of archaeological artifacts found at the site.

Monte de São Romão. www.csarmento.uminho.pt. ✆ **25/341-59-69.** 3€. Daily Apr–Sept 9am–6pm; Oct–Mar 9am–5pm.

Largo da Oliveira ★★ PLAZA At the center of the old city is Guimarães' most distinctive plaza. "Olive tree square" is surrounded by brightly painted three-story houses in typical Minho style, with an arcade at street level to allow pedestrians to pass by in the dry during the winter rainy days responsible for the region's famed greenery. The square's Gothic shrine was built to commemorate a 14th-century victory over the Emirate of Granada. Other medieval monuments include the multi-arched former city hall and the **Igreja de Nossa Senhora da Oliveira** church, both Gothic works from the 14th century. For all its ancient, history, the square remains a center for social life and is lined with bars and cafes. In old monastery buildings attached to the church is the **Alberto Sampaio Museum** (www.culturanorte.gov.pt; ✆ **25/342-39-10;** open Tues–Sun 9am–5:45pm; admission 3€). The collection of silverware, ceramics, and medieval sculpture includes the chainmail tunic worn by King João I at the fateful battle of Aljubarrota, where Portugal secured its independence from Spain in 1385.

Largo do Tourel ★ PLAZA This spacious square was laid out in the 18th century and contrasts with the narrow, medieval streets around Largo da Oliveira and Largo de São Tiago. Its eastern edge is lined with tall, glass-fronted houses that glitter in the evening light. The plaza is a city meeting place where folks gather to talk, get a shoeshine, grab an almond pastry from the 60-year-old **Pastelaria Clarinha** cake shop, or take a coffee at the timeless **Café Milenário,** which opened in 1953, the year Guimarães celebrated 1,000 years since its founding. Next door, the slogan "Here Portugal was Born" adorns one of the surviving towers of the **city walls** standing among a row of houses covered with multicolored ceramic tiles.

Paço dos Duques de Bragança ★ PALACE This massive, four-winged palace was built in the early 15th century by an illegitimate son of King João I as a love nest for his mistress. With its stone towers, soaring chimneys and steeply sloped tile roofs, it's an unusual example of a French-style Renaissance palace on the Iberian Peninsula. The place fell into disrepair when the Braganza family moved elsewhere, but it was heavily restored in the 1930s when dictator António de Oliveira Salazar turned it into his northern retreat. Today, it's a museum where you can view royal portraits, medieval weapons, Persian hangings, Indian urns, and Chinese porcelain. Enormous tapestries depict warlike Portuguese activity in North Africa. There's also a room dedicated to José de Guimarães, one of Portugal's best-known modern artists.

Rua Conde Dom Henrique. www.pacodosduques.gov.pt. ✆ **25/341-22-73.** 5€, 2.5€ over 65s and students with ID, free for children under 12. Daily 10am–5:30pm.

Rua de Santa Maria ★★ NEIGHBORHOOD If you'd like to step into the Middle Ages for an hour or two, stroll down Guimarães' oldest street, built to link the castle to the convent opened by Countess Mumadona in the 10th century. The narrow lane is flanked by solid granite houses both noble and humble. There are plenty of fascinating shops and cafes to stop in along the way: The **Casa Costinhas** at No. 70 is a cafe/pastry shop founded by nuns that still sells almond-and-pumpkin treats based on recipes from the neighboring Santa Clara convent; **Chafarica** at No. 29 is an emporium of local textile products; **Meia Tigela** at No. 35, in the shadow of the stone arch over the street, specializes in ceramics and other handicrafts. Rua de Santa Maria passes through a succession of pretty plazas like **Largo do Cónego,** where the baroque convent is now occupied by city hall; or **Largo de São Tiago,** lined with 16th- and 17th-century homes fronted by handcarved wooded balconies, usually hung with flowers or washing. Much of the city's nightlife is around Largo de São Tiago, with bars like **Tasquilhado**, Rua Santa Maria 42, and **El Rock,** Praça de São Tiago 31, among the hotspots.

Where to Stay

MODERATE

Casa de Sezim ★★★ This extraordinary country manor has been in the same family since 1376. The center of an estate producing *vinho verde* wines, it is 4km (2½ miles) outside Guimarães. Behind the noble, rose-painted facade, the interior decoration is notable for its murals—intensely colored paintings showing scenes of colonial life in India and the Americas, or historic events. Antique furnishings, traditional Portuguese fabrics, subtle lighting, fresh flowers from the garden, and a library of venerable leather-bound volumes (where you'll take breakfast—unless it's warm enough for the veranda) all combine to make this a very special place to stay. Guest rooms are spacious and decorated in tune with the house. There's a winery and bougainvillea-rich garden to explore, and a warm welcome from the owners. There's no restaurant, but evening meals can be taken in the dining room if ordered in advance. You'll need to book early, because it fills up fast.

Rua de Sezim, São Tiago de Candoso. www.sezim.pt. ✆ **25/352-30-00.** 8 units. 123€–215€ double. Free parking. **Amenities:** Garden; terrace; tennis; bike hire; outdoor pool; massage service; bar; games room; free Wi-Fi.

Pousada Mosteiro Guimarães ★★★ Overlooking the city on the slopes of the Penha hill, this luxury inn is located in a monastery dating back to the origins of Portugal. It once belonged to Queen Mafalda, wife of the country's first king. There's history all around you. Noble salons and the old library feature oak paneling and portraits of local nobles, vast panels of *azulejos* (tiles) show scenes of battles and hunting, ancient stonework frames the doors and windows, and antique furniture lines the bar, restaurant, and other public rooms. The attached church is a flamboyant granite-and-gold baroque wonder. Esplanades give views over the lights of Guimarães and the hotel's 10 hectares (25 acres) of garden and woodland. Guest rooms blend old stonework, regional fabrics, and Portuguese lithographs. About half are in a modern wing (added in 1985); ask to stay in the original house. The restaurant is renowned for its take on traditional Minho cooking served under medieval stone arches.

Largo Domingos Leite de Castro. www.pousadas.pt. ✆ **25/351-12-49.** 51 units. 84€–240€ double. Free parking. **Amenities:** Garden; terrace; outdoor pool; massage services; restaurant; bar; free Wi-Fi.

INEXPENSIVE

Casa do Juncal ★★ This noble 18th-century manor in the heart of the old city has been transformed into a chic boutique hotel, with wooden floors, natural stone or pure white walls, and soft gray fabrics. Its modern, glass-fronted breakfast room opens onto a garden—the ideal place to relax after a hard day's sightseeing. Modern design and art installations contrast with historic framing. The hotel is suite-only and units range from 28 to 32 sq. meters (300 sq. ft.–344 sq. ft.). Some are split level, with the beds upstairs. Sheets are Egyptian cotton and duvets are stuffed with Hungarian goose down.

Rua Dr. Avelino Germano, 65. www.casajuncal.com. ✆ **25/204-21-68.** 6 units. 90€–135€ double. Free parking nearby. **Amenities:** Garden; terrace; massage service; free Wi-Fi.

Hotel da Oliveira ★★ If you want to be in the thick of things, this is the place. Occupying a landmark 16th-century building overlooking Largo da Oliveira in the heart of the historic center, this sophisticated option was recently renovated by interior designer Paulo Lobo under the slogan "Feel Guimarães." Rooms are themed around a character or event out of the city's history. Original stone doorways and wooden ceiling beams are combined with stacks of old books, modern art, and natural cotton and linen bedclothes to create an ambience that is cool but comfy, and jibes with the history of the house. The ground-floor restaurant serving regional and international food has a terrace spilling over onto the square. Orchids and scented Portuguese toiletries in the bathrooms are a thoughtful touch.

Largo da Oliveira. www.hoteldaoliveira.com. ✆ **25/351-41-57.** 20 units. 70€–146€ double. Free parking, reservations required. **Amenities:** Terrace; bike hire; restaurant; bar; library; free Wi-Fi.

Where to Eat

Cor de Tangerina ★ VEGETARIAN A surprise amid the meat-driven traditional restaurants of the region, this delightful organic-vegetarian place is set in an old house beside the castle. Decor is rustic chic, with raw wooden floors and furniture; there's a splendid garden out back, perfect for summer lunches. As much as possible, they grow their own food or source locally (the delicious breads and pastries are baked on-site). Inventive dishes include

LAND OF green wine

There is some question over how ***vinho verde*** got its name. *Verde* means "green" in Portuguese, but although the crisp, fresh wines produced in the Minho region come in white, rosé, and red varieties, none are green. Some say *verde* in this case means "young" or "immature," since the wines are generally consumed shortly after bottling rather than being left to mature for years. Others suggest the name comes from the landscape where the vines are grown—**verdant hills** facing the Atlantic that owe their lush green hues to the winter rain.

Whatever the interpretation, the wines are a pleasure to drink and the **region ★★★** that produces them is a pleasure to explore. Portugal's biggest wine region covers almost the entire historic Minho province and spills over its borders. The vines are often grown on trellises that cover the hillsides, interspersed with forests or fields of corn. Scattered through the region are pretty towns and **aristocratic wine estates** known as *solars* or *quintas*, many dating back centuries and offering boutique accommodations to travelers.

Most *vinho verde* is white, usually blends of the Alvarinho, Arinto, Avesso, and Loureiro grape varieties, although single-variety wines—particularly **Alvarinhos**—are often considered the best. Some *vinho verdes* are slightly bubbly. The producers' association **CVRVV** has an informative website explaining about the wine and giving tips on where to stay, visit, and taste in the region: www.vinhoverde.pt.

The perfect base is **Ponte de Lima ★★**, one of the oldest and most charming towns in Portugal. Made of two halves linked by an ancient stone bridge over the River Lima, the town has existed since Roman times, when wine was already being produced around here. The view of the elegant riverside church of Santo António beside the bridge is one of Portugal's most iconic. Ponte de Lima is filled with historic mansions whose verandas brim with summer flowers. The surrounding hills are packed with wine estates. Among those where you can stay is **Paço de Calheiros ★★** (www.pacodecalheiros.com; ✆ **25/894-71-64**), where Count Francisco welcomes guests to the manor that's been his family's home since the 16th century.

Another must-see estate is the **Palácio da Brejoeira ★★★** (www.palaciodabrejoeira.pt; ✆ **25/166-61-29**), a magnificent palatial residence built in 1806 near the fortified border town of **Monção.** It doesn't have accommodations, but visitors can tour the house and vineyards, which produce one of the best Alvarinho wines and some tasty brandy.

Along the valleys of the Lima and Minho rivers, visit enchanting wine towns like **Arcos de Valdevez ★**, **Melgaço ★**, or **Ponte da Barca ★**, where you should try a steak from the locally raised Barrosã cattle breed in **O Moinho ★** (www.restauranteomoinho.pt; ✆ **25/845-20-35**), a restaurant in an old water mill. Don't miss the fortified frontier town of **Valença ★★**, which stares across the River Minho at its Spanish twin **Tui** on the north bank.

creamy rice with wild mushrooms and cheese from the Azores, followed by carob mousse with pineapple, coconut cream, nuts, and dehydrated beet.

Largo Martins Sarmento, 89. www.cordetangerina.pt. ✆ **96/687-61-65.** Mains 13€. No credit cards. Tues–Sat noon–3:30pm, 7:30–10pm; Sun 12:30–3pm.

Florêncio ★★ PORTUGUESE Entering this restaurant in the northern suburbs is a bit of a shock. From outside, it's a rustic house built of massive blocs of stone but walk through the door and you're amid sophisticated modern decor, with walls in crimson and lemon-yellow, decorated with award certificates, press clippings, and row upon row of wine bottles. There's no confusion about the food, though: This is a bulwark of traditional Minho cooking. Pork offal dishes such as *bucho* (stuffed stomach) and *rojões* (cubes of marinated pork fried with blood sausage and tripe), or salt-cod in a cornbread crust are among the treats that secure its loyal local following. Many dishes are cooked in a wood-fired oven.

Madre-de-Deus, Azurém. www.restauranteflorencio.pt. ✆ **25/341-58-20.** Mains 7€–16€. Mon–Sat noon–10pm; Sun noon–3pm.

São Gião ★★ PORTUGUESE The village of Moreia de Cónego is a 20-minute drive south from downtown, but it's worth the trip to eat in this restaurant that many consider the region's best. Chef Pedro Nunes' cooking is firmly rooted in northern Portuguese traditions, but he brings his own touch to the classics or experiments with some French or Italian touches. The restaurant has its own smokery, making hams and sausages served as appetizers. The roast kid and wine-stewed pigs' cheeks are famed, and there are game dishes and fresh river fish in season. A classic.

Avenida Comendador Joaquim Almeida Freitas 56, Moreira de Cónego. www.restaurantesaogiao.pai.pt. ✆ **25/314-10-86.** Reservations recommended. Mains 13€–24€. Tues–Sat 12:30–3pm, 7:30–11pm; Sun 12:30–3pm.

Solar do Arco ★ PORTUGUESE A solid choice in the historic center, the dining room is in an antique house under the stone arches that give the place its name. White-painted wood panels are covered with big black-and-white pictures of city sights. The food is based on local products. *Vitela assada* is a signature dish. *Vitela* is usually translated as "veal," but is actually beef from a younger animal, rather than the white meat of very young calves served as veal in France or Italy. Here it's oven roasted and served with the traditional accompaniments of roast potatoes and greens. Other recommended dishes include salt-cod with cornbread and rice with octopus. As with many Portuguese restaurants, portions will be huge, and it's perfectly okay to ask for a half-portion (*meia dose*) or to share a main.

Rua da Santa Maria 48–50. ✆ **25/303-52-33.** Reservations recommended. Mains 8€–15€. Wed–Mon noon–3:30pm, 7–11pm.

Shopping

Guimarães and the surrounding area is a center for the textile and shoe industries, as well as being home to a strong handicraft tradition. There are several stores selling homemade gifts in the historic center, but the city-run **Loja Oficina,** Rua Rainha D. Maria II, 126 (www.aoficina.pt; ✆ **25/351-52-50;** Mon–Sat 10am–1pm, 2–7pm), stands out for promoting local products like embroidered linen and the red-clay *cantarinhas dos namorados* jugs traditionally offered by young men to their intended fiancés. Portugal is second only to Italy in exporting high-quality shoes, and Guimarães is a good place for fashionistas to bag a bargain. The **Kyaia** factory store, Rua 24 de Junho 453, Penselo (www.kyaia.com; ✆ **25/355-91-40;** Mon–Sat 10am–1:30pm, 3–6pm), selling shoes from the hip Portuguese brand **Fly London,** is just outside the city in the village of Penselo. Downtown, **Fenui,** Rua Dr. Avelino Germano 84/86 (www.fenuishoes.com; ✆ **91/993-43-02**; Mon–Fri 10–7pm; Sat 10am–1pm and 2:30–6pm), sells a range of handmade Portuguese shoes.

BRAGA ★★

55km (35 miles) N of Porto; 370km (230 miles) N of Lisbon

The Minho's capital manages to be one of Europe's oldest and youngest cities: Oldest because it was founded by the Romans as Bracara Augusta in 20 B.C. on a site already occupied by Celtic tribes; youngest because of its youthful population—almost one-third are under 25—thanks in part to the University of the Minho, which injects a fresh vitality into the city's cultural life. The arrival of a significant Brazilian immigrant community over the past 10 years has brought a tropical vibe to the northern city.

Since Roman times, Braga has been a center for Christianity. It's been the seat of a bishopric since A.D. 45 and remains one of Portugal's three archdioceses, along with Lisbon and Évora. A Portuguese saying has it that Braga prays, while Coimbra sings, Porto works and Lisbon has fun. There are churches everywhere, some dating back to the early Middle Ages. It has Portugal's oldest cathedral, as well as several splendid baroque temples among the hilltop Bom Jesús do Monte, a UNESCO World Heritage Site. Easter Week celebrations are the most intense in Portugal, culminating in processions led by barefoot, black-hooded penitents.

Braga, however, is much more than a religious center. As the biggest city north of Porto, it's an important regional hub. Within the city walls are bright, sunny plazas filled with flowers; cobbled alleys, and streets of sturdy granite houses, many clad in *azulejos*. There are cozy old cafes, trendy boutiques, and one of the world's oldest soccer stadiums carved into a mountainside.

Essentials

ARRIVING

BY TRAIN It takes about 1 hour from Porto's Campanhã station to Braga, with about 30 trains making the trip daily. Tickets usually cost 3.25€, unless you take one of the six fast express trains that make the trip in 39 minutes with fares of up to 14.70€. There are four daily Alfa trains direct from Lisbon. The fastest takes just over 3 hours and costs 33.70€.

BY BUS The bus journey from Lisbon lasts about 4 hours and costs 20.90€ with **Rede Expressos** and there are about 20 buses making the trip daily. From Porto there are around 30 daily buses with the same company. The trip takes 1 hour and costs 6€. **Get Bus** (www.getbus.eu; ✆ **25/326-23-71**) makes up to 12 daily trips direct from Porto airport for 8€ for adults, 4€ for children aged 4 to 13, and free for younger kids.

BY CAR From Porto, the drive takes about 45 minutes on the A3 toll highway. The journey from Lisbon is about 3½ hours. Guimarães is 30 minutes away on the A11.

VISITOR INFORMATION

The **Braga Tourist Office** is in a lovely 1930s building at Av. da Liberdade 1 (www.cm-braga.pt; ✆ **25/326-25-50;** open Mon–Fri 9am–1pm and 2–6:30pm; Sat–Sun 9am–1pm, 2–6pm). The **Braga Cool** website (www.bragacool.com) has up-to-date info on the city.

Exploring Braga

Braga is an easy place to explore on foot, with most of the sights in the historic center between the gardens of Praça da República in the east and Jardim da Casa dos Biscaínhos to the west. Beside the main sights, the streets are perfect for strolling among the old granite townhouses and retro stores.

Capela de São Frutuoso ★ CHURCH Amid modern high-rise housing projects in Braga's northern suburbs there is a cluster of stone-built religious buildings. Some are were built as part of a 17th-century baroque convent but among them is this gem of a chapel, dating back to the 10th century or even earlier. It was built by the German tribes who settled in northern Portugal during the decline of the Roman Empire. It's a rare example of church architecture of that era, built on a Greek-cross layout with four stubby arms. Inside there are traces of Byzantine, Islamic and Visigoth-influenced decoration. The University of the Minho is seeking funds to rehabilitate the site. At the moment, it's largely abandoned, and you'll need to call ahead to visit the interior.

Avenida São Frutuoso. www.culturanorte.pt. ✆ **92/721-18-12.** Free. Daily 2–4pm with reservation.

Mosteiro de São Martinho de Tibães ★★ MONASTERY This sprawling monastery is a 15-minute drive from downtown. It was founded in the 11th century and in 1569 became the headquarters of the Benedictine order in Portugal and Brazil. The buildings you see today date mainly from the 17th and 18th centuries and make up one of the biggest and most spectacular religious complexes in Portugal. On the grounds are armies of baroque statues; a rococo church adorned with gold, silver, and marble; and cloisters lined with *azulejos* and carved wooden ceilings. Beyond the opulence of the decoration, a visit also gives visitors the opportunity to glimpse the lives of the monks who lived there, peeping into their cells, dining rooms, even the barber's. It's located in acres of landscaped parkland.

Rua do Mosteiro, Mire de Tibães. www.culturanorte.pt. ✆ **25/362-26-70.** 4€ adults, 2€ students and seniors. Tues–Sun Apr–Oct 10am–7pm; Nov–Mar 10am–6pm.

Museu dos Biscainhos ★ MUSEUM How did the other half live in the 18th century? This well-preserved noble home has some answers. You'll stroll below ornamented ceilings and past walls with panels of tiles and paintings, through collections of Portuguese furniture, glass, silverware, textiles, and porcelain. Most impressive: the entry hall, with geometric patterns carved into its granite floor and the vaulted painted ceiling of the ballroom. You can walk for free through to gardens filled with sculptures, pavilions, and fountains among vegetation, which includes a 300-year-old American Tulip tree that bursts into flame-colored flower every spring. It also hosts regular events from exhibitions to chamber music concerts, jazz in the gardens to seminars on current affairs.

Rua dos Biscainhos. www.culturanorte.pt. ✆ **25/320-46-50.** 2€, 1€ seniors and youngsters 15-25, free for children under 15. Free access to gardens. Tues–Sun 10am–12:45pm and 2–5:30pm.

Praça da República ★★ PLAZA A broad, garden-filled plaza, the Praça da República is flanked by stately old buildings housing stores, cafes and restaurants, plus the occasional grand bank or 18th-century church. In a splendid 1700s silk merchant's house, you'll find the **Centésima Página ★★** (www.centesima.com; ✆ **25/326-76-47**) bookstore, cafe, and cultural hub. Just around the corner, **ID Concept Store ★★**, at Praceta Santa Bárbara 3 (✆ **92/571-21-94;** Tues–Sat 11am–7pm), offers an extensive collection of Portuguese fashion and design.

Tunnels built in the 1990s took traffic underground, so the square is again a place to stroll, window-shop or admire the flowers and fountains. Locals refer to the plaza simply as *Arcada,* referring to the arcades running along the neoclassical building on the western edge of the square.

Under those arcades are a couple of the city's historical cafes: **Café Vianna ★★** (✆ **25/326-23-36;** Sun–Thurs 9am–midnight, Fri–Sat 9–2am), opened in 1871, and its neighbor **Café Astória ★** (✆ **91/901-18-90;** Sun–Thurs 9am–midnight, Fri–Sat 9–2am), a relative newcomer from 1928. The square is particularly charming when the lights come on at dusk.

Rua do Souto ★★ NEIGHBORHOOD Braga's most iconic cafe is just west of Praça da República in a building covered in deep blue *azulejos*. **A Brasileira ★★**, Largo do Barão de São Martinho 17 (✆ **25/326-21-04;** Sun–Thurs 8am–midnight, Fri–Sat 8–2am), has been serving up shots of coffee since it was opened in 1907 by a trader importing beans from Brazil. It remains the city's favorite meeting place.

Beyond A Brasileira, **Rua do Souto,** the long, pedestrian-only street, is a center of social and commercial life. It and the lanes and plazas off it are packed with cute stores, cafes, and restaurants. For real local color, pop into **Mercado de São João ★★**, Rua de São João 5–9 (www.bacalhau-portugal.com; ✆ **96/674-54-33;** Mon–Fri 9am–7pm and Sat 9am–1pm), a grocer since 1894 where, among the spices, freshly ground coffee, and dried fruits, is where locals come to buy *bacalhau.* The salted cod is a staple across Portugal and a particularly important part of the diet in Braga, where it's traditionally served pan-fried with onions and olive oil.

BRAGA'S modern side

Ancient it may be, but it would be a mistake to leave Braga without a glimpse at its modern side. The capital of the Minho has cutting-edge architectural surprises and a bubbling contemporary arts scene. A good place to start is **GNRation,** Praça Conde de Agrolongo 123 (www.gnration.pt; ✆ **25/314-22-00;** Mon–Fri 9:30am–6:30pm, Sat 10am–6:30pm), a hip space for digital art exhibitions, modern dance, and concerts, set in a former National Guard headquarters, which the architects transformed by fixing dozens of potted plants to the patio walls.

Braga's soccer stadium is unique: the **Estádio Municipal,** Parque Norte, Dume (www.scbraga.pt; ✆ **25/320-68-60**), offers guided tours in winter Monday to Friday at 10:30am and 3pm, in summer at 10:30am, 2:30, and 3:30pm; 6€, 4€ seniors 3€ youngsters 4 to 18, reservation needed. It was built by Pritzker Prize–winning architect Eduardo Souto Moura in 2003. He carved a space out of a hillside, leaving a wall of rock behind one goal. It's picked up more international prizes than the local club Sporting Braga.

In complete contrast is the *Árvore* **da Vida** (Tree of Life), Largo de Santiago 47 (✆ **25/320-33-00;** Fri 5–6pm), a tiny chapel crafted of 20 tons of bare wooden planks, fitted together without nails to build an intimate place of worship within the vast 16th-century *São Pedro e São Paulo* seminary. Local architects worked with a Norwegian sculptor to build the interlocking curving timbers; the chapel was voted 2011's religious building of the year worldwide by the website ArchDaily.com.

Braga's modern art galleries include **Zet Gallery,** Rua do Raio 175 (www.zet.gallery/zet-gallery; ✆ **25/311-66-20;** Mon–Sat 10am–7pm; free admission), which promotes local and international artists working with other galleries around Europe through online exhibitions and art sales. On a hillside just north of Braga, **Galeria Mário Sequeira,** Rua da Galeria, 129, Parada de Tibães (www.mariosequeira.com; ✆ **25/360-25-50;** Mon–Fri 10am–1pm, 3–7pm; free admission) has showcased international names such as Andy Warhol, Anish Kapoor Long, and Gilbert and George, as well as leading Portuguese artists. The works are handsomely presented in a cool, low white building fused into the surrounding gardens, and a 19th-century farmhouse.

Also worth noting along the street: the **Arco da Porta Nova ★**, a baroque triumphal arch; the **archbishop's palace ★**, dating back to the 14th century and the neighboring **Santa Barbara gardens ★**. The **Casa do Passadiço ★**, Largo de São João do Souto (www.casadopassadico.com; ✆ **25/361-99-88;** Mon–Sat 10am–7pm), one of the city's finest old mansions, now houses a stylish interior design store.

Santuário Bom Jesús do Monte ★★★ CHURCH This hilltop pilgrimage site is Braga's best-known landmark and, since 2019, a World Heritage Site. It's 300m (983 ft.) above the city, but you can reach it by car up a tree-lined drive; take the oldest funicular in the Iberian Peninsula (for 1.50€), which is powered by a water counterweight system and was opened in 1882; or climb on foot up the **monumental granite double staircase ★★★** dating from the 18th century, pausing to admire the baroque sculptures representing the senses and the virtues, chapels and grottoes along the way. At the top is a twin-towered neoclassical church in white plaster and gray stone built in 1725. Its chapels feature shockingly realistic and full color sculptures of the Crucifixion. The views from outside are magnificent. There is also a leafy park with a boating lake, wishing well, gazebos, and shady spots where locals come to picnic.

Bom Jesús do Monte, Tenões. http://bomjesus.pt. ✆ **25/367-66-36.** Free. Summer 8am–7pm; winter 9am–8pm. Funicular summer 9am–8pm; winter 9am–7pm.

Sé ★★ CHURCH When something is very old, Portuguese will say "It's older than Braga cathedral." It's older than the country, an 11th-century building whose towers loom over downtown, it was built by Count Henry of Burgundy and his wife Dona Teresa, parents of Portugal's first king, Afonso Henriques. Their tombs are in the Gothic Chapel of Kings. Architecture buffs can read history in the building: the Romanesque structure has accumulated add-ons in just about every style over the centuries, from Gothic-arched entrances to the frame of Manueline cupolas topping the towers. Among the greatest treasures inside are the choir benches, made from ornately carved Brazilian hardwood coated with gold; and the magnificent organ installed in the 1730s. The cathedral's position as an integral part of downtown is increased by the habit locals have of using its front and side entrances as shortcuts when walking around the city. Attached to the cathedral is the **Museu do Tesouro da Sé,** containing a rich collection of religious artifacts, including the **iron cross** carried by Pedro Álvares Cabral when he discovered Brazil and used in the first mass held there in 1500.

Rua Dom Paio Mendes. www.se-braga.pt. ✆ **25/326-33-17.** 2€ for the cathedral, 3€ for the treasury museum. Children under 12 go free. Daily 9:30am–12:30pm, 2:30–5:30pm; in summer until 6:30pm.

Where to Stay

EXPENSIVE

Vila Galé Collection Braga ★★ Opened in 2018, this really filled a gap by giving Braga an historic, luxury downtown hotel. The landmark 16th-century building it occupied was Portugal's oldest purpose-built hospital, founded in 1508, where babies were still being born until 2011. The Vila Galé has restored the core of the historic building for this hotel, which is ideal for travelers with children, containing 20 family rooms and 15 suites. Rooms, decorated in cream and burgundy, are comfortable if rather impersonal. There's a splendid baroque church integrated into the building and cloister where you can dine overlooking flower beds and a trickling Renaissance fountain.

Largo Carlos Amarante, 150. www.vilagale.com. ✆ **25/314-60-00.** 123 units. 110€–212€ double, 172€–248€ suite. Free parking **Amenities:** Garden; indoor and outdoor pools; spa; fitness room; 2 restaurants; bar; games room children's play area; free Wi-Fi.

MODERATE

Hotel do Parque ★ One of Braga's oldest hotels, opened in 1870 up on the Bom Jesús do Monte hilltop overlooking the city, features the original granite-and-white facade with an interior that's a showcase for modern design. The rooms are bright and airy, and most offer views over the gardens, hilltop church, and city below. Decor is predominately soft grays and cream, with rich textile features in mauve or crimson. The lounge, games room, and spa offer a modernized take on grand-old-hotel elegance. The gardens, filled with palm trees, statues, and grottoes, are a treat. Guests can also use the wellness center at the next-door Hotel do Templo, which belongs to the same group.

Parque do Bom Jesús do Monte, 4700 Braga. www.hoteisbomjesus.pt. ✆ **25/360-34-70.** 47 units. 70€–115€ double, 128€–258€ suite. Free parking (reservation recommended). **Amenities:** Sauna; hammam; massage service; bar; games room; free Wi-Fi.

Villa Garden ★★ A palatial 19th-century villa surrounded by gardens about 20 minutes' walk from the cathedral, the Villa Garden is an island of calm in the city. Rooms, divided between the main house and a modern garden wing, are spacious, with rich, dark fabrics contrasting with the overall white, modern design. Throughout the hotel there's a scattering of antiques and (sometimes rather racy) modern artworks, along with vintage tiled floors, hardwood staircases and chandeliers. In some bathrooms, the bare stone of the original walls has been exposed. The bar has a clubby feel with dark wood panels and black-and-white photos. Next door, there's a separate restaurant run by the hotel. In summer, the garden pool is a major attraction. Suites and family rooms are available. Be sure to visit the charming multilevel chapel. Breakfast service can be a little lackadaisical.

Largo de Infias. www.villagarden.pt. ✆ **25/368-00-20.** 26 units. 69€–120€ double, 130€–161€. Free parking. **Amenities:** Garden, terrace; bike hire; outside pool; restaurant; bar; free Wi-Fi.

INEXPENSIVE

Domus Guesthouse 26 ★★ Smack in the center of town, this sweet little B&B is a great bargain. It has just four rooms, each individually furnished in pastel shades featuring wallpaper with subtle floral or geometric patterns, all set in a restored, cream-colored, four-story 19th-century house adorned with flower-filled balconies. The welcome is friendly with great attention to detail, from scented made-in-Porto Castelbel soaps and body creams in the bathrooms, to orchids in the lounge and homemade preserves with breakfast. All rooms have cable TV, tea and coffee facilities, plus a sound system where you can plug in your tablet or smartphone. We recommend the Cathedral room, which has the most space and a view over the facade of Portugal's oldest cathedral.

Avenida São Miguel o Anjo, 26. www.domus26guesthouse.pt. ✆ **91/733-90-95.** 4 units. 62€–75€ double. **Amenities:** Free Wi-Fi.

InBraga Hostel ★ Braga's reputation as a lively student town and its location on the pilgrimage route to Santiago de Compostela across the border, in Spain's Galicia region, means there's plenty of good, cheap hostel accommodations. Among the advantages of this place is a central location—just around the corner from the Biscainhos museum—friendly welcome and peaceful garden out back. Cheap, cheerful, and youthful, the hostel is housed in a restored 19th-century row house. Beds are covered with bright colored duvets. The lounge, opening onto the garden, is filled with recycled wooden furniture. Previous guests have left multilingual graffiti messages on the walls. There are mixed and female-only dorms with private lockers and bunks, plus a couple of small private rooms.

Rua da Boavista, 21. www.inbragahostel.com. ✆ **25/303-35-46.** 5 units. 26€–34€ double; 13€–15€ bunk in dorm. Breakfast 2.50€ per person. **Amenities:** Garden; terrace; barbeque; shared kitchen; bike hire; games room; free Wi-Fi.

Where to Eat

Arcoense ★★ PORTUGUESE For 30 years, this has been hallowed ground for fans of traditional Portuguese food. Fresh fish is brought in daily from the coast, the pork comes from their own hand-raised pigs, and the wine selection is enormous. It's hidden away on a nondescript side street in a modern neighborhood 20 minutes by foot from the cathedral but is well worth the trip. The roomy interior is modern and refined, with wooden floors, wall paneling and plenty of glass cabinets showing off all that wine. Braga-style cod with onions, mixed grill with baked rice, and ox stew are among the specialties. Most dishes come with a half-portion option (which is often enough for two people).

Rua Eng. José Justino de Amorim, 96. www.arcoense.com. ✆ **25/327-89-52.** Reservations recommended. Mains 10€–20€. Mon–Sat 12:30–3pm and 7:30–10pm, Sun 12:30–3pm.

Félix Taberna ★ PORTUGUESE There's a quirky bohemian feel to the pair of bric-a-brac–filled dining rooms that make up this restaurant in an old, yellow-painted house in the heart of Braga's old town. This is another holdout of the city's robust local cuisine; aficionados wax lyrical over its sardines with black-eyed peas or oven-baked rice with duck and *chouriço* sausage (*arroz de pato*). In summer, the outside tables offer a chance to dine alfresco on one of Braga's most agreeable plazas.

Largo da Praça Velha 18/19. ✆ **25/361-77-01.** Mains 7€–13€. Mon–Fri noon–3pm and 7pm–midnight, Sat 7pm–midnight.

Ignácio ★★ PORTUGUESE In an old stone building just outside the Arco da Porta Nova city gate, a restaurant called O Inácio has been thriving since 1934 by providing authentic Minho regional cuisine. In 2018, much-traveled (and TV famous) chef Paula Peliteiro took over, added a "g" to the name and a touch of refinement to the decor and food. The rugged stone walls and ceiling beams from the 1700s are still there, but there's less clutter and a fresh gleam to the place. On the menu, the likes of shrimp-and-avocado cocktail shoulders with "grandma's-style" *sarrabulho* (pork, cumin, and cornmeal mush). Delicate fillets of market-fresh fish come with a tomato and pepper sauce with clams, but the old Sunday lunch special of roast kid still holds pride of place.

Campo das Hortas 4. ✆ **25/361-32-35.** Reservations recommended. Mains 12€–19€. Wed–Mon noon–3pm and 7:30–10pm.

BARCELOS ★

23km (14 miles) W of Braga; 60km (37 miles) N of Porto; 380km (235 miles) N of Lisbon

Barcelos is an attractive riverside town ringed by green hills. Within its walls are a scattering of medieval and baroque churches, stately palaces, and fine houses. But the town is best known for its outdoor markets, handicrafts and the legend that bequeathed Portugal one of its most enduring symbols—*O Galo de Barcelos* (the Rooster of Barcelos). The black cockerel with a red crest and flower-and-heart bedecked wings and tail is found transformed into refrigerator magnets, key rings, and ceramic statuettes of every size in souvenir shops around the country.

Essentials

ARRIVING

BY TRAIN There are trains through the day from Porto. The fastest take around 40 mins and cost 4.80€.

BY BUS The station is on Avenida das Pontes (✆ **25/382-58-15**). The **TransDev** company (www.transdev.pt; ✆ **22/510-01-00**) operates buses hourly from Braga between 7am and 7pm on weekdays. The journey takes an hour and costs 3.35€. **Rede Expressos** has three buses a day from Porto taking at least 1½ hours with a change in Braga for 7.60€

BY CAR From Braga it's 25 minutes on the A11 toll highway. From Porto it takes 50 minutes north on the A28, then east on the A11.

VISITOR INFORMATION

The **Barcelos Tourist Office** is at Largo Dr. José Novais 27 (www.cm-barcelos.pt; ✆ **25/381-18-82;** open Mar 15–Sept 30: Mon–Fri 9:30am–6pm; Sat 10am–1pm, 2–5pm; Sun 10am–1pm, 2–4pm; Oct 1–Mar 14: Mon–Fri 9:30–5:30pm; Sat 10am–1pm, 2–5pm).

Exploring Barcelos

Try to visit Barcelos on Thursday, when the **weekly outdoor market ★★★** (7am–6pm) takes over the vast **Campo da República.** The market dates back to the Middle Ages and draws busloads from around Portugal. Farmers bring in their produce, Roma women hawk cut-price clothes and stands offer roast sausage and cups of local *vinho verde* wines. What interests most visitors are the handicrafts for which Barcelos is famous—rugs, shawls, embroidered linen, painted wooden ox yokes, handwoven baskets and, most of all, pottery. Local earthenware plates, pots, and jugs in red or yellow clay are renowned, but the real attractions are the **sculptured figures:** brightly colored marching bands, guitar-playing oxen, grotesque demons, and saints with oversize heads.

PORTUGAL'S wild north

Mountain ranges, bleak plateaus, forests where wolves roam, stone villages where time seems to have stood still—these are the hallmarks of the far north. The biggest and best wilderness area is the **Parque Nacional da Peneda-Gerês ★★★**. Portugal's only national park covers over 700 square km (over 270 sq. miles) curled around the Spanish border northwest of Braga. Its mountains soar 1,559m (5,115 ft.), sheltering plunging waterfalls, flower-filled valleys, crystalline lakes and enigmatic ruins.

Unmissable sights include the **Miradouro Pedra Bela ★★**, a rocky outcrop providing breathtaking views over the forests and lake below; the **Cascatas do Tahiti ★★**, a series of waterfalls ending in a pool of translucent water; the 500-year-old **Ponte da Ladeira ★** bridge; and the villages of **Lindoso ★★** and **Soajo ★**, hewn from the rock and surrounded by ***espigueiros***—spooky tomblike granite structures that are actually grain stores, raised off the ground on pillars to deter vermin.

You may catch a glimpse of golden eagles, **gray wolves,** or Spanish ibex. More likely, you'll bump into the local long-horned cattle or the powerful ***cão de Castro Laboreiro*** dogs, used by local herdsmen to keep the wolves at bay. You'll also likely spot the ***garrano*** ponies that roam wild here.

There are plenty of great places to sleep in and around the park. Cream of the crop is the **Pousada Mosteiro Amares ★★★** (www.pousadas.pt; ✆ **25/337-19-70**), situated in a former monastic retreat dating back to the 12th century. Just slightly more modest is its sister hotel, the **Pousada do Gerês-Caniçada ★★** (www.pousadas.pt; ✆ **21/040-76-50**), a rock-hewn luxury hilltop hideaway. Alternatives include the **Quinta da Mouta ★★** (www.quintada-mouta.com; ✆ **93/735-29-42**), a family-run guesthouse in a restored farm complex, or the **Quinta do Bárrio ★** (www.quintadobarrio.pt; ✆ **25/310-76-60**), an old stone mansion with an infinity pool overlooking the mountains.

If you can't make it on a Thursday, look for the ateliers around town and in the surrounding villages. The tourist board has a list and can help organize visits. **Júlia Ramalho** is a leading artist who carries on a tradition started by her grandmother, Rosa Ramalho (1888–1977), considered the greatest of the clay sculptors. Her studio in the village of Galegos São Martinho can be visited by appointment (✆ **93/650-44-26**). There's a list of artists with contact details on http://artesanato.barcelos.pt. Another option is to drop into the **Museu de Olaria ★** or Pottery Museum, Rua Cónego Joaquim Gaiola (www.museuolaria.pt; ✆ **25/382-47-41;** Tues–Fri 10am–5:30pm, Sat–Sun 10am–12:30pm and 2–5:30pm; free admission). It showcases local artists, giving an overview of the handicraft traditions, as well as organizing regular temporary exhibitions and workshops.

One unavoidable handicraft item is the **Galo de Barcelos.** Reproductions of the renowned rooster are everywhere around Portugal. The country's best-known contemporary artist, Joana Vasconcelos, in 2016 created what's believed to be the biggest ever—10m (33 ft.) high—and covered with thousands of ceramic tiles and LED lights. It's on a world tour that's taken in Beijing and Barcelos (www.popgalo.com).

The legend that launched a million souvenir roosters is set in medieval Barcelos. It seems a pilgrim passing through town was accused of stealing and sentenced to hang. The man pointed to a cockerel carcass being prepared for the judge's table and said the deceased bird would crow three times to proclaim his innocence. Surprise, surprise: As the rope was placed around the pilgrim's neck, the judge's lunch produced a cock-a-doodle-do that won the man a reprieve. The Barcelos rooster became a symbol of justice restored. If you buy one, better to get a handcrafted version made by a local artist in the hometown of this miraculous poultry, rather than any of the countless mass-produced varieties found in tacky stores nationwide.

A medieval stone cross, with carvings depicting the story, is said to have been erected by the pilgrim himself on a return visit. It can be seen in the archaeological museum, **Museu Arqueológico ★**, Rua Dr. Miguel Fonseca (✆ **25/380-96-00;** open daily summer 9am–7pm, winter 9am–5:30pm; free admission). More ruin than museum, it's housed within the remains of the Counts' Palace (**Paço dos Condes**), a medieval hangout of the Braganza family, who went on to become kings of Portugal. Still one of the town's most distinctive sights, it overlooks the fast-flowing River Cávado and the **14th-century stone bridge** that crosses it.

Adjoining the palace is the **Igreja Matriz ★** (parish church), whose interior contains an unusual and lovely mix of stone Gothic arches framed with blue painted tiles.

Barcelos' other notable church buildings include the 18th-century **Igreja de Nossa Senhora do Terço ★**, Av. dos Combatentes da Grande Guerra (www.igrejadoterco.org; ✆ **25/381-70-91;** daily 9am–5pm; free admission), a church that boasts a spectacular gold and *azulejo*-filled interior beneath a ceiling covered with painted wooden panels depicting biblical scenes. Nearby is the small octagonal **Igreja do Bom Jesús da Cruz ★**, Largo da Porta Nova (✆ **93/918-70-71;** daily 7:30am–7pm; free admission), which shows the Italian influence on Portuguese architecture in the 1700s and features a sumptuous crystal, marble and gilt interior. The church is the hub of one of the Minho's most important pilgrimages in late April and early May, the **Festa das Cruzes ★★**, accompanied by a week of festivities, when the city is strung with fairy lights, streets are strewn with flowers, fireworks light up the river and big-name singers come to play in town. Check with the tourist office for dates and details.

Where to Stay

Quinta do Convento da Franqueira ★ Barcelos isn't overflowing with good places to stay, and this sensitively restored 16th-century convent set among gardens and woodland just south of town is the best bet. The outdoor pool is filled by natural spring whose waters were priced for healing qualities. From it you can look over the treetops to the mountains up on Portugal northern border. The place was bought in the 1960s by a retired British naval officer whose family continues to run it. Rooms are pastel painted filled with a mix of English antique furnishings and Portuguese ceramics and textiles. There's a cozy lounge and a kitchen complete with refrigerator stocked with *vinho verde*. Aside from the rooms, there are two self-catering units for weekly rent. They are closed from November through to early April.

Travessa do Senhor Fonte de Vida189, Pereira. www.quintadafranqueira.com. ✆ **25/383-16-06.** 6 units. 100€–115€ double. Free parking. **Amenities:** Garden; terrace; outdoor pool; free Wi-Fi.

Where to Eat

Pedra Furada ★★ PORTUGUESE A 15-minute drive south from downtown is the village of Pedra Furada, with this eponymous restaurant that has become a local legend—not least because of its roast rooster, a dish inspired by the bird that put Barcelos on the map. The beast is cooked slowly, filled with a smoked meat stuffing, and served with roast potatoes. They say one bird will feed six people, but you can order a half. It's only on the menu on Friday and Saturday lunchtimes, but Senhor António will make one special if you order a day in advance. Other specialties, served between the handicraft-laden granite walls of the cozy dining room, include marinated pork (*rojões*) and the traditional boiled dinner of meats, smoked sausages, and vegetables (*cozido*). Open since the 1940s, the place is a traditional stopover for pilgrims headed for Santiago de Compostela, the Spanish city 200km (120 miles) to the north.

Rua Santa Leocádia, 1415. Pedra Furada. www.pedrafurada.com. ✆ **25/295-11-44.** Mains 10€–19€. Tues–Sun noon–3pm, 7–10pm; Mon noon–3pm.

VIANA DO CASTELO ★★

75km (50 miles) N of Porto; 390km (240 miles) N of Lisbon; 60km (40 miles) W of Braga

The highlight of the Minho coast, Viana do Castelo is a fishing port at the mouth of the River Lima. It's an appealing hodgepodge, with an historic downtown filled with medieval and Renaissance buildings overlooked by a spectacular mountaintop basilica; some of northern Portugal's best beaches on its doorstep; great seafood; and a vibrant folk tradition that sees female locals take to the streets in an August festival clad in layers of golden jewelry over gloriously colorful costumes. On top of all that, the maritime city in recent years has sprouted some of Portugal's most noteworthy modern architecture.

Essentials

ARRIVING

BY TRAIN There are nine direct trains a day from Porto. The trip lasts around 1 hour and 20 minutes, and costs from 7.20€. Some trains are operated by the Spanish rail company **Renfe** and after Viana head north into Spain's Galicia region.

BY BUS **Rede Expressos** line has up to 14 daily journeys from Porto. The quickest lasts 1 hour and costs 7.60€.

BY CAR From Porto the A28 toll highway gets you to Viana in about 1 hour.

VISITOR INFORMATION

The **Viana Welcome Center** is on Praça do Eixo Atlântico (© **25/809-84-15;** open Jul–Aug: daily 10am–7pm; Mar–June, Sept–Oct: Tues–Sun 10am–1pm, 2–6pm; Nov–Feb Tues–Sun 10am–1pm, 2–5pm). The city council has a useful, multilingual website: www.cm-viana-castelo.pt.

Exploring Viana do Castelo

The place to start is **Praça da República ★★**, one of Portugal's best-looking city squares. At its heart is the much-photographed 16th-century **Chafariz Fountain.** The most striking building is the **Igreja da Misericórdia ★★** (© **25/882-79-30;** admission 1€ Mon–Fri 9:30am–12:30pm and 1:30–6pm Sat 10am–10pm). Beyond its three-tiered Renaissance facade, the inside is a riot of baroque gold work, floor-to-ceiling blue-and-white tiles showing scenes of biblical charity, and a glorious painted ceiling.

The other building dominating the square is the 1502 **Antigos Paços do Concelho ★** (© **25/880-93-51;** Mon–Sat 10am–6pm). This fortress-like former town hall is constructed over an arcade made up of three wide, low, Gothic arches. The crenulated facade displays a royal coat of arms and wrought-iron balcony windows above each arch. Nowadays, it is used to host art shows.

Praça da República and the narrow streets running from it are a center for the **Romaria de Nossa Senhora d'Agonia ★★★** (www.vianafestas.com), the city's biggest party. Built around a religious pilgrimage dating back at least to the 17th century, the 4-day festival takes over the city in late August. Streets are covered with flower petals and churches strung with lights, a flotilla of flower-decked fishing boats carries holy statutes to bring blessings to the sea, giant figures with papier-mâché heads stumble around the square, and fireworks light up the harbor. The main attraction is the procession of **Mordomas,** where over 500 local women parade in the local costume: a blaze of color with bodices, embroidered blouses, striped skirts, shawls wrapped around their heads, and layer upon layer of necklaces laden with the region's filigree gold work. It is a spectacular sight.

To find out more about Viana's costumes, jewelry, and rich folk tradition, visit the costume museum, **Museu do Traje ★**, Praça da República (© **25/880-93-06**; Tues–Sun 10am–1pm and 3–6pm [7pm in summer]; admission 2€ adults, 1€ students and seniors, free for children under 12). Located in a 1950s former bank building, the museum showcases the costumes and explains their place in the city's history and culture.

Viana's downtown is ideal for strolling. Among the lanes there's plenty to please the eye: the 15th-century **Igreja Matriz ★**, which serves as the town's cathedral; the mighty **Castelo de Santiago da Barra ★** fortress guarding the mouth of the River Lima since 1589; a cluster of palaces and churches, among which standouts include the 16th-century **Igreja de São Domingos ★** and the **Capela das Malheiras ★**, a little baroque gem. There's also an iron bridge across the Lima built in 1878 by the firm of Gustave Eifel. To understand

Viana's position as the base for fishing armadas that once trawled the farthest reaches of the north Atlantic in search of cod, visit the **Gil Eannes ★**, Doca Comercial (www.fundacaogileannes.pt; ✆ **25/880-97-10**; daily 9:30am–6pm in winter, until 7pm in summer; admission 4€, children under 6 free), a former hospital boat that accompanied the cod fleets on their journeys to Greenland or Newfoundland. Now it's a floating museum moored in the harbor.

For one of the great panoramas in the north of Portugal (in fact, *National Geographic* called it one of the greatest views in the world), you can visit the **Miradouro de Santa Luzia ★★★**, a belvedere on the hill of Santa Luzia, to the north of the town where the view of Viana is especially stunning at night when all the lights go on. The viewpoint is topped by the **Basilica de Santa Luzia** (www.templosantaluzia.org; ✆ **25/882-31-73**) constructed in a neo-Byzantine style in the early 20th century; its towers and domes recall Paris' Sacré-Coeur. For an even better view over the city and coast, climb the 142 steps up to the cupola, open summer 8am to 6pm (until 8pm in August), winter 8am to 5pm; admission free. Portugal's longest **funicular railway** (✆ **25/880-93-33**) will haul you the 650m (2,130 ft.) to the hilltop for 2€ one-way. It starts at Avenida 25 Abril (June–Sept: daily 9am–8pm; Mar–May, Oct: Mon–Fri 10am–noon and 1–5pm, Sat–Sun 9am–6pm; Nov–Feb; Tues–Fri 10am–noon and 1–5pm, Sat–Sun 10am–5pm).

Lately, Viana has gained a reputation for its **modern architecture,** with internationally celebrated designers of the Porto school laying down major new works in the city. Highlights include the riverside **Praça da Liberdade ★** plaza by Fernando Távora; the **municipal library,** Alameda 5 de Outubro (✆ **25/880-93-40;** Mon–Fri 9am–7pm, Sat 10am–7pm) designed by Álvaro Siza Vieira; and the **Centro Cultural,** Praça Marques Júnior (✆ **25/880-93-51**), opened in 2013 by another Pritzker Prize laureate from Porto, Eduardo Souto de Moura. It is used for concerts and theater performances.

Where to Stay

MODERATE TO EXPENSIVE

Casa Melo Alvim ★★ The oldest urban mansion in Viana do Castelo is today an inn of antique charm. Built in the Manueline style in 1509, it retains its baroque stairwell, which features a row of original stone pillars. Rooms are individually decorated to illustrate the evolution of Portuguese styling from 17th-century baroque to contemporary. That might mean chestnut furniture typical from the region or rooms in the colonial Indo-Portuguese style using tropical hardwoods. A peaceful garden and a restaurant serving regional dishes with a classical French influence add to the inn's allure. Breakfast features local cold cuts, cheeses, fresh fruit, and breads. The hotel displays an extensive collection of Viana's filigree gold jewelry. Five apartments and a pool were added in 2019.

Av. Conde da Carreira 28. www.casameloalvim.com. ✆ **25/880-82-00.** 25 units. 78€–123€ double, 101€–173€ suites and apartments. Public parking nearby, 10€ daily. **Amenities:** Garden; free bikes; outdoor pool; restaurant; bar; library; babysitting; free Wi-Fi.

THE green COAST

North and south of Viana, the Minho's shoreline is known as the **Costa Verde ★★**, or "Green Coast," named for the forests and fields that spread down to the broad sandy beaches. The area has a reputation for chilly water and strong surf, but it has some beautiful, uncrowded beaches. Just keep an eye on the lifeguards to see if the currents are making it unsafe for swimming—red flags mean keep out of the water, yellow means take care, green indicates it's safe to go in and have fun. The beaches have always been popular with families from Porto and other northern cities, but they are increasingly drawing an international following—not least among surfers and other water sports enthusiasts.

Many rate **Praia de Moledo ★★★** as the region's best. It's Portugal's northernmost beach and draws a fashionable crowd from Porto. The wide sandy strand curls southward from the River Minho, which forms the Spanish frontier. Beyond is the conical Mount Santa Tecla, and there's a 15th-century fort on a small offshore island just to add to its scenic appeal. If all that sea air gives you an appetite, the **Pra Lá Caminha** (✆ **25/872-26-06**) beach bar is renowned for its sandwiches.

The nearby town of **Caminha ★** has a lovely location where the River Minho meets the ocean. Its picturesque center reflects a golden age trading with Portugal's Africa and Asian outposts during the 15th and 16th centuries. Staying the night? **Design & Wine Hotel ★★**, Praça Conselheiro Silva Torres (www.designwinehotel.com; ✆ **25/871-90-40**) offers a cool mix of 18th-century and ultra-modern buildings on the waterfront, with a spa and a wine cellar that serves as a reminder that we're still in *vinho verde* territory.

Other top beaches include **Praia de Ofir ★★**, backed by dunes and pine forests (and a trio of ugly tower blocks) just south of the resort town of Esposende, and **Praia de Afife ★★**, an endless stretch of fine white sand north of Viana, which boasts a celebrated restaurant, **Mariana ★★** (✆ **25/898-13-27**), serving divine sea bass steamed with algae.

Fábrica do Chocolate ★★ Yep, this is a hotel in a chocolate factory—the ideal place to unleash your Willy Wonka fantasies. In fact, there's a Willy Wonka–themed room featuring a giant mural inspired by Roald Dahl's character and a bedstead in the form of his "golden ticket." Rooms are all chocolate-themed, ranging from romantic to playful. One is inspired by the movie *Chocolat* staring Juliette Binoche and Johnny Depp. A suite with families in mind is made up like the candy house from Hansel and Gretel. It's all in a restored chocolate factory built in 1914, which also includes a chocolate museum, a store and a workshop for chocolate-making classes. There's even a spa with "chocotherapy" treatments. It's nicely located on a quiet street a block from the riverside gardens and a short walk to Praça da República.

Rua do Gontim 70 a 76. www.fabricadochocolate.com. ✆ **25/824-40-00.** 18 units. 64€–130€ double, 104€–185€ suite. Public parking nearby from 8€ per day. **Amenities:** Terrace; spa; massage service; babysitting; free Wi-Fi.

Flôr de Sal ★★ This modern three-story hotel in steel and glass stands right at the edge of the Atlantic and most of its rooms have balconies with wooden decks offering uninterrupted ocean views. The others look up to Santa Luzia mountain. They are elegant, tasteful, and supremely comfortable, with state-of-the-art bathrooms. An excellent spa and fitness center make it fun to sweat: You can gaze out over the waves from the Jacuzzi or running machines. If it's too chilly for the beach, the hotel has two heated, indoor saltwater pools. The restaurant provides regional cooking with a seafood accent and more panoramic sea views.

Avenida de Cabo Verde 100, Praia Norte. www.hotelflordesal.com. ✆ **25/880-01-00.** 60 units. 115€–170€ double, 150€–210€ suite. Free parking. **Amenities:** Garden; terrace; free bikes; 2 indoor pools; gym; spa; sauna; hammam; Jacuzzi; massage service; babysitting; free Wi-Fi.

Pousada Viana do Castelo ★★★ A jewel in the Pousada chain of luxury boutique digs, this Belle Epoque palace is surrounded by lushly landscaped gardens and boasts some of the finest views in Portugal, looking down on the domes of Santa Luzia church with Viana, the River Lima and the sweeping curve of the Atlantic coast laid out before you. It will be hard to drag yourself away from your balcony, but rest assured that you can also enjoy the panorama from the outdoor pool, while getting a massage in the gardens, or from amid the crystal and chintz of the spacious lounge and gourmet restaurant. Built in 1895, the hotel has neoclassical details and granite balconies and looks especially good when floodlit at night. Winding cobblestone roads run through a forest to the entrance, which is a 15-minute taxi ride from downtown.

Monte de Santa Luzia. www.pousadas.pt. ✆ **25/880-03-70.** 51 units. 84€–204€ double. Free parking. **Amenities:** Garden; terrace; bike hire; outdoor pool; restaurant; bar; free Wi-Fi.

Where to Eat

A Laranjeira ★ PORTUGUESE A friendly, family-run restaurant in the heart of downtown, the "orange tree" is devoted to preserving traditional Minho cooking, with recipes handed down from generation to generation. Menus change with the season, but signatures include deep-fried hake filets with Russian salad, roasted salt-cod with kale, or pork with chestnuts. Vegetarian options are available, and a dessert trolley loaded with temptations ("golden soup" is a must-try) makes the rounds at the end of the meal. The decor is bright and modern. It's located in a town house fronted with green ceramic tiles that also contains Viana's oldest guesthouse, whose recently restored rooms provide bargain accommodations. There's an excellent wine list with a focus on local *vinho verde* and Douro reds.

Rua Manuel Espregueira, 24. www.olaranjeira.com. ✆ **25/882-22-58.** Mains 9€–15€. Thurs–Tues noon–3:30pm and 7–10:30pm.

Camelo ★★ PORTUGUESE Nationally renowned for its Minho cuisine, this country-style house on the road leading east out of Viana is located where the suburbs start to give way to vine-covered hills. The vegetables come from the owners' plot owners and they raise their own pigs. Some 350 people can fit in the dining rooms, which quickly fill with families gathering for Sunday lunches or workmates out for celebration. In summer, the coveted tables are in the vine-shaded back garden. Camelo always has fresh fish, but salt-cod and roast meat dishes are what the place is best known for, along with seasonal specials like marinated pork served with blood-thickened rice or lamprey—an eel-like fish that's pulled from the rivers of the Minho between January and April. It might be ugly, but it's a big favorite up here.

Rua de Santa Marta 119, Santa Marta de Portuzelo. www.camelorestaurantes.com. ✆ **25/883-90-90.** Main courses 10€–25€. Tues–Sun 11am–10:30pm.

CHAVES ★

125km (77 miles) E of Braga; 150km (96 miles) NE of Porto; 440km (275 miles) N of Lisbon

High up on the Spanish border, Chaves has its roots in Roman times. It was founded by Emperor Flavius Vespasian in A.D. 79 and prized by the Romans both as military strongpoint and bath resort, thanks to its hot springs. The arched bridge across the River Tâmega, which is still a symbol of the city, was built during the reign of the Iberian-born Emperor Trajan. Today Chaves is an attractive town of narrow streets and noble buildings clustered on the riverbank beneath the keep of its 14th-century castle. It's renowned for culinary delights such as smoked ham and puff-pastry meat pies, but the main attraction are those hot springs, making Chaves, and its surrounding resorts, a major spa center.

Essentials

ARRIVING

BY BUS There's no rail link, but **Rede Expressos** makes about a dozen daily trips from Porto in just over 2 hours. Ticket's cost 13.30€. From Lisbon it costs 22.80€ and takes around 6 hours with a change in Porto.

BY CAR From Porto, it should take about 1½ hours along the A3 and A7 toll highways passing by Guimarães. From Lisbon, the journey is 4 hours: take the A1 to Coimbra, the IP3 to Viseu, and the A24, which takes you to Chaves. If you are coming from the Douro Valley wine region, the A24 gets you from Peso da Régua in less than 1 hour.

VISITOR INFORMATION

The **tourist office** is at Praça de Camões 1 (www.chaves.pt; ✆ **27/634-81-80;** open Apr–Sept: daily 9:30am–1:30pm and 2:30–6:30pm. Oct–Mar: daily 9:30am–1:30pm and 2:30–6pm).

Exploring Chaves

Start out on the **Ponte Romana ★★**, or Roman Bridge, which runs for 150m (almost 500 ft.) over 12 arches across the Tâmega. It was built on the orders of Emperor Trajan in A.D. 104 and was a major link between the Roman cities of Braga and Astorga (in Spain). Today it's pedestrian-only and the perfect place to admire the outline of old Chaves with its churches, fortifications, and mansions on the west bank; the quaint **Madalena** neighborhood to the east; and leafy riverside gardens on both sides. In the center of the bridge are two engraved **Roman columns** dedicated to the city, which the Romans called *Aquae Flaviae* (Flavius' Waters) in honor of its founding emperor and the hot springs. For the adventurous, an alternative way across the river is the row of stepping stones or **Poldas** ★ just downstream, which locals have long used as a shortcut.

From the bridge, the **Rua de Santo António** ★ is the main commercial street running up to the center of town. It's lined with brightly painted granite-and-glass town houses dating back to the 18th century and earlier. At the top is the **Forte de São Francisco** ★, Rua do Terreiro da Cavalaria (www.fortesaofrancisco.com; ✆ **27/633-37-00**), a mighty, star-shaped fortress built around a 15th-century convent in 1658 to bolster the frontier defenses during the war against Spain to restore Portugal's independence. It was the scene of a notable battle in 1809, when Portuguese troops dislodged Napoleon's invading French troops. These days, the hilltop fortress contains a hotel, but non-guests are welcome to pay a discreet visit inside the battlements.

Heading back downtown, many of the houses are cracked with age and maintain centuries-old wooden verandas decorated with flowers on the upper floors. **Rua Direita** ★ is one of the best places to spot them. **Praça de Camões** ★ is the city's monumental heart. It contains the **Igreja de Santa Maria Maior** ★ (✆ **27/632-13-84;** daily 9am–6pm; free admission), a church dating back to the 12th century, on the site where a Roman temple and a Swabian basilica once stood. There's also the handsome 19th-century **City Hall,** the baroque facade of the **Igreja da Misericórdia** and the imposing **Paço dos Duques de Bragança,** a ducal palace built between the 15th and 18th centuries and now housing the **Museu da Região Flaviense** ★ (✆ **27/634-05-00;** Mon–Fri: 9am–12:30pm and 2–5:30pm, Sat–Sun: 2–5:30pm; admission 2€ adults, 1€ students and seniors, free for children under 12), a museum containing Roman and prehistoric artifacts from around the region. The museum ticket also includes entry to the nearby military, religious arts, and railway museums.

Next door to the museum are the remains of Chaves' medieval castle, also built to deter Spanish incursions. Its 14th-century donjon, the **Torre de Menagem** ★, rises out of neatly tended gardens. It contains a military museum, but its main attraction is the view from the ramparts. Admission is included in the price of the regional museum and it keeps the same hours.

If you are not staying at one of the spa hotels, you can sample the benefits of Chaves' hot springs by popping into the **Termas de Chaves** ★, Largo das Caldas (www.termasdechaves.com; ✆ **27/633-24-45;** Mon–Sat 9am–12:30pm, 2–7pm, Sun 9am–12:30pm), the modern municipal spa, which offers a range of health treatments and wellness packages using the waters that spring to the surface here at a constant 73°C (163°F). Day-long spa packages cost from 58€; a 45-minute massage, 45€; a 15-minute sauna, 15€. In the rotunda outside, you can drink the mineral-rich waters, said to be very good for the health, if not so easy on the taste buds.

Where to Stay

Forte de São Francisco ★★ The best choice in the center of town, this family-run hotel sits within the massive walls of the 17th-century fortress built to defend Portugal's northern borders. The rooms are decorated in a restrained modern style, but with antique touches such as wooden bedsteads. Rooms are mostly in the old convent around which the defensive complex was raised. The broad parade grounds now hold gardens with palm, olive, and citrus trees; a tennis court; and an outdoor dining area. One of the bastions has an outdoor pool built into the roof that offers views over the city and surrounding hills.

Rua do Terreiro da Cavalaria. www.fortesaofrancisco.com. ✆ **27/633-37-00.** 58 units. 56€–110€ double, 109€–150€ suite. Free parking. **Amenities:** Garden; tennis; bike hire; outdoor pool; 2 restaurants; 2 bars; games room; kids play area; babysitting; free Wi-Fi.

Hotel Casino Chaves★ For a touch of Vegas in Trás-os-Montes, this brash modern place has roulette, blackjack, poker and lots of slots. Just north of downtown, it's 8km (5 miles) from the border and popular with visitors from Spain, who nip over for a flutter. They can hardly miss it; the architecture resembles a pile of irregular shaped white boxes balanced precariously on top of each other. Inside, it's a riot of color. Rooms come in bright candy hues, while black and amber shades predominate in the bathrooms. All offer city or mountain views. There's a seriously large outdoor pool from which you can gaze across the hills, and a wide range of spa, fitness, restaurant, and bar options. Big-name Portuguese music stars frequently perform.

Lugar do Extremo, Valdanta. www.solverde.pt. ✆ **27/630-96-00.** 78 units. 62€–176€ double, 62€–176€ suite. Free parking. **Amenities:** Garden; terrace; bike hire; outdoor and indoor pools; spa; sauna; hammam; Jacuzzi; fitness room; squash courts; 3 restaurants; 6 bars; games room; babysitting; free Wi-Fi.

Pedras Salgadas Spa & Nature Park ★★★ Wherever you go in Portugal, cafes serve little green bottles of sparkling mineral water called "Água das Pedras." This is where it comes from, a spa resort that was all the rage in the years before World War I, set in a forest of redwood, pine, and cypress, about 30 minutes' drive south from Chaves. Revamped and reopened in 2012, its accommodations comprise slate-covered treehouses—space-age, tubular contraptions propped up among the branches. It's not exactly living Tarzan-style, however: the houses come will all mod cons, including lounges and kitchenettes, all decked out in Nordic-style minimalism. Vertigo sufferers can relax, there are also roomy ground-based "eco houses" in a similar style planted among the trees. The resort includes a scattering of delightful original buildings, like the pink-painted former casino and the white stucco spa pavilion from 1912, renovated by Pritzker-Prize–winning architect Álvaro Siza Vieira, which provides posh pampering. A museum was added in 2018 explaining the history of the waters.

Parque Pedras Salgadas, Bornes de Aguiar. www.pedrassalgadaspark.com. ✆ **25/943-71-40.** 14 units. 122€–270€ double. Free parking. **Amenities:** Garden; tennis; free bikes; indoor and outdoor pools; spa; sauna; hammam; Jacuzzi; restaurant; bar; games room; free Wi-Fi.

Vidago Palace ★★★ This extraordinary place was commissioned in 1908 on the orders of King Carlos I, who wanted Portugal endowed with a grand spa resort to compete with the best of Europe. He never saw it completed, assassinated by gunmen later that year in Lisbon. Portugal became a republic the year it opened in 1910. Over the next century, the palace had its ups and downs, but it reopened in 2010, restored to all its Belle Epoque glamour, and is one of the best hotels in the country. Siza Vieira oversaw the restoration of the spa and Club House bar and restaurant. Behind the 100-plus windows of its vast salmon-pink facade, there are monumental staircases, marble columns, silk wall hangings, rooms fit for royalty and chandelier-lit restaurants in the hands of star chef Vítor Matos. Outside are 100 hectares (250 acres) of forested parkland and a golf course laid down in 1935 by the legendary Scottish designer Philip Mackenzie Ross. It even gave its name and location to a *telenovela.*

Parque de Vidago, Vidago. www.vidagopalace.com. ✆ **27/699-09-20.** 70 units. 147€–405€ double, 328€–800€ suite. Free parking. **Amenities:** Garden; tennis; golf; free bikes; indoor and outdoor pools; spa; sauna; hammam; Jacuzzi; 3 restaurants; 3 bars; games room; kids' play area; babysitting; free Wi-Fi.

Where to Eat

Adega Faustino ★★ PORTUGUESE Over a century ago, this solid, single-story stone building opened as a wine store and tavern. It's still in the same family and the great oak wine casks still stand proudly behind the bar, but its role has evolved over the decades. These days, Faustino serves up hearty plates of homemade local *petiscos*—Portugal's version of tapas. It's a no-frills place with plain whitewashed walls, cobbles on the floor, and plastic cloths on the long wooden tables. But the food is an authentic taste of Trás-os-Montes (with the occasional dish from Angola showing up sometimes on the menu—a reminder of many Portuguese families' links with the African country). Liver with bacon, garlicky *alheira* sausages, lamb chops, and tripe with chickpeas are some of the treats you can wash down with a jug of red wine from those casks.

Travessa Cândido Reis. www.adegafaustino.pt. ✆ **27/632-21-42.** *Petiscos* 2€–10€. Mon–Sat noon–3pm, 7–10:30pm.

Carvalho ★★ PORTUGUESE Occupying the ground floor of a modern apartment block next to the thermal baths, this restaurant doesn't look like much on the outside. Inside, too, the decor is not that exciting unless floral tablecloths and a collection of oversized clocks are your thing. The food, however, is something else. The mother and daughter team in the kitchen have made this place the restaurant of reference for regional cooking in Chaves for over 30 years. There's always fresh fish for the grill and typical dishes based on locally raised livestock. Specialties include *Naco de vitela* (a hunk of young beef) with rice baked with smoked meats, salt-cod broiled over hot coals or roast kid. The guestbook bears witness to Carvalho's fame—from

ROSÉ palace

If you discovered wine in the 1960s or 1970s, chances are you're already familiar with the **Casa de Mateus** ★★★ (www.casademateus.com; ✆ **25/932-31-21**), a wonderful baroque palace just outside Vila Real on the road between Chaves and Régua. Back then, a slightly sweet pink fizz called **Mateus Rosé** was the world's best-selling wine. Fans ranged from Jimi Hendrix and Queen Elizabeth II to countless students for whom Mateus was the beverage of choice for first dates—cheap sophistication with an exotic curved bottle you could convert into a romantic candle holder. Tastes have evolved and, although Mateus has made something of a comeback as an icon of 1970s nostalgia (and still sells 20 million bottles a year in 120 countries), serious wine buffs tend to be scornful. The palace that inspired its label, however, has a timeless appeal.

Built in the early 18th century, it is the most perfect of all the country's baroque manors. In contrasting white-painted plasterwork and soft gray granite, the main building is accessed by a balustraded double staircase flanked by twin wings advancing toward an ornamental pool that perfectly reflects the facade. A flurry of chimneys, decorative pinnacles, and pediments project over the roof. There's a splendid chapel off to one side and a row of stately cypress trees providing shade along the path from the remarkable **gardens.** The architect is unknown, but Nicolau Nasoni, the Italian behind much of Porto's baroque skyline, is thought to have had at least a hand in the design.

Inside, the house is richly furnished with silk hangings, high wooden ceilings, paintings of bucolic scenes and an early illustrated edition of the Portuguese classic poem *Os Lusíadas*. Descendants of the original owners still live in one wing, but the rest of the house and the gardens are open to the public. Regular concerts of jazz, classical and Portuguese music take place here during the summer.

It's located at Largo Morgados de Mateus in the village of Mateus, just over 3km (almost 2 miles) east of Vila Real. It's open daily 9am to 7pm. Admission to the house and gardens is 13€ including a guided tour; just the gardens is 9.50€. The estate sells port wines in its store but don't expect to find Mateus Rosé; it's made elsewhere.

Olympic champions to presidents of the republic—everybody eats here when they're in town.

Alameda de Tabolado, Largo das Caldas 4. www.restaurante-carvalho.com. ✆ **27/632-17-27.** Reservations recommended. Main courses 15€–19€. Tues–Sat noon–3pm and 7–11pm; Sun noon–3pm.

BRAGANÇA ★

210km (130 miles) E of Porto; 490km (310 miles) NE of Lisbon

Bragança (or Braganza, as it's sometimes written) is the historic capital of Portugal's Trás-os-Montes region. The heart of the city is a fortified citadel built in the early 1100s. From its sturdy walls you get a view across the forests, desolate plateaus, and hill ranges that are snow-covered in winter. Natives call the country here *terra fria* (cold land). Inside the battlements are the narrow lanes of one of Portugal's best-preserved medieval cities, where ancient buildings and traditions survive. Despite its remoteness, Bragança played a key role in Portugal's history: Local lords bearing the city's name formed Portugal's royal family from 1640 until the fall of the monarchy in 1910.

Essentials

ARRIVING

BY BUS The rail network doesn't make it up here. **Rede Expressos** runs around a dozen daily buses from Lisbon. The trip takes around 6 hours and 40 minutes and costs 23€. From Porto, there are some 10 daily buses making the 3-hour trip for 14.30€.

BY CAR In their 1980s hit *Para ti Maria*, Portugal's greatest rock band Xutos e Pontapés complain that it takes 9 hours to get from Lisbon to Bragança (where girlfriend Maria is waiting). Since then, European Union money has laid down a network of highways that has cut that by half. Take the A1 to Coimbra, the IP3 to Viseu and the A24 to Vila Real, where you pick up the A4. From Porto it's just over 2 hours from along the A4 toll highway.

VISITOR INFORMATION

The **tourist office** is at Avenida Cidade de Zamora (www.cm-braganca.pt; ✆ **27/338-12-73;** open Mon–Fri 9:30am–1pm and 2–5:30pm).

Exploring Bragança

The **Cidadela ★★** is the place to start. Fortified in the 12th century and strengthened in the 15th, it was long a stronghold to deter incursions from Spanish neighbors. Within the walls the medieval atmosphere is preserved. One- or two-story homes, with gray stone doors and window frames, whitewashed walls, and clay-tiled roofs cluster beneath the donjon, the **Torre de Menagem ★**, which broods over the city and the surrounding plateau. An army outpost until the 1920s, it now holds a military museum, the **Museu Militar** (✆ **27/332-23-78;** open Tues–Sun 9am–noon and 2–5pm; admission 2€), with displays that range from medieval suits of armor to a mockup of a World War I trench and material from Portugal's colonial wars in Africa. As much as the exhibits, it's worth paying the admission price to see the medieval architecture from the inside and climb to the roof for the stunning views.

In the garden besides the tower is a Gothic **stone pillory ★**. Such symbols of municipal power are found in towns across Portugal. This one stands out because it emerges from a statue of a *berrão*—an ancient statue representing a boar, sculptured by tribespeople who inhabited these lands before the Romans. Hundreds of them were planted in the northwest of the Iberian Peninsula between the 4th and 1st centuries B.C. This is one of the best preserved. Nobody is quite sure what they meant to the Iron Age people who made them.

Another historical mystery is in the nearby Municipal House, or **Domus Municipalis ★,** Rua da Cidadela (✆ **27/332-21-81;** open Tues–Sun 10am–6pm). A squat granite structure ringed with little arched windows, it is a rare surviving civil building from the Romanesque era of the early Middle Ages. Its original use is uncertain. One theory is that the first floor served as a cistern for the town water supply, while the chamber above was a meeting place for a prototype municipal council. Before leaving the walled upper town, cast your eyes inside the citadel's church, **Igreja da Santa Maria ★** (✆ **27/332-55-10;** Tues–Sun 10am–5pm; free), distinguished by its twisted columns and vividly painted barrel-vaulted ceiling.

Down the hill from the castle, the lower part of Bragança's old town is a pleasing mix of handsome plazas, granite mansions, and white-painted churches. Its wealth reflects the 16th-century influence of the Bragança family and the city's establishment as the region's main administrative and religious center following a devastating Spanish attack on the border town of Miranda do Douro in 1762. **Praça da Sé ★** is the main square flanked by the 18th-century **Sé Velha,** or Old Cathedral, used as a cultural center since a new cathedral was built in 2001. The square forms a hub for the city's main commercial streets. A yellow building with the rounded facade and balcony at the eastern end of the square houses the **Chave d'Ouro** cafe, where locals have gathered to sip coffee, gossip, and argue soccer and politics since the 1920s.

Close by are a couple of museums that are well worth a visit. The **Museu Abade de Baçal ★,** Rua Abílio Beça 27 (✆ **27/333-15-95;** Tues–Sun 9:30am–12:30, 2–6pm; admission 3€), occupies a former bishop's palace built in the late 1600s. The expertly presented collection ranges from masks and costumes used in local folklore to Renaissance church sculptures; prehistoric boar statues, regional landscape paintings, silver plates, antique furniture and ceramics. Down the road is the **Centro de Arte Contemporânea Graça Morais ★**, Rua Abílio Beça, 105 (http://centroartegracamorais.cm-braganca.pt; ✆ **27/330-24-10;** Tues–Sun 10am–6:30pm; admission 2.08€, 1.04€ students and seniors, free for children under 10), a modern gallery dedicated to one of Portugal's best-known living artists, Graça Morais (b. 1948), who was born in Trás-os-Montes and frequently takes her inspiration from the region's landscapes, people and traditions. It also shows works by other contemporary artists and runs regular temporary exhibitions.

Bragança sits on the southern edge of the **Parque Natural de Montesinho ★★**, a forbidding but beautiful nature reserve of rolling hills and high plains, covered with forests of oak and chestnut. Almost 10% of the world's chestnut forest lies in Portugal, and 80% of the country's production is in Trás-os-Montes. Through fall and winter, carts of roasting chestnuts are a common street-corner sight in cities around the country. The park, which stretches almost 750 sq. kilometers (290 sq. miles) along the Spanish border, has some of southern Europe's wildest terrain. Temperatures range from -12°C (10°F) in winter to searing summers of 40°C (104°F). The Iberian wolf and rare black stork are among the wildlife. In the granite-and-slate villages spread through the park, shepherds, cattle herders, and small landholders eek out an existence, many continuing centuries-old communal farming practices. Information,

BUONOS DIES miranda

Portuguese is the world's sixth-most-spoken language, used by 250 million people from Mozambique to Macao, Brazil to Braga. Up in Portugal's remote northeast, however, a few speak something different. The country's second official language is **Mirandese,** spoken by 15,000 people living around the city of **Miranda do Douro ★★**.

The language is closely related to Portuguese: "Good day" is *buonos dies* rather than *bom dia;* "thank you" is *oubrigado* instead of *obrigado.* But local people are proud of their distinct tongue, which has been making a comeback since schools began teaching it in the 1980s.

Miranda sits high above the Douro. Up here the river carves a deep canyon into the land, forming the border between Portugal and Spain. Once a thriving regional center, the city slipped into obscurity after 1762, when most of it was destroyed by shelling from an invading Spanish army during the Seven Years' War. Local bigwigs decamped to Bragança, farther from the frontier, and Miranda was left to its own devices.

Isolation maintained not only the language, which still resounds within the surviving medieval streets around the 16th-century canyon-side **Cathedral ★★**, but also other traditions. Inside the cathedral, look for the tiny statue of a boy sporting a top hat, frock coat, and sword strapped to his belt. Revered by locals, the **Menino Jesús de Cartolinha** is supposed to represent a youthful Jesus who, legend has it, appeared in the city in the 17th century waving a sword to inspire resistance against besieging Spaniards. An even older bellicose tradition are the ***pauliteiros* ★★** (www.pauliteiros.com), groups of men who perform a war dance that involves bashing sticks together while dressed in frilly white skirts, striped stockings, and brightly colored shawls to a beat of drums and bagpipes. The origins are lost in time, but the local museum, **Museu da Terra de Miranda ★**, Praça D. João III 2 (www.culturanorte.pt; ✆ **27/341-72-88;** open Wed–Sun 9am–1pm and 2–8pm, Tues 2–6pm; admission 2€) explains the dance and other local traditions. Check your hotel or the local tourist office, Largo do Menino Jesús da

maps and ideas for car, bike, or hiking tours can be found at the tourist office in Bragança or from the park authorities (www.natural.pt; ✆ **27/330-04-00**).

Other attractions close to Bragança include the **Basílica Menor de Santo Cristo ★** (✆ **96/004-15-67**), an outsize baroque church that towers over the tiny village of Outeiro. It was built in 1698 to celebrate a miracle reported in the village when blood was supposed to have seeped from a statue of Christ. It's a 20-minute drive southeast from the city. Opening hours can be unpredictable, so it's best to call ahead if you want to view the golden altar and painted wooden panels inside. Just to the west of Bragança, the village of **Castro de Avelãs** contains a **church ★** built partly in the 12th century that is one of the best-preserved examples in Portugal of the Mudéjar style of Christian buildings influenced by Arab architecture. Check opening times with the Bragança tourist office, but it's the exterior of the building that is most striking.

Cartolinha (www.cm-mdouro.pt; ✆ **27/343-00-25**), for dates of *pauliteiro* performances.

The climate here is extreme. Locals say they get *nove meses de inverno e três de inferno* (9 months of winter and 3 of hell). Snow frequently covers the austere landscape of rocky plateaus and rolling hills. Stretching for 130km (80 miles) along the Portuguese bank of Douro is a nature reserve, the **Parque Natural do Douro Internacional ★★** (www.natural.pt). It's a paradise for birdwatchers. They can spot shaggy-headed Egyptian vultures, black storks, pink hoopoes and blue rock thrushes. For the most spectacular ornithological encounters, head to **Penedo Durão ★★★**, a rocky outcrop towering over the river, which is a favored hangout for Griffon vultures, one of the largest raptors. You can look them in the eye as they glide past on 3m (9-ft.) wingspans.

Many of the villages around here have kept winter festivities rooted in ancient pagan rites. Around Christmas, Twelfth Night, or Mardi Gras, young men dress up in devilish masks and outlandish costumes and run riot through the streets. The most remarkable is in the village of **Podence,** a half-hour drive south of Bragança, where during the week of Mardi Gras, a masked, bell-ringing gang called the ***carretas* ★★** take the streets, making merry mischief while draped in shaggy hooded suits striped with yellow, green, and scarlet.

The best place to stay in Miranda is the **Hotel Parador Santa Catarina ★**, Largo da Pousada (www.hotelparadorsantacatarina.pt; ✆ **27/343-10-05**), where the rooms have plunging views over the canyon. Among the many eateries serving the local delicacy *posta mirandesa* (a thick-cut steak from the local breed of cattle), try **La Balbina ★**, Rua Rainha Dona Catarina 1 (✆ **27/343-23-94**), where they grill them in the fireplace while you watch. The region's most original accommodation is 40km (25 miles) south of Podence, **Bela Vista Silo Housing ★★**, Quinta da Bela Vista 176, Eucisia, Alfândega da Fé (www.belavistasilohousing.pt; ✆ **27/946-32-80**), which has rooms in converted grain silos. Go in late February and March and it will be too cold for the outdoor pool, but perfect for seeing the countryside whitened by the blooming of countless almond trees.

Where to Stay

A Montesinho ★ In the riverside village of Girmonde, a 15-minute drive from the center of Bragança at the entrance of the Montesinho Natural Park, the owners of a famed local restaurant have restored a bunch of scattered rural dwellings that are now guesthouses. You can rent rooms or a whole house. Casa da Mestra, once the schoolteacher's house, has five double rooms. The solid stone building was given a daring makeover, with a glass and wood-board front revealing a display of local handicraft products. It's not grand luxury, but makes a cozy, inexpensive base for exploring the park (the owners will be happy to guide your treks). There's a shared kitchen and a lounge that integrates the bare stone walls into a modern design, warmed by a blazing fireplace. In summer, guests can use the outdoor pool belonging to another of the family's properties in the village. Dine at Dom

Roberto's restaurant. A tavern since the 1930s, it does wonders with local meat, trout, and game.

Rua Coronel Álvaro Cepeda, 1, Girmonde. www.amontesinho.pt. ✆ **27/330-25-10.** 22 units. 63€–65€ double, 66€–75€ suites. Free parking. **Amenities:** Garden; terrace; bikes hire; outdoor pool; sauna; Jacuzzi; restaurant; bar; games room; kids' play area; babysitting; free Wi-Fi.

Pousada Bragança ★★ On the heights of the Serra da Nogueira, with panoramic views of Bragança castle and the old city, this lodging is at its best at night or emerging from the morning mist. The *pousada* was built in the 1950s, using local stone and natural wood. A vintage feel is maintained with furniture and artwork from that period. The spacious guest rooms are well furnished and maintained, with private balconies. Beds feature covers with traditional Tràs-os-Montes patterns. Bathrooms come in granite and marble. In winter the open fireplace (and in summer the outdoor pool) is much appreciated. The G restaurant holds a Michelin star for its modern take on regional cuisine. It's a 15-minute walk to downtown.

Estrada de Turismo. www.pousadas.pt. ✆ **27/333-14-93.** 28 units. 90€–219€ double, including breakfast. Free parking. **Amenities:** Garden; terrace; outdoor pool; restaurant; bar; kids' play area; free Wi-Fi.

Solar de Santa Maria ★ In the center of town, this graceful house built in 1639 served as a convent, school and residence for the district police chief before being turned into a guesthouse. It still has the feel of a noble family home and is packed with antique wooden furniture, framed prints, and comfortable sofas. Rooms are a decent size, with wooden floors and high ceilings. The patio garden, with its Renaissance arcades and shady orange trees, is a treat. Fresh bread, cheeses, homemade cakes, and jams are served at breakfast.

Rua Eng. José Beça, 39. www.solarsantamaria.pt. ✆ **27/333-31-61.** 5 units. 65€ double, breakfast 5€ per person extra. Free public parking nearby. **Amenities:** Garden; library; free Wi-Fi.

Where to Eat

O Javali ★★ PORTUGUESE The name means "the wild boar," and the highland cooking here is game-heavy. Partridge pie and boar steak on the wood-fired grill are specialties. In Europe, chestnuts were a staple before traders introduced the potato from the New World. Here they still are. You can start your meal with chestnut soup and finish with chestnut pudding. Naturally, there's a boar's head mounted on the wall. If neither boar nor chestnuts are to your taste, they serve trout from the fast-flowing local streams and baby goat raised in the hills of Montesinho. Portions are massive; you may want to share a main. The place recently got a facelift, adding new light to the dining room and a spacious terrace outside; plus they opened a downtown offshoot Taberna do Javali.

Estrada do Portelo, km 5. ✆ **27/333-38-98.** Mains 13€–21€. Wed–Mon noon–3:30pm, 7–11pm.

Solar Bragançano ★★★ PORTUGUESE A legend. For many, this is the epitome of what a Portuguese regional restaurant should be. Located in a 3-centuries-old house on the main square of town, it serves the best, most flavor-filled regional dishes with a true taste of Trás-os-Montes. A tiled stairway leads to a dining room lined with cabinets filled with wine and crystal. There are handwoven regional rugs and the occasional stag's head, sword or portrait of a local notable on the walls. It's fabulous to eat here at any time, but autumn and winter are when game takes over the menu—the pheasant with chestnuts or hare with rice draw fans from all over the country. In summer, you can dine in the leafy garden.

Praça da Sé. ✆ **27/332-38-75.** Reservations recommended. Mains 9€–19€. Tues–Sun noon–3pm and 6–10pm.

MADEIRA & THE AZORES

15

Portugal's Atlantic islands have some of the country's most spectacular landscapes and intriguing culture. Far from the mainland, these volcanic archipelagos surge from the ocean in dramatic peaks, the tips of giant underwater mountains. Madeira is closer to Africa than mainland Europe. Its subtropical climate, forested slopes, and fine wines have long attracted travelers. By contrast, weather in the Azores is mild, but notoriously unpredictable. It's warm enough to grow pineapples and tea, but prone to gusting downpours. The rugged, remote beauty of the nine islands is just beginning to draw more international visitors.

Madeira's sobriquet of "Pearl of the Atlantic" is well deserved. It enjoys a year-round springtime climate, nourishing an abundance of exotic fruits and flamboyant flora; mountains covered with ancient forests soar from a sea of deepest blue. A tourist attraction since the days of tall ships, it's packed with refined and historic hotels, the seafood is superlative, and its unique wines famed since before America's founding fathers chose them to toast the Declaration of Independence.

Madeira's capital, **Funchal,** is a lively, cosmopolitan city rising up in a crescent of hills from its historic core that dates from the 15th century. Its **farmers' market** and **botanical gardens** are a riot of color, and there's a string of first-class waterfront hotels.

Inland, a series of jagged peaks pierce the clouds, reaching over 1,800 meters (6,000 ft.) at its highest points. Views from majestic **Pico Ruivo** are stunning. The island's indigenous **laurissilva** forest is a UNESCO World Heritage Site. Many of the ***levada*** hiking tracks that crisscross Madeira pass through this lush vegetation, revealing panoramic vistas or hidden waterfalls.

Around the coast, highlights include **Câmara de Lobos,** a fishing port that charmed Winston Churchill. Nearby, the **Cabo Girão** skywalk will take those brave enough over one of Europe's highest sea cliffs. **Santana** in the north is the place to see traditional thatched cottages, while **Porto Moniz** has a seawater bathing spot integrated into black volcanic rock pools. If you crave a real beach, head to the nearby island of **Porto Santo;** its 6.5km (4 mile) stretch of golden sand is one of Portugal's best.

In the Azores, there are nine islands to choose from. They stretch 600km (375 miles) across the North Atlantic from Santa Maria in the southeast to Corvo in the northwest. **São Miguel** is the largest. Its capital **Ponta Delgada** is the archipelago's largest city and main gateway. The mountainous landscape here is marked by beautiful crater lakes, of which **Lagoa das Sete Cidades** is the most famed. In **Furnas** you can soak in natural pools heated by a volcano.

The city of **Angra do Heroísmo** on the island of **Terceira** is the Azores' main urban attraction. A UNESCO World Heritage Site, its colorful Discoveries Era streets served as a model for colonial towns across Latin America. The island has rich traditions from village **bull running** to its unique devotion to the Holy Spirit. Also in the central group of islands, **Pico** holds Portugal's highest mountain: a conical volcano rising dramatically out of the ocean. The second-largest island has a rich wine heritage, and its historic whaling ports are now centers for whale watching. Across the narrow strait, **Faial** has long been an Atlantic crossroads, from sailing boats and seaplanes to today's yacht crews who gather in the storied **Peter Café Sport.**

MADEIRA ★★★

853km (530 miles) SW of Portugal; 564km (350 miles) W of the African coastline

Essentials

ARRIVING

Madeira does not have direct flights from North America. However, you can fly there using TAP Air Portugal's **stopover** (p. 466) system, which allows you to spend up to 5 days on the Portuguese mainland, via Lisbon or Porto, before picking up a connecting flight to the island. Overwise, there are plenty of flights from mainland Portugal and the rest of Europe. TAP (www.flytap.com) has eight daily flights making the journey of 1 hour 45 minutes from Lisbon to Funchal, plus two direct flights from Porto. **EasyJet** (www.easyjet.com) also has at least two daily flights from Lisbon. Book in advance and, at low season, you can get round-trip tickets for well below $100, although prices go up sharply in summer and around New Year. TAP also has direct flights from Lisbon to **Porto Santo,** although the frequency decreases outside summer.

A range of companies operate scheduled flights to Madeira from other European cities including London, Paris, Frankfurt, and Brussels. There are also frequent charter flights.

The island's gateway was officially renamed **Madeira International Airport Cristiano Ronaldo** (www.aeroportomadeira.pt; ✆ **29/152-07-00**), in 2016 to honor the Funchal-born soccer star. Fortunately, the much-mocked bust of the player by amateur sculptor Emanuel Santos was replaced in 2018 with a more realistic representation of the famous face.

Sandwiched between the sea and the mountains, Funchal airport is reputed to be one of the world's most challenging for pilots, but successive runway extensions have made it safer. The terminal was given a major facelift in 2016.

Local bus company **SAM** (www.sam.pt; ✆ **29/120-11-51**) operates an **Aerobus** shuttle from the airport to downtown Funchal and onward to the seaside district of Praia Formosa, with stops at major hotels. The bus takes about 30 minutes to the city center and costs 5€ single or 8€ return. You can buy tickets on the bus. Drivers will help you find the right stop for your hotel. The company also runs occasional buses from the airport to other locations around the island. A **taxi** should cover the trip into town in around 20 minutes with prices starting at 20€.

In July, August, and September, a ferry service (www.madeira-ferry.pt; ✆ **29/121-03-00**) links Madeira to mainland Portugal and to Spain's Canary Islands. Ticket prices start at 85€ for adults for the 23-hour sea journey from Portimão in the Algarve.

WHEN TO VISIT

Madeira is called the island of eternal springtime for its year-round mild climate. Funchal averages 23°C (73°F) in August and 17°C (62°F) in February. Sea temperatures are more or less the same. Rainfall is heaviest October through March, but the rain rarely lasts for long and the mountainous terrain means that when there's a downpour on the north coast, it's sunny in Funchal. Many Europeans like to come in winter to escape the northern cold. In high summer, low clouds known as the *capacete* (helmet) can occasionally shut out the sunshine. The island blossoms in spring, holding a renowned April **Flower Festival.** Visitors also flock to the island on New Year's Eve for one of the world's biggest **firework displays** over Funchal harbor. There are more pyrotechnics in June for a month-long **Atlantic Festival** of arts and music. **Carnival** is also big in Funchal, with a Rio-like procession of samba schools and much downing of *poncha*.

VISITOR INFORMATION

The main **Madeira Tourist Office** is on Av. Arriaga 16, in Funchal (www.visitmadeira.pt; ✆ **29/121-19-02;** open Mon–Fri 9am–7pm and Sat–Sun 9am–3:30pm). There are six others dotted around the island, plus one in Porto Santo. Its website is a mine of information.

Madeira in Context

Madeira has enchanted travelers for centuries. "The climate is so fine that any man might wish it in his power to live here," wrote botanist Sir Joseph Banks when he passed through in 1768. "In the Sahara of the sea, it is impossible to imagine a more grandiose oasis," was the view of Jules Verne in 1908. "Nowhere else in the world does vegetation flourish so well."

Yet this speck of green surging out of the blue subtropical waters long had something of an image problem. "Dreary, stuffy little place. Nobody goes there but very old ladies," writer Paul Bowles was told by an acquaintance back in the 1950s. The globe-trotting Bowles ignored him and fell in love with Madeira. It's true that the lower gardens, sweet wines, and gentle weather have always appealed to older, well-heeled visitors, but squeezed within its

Madeira

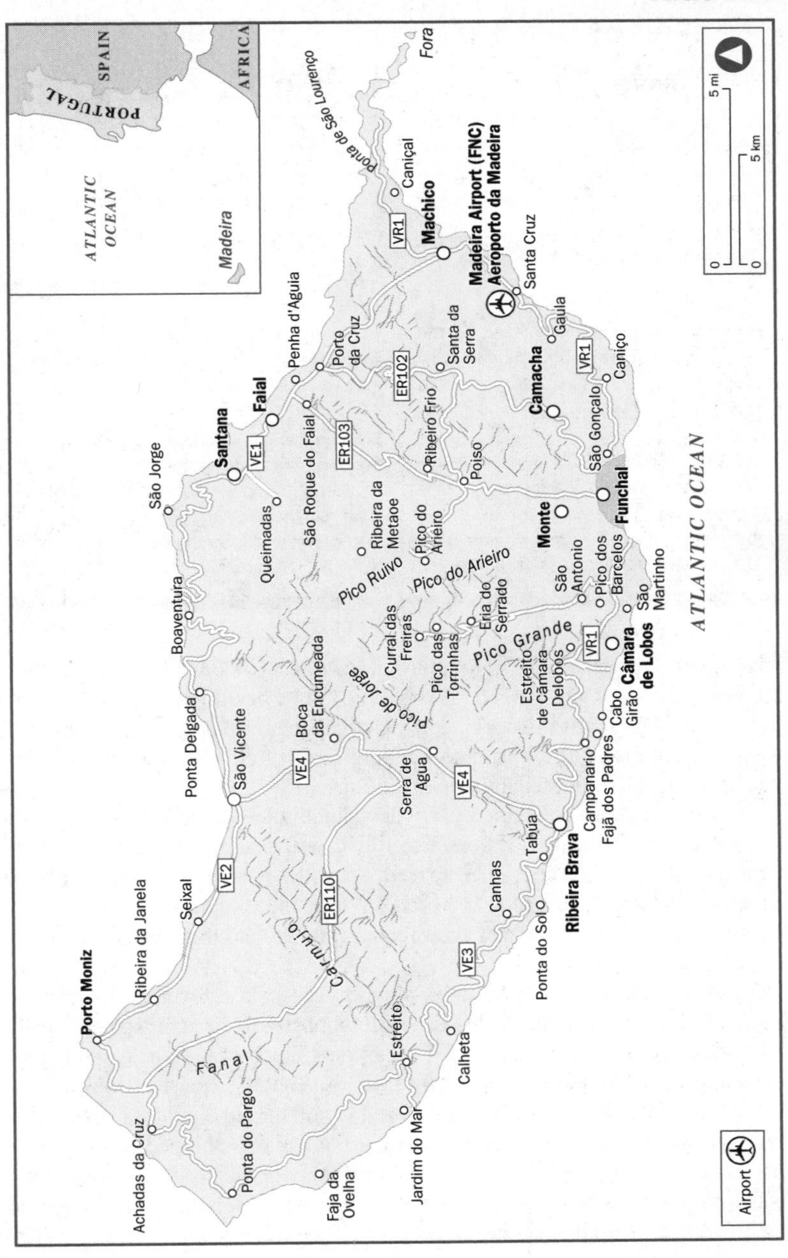

PORTUGAL
SPAIN
AFRICA
ATLANTIC OCEAN
Madeira
Fora
Ponta de São Lourenço
Caniçal
Machico
VR1
Madeira Airport (FNC)
Aeroporto da Madeira
Santa Cruz
Penha d'Aguia
Porto da Cruz
Santa da Serra
Gaula
Caniço
Camacha
São Gonçalo
ER102
Ribeiro Frio
Poiso
Faial
São Roque do Faial
ER103
Santana
VE1
São Jorge
Queimadas
Ribeira da Metaoe
Pico do Arieiro
Funchal
Monte
Pico Ruivo
Pico do Arieiro
São Antonio
Pico dos Barcelos
São Martinho
ATLANTIC OCEAN
Boaventura
Curral das Freiras
Eria do Serrado
Pico Grande
Pico das Torrinhas
Estreito de Câmara Delobos
Câmara de Lobos
Cabo Girão
Pico de Jorge
Boca da Encumeada
Ponta Delgada
São Vicente
VE4
Serra de Agua
Campanario
Fajã dos Padres
Ribeira Brava
Tabúa
VE2
Seixal
ER110
Canhas
Ponta do Sol
Ribeira da Janela
Carmujo
VE3
Porto Moniz
Estreito
Calheta
Fanal
Achadas da Cruz
Ponta do Pargo
Jardim do Mar
Faja da Ovelha
Airport
0
5 mi
5 km

FROMMER'S favorite MADEIRA EXPERIENCES

Becoming a highspeed basket case. A Madeira must-do, since the 1800s, is sliding into Funchal from the hillside suburb of Monte on a *carro de cesto*—a wicker toboggan guided by two drivers sporting straw boaters. The joy ride lasts around 20 minutes.

Basking on the beaches of Porto Santo. Madeira is the island that has it all—except beaches. Fortunately, it's a short boat or plane trip to Porto Santo and its 6.5km (4 miles) of golden sand gently lapped by the Atlantic.

A morning at the market. Funchal's daily *Mercado dos Lavradores* is a riot of color, from flower vendors in rainbow-striped skirts and bunches of bananas and piles of passionfruit, to fishmongers wielding machetes to slice giant tuna.

Hitting the road. Public works in the 1990s gave Madeira a highway and tunnel network that makes driving around the island a breeze, but the old roads are a scenic joy—if you're brave enough for the cliff-hugging curves.

Walking *levada* trails. A web of over 1,400km (870 miles) of narrow stone irrigation channels known as *levadas* crisscross Madeira's mountainous countryside. Running alongside them are wonderful hiking trails. Among our favorites: Levada do Caldeirão Verde leads to a 100-meter (330-ft.) waterfall.

Sipping *poncha*. Madeira's wines may be world-famous, but the islanders' preferred tipple is *poncha*, a potent mix of local rum, honey, and lemon juice. It tastes best watching the harbor lights twinkle in Câmara de Lobos.

737 square kilometers (285 sq. miles), Madeira has an array of spectacular scenery to impress any traveler. The variety can be bewildering: banana plantations on south coast hillsides appear Caribbean; verdant clifftops in the far west look like Ireland; black peaks poking through cloud cover around Pico do Arieiro recall Chinese landscape paintings.

In 2019, Madeira celebrated 600 years since its discovery by Portuguese navigator João Gonçalves Zarco. The island was deserted and covered with thick forest when Zarco's men arrived, so without much imagination they called it Madeira, which means "wood." Where the island's capital would be founded, they stumbled across wild fennel (*funcho*), so they called the place Funchal.

Madeira was the first step in Portugal's Age of Discoveries, guided by Prince Henry the Navigator. He sent settlers mostly from mainland Portugal, with some from Northern Europe. They burned much of the forest and began to clear the land for cultivation. By the late 15th century, the island was booming thanks to sugar cane, which thrived in the hot, humid climate. The population grew to 180,000 in 50 years—among them slaves shipped from Africa. Merchants from around Europe arrived for a share of the profits. Among them was a young man from Genova named Christopher Columbus who married the governor's daughter on Porto Santo and stayed for 2 years.

Ironically, the expansion of Portugal's overseas empire became Madeira's downfall, when Brazil's vast sugar plantations replaced it in satisfying Europe's sweet tooth. As decline set in, the island fell prey to pirates. French corsairs went on a 13-day rampage in 1566. Portugal's long relationship with England would eventually come to the island's aid. As well as taking tea and marmalade to the English when she married King Charles II, Princess Catarina de Bragança introduced London society to Madeira wines and granted English merchants special trading rights. Wine production took off, with Germany, Russia, and North America joining the Brits as the main customers. Thus in 1776, Franklin, Jefferson, and Co. would toast Independence with Madeira wine.

Disease wiped out most of the vines in the late 19th century, triggering a new cycle of poverty for the island. Thousands emigrated. Today there are large Madeiran communities in South Africa, Venezuela, Britain, and the United States. Among those to settle in the States was the father of writer John dos Passos and Manuel Nunes, who was credited with introducing the ukulele (*cavaquinho* in Portuguese) to Hawaii.

Although wine production eventually recovered, the economy became increasingly based on tourism. Again, the British led the way, making the island a stopover on the route to their colony in India. As word of Madeira's healthy climate spread, it became a *de rigueur* destination for European aristocracy. Luxury hotels, casinos, and country homes were built to cater to them. Funchal became a cosmopolitan place famed for lavish parties and royal visits. Tourism remains the main business for the island of 270,000 people, despite efforts to diversify through the creation, in 1986, of the Madeira International Business Center. The World Travel Awards voted it the "World's Leading Island Destination" for 4 consecutive years up to 2018. Funchal's lively arts and nightlife scene and the development of big wave surfing and other extreme sports have definitely wiped out any vestiges of the stuffy image.

Together with Porto Santo and some uninhabited islands, Madeira forms an autonomous region with a large degree of self-governance within Portugal.

Getting Around Madeira

BY BUS Buses are a cheap, but slow, way of getting around the island. Among local companies, **Horários do Funchal,** or HF (www.horariosdofunchal.pt; ✆ **29/170-55-55**), operates in the greater Funchal area, ideal for getting up to Monte or the botanical gardens. Tickets bought on board are 1.95€ per trip or 1.35€ if you buy a rechargeable pre-paid card available from newsstands, post offices, and other stores around town. You can also get tickets offering unlimited travel from 4.50€ for one day, up to 21.50€ for a week. In the city center, HF operates **Linha Eco,** environmentally friendly minibuses that you can hail in the street. HF also runs longer distance buses in the eastern part of the island, including to Machico, Santana and Curral das Freiras. **SAM,** which runs the airport bus, also has routes around the east, for

A hike TO REMEMBER

Madeira is heaven for hikers. Walking trails follow over 1,400km (870 miles) of irrigation channels known as *levadas*. Many run through the indigenous *laurissilva*, cloud forests that cover 15,000 hectares, (37,000 acres) in the northern hills. There are also mountain paths known as *veredas* crossing some of the most dramatic island uplands. The tourist board has details of walking routes in the "what to do" section of its website (www.visitmadeira.pt). There's more information on www.walkme.com.

Among our favorite walks: **Levada do Caldeirão Verde** twists for 6.5km (3.7 miles) through the laurissilva, passing plunging ravines before reaching a 100-meter (330-ft.) waterfall; **Vereda do Pico Ruivo** climbs to Madeira's highest peak, often in the clouds at 1,860m (6,102 ft.), a 5.4km (3.3-mile) round trip; **Vereda dos Balcões** is short but very sweet, leading from Ribeira Frio trout farm to a belvedere with endless vistas of green peaks; **Levada das 25 Fontes** links 25 waterfalls; and **Vereda da Ponta de São Lourenço** trails over the starkly beautiful eastern cape.

You can walk with a guide, arrange taxi transport, or navigate bus routes to trail departure points. Walks are generally safe, but it's always best to take a cellphone, flash light, water, and a companion.

example charging 3.50€ for the 50-minute trip to Machico. In the west, the main operator is **Rodoeste** (www.rodoeste.pt; ✆ **29/122-0-48**), which heads from Funchal to Câmara de Lobos, Calheta, Porto Moniz and other towns. A one-way ticket for the 20-minute trip from Funchal to Câmara de Lobos is 2.20€.

BY TAXI Madeira's taxis are painted in the bright yellow and blue of the island flag. In Funchal they are easy to hail in the street, or pick up from numerous ranks, for example next to the Jardim Municipal, the market, or in front of City Hall. You can also call one from a number of operators such as **Radio Taxis** (www.taxismadeira.com; ✆ **96/877-87-22**). Funchal taxis work on a meter, with a minimum charge of 2€ up to 2.40€ at nights, weekends, and holidays. Outside the capital, taxis operate on a fixed per kilometer rate. Ask in advance how much you should pay. Most taxi operators run fixed-rate excursions and bespoke tours. **AITRAM** (www.aitram.pt; ✆ **29/176-57-60**), for instance, has a voucher system that you can use to pre-book excursions. A 7-hour tour from Funchal west through Câmara de Lobos, Ribeira Brava, Santana, and a number of other beauty spots costs 140€ for up to four people. **Taxi Madeira** (www.taximadeira.com; ✆ **91/200-06-25**) has a similar service. They also do drop-offs and pickups for *levada* walks. At time of writing, ride-hailing apps had yet to take off.

BY CAR Major international car hire companies operate from Madeira Airport including **Avis** (www.avis.com; ✆ **29/152-43-92**), **Sixt** (www.sixt.pt; ✆ **25/578-81-99**), and **Hertz** (www.hertz.com; ✆ **21/942-63-00**). Established local companies include **Madeira Rent** (www.madeirarent.pt; ✆ **29/152-33-55**) and **Rodavante** (www.rodavante.pt; ✆ **29/152-47-18**). Most have offices in downtown Funchal too, in case you prefer to spend a few days strolling in the capital before getting on the road.

A web of fast highways and tunnels built since the 1990s means that it's now easy and quick to drive around the island. Cruising the old roads that wind through the mountains or hug the coast, passing by spectacular *miradouros* (viewpoints) is, however, one of the island's great pleasures. Care is, of course, needed on the twisting roads.

BY PLANE & BOAT The 2-hour, 15-minute sea journey to Porto Santo can be made with **Porto Santo Line** (www.portosantoline.pt; ✆ **29/121-03-00**), whose ferry leaves Funchal port at 8am and makes the return trip at 7pm. Round trips for non-residents start at 48€. The ship has a restaurant, bars and a cinema. There are great views from the deck and dolphins frequently swim alongside. If you're pressed for time, Spanish airline **Binter Canarias** (www.bintercanarias.com) flies twice a day on the 25-minute route Madeira to Porto Santo. Prices vary but return fares for non-residents usually start from 112€.

ORGANIZED TOURS There's a huge range of organized tours to choose from, by bus, car or on foot. In Funchal, **Yellowbus** (www.yellowbustours.com; ✆ **21/850-32-25**) offers hop-on-hop-off trips by open-topped double-deckers, taking in sights of the capital and beyond. Aside from the taxi services mentioned above, **Daniel Madeira Táxis** (www.danielmadeirataxis.com; ✆ **91/979-12-89**) has a series of personalized half- and full-day tours, including drop-and-fetch for 10 *levada* routes. Among companies running trips up into the mountains, **Hit the Road Tours** (www.hittheroadmadeira.com; ✆ **96/946-63-59**) specializes in small-group tours in Land Rovers, going off road to explore remote beauty spots. Their tours can include *levada* walks and sea swimming if the weather's right. **Mountain Expedition** (www.mex.pt; ✆ **96/967-76-79**) also offers off-road trips in 4×4s guided by island experts through less-explored parts of the island. Their full-day Jeep-and-catamaran tour starts at 70€ per person including a picnic lunch. In Funchal, students from the University of Madeira lead specialist walking tours under the name **History Tellers** (www.madeiranheritage.pt; ✆ **93/501-07-79**). They cover the old neighborhoods and key buildings such as the Jesuit College. Tours run Monday to Friday, 10am to 6pm. A 2-hour old town tour costs 10€ for adults.

[FastFACTS] MADEIRA

ATMs Available 24 hours a day throughout the island.

Business Hours As on the mainland, **shops** are usually open from around 9am till 6pm, although it varies by an hour or so. Many stores will close Saturday afternoon and most shut down Sundays. Some close for lunch. **Municipal buildings** are mostly open Monday to Friday 8:30am to 4:30pm. **Banks** Monday to Friday 8:30am to 3pm.

Consulates Citizens of the United States, Canada, and the UK should contact consulates in Lisbon (p. 473).

Dentists The **Malo Clinic** provides ultra-modern dental services on Rua de Leichlingen 26-28 (www.maloclinics.com; ✆ **29/123-12-77**), in Funchal's main seaside hotel zone.

Doctors The main public hospital is **Hospital Dr. Nélio Mendonça** on Av.

Luís de Camões 6180 (✆ **29/170-56-00**). Private clinics with English-speaking GPs and a wide range of specialists include: **Madeira Medical Center** (www.grupohpa.com; ✆ **29/100-33-00**) on Rua do Hospital Velho, 2; and **Hospital da Luz** (www.hospitaldaluz.pt; ✆ **29/170-00-00**) on Rua 5 de Outubro, 115-116.

Drugstores Pharmacies usually open Monday to Saturday 9am to 7pm, although times vary. Some close for lunch or on Saturday afternoons. The **Holan** group (www.farmaciasholon.pt) has a website in English listing its pharmacies around Portugal, including the islands, with hours and contact details. Serving Funchal's British community (and not only) since 1876 is **Farmácia Luso-Britânica** (✆ **29/122-25-29**), while **Farmácia Funchal** (✆ **29/123-11-74**) is open 9am to midnight in two Funchal shopping malls, La Vie and Madeira Shopping. Rotating **after-hours pharmacies** are listed (in Portuguese) on www.farmaciasdeservico.net.

Emergencies Call ✆ **112** for a general **emergency.** Funchal police are on ✆ **29/120-84-00.**

Post Office Funchal's main **Post Office** (Correios) is at Av. Zarco 9 (✆ **70/726-26-26;** open Mon–Fri 9am–7pm). There's another in the main hotel district at Estrada Monumental 318 (open Mon–Fri 9am–6pm).

Safety Madeira is a generally safe destination, with less crime than mainland Portugal. Still, it pays to use usual common sense and take care of valuables.

Taxes As we were going to press, authorities were considering a tourist tax of 1€ a night for the first seven nights of stays in Funchal and Porto Santo. Such a tax was introduced in 2017 in Santa Cruz for summer stays. Madeira has slightly lower rates of sales tax (VAT) than the mainland.

Tipping Similar to the mainland, there's no obligation to tip. But rounding a bill up by 5% or 10% is common if service is good.

Exploring Madeira

FUNCHAL ★★★

Funchal has an outstanding location. Facing the ocean to the south, it is surrounded by a natural amphitheater of hills rising up to 1,200 meters (4,000 ft.). Its climate is balmy, allowing the many gardens and parks to abound with flowers. With 112,000 people it is Portugal's 6th largest city, a dynamic, cosmopolitan place that has welcomed international visitors for centuries. The downtown heart is marked by Discoveries Era buildings like the **Sé** cathedral, **Paço Episcopal** (bishop's palace) or **Palácio de São Lourenço** fortress. The main shopping and business district is centered here.

Around the colorful **Mercado dos Lavradores** market, the **Zona Velha** (old zone) is undergoing a renaissance as a hub for nightlife and the arts. Along the coastal road to the west the **Estrada Monumental** links to the big hotels and bathing areas. Inland, streets rise steeply to the districts of Monte, São Pedro and São Gonçalo with their **sub-tropical gardens** and **elegant mansions**.

Strolling its cobbled streets will bring you to venerable wine lodges, elegant cafes, and timeless stores selling handcrafted goodies ranging from embroidered linen to molasses cakes.

Avenida Arriaga ★★ NEIGHBORHOOD This thoroughfare leading west from the Cathedral is a favorite place for city stroll, especially in April and May when the **jacaranda trees** bloom purple. Its broad sidewalks are decorated in typically Portuguese black-and-white stones. You'll pass the mighty fortress of de São Lourenço, a statue of island discoverer Zarco, and swanky old cafes like **Golden Gate** (www.goldengate.pt) and **The Ritz Madeira** (www.theritzmadeira.com). The **Teatro Baltazar Dias** has been a cultural focus since the 1880s in front of the **Jardim Municipal** with its flowering coral and kapok trees. **Blandy's Wine Lodge** is the place to discover—and buy—island tipples (p. 424).

Jardim Botânico ★★ GARDEN The geometric flowerbeds and inch-perfect topiary of this garden rising 350 meters (1,150 ft.) above Funchal are a symbol of the island. Views and floral displays are spectacular, but the garden—founded in 1880 by the Reids hotel family—also plays an important role conserving Madeira's unique plant life. There are 200 native species, plus over 3,000 exotic imports. Many are extremely rare. It's wonderful for walking. There's a section with island crops like sugar cane and papaya, and a quirky little natural history museum. The outdated institutional website doesn't do it justice. You can arrive by **cable car** (www.telefericojardim botanico.com; ✆ **29/121-50-70**), a chance for yet more breathtaking views.

Caminho do Meio, Bom Sucesso. http://ifcn.madeira.gov.pt. ✆ **29/121-12-00.** 6€ adults, 2€ children 6–12, free for under 6s (no credit cards). Daily Apr–Sept 9am–6:30pm; Oct–Mar 9am–5:30pm. Bus: 29, 31, 31A.

Mercado dos Lavradores ★★★ MARKET If you have just 1 hour in Funchal, spend it amid the sensorial feast in this daily farmers' market. Housed in a distinctive 1940s building, it has flower sellers in the kaleidoscopic traditional costume; and fishmongers dealing strange and wonderful denizens of the deep, from huge tuna and swordfish to the toothy, snake-like black scabbard fish so popular on island menus. Fruit is the main attraction though: local bananas crammed with flavor, a bewildering array of passion fruits; tamarillos, custard apples and something called *monstera deliciosa* that looks and tastes like pineapple crossed with banana. Around the market are stand-up bars serving *poncha*, local Coral beer and snacks like scabbard-fish sandwiches (**Snack Bar Coca Cola** is our favorite). Behind the market, the once rundown **Zona Velha** has turned hip. Buzzing at night, it's also developed a flourishing art scene. Check out the graffiti and galleries on **Rua Santa Maria**.

Largo dos Lavradores. ✆ **29/121-40-80.** Mon–Thurs 8am–7pm, Fri 7am–8pm, Sat 7am–2pm. Bus: 2, 22, 26, 36, 36A, Linha Eco Variante 1.

Monte ★★ NEIGHBORHOOD Climbing to 1,300 meters (4,260 ft.) above Funchal, this clement suburb has long been a retreat for the city elite. Leafy lanes are lined with aristocratic *quintas*. Among the beautiful gardens is **Quinta Jardins do Imperador** ★★ (Caminho Do Pico, Mon–Sat 9:30am–5:30pm, Sun 10:30am–5:30pm) named for Karl I, last Emperor of Austria, who died in exile here in 1921. He's buried in the twin-towered **Nossa Senhora do Monte** ★ church dating from the 1740s. The **Monte Palace Tropical**

HISTORY IN A glass

Madeira wine was a favorite tipple for America's revolutionary armies, Russia's czars and sailors on the ship that discovered Australia. George Washington reputedly downed a pint a day and England's King George IV would drink no other wine. Like the island itself, Madeira wine went out of fashion for a while, decried as old-fashioned and stuffy. Now, its unique qualities are again highly sought after. Rare bottles auction for $10,000. Fortunately, you can enjoy excellent Madeiras for much less. Like port, Madeira is fortified by adding brandy. Then the wine is left to ferment naturally in hot rooms called *estufas*. The youngest Madeiras are 3 years old, with at least two spent in wooden casks. The oldest vintages still around date to 1715. The most common types are: *sercial*, light, dry and served as an aperitif; *verdelho*, golden and medium-sweet; *boal* with chestnut tones and honeyed sweetness to accompany desserts; and *malmsey* or *malvazia*, the darkest and caramel sweet.

Several lodges and specialist stores allow you to discover more about Madeira wines and sample a few. For a full immersion, head to **Blandy's Wine Lodge** ★★ (www.blandyswinelodge.com; ✆ **29/122-89-78**) on Funchal's Avenida Arriaga. The cellars were installed by a British wine family in the 19th century in a former convent built 300 years earlier. Witty, informative, and multilingual guides take you through the historic lodge and museum, explain the production process and offer a tasting. Don't miss the wonderful 1920s murals by German artist Max Römer or the Blandy family's collection of rare vintages. Tours start from 9€ and run all day weekdays and mornings on Saturday.

Also worth a visit is **D'Oliveiras** ★, Rua Ferreiros, 107 (✆ **29/174-01-00**). It's one of the oldest producers. You can enjoy a tasting in the atmospheric store/cafe in the old warehouse. Open Monday to Friday 9am to 6pm, Saturday 9:30am to 1pm.

Garden ★★ (www.montepalace.com; garden open daily 9:30am–6pm, museum 9:30am–4:30pm; admission 12€, free for under 12s) encloses not only extravagant displays of flora, but also African and Asian art, plus Portuguese *azulejos* dating back to the 15th-century.

You can reach Monte by bus, taxi or **cable car** ★ (www.madeiracablecar.com; 11€ adult one-way), but to get back downhill try the ***carros de cesto*** ★★ . Described by CNN as the world's coolest commute, they are sleds made like wicker baskets, originally designed for a wealthy Englishman keen to reach his downtown office. Today, tourists line up for the 20-minute slide over the cobbles cushioned in passenger seats. Two strong guys in cricketers' whites and boater hats will guide your way. The story that Ernest Hemmingway described it as one of the most interesting experiences of his life may be a local myth, but it's definitely a fun trip (www.carreirosdomonte.com; ✆ **29/178-39-19;** Mon–Sat 9am–6pm; 30€ for two). Be warned: The toboggans only take you halfway down, so it's a long walk. But you can take a bus or taxi back to the city center.

Museu da Quinta das Cruzes ★ MUSEUM Although much changed over the centuries, this old mansion was once home for João Gonçalves Zarco, who discovered Madeira in 1419. The museum houses an eclectic collection ranging from sketches by early English tourists and China-trade porcelain to exquisite Indo-Portuguese furniture from the 16th century. The gardens are an urban oasis with high trees and rare orchids. A short walk from downtown in the São Pedro neighborhood, which is chockablock with lovely old buildings including the 500-year-old **Santa Clara** ★ convent and its beautiful *azulejo* tiles.

Calçada do Pico 1. http://mqc.madeira.gov.pt. ✆ **29/174-06-70.** 3€, 1.50€ seniors, free for children and students and for all on Sun. Tues–Sun 10am–12:30pm and 2–5pm. Bus: 50, Linha Eco Variante 2.

Museu de Arte Sacra ★★ MUSEUM In the early days of settlement, Madeira grew rich exporting sugar to northern Europe. Among the best customers were merchants in Antwerp and Bruges, setting up a connection that filled the island's churches with artworks by Dirk Bouts, Gerard David and other Flemish masters. Many of them are now gathered in this fine museum housed in the 16th-century Bishop's palace. It also contains some gloriously gilded saintly statues, including a Last Supper group decked out in colorful floral tunics.

Rua do Bispo 21. www.masf.pt. ✆ **29/122-89-00.** 5€, free for under 12s. Mon–Fri 10am–5pm, Sat 10am–1pm. Bus: 12, 20, 21, 27, 49, EcoLinha variante 2.

Sé (Cathedral) ★★RELIGIOUS SITE The tower and plain Gothic facade of the cathedral has been a downtown landmark since 1517, but its real glory lies inside. The building is packed with gilded statues, a shimmering altarpiece, Flemish paintings and, best of all, the extraordinary cedarwood ceiling carved and inlaid in the Arab-influenced Mudéjar style. Look out for the silver cross, a gift to the island from King Manuel I and considered a masterwork of the Manueline style.

Rua do Aljube, Funchal. www.sefunchal.com. ✆ **29/122-81-55.** Free; donation suggested. Daily 7:30am–noon and 4–7pm. Bus: 1, 2, 4, 9, 12, 15.

WESTERN MADEIRA ★★★

The wild mountainous ridge running down the spine of Madeira flattens out a bit in the west to form the scrubby **Paul de Serra** plateau, a striking but rarely visited landscape. Around it the land falls away to the coast in vertiginous cliffs. Most people live in the valleys and ravines, which are often covered with banana plantations. A string of picturesque towns and villages cling to thin strips of coastal lowland.

Curral das Freiras ★★

A village with a spectacular location, you can reach it by a scenic road that snakes inland through forests of pine and eucalyptus or take a new tunnel that cuts through the mountains. Either way, be sure to stop at one of the viewpoints at **Eira do Serrado** or **Paredão** to look down on the isolated settlement at the bottom of a valley encircled by almost perpendicular mountains. The name, meaning "Nuns' Corral," comes from the 1500s when sisters fled here from French pirates pillaging the coast. Close up, the village loses something of its charm, with modern houses and some tacky stores catering to coach trips. Still the views looking back up at the hills are impressive and the cafes serve tasty pastries made from local chestnuts.

Câmara de Lobos ★★

First stop on the coast road out of Funchal is Câmara de Lobos, a 10-minute drive. It is a place of great charm which captured the heart of Sir Winston Churchill. He came here in the 1940s to relax and paint the jumble of white, red-roofed houses circling up from the horseshoe-shaped bay and the brightly painted boats bobbing in the harbor. Most of the black scabbard fish eaten on the island will have been plucked from the depths by fishing boats sailing from here using nylon lines a kilometer (3,300 ft.) long. Beyond the village, hills rise up in a steep semi-circle covered with vines and banana plantations. It's pretty anytime, but come at night to when the harbor lights glow, and the mood livens up in quayside bars making the island's best *poncha.* The name means "chamber of wolves" after seals called *lobos-marinhos* (sea wolves) once common there.

Cabo Girão ★★★

Just beyond is the lofty headland of Cabo Girão, claimed to be the highest sea cliffs in Europe. Although that's contested in Ireland and Norway, it's clear this is not for vertigo sufferers. The precipice rises vertically 570m (1,870 ft.) from the waves. In 2012, the site was made even more scary with the construction of a glass **Skywalk** jutting out over the drop. If it doesn't freak you out, the views are amazing, especially at sunset. It's open all day and entry is free.

Calheta ★★

The southwest coast is the sunniest part of the island. As you continue on the shore hugging road, you'll pass ravines planted with banana trees and sugar cane and a succession of pretty coast towns like **Ribeira Brava**, **Ponta do Sol**—the ancestral home of writer John dos Passos—and **Madalena do Mar**. Calheta was once a sugar town and still has a working mill producing rum and molasses, run by the **Sociedade dos Engenhos da Calheta** ★, where you can visit, drink and shop (Avenida Dom Manuel I; ✆ **29/182-22-64;** Mon–Fri 8am–7pm; Sat–Sun 10am–7pm). Wedged between the mountains and the sea, Calheta also boasts that Madeira rarity: a **beach** of golden sand, although it's artificially built with sand shipped in from overseas. The main attraction is the **MUDAS Arts Centre** ★ (Vale dos Amores, Estrela à Baixo; www.facebook.com/pg/MUDASmuseu; ✆ **29/182-09-00**) a startlingly piece of contemporary architecture in volcanic stone on a hilltop overlooking the village and the Atlantic. It showcases contemporary artists from Madeira and mainland and holds regular concerts. It's open Tuesday through Sunday 10am to 7pm. Nearby **Jardim do Mar** has a growing reputation as a surf spot, but it is not for beginners.

Porto Moniz ★★

For a gentler encounter with the ocean, head to Porto Moniz on the northwest coast. Its **natural pools** ★★ are a wonderful place to take a dip. They were formed over 6,000 years ago by a volcanic eruption that poured molten lava into the sea, where it solidified, creating black rook pools. The serrated rocks shelter bathers from the waves, although the occasional roller does send over a shower of cooling spray. They cover a surface bigger than three Olympic-size pools and there's a sun terrace from which to admire the cliffs soaring above the village. The main bathing area is open 9am to 7pm in summer, 10am to 5:30pm. It costs 1.50€, though there are "untamed" pools along the coast which are free. A short walk away there's a fort built in 1730 to deter pirates that houses an **aquarium** ★ showing Atlantic life (open daily 10am–6pm; admission 7€, or 4€ for over 65s and children 6–14, free for under 6s).

São Vicente ★★

The **old coast road** ★★ from Porto Moniz to the town of São Vicente is the most spectacular along Madeira's shore, even if parts of it have been closed as too dangerous and replaced by a modern highway with tunnels. Carved from the cliff face in the 1950s, it was nicknamed the "gold route" because of the cost. It clings to the coast and is occasionally soaked by waves and waterfalls. The closed sections can be walked and the views are staggering. São Vicente is one of a string of idyllic small towns along the north coast. Its whitewashed homes are wedged between brooding triangular peaks and the immensity of the Altantic. As well as being the starting point for *levada* walks into the UNESCO World Heritage laurissilva forest, it has some fine **volcanic caves** with an underwater lake and **Volcanism Center** ★ (www.grutasecentrodovulcanismosaovicente.com; ✆ **29/184-24-04**) explaining how the island was founded by undersea eruptions 6 million years ago. The caves and center can be visited together. Open daily 10am to 6pm; admission 8€, 6€ children 5 to 14 and over 65s, free under 5s.

EASTERN MADEIRA ★★★

The east coast is more developed, containing the airport, golf courses, the ports of Santa Cruz and Machico, and coastal and hill retreats long been popular with British and German expats. Drive inland, however, and you soon become aware of Madeira's wild side. Jagged peaks reach up to 1,860m (6,102 ft.). Dense forest burst with plant life. On the north coast, old traditions linger amid high cliffs that surge from the surf. At the northwestern tip, the remote São Lourenço peninsula presents a stark contrast with the island's trademark greenery.

Pico do Arieiro ★★★

Drive north out of Funchal and after Monte you soon leave the pampered gardens and delicate tea pavilions behind and penetrate Madeira's untamed heart. The road twists through bleak moors and forests of pine and cedar. It's not just the landscape that changes as you climb: the weather frequently shifts through patches of mist, cloud and sun. Take the turning to Pico do Arieiro and you'll emerge on to a stripped landscape of rocks and heather. This is Madeira's third-highest summit and gives endless vistas over lesser peaks below. There's a cafe, useful for sustenance if you plan to hike the 8km

(5-mile) trail to **Pico Ruivo ★★★**, the island's highest point. Alternatively, you can drive toward Pico Ruivo from Santana and take an easier, but no-less awe-inspiring walk to the high spot.

Santana ★★

Over the central ridge, the ER103 road from Funchal to the north descends in a string of hairpins. The profuse forest here is protected as part of Madeira's botanical heritage. Several walking paths lead out from the hamlet of **Ribeiro Frio ★**, which is also home to a trout farm. The road hits the coastal plateau at Santana which is famed for red-white-and-blue triangular thatched cottages, a symbol of the island. The *palheiros* are no longer lived in, a few are used as sheds but most are preserved as tourist attractions, including some in the town center where the interiors are open to show how life used to be. There are also several in **Madeira Theme Park ★**, Estrada Regional 101, Fonte da Pedra (www.parquetematicodamadeira.pt; ✆ **29/157-04-10**), which is dedicated to rural life on the island with a traditional restaurant and working artisans. It also has a boating lake and kids' playground. It's open Tuesday to Sunday 10am to 7pm. Admission is 6€, 4€ for over 65s and children ages 5 to 14; children under 5 go free.

Machico ★

Lying in a curved bay, this appealing port was Madeira's first settlement. According to legend, there were Europeans here even before the Portuguese: a pair of star-crossed lovers are said to have been marooned in the bay after eloping from England in the 14th century. Machico has good seafood restaurants (try **Maré Alta ★★** on the seafront) and two contrasting beaches. On one side of the little river is a natural pebble beach; on the other, golden sand imported from Morocco. Inland, the highland village of **Santo da Serra ★** is renowned for a Sunday farmers' market and its championship golf course (p. 429). North of Machico, **Ponta da São Lourenço ★★** is an undulating finger of barren land poking into the Atlantic. Its strange, bare scenery is traversed by hiking trails. A swish resort and marina sits on the south coast of the once-deserted peninsula (www.quintadolorde.pt).

PORTO SANTO ★★

Just 50 kilometers (30 miles) away, Madeira's little sister presents quite a contrast from the lush green hills of the main island. Like a chunk of the Sahara that's drifted into the Atlantic, Porto Santo is arid and sandy with a harsh beauty. There are hills at either end, reaching 509m (1,670 ft.) at **Pico do Facho ★**, and trails for hiking and biking. The big attraction however is the **beach ★★★**. Running for 6.5km (4 miles), the strip of fine sand along the southern shore is one of the best in Portugal and a paradise for sun worshipers. The place fills up in high summer, not least because Madeira islanders head here to soak up the rays. Outside peak times, Porto Santo remains a sleepy place despite an extension of the airport that brings in occasional charter flights from Europe. In winter, you can have temperatures well over 20°C (70°F) and stretches of beach to yourself.

The best-known landmark in the tiny capital Vila Baleira is the **Casa Colombo** ★ museum, 4 (✆ **29/198-34-05**) located in the house where a young Christopher Columbus is reputed to have lived for 2 years after marrying the governor's daughter. The Genovese navigator is supposed to have sailed here to trade in "dragon's blood," a red dye extracted from the fruit of the spiky dragon trees that flourish in the dry climate. Another Vila Baleira attraction is **Lambeca's** ice-cream parlor (✆ **29/199-90-00**) offering handmade gelato on the main square for half a century. Porto Santo makes an easy day trip from Madeira (p. 428) or a longer-stay *far-niente* destination for beach bums. You can rent cars and scooters in Vila Baleira, but for heading up and down the coast bikes are a good option. **Colombo Rental** (www.aacolombo.com; ✆ **29/198-44-38**) has a good selection from 10€ a day.

Madeira Sports

GOLF There are two championship courses on Madeira and another on Porto Santo. Designed by Spanish superstar Seve Ballesteros, **Porto Santo Golfe** (www.portosantogolfe.com; ✆ **29/198-37-78**) course starts by the beach, then runs into a specular cliff-top back nine. The **Clube de Golf Santo da Serra** (www.santodaserragolf.com; ✆ **29/155-01-00**) is where golf began in Madeira in the 1930s. It's over 300 meters (1,000 ft.) up in the hills which can mean playing over the clouds. Designed in 1991 by legendary architect Robert Trent Jones, it now has 27 holes. Every hole on **Palheiro Golf Course** (www.palheironatureestate.com; ✆ **29/179-01-20**), in the hills above Funchal, provides magnificent views over the city, the ocean, and the offshore Desertas islands. It's bordered by forest and glorious subtropical gardens.

MOUNTAIN ACTIVITIES Belying its once-staid reputation, Madeira is now a hot place for the adventurous. Trail running, mountain biking, rock climbing and paragliding are just a few of the extreme sports available up in the hills. **Go Trail Madeira** (www.gotrailmadeira.com; ✆ **96/283-54-42**) organizes epic runs and **Madeira Outdoors** (www.madeiraoutdoor.com; ✆ **96/623-02-12**) has a wide range of heart-pumping activities.

WATERSPORTS Whether you want to fish for blue marlin, surf Atlantic swells or scuba dive in crystalline waters, Madeira is the place. Its deep waters mean there are big fish close to shore. May to October is peak marlin season. Veteran skipper **Peter Bristow** (www.fishmadeira.com; ✆ **91/759-99-90**) has made record-breaking catches and operates a catch-and-release policy on billfish. Without sandy beaches, Madeira was slow to take off as a surf destination, but with regular waves around 5 meters (15 ft.) the west coast is now a big draw for experienced boarders. Beginners will prefer the north coast or Porto Santo. **Calhau Surf School** (www.madeiracalhausurfschool.com; ✆ **92/618-98-94**) on the north coast is the island's oldest. For diving, Madeira has wide range of options including around ships wrecked off the rocky sure. **Focus Natura** (www.focusnatura.com; ✆ **91/640-97-80**) has options for beginners or pros. If coasteering or canyoning is your chosen adrenaline rush, try **Epic Madeira** (www.epicmadeira.com; ✆ **93/366-82-28**).

Where to Stay

The best of Madeira's hotels tend to break down between modern resorts with big pools, extensive amenities and clifftop locations, or discreet country homes (*quintas*) that have been transformed into boutique accommodation. The former are concentrated in Funchal's western shore running out along Estrada Monumental. The latter are scattered in the hills surrounding downtown. There are few hotels in Funchal city center. Prices skyrocket at New Year when hotels are often booked months in advance. There's also a growing range of excellent hotels outside the capital. All prices below include breakfast.

FUNCHAL

Belmond Reid's Palace ★★★ The most iconic place to stay in Funchal, opened in 1891 by a Scottish family, has long been regarded as one of the world's finest hotels. It's located on a rocky outcrop amid 4 hectares (10 acres) of terraced subtropical gardens offering gorgeous views along the coast. George Bernard Shaw learned dance steps on the terrace; Winston Churchill (a regular visitor) painted from his balcony; generations of aristocrats and movie stars enjoyed the cocktails and afternoon teas. Today's hotel manages to fuse that vintage elegance with outstanding modern facilities, from the world-class spa to the Michelin-starred **William** restaurant or the clifftop swimming pools. Rooms all have ocean views and a light airy decor featuring floral motifs and marble bathrooms. It's all in a "very British" good taste. Breakfast is fabulous.

Estrada Monumental, 139. www.belmond.com. ✆ **29/171-70-30.** 158 units. 319€–735€ double; 731€–2,711€ suite. Free parking. **Amenities:** 4 restaurants; 2 bars; babysitting; children's programs; concierge; health club and spa; massage and beauty treatments; 3 outdoor pools; 2 outdoor tennis courts; watersports; bicycle rental; gardens; free Wi-Fi.

Casa Velha do Palheiro ★★★ The old house was built in 1804 as a hunting lodge for the Count of Carvalhal and it maintains an air of noble elegance 500 meters (1,640 ft.) up in the hills above Funchal. It's surrounded by one of Europe's most beautiful gardens, 120 hectares (300 acres) of flora cared for by generations of the wine-producing Blandy family, who've owned the estate since 1885. There's a par-71 championship golf course on the doorstep, indoor and outdoor pools, a fully equipped spa, and over 20km (12 miles) of walking paths. Rooms in the main house or newer wings overlook the garden and are decorated in a restrained, English country house-style, with soft furnishings and floral prints. You can dine in style in the old house restaurant or the golf course club house, which has great views over Funchal. The hotel has a motor yacht available for game-fishing hires.

Rua da Estalagem 23, São Gonçalo. www.palheironatureestate.com. ✆ **29/179-03-50.** 37 units. 149€–357€ double. Free parking. **Amenities:** Restaurant; bar; babysitting; fitness room; golf course; garden; sun terrace; outdoor heated pool; spa and wellness center; games room; bicycle rental; free Wi-Fi.

Funchal

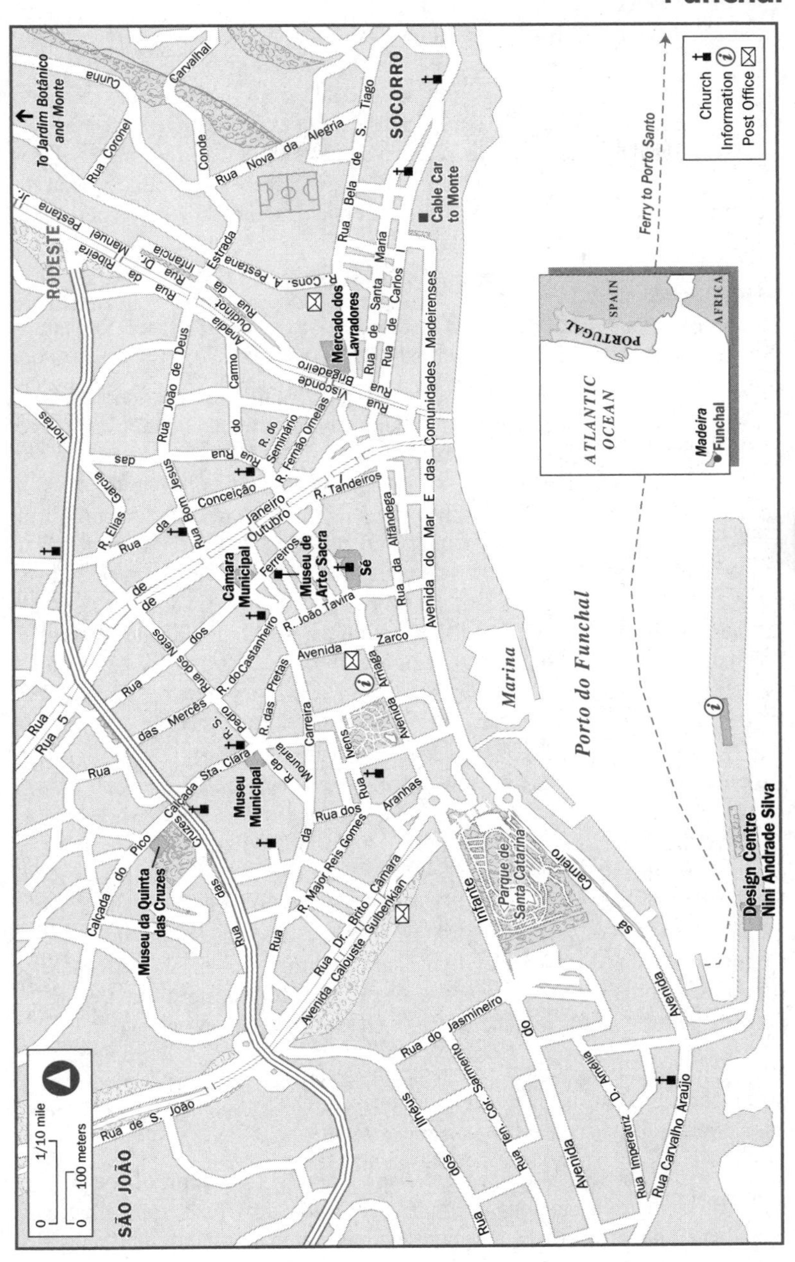
To Jardim Botânico and Monte
RODESTE
SOCORRO
SÃO JOÃO
Church
Information
Post Office
Ferry to Porto Santo
Cable Car to Monte
Mercado dos Lavradores
Câmara Municipal
Museu de Arte Sacra
Sé
Museu Municipal
Museu da Quinta das Cruzes
Parque de Santa Catarina
Marina
Porto do Funchal
Design Centre Nini Andrade Silva
ATLANTIC OCEAN
PORTUGAL
SPAIN
AFRICA
Madeira
Funchal
Rua Nova da Alegria
Rua Bela de S. Tiago
Rua de Santa Maria
Rua de Carlos I
Avenida do Mar E das Comunidades Madeirenses
Rua da Alfândega
Rua João de Deus
Rua do Carmo
Rua da Conceição
Rua Bom Jesus
Rua dos Netos
R. do Castanheiro
R. das Pretas
R. da Mourana
Rua das Mercês
Calçada do Pico
Calçada Sta. Clara
Rua das Cruzes
R. João Tavira
Avenida Zarco
Avenida Arriaga
Rua dos Aranhas
R. Major Reis Gomes
Rua Dr. Brito Câmara
Avenida Calouste Gulbenkian
Rua do Jasmineiro
Avenida do Infante
Rua Imperatriz D. Amélia
Rua Carvalho Araújo
Rua de S. João
1/10 mile
100 meters

Pestana Carlton Madeira ★★ Built in 1972, this glass-fronted, 18-story tower was a prototype of the mid-range hotels that have sprung up along the oceanfront road west from downtown. Some of the rooms in this family-friendly place need a facelift, and the paid parking is a bore, but nothing can take away the views across the Atlantic from the breakfast room terrace or sea-facing rooms. The curves and palm trees of the huge saltwater pool overlook Reid's gardens. There are also steps leading down the rocks if you want to take a dip in the ocean itself. Try to get a sea-view room, those at the back look out toward the hills, but the waterside panorama is much better. It's a 15-minute walk to the city center.

Largo António Nobre. www.pestanacarltonmadeira.com. ✆ **29/123-95-00.** 287 units. 100€–422€ double; 176€–529€ suites. Paid parking, average .60€ per hour. **Amenities:** Restaurant; bar; babysitting; children's playground; game room; outdoor and indoor pools; massage services, fitness room; hairdresser; sauna; free Wi-Fi.

Pestana CR7 Funchal ★★ Opened in 2016, this sleek harborside hotel is a collaboration between two of Madeira's biggest names, the Pestana hotel group and soccer superstar Cristiano Ronaldo, aka CR7. The hotel offers a glimpse of the player's lifestyle with frequent DJ parties beside the rooftop pool, rooms full of tech gadgets (they are soundproofed in case you don't want to share the parties), a fitness room and breakfast packed with power foods. It draws a younger crowd, but views from the seafront rooms and especially from the roof will appeal to anyone. It's a short walk to downtown along a seaside promenade. Fans will love the striker's pictures, memorabilia, and larger than life statue outside. Guests get free entrance to the next-door **CR7 Museum.**

Av. Sá Carneiro/Praça do Mar. www.pestanacr7.com. ✆ **29/114-04-80.** 49 units. 90€–207€ double. Public parking nearby 10€ per day. **Amenities:** Restaurants; rooftop bar; DJ sets; exercise room; outdoor pool; sun terrace; Jacuzzi; free Wi-Fi.

Quinta Jardins do Lago ★★ Another elegant *quinta* reflecting Madeira's British ties—Gen. William Beresford had his residence here when his garrison defended the island from Napoleon. It lies in the São Pedro district on one of the hills enveloping the city. There's a 30-minute walk downhill into town, but the hotel operates a free shuttle bus. The wonderful gardens surrounding the 18th-century house contain over 500 plant species and one giant tortoise called Colombo. Rooms are bright and spacious, featuring botanical prints, antique furniture, embroidered linen sheets, and (in some) four-poster beds. Beside the pool are an excellent bistro and a terrace shaded by palm and mango trees.

Rua Dr. João Lemos Gomes 29, São Pedro. www.jardinsdolago.com. ✆ **29/175-01-00.** 41 units. 185€–382€ double; 280€–716€ suite. Free parking. **Amenities:** 2 restaurants; bar; exercise room; hammam; sauna; Jacuzzi; outdoor freshwater heated pool; croquet court; garden; games room; sun terrace; free Wi-Fi.

Quinta da Penha de França ★★ There's something of the best of both worlds here: a gracious old *quinta* surrounded by lush tropical gardens but situated near the city center in a fabulous waterfront location. It's divided between the antique-filled main house and modern annexes. A footbridge connects to the most recent part. The cheapest rooms in the attic lack air-conditioning and Wi-Fi and in some others the decor is dated. The best with ocean views in the modern part are jauntily attired with pastel striped walls and floral throws. There are two ocean-facing swimming pools. **Joe's Billiards** bar is a Funchal institution, with a pub atmosphere and good food.

Rua Imperatriz Dona Amélia, 85. www.penhafrancahotels.com/m/en/home. ✆ **29/120-46-50.** 109 units. 60€–198€ double; 119€–232€ junior suite. Free parking. **Amenities:** 2 restaurants; 2 bars; babysitting; outdoor seawater heated pool; diving center; garden; sun terrace, games room; free Wi-Fi (most rooms).

WESTERN MADEIRA

Aqua Natura Madeira Hotel ★★ Be prepared for outstanding views when you check into this modern, white-painted hotel squeezed between the soaring cliffs and volcanic rock pools that make Porto Moniz one of Madeira's most attractive villages. There's no pool, but the hotel boasts a Jacuzzi with a view, and guests have free access to the natural bathing spots among the black rock. Rooms are in bright primary colors reflecting the deep blue of the Atlantic and the verdant surrounding hills. The place has a youthful, relaxed feel. It's a great base for exploring Madeira's natural beauties: *Levada* trails heading into the *laurissilva* start nearby and you can go scuba diving among the sharks and rays of the Madeira Aquarium.

Rotunda Da Piscina #3, Porto Moniz. www.aquanaturamadeira.com. ✆ **29/164-01-00.** 25 units. 80€–156€ double. Free parking. **Amenities:** Restaurant; bar; babysitting; sun terrace; garden; bike rental; sauna; Jacuzzi, massage service; scuba diving; fitness room; free Wi-Fi.

Pestana Churchill Bay ★★ The newest addition to the Pestana empire sits on the quayside in the fishing village of Câmara de Lobos, a favorite spot of Sir Winston Churchill, who was a repeat vacationer in Madeira in the years after WWII. It opened in 2019 and its pastel-painted facade fits into the seafront, partly located in a former fish market. Rooms overlooking the bay feature sober grey pinstriped fabrics and natural wood floors, but their main features are the wall-size reproductions of a colorful Churchill watercolor showing the village. The roof-top features a lime-green pool and views reaching across the sea to the banana-tree covered slopes enclosing the bay.

Rua da Nossa Senhora da Conceição, 17, Câmara de Lobos. www.pousadas.pt. ✆ **21/844-20-01.** 57 units. 104€–265€ double. Free parking nearby. **Amenities:** Restaurant; bar; terrace; outdoor rooftop pool; massage service; sauna; free Wi-Fi.

Savoy Saccharum Resort & Spa ★★ Behind a rather forbidding facade you'll encounter the island's most-lavish pampering. Opened in 2015, its startling interior is the work of Madeira-born designer Nini Andrade Silva who took her inspiration from the sugar refining industry that once thrived in Calheta. Metallic finishes recall rum stills, and photos of cane fields abound. The spa is a hedonist's delight. It has four treatment and massage rooms, a heated indoor pool, sensorial showers, sauna, hammam, and more. There are three outdoor pools, including an edge-of-the-cliff infinity pool. Rooms are decorated in earth tones. Try to get one with a sea-view balcony. Calheta's beaches are on the doorstep.

Rua Serra de Água, 1, Arco da Calheta. www.savoysignature.com. ✆ **29/182-08-00.** 243 units. 130€–218€ double; 144€–523€ suite. Parking, 8€ per day. **Amenities:** 2 restaurants; 2 bars; babysitting; 3 outdoor and 1 indoor pool; kid's playroom; squash court; sun terrace; massage service; spa; gym; free Wi-Fi.

EASTERN MADEIRA

Portobay Serra Golf ★★ Centered on a cornflower blue 1920s villa with Art Nouveau features, this charming family hotel is set on Madeira's top golf course, high in the hills above the east coast. There are two superior rooms and a suite in the main house decorated in rustic style with natural wood and rugs. In a more modern wing, rooms have creamy shades and floor-to-ceiling windows opening on to the garden. Marble bathrooms feature Rituals toiletries. There's a cozy indoor pool and spa. If you're making a tour of the island, this is a handy last stop before the airport. On Sundays there's a fascinating market in the village of Santo da Serra.

Sítio dos Casais Próximos, Santo da Serra. www.portobay.com. ✆ **29/155-05-00.** 21 units. 79€–150€ double. Free parking. **Amenities:** 2 restaurants; 2 bars; babysitting; 3 outdoor and 1 indoor pool; children's playroom; squash court; sun terrace; massage service; spa; gym; free Wi-Fi.

Quinta do Furão ★★★ On a dramatic stretch of the north coast, this mustard-colored mansion sits amid a clifftop wine estate. Its restaurant alone is worth a visit. Dishes like chestnut soup or tuna with algae and fried maize make it a gourmet treat. Appetites will be enhanced by panoramic views up the coast and across to Porto Santo. There's also a pub and wine cellar for tasting the full range of island styles. Spacious rooms come in pastel colors with antique-style furnishings, with balcony views over the ocean or mountains. The gardens grow herbs and fruits as well as vines.

Estrada Quinta do Furão 6, Santana. www.quintadofurao.com. ✆ **29/157-01-00.** 45 units. 90€–175€ double. Free parking. **Amenities:** Restaurants; bars; wine cellar; outdoor pool (covered in winter); game room; terrace; garden; massage service; Jacuzzi; fitness room; free Wi-Fi.

PORTO SANTO

Pestana Ilha Dourada Hotel & Vilas ★ This modern lodging is at the far end of the island from the ferry, a 5-minute stroll to a stretch of beach which is among the least crowed in summer. The streamlined glass-and-white architecture of the main two-story building is built in a flat "v" around the lawn, pool, and sun terrace. There are also 32 villas with lounges and mini-kitchens. All around is the arid, desert-like landscape of Porto Santo, so different from lush, green Madeira less than 50km (30 miles) away. Like many on the island, it operates on a half-board basis.

Rua Ponta dos Zambujeiros. www.pestana.com. ✆ **21/011-44-33.** 49 units. 105€–216€ double; 179€–357€, rates include breakfast and dinner. **Amenities:** Restaurant; 2 bars; babysitting; exercise room; outdoor pool; sauna, hammam; Jacuzzi; massage service; garden; terrace; free Wi-Fi in public areas.

Torre Praia Hotel ★★ Most people come to Porto Santo to get up close and personal with the miles and miles of golden sand and this place certainly helps you do that. Step down from the terrace bar and you've got the golden stuff between your toes. The architecture incorporates a tower that belonged to a cement factory that once existed on the site. Decor in the rooms and public areas is bold and bright with geometric designs and primary colors. Most rooms have ocean views. It appeals to a younger crowd and families with children, so can get a bit noisy around the bar and poolside.

Rua Goulart Medeiros. www.portosantohotels.com. ✆ **29/198-04-50.** 66 units. 108€–235€ double; 155€–226€ suite. Free parking. **Amenities:** 2 restaurants; 3 bars; babysitting; exercise room; Jacuzzi; outdoor pool; sauna; free Wi-Fi in public areas.

Where to Eat

Madeira's deep coastal waters teem with life, so seafood plays a key part in the distinctive regional cuisine. Tuna and octopus are important, grilled limpets are a common starter, but the fish most associated with the island is a nightmarish-looking creature called black scabbard fish. It may be ugly, but its white flesh is delicious, often served accompanied with locally grown bananas. A visit to Funchal market shows the variety of fruits and vegetables thriving in the warm climate. The island's signature dishes, however, are meaty: *espetada* involves flame-grilling chunks of beef skewered on laurel sticks; *vinho d'alhos* is a festive dish of marinated pork served with sweet potato and cubes of deep-fried cornmeal. Those with a sweet tooth must try *bolo de mel,* a sticky cake made with sugarcane molasses. It goes down well with sweet Madeira wines.

FUNCHAL

Design Centre Nini Andrade Silva ★★ INTERNATIONAL World-renowned designer Nini Andrade Silva returned to her home island to turn a harborside fortress into a happening cultural hub featuring an art gallery, boutique, lounge bar, and a rooftop restaurant with stunning views across the bay to the lights of Funchal. The menu fuses island products with cutting-edge cooking and exotic imports, producing dishes like black scabbard fish tortellini with sage and olive butter; scallops in creamy fish sauce and horse mackerel caviar; or a mango and passionfruit rice pudding accompanied with sweet-potato ice cream. All this in a dining room whose stripped-down design maintains an intimate feel, even as its glass walls open up to the endless vistas outside.

Estrada da Pontinha, Forte de Nossa Senhora da Conceição. www.ninidesigncentre.com. ✆ **29/164-15-51.** Reservations recommended. Main courses 21€–27€; fixed menus 55€–140€. Daily 7–11pm.

Doca dos Cavacos ★★★ SEAFOOD Jutting over the ocean like the prow of a cruise liner, the blue-and-white terrace of this simple seafood joint curves toward the bay of Praia Formosa, a popular bathing spot on Funchal's western oceanfront. You can sit beneath a starlit sky, as waves lap below, and tuck into skillfully grilled fish just pulled from the water. Start with *lapas*—chewy limpets broiled in butter and garlic. Then take catch-of-the-day if you're lucky they'll have scarlet-scaled *bodião* (parrot fish, which is much sought after in these waters) served with sweet potatoes and seasonal vegetables. Finish up with passionfruit pudding.

Rua da Ponta da Cruz 66. ✆ **29/176-20-57.** Mains 11€–23€. Tues–Sun 10:30am–midnight.

Gavião Novo ★★ PORTUGUESE/SEAFOOD In the heart of the hopping old town, this is where in-the-know Portuguese from the mainland head when they want Madeiran seafood. It's the perfect place to try the island's signature dish of fried black scabbard fish (*peixe espada*) with banana. Or you can ignore the menu and let the staff show you the parrot fish, amberjack, grouper, or whatever else the fishermen have brought in that day. Rest assured it will be expertly grilled. If you have trouble choosing, share a fish mixed grill. There's a wide range of meaty options for non-piscivores.

Rua de Santa Maria 131. www.gaviaonovo.com. ✆ **29/122-92-38.** Mains 11€–20€. Daily 11am–11pm.

Il Gallo d'Or ★★★ FINE DINING/INTERNATIONAL French chef Benoît Sinthon has created one of the finest dining experiences in the Atlantic at this sophisticated place overlooking the ocean in the uber-posh **Cliff Bay Hotel.** The two-star Michelin restaurant combines island produce with treats from farther afield in dishes that look more like abstract art than stuff you eat. The menu constantly changes but could include *foie gras* with Madeiran banana; lobster with asparagus and orange vinaigrette; or a jellied pyramid of passion fruit. If it's a balmy evening, ask to be seated outside on the terrace (a sexier space than the classic dining room). Award-winning sommelier Sérgio Marques guarantees perfect wine matches.

The Cliff Bay, Estrada Monumental 147. www.ilgallodoro.portobay.com. ✆ **29/170-77-00.** Reservations required. Mains 18€–70€; tasting menus 105€–350€. Mon–Sat 7–9:30pm.

WESTERN MADEIRA

Fajã dos Padres ★★★ MADEIRAN/PORTUGUESE Getting here is an adventure, but it's so worth it. A *fajã* is a lick of land at the foot of a cliff. This one is at the foot of one of Europe's highest cliffs and was settled by wine-producing Jesuit priests seeking solitude in the 16th century. Unless you have a boat or are a rock-climber, the only way down is by a cable car that descends 300 meters (and adds 10€ to your bill). At the bottom, Chef Amândio Gonçalves serves up (lunch only) plates of grilled limpets, smoked swordfish, and grilled tuna with aromatic herbs as you sit beneath shady palms beside the pebble beach. Don't be surprised if a fisherman appears with a basket full of his latest catch. The fruits, vegetables, and herbs are grown organically in the *fajã*'s fertile gardens, including more than 20 varieties of mango and *pitanga,* a cherry-like tropical fruit that Gonçalves turns into a tangy ice-cream. Simply magical, and there are rooms where you can stay overnight (doubles from 65€–115€, 2-night minimum).

Estrada Padre António Dinis Henriques 1, Quinta Grande. www.fajadospadres.com. ✆ **29/194-45-38.** Reservations recommended. Mains 11€–16€. Daily 10am–6pm (closes 5pm in winter).

Vides ★★ MADEIRAN Okay, so there's a menu, but people come here for one thing only: *espetada.* Madeira's signature dish has its roots in this village high in the hills above Câmara de Lobos when skewers of beef were grilled over burning vine stalks. This rustic place has been serving up cubes of tender meat on spears of laurel wood since 1950 and is many people's favorite among several in the village. Order the meat by weight and choose what goes with it: fried cornmeal, salad, fries with garlic and oregano, and *bolo de caco* bread rolls are the norm. It's a carnivore's delight. Islanders will knock down cold beer or red wine with this, but given the winding road down the hill, one of you should stick to Brisa (Madeira's cherished passionfruit soda).

Rua da Achada 17, Estreito de Câmara de Lobos. ✆ **29/194-52-22.** Mains 10€–15€. Daily noon–4pm and 7–10:30pm.

EASTERN MADEIRA

Abrigo do Pastor ★★ MADEIRAN/PORTUGUESE Once a highland refuge for shepherds and hunters, this rough-hewn stone-and-wood cabin serves hearty mountain food, like boar steaks or rabbit slow-stewed in clay pots. If you find yourself up in the forests around Ribeira Frio on one of those days when a chilly mist settles over the mountains, this is the place to warm up beside the fireplace with a glass of *poncha.* There's also a bar serving "light" snacks like mugs of homemade chicken soup or steak slices in *bolo do caco* flatbreads.

Estrada das Carreiras 209, Camacha. www.abrigodopastor.com. ✆ **29/192-20-60.** Mains 9€–22€. Wed–Mon 10am–11pm.

Cantinho Da Serra ★★ MADEIRAN This homey restaurant offers a treasure trove of hard-to-find Madeira highland specialties, with a focus on slow-cooked meat dishes. Kick off with a selection of appetizers, which could include tuna pâte, pork marinated in garlic and vinegar, or fava-bean salad. Then turn to rabbit stewed with sage and wild onions or roast kid (young goat). Mop up the sauce with sweet-potato bread. For dessert, choose between seasonal fruit or treats like curd cheese with pumpkin preserves. It's all set in a rustic-but-refined country house on the road down from the highest island peaks, making this the perfect place to replace calories burned on a mountain hike. Service can be slow.

Estrada do Pico das Pedras 57, Santana. www.cantinhodaserra.madeiratravelbook.eu. ✆ **29/157-37-27.** Mains 13€–15€. Mon–Tues noon–3pm and 6:30–10pm; Wed–Sun noon–10pm.

PORTO SANTO

Pé na Água ★★ MADEIRAN/PORTUGUESE The name means "foot in the water" and that's what you get here. The tables of this beach restaurant are so close to the water that the waves are almost lapping at your flip-flops. If the sun's too hot outside, head to the cool (in both senses) interior with its high plank ceiling and wicker chairs. As you'd expect, seafood dominates, with baked octopus and grilled tuna with sweet potato among the specialties. There's a range of good steak options too.

Estrada Nacional 111. www.penaagua.pt. ✆ **29/198-52-42.** Mains 12€–40€. Wed–Mon 10am–11pm.

Ponta da Calheta ★★ MADEIRAN/PORTUGUESE Yet another excellent beach restaurant, this one is set at the far end of Porto Santo's magnificent strand. It overlooks the islet of Cal and the mountains of Madeira on the horizon. The decor—an all-white interior with big beachscape photos—and the food elevate this above the average beach shack. Peppery octopus-and-bean stew and fried scabbard fish with banana, and the tart island passionfruit are among the standouts. Rent a bike in Vila Baleira town, and this makes a perfect (and flat) 7km (4½ mile) ride beside the beach.

Ponta da Calheta. ✆ **29/198-53-42.** Mains 12€–15€. Daily 10am–11:30pm.

Shopping

Aside from wine (p. 424), Madeira's best-known consumer goodie is embroidered cotton and linen. The tradition dates back to the early days of settlement, but it took off in the 19th century when *broderie madère* became a must-have for fashionistas in Victorian Britain. Asian copies abound, so make sure your purchase has a made-in-Madeira seal. There are no imitations in **Bordal** ★ (www.bordal.pt; ✆ **29/122-29-65**). Its factory and main store is at No. 77 Rua Dr Fernão Ornelas 77, a street across from Funchal's farmers' market with several cute traditional stores. The firm was founded in 1962 and produces exquisite table linen, bedding, blouses, nightshirts, and accessories. Visitors can watch artisans in action, see exhibitions tracing the history of the art and even learn to embroider themselves. Wickerwork baskets, furniture and decoration are another specialty. Choose yours over a drink at **Café Relógio** ★ (www.caferelogio.com; ✆ **29/192-27-77**) in the hill village of Camacho northeast of Funchal. The factory is connected to the cafe and store. They commission artists for contemporary basket work. Since 2017, Funchal has a one-stop shop for handicrafts, the **Loja do Artesanato da Madeira** ★ (http://ivbam.gov-madeira.pt; ✆ **29/120-46-00**) in the 19th-century home of a British wine merchant, Rua dos Ferreiros, 152.

For contemporary styling head to the **Design Centre Nini Andrade Silva** ★★ (www.ninidesigncentre.com; ✆ **29/164-87-80**), which has a store selling items created by the island-born designer as well as exhibition spaces, a bar and restaurant (p. 435) in a quayside fortress. Young Madeiran stylist Mariana Sousa retails sunny, handcrafted clothes and accessories at her store **Sous** ★ (www.sous.pt; ✆ **968 375 224**) in the Oudinot Shopping Center near the farmers' market.)

For gourmet gifts, go for *bolo de mel*, Madeira's rich and sticky molasses cake. Among the best are those produced in the **Fábrica Santo António** ★ (www.fabricastoantonio.com; ✆ **29/122-02-55**) bakery downtown on Travessa do Forno 27-29. It's been around since 1893, and also makes a selection of cookies, candies, and preserves.

Madeira Entertainment & Nightlife

The **Zone Velha** ★★ district behind the market has emerged as the hip nightlife area, with its narrow streets often packed with nocturnal crowds moving among the bars and restaurants. In the heart of it on Rua Santa Maria, **Venda Velha ★** (✆ **91/475-89-75**) is an old-style Funchal tavern that fills up with a young crowd eager for freshly made *poncha*—a traditional blend of local rum and lemon juice, although passionfruit, tamarillo and other island fruits are also used. Open Sunday to Thursday 4pm to 1am, Friday to Saturday 4pm to 2am. Between the old town and the ocean, **Barreirinha Bar Café ★** (✆ **29/162-74-18;** Mon–Sat 9am–2am, Sun 9am–1am, at Largo do Socorro, 1) has great sunsets followed by live music and DJ sets.

Contrasting with the streetwise old town scene is the glittering **Casino de Madeira ★** on Avenida do Infante (www.casinodamadeira.com; ✆ **29/114-04-24**). In a distinctive 1960s building by Brazilian architect Oscar Niemeyer, it offers gaming from slots to roulette and Texas Hold'em, plus cocktail bars, restaurants with dance shows, and the **Copacabana** discotheque, maybe the hottest spot east of Havana. It also has the outdoor **Garden** dance club. Over 18s only and ID required. The dress code rules out beach and sportswear. It's open Sunday to Thursday from 3pm to 3am, Friday and Saturday 4pm to 4am.

Outside the casino, Funchal's best-known dance spot is **Vespas ★**, Av. Sá Carneiro 7 (✆ **29/123-48-00**). Its turntables have spun since the days of *Saturday Night Fever,* but it remains a top spot with DJs from the island and mainland Portugal. The rooftop at the **CR7 hotel** (p. 432) also hosts regular dance parties, where the island's most famous soccer player occasionally makes an appearance. Outside Funchal, the harbor at Câmara de Lobos is a great place to spend an evening, with a jumble of *poncha* bars. We have a soft spot for **Bar No. 2 É prá a Poncha ★★** (✆ **29/194-25-54**).

THE AZORES ★★★

Roughly 1,500km (900 miles) W of Portugal; 4,300km (2,600 miles) E of New Jersey

Essentials

ARRIVING

Unlike Madeira, the Azores has direct flights from North America. **Azores Airlines** (www.azoresairlines.pt) flies daily flights from Boston to **Ponta Delgada Airport** (www.aeroportopontadelgada.pt) on the island of São Miguel and **Lajes Airport** (http://aerogarelajes.azores.gov.pt) on Terceira. It also runs four flights a week from Toronto to both islands, as well as seasonal flights from Montreal and Oakland. **Delta** is also flying non-stop from New York JFK to Ponta Delgada. Flights from mainland Europe to Terceira and São Miguel are also increasing and become cheaper. **Ryanair, TAP Air Portugal,** and **Azores Airlines** all fly from the Portuguese cities of Lisbon and Porto, and there are direct flights to London, Frankfurt, Manchester, and Madrid. Book in advance and you can get a Lisbon-Ponta Delgada return for less than $50. Azores Airlines also links to Madeira, the Canaries, and Cape Verde. It operates a **stopover program** enabling you to stay for up to 7 days in the islands on your way to one of its destinations in Europe or Cape Verde.

An added bonus for passengers flying from mainland Portugal or Madeira is the ***encaminhamentos*** system (www.encaminhamentos.sata.pt) operated by **SATA Air Açores,** which offers a free onward flight to any of the other Azores islands if you stay less than 24 hours on the island where you first arrive. For example, if you arrive in Terceira on the 9am flight from Lisbon, you can fly for free to Faial at 8:30 the next morning. The same service works on the return flight, again if you spend less than 24 hours in the island you're leaving from. SATA, the parent company of Air Azores, operates regular island-hopping flights around the archipelago.

Ponta Delgada Airport is 3km from the city, but at time of writing there was no bus service. **Taxis** can be picked up at arrivals or pre-booked (www.taxis pdl.com) for a fixed rate of 12€ for downtown hotels. On Terceira, the **EVT** bus company (www.evt.pt) runs buses roughly twice an hour from the airport to Angra do Heroísmo for 2.50€. The journey takes just over an hour. By taxi it's 20 minutes and 20€.

WHEN TO VISIT

Azores weather is unpredictable. It rains a lot but is always mild. Locals joke that while some places get four seasons in one a day, here you can get them all in an hour. Generally, there's less rain in the summer months of June, July and August when daytime temperatures enjoy average highs around 20°C (70°C). Rainfall is highest November to March but, even in winter, temperatures rarely drop below 10°C (48°C) except in the hills. Pico Mountain is often capped with snow between January and April.

July is the best time to see the **hydrangeas** whose blooms line roads around the islands, particularly on Faial, earning it a "blue island" nickname. You can spot sperm whales and dolphins on **whale-watching** trips year-round, but mid-April to mid-May is the best time to catch the really big species as they migrate past the islands. For **game fishing**, July to September is marlin season. Terceira's village **bull runs** are held from May through September. The island's **Sanjoaninas** festival involves 2 weeks of parties starting on June 21 (www.sanjoaninas.pt). São Miguel hosts an annual festival of contemporary arts in July called **Walk & Talk** (www.walktalkazores.org). In the 50 days between Easter and Pentecost, villages across the Azores will celebrate the **Holy Spirit** with processions and religious ceremonies but also communal lunches and festivities. The **Senhor Santo Cristo dos Milagres** festivities, held the fifth Sunday after Easter in Ponta Delgada, are another major religious celebration.

VISITOR INFORMATION

The regional tourist office has broad information on the islands on its website (www.visitazores.com). There's a tourist information office in Ponta Delgada, on Avenida Infante D. Henrique (✆ **29/630-86-25**) open daily from 9am to 7pm. In Angra do Heroísmo, the tourist office is on Rua Direita 74 (✆ **29/540-48-10**). Contacts for tourist offices in the other islands can be found on the Visit Portugal website (www.visitportugal.com).

São Miguel

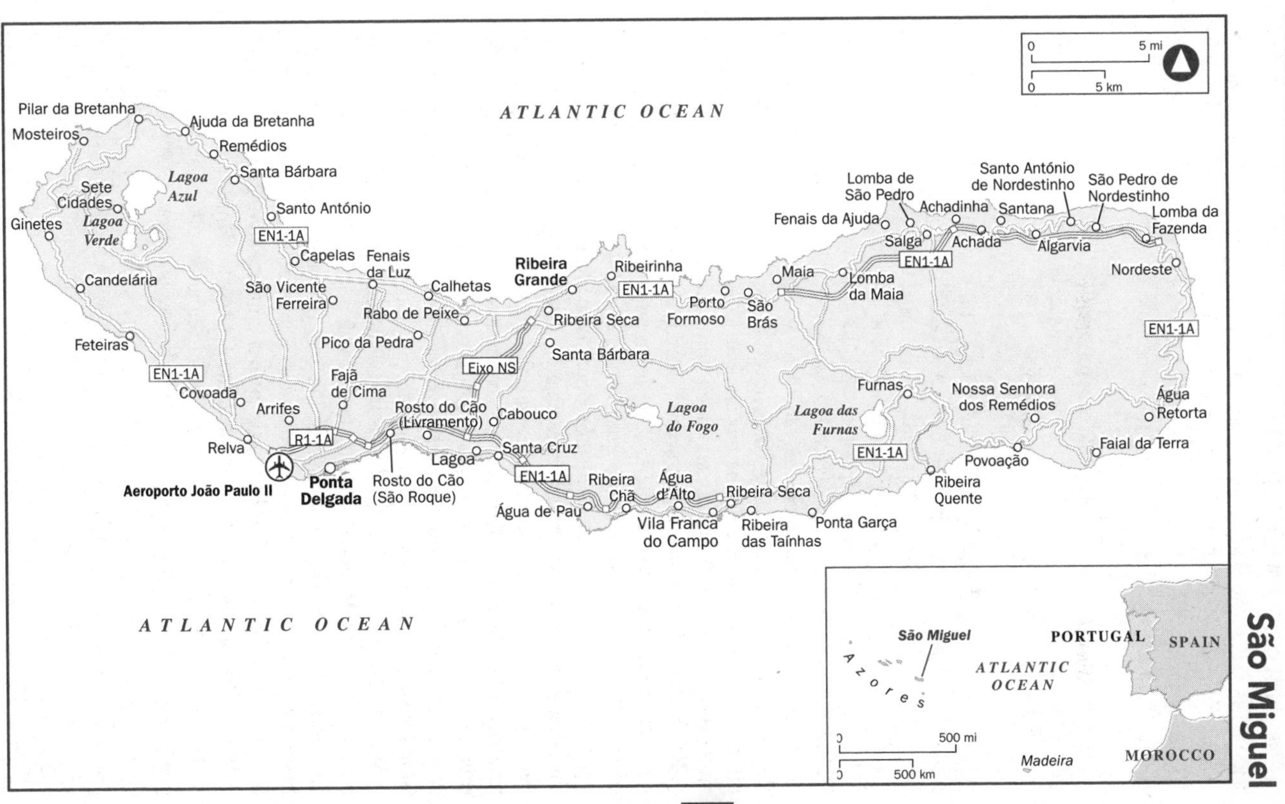

0
5 mi
0
5 km
ATLANTIC OCEAN
Pilar da Bretanha
Mosteiros
Ajuda da Bretanha
Remédios
Santa Bárbara
Sete Cidades
Lagoa Azul
Lagoa Verde
Ginetes
Santo António
EN1-1A
Capelas
Fenais da Luz
Calhetas
Ribeira Grande
Ribeirinha
Candelária
São Vicente Ferreira
Rabo de Peixe
Ribeira Seca
Porto Formoso
São Brás
Maia
Lomba da Maia
Fenais da Ajuda
Lomba de São Pedro
Salga
Achadinha
Achada
Santo António de Nordestinho
Santana
Algarvia
São Pedro de Nordestinho
Lomba da Fazenda
Nordeste
Feteiras
Pico da Pedra
Santa Bárbara
Eixo NS
Covoada
Arrifes
Fajã de Cima
Rosto do Cão (Livramento)
Cabouco
Lagoa do Fogo
Lagoa das Furnas
Furnas
Nossa Senhora dos Remédios
Água Retorta
Faial da Terra
Relva
R1-1A
Lagoa
Santa Cruz
Povoação
Ribeira Quente
Aeroporto João Paulo II
Ponta Delgada
Rosto do Cão (São Roque)
Ribeira Chã
Água d'Alto
Ribeira Seca
Água de Pau
Vila Franca do Campo
Ribeira das Taínhas
Ponta Garça
ATLANTIC OCEAN
São Miguel
Azores
PORTUGAL
SPAIN
ATLANTIC OCEAN
0
500 mi
0
500 km
Madeira
MOROCCO

The Azores in Context

The Azores are sometimes described as Europe's Hawaii. Nine shards of emerald sprinkled for 600km (375 miles) across the Atlantic. Besides endless shades of green, the dominant colors are black from the rocks formed by the islands' volcanic geology and blue from the blooms of hydrangeas and agapanthus, and the waters of the ocean and many crater lakes. That's when you're lucky. The islands are green for a reason. It rains a lot and sometimes the skies and seas will be grey, with low cloud covering the peaks. Still, the rain rarely lasts for long, at least in summer.

The Azores are a paradise for nature lovers. They are one of the world's best places for watching whales, and offer miles of hiking trails through primeval forests, verdant pasture or rugged hills. Above all they offer a change in the pace of life—a laid-back rhythm with great food, countless village festivities, and time to unwind amid the extraordinary landscapes.

Legends have it that Visigoth knights, Irish saints, Viking adventurers, and the lost city of Atlantis all inhabited the Azores back in the mists of time. By the time Portuguese explorers arrived there around 1427, the islands were deserted. The archipelago's name is believed to result from an ornithological error: some seadog mistaking the buzzards he saw swooping over the islands for goshawks (*açor* in Portuguese) which don't actually live there.

Prince Henry the Navigator, however, quickly understood the island's strategic importance and sent settlers from the mainland to establish Portuguese control. They were joined by migrants from Flanders and the Netherlands, which helps explain the prevalence of Dutch names and blonde islanders.

Atlantic wind patterns meant the islands, particularly the port of Angra, became a key staging post as Portugal built a trading empire that stretched from Brazil to Africa and Asia. On his voyage back from discovering the searoute to India, Vasco da Gama stopped in Angra in the forlorn hope of saving his sick brother, fellow sea captain Paulo da Gama, who is buried in the city's Convent of São Francisco.

When Spain's king Philip II grabbed Portugal in 1581, Angra briefly became capital of breakaway Portuguese kingdom, until the Spanish stamped out Azorean resistance. Again, during the Portuguese civil war in the 1830s, Angra was for several months the capital of King Pedro IV as he sailed from Brazil with a liberal army to battle his upstart conservative brother Miguel I.

When sail gave way to steam, a decline set in, but Horta on Faial island remained an important staging point for transatlantic cables and for flying boats, including PanAm's Clipper fleet heading to and from Europe. In 1943 the British secured base rights in the Azores to fight Nazi U-boats and the Lajes Airbase on Terceira was a major U.S. facility during the Cold War. In 2003, President George W. Bush met European allies there to discuss the impending war in Iraq.

The airbase is just one of the Azores links to the U.S. Waves of emigration mean the around 1 million North Americans of Azorean origin far outnumber the island population. The diaspora is often referred to as the 10th island, and

FROMMER'S favorite AZORES EXPERIENCES

Enjoying a volcanic soak. You are never far from a volcano in the Azores. In São Miguel's eastern hills, volcano-heated hot springs bubble to the surface allowing restaurants to cook a renowned thermal stew. Visitors can also stew themselves in thermal pools. Our favorites include **Dona Beija** pools in Furnas or the waterfall-fed pool among the tropical forest of **Caldeira Velha.**

Soaking up history in Angra. Angra do Heroísmo may be the most beautiful city in Portugal. Its fortresses fought off pirates like Sir Francis Drake; its streets of brightly painted churches, mansions, and stores were a lynchpin of Portugal's trading empire; and it earned its heroic name for defending the liberal cause during a civil war in the 1830s. It has fine cafes and a sandy urban beach.

G&T with a view. Peter Café Sport is one of the world's great bars, a meeting place for transatlantic travelers since 1918. Its wood paneled interior is decorated with flags and memorabilia left by generations of sailors. From the windows or harborside terrace you sip one of its signature gin and tonics while watching the sun play on the vast conical silhouette of Mount Pico, Portugal's highest mountain just across the channel. Upstairs there is a museum of scrimshaws—engraved whale teeth.

Hiking the lakes. São Miguel is potted with lakes nestled in the craters of volcanos. You can drive up to *miradouros* (viewpoints) to enjoy panoramic visits, but there are also hiking trails that will take you through startling landscapes, from forests of towering Japanese cedar to heather covered moors or isolated shoreline churches. The biggest lake is **Sete Cidades;** if the light is right it will be part blue, part green.

Feasting on fish you've never heard of. The ocean around the Azores teems with life and seafood that is an integral part of island cuisine. Go to the markets and you'll see species like you've never seen with names like almaco jack, bluemouth rockfish, or greater forkbeard.

Discovering whale culture past and present. The Azores are among the world's best places for whale watching, particularly the islands of Pico and Faial. Before whales were watched they were hunted. In **Lajes do Pico, São Roque do Pico** and **Horta** there are good museums recounting the whaling heritage from the hunt to the gruesome business of extracting valuable oil from the carcasses.

family ties are strong to communities mostly centered in New England and California. English is widely understood.

Since 1976, the Azores, like Madeira, have the status of a special autonomous region within Portugal, electing their own regional government and parliament meeting in Ponta Delgado with broad powers of local affairs.

As the volcanic islands astride the three-way continental divide between America, Europe and Africa, the Azores remain subjected to seismic activity. A 13-month volcanic eruption began in 1957 and destroyed 300 homes in Faial, prompting President Dwight Eisenhower to welcome in hundreds of Azorean refugees. The new land created by the eruption is now a popular attraction. More devastating was the 1980 earthquake centered on Terceira and São Jorge, killing over 60 and damaging 70% of island homes.

The population of the islands is 250,000, with just over half living on São Miguel. Over the years, orange production and whaling provided major contributions to the islands' economy. These days tourism is of growing importance, alongside fishing and agriculture with a strong focus on dairy farming. Azorean milk, butter and cheese is widely exported to mainland Portugal.

The nine islands are divided into three groups. In the east is São Miguel and Santa Maria. Terceira and Graciosa make up the central group along with triangle of Faial, Pico and São Jorge. Flores and tiny Corvo form the remote western group. Thanks to the warm, damp climate all have lush, green landscapes with rich pastureland, thick forests, and moors on the volcanic uplands. They are dotted with homes combining whitewash, black rock, and brightly colored paintwork.

The islands have their own time zone, 1 hour behind continental Portugal and Madeira.

Getting Around the Azores

BETWEEN THE ISLANDS Island hopping by plane is easy. **Azores Airlines** operates flights to all islands using Canadian-built De Havilland Dash turbo prop planes. On the 40-minute route between São Miguel and Terceira, for example, there are up to six flights a day. Prices vary but usually cost between 50€ and 100€ each way. The airports are small, and check-in is usually quick and hassle-free. Islanders joke the little planes are their busses. If you have more time, **Atlânticoline** (www.atlanticoline.pt) connects all the islands by ferry. The crossing from Horta across the strait to Madalena on Pico island is the most popular. It takes 30 minutes and costs 3.60€. The 40-minute trip from Flores to Corvo costs 10€. Be aware that unpredictable weather can complicate travel by sea and air. Just one of the line's four boats takes vehicles; check with your rental company if you want to take a hire car by boat between the islands.

BUSES & TAXIS **Bus** companies operate on most of the islands, but services can be slow and infrequent, using backroads to visit villages along the way. On Pico, for example, the bus from Madalena to Lajes do Pico lasts at least an hour but is doable in 35 minutes by car. The bus is cheap however: a ride from Angra to Terceira's second city of Praia da Vitoria costs 2.52€. Ponta Delgada operates a **minibus** service within the urban area for just 0.50€ a ride and Angra and Horta have similar systems for just 0.30€.

Taxis are plentiful and reasonably priced. On São Miguel the taxi drivers' association has an efficient website for booking rides (www.taxispdl.com) and also operates excursions: A 3-hour tour to the Sete Cidades lake costs 49€. Taxis often don't run meters, so check the price before setting off.

BY CAR Renting a car is the best way to really explore the islands. Because everybody arrives by plane, there are a plethora of rental companies to choose from at the island airports (except in tiny Corvo, where there's only one road). The oldest and biggest in the islands is Ilha Verde (www.ilhaverde.com) which also represents Avis in the Azores. Other international rental companies such as Hertz and Sixt operate at the island's main airports either directly or through local partners.

Recent investment supported by the European Union has vastly improved roads, giving São Miguel a network of fast highways and Terceira a two-lane road from Angra to Lajes airport. Still normal care should be taken, particularly on twisting roads through the hills where low clouds, sudden rain, and fog can make driving difficult.

ORGANIZED TOURS There's a big range of tour operators offering everything from hiking to boat trips and bus excursions. The tourist board has a list for each island under the "Getting Around" section of their website (www.visitazores.com). Among the most reputed are **Futurismo** (www.futurismo.pt) which offers a range of tours and packages by Jeep, van, bike, or boat mostly in São Miguel, or **Azores On Travel** (www.azoresontravel.com), which operates across the archipelago, for example running a day-long discovery of São Jorge from tip to mountainous tip including visits to a dairy farm and a coffee plantation for 90€ including lunch. For a personalized walking tour of the historical treasures of Angra do Heroísmo, we recommend freelance guide Paula Ferreira (✆ **96/358-38-63**).

[FastFACTS] AZORES

ATMs Available 24 hours a day in all but the smallest villages.

Business Hours As on the mainland, **shops** are usually open from around 9am till 6pm, although it varies by an hour or so. Many stores will close Saturday afternoons and most shut down Sundays; some close for lunch. **Municipal buildings** are mostly open Monday to Friday 8:30m to 4:30pm. **Banks** Monday to Friday 8:30am to 3pm.

Consulates **U.S.:** Avenida Príncipe de Mónaco, 6-2 F, Ponta Delgada (✆ **29/630-83-30**). **Canada:** Rua D'Água 28, Ponta Delgada (✆ **29/628-14-88**).

Dentists **Espaço Riso** (www.espacoriso.pt; ✆**29/670-67-13**) R. Dr. Hugo Moreira, 52, Ponta Delgada, is a modern clinic with English-speaking staff.

Doctors The **Clínica do Bom Jesus** (www.clinicabomjesus.org) offers a wide range of health services and English-speaking staff. Avenida Príncipe Mónaco, Ponta Delgada, near the airport (✆ **29/628-53-52**).

Drugstores Pharmacies are usually open Monday to Saturday 9am to 7pm, although some close for lunch or on Saturday afternoons. The **Holan** group (www.farmaciasholon.pt) has a website in English listing its pharmacies around Portugal, including the islands, with hours and contact details. Rotating **after hours pharmacies** are listed (in Portuguese) on www.farmaciasdeservico.net.

Emergencies As in the mainland, call **112** for a general **emergency,** ✆ **29/620-55-00** for the Ponta Delgada **police**.

Post Office The central **Post Office** (Correios) in Ponta Delgada is on Rua Conselheiro Luis Bettencourt, 10A (✆ **29/630-40-71**). In Angra it's at Rua do Palácio (✆ **29/520-45-80**). Both open Monday to Friday 9am to 6pm.

Safety Crime levels are lower than in Lisbon, Porto and the Algarve, but there has been an increase in pickpocketing, particularly in São Miguel, so normal care should be taken.

Taxes Sales taxes (IVA) are lower than on the mainland or Madeira with rates on goods and services between 4% and 18%.

Tipping Similar to the mainland, there's no obligation to tip. But rounding up a bill, up to a 10% maximum is common if service was good in a restaurant or taxi.

Exploring the Azores

SÃO MIGUEL ★★★

Portugal's biggest island (it beats Madeira by 20 sq. km/8 sq. miles) is shaped roughly like a slightly bent arm. It runs over 60km (38 miles) east-west but is just 8km (5 miles) wide at its narrowest point. With 140,000 people, it has over half the Azores' population. Ponta Delgada, on the south coast, is the archipelago's capital and largest city, with handsome black and white buildings in its 16th-century heart. São Miguel's main attractions lie outside the city, however, in a landscape marked by volcanic ranges to the west and east, crystalline crater lakes, waterfalls plunging from tropical forests, and steaming thermal parks.

Ponta Delgada ★★

The best place to start a visit to the Azores capital is beneath the **Portas da Cidade** ★, the triple arched 18th-century gates that have become the symbol of the city. Like the surrounding cityscape they are a contrast in black volcanic rock and white-painted plaster. In front, the arcaded facades and black-and-white paving of Praça Gonçalo Velho stretch down to the quayside. To the right is the 17th-century City Hall whose **bell tower** ★ offers an excellent view over the city for those energetic enough to tackle the 106 steps (Mon–Fri 9:30am–5pm, free entry).

Inland from the gates, the **Igreja de São Sebastião** ★ is the city's main church, a monochrome confection of Gothic, baroque, and Manueline styles. It contains a rich collection of religious art (daily 8am–7pm except during services, free entry). An even more spectacular church is the **Convento de Nossa Senhora da Esperança** ★★, which is still in use as a convent behind the thickly barred windows of its five-story tower. The church contains magnificent 17th-century *azulejos* and gold-covered wood carvings. It also holds the statue of Santo Cristo dos Milagres, which is venerated by Azorean Catholics and is carried in procession through the city as part of festivals held every spring (www.senhorsantocristo.com; daily 7:30am–5:30pm; free entry).

To get a picture of the island's varied produce head to **Mercado da Graça** ★, a daily food market in the city center (Mon–Wed 7:30am–6:30pm, Thurs 7:30am–7:30pm; Fri 7am–7pm, Sat 7am–2pm, free entry) which has been running since the 1840s. Pineapples take pride of place among the fruit and veg, but there are also bananas, yams, pots of homemade fig and blackberry jam. Butchers sell local beef and traditional sausages while the pungent aroma will draw you to **O Rei dos Queijos** (www.oreidosqueijos.com) offering 42 varieties of Azores cheese. Ponta Delgada's hip side can be found in around Rua D`Água, Rua Pedro Homem and Rua Carvalho Araújo which are filled with cafes, boutiques and galleries like **Miolo** (www.miolostore.ecwid.com).

Lagoa das Sete Cidades ★★★

"Seven cities lake" is one of the iconic sites of Portugal. To fully appreciate its beauty, hire a car or join a tour up to the **Miradouro da Vista do Rei** ★★★ viewpoint where, on a hillside blue with hydrangeas, you can gaze upon this

PICK UP A pineapple

Once the Azores were a major exporter of oranges to northern Europe. When disease killed the crop, planter Augusto Arruda decided to try something new, making commercial use of a plant that islanders had long ago introduced from Brazil as a garden curiosity. As a result, São Miguel is today's Europe's only significant pineapple grower, producing around 1,000 tons a year under greenhouses centered in the suburban slopes of Ponta Delgada. **Arruda's original plantation ★** is open for visits where you can follow the fruit's 2-year journey to juicy maturity. After that, sample pineapple cakes, ice cream, or *pina coladas* in a leafy garden next to the plantation house; examine a collection of 800 pineapple-themed objects; or buy pineapple liquor, jam, chutney or other non-fruity regional souvenirs in the plantation's classy store (www.ananasesarruda.com; © **29/638-44-38;** open daily 9am–10pm Apr–Sept, 9am–6pm Oct–Mar; free admission).

shimming expanse of water surrounded by the wooded slopes of a volcanic crater. The lake takes the form of a figure-8 with a narrow bridge across its waist. If skies are clear, the two halves will take on different colors: one deep green, the other sapphire blue. According to legend they were filled by the tears of a blue-eyed princess and her green-eyed lover after her dad ended the affair. In reality, the phenomenon is caused by unromantic algae-related stuff, but that does nothing to detract from the beauty. You can get more views heading uphill where there are more, smaller lakes; or down to the lakeside village. This protected natural reserve area is crisscrossed by hiking trails if you prefer to view its delights by foot.

Ribeira Grande ★

The main city on São Miguel's dramatic north coast has an attractive center dissected by a fast-flowing stream running down from the hills. There are impressive buildings like the city hall dating from 1507 and the ornate Espírito Santo church. Its main attractions, however, lie on the outskirts: **Areal de Santa Bárbara beach ★★**, one of the best in the Azores and a surfers' favorite, and the **Arquipélago – Contemporary Arts Center ★★**. Opened in 2015 in a derelict tobacco and liquor factory, the center's cutting-edge design was shortlisted for Europe's top architecture prize. It aims to promote culture on the island and showcase artists from the Azores and beyond (www.arquipelagocentrodeartes.azores.gov.pt; © **29/647-01-30;** open Tues–Sun 10am–6pm). Admission is 3€, free for under-14s and for all on Sundays. There's open-air art in the neighboring fishing port of **Rabo de Peixe** where world-renowned Lisbon street artist **Vhils** has carved portraits of local men into the side of housing blocks on Rua do Porto.

Lagoa de Fogo ★★★

Here's another amazing crater lake, over 570 meters (1,880 ft.) up in the central volcano range. To get the best views, drive up to **Miradouro do Pico da Barrosa** or **Miradouro Lagoa de Fogo** on the crater rim (although beware at this height, clouds can come down to spoil the picture). The area is a protected reserve with little signs of human activity amid the indigenous vegetation and abundant bird life. There's a pleasant hike down from the Lagoa de Fogo viewpoint down to the lakeside—harder on the way back up. On the way to the lake from the north coast, stop of at the **Caldeira Verde ★★** natural park. Squeezed into a ravine packed with exotic vegetation—the towering tree ferns introduced from New Zealand are especially eye-catching. At its heart is a thermal pool fed by a waterfall of warm water emerging from the volcanic hillside. You can take a dip there or in a number of smaller man-made tubs downstream. Just take care not to wander past the barriers sealing off one pool that bubbles to the surface at close to boiling point. There's a visitor center explaining all the nature. The park is open June to September 9am to 9pm; April, May, and October 9am to 8pm; and November to March 9:30am to 5:30pm. Admission 8€ if you plan to dip in the pools, 3€ just to visit, free for children under six, reductions for older children, seniors and families (http://parquesnaturais.azores.gov.pt; ✆ **29/670-46-49**).

Fábrica de Chá Gorreana ★★

São Miguel has Europe's only **tea plantations**. Once the leaves were a major crop on the north coast, but now there are only two producers. This is the oldest and largest. It occupies a privileged location overlooking the ocean. Rows and rows of the little bushes cover the gentle slopes around a factory founded in 1883. The visit is a delightfully informal affair. Schoolkids at the gate will take you around for tips, or you can simply wander in among the men and women working on rolling, drying and bagging up tea leaves using machines imported from England over 100 years ago. There are refreshment stations throughout where you can help yourself to a free cup of black or green tea. Walking paths lead off around the plantation. The place is run by the 6th generation of the family of German origin that moved to the islands in the 1800s. The brew is excellent and makes an original souvenir (www.gorreana.pt; ✆ **29/644-23-49;** Mon–Fri 8am–6pm; Sat–Sun 9am–6pm; free admission).

TERCEIRA ★★★

While the natural landscapes are the main attraction elsewhere in the Azores, here the amazing city of Angra de Heroísmo is the top draw. Severely damaged in a 1980 earthquake, its historic center was meticulously reconstructed, becoming the first city in Portugal to attain UNESCO World Heritage status. That's not to say the rest of this oval-shaped island is to be ignored. A third of its territory is protected natural habitat. There are plenty of spectacular volcanic rim viewpoints, and you can even head underground into the entrails of the mountains. Terceira is also rich in cultural traditions, including the Espírito Santo cult which has graced the island with dozens of colorful chapels, and village bullfights that leave the animal, but not always the human participants, unscathed.

Angra do Heroísmo ★★★

Angra received its "heroism" title after the island of Terceira took the liberal side in Portugal's civil war in the 1830s, bravely fighting off the conservative forces of King Miguel I. Its citizens are proud of the city's beauty and of its valiant history of bouncing back after pirate raids, earthquakes, invasion and economic adversity.

A stroll through the old town is a delight. In contrast to the black and white that predominates in other Azorean cities, Angra paints its houses from a palette of 18 authorized shades. The result is a riot of pastel facades and frames. The city was originally built on a hilltop above the current site. But after fortresses were built to protect the harbor from buccaneers a new, modern city was laid out on a grid pattern downtown. It would provide the inspiration for New World cities like Cartagena in Colombia, Salvador in Brazil, and San Juan, Puerto Rico.

A good place to start any tour is the **Igreja da Misericórdia**, a harborside church whose soaring 18th-century facade was confected in sky-blue and white on the site of a Discoveries Era hospital where sick sailors were brought on their way back from Asia, Africa and the Americas. **Vasco da Gama** nursed his dying brother here when he returned from the first sea journey round Africa to the east. A statue of the navigator stands by the quay.

The straight streets of Angra's **downtown** run inland from here. Among the prettiest are Rua Direita and Rua de São João lined with colorful houses, often with flowers flowing from wrought-iron balconies. The **Sé,** or cathedral, was built in the late 16th century during the 60 years of Spanish rule. Its peaches-and-cream facade was rebuilt twice after the 1980 earthquake and a fire four years later. Another outstanding religious exterior is the old Jesuit college **Igreja do Colégio,** painted in mustard and white.

If you visit just one church in Angra, however, go to the **Convent and Church of San Francisco ★★**, which now houses the city museum. The marble-and-gold interior is a blaze of color. It holds the tomb of explorers Paulo da Gama and João Vaz Corte-Real who, some historians say, reached the coast of Canada 20 years before Columbus first sailed to the Americas. Concerts are held at 11am Sunday mornings on the giant church organ made in 1788. Inside the convent the museum is a fascinating and well-presented mix of art and local history whose exhibits range from WWI cannons to Renaissance painting and traditional island costumes. Open Tuesday to Sunday, 10am to 5:30pm from April to September, opening and closing 30 minutes earlier in winter. Admission 2€, free for under-14s, 1€ for under-25s and over 65s (http://museu-angra.azores.gov.pt; ✆ **29/524-08-00**).

If you've built up an appetite with all the culture, head to one of Angra's fine cafe-pastry shops. The city's long association with the spice trade has left a tradition of conjuring up sweet wonders with cinnamon, cloves and vanilla. Try *bolos Dona Amélia*, a little cake named after a Portuguese queen and the city favorite tidbit, at **O Forno ★**, on Rua de São João (✆ **29/521-37-29;** open Mon–Sat 8am–7pm).

Walk off the calories in the **Jardim Duque da Terceira ★** gardens filled with exotic plants and shaded walkways laid out in 1882 (open daily 8am–6pm). You can climb through the garden to the **Alto da Memória ★** a strange, elongated pyramid that dominates the skyline (daily 8am–8pm). It was erected by a local nobleman in honor of King Pedro IV, leader of the liberal cause in the civil war and first emperor of Brazil. There are spectacular views to be had from up here across the city to **Monte Brasil ★★**, the volcanic headland that dominates Angra harbor. Most of it is a nature reserve, popular with hikers and picnicking families. It is another great place for views. Surrounding it are the walls of the **Fortress of São João Baptista ★★**, one of the world's largest forts, built in the 1500 to keep out English corsairs like Sir Francis Drake and the Earl of Essex, who both tried to assault the island. Part of it is still used as an army base, but there is an interesting **Military Museum ★** built into the ramparts. It's part of the city museum (see above) with the same opening hours and one ticket will get entry to both. In 1896, **King Ngungunhane** of Gaza who led resistance to Portuguese conquest in what is now Mozambique was sent to exile on Monte Brasil. He died there 10 years later.

Algar do Carvão ★

This is your chance to get inside a volcano. The **natural cave** was a tube through which lava once spouted. It drops down under the ground for 100m (330 ft.) reaching a depth of 90m (300 ft.). The domed subterranean space has rocks of many colors, a transparent lake and glistening stalactites, making for a strange and atmospheric space (www.montanheiros.com; ✆ **29/521-29-92;** open daily June–Sept 2–6pm, Mar–May 2:30–5pm; Tues, Wed, Fri and Sat Oct–Mar 2:30–5:30pm). Admission 8€, free for under 12 if accompanied by an adult. Nearby are walkways among bubbling sulfur pits, a reminder that the volcanos are still active. The same ticket will also give you access to another cave, up high on the Santa Barbara volcano in the west of the island called **Gruta do Natal ★** where mass is held on Christmas Eve. Access is harder here (visitors must wear hard hats), but volcano buffs will love following tracks made by lava flows.

To admire Terceira's volcanic landscape from the outside, visit the **Santa Barbara Natural Reserve ★★** with its unique cloud-forest vegetation and sweeping views across to other islands in the central group, or the **Miradouro da Serra do Cume ★★★** which offers the best view of all from the 15km (9-mile) rim of an extinct volcano. Below are endless green meadows divided by black stone walls.

Biscoitos ★

A scenic road runs north from Angra over the highland heart of the island to the north coast village of Biscoitos. On the way you'll past dairy herds that remind you that there are more head of cattle than people on Terceira. Higher up **black bulls** graze semi wild, the stars of the island's bull running tradition. Biscoitos has two claims to fame: bathing and **wine.** Both involved the jagged basalt rock that covers the landscape. On the coast, **natural rock pools** are famed spot for a dip in Atlantic waters warmed by the Gulf Stream. Just inland, vines grow clinging to black stone walls producing distinctive white wines that match well with local seafood.

DON'T HURT THE bull

Terceira's form of bullfighting is called *tourada à corda* and takes place across the island from April to September. Unlike Spanish bullfighting where the animal is killed, or the mainland Portuguese version where bulls survive but are stabbed with spears, the bulls are not harmed in Terceira—although human participants certainly risk injury. It works like this: village males known as *pastores* will select four bulls from one of the island's herds. On the chosen day, the animals are set loose on the main street. Reckless locals will test their manhood by baiting the bulls with rags, umbrellas and their sheer bravado, aiming to get as close as possible without getting railroaded by a ton of raging flesh. Teams of *pastores* try (with limited success) to restrain the animal at the end of a long rope. The mayhem provides amusement for spectators who look on with beer and street food from a safe(ish) distance.

Along the coast at the village of **Quatro Ribeiras** is one of the most beautiful ***impérios*** ★★★—small chapel-like constructions that are sprinkled around the island and are often painted in brilliant colors. They are used by local brotherhoods who celebrate the Holy Spirit by carrying out charitable work and organizing festivities in the weeks following Easter. There are more than 70 such buildings on Terceira. Quatro Ribeiras' was built in 1885 and painted blue, yellow, and white. Other notable *impérios* can be found in **Figueiras do Paim** and **São Sebastião.**

FAIAL ★★

Separated from Pico by a narrow channel, Faial is slightly larger than New York's Staten Island and vaguely has the form of a turtle, its nose pointing westward. That nose grew by a couple of square kilometers (miles) in the 1950s, when a 13-month volcanic eruption spewed magma into the Atlantic. That desolate landscape is now a major attraction. In contrast are the lanes lined with hydrangeas which bloom through the summer and earn Faial its "blue island" tag. What draws most visitors, however, is the magnificent harbor of the capital Horta, a crossroads for transatlantic travelers with its bustling marina and the legendary sailors' bar **Peter Café Sport.** Faial has a long history of relations with the United States. Its menfolk served on New England whalers in Moby Dick days; Pan Am clippers paused here on their way to Europe and thousands of islanders emigrated across the ocean. Heading the other way, the Dabney family arrived from Boston in 1806 and had a major impact on the history and culture of the island.

Horta ★★★

Drive to Horta's waterfront from the airport and the first thing that strikes you is the **view** ★★★. Beyond the harbor, just 8km (5 miles) of strait separate Faial from Pico and its volcano rising up 2,000 meters over the ocean. It is an awe-inspiring site.

The word horta means vegetable garden in Portuguese, but the city actually gets its name from **Josse van Huerter,** a Flemish nobleman who the king of Portugal named as first governor of the island in 1468. Many islanders are descended from the Flemish settlers he brought with him. Horta soon developed as an important trading post for the Portuguese empire but was vulnerable to attack from pirates and rival powers. Sir Walter Raleigh sacked the city in 1597 when it was under Spanish rule.

The main fortress, now a luxury hotel (p. 456) and many of the striking black and white stone churches and mansions of the city date from that period. The old city looks little changed since Mark Twain passed through in 1867, noting: "No village could look prettier or more attractive."

Even after the age of sail, Horta remained an important international center for the laying and maintenance of transatlantic cables and for flying boats that would land to refuel in the harbor. Today it remains a cosmopolitan place. You'll hear a babble of languages in the streets, bars and restaurants thanks to the **marina ★★**, which is a favorite for yachters who make it one of the world's busiest. Tradition has it that passing crews have to leave their mark, so the harbor walls and walkways are painted with an extraordinary collection of designs recalling the passage of mariners from Norway to New Zealand and just about every port between.

Since 1918, sailors have whetted their whistles in the mythical **Peter Café Sport ★★★** (p. 443). Above the cafe is the fascinating **Scrimshaw Museum ★★** which contains one of the best collections of inked and engraved sperm whale teeth, an art form that developed and thrived among whalers and sailors in the 19th century. Some of the scrimshaws collected over the years by the family of the original "Peter" who still owns the bar show a high-level of artistry. Grimmer reminders of Faial's whaling past can be found in the modern **Fábrica da Baleia museum ★** which opened in 2018. It's set in the restored waterfront "whale factory" and tells in gruesome detail how, for over 100 years, sperm whales were harpooned, butchered and processed into oil and meal. Hunting continued here until the 1980s. The museum tells of the bravery of the men who risked their lives to hunt the whales in small open boats but is also focused on contemporary efforts to preserve the gentle mammals and the rest of the Azores sea life. Admission 4€; 2€ for over-65s and children 7 to 14; free under 6s (www.oma.pt; ✆ **29/229-21-40;** open daily 10am–6pm Apr–Sept; Mon–Fri 10am–5pm Oct–Mar.).

Today, **whale-watching ★★★** is big on the island. A number of operators organize boat trips, including the owners of Peter's bar, which runs twice daily 4-hour trips, or whale-watching holidays of up to a week.

The old whaling station sits on the edge of **Porto Pim bay ★★** whose crescent of gently sloping sand offers the city's best bathing and some of the best views of Pico.

Capelinhos ★★

Faial's verdant scenery changes dramatically when you head out to its western extremity. The cape here remains marked by the 1957-8 volcanic eruption that created a new headland of 2.4 sq. km (1 sq. mile). It's a desolate, dramatic sight where a ruined lighthouse looms out of the ash and lava. Gradually plant life is taking hold creating a feel of primeval life. There are hiking trails around the now dormant volcano starting from the lighthouse which holds an award-winning visitors' center (http://parquesnaturais.azores.gov.pt; ✆ **29/220-04-70;** the center is open daily Apr–Oct 10am–6pm; and from Nov–Mar Tues–Fri 10am–5pm, Sat–Sun 2–5:30pm). Admission is 10€; 5€ for over-65s and children 7 to 14; free for under 6s.

Cabeço Gordo ★★

"Fat Head" is the island's highest mountain at 1,045m (3,422 ft.). On days when it's not covered by clouds there are magnificent views over Faial and the neighboring islands. You can also look down into the swampy bottom of the volcanic **caldera.** There are places around here where steam and warm water still bubble to the surface as a reminder that the volcano may be dormant but is by no means dead. There are plenty of viewing points and hiking trails. On the way up or down, take the road between Cabouco and Ribeirinha which, in summer, is flanked by some of the most exuberant displays of the **hydrangeas ★★** (aka hortensias) for which the "blue island" is famed.

PICO ★★★

Pico is unlike the other islands. It is dominated by the brooding cone of Portugal's highest mountain. Mount Pico surges menacingly out of the ocean for 2,351 meters (7,713 ft.). The mountain is a constantly changing spectacle, at times invisible behind a shroud of clouds, at times poking above the cloud cover, or reflecting the light in tones of green, black or mauve. The Azores' second-largest island's trilogy of attractions is made up of volcanos, wine and whales. Its wine-growing area is a UNESCO World Heritage Site, and its former whaling villages are now centers for whale watching. There's an airport connecting to other islands, but the best way to arrive is by the 30-minute ferry crossing from Horta.

The Vineyard Landscapes ★★★

Drive south on the coast road from the island capital of Madalena and you are quickly among the unique Pico wine-growing landscape. The vines grow among hundreds of tiny plots (*currais*) divided by dry-stone walls made from pilling up the volcanic rock that cover much of the island. The black stone reflects the heat and mitigates the effect of sea breezes, giving a special taste to the wines. Areas around the villages of **Criação Velha** and **Candelaria** are among the most striking, with the vineyards between the volcano and the sea. For the perfect Instagram moment, head to the scarlet-painted Moinho do Frade **windmill** amid the *lajido* (lava field) of Criação Velha. Pico has been growing wines since the 15th century and nectars where once exported to the czars of Russia. These days there are almost 1,000 hectares (almost 2,500 acres) under cultivation. Its crisp whites and fortified sweet wines are the best. There's a **Wine Museum ★** in Madalena housed in a 17th-century convent and surrounded by vines and dragon trees (http://museu-pico.azores.gov.pt; ✆ **29/262-21-47;** open Tues–Sun: Apr–Sept, 10am–5pm; Oct–Mar 9:30am–5pm; free admission).

THE smaller ISLANDS

Santa Maria is the westernmost Island. It's green and mountainous, but in many ways the least Azorean-looking. Its whitewashed houses with their painted windows and high chimneys look distinctly Algarvean. Like the Algarve, it has fine beaches: **Praia Formosa** is considered the best in the archipelago. It also has the Azores' mildest climate and sea temperatures, warmer than the Algarve.

São Jorge is spectacular. Crocodile-shaped, its coast is comprised of high cliffs topped by a long, narrow plateau. Most people live on small flat areas at the bottom of the cliffs known as *fajãs.* Its cows produce the region's best cheese, which can be pungently parmesan-like. Tinned tuna and Europe's only coffee plantation are other specialties. **Fajã da Caldeira de Santo Cristo** is a stunningly beautiful bathing spot.

North of Terceira, **Graciosa** is the least-visited of the central group, despite its name which means "elegantly beautiful." The whitewashed capital **Santa Cruz** is a delight: It makes excellent wines and pastries, and is 100% run on renewable energy.

The two islands in the remote western group lie about 230km (140 miles) from Faial and are technically part of the American continent. Many consider **Flores** (pop. 3,800) to be the most beautiful island, with its soaring peaks, forested ravines and abundance of lakes and waterfalls. Its star attraction is the **Poça da Alagoinha** where over a dozen parallel waterfalls cascade into a dark, green lake. Finally, **Corvo,** the smallest, remotest island, is inhabited by just 450 people. There's only one road heading from the tiny capital **Vila do Corvo** to the lake-filled volcanic crater at the island's heart.

Mount Pico ★★★

The giant volcano last erupted in 1720, leaving swathes of land covered with black lava which islanders call *mistérios* (mysteries). It's dormant but getting to the top is a challenge.

You can go halfway up by car. At the end of the road is the **Mountain's House** (*Casa da Montanha*) visitor center (http://parquesnaturais.azores.gov.pt; ✆ **96/730-35-19**). Hiking from there to the summit and back is a demanding 7 to 9 hours. If you're feeling fit enough, you have to pay a 20€ fee for the summit, or 15€ to the crater rim. There's an additional 10€ fee for camping overnight on the peak. Staff give you a tracking device in case of trouble but, be warned, there's a 1,000€ fee for rescues. Stick to the trail, which is marked by 47 poles leading to the top, and you should be okay. There's a limit of 160 people at any one time, so it's best to arrive early.

You can reserve a slot by booking an **authorized guide** through outfits such as **Épico** (http://epico.uractive.com; ✆ **96/295-61-96**) whose fees start at 50€, or **Fonte Travel** (www.bookingpico.com; ✆ **29/267-95-05**) from 60€ per person. Most guides also offer night-time climbs for a higher price.

If the weather is erratic everywhere in the Azores, it is doubly so on the mountain. You will need warm clothes and sturdy shoes. The peak gets covered with snow in winter and is always much colder than on the coast. After all those warnings, the rewards can be immense, with clear weather providing fabulous views across to all the islands of the central Azores.

The Mountain's House is open June to September daily 24 hours; in May and October 8am to 8pm; and November to April 8am to 6pm. If you're content to contemplate the peak from a distance, the EN3 road known locally as the ***longitudinal*** ★★ offers great views, particularly from the little **Lagoa do Capitão** lake.

Lajes do Pico ★

This little town on the south coast is all about whales. Up until 1987 it was a whaling port where local men would rush to little boats and grab their harpoons when pods were spotted offshore. Now it is a world-renowned center for **whale watching** ★★★.

Frenchman Serge Viallelle played a key role in the turnaround, hooking up with former whalers to set up the first whale watching trips and to monitor and protect the marine environment. His **Espaço Talassa** (www.espacotalassa.com; ✆ **29/267-20-10**) base remains one of the best whale-watching operations. Based on Lajes quayside, its offer ranges from 3-hour trips starting at 39€ to weeklong trips for over 1,000€, tracking the biggest species as they migrate in April. Springtime is best for the big whales, but there are also dolphins and sperm whales. Viallelle has a 98% success rate in spotting whale or dolphins on his trips but warns that bad weather forces around one-in-ten trips to be cancelled.

Just around the corner on a row of old boat houses, the excellent **Museu dos Baleeiros** ★★ or whalers' museum traces the history of an industry that left a deep mark on the culture of the island (http://museu-pico.azores.gov.pt; ✆ **29/262-21-47;** open Tues–Sun: Apr–Sept, 10am–5pm; Oct–Mar 9:30am–5pm; free admission).

Where to Stay

Since the Azores are relative newcomers to tourism, they lack Madeira's range of options, but a recent expansion ensures there's a good selection from luxury hotels to eco-resorts and heritage homes converted into boutique accommodations.

SÃO MIGUEL

Hotel do Colégio ★★ Smack in the historic center of Ponta Delgada, the heart of this boutique option sits pretty in a mansion built at the height of the island's 19th-century orange exporting boom. More rooms were added after a 2017 makeover. Many have a musically themed decor, including traditional instruments on display, to recall its previous use as a music school. The cozy lounge features an arched ceiling made from black local stone. The pool built into the school's former recreation yard is a haven of peace in the city. Refined cuisine based on Azorean products is the signature of the restaurant, which has become a firm local favorite.

R. Carvalho Araújo 39, Ponta Delgada. www.hoteldocolegio.pt. ✆ **29/630-66-00.** 59 units. 65€–165€ double. Limited free parking. **Amenities:** Restaurants; bars; outdoor pool; free Wi-Fi.

Pedras do Mar ★★ Opened in 2016, this five-star option occupies a four-story bloc perched on the clifftop on an open stretch of the north coast. Natural materials abound, including cork cladding, volcanic stone features and wall panels of locally grown Japanese cedar in the rooms. It's worth paying extra for a sea-view room filled with natural light and enjoying infinite balcony views. The glass-walled bathroom is great for soaking in the tub with a view, less so for privacy. There's an outdoor pool in gardens overlooking the ocean and a small indoor pool downstairs in the spa. An excellent breakfast features local produce—go for island cheese on toasted *bolo lêvado* flatbreads.

Rua da Terça, 3, Fenais da Luz. www.pedrasdomar.com. ✆ **29/624-93-00.** 92 units. 85€–240€ double; 116€–315€ suite. Free parking. **Amenities:** Restaurants; bar; playground; health club and spa; indoor and outdoor pools; tennis; bike rental; terrace; free Wi Fi.

Santa Barbara Eco Beach Resort ★★★ The coolest place on the island was built in 2015 by a pair of buddies who fell in love with the Azores. It's constructed of natural materials: Japanese cedar, volcanic stone, cork cladding from mainland Portugal. Spacious villas and studios all have kitchens and living spaces. There are tables carved from logs, handwoven throws and rugs, natural stone bathrooms. But the decor is overshadowed by the views. The single-story structures are integrated into a low cliff overlooking one of the Azores' best beaches, a kilometer-long stretch of soft grey sand that's renowned for its surf (there's a surf school next to the resort). Aside from the regular infinity pool, some of the studios enjoy outdoor Jacuzzies on their private terraces. In the seafront restaurant and bar, you can eat sushi made from Azorean fish, sip local white wines, and be thankful you're here.

Estrada Regional 1, 1 Morro de Baixo, Ribeira Seca. www.santabarbaraazores.com. ✆ **29/29/647-03-60.** 26 units. 119€–388€ 1-bedroom villa for 2; 180€–355€ studio. Free parking. **Amenities:** Restaurant; bar; beach club; outdoor pools; garden; terrace; bike hire; massage service; free Wi-Fi.

Terra Nostra Garden Hotel ★★★ A dreamy spot tucked away in tropical gardens by the thermal resort of Furnas, the hotel was built in the 1930s and its core retains the Art Deco style. The surrounding park was created 200 years ago by a merchant from Boston who built a hideaway known as Yankee House. Plants from around the world thrive here around a splendid thermal pool naturally heated at 37°C (99°F) and tinted red by its flow through underground minerals. Rooms are in soft earth tones with murals that reflect the flowers and ferns outside.

Rua Padre José Jacinto Botelho, 5, Furnas. www.terranostra-gardenhotel.com. ✆ **29/654-90-90.** 86 units. 102€–329€ double; 298€–426€ suite. Free parking. **Amenities:** Restaurant; bar; spa; games room; garden; bike hire; fitness room; thermal pools; indoor and outdoor swimming pools; garden; free Wi-Fi.

TERCEIRA

Pousada Forte Angra do Heroísmo ★★ Plunge into history with a stay at this 16th-century fortress guarding the bay to Angra. Over the years it fought off French and English corsairs, including Sir Francis Drake. The British set up a strategic base here during WWII. Converted into a hotel in 2006, its modern rooms open up over the garden and pool within the ramparts and most enjoy glorious views up the coast. Decor combines soft grey stone matching the local volcanic basalt combined with natural wood floors and furnishings. The sober, stone theme continues in the well-equipped bathrooms. There's a cozy bar and garden terrace. If you check out too early for breakfast in the award-winning restaurant, staff will make up a lunchbox with sandwiches and fresh fruit. It's a short walk to the harbor and downtown.

Rua do Castelinho. www.pousadas.pt. ✆ **29/540-35-60.** 29 units. 80€–190€ double. Free parking. **Amenities:** Restaurant; bar; outdoor pool; garden; free Wi-Fi.

Quinta das Mercês★★ In a neighborhood packed with posh mansions dating from Angra's golden age as a staging post on the spice routes to the Orient, this aristocratic 16th-century country house stands out. Its mustard-and-white walls overlook the Atlantic amid 3.5 hectares (8.6 acres) of gardens, through which you can wander to the ocean-view pool or the tennis court. Rooms are decorated period style with cream tones and floral motives. Furniture harks back to the Portuguese Dona Maria style of the late 18th century. Impeccable service and discretion have made this a hideaway for TV stars and European royalty.

Caminho De Baixo, São Mateus. www.quintadasmerces.com. ✆ **29/564-25-88.** 13 units. 115€–140€ double; Free parking. **Amenities:** Outdoor pool; garden; dinner on request; Jacuzzi; fitness room; bike hire; tennis; free Wi-Fi.

Terceira Mar ★★ This is all about wide horizons. The spacious rooms all have balconies looking out over the Atlantic, the view framed by the wooded slopes and mighty fortress of Monte Brasil. Opened in the 1980s, its style is a little dated but the panoramas more than compensate, especially from the sweeping terrace of the bar, or the lawns that surround the sizable seafront pool. There's a basement gym and small indoor pool too. It's popular with European tour groups and with Azorean-Americans visiting the old country. It's a 15-minute walk into Angra's historic center.

Portões de São Pedro, 1 Angra do Heroísmo. www.bestazoreshotels.com. ✆ **29/540-22-80.** 139 units. 59€–146€ double. **Amenities:** Indoor and outdoor pool; gym; sauna; Jacuzzi; garden; parking; restaurant; bar; free Wi-Fi.

FAIAL

Hotel Do Canal ★ This modern harborside hotel features four stories in while wash and basalt. Rooms are spacious with cotton sheets, comfy fabric-covered armchairs, and rather ugly carpets. It's worth paying extra to get an ocean-view room with a balcony looking across the strait to Pico Mountain. The lobby is dominated with a map showing vintage Pan Am routes and a model Clipper flying boat, a reminder of the days when Horta was a crucial stopping off point for transatlantic flights. The buffet breakfast features local cheeses and harbor views.

Largo Dr. Manuel de Arriaga, Horta. www.bensaude.pt. ✆ **29/220-21-20.** 103 units. 50€–170€ double. Free parking. **Amenities:** Restaurant; bar with terrace; gym; spa; parking; free Wi-Fi.

Pousada Forte da Horta ★★ Part of the pousada chain of historic hotels, this one is set in a 16th-century fortress, a veteran of battles with Spanish armadas and raids by English corsairs, including Sir Walter Raleigh who attacked in 1597. Today its ivy-covered ramparts shelter a haven of peace, immensely comfortable (even if the decor is a little dated). The poolside lawns and many of the rooms offer great views of Horta's colorful marina and the looming summit of Pico Mountain across the channel.

Rua Vasco da Gama, Horta. www.pousadas.pt. ✆ **21/040-76-70.** 28 units. 80€–240€ double. Free parking. **Amenities:** Restaurant; bar with terrace; outdoor pool; game room; free Wi-Fi.0

PICO

Aldeia da Fonte ★★★ A magical place on the south coast of the island, this hamlet of traditional homes is constructed from black volcanic rocks hidden among the dense, semi-tropical forest that clings to the steeply sloping shoreline. Standard rooms are simple, but all offer views over the ocean or the lush surrounding vegetation. Paths twist through the trees leading to the cliff-top pool, or stairs cut into the rock enabling guests to swim in the hotel's own bay. There's an excellent bar and restaurant where locals and visitors mingle beneath a canopy of plane trees to sip Pico wines and eat divine local food—try the octopus stewed in spiced white wine, followed by honey cake with lemon sorbet.

Caminho de Baixo, Lajes do Pico. www.aldeiadafonte.com. ✆ **29/262-91-35.** 8 units. 72€–104€ double; 124€–150€ suite. Free parking. **Amenities:** Restaurant; bar; exercise room; sauna; outdoor pools; garden; private ocean access; free Wi-Fi.

Pocinho Bay ★★ Between the ocean and Pico's UNESCO World Heritage wine landscape, this island of tranquility is comprised of traditional basalt homes tastefully decorated using bare wood and ethnic arts from the Azores and way beyond. It has a village atmosphere set amid 3 hectares of waterfront gardens. The rooms have views of the sea or of Pico Mountain. Extra luxury was added in 2018 with a two-bedroom villa featuring a fireplace and private outdoor Jacuzzi.

Pocinho do Monte, Monte. www.pocinhobay.com. ✆ **29/267-95-00.** 8 units. 155€–215€ double; 490€–545€ 2-room villa/cottage. Free parking. **Amenities:** Bar, outdoor pool; garden; free Wi-Fi.

Whale'come ao Pico ★ If whale watching is what you've come for, this is the place. It's run by Frenchman Serge Viallelle who arrived in the 1980s and played a key role in the Azores switch from hunting to observing the marine mammals (p. 455). The quayside hotel is part of his Talassa Center which organizes the whale watching trips. The ground floor cafe and breakfast room is a meeting place for the international whale following community in Lajes. Offering simple, affordable accommodation in rooms featuring while linen and bare stone walls, they also have traditional homes to rent in and around the village.

Rua dos Baleeiros, Lajes do Pico. www.espacotalassa.com. ✆ **29/267-95-00.** 12 units. 43€–81€ double. **Amenities:** Bar, snacks; free Wi-Fi.

Where to Eat

Foodies will love the Azores. The surrounding seas teem with fish, from exotic species integral to the islanders' diet to familiar tunas, octopus, and swordfish. Cattle-raising is key to the economy, producing excellent beef and fine cheeses, particularly in São Jorge. Fresh fruit abounds, including pineapple on São Miguel, bananas and Pico blackberries. There's a rich tradition of cinnamon-scented pastry dating back to the spice trading days, and some crisp white wines are produced on Pico's volcanic slopes.

SÃO MIGUEL

Alcides ★★ AZOREAN/PORTUGUESE A meeting place for Ponta Delgado gastronomes since 1956, this elegant dining room in the heart of the old city is famed above all for its steak, served the way they like it here with lots of garlic and spicy *pimenta da terra* sauce. Still run by the founder's family, its treatment of local seafood is also renowned with dishes like baked forkbeard (*abrótea*) with new and sweet potatoes, or fried tuna with onion. Start out with an appetizer of blood sausage served with São Miguel pineapple.

R. Hintze Ribeiro 67, Ponta Delgada. www.casavelharestaurant.com. ✆ **29/628-26-77.** Mains 9€–21€. Mon–Sat Daily noon–3pm and 7–10pm.

Associação Agrícola de São Miguel ★★ AZOREAN Sometimes it's best to go to the source. São Miguel's farmers' association set up this restaurant to showcase their products, principally beef. It's a big, modern room with raw wood paneling and huge wickerwork lampshades hanging overhead. Service is brisk and efficient. Ask the waiter to pick you a hearty red from the vast selection of Portuguese wines. Steak is the thing here. You can choose your cut, weight and preparation. If you're brave enough, go for a monster 400g (14 oz.) slab served "association style"—swimming in a white-wine, garlic, and red pepper sauce. For dessert, try a pudding make from local tea.

Recinto da Feira, Campo de Santana, Ribeira Grande. www.restauranteaasm.com. ✆ **29/649-00-01.** Mains 9€–25€. Daily noon–11pm.

Õtaka ★★ JAPANESE/PERUVIAN An exotic new star in Ponta Delgada's bubbling restaurant scene, Õtaka takes the best Azorean seafood ingredients and turns them into dishes reflecting the Japanese-Peruvian Nikkei tradition made internationally famous by the Nobo chain. It's best to reserve ahead, because fans are lining up for dishes like black cod with turnip greens and miso crush, or tuna tataki with jalapeño ponzu. To get the full experience go for one of the tasting menus offering 7 to 10 courses.

Rua Hintze Ribeiro 5, Ponta Delgada. http://otaka-restaurant.negocio.site. ✆ **91/931-20-80.** Mains 9€–25€. Tues–Sat 7–10:30pm.

Vale Das Furnas ★★★ AZOREAN *Cozido* is Portugal's national dish. Every region has its own take on this one-pot boiled dinner of meat, sausage, and vegetables, but nothing beats the unique version in the thermal resort of Furnas. Here the mix is slow-cooked for hours in pits dug into the ground, where volcano-heated water bubbles and boils. Flavors blend to perfection, meats are fork-cutting tender. Volcano-cooked *cozido* is a magnet for mainland tourists, but while many places heave with coach-trippers, this place—in the local campsite—keeps its character and its flavors. Views of the cedar-covered slopes are a bonus.

EN1-1A, Parque de Campismo, Furnas. www.casavelharestaurant.com. ✆ **29/658-43-07.** Mains 9€–14€. Daily 9am–10pm.

TERCEIRA

Beira Mar ★★★ AZOREAN Overlooking the pretty fishing harbor of São Mateus, a short, scenic drive from Angra, this bustling local favorite serves the island's freshest seafood. Choose your main from the catch of the day displayed by the kitchen. Local species like *goraz* (blackspot seabream) or *lírio* (greater amberjack) will be grilled to perfection. To start try seafood soup served in a hollowed out loaf, or *cracas*, local barnacles that need careful extraction from their rocky shells. The rooms and terrace are almost always full, so book in advance.

Canada do Porto, São Mateus da Calheta. ✆ **29/564-23-92.** Reservations advised. Mains 7€–15€. Tues-Sun noon–3pm and 6:30–11pm.

O Chico ★★ AZOREAN/PORTUGUESE This no-nonsense family-run restaurant serves traditional cooking in a simple, tile-lined dining room decorated with period photo and the occasional framed fish. Locals recommend the *alcatra*, a Terceira specialty of beef cooked slowly in a clay pot with white wine. If you prefer seafood (since the Atlantic is a couple of steps away), their battered fillets of forkbeard (a local favorite that's related to hake) is excellent. It fills up quickly with locals and visitors from the Portuguese mainland and doesn't take reservations.

Rua São João 7, Angra do Heroísmo. ✆ **29/533-32-86.** No reservations. Mains 7€–12€. Mon-Sat noon–3pm and 6:30–11pm.

Tasca das Tias ★ AZOREAN/PORTUGUESE "Aunties' Tavern" was opened up in 2014 by a group of friends who came together to cook up snacks for a local festival. It's now a firm fixture in one of Angra's historic central streets. The contemporary decor features wooden tables and floor-to-ceiling photos of smiling local old timers. There's a good snack (*petisco*) menu that includes garlicky grilled limpets (*lapas*) or a selection of Azorian cheeses (tangy São Jorge is best). More substantial mains include

Azores-style tuna and a range of steak cuts. Relaxed cosmopolitan atmosphere; service with a smile.

Rua São João 117, Angra do Heroísmo. ✆ **29/562-80-62.** Mains 10€–19€. Daily 11:30am–11:30pm.

FAIAL

Café Sport "Peter's Bar" ★★★ AZOREAN/INTERNATIONAL Simply a legend, the world's most famous sailors' bar has been a joyous meeting place for transatlantic travelers since 1918. The polished wood interior has walls and ceiling covered with yachting memorabilia left by generations of seadogs from around the world. The bar is globally renowned for its gin & tonics and now has its own passionfruit-infused gin. They also serve tasty, uncomplicated local food which you can enjoy in the bar or on the harborside terrace overlooking Pico Mountain. Dishes include black pudding and spicy sausage served with yams or fried blue jack mackerel (*chicharros*) with sweet potatoes and a vinegary sauce. There's live music on Friday and Saturday nights.

Rua José Azevedo (Peter), 9, Horta. ✆ **29/229-23-27.** Main courses 8€–25€. Sun–Fri 8am–1am; Sat 8am–2am.

Genuíno ★★ AZOREAN In 2008, islander Genuino Madruga became only the 10th helmsman to sail solo round the world via Cape Horn. He returned from his wanderings with a boatload of souvenirs and a longing for the traditional cooking of the Azores. The result is one of the archipelago's best-known restaurants. Its glass facade overlooks Porto Pim bay; its walls and tables are decorated with mementos picked up on his two circumnavigations; and the menu's loaded with beef raised on the islands' green pastures and fish scooped from offshore waters. Fried tuna with a tart, peppery sauce and sweet potato, and grilled swordfish are among the tastiest offerings. Try yam pudding for desert and citric Pico white wines. The old salt himself will likely be on hand to share a yarn as you settle the check.

Areinha Velha, 9, Horta. www.genuino.pt. ✆ **29/270-15-42.** Reservations advised. Mains 9€–31€. Thurs–Tues noon–3pm and 6:30–10pm.

PICO

Ancoradouro ★★ AZOREAN/PORTUGUESE Pico's best-known restaurant enjoys a splendid south-coast location amid the vineyards looking out across the sea to Faial. As the waves lap against the rocks outside tuck into freshly grilled catch of the day, or dishes like parrot fish (*veja*) with almonds and tuna stew (*caldeirada de atum*). The dining room is modern and light-filled, with shelves showcasing local wines and old photos recalling the islands piscatorial past.

Rua Rodrigo Guerra 7, Areia Larga. ✆ **29/262-34-90.** Reservations advised. Mains 14€–18€. Tues–Sun noon–3pm and 7–10pm.

Cella Bar ★ AZOREAN/INTERNATIONAL Worth a visit for the award-winning architecture alone, made of part traditional volcanic-stone house, part avant-garde shack with planks curved to resemble wine barrels. The views across the channel to Faial are breathtaking, especially from the terrace on sunny days. It's a wine bar, wine shop, late-night drinking joint and a restaurant serving full meals and snacks. For a light lunch at weekends, try the fish soup or grilled *linguiça* sausage with puréed yam. As well as local wines, they serve Azorean craft beers.

Lugar da Barca, Madalena. www.facebook.com/cellabar. ✆ **29/262-36-54.** Mains 8€–20€. Mon–Thurs 4pm–midnight; Fri 4pm–2am; Sat noon–2am; Sun noon–midnight.

Lagoa ★ AZOREAN/PORTUGUESE A simple, family place by the harbor of the old whaling town of Lajes do Pico, the dining room here is bright and decorated with glossy color photos of island life. There's a hearty all-you-can-eat buffet with local favorites like *alcatra* beef stew or deep-fired forkbeard fish (*abrótea*). If you go a la carte, ask for the catch of the day and tuck into expertly grilled local critters like offshore rockfish (*bagre*) or blue jack mackerel (*chicharro*).

Rua de São Pedro, Lajes Do Pico. ✆ **29/267-22-72.** Mains 8€–16€. Daily noon–midnight.

Azores Sports

DEEP-SEA FISHING As the peaks of huge underwater mounts where sea depts plunge to 1,000m very close to shore, the Azores offer excellent conditions for sports fishing. Marlin and tuna are the main targets. Fishing charters operate in the main ports. **Oceanic** (www.azores-oceanic.com; ✆ **96/6783101**) on the waterfront in Horta operate a sustainable catch-and-release approach to game fishing and monitors marine life in collaboration with the University of the Azores.

GOLF There are three courses in the Azores. The oldest and most-renowned is **Furnas Golf** (✆ **29/658-46-51**) on São Miguel, whose first nine holes were designed by renowned Scottish architect Philip Mackenzie Ross. It sweeps through an undulating valley surrounded by Japanese cedar and other exotic trees. The 27-hole **Batalha Golf** (✆ **29/649-85-59**) course also on São Miguel offers long, broad tree-lined fairways. For information on both: www.azoresgolfislands.com. The **Terceira Island Golf Club** (www.terceiragolf.com; ✆ **29/590-24-44**) was originally built for military personal on the nearby U.S. base at Lajes. It's considered the least challenging in the archipelago.

SWIMMING Portuguese from the mainland tend to be a bit sniffy about the black or greyish beaches formed by the Azores' volcanic nature. Yet there are some outstanding beaches on the islands. **Praia Formosa** on Santa Maria is many people's favorite, but **Praia de Caloura** on the south coast of São Miguel and the surfer hangout of **Areal de Santa Bárbara** on the north shore are both excellent, as are the gentle sands of Praia **de Porto Pim** on Faial. There are also dozens of bathing spots built into rocky shorelines, notably the lava pools at **Biscoitos** on the north coast of Terceira. Thanks to the Gulf Stream, water temperatures are generally warmer than on the mainland.

Bathers should watch out for **jellyfish,** particularly the purple Portuguese man o' war, which packs a painful sting. Because they are brightly colored and float on the surface, they are usually easy to spot.

Shopping

The islands have a rich tradition of embroidery, basketmaking and ceramics. In Ponta Delgada and particularly the center of Angra, there are souvenir shops offering such things, but be careful to get the genuine article. The regional government has an "**Artesanato dos Açores**" brand for island-produced material handicrafts. Among the authentic places is the **Cerâmica Vieira** factory in Lagoa (✆ **29/691-21-16**), on the south coast of São Miguel, that has been producing distinctive blue-and-white pottery since 1892; and **Açorbordados,** selling hand-embroidered linen in Angra (✆ **29/521-42-39**).

Culinary souvenirs abound, from **tea** (p. 448) and **pineapple**-derived products (p. 447) from São Miguel, to **cheese** from São Jorge and other islands (p. 454), or **Pico wines** (p. 453). Another original gift is canned fish, which you can buy in stores around the islands, online or at the source, such as the **Santa Catarina** cannery on São Jorge (www.atumsantacatarina.com; ✆ **29/541-62-20**).

To remember your trip to the world's greatest sailor's bar, **Peter Café Sport** (p. 443) has a number of outlets selling nautical clothing with their whale logo, passion-fruit flavored gin and other products in Angra and Ponta Delgada, as well as next to the bar in Horta (✆ **29/239-18-37**). Farther up the Horta harbor front, the **Oceanic** store sells extraordinary prints of Azores marine life drawn by graphic artist Les Gallagher (www.azores-oceanic.com; ✆ **96/678-31-01**). The multilingual guide to local fish is practical as well as beautiful, if you plan to navigate local seafood menus.

If you don't want to haul your Azores gifts home, Terceira-based **Made In Azores** (www.madeinazores.eu) sells island goodies online.

Azores Entertainment & Nightlife

The Azores are more for strolling under the starlight rather than carousing the night away, but there is some interesting nightlife, mainly in Ponta Delgada. **Raiz Club** which blends hot cocktails with an eclectic mix of life music and DJs, is the best known in the city center (www.facebook.com/raizclube; ✆ **96/691-94-10;** open Tues–Thurs 10pm–3am; Fri–Sat 10pm–5:30am). More chilled is **Lava Jazz** with drinks, snacks and regular live shows (www.lava jazz.com; ✆ **91/735-04-18;** open Tues 6–10pm, Wed–Thurs 6–11:45pm, Fri 6pm–1am; Sat 8pm–1am).

On Horta, **Peter Café Sport** (p. 443) is a natural nightlife focus with regular live music on Fridays and Saturdays starting 11pm. There's also a lively scene, craft beers, and weekend bands up the road amid the splendid natural wood decor at **Oceanic** (www.azores-oceanic.com; ✆ **96/678-31-01;** open Sun–Thurs 6pm–2am and Fri–Sat 6pm–4am).

Ponta Delgada's **Teatro Micaelense** (www.teatromicaelense.pt; ✆ **29/6 30-83-50**) is a major cultural institution with music, dance and theater performances that bring in top performers from the Portuguese mainland and beyond as well as promoting local talent. The regional capital also got a **casino** in 2017, situated in the **Azor Hotel** (www.azorhotel.com; ✆ **29/624-99-00**) in the modern, oceanfront Portas do Mar neighborhood. It spins Sunday to Thursday 6pm to 1am, Friday and Saturday 6pm to 3am.

Several islands host summer festivals of rock, jazz, and electronic music as well as local traditional celebrations that often involved carousing into the night. To check on what's on: www.agendacores.pt.

PLANNING YOUR TRIP

16

This chapter addresses the where, when, and how of visiting Portugal—all the logistics of putting your trip together and taking it on the road.

GETTING THERE

By Plane

Air transport to Portugal and its islands has increased dramatically in the last five years. **TAP Air Portugal, United Airlines, Delta,** and **Air Canada** are among those operating more flights to and from North America, and there has been a significant upsurge of flights from Brazil and European cities.

Portugal has five international airports: three on the mainland, the others on Madeira and the Azores. The biggest is Lisbon's **Aeroporto Humberto Delgado** (LIS; www.aeroportolisboa.pt). **Porto's Francisco Sá Carneiro Airpor**t is the second largest, serving the north (OPO; www.aeroportoporto.pt), followed by **Faro** (FAO; www.aeroportofaro.pt), gateway to the Algarve's beaches.

In the Azores, **João Paulo II Airport** (PDL; www.aeroportopontadelgada.pt), serving **Ponta Delgada,** the island, and **Lajes Airport** (TER: www.aerogarelajes.azores.gov.pt) on Terceira island have seen a big increase in traffic thanks to an opening up to European low-cost carriers. They also receive direct flights from North American cites, most frequently Boston and Toronto.

Madeira's recently renamed **Cristiano Ronaldo Madeira International Airport** (FNC, www.aeroportomadeira.pt) lies just outside the capital city of Funchal and is famous for its sea-level runway.

Most flights from North America land in Lisbon, which is operating at capacity. From the summer of 2020 Portuguese carrier **TAP Portugal** (www.flytap.com; ✆ **21/843-11-00**) was due to operate two daily roundtrip flights between Lisbon and New York's JFK and daily flights linking the Portuguese capital to Newark, Boston, Toronto, Chicago, and Washington, DC. They also have several flights per week from Miami and San Francisco, and a daily Newark-Porto service.

TAP is a member of the **Star Alliance** frequent flyer program, to which United Airlines and Air Canada also belong. TAP is also strong on African and Latin American routes, particularly to Brazil.

United flies to Lisbon direct from Newark and runs seasonal Lisbon-Washington and Porto-Newark flights; **Delta** flies to Lisbon from JFK and seasonally from Boston. **American Airlines** has seasonal flights from Philadelphia to the Portuguese capital. Portugal's **Azores Airlines** (www.azoresairlines.pt; ✆ **29/620-97-20**) also has flights from Boston to Lisbon and to Ponta Delgado.

Canada's **Air Transat** and, in season, **Air Canada Rouge,** operate flights to Portugal from Montreal and Toronto.

TAP operates a **stopover program** which enables travelers planning a two-stop vacation to spend up to 5 nights in Lisbon or Porto for no extra cost before flying on to another destination in Europe or Africa. The program also offers cut-rate prices at selected hotels, restaurants and attractions. Check out www.flytap.com for details. Azores Airlines runs a similar program for stopovers in the Atlantic islands.

Portugal is very well connected with flights to the rest of Europe. Lisbon, for example, has over 20 daily flights to London. Porto has a similar number of daily nonstop flights to Paris. Low-cost companies led by Ireland's **Ryanair** (www.ryanair.com) and Britain's **EasyJet** (www.easyjet.com) have many flights from cities around Europe to Portugal, making it easy and cheap to connect. Ryanair has flights from Lisbon to around 25 European destinations in 10 countries from as little as 15€.

Lisbon airport is conveniently close to the city center. There is a metro line heading into town and a convenient and relatively fast shuttle bus, which is not part of the regular bus network. There are plans to expand capacity at Humberto Delgado and to build a second Lisbon airport by 2022 at Montijo military base south of city. It should be linked by fast ferries across the River Tagus and dedicated bus lanes on the Vasco da Gama bridge

Porto airport also has good subway and bus links to the city center.

From Faro airport you can catch a city bus that connects the train and bus station, where you can catch lines running to resorts along the coast, if your hotel does not offer a pickup service.

If you are traveling in a group, taxis—which are relatively cheap compared to most other European countries—can be a convenient alternative without adding too much to the cost. For details, see regional chapters.

By Car

There are **fast highways** linking Portugal to the rest of Europe. If you are making the 2,180km (1,355-mile) drive from London to Lisbon, after crossing into France, you take the A16 and A28 *autoroutes* toward Rouen, then onward south via Le Mans and Tours. There, you join the A10 that takes you to Bordeaux, then the A63 to the Spanish border at Hendaye. From there, take the A8 along the Basque coast, before turning south to Burgos on the AP-1. From

Burgos, turn west on the A62 that takes you all the way to the Portuguese border via Valladolid and Salamanca. If you are heading to Porto and the north, turn off at Burgos onto the A231 towards León.

Beware that the French and northern Spanish highways can be very crowded at peak seasons, particularly in August, when vacationers head south. Especially long lines can build up at the toll booths on the *autoroute*.

From London, the trip will cost you around 120€ in **highway tolls** and 270€ in fuel. If you have time, you can avoid the toll roads, but it will add at least another day to your trip. There are plenty of splendid places—from the pastures of Normandy to the mountains of the Basque Country—where you can break the trip.

If you are driving to the Algarve, turn south at Salamanca toward Cáceres and Seville.

There is also a direct highway linking Madrid to Lisbon in 6½ hours.

One way of reducing the drive is by taking a car ferry from England to the north coast of Spain. **Brittany Ferries** (www.brittany-ferries.co.uk; ✆ **44 330 159 7000**) operates seven weekly crossings from Plymouth and Portsmouth on the English south coast to the Spanish ports of Santander and Bilbao. The crossing time is around 24 hours. From Santander, it's a 6-hour drive to Porto; 8 hours to Lisbon.

By Train

International rail connections are limited. Portuguese governments have been talking for years about building a high-speed train line that would link into the European system in Madrid, but the plans have yet to get off the drawing board.

You can travel on France's high-speed train network to Irun/Hendaye on the France-Spain border and connect with the **Sud Expresso** sleeper train that runs nightly to Lisbon, operated by the Portuguese rail company **CP** (www.cp.pt; ✆ **70/721-02-20**). The journey takes around 12 hours. There's a dining car and first-class private cabins for two with showers; cheaper berths are available in four-person cabins. One-way prices range from 69€ for a seat to 198€ for a "grand class" single cabin complete with private bathroom. Adult prices on the French **TGV** high-speed train from Paris to Hendaye start from 91€.

If you are coming from Madrid, the train can be a good option. The regular single tariff for the 10-hour Madrid-Lisbon overnight **Lusitania Comboio Hotel** ranges from 62.50€ to 180.50€, depending on whether you get a regular seat or a luxury sleeping berth. You can get promotional basic tickets for less than 25€.

Cut-rate ways of touring in Europe include **Eurail** (www.eurail.com) for non-European residents, and **Interrail** (www.interrail.eu) for European residents, which offers passes allowing for unlimited rail travel in a number of countries for a specific period of time. Eurail, for example, offers a family 10-day pass for two adults and two children for $910 that can be used over 2 months. Interrail has an adult monthly pass for up to 30 countries for 670€. There are discounts for young people and seniors.

By Bus

If you're not in a hurry or you really don't like flying, the bus can be a cheap alternative for getting to Portugal from other parts of Europe: for example, **Eurolines** (www.eurolines.com) has four daily buses leaving from Paris to Lisbon. The journey takes at least 22 hours; one-way adult tickets cost around 65€. **Alsa** (www.alsa.com) has several buses making the daily trip from Barcelona to Lisbon with a change in Madrid for around 50€, taking around 20 hours. To get an overview of routes and make bookings: www.checkmybus.com.

GETTING AROUND

By Car

Portugal has one of Europe's highest densities of motorways, most built in the last 30 years or so thanks to European Union investment funding. That means it's usually quick and easy to get between the main cities. Beyond them, drivers used to long, straight North American highways may find some of the narrower country roads and the intricate street patterns of city centers a challenge.

The fastest roads are ***autostradas,*** toll highways mostly four- or six-lane, linking the main cities. They are designated by an A; for example, the A1 links Lisbon to Porto via Coimbra and Aveiro, the A2 runs from the capital to the Algarve, the A3 heads north from Porto to Braga and on to the Spanish border at Valença, and so on.

Other major roads are designated *itinerários principais* (IP) or *itinerários complementares* (IC), which may involve sections of highway and stretches of single track. They mostly don't carry tolls. *Estradas nacionais* (EN) tend to be older roads, less used and replaced by highways, although many drivers prefer to use them to avoid tolls. *Estradas regionais* (R) connect smaller towns.

Confusingly for the uninitiated, Portugal has two types of **toll systems** on its roads. In the classic type, used, for example, on the A1 Lisbon-Porto autostrada or the A2 Lisbon-Algarve road, there are **toll booths** where you pick up a ticket when you enter and pay when you leave, either by handing over cash to a cashier or paying by credit card at a machine. Toll gates will usually have one or two lanes marked by green signs bearing a white V standing for **Via Verde.** They are reserved for vehicles fitted with automatic electronic toll collection, a system pioneered by Portugal in the 1990s. If you are renting a car in Portugal, check whether your vehicle is fitted with Via Verde. If it is, you won't have to stop to pay at toll gates, but the toll will be added to your rental bill.

In 2011, Portugal introduced an exclusively **electronic toll system** on a number of highways, including the A22 running east-west along the Algarve coast and the A25 leading to Aveiro from the Spanish frontier. Here there are no toll gates, but electronic sensors are posted over the road. Once again, if you are renting a car, you should check that it is equipped with a Via Verde mechanism so you can travel on these roads; most are, and in that case the tolls will be added to your rental bill. If you are driving into Portugal on a highway from Spain, the best way to deal with the system is to stop off at one of the **"Welcome Points"** just past the border posts and register your license plate and credit card. Tolls you incur will be charged directly to your card. Alternatively, you can buy a **pre-paid toll card** online on www.tollcard.pt, which will be activated by a cellphone text message. The highway authority explains the whole system at www.portugaltolls.com, and there is an information line at ✆ **70/750-05-01** from within Portugal or ✆ **+351 212 879 555** from outside.

Lisbon to Porto on the A1 costs around 22€ in tolls; Lisbon to Faro on the A2 and A22, 22.50€; and a trip along the Algarve coast from Lagos to Castro Marim on the Spanish border, 9€. Fuel prices in Portugal are among Europe's highest. In August 2019 a liter of unleaded gasoline averaged 1.56€. Diesel is slightly cheaper at 1.4€ per liter. If you're driving from Spain, you'll save by filling up before you cross the border.

The minimum age for driving a car in Portugal is 18. If you are a European Union citizen and are over 18, your license is valid for Portugal. U.S. and Canadian licenses are also valid for 180 days driving in Portugal. You may want, but are not obliged, to get an **International Driving Permit,** which contains a translation of your license in various languages. You can get it for $20 from the **AAA** (www.aaa.com) in the United States, or $25CDN from the **CAA** (www.caa.ca) in Canada.

DRIVING RULES Although there has been a marked improvement in road safety over recent years, due to better highways and stricter law enforcement, Portugal's roads remain dangerous compared with most places in Western Europe. The death rate is above the European Union average and more than double that of the safest countries like Sweden or Britain. Care is therefore needed when driving, particularly on narrower rural roads and on busy suburban highways. Speeding and tailgating on highways are particular problems.

The official **speed limits** are 120kph (75 mph) on most highways, 90kph (54 mph) on two-lane roads, and 50kph (31 mph) in urban areas. Although they are frequently disregarded, if you are caught speeding fines can be high, from 60€ to 2,500€ depending on how fast you are going and where. As with other traffic violations, the police can fine you on the spot. If you don't have cash, they carry credit card–reading machines. You also must carry your passport or ID cards, as well as ownership documents for the vehicle, and proof that it's insured, as well as your license.

Speed limit signs are round with black numbers on a white background in a red circle. The end of a speed zone is a round white sign with a black slash.

Drivers and passengers must wear **seatbelts** in front and back seats. Children under 12 or shorter that 135cm (53 inches) must ride in the back and in special **child seats.** Exceptions are made for children under 3, who can sit in the front if they have a proper child's seat and the airbag has been deactivated.

It is also obligatory to carry a red **warning triangle** and a yellow or orange **reflective vest,** which must be worn if you have to get out of the vehicle on the highway. Drivers are not allowed to use mobile phones.

Portugal's **drunk driving** rules are strict, with a maximum of 0.5%, less than in England or most U.S. states; it means a single drink may push you over the legal limit.

PARKING Street parking is difficult in big city centers. You'll often need to pay by purchasing a ticket from coin-operated dispensing machines. There is normally a 2-hour maximum limit. Common in many cities are people, often homeless, who will guide you to a parking spot. Usually they are content with a few cents in return, but in some places—Aveiro has been a black spot—gangs have taken over, aggressively demanding several euros. They also have no scruples in guiding unsuspecting drivers to illegal places, where they face fines. **Parking lots** are plentiful but can be expensive. A city-run car park in central Lisbon could charge 1.50€ for an hour, with a daily maximum of 25€. Exit booths in car parks are usually automatic. You'll need to exchange the ticket you pick up at on your way in for an exit ticket after paying at a coin- or card-operated automated payment machine before returning to your vehicle.

RENTALS Generally you'll get the best rates if you book your car 6 to 8 weeks in advance. Major international rental companies are present in Portugal, including Avis (www.avis.com; ✆ **21/754-78-25**), Budget (www.budget.com.pt; ✆ **21/754-78-25**), Sixt (www.sixt.pt; ✆ **25/578-81-99**), and Hertz (www.hertz.com; ✆ **21/942-63-85**). As well as booking directly, you can search for rental bargains through websites such as www.autoeurope.com, www.rentalcars.com, or www.kayak.com. If you are unfamiliar with manual transmissions, don't forget to request an automatic, although that may be considerably more expensive, especially if you are renting a compact or mid-range model. Drivers below 25 are likely to face a surcharge of around 10€ a day.

BREAKDOWNS Rental car companies will usually offer 24-hour breakdown service. Otherwise, if you belong to major automobile club such as AA, CAA, or AAA, you can get aid from the **Automóvel Club de Portugal** (www.acp.pt; ✆ **80/822-22-22**). Check also if your credit card or insurance company offers free breakdown assistance.

By Plane

Portugal is a small country, but there are regular internal flights between the three mainland airports and to the islands. TAP runs hourly shuttle flights between Lisbon and Porto, sometimes for less than 40€ each way. Ryanair has fewer flights on the same route, but can be even cheaper. TAP also has three daily flights to Faro. Check regional chapters for more details.

By Train

Trains are operated by the **CP** rail company (www.cp.pt; ✆ **70/721-02-20**). There are regular, fast, and comfortable trains between Lisbon and Porto, particularly the **Alfa Pendular** service that links the two cities in 2½ hours, stopping in Coimbra and Aveiro.

Elsewhere, the mainline system is limited. Porto is a hub for trains heading farther north to Guimarães, Braga, and up to Vigo in Spain. The picturesque line connecting the wine towns along the Douro River is an excellent way to discover the region. There are occasionally special trains along the Douro that use historic cars and serve gourmet lunches.

The Beira line heading inland from Coimbra to Guarda and occasionally to Madrid is slow, but provides an alternative to driving.

To get to the Algarve, there's a train from Lisbon that takes just over 2½ hours to reach the junction from Tunes, where the mainline connects with the line running along the south coast from Vila Real de Santo António, on the Spanish border, to the western town of Lagos.

There are also trains that chug through the countryside from Lisbon to the inland cities of Évora, Beja, Portalegre, Castelo Branco, and Covilhã.

Both Lisbon and Porto have extensive networks of urban electric trains running out to the suburbs. In Lisbon, the lines to Cascais from the **Cais do Sodré** station and to Sintra from the **Rossio** station are the most useful for visitors.

Many of Portugal's railway stations are decorated with beautiful *azulejos* (tiles) that make them attractions in their own right. São Bento in Porto is the most spectacular, but many small rural stations, particularly those along the Douro, are worth stopping to look at, if you are not rushing.

See regional chapters for more details of services, times, and prices.

CP offers significant discounts for tickets purchased in advance and for young and senior passengers. Full details can be found on the company's excellent English-language website (above), where you can also buy tickets online.

By Bus

The **Rede Expressos company** (www.rede-expressos.pt; ✆ **70/722-33-44**) runs a national network of intercity buses, which are a cheap, air-conditioned way of getting around. Lisbon to Bragança, in the far northeast, takes just less than 7 hours and costs 23€; to reach Tavira in the Algarve takes just over 4 hours and costs 20€. There are also regional networks such as **EVA** (www.eva-bus.com; ✆ **28/951-36-16**) in the Algarve, which, for example, runs a 2-hour route from Faro to Lagos from 5.38€ one-way.

See regional chapters for more details.

[Fast FACTS] PORTUGAL

Area Codes The country code for Portugal is ✆ **351.** Portugal scrapped area codes and incorporated them into subscribers' numbers. Portuguese fixed numbers are nine digits long. Fixed numbers generally begin with a 2, mobile numbers with a 9.

Business Hours Banks generally are open Monday to Friday from 8:30am to 3pm. Avoid lunch hours when small branches may take a break or will be thinly staffed. Shop hours vary. In the center of big cities, they tend to open Monday to Saturday between 9 and 10am and stay open until 7 or 8pm. Shopping malls stay open longer, often until 11pm, and are usually open Sundays. Out of centers and in rural areas, stores tend to close earlier, around 5 to 6pm, and close on Saturday afternoon and Sunday.

Note that almost all museums are closed on Mondays. The Gulbenkian in Lisbon is a notable exception, taking its weekly break on Tuesday. For the rest of the week, museums are generally open 10am to 6pm, although some smaller ones may break for lunch.

Most restaurants serve lunch from noon until 3pm and dinner from 7:30 until 10pm, although in cities it's not hard to find places that serve food all day and until midnight or later. On Sundays, many restaurants close or only open for lunch. Several take their weekly break on Mondays. Many nightclubs open at 10pm, but the action doesn't really begin until after midnight and often lasts until between 3 and 5am.

Customs Travelers from outside the European Union should declare any currency above 10,000€ when they are leaving or 5,000€ when entering Portugal. Duty-free goods you can carry into Portugal include a maximum of 4 liters of wine or 1 liter of spirits; 200 cigarettes or 50 cigars. You are generally not allowed to bring meat or dairy products from non-EU countries.

There are few restrictions when traveling to or from another EU country, but you may face questioning if you are carrying more than 10 liters of spirits, 90 liters of wine, or 800 cigarettes.

Heading home to the United States, you are required to declare food products. You'll generally be okay with things like olive oil, hard cheese, canned fish, honey, and cakes. Hams and sausage may be more problematic; certain types of hams and cured deli products are allowed, others are illegal. Be sure to look at the U.S. Customs' website before purchasing and check federal and state rules on bring back booze. Canada has similar rules. Remember that any liquids will have to be packed in your checked luggage.

Doctors & Hospitals European Union citizens should apply for the free **European Health Insurance Card.** It grants access to medically necessary, state-provided health care in Portugal and the other EU nations under the same conditions as local people. That means free or low-cost treatment under Portugal's **national health service.** It won't give you access to private health care or repatriation services.

Travelers from the U.S. and other non-EU nations should check with their insurer to see what coverage they have; most U.S. insurance plans do not cover accidents in Europe, so it's a good idea to get medical insurance before you hit the road.

Portuguese doctors and nurses are much sought after in other countries, but years of underfunding mean state hospitals and health centers, although generally well equipped in the big cities, often have long waits for all but the most urgent cases.

If your insurance covers it, private hospitals in big cities are often very well equipped with English-speaking staff, and many offer 24-hour emergency services. Among the best prepared for international visitors are **Hospital da Luz** (www.hospitaldaluz.pt; ✆ **21/710-44-00**), which is based in Lisbon but operates a number of hospitals and clinics around the country; **CUF** (www.saudecuf.pt; ✆ **21/392-61-00**); and **Lusíadas** (www.lusiadas.pt; ✆ **21/770-40-40**).

The U.S. embassy has a list of hospitals and doctors in Lisbon and the Azores (https://pt.usembassy.gov/u-s-citizen-services/doctors).

Drinking Laws The legal age for drinking in Portugal is 18. Beer, wine, and liquor are on sale in markets, cafes, restaurants, and liquor stores. There are no restrictions on when you can purchase alcohol. In an effort to curb noise and antisocial behavior, Lisbon city council bans drinking in the street after 1am in areas with a high concentration of bars like Bairro Alto and Cais do Sodré, but the rules are rarely enforced.

Drugs In 2001, Portugal decriminalized possession of drugs for personal use. That's all drugs, from cannabis to heroin. The law was ground-breaking, but it does not mean that drugs are legal. If you are caught with small amounts you will not be arrested or prosecuted, although you may have the drugs confiscated, receive a citation, and be ordered to attend counseling sessions. You can also be fined and have other "administrative" restrictions, such as being banned from attending bars and clubs, or being suspended from working in certain professions.

Supporters of the policy claim it has been successful in reducing HIV infection, overdose deaths, and addiction rates by encouraging users to seek medical treatment. Portugal's drug-induced death rate is five times lower than the EU average.

There are still strict criminal penalties for selling, producing, or trafficking drugs, including prison terms of up to 12 years. Nevertheless, in Lisbon, Porto, and some other places, it is quite common for foreigners to be approached by shady-looking characters in the street, even in broad daylight, offering to sell cocaine or marijuana. Often what they sell is fake—making it hard for police to prosecute them. They will usually move on if you say no or ignore them.

Electricity Voltage is 200 volts AC (50 cycles) as opposed to the U.S. 110-volt (60 cycles) system. Portugal uses plugs with two round pins like the rest of continental Europe. You'll need a simple converter for devices using flat-pin North American plugs or the UK-style three-pin plugs. Most electronics are dual-voltage—check to see if they have 110–220 on the plug. If not, you may want to buy a current converter. Hardware stores, travel and luggage shops, and airports should be able to meet your converter needs before you leave.

Embassies & Consulates The **U.S. Embassy** in Lisbon on Avenida das Forças Armadas (https://pt.usembassy.gov; ✆ **21/727-33-00**) is open Monday through Friday from 8am to 5pm. For U.S. citizens' consular services, call ✆ **21/770-21-22.** There is also a U.S. Consulate on São Miguel island in the Azores, Avenida Príncipe do Mónaco, 6-2 F, Ponta Delgada; ✆ **29/630-83-30;** open Monday to Friday, 8:30am to 12:30pm and 1:30 to 5:30pm.

The **Canadian Embassy** in Lisbon is at Av. da Liberdade 198–200, 3rd Floor (www.canadainternational.gc.ca; ✆ **21/316-46-00**). Open Monday to Thursday from 8am to 12:30pm and 1 to 5:15pm; Friday 8am to 5pm. Consular services for Canadians are open Monday to Friday, 9am to noon. Canada also offers consular services in the Algarve at Rua Frei Lourenço de Santa Maria 1, 1st Floor, Faro; ✆ **28/980-37-57;** open Monday to Friday 2 to 5:30pm; and in the Azores at Rua Carvalho Araujo, 94, Ponta Delgada on São Miguel island; ✆ **29/628-14-88;** Monday to Friday 9:30am to noon and 2 to 4pm.

The **U.K. Embassy** in Lisbon is on Rua de São Bernardo 33 (www.gov.uk; ✆ **21/392-40-00**), open Monday to Friday 9am to 1pm and 2:30 to 5:30pm. There is a British Vice Consulate in the Algarve in Portimão at Edificio A Fábrica Avenida Guanaré (✆ **28/249-07-50**), open 9:30am to 2pm.

The **Irish Embassy** is at Av. da Liberdade 200, 4th Floor, Lisboa (✆ **21/330-82-00**), open Monday through Friday 9:30am to 12:30pm. The **Embassy of Australia** is in the same building, Av. da Liberdade 200, 2nd Floor, Lisboa (www.portugal.embassy.gov.au; ✆ **21/310-15-00**), open Monday through Friday 10am to 4pm. **New Zealand** handles it's affairs through the embassy in France (www.mfat.govt.nz/france; ✆ **+33 1/450-14-343**) but has an honorary consulate at Rua da Sociedade Farmaceutica No 68, Lisbon (✆ **21/314-07-80**).

Emergencies For emergencies needing police, ambulance, or firefighters, call ✆ **112,** the European Union–wide equivalent to North America's 911.

Family Travel Portugal is a good place to travel with kids. Most beaches on the south coast are gently sloping with shallow water and small waves. On the west coast, you'll need to be aware that there can be heavy surf and riptides; check with the lifeguards, and never let your children (or yourself) go into the water if red flags are flying. They should also be protected against the sunshine, which will beat down hard during the middle of the day in summer.

Portugal has enticing attractions and activities for children, from the delights of the **Oceanário** in Lisbon, where kids can overnight next to the shark tank, to dolphin safaris or surf school in the real-life ocean. Most museums offer free entry to small children and half-price admission to students.

Portuguese families eat out with their children, particularly on weekends. Kids usually get a warm welcome, with most places offering special kids' menus and almost all offering half-portions of dishes on the menu.

Children get discounts on public transport. On the **CP** rail network, for example, children under 3 travel free if they don't take up a seat. Kids age 4 to 13 pay half-price.

Many hotels have family rooms, suites, or apartments and babysitting services. Particularly along the coast, there are family-friendly resorts. The wide availability of self-catering accommodations, both in traditional aparthotels and villas, and through agencies like **Airbnb**—which is thriving in Portugal—makes it easier to travel with kids.

Children need a **passport** to travel to Europe. Minors under 18 must be accompanied by a parent or guardian to enter Portugal or be met at the airport by a parent or guardian. If not, they will need a **letter of permission** to travel signed by their parents or guardians. Children traveling with just one parent should have a letter dated and signed by the other parent. In both cases the letter should be authorized by a notary. U.S. Customs and Border Protection offer advice on how to draft such a letter (www.cbp.gov/travel/us-citizens/know-before-you-go/your-trip), as do the authorities in Canada (www.travel.gc.ca/travelling/children). If in doubt, it's best to contact the Portuguese Embassy in your country.

Health You should encounter few health problems while traveling in Portugal. The tap water is generally safe to drink, milk is pasteurized, and health services are good. Occasionally, the change in diet can cause stomach upsets, so you might want to take along some anti-diarrheal medicine.

There is a very wide network of **pharmacies** (*farmácias*). They are normally open Monday to Friday 9am to 7pm and Saturdays 9am to 1pm. However, they take turns staying open later and on Sundays, serving as *farmácias de serviço*. These are listed on a notice posted in the windows of all pharmacies and on the website, www.farmaciasdeservico.net, which is in Portuguese only, but quite straightforward since you only have to click on the name of towns and districts to get a list. The site also lists a number of pharmacies that are routinely open until late at night or 24 hours.

Insurance For information on traveler's insurance, trip cancellation insurance, and medical insurance while traveling, please visit www.frommers.com/planning.

Internet Access Portugal is a wired-up country. Most hotels and hostels have free Wi-Fi in rooms and public spaces. It's also common in cafes and restaurants; just ask the staff for the password. Museums, libraries, railway stations, and other public spaces will have it. In most airports, there is unlimited free Wi-Fi, although you will need to set up an account to access it. Public transport networks such as the buses in Porto, Lisbon metro, and certain CP trains offer free Wi-Fi, although the connection can be up-and-down when busy. If you buy a Portuguese SIM card or don't mind paying roaming charges, you can connect with tablets and smartphones via 3G or 4G in all but the most remote places.

Language English is widely spoken, especially among younger people in the cities, much more so than in France, Spain, or Italy. If you speak Spanish, most people will understand you and reply in a hybrid, jokingly known as *portunhol*.

LGBTQ Travelers Portuguese attitudes to homosexuality have undergone a sea change in the past couple of decades. It was one of the first countries in Europe to outlaw workplace discrimination based on sexual orientation, and legalized **gay marriage** in 2010. In 2016, gay couples were given equal adoption rights and lesbians granted access to medically assisted fertilization. The year 2018 saw parliament pass a law making it easier for people to change gender from 16 and up. Lisbon, Porto, and the Algarve have thriving gay scenes. Overt homophobia and hate crimes are rare. Attitudes tend to be more conservative in rural areas. The annual **Pride** festivals are major events on the Lisbon and Porto social calendars, and **Queer Lisbon** (www.queerlisboa.pt), every September, is the city's oldest film festival. The main gay rights organization, **ILGA Portugal** (www.ilga-portugal.pt), apologizes for not having all of its website translated into English, but welcomes calls (✆ **21/887-39-22**) and promises to answer emails (ilgaportugal@ilga-portugal.pt). The site www.gay.portugalconfidential.com also offers information for LGBTQ travelers in Portugal.

Mail & Postage Sending postcards and standard letters from Portugal costs 0.86€ to elsewhere in Europe, 0.91€ to the rest of world. Post office opening hours vary, but bigger branches are usually open 9am to 6pm; smaller ones close for an hour at lunchtime. The mail company CTT (www.ctt.pt) has a list of post offices on its website and a phone line for enquiries in English (✆ **70/726-26-26**).

Mobile Phones Most modern North American cellphones will work in Europe, but roaming charges can be high. Check with your provider to make sure yours will work and if you can activate their international service to cut costs.

If you plan on making regular calls in Portugal, it can be cheaper to buy a local phone or a Portuguese SIM card. The process is generally hassle-free and offered by the three main telecom companies: Vodafone (www.vodafone.pt), MEO (www.meo.pt), and NOS (www.nos.pt), which have shops around the country, including in airport arrival lounges. Meo and Vodafone have an easy-to-understand English language section on their websites that explain what you need to do and how much it costs. A prepaid, rechargeable Vodafone SIM card with 500 minutes/text messages to Portuguese numbers and 5 gigabytes of data costs 20€.

Money & Costs Frommer's lists exact prices in the local currency. The currency conversions quoted below were correct at press time. However, rates fluctuate, so before departing, consult a currency exchange website such as **www.xe.com** to check up-to-the-minute rates.

Portugal is one of 19 countries in the euro-zone. The **euro** is divided into 100 cents. Euro coins are issued in denominations of 0.01€, 0.02€, 0.05€, 0.10€, 0.20€, 0.50€, 1€, and 2€; bills come in denominations of 5€, 10€, 20€, 50€, 100€, 200€, and 500€.

The easiest way to get **cash** is to take it directly from your bank account in euros by using your debit

THE VALUE OF THE EURO VS. OTHER CURRENCIES

Euro (€)	US$	UK£	C$	AUS$	NZ$
1	1.08	0.84	1.43	1.58	1.69

WHAT THINGS COST IN LISBON (HOTEL PRICES ARE HIGH SEASON)	EURO €
Bus ticket (bought on board)	2.00€
Double room with breakfast at Pestana Palace (expensive)	250.00€
Double room with breakfast at Hotel Britania (moderate)	160.00€
Double room at Casa São Mamede (inexpensive)	100.00€
Dinner for one with wine at Belcanto (expensive)	230.00€
Dinner for one with wine at Ramiro (moderate)	35.00€
Dinner for one with wine at Cantinho do Aziz (inexpensive)	20.00€
Pastel da nata at Manteigaria	1.00€
Espresso at A Brasileira (at bar/seated outside)	0.70€/1.50€
Glass of wine at Pensão Amor	3.50€–6€
Adult admission to Oceanário	16.00€
Stall seat for an opera at São Carlos theater	65.00€

card at one of Portugal's 12,000 **ATMs.** They have multilingual machines that enable you to carry out transactions in English; they are found in shopping malls, railway stations, airports, and other public spaces as well as in banks. Your bank may charge you a small commission (around 1 to 3%) on the exchange. Rates are less favorable if you exchange money at exchange bureaus and even worse if you use hotels or stores.

Credit cards are accepted almost everywhere, apart from some budget and remote places. Visa and MasterCard are the most widely used. You will sometimes see MULTIBANCO FORA DE SERVICO signs up in some places, meaning the card service is out of order. Some stores won't allow card transactions for less than 5€. Credit card transactions in Europe are usually by the "chip and PIN" system, meaning you type in your PIN code rather than signing a receipt. Most places will still allow signature payments by U.S. cardholders, but you should check with your bank to make sure you have your four-digit PIN code. It's always a good idea to let your bank and credit card provider know when you are traveling to avoid them blocking the card through fear that it's being used fraudulently.

Newspapers & Magazines There's a weekly English-language newspaper, the ***Portugal News,*** which updates national events and focuses mostly on the British community in the Algarve and around Lisbon. It's distributed free in some hotels and stores in the Algarve and other areas and is available online at www.theportugalnews.com. British newspapers and *The New York Times, Wall Street Journal,* and *USA Today* are widely available at newsstands in the big cities and in the Algarve. Many newsstands in Lisbon and Porto have a range of international magazines (e.g., **Tabacaria Monaco** in Lisbon's Rossio square, selling the news since 1875).

Passports & Visas For visits of less than 3 months, U.S., Canadian, Irish, Australian, New Zealand, or British citizens need only a valid passport.

Police Portugal has three main police bodies. The **Public Security Police** (PSP), in dark-blue uniforms, are the ones you are most likely to see patrolling the streets and take a lead role in law enforcement in cities. The **National Republican Guard** (GNR), who wear gray, are a paramilitary unit and generally perform more "high-end" public-order work, such as riot control, and are also active in traffic policing, particularly in rural areas. The **Judicial Police** (PJ) is a plainclothes investigative force. In emergencies, call ✆ **112.** The PSP run special **tourist police** units for dealing with travelers' problems. In Lisbon they are based in the **Palácio Foz** building in Praça dos Restauradores (✆ **21/342-16-23** or 21/340-00-90); in Porto they are near City Hall at Rua Clube dos Fenianos, 11 (✆ **22/208-18-33**).

Safety Portugal is a low-crime country. Violent crime against tourists is rare. **Pickpocketing** and theft from parked cars are the biggest problems. Don't leave valuables in cars, even during daylight. Pickpockets and bag snatchers tend to focus on crowded areas where there are lots of tourists. The Chiado district and the Portas do Sol viewpoint in Lisbon are hotspots. They also operate on public transport: take special care on packed Lisbon streetcars. If you're robbed, report it to the police. They may not put out an all-points alert for the culprit, but they will return stolen documents, which frequently show up dumped by criminals after they've emptied purses of cash.

In the summer season, almost all of Portugal's beaches are staffed with **lifeguards.** They hoist red flags or yellow flags if the water is deemed dangerous for bathing: Red means don't go in the water at all; yellow allows you to walk into the water, but swimming is not allowed. Follow their advice. As a general rule, south coast beaches tend to be gentle and sheltered; some of the more exposed places on the west can have strong currents and big waves. Jellyfish (*alforreca*) can be an occasional annoyance, as are **weaver fish** (*peixe aranha*). These small fish live along the western and southern coasts of Europe. They live close to the sand but have venomous spines exposed on their back. Stepping on one is very painful, but generally not dangerous. If it happens, go to the lifeguard. Plunging the foot in hot water usually brings quick relief. In rare cases, fever, chills, or nausea occur. If so, head to a hospital.

Senior Travel Portugal has long been a draw for senior travelers. Madeira, the Algarve, and the Cascais area west of Lisbon, in particular, have attracted retirees from Britain, other places in Northern Europe, and recently France and Italy, with their mild climate, relaxed lifestyle, and plethora of golf courses. Many decide to stay, buying vacation or retirement homes there, Portugal's generous tax breaks for so-called "non-habitual residents" often help with that decision.

Those over 65 can travel for half-price on Portugal's **CP rail network** and get significant reductions on **Rede Expresso**'s buses. There are also discounts of up to 50% on admission to most museums and attractions. In all cases, you must show a valid ID proving your age.

Smoking Smoking is banned in most public buildings and transport. Under certain conditions, restaurants and bars can set aside smoking rooms, and hotels can assign up to 40% of rooms for smokers. The rules are generally applied strictly in restaurants, less so in some bars. If you want to dine or drink alfresco, be aware that many smokers will head to outside tables to escape the ban.

Student Travel Students can get discounts on everything from museums to haircuts. In most cases your university's student ID will work, but to be on the safe side, get an **International Student Identity Card** (www.isic.org). In some places, you must be under 30 to get the discounts. Trains in Portugal don't offer discounts for students, but if you are under 25, you get a 25% reduction. To get reductions on **Rede Expresso** buses, you need to be below 30.

Taxes Sales tax, known as **IVA,** is included in the price of almost everything you buy in Portugal. The standard rate is 23%, although reduced rates apply to some purchases. In restaurants, for example, the rate on food is 13%, but on liquor the full 23% rate will apply. Your receipt will usually tell you how much you've given to the government. Residents outside the EU can get **a sales tax refund** when they leave on purchases, they are taking home over 53€ to 61.50€ depending on the type of product. Look for stores displaying tax-free shopping signs and ask them to hand you a refund form. In some places, you can be refunded in the store. In others, you'll need to get the form stamped by a customs official at the airport and pick up your money from a refund desk in departures. For more details, check out **www.premiertaxfree.com** or **www.globalblue.com**.

Taxes are usually included in the price of your hotel room, but in Lisbon, the City Hall has introduced a special **tourism tax,** there's a 1€ per person per night added to your bill, up to a maximum of 7€. It does not apply to children under 13.

Time Portugal keeps the same time as Britain and Ireland, an hour behind Spain and most of western Europe. It is 5 hours ahead of U.S. Eastern Standard Time. Portugal has daylight saving time. It moves its clocks ahead an hour in late spring and an hour back in the fall. Exact dates vary.

Tipping Service charges are rarely included in restaurant bills, but tipping is optional. In fancy places, people may leave up to 10%; elsewhere, rarely more than 5%, and only then if you've appreciated the service. Often people will just use a couple of coins or nothing. In bars and cafes it's rare to tip more than a few coins. In taxis, too, tipping is optional, although people will often round up the bill to the nearest euro or two, likewise with hairdressers or barbers. In hotels with porters or valet parking, you might want to tip 0.50€ or 1€.

Toilets Public toilets exist but are rare. If you are in need, nip into a cafe, buy a coffee or a bottle of water, and use facilities as a paying customer.

Travelers with Disabilities With their steep hills and cobbled sidewalks that are often narrow, uneven, and blocked by scaffolding or illegally parked cars, the centers of Lisbon, Porto, and other Portuguese cities can be challenging for people with disabilities. Portuguese authorities woke up late to the idea of accessibility, but there has been significant progress in recent years.

Many more modern hotels and other forms of accommodation have accessible rooms. The **Associação Salvador** (www.portugalacessivel.beta.due.pt; ✆ **21/318-48-51**) has information in English on the accessible options in hotels, transport, beaches, and so on.

There are also travel agencies that specialize in travel for people with disabilities that can help plan trips to Portugal. Many are based in the UK, where Portugal has long been a popular destination. They include **Enable Holidays** (www.enableholidays.com) and Disabled Holidays (www.disabledholidays.com). Within Portugal, **Adapted & Senior Tours** (www.adaptedtoursportugal.com; ✆ **91/619-04-14**), **Portugal 4 All Senses** (www.portugal4allsenses.pt; ✆ **96/336-43-59**), and **Accessible Portugal** (www.accessibleportugal.com; ✆ **92/691-09-89**) organize tours and transfers.

The "**Praia Acessível – Praia para Todos!**" (Accessible Beach – Beach for All) program launched in 2005 covers 214 beaches as of 2019 (just about ⅓ of the total), which means they must have accessible parking spaces, toilet facilities, lifeguards, and unimpeded access (usually wooden pathways leading to the water). Many also have amphibious wheelchairs, available from the lifeguards, to ease entry into the sea.

Lisbon's public bus company **Carris** (www.carris.pt/en/reduced-mobility) says 88% of its vehicles are equipped with ramps for wheelchair users, and 50% also have spaces for wheelchairs. All buses have seats reserved for disabled travelers. Carris also has adapted minibuses at the disposal of special-needs passengers, but they must be reserved 2 days in advance (✆ **21/361-31-41**). Lisbon's **Metro** stations have wide access gates for disabled customers and ticket vending machines are adapted for visually impaired users. Newer stations have elevators. The company says all of its stations offer street-to-platform wheelchair accessibility.

The railway company **CP** has a 24-hour helpline for passengers with special needs (✆ **70/721-07-46;** or go to www.cp.pt/passageiros/en/passenger-information and select "special needs customers"). It also offers discounts of up to 75% on tickets for disabled passengers and smaller discounts for fully able companions. Most taxi companies have adapted vehicles available. **Cooptaxis,** which operates in Lisbon and the Algarve (www.cooptaxis.pt; ✆ **21/799-64-75**) is among the best equipped. In Porto, try **Raditaxis** (www.raditaxis.pt; ✆ **22/507-39-00**).

Water Tap water is drinkable throughout Portugal, but many people prefer the taste of bottled water and it's commonly drunk and served in restaurants and cafes. Portugal's wealth of springs means there are a variety of still brands on the market. If you order water (*água*) in a cafe, you'll always be asked if you want still (*sem gás*) or sparking (*com gás*), chilled (*fresca*) or room temperature (*natural*).

Most beaches in season fly a blue flag signaling the water has been certified as clean for bathing by European Union inspectors and has adequate lifeguard services. Several inland bathing spots on rivers and lakes have similar blue-flag certification.

Websites The national tourist board has a good multilingual website, **www.visitportugal.com**. The quality of regional tourism sites is patchy. Among the best are www.visitcentro.com on the center, www.visitmadeira.pt, www.visitportoandnorth.travel, www.visitazores.com, www.visitalgarve.com, and www.visitlisboa.com. There's excellent information on the country's protected parks and nature reserves at www.natural.pt, despite the unreliable English.

Some interesting blogs and private guides in English giving tips and insight into the country include **www.saltofportugal.com**, which is produced by a group of enthusiastic young Portuguese and offers tips on everything from poetry to *pasteis da nata;* **www.portugalconfidential.com**, which claims to cover "everything cool in Portugal;" and **www.nelsoncarvalheiro.com**, for great food, recipes, and travel ideas.

Index

See also Accommodations and Restaurant indexes, below.

General Index

A

B

C

D

E

Q

R

S

Accommodations

Restaurants

Map List

Photo Credits

p. i: Pauline Frommer; p. ii: Pauline Frommer; p. iii: Photo and Vector / Shutterstock.com; p. iv: Pauline Frommer; p. v, top: ESB Professional; p. v, bottom left: Meghan Lamb; p. v, bottom right: Daniel Vine Photography / Shutterstock.com; p. vi, top: Anup subedi / Shutterstock.com; p. vi, bottom left: Alex McCarten; p. vi, bottom right: Sergio Azenha / Alamy Stock Photo; p. vii, top: travelview; p. vii, middle: Pauline Frommer; p. vii, bottom: ribeiroantonio / Shutterstock.com; p. viii, top left: dynamosquito; p. viii, top right: Pauline Frommer; p. viii, bottom: Junior Braz / Shutterstock.com; p. ix, top: Filipe Pimentel; p. ix, middle: Rolf E. Staerk; p. ix, bottom: Pauline Frommer; p. x, top: Nacho Pintos; p. x, middle: Vector99; p. x, bottom: Nido Huebl / Shutterstock.com; p. xi, top left: Landscape Nature Photo / Shutterstock.com; p. xi, top right: Agnieszka Skalska / Shutterstock.com; p. xi, bottom left: Benny Marty / Shutterstock.com; p. xi, bottom right: Jessica Spengler; p. xii, top: Aki Shi / Shutterstock.com; p. xii, middle: Anton_Ivanov / Shutterstock.com; p. xii, bottom: LuisCostinhaa / Shutterstock.com; p. xiii, top: Tatiana Popova; p. xiii, bottom left: Mauro Rodrigues / Shutterstock.com; p xiii, bottom right: Cenz07 / Shutterstock.com; p. xiv, top left: zi3000; p. xiv, top right: Caron Badkin / Shutterstock.com; p. xiv, bottom: Pawel Kazmierczak; p. xv, top: Benny Marty / Shutterstock.com; p. xv, middle: saiko3p; p. xv, bottom: Steve Photography; p. xvi, top: Aureliy; p. xvi, middle: AngeloDeVal / Shutterstock.com; p. xvi, bottom: Sergio Stakhnyk.

Frommer's Portugal, 24th Edition

Published by
FROMMER MEDIA LLC

ISBN 978-1-62887-505-8 (paper), 978-1-62887-506-5 (ebk)

Editorial Director: Pauline Frommer
Editor: Elizabeth Heath
Production Editor: Erin Geile
Cartographer: Liz Puhl
Photo Editor: Meghan Lamb
Assistant Photo Editor: Phil Vinke
Indexer: Maro Riofrancos
Cover Design: Dave Riedy

Front cover photo: A historic facade in Porto, decorated with traditional azulejo tiles. Credit: Mirifada / Shutterstock.
Back cover photo: A beautiful cove beach near Lagos, Algarve. Credit: Kite_rin / Shutterstock.

For information on our other products or services, see www.frommers.com.

FrommerMedia LLC also publishes its books in a variety of electronic formats. Some content that appears in print may not be available in electronic formats.

Manufactured in the United States of America

5 4 3 2 1

ABOUT THE AUTHOR

Paul Ames has been enchanted by Portugal since he first arrived as a child in 1975 and found the country gripped by revolutionary fervor. He lives in Lisbon, works as a freelance journalist, and never tires of exploring the delights of his adopted homeland, from the vine-covered hills of the Minho to Madeira's rocky shores and all the beaches in between.

ABOUT THE FROMMER TRAVEL GUIDES

For most of the past 50 years, Frommer's has been the leading series of travel guides in North America, accounting for as many as 24% of all guidebooks sold. I think I know why.

Though we hope our books are entertaining, we nevertheless deal with travel in a serious fashion. Our guidebooks have never looked on such journeys as a mere recreation, but as a far more important human function, a time of learning and introspection, an essential part of a civilized life. We stress the culture, lifestyle, history, and beliefs of the destinations we cover, and urge our readers to seek out people and new ideas as the chief rewards of travel.

We have never shied from controversy. We have, from the beginning, encouraged our authors to be intensely judgmental, critical—both pro and con—in their comments, and wholly independent. Our only clients are our readers, and we have triggered the ire of countless prominent sorts, from a tourist newspaper we called "practically worthless" (it unsuccessfully sued us) to the many rip-offs we've condemned.

And because we believe that travel should be available to everyone regardless of their incomes, we have always been cost-conscious at every level of expenditure. Though we have broadened our recommendations beyond the budget category, we insist that every lodging we include be sensibly priced. We use every form of media to assist our readers, and are particularly proud of our feisty daily website, the award-winning Frommers.com.

I have high hopes for the future of Frommer's. May these guidebooks, in all the years ahead, continue to reflect the joy of travel and the freedom that travel represents. May they always pursue a cost-conscious path, so that people of all incomes can enjoy the rewards of travel. And may they create, for both the traveler and the persons among whom we travel, a community of friends, where all human beings live in harmony and peace.

Arthur Frommer